D1717003

American Silver at Winterthur

American Silver at Winterthur

IAN M.G.QUIMBY

WITH

DIANNE JOHNSON

A WINTERTHUR BOOK

DISTRIBUTED BY
THE UNIVERSITY PRESS OF VIRGINIA

To Maureen, Sean, and Patrick, who have so enriched my life.

Generous funding for research and publication was provided by
the Henry Luce Foundation, Inc.

Copyright 1995, The Henry Francis du Pont Winterthur Museum, Inc.

All rights reserved. No part of this publication may be reproduced or transmitted in
any form or by any means, electronic or mechanical, including photocopying, recording,
or any information storage retrieval system, without written permission of Winterthur
Publications, Winterthur, Delaware, 19735.

Library of Congress Cataloging in Publication Data
Quimby, Ian M.G.
    American Silver at Winterthur / by Ian M.G. Quimby with Dianne Johnson
      p. cm.—(A Winterthur book)
    Includes bibliographical references and index.
    ISBN 0-912724-32-3
    1. Silverwork—United States—Catalogs. 2. Silverwork—Delaware—
Winterthur—Catalogs. 3. Henry Francis du Pont Winterthur Museum—Catalogs.
I. Johnson, Dianne. II. Henry Francis du Pont Winterthur Museum. III. Title.
NK7112.Q56 1995
739.2'3774'0747511—DC20   95-14228
                                CIP

Printed in Hong Kong

Cover: Salver by John Heath; see no. 209
Frontispiece: Sugar box by Edward Winslow; see no. 140

Contents

List of Makers

❧ PENNSYLVANIA AND THE SOUTH

Foreword

I came to Winterthur in 1966 as a graduate student in the Winterthur Program in Early American Culture and, subsequently, served as a curator. I can recall numerous fascinating lunchtime conversations with Ian Quimby about his interest in American silver and his determination to produce a catalogue of Winterthur's great silver collection.

Ian began the project while serving as full-time director of publications and saw it to completion after taking early retirement in 1991. During his tenure, a bonanza of Winterthur catalogues was produced. These include Charles F. Montgomery's *History of American Pewter*, E. McSherry Fowble's *Two Centuries of Prints in America, 1680–1880*, and Benno M. Forman's *American Seating Furniture, 1630–1730*, which have all become standard references in their field.

It gives me great personal pleasure to welcome Ian Quimby's new catalogue, *American Silver at Winterthur,* to the distinguished series documenting the collections created by Henry Francis du Pont and expanded over the years by staff, donors, and trustees. It was well worth the wait!

Dwight P. Lanmon
Director

Acknowledgments

In a project of this size and duration, one incurs many debts—too numerous, in fact, to list completely. There were those who provided leads, clues, and suggestions as well as support in other forms. To the silver historians whose works are mentioned repeatedly, I am tremendously grateful. I cannot think how I would have managed without the publications of Kathryn C. Buhler, Graham Hood, Martha Gandy Fales, Patricia E. Kane, Deborah Dependahl Waters, and Barbara McLean Ward and Gerald W. R. Ward. Conversations with the Wards, first in Delaware and later in New Hampshire, helped more than they know. They also generously allowed me to stay with them on several occasions when I was in New England conducting research. Others whose scholarship is reflected in this catalogue include Louise Conway Belden, Charles H. Carpenter, Donald L. Fennimore, and Jennifer Faulds Goldsborough.

I am particularly grateful to David Low, who spent the summer of 1976 collecting information on New York silversmiths and their patrons—research that subsequently proved very useful. Margie Cist also came forward to help during the summer of 1980. The Winterthur Fellows who wrote papers on silver for their connoisseurship classes deserve recognition as well. Those papers, now in the object files of the Registration Division at Winterthur, were valuable on several occasions.

I am grateful for the assistance rendered by the staffs of the following organizations: American Antiquarian Society, Essex Institute, Historical Society of Pennsylvania, Maine Historical Society, Massachusetts Historical Society, New England Genealogical Historical Society, New-York Historical Society, Old Sturbridge Village, Rockingham County Probate Records Office and Public Library (Exeter, New Hampshire), and Suffolk County Probate Court (Boston).

Obviously this project would not have been possible without extensive institutional support. Thanks to former Winterthur director Charles van Ravenswaay and former deputy director John A. H. Sweeney, who secured for me a travel-study grant during the summer of 1971 to visit British and Continental museums that have important silver collections. Although primarily useful as background, research in the Burgerbibliothek in Bern, Switzerland, is reflected in the biography of Daniel Christian Fueter. More research on Fueter, at the Moravian Archives in Bethlehem, Pennsylvania, in 1980 was also supported by Winterthur.

Early in 1985 the Henry Luce Foundation for American Art invited Winterthur to apply for a grant to support research and publication costs for a catalogue of one of its major collections. Scott T. Swank, then deputy director for interpretation, and Charles F. Hummel, then deputy director for collections, nominated the silver catalogue, and William Ayres used his considerable skills as development officer to fine-tune the grant proposal and shepherd it to a successful conclusion. There is no question that the Luce grant moved the silver project to the front burner, and I am deeply grateful for their support.

Over the next several years, thanks to the Luce grant, I was able to employ a research assistant. Eleanor Southworth Thompson, then a recent graduate of the Winterthur Program in Early American Culture, did yeoman service in building the research files, particularly in reconstructing H. F. du Pont's acquisition records. Eleanor was succeeded by Dianne Johnson, a graduate student in art history at the University of Delaware, who had recently been employed at Yale University Art Gallery. Dianne worked intermittently for about four years, between the demands of graduate study and bearing her first child. She produced a variety of databases that became the controls for the hundreds of silver pieces we had to deal with. She arranged for the spectrographic analysis and weighing of each item, for moving all pieces to a workroom, and for measuring each object. She prepared worksheets for almost all of the spoon entries. The two of us spent many days examining hollowware and drafting the descriptive entries. I cannot thank her enough for using her good eyes and growing knowledge of silver to help me through this process. She was unfailingly cheerful, even when the work grew tedious. Dianne's contributions to this project are exceeded only by the warmth of her personality and her decency as a human being. I feel privileged to have gained her friendship.

By 1990, with the New England portion of the catalogue completed, it became clear that completion of the project would require blocks of free time. That summer, following vacation with my family in Maine, I stayed on for several weeks of uninterrupted writing. Subsequently, with the administration's blessing, I was granted research leave, and the following January I moved my files and computer to Hagley Museum and Library, where Patrick Nolan, head of the Center for the History of Business, Technology, and Society, had generously offered me office space. There it was possible to write without interruption. During the spring of 1991, while still on leave, I accepted Winterthur's early retirement option, effective August 31. By this time I had drafted all the entries but still needed to fill in missing information and compose the introductory essays. Much of this work was completed under contract over the next ten months on a part-time schedule, as I had assumed the editorship of the *Pennsylvania Magazine of History and Biography* in September 1991.

In addition to Winterthur staff already mentioned, there are others who contributed to the project. Although some of the photos were made from negatives on file, Wayne B. Gibson was responsible for all new photography. Because of his experience at Winterthur, he did not need a lot of coaching. For this and for the quality of his work, I thank him. The staff of the Registration Division, headed by Karol A. Schmiegel, moved hundreds of objects. My gratitude for their cheerful cooperation goes to Karol, Susan Ishler Newton, Douglas MacDonald, and their colleagues.

I have had the pleasure of working for many years with Winterthur's analytical laboratory, headed initially by Victor Hansen but for most of the duration of this project by George Reilly, ably assisted by Janice Carlson and Maruta Skelton. Their resourcefulness in providing hundreds of analyses and weights is deeply appreciated. George's important work on measuring the wall thickness of hollowwares appears in the appendix.

I used no resource at Winterthur more frequently than the Printed Books and Periodicals Collection, under the direction of my good friend Neville Thompson, whose kindness and cooperation knows no bounds. I also frequented the Visual Resources Collection, managed by Bert L. Denker, and the Joseph Downs Collection of Manuscripts and Printed Ephemera, formerly headed by Bea Taylor and, more recently, by E. Richard McKinstry. Visiting scholars often sing the praises of the Winterthur library, and I found out why. Not only are all its collections eminently accessible, but the staff is always ready to assist. The library also provided me with office space for the project in 1986 and for portions of 1991–92.

Without the help of Lin Hardy and others in Information Systems Division, I might not have attained my modest degree of computer literacy. Lin was helpful in many crises, and she always came to my aid with good humor. I acknowledge with gratitude the staff of the Word Processing Center, under the direction of Anne Marie Keefer, who entered the first third of the book into the computer using my rough copy drafted on a typewriter.

I am grateful to Winterthur's Publications Division, particularly Onie Rollins and Susan Randolph, for overseeing editing and production of this book. I also cannot thank enough the several secretaries in that office who, over the years, indulged my whim for incessant photocopying from magazines and books. Thanks also to Katy Homans and Deborah Zeidenberg, who designed and typeset the book.

Lastly, I am indebted to my wife, Maureen, for her support, encouragement, and understanding when research or writing kept me away from the family. She always remained a true believer—even on those occasions when I doubted the wisdom of having undertaken this endeavor.

Ian M. G. Quimby

Preface

I will never forget the day in late autumn 1961 when Charles F. Montgomery held his connoisseurship class on the East Terrace at Winterthur. It was a bright and blustery afternoon as dried leaves swirled around a long table filled with New York and Boston silver tankards—unthinkable classroom conditions today. I had never seen such a sight. Charles talked about the tankards as if they were old friends. It seemed like a strange way to relate to things, but he was unselfconscious—he really loved them. He once said that, as a dealer, many great objects had passed through his hands, but he did not regret their departure because he would always own them in his heart. And so he lived not clinging to a collection of precious objects of his own but in a universe of things that had been part of his life and the lives of others. He contributed to building the silver collection at Winterthur in his capacities as a dealer in Wallingford, Connecticut, and as curator and director of Winterthur from 1956 to 1961. He contributed even more to our understanding of things as a teacher and mentor from 1961 until 1970, when he departed for Yale to inspire yet another generation of students.

In January 1965 I joined the Winterthur staff as assistant registrar under Milo M. Naeve. My first assignment was to help in cataloguing the entire collection. I had the good fortune to begin my work in the Queen Anne Dining Room, where I was greatly taken by the New York silver in general and by the Daniel Christian Fueter teapot in particular. Intrigued by this beautiful object and by its elusive Swiss maker, who worked in America for fifteen years, I made a mental note to look deeper into both when the opportunity presented itself. Meanwhile, within three weeks of my starting work, Naeve had been appointed full-time editor of *Winterthur Portfolio*, and I took over his duties as registrar, which fully occupied my time, ending my brief career as a cataloguer.

Later that year, when it came time to choose a portion of the collection for Henry Francis du Pont's annual gift, I recommended the silver. (Du Pont had retained title to the collection when he gave the museum building to the Winterthur Corporation, and each year he gave a portion of the collection as dictated by his tax situation.) Du Pont agreed, and I proceeded to arrange for the appraisal of the silver. With two independent appraisals required, I selected Bernard Levy, from the firm of Ginsburg & Levy in New York City, and Charlotte and Edgar Sittig, dealers from Shawnee-on-Delaware, Pennsylvania. All had been in business for many years and had sold numerous items to Harry du Pont (as they called him). Levy started in the antiques business as a child in his father's shop, and he knew just about every collector and curator in the American field. Like most good dealers, he had incredible visual recall. He also had an unlimited fund of anecdotes. Virtually every time we rounded a corner in the museum, he recognized furniture, silver, or something else that had passed through the family shop, and a new story began. Before Montgomery, I had never known anyone for whom objects could be so stirring. But then, the Sittigs responded similarly, although their method of setting prices required friendly bickering, and thus the process took a little longer. On their way through the museum, they too recognized many old friends. My experience with this engaging couple proved equally enjoyable. With the Sittigs and Levy I had to repress my panic when they insisted on handling silver without gloves. That is simply how they were used to doing it. They shared many stories of not having charged enough or of missed opportunities, but, as with Montgomery, there was genuine affection for the objects and abiding love for their vocation. For me, the enthusiasm of Montgomery, Levy, and the Sittigs, plus my own brief encounter with a particularly intriguing object, lent a new importance to American silver that, in some mysterious way, ultimately led to this book. I am profoundly grateful to all of them.

The enormous task of cataloguing the collection at Winterthur in the 1960s had as its goal the recording of every object so that when du Pont passed away there would be a record of all that he had collected. Meanwhile, a publications program had been launched by John Morse at the behest of museum director Edgar P. Richardson. Called the National Extension Program, its purpose was to share the collection with a national audience through books, catalogues, films, filmstrips, and a bookstore. Morse needed authors and titles in order to have a program, and so he convinced several of us to sign contracts.

It struck me then, as it does today, that American silver could serve as a kind of index to early American culture. Having been buoyed as a graduate student by the heady interdisciplinary rhetoric of professors Frank Sommer and Alan Gowans, I thought it possible to produce not just a conventional catalogue but an interpretive work that would transcend the genre. In the 1960s the existing literature on American silver was basically antiquarian, aimed at collectors and dealers. Most academic scholars eschewed not only silver but the field of decorative arts in its entirety. Art historians referred contemptuously to the "minor arts." The 1968 Winterthur conference—"Spanish, French, and English Traditions in the Colonial Silver of North America"—suggested new possibilities, however.

All presentations at the conference were valuable, but three stood out for their originality: George A. Kubler's "Time's Perfection and Colonial Art," Anthony N. B. Garvan's "American Church Silver: A Statistical Study," and Frank H. Sommer's "The Functions of American Church Plate." Kubler's piece was a meditation on the qualities of colonial art and how time changes our perception of all art—using art in its very broadest sense. The irrepressible Tony Garvan, aided by three of his graduate students, presented an analysis of silver holdings, by form, in the various denominations of American churches. He used as a database E. Alfred Jones's magisterial *Old Silver of American Churches* (1913). Sommer explained the influence of the Reformation on ecclesiastical forms used in celebrating the Lord's Supper and, in particular, the trend toward secular vessels among the dissenting churches, especially those of New England. Brief though it was, Sommer's presentation remains the clearest explanation for the selection of particular forms found in churches of seventeenth- and eighteenth-century colonial America. What all three presenters did so well was to provide significant contexts for artifacts, illustrating the overwhelming importance of historical and cultural knowledge for their interpretation. Although we can "read" an artifact to extract certain information, like any other document we cannot go very far without a knowledge of the context in which it existed, nor indeed without having an interpretive mechanism for understanding the past. In the words of Immanuel Kant, "Concepts without percepts are empty; percepts without concepts are blind."[1]

The catalogues of specific collections at Winterthur had to wait, however, in the face of such pressing matters as the inevitable reorganization of Winterthur following the death of H. F. du Pont in 1969 and the damaging inflation of the early and mid 1970s—not to mention new assignments for me as editor of *Winterthur Portfolio* and director of publications. Following his assumption of the directorship of Winterthur in 1976, James Morton Smith revived the catalogue publishing effort. Assignments were made, and a schedule was developed. Because it was still in the early stage of research and because of my commitments in the area of museum publications, the silver project remained a low priority. There was, understandably, greater interest in moving forward Louise Belden's *Marks of American Silversmiths in the Ineson-Bissell Collection*, which appeared in 1980. Not until a grant was secured from the Henry Luce Foundation in 1985 did the silver project take center stage. By that time, however, the silver collection had expanded enormously, at least threefold beyond what it had been when H. F. du Pont died in 1969. Several important books had appeared during the 1970s, among them the catalogues of the silver collections at Yale University Art Gallery and the Museum of Fine Arts, Boston and two important volumes by Martha Gandy Fales: *Early American Silver* and *Joseph Richardson and Family: Philadelphia Silversmiths*. Charles H. Carpenter's books on Tiffany and Gorham expanded the canon, and the innovative *Silver in American Life*, edited by Barbara McLean Ward and Gerald W. R. Ward, showed the range of possibilities in the study of silver.[2] Important dissertations on networks of silversmiths were completed in the 1980s by Barbara Ward and Deborah Dependahl Waters, and Patricia E. Kane provided the definitive study of John Hull and Robert Sanderson. These works plus a number of others made available an enormous amount of information. By the mid to late 1980s, the secondary literature on American silver had grown significantly in both number and quality.

The Winterthur silver project clearly benefited from the delays attending its execution. The expansion of knowledge about makers, users, and environments and the publication of so many collections provided detailed information and links to related objects elsewhere that would have been infinitely harder to come by when the project was originally proposed. The greatly expanded number of objects at Winterthur demanded more research, examination, and analysis as well. My attempts to provide contexts for the silver at Winterthur have produced uneven results. Some entries and biographies were enriched by the extensive information found; others are bare-bones affairs because little or nothing could be unearthed or because so many objects were unaccompanied by histories. The New England silver, a number of pieces of which came with family associations, yielded the richest results. Thanks to the large number of secondary sources and the survival of so many probate records, it was possible to expand a number of these clues into narratives that, I trust, provide a sense of the lives of the persons whose names are stamped on the silver and of the owners, patrons, and donors. These objects were made, used, and cherished by real people. It helps us to understand these people and the world they lived in if we also have a sense of who they were or who they aspired to be.

I have elected to provide detailed descriptions of objects on the grounds that a picture does not necessarily tell us everything we need to know. It is not apparent to everyone how a silver teapot or tankard was made, and, indeed, processes changed over time. By including detailed descriptions incorporating production techniques and by noting the presence or absence of centerpunches, engraving, and scratched information, I have provided the reader with all of the information that could be gleaned from examining the object directly. Not everyone will need this level of detail, but it is there for those who do. Notwithstanding the desire to create a more interpretive work, a catalogue is still primarily a compilation of descriptive and background information. The nature of the beast—and the number of objects—serve to limit the possibilities for interpretation. I would like to think that the results of my labor provide at least a starting point for broader and deeper interpretive efforts. I can hear Charles Montgomery's response, "Well, let's get on with it."

NOTES   1. Edward Caird, *The Critical Philosophy of Immanuel Kant*, 2 vols. (1889; reprint, New York: Kraus, 1968), 1:591. Winterthur conference papers are published in *Spanish, French, and English Traditions in the Colonial Silver of North America* (Winterthur, Del.: Henry Francis du Pont Winterthur Museum, 1969), pp. 7–12, 73–104, 105–9.

2. Charles H. Carpenter, Jr., with Mary Grace Carpenter, *Tiffany Silver* (New York: Dodd, Mead, 1978); Charles H. Carpenter, Jr., *Gorham Silver, 1831–1981* (New York: Dodd, Mead, 1982); Barbara McLean Ward and Gerald W. R. Ward, eds., *Silver in American Life: Selections from the Mabel Brady Garvan and Other Collections at Yale University* (Boston: David R. Godine, 1979).

On the Nature and Use of Silver

Silver occupies a unique niche among the many natural materials that man has manipulated to his needs. Although it shares many of the same physical properties as gold, it has the virtue of being more abundant and therefore less expensive. Aside from appearance, the four most important physical qualities of silver are that it is malleable, ductile, conductive, and fusible. Because it is malleable, silver can be worked and shaped with simple tools. Lead is malleable too, but it lacks ductility, the capability to be stretched without breaking. It is possible, for example, for one gram of pure silver (1/28 ounce) to be drawn into a wire a mile long—so thin that it is invisible except under magnification. Only gold is more malleable and ductile. Silver is also an excellent conductor of heat and electricity. Because heat flows quickly through silver, wooden handles are required on silver teapots. A silver handle, unless insulated, would be too hot to touch. Efficient heat conduction also means that tea in a silver container cools relatively quickly. The superb ability of silver to conduct electricity—even better than copper—has resulted in its widespread use in circuit boards and other electrical and electronic applications. Lastly, silver is fusible, one part is easily joined to another by soldering.

Silver has one additional quality that has led to its largest single use: mixed with nitric acid and certain salts, it absorbs light. In 1991, 51.7 percent of American silver usage was for the production of photographic film and 16.7 percent was used in electrical and electronic applications. Only 6.5 percent went into sterling, silver-plated wares, and jewelry.[1] While not recognized as an important attribute in scientific circles, silver has yet another quality that is important to its use as tableware; unlike most metals it is tasteless and therefore ideal for eating and drinking vessels.

It is, of course, its appearance—its whiteness and reflectivity—that has made silver so desirable for millenia. In an age before stainless steel, polished aluminum, Britannia (an alloy of tin, antimony, and copper), nickel silver, and paktong (an alloy of nickel, copper, and zinc), the brilliance of hand-wrought silver was unique. Silver was not intended to exist in isolation as it so often does in museum cases today. It is at its best when it reflects richly appointed surroundings and light sources. The reflection and refraction of light in the depths of polished metal enchants and delights. Silver was one of the earliest materials capable of taking a high finish.[2] The aesthetic of the high finish flourished in the eighteenth century and is epitomized by the discovery and exploitation of the formula for true porcelain. The visual qualities of silver fit this aesthetic, and new forms exploiting the alloy's smoothness, whiteness, and reflectivity were developed. A different aesthetic emerged during the nineteenth century, one based on complexity of surface and an eclectic approach to style. Ornament flowed over forms, the more elaborate the better, often as a tour de force to demonstrate a mastery of materials and technical proficiency. Design reform movements, starting with the arts and crafts movement, reacted against what were considered the excesses of Victorian decorative design. But instead of returning to the high-finish aesthetic of the eighteenth century, arts and crafts devotees frequently emphasized the unfinished look, epitomized by hammer marks deliberately left in silver—sometimes introduced where they did not exist—to suggest the craft products of medieval times. The international style, with its wholesale adoption of smooth machine-made surfaces and a near total rejection of ornament, completed the movement for stylistic reform. Because it can be shaped into an infinite variety of forms and take on many different surface textures, silver was easily adapted to all these whims of fashion.

COMPOSITION

Pure silver is too soft for practical use. The addition of 5.0 to 15.0 percent copper provides the requisite structural qualities and lends a touch of warmth to the stark whiteness of the metal. Since variations in the amount of copper in the alloy affect its value, one of the first statutes regulating the industry, enacted in England in 1238, called for silver wares to contain at least as much silver as coin of the realm. By an act of Parliament passed in 1300 under Edward I, all wrought silver had to be 92.5 percent pure and be stamped with a leopard's head, indicating its adherence to the sterling standard. As assay offices were established in other English cities, the leopard's head came to indicate only that the silver had been made in London. By about 1544 an additional stamp, a lion passant, was required as the guarantee of sterling quality.[3] This stamp remains in use today by all English assay offices: London, Birmingham, and Sheffield.

Although the fineness of silver was controlled by guilds in British and Continental cities, British America was another matter. There were neither guilds nor any effective local or provincial laws governing the silversmiths' trade practices, although there were several attempts to establish controls. Analyses of thousands of examples of early American silver show wide fluctuations in their silver content: from 85.0 to 95.0 percent. Generally speaking, however, early American silver falls below the sterling standard. This does not necessarily mean that American silversmiths were deliberately cheating their customers. The variations in content probably had more to do with what went into the melting pot: old wrought plate and coins from many different countries. Spanish dollars, the most widely circulated silver coins in colonial times, fluctuated in silver content but were generally about 90.0 percent pure. Moreover, the standard established in 1792 for United States silver currency was 89.2 percent, raised in 1837 to 91.7 percent. In other words, "coin silver" was not sterling.[4] Baltimore established an assay office in 1814 and even had a system of stamps resembling those used in England, but the standard required under the new law was still only 91.7 percent. A sterling stamp, normally the word itself, was used occasionally by certain American silversmiths early in the nineteenth century, but it was no guarantee of purity. In 1851 Tiffany & Company adopted the sterling standard at a time when most silver was stamped "coin," "dollar," or "standard." From 1854 to 1870, Tiffany silver was stamped "English sterling" and after that date "sterling silver." The attempt to emulate English quality (without government or guild coercion) was a successful marketing ploy aimed at upscale customers. The Gorham Company adopted the sterling standard in 1868, followed by most of the industry. Not until 1906, however, did the United States government require that silver stamped "sterling" actually be 92.5 percent fine.

In early America, fluctuations in silver content rarely seem to have been an issue. Most silver made prior to the American Revolution bore a stamp with the initials of the maker/seller; in postrevolutionary years the last name was often spelled out. (In New England the practice of using the entire last name began early in the eighteenth century, as in the works of Knight Leverett and John Burt.) In each case such identification was itself a kind of guarantee or certification of quality. As markets expanded, the name of the town or city was sometimes added. One of the first to adopt this practice was Daniel Christian Fueter, whose work usually carried "N:York" in addition to his initials.

TECHNICS

Silversmithing is an ancient craft that dates at least to the beginning of recorded history. The physical properties of silver allow it to be worked with relative ease, and a respectable silver vessel can be produced using a few simple tools. The most common technique for creating hollowware in preindustrial times was raising. The smith started with a disk of silver, marked its center with a punch, and hammered a series of concentric circles, working out from the center. As the silver near the center was thinned and stretched by hammering, the sides rose to give the whole piece a bowl-like configuration. Even a novice could make a primitive bowl in this manner. The accomplished craftsman could, of course, control this forming process to create many different shapes. More sophisticated shapes required a variety of specialized hammers, stakes, and anvils. Repeated hammering made the silver harder, and it eventually became brittle. To relieve stresses and prevent fractures, the silver was annealed (heated until it was cherry red) and quenched (dunked in cold water). It was then ready for further hammering. This process was repeated many times in the course of making a piece of hollowware.

During the eighteenth century there were two important innovations in silvermaking. One was the development of rolling mills that made it possible to roll out thin sheets of silver. A piece of appropriate dimensions then was cut from the sheet, bent into a circular or oval shape, and the edges soldered together at the seam (hence the term *seamed*)—an ideal forming method for certain pieces in the early neoclassical style. The labor of hand raising was circumvented, greatly shortening the time required to make a piece of hollowware. A related development was the invention, around 1742, of fused plate, sometimes called Sheffield plate for the city that produced so much of it. In the eighteenth century most of the cost of finished wrought silver came from the metal; the cost of labor was small in comparison. Hence, if the cost of the silver could be reduced, the finished product could be sold at a lower price and to a far wider market. The solution was found in the fusibility of silver and copper, the latter a much cheaper metal. A thin bar of silver was bound to a thick bar of copper, heated, and passed through a rolling mill. Under heat and pressure and with repeated passes through the mill, the bars fused and flattened into a sheet, with copper on one side and silver on the other. The sheet could then be cut, bent, and seamed, as with silver, except that the cost of materials was now greatly reduced. The fused plate industry boomed, and its products were shipped throughout the Atlantic world. They looked like silver but cost less. So many different versions of the same forms were available that pattern books were printed and distributed. Both fused plate wares and pattern books became influential carriers of the neoclassical style. The disadvantage of fused plate, however, was that the thin layer of silver easily wore through to reveal the copper body beneath.

The 1830s brought the ultimate refinement in producing ersatz silver when it was discovered that a microscopically thin layer of silver could be deposited on a base metal by electrolysis. Hollowware could be made out of an inexpensive metal like Britannia or German silver (an alloy of copper, nickel, and zinc) and then plated. The bodies of these pieces, or portions thereof, were formed in minutes by spinning on a lathe, another innovation of the period, and the ancillary parts soldered on. Many pieces made in this manner carry the initials "EPNS," which mean electroplated nickel silver. The plated silver industry was founded in England and enjoyed international success long before it came to America. Some of the new forming processes were adopted by American silversmiths, but many pieces continued to be made in a traditional manner.

Using traditional methods, forming the body was only the first step in making a piece of hollowware. In the coffeepot by Myer Myers (no. 230), for example, the body, lid, and pedestal were raised. The finial, gadrooned edge around the lid, handle sockets, and spout were all cast by pouring molten silver into sand molds that had been impressed by hand-carved wooden patterns. With the exception of porringer handles, which were molded in one piece, such cast parts were usually molded as halves, soldered together, and then filed and finished before being soldered to the body. Occasionally entire pieces were made of cast parts, as in the candlesticks by John Burt (no. 20) and Nathaniel Morse (no. 99), but this was rare because of the amount of silver required.

The base of the Myers pot was given its shape by raising, but the decorative pattern was created by chasing, which involves using punches of various shapes. Unlike engraving, chasing removes no metal. Engraving, which creates a furrow in the metal, was usually executed last. It is important to be aware that engraved inscriptions are not necessarily contemporary with the object. Inscriptions and coats of arms were often added by later owners.

Other techniques for forming ancillary parts are drawing and punching, neither of which is a very descriptive term. Drawing is accomplished by pulling a small bar or rod of silver through a hole in a steel plate, the shape of the hole being imparted to the silver. In this manner the silver can be transformed into a molding that can be wrapped around, say, a tankard (see base and midband on the Paul Revere tankards, no. 111). Because of the force required, drawing was done on a draw bench that had a large wheel to provide leverage.

A piece of silver can be decoratively shaped on one side, without the design showing through on the other, using swages. These are steel dies with the design cut into one half of a die shaped to fit one side of the object and the other half of the die shaped to fit the other side of the object. With the silver between the two dies, a sharp blow of a hammer imparts the design to one side but not the other. Drops and shells on the backs of spoons (no. 60) and the more complicated king's pattern on spoon handles (no. 72) were formed in this manner. In the nineteenth century the same principle was applied on a larger scale to factory-produced hollowwares in a process that became known as drop stamping. One of the two dies was allowed to fall in a controlled path from a height of several feet, with gravity providing the necessary force to shape these larger pieces of metal.

A highly effective decorative technique used in the eighteenth century was piercing. It involves drilling a small hole in the silver and then enlarging it into the desired shape with a special saw. Of course there had to be many such voids, all carefully arranged in a pattern, for the technique to be visually effective. The effectiveness of the technique can be seen in the chafing dish by John Potwine (no. 106).

Porringer handles were also pierced to form attractive patterns, like the ubiquitous keyhole and geometric configurations seen in the works of Samuel Vernon (no. 126) and Edward Webb (no. 132). In these cases, however, the voids were not cut but cast.

Yet another decorative technique is cut-card work. Sheet silver, laboriously hammered by the silversmith's apprentice or journeyman, is cut into shapes, sometimes chased or engraved in a pattern, and then soldered to the body. A Jeremiah Dummer tankard (no. 45) has a cut-out piece, on its top, that greatly resembles a furniture escutcheon. A better-known use of cut-card work is found in early eighteenth-century New York tankards, which often have a band of leaflike decoration just above the base molding (no. 221). Similar decorative bands are found on silver-mounted exotic materials from seventeenth-century England.[5]

FUNCTION
Aside from the fact that silver imparts no taste, there is no functional reason not to make objects for food and drink in other materials. Indeed, every silver form exists in some other material, such as pewter, glass, ceramic, or wood. Many silver objects derive their form from objects first made in other materials. Straight-sided silver tankards, for

example, take their tapered shape from ancient tankards made from wooden staves. Of course, common forms are ennobled when rendered in a precious metal, and they cease to be used in quite the same way. While a great deal of silver was made for the table, it was not for everyone's table. It set off the owner from the majority who could not afford it, thereby becoming an index of status.

Conspicuous display historically has been one of the major functions of secular silver. The medieval dresser was developed solely to showcase household plate. By 1608 an English traveler in Paris was startled to see dressers filled with silverware moved into the street in front of owners' houses. Samuel Pepys, the English diarist, gloated over the envy of his friends as "they looked upon all my fine plate," adding, "for I made the best show I could." The oft-quoted remark of William Fitzhugh of Virginia (1676–1701) explains: "I esteem it as well politic as reputable to furnish myself with an hansom Cupboard of plate which gives my self the present use & Credit, is a sure friend at a dead lift, without much loss, or is a certain portion for a Child after my decease." Fitzhugh ordered huge quantities of silver from London and Bristol. In one letter of 1698, he requested two large silver dishes, "80 or 90 ounces each dish," a dozen silver plates, a pair of silver candlesticks "large and fair," two bread plates, and a pair of snuffers and stand. Moreau de St. Méry noted during his sojourn in Philadelphia from 1794 to 1798 that "before and all during dinner, as is the English custom, all the silver one owns is displayed on the sideboard in the dining room."[6]

If silver was useful for conspicuous display, it was also a liquid asset or, as Fitzhugh put it, "a sure friend at a dead lift." Prior to the existence of banks, a portion of an individual's wealth was invested in plate, which was tantamount to having a substantial cash reserve. Of course there was the same risk involved as having cash lying around the house. Silver was portable and easily stolen. That it tended to disappear is attested to by the frequency of advertisements in colonial newspapers describing lost or stolen items and offering rewards for their return. Caution, therefore, became one of the reasons for personalizing silver with initials, inscriptions, or armorial devices through which it could be linked to the owner. George Burns of New York City advertised in February 1764: "Stolen on Friday last, out of the house of George Burns, at the New York Arms in the Broad-way, a silver pint can, stamped on the bottom TH and has a coat of arms at the front of three arrows level, crest a mermaid on a crown and cushion." With such a detailed description there would be no mistaking the cann if it turned up. In the same year, Baltus Van Kleck advertised his loss by burglary of "a silver tankard marked BVKS, the maker's name TS."[7]

The term *marked* in this context usually refers to the owner's initials and not to the identity of the maker. The silversmith's touch is always referred to as the *stamp* (which is how it is used in this catalogue). Thus the "TH" stamp on Burns's cann undoubtedly referred to silversmith Thomas Hammersly, while the "TS" stamp on Van Kleck's tankard probably signified the work of Thomas Shields. These notices appeared with sufficient frequency to suggest that urban crime is not exactly a recent phenomenon. Not that the aggrieved owners expected the thief to return the stolen silver, although rewards sometimes made that a possibility; what they hoped to do was alert silversmiths and others to whom the thief might try to sell the merchandise. The value of silver and gold artifacts was determined by the locally accepted rate of exchange for the metal based on the price per ounce, which varied depending on economic conditions. The same process applied to coins. The value of everything was negotiable. Cash holdings in the seventeenth and eighteenth centuries more often than not consisted of a polyglot collection of currencies, financial instruments, and precious metal artifacts. Stolen from the sleeping chamber of John Walker of New York City was "a small red leather English gilt trunk, containing upwards of £300, Eighty pounds of which were in bills of credit of this province, as half Johannes, 2 English guineas, 1 Spanish pistole, about £25 sterling in English silver, 1 Boston shilling, and several pieces of French silver, 8 or 9 pairs of silver shoe and knee buckles, one pair of which was very large wrought silver marked PMW and one pair of plain knee buckles marked EB."[8]

MONEY AND CREDIT

Business transactions were complicated by the different mediums of exchange. Provincial currencies were not as valuable as their English counterparts, and the content of silver in both coinage and artifacts varied. Merchants had to know the fluctuating worth of French *ecus, livres,* or *Louis d'or;* Dutch *gulden* or *florin;* Portuguese *cruzados, moedas, Johannes* ("Joes"); and Spanish *pesos* ("pieces of eight" or "dollars") or *pistoles* (gold doubloons), to name the more common coins. For British North America, all of these were measured against the pound sterling and then translated into the local colonial currency. Coins constituted real money, but most business transactions were carried out with imaginary money, also called moneys of account. (Ironically, there was no pound sterling unit of currency until the nineteenth century; it was an imaginary unit equal to 20 shillings.) The principal instrument for imaginary money was the bill of exchange, which was used to settle a financial obligation with someone in a distant location. It could, but usually did not, involve the transfer of specie. In seventeenth-century New England the supply of silver coinage was seriously depleted by transfers to the mother country. More commonly throughout the colonial period, a kind of sophisticated barter system using bills of exchange prevailed in international trade.[9]

By far the most common coin of the seventeenth and eighteenth centuries was the Spanish peso. Pesos were produced in mints established by the Spanish in the New World near the silver mines of Mexico, Peru, and Bolivia. The quantities are staggering; during the 1760s the Mexico City mint was striking twenty million Spanish dollars a year. It has been said that the silver that flowed from the New World to the Old World during the sixteenth and seventeenth centuries financed the expansion of Europe and the growth of capitalism. Portions of the Spanish treasure found their way into the melting pots of American silversmiths. The great silver deposits of Central and South America were discovered early in the sixteenth century and exploited for the next several centuries, but the story was different in North America. The prospect of quantities of gold and silver in the northern provinces of New Spain haunted the Spanish imagination and resulted in several abortive attempts to discover new wealth. The Indians of what is now the American Southwest found that one way to get rid of the Spanish was to tell them about far-away fabled cities of gold, such as the Seven Cities of Cibola.[10] Francisco Vasquez de Coronado was the most well-known explorer to fail in the search for precious metals. Not until the middle of the nineteenth century would the substantial gold and silver deposits of the North American West finally be found in California, Nevada, and Colorado.

These discoveries, along with improved refining methods, made it economically feasible to extract silver from hitherto unusable ore, causing the value of silver relative to gold to drop dramatically. In 1750 the value ratio of silver to gold was 1 to 6; in 1988 it was 1 to 65. Silver has almost ceased to be a precious metal. Its industrial applications have far outdistanced its decorative uses. Nor does it carry the cachet that it once did. By 1990, 60 percent of flatware sales were stainless steel, and brides no longer feel compelled to acquire sterling silver place settings, as had been the case with their mothers and grandmothers. As a consequence, one of the oldest of the major silverware companies, Towle Manufacturing, closed its Newburyport, Massachusetts, plant in 1990.[11] From relative scarcity in the seventeenth and eighteenth centuries through the cornucopia of increasing abundance in the nineteenth and early twentieth centuries to its status today as a modest luxury item, the social value of silver has declined along with its relative monetary value. Clearly, the function of silver in society has changed dramatically from the days of William Fitzhugh.

NOTES

1. Robert G. Reese, "Silver," in *Minerals Yearbook* (Washington, D.C.: Dept. of Interior, U. S. Bureau of Mines, 1991), pp. 1389–1412. It is important to distinguish between refined silver produced and silver actually used in industrial applications. For 1991, 3,972 metric tons of silver were used, but only 3,743 tons were produced. The large quantites of silver held by investors and in government and industrial stockpiles are also a source of the metal. Production of silver is not simply a matter of supply and demand. Much of it is produced as the by-product of mining for other nonferous metals. A significant amount of silver is also recycled from scrap.

2. As silver ages, its appearance changes, and connoisseurs admire old silver for its patina; see B. Seymour Rabinovitch, "The Patina of Antique Silver: A Scientific Appraisal," *Silver Society Journal* (Winter 1990): 13–22. After exploring other possible causes, Rabinovitch concludes that the patina of old silver is the result of thousands of minute scratches acquired from "wear-and-care."

3. *Touching Gold and Silver* (London: Goldsmiths' Company, 1978), pp. 14–16. See also Charles James Jackson, *English Goldsmiths and Their Marks* (1921; reprint, New York: Dover Publications, 1964), chap. 2.

4. See Robert B. Barker, "Proposals for an Assaying System in Pennsylvania, 1753–1770," *Silver Society Journal* (Winter 1991): 75–79. The bills proposed in 1767, 1769, and 1770 were all entitled "An Act for the Prevention of Frauds and Abuses in Gold and Silver Wares Made and Sold in This Province." Owen Biddle, Edward Duffield, and John Jennings, not one of them a working or retailing silversmith, were put forward as potential assay masters. In a 1975 test conducted in Winterthur's analytical lab, silver content in objects stamped "coin" varied from 84.4 to 91.3 percent; those stamped "pure coin" ranged from 83.0 to 91.9 percent, those stamped "premium" fell between 87.0 and 90.0 percent; and silver marked "standard" ranged from 84.5 to 92.2 percent.

5. For a serpentine tankard equipped with silver mounts, see *Octagon* 12, no. 3 (Autumn 1975): 13. The silver mounts were made by John Plummer of York about 1657.

6. Fernand Braudel, *The Structures of Everyday Life: The Limits of the Possible*, vol. 1 of *Civilization and Capitalism, Fifteenth to Eighteenth Century* (New York: Harper and Row, 1981), pp. 304–5. *The Diary of Samuel Pepys*, trans. Robert Latham and William Matthews, 11 vols. (Berkeley and Los Angeles: University of California Press, 1974–83), 8:157; Richard Beale Davis, ed., *William Fitzhugh and His Chesapeake World, 1767–1701* (Chapel Hill: University of North Carolina Press for the Virginia Historical Society, 1963), p. 246; *Moreau de St. Méry's American Journey*, trans. Kenneth Roberts and Anna Roberts (New York: Doubleday, 1947), p. 266. See Grahame Clark, *Symbols of Excellence: Precious Materials as Expressions of Status* (New York and London: Cambridge University Press, 1986), esp. chap. 4. Clark is concerned primarily with ancient and premodern cultures.

7. *New York Mercury*, February 27, October 1, 1764.

8. *New York Mercury*, July 27, 1761.

9. See John J. McCusker, *Money and Exchange in Europe and America, 1600–1775: A Handbook* (Chapel Hill: University of North Carolina Press for the Institute of Early American History and Culture, 1978), esp. chaps. 1, 3.

10. Earl J. Hamilton, *American Treasure and the Price Revolution in Spain, 1501–1650* (Cambridge: Harvard University Press, 1934). See also Jeanne Prial Gordus, "American Silver and European Coinage in the Sixteenth and Seventeenth Centuries" (Ph.D. diss., University of Michigan, 1979). Marc Simmons, *New Mexico: An Interpretive History* (Albuquerque: University of New Mexico Press, 1988), chap. 1.

11. *New York Times*, January 7, 1990; *Portland Press Herald* (Maine), July 27, 1990.

Silver and Material Culture

The study of material culture is based on the proposition that objects are a valid reflection of the culture that produced them and, therefore, that the study of objects can tell us a good deal about the people who made, sold, or used them. Artifacts (as anthropologists call them), like all historical documents, are messages from the past. As art historian George A. Kubler put it, they are like the light from distant stars that is old by the time it reaches earth. What we see in starlight, therefore, is a past event. So too are objects past events locked in material form. An artifact is a record of human will in action—not simply an accidental impression but a purposive event, matter given shape by the mind.[1] Thus, if we can learn how objects were made and distributed, who owned them and why, and what they signified to their owners and their contemporaries, we will gain useful insights into the past. This is not to assert the primacy of objects over documents; it is rather to assert that through artifacts we contact the past in a unique, affective way. Objects are made by and for people. They are not apart from but are part of society. Man the artificer makes artifacts for a variety of reasons, sometimes to fulfill basic needs but more often to say something about his place in the world; his aspirations; his relation to nature, God, and his fellow man; and his love of form and materials for their own sake. Artifacts incorporate the cultural baggage of previous generations through both unselfconscious tradition and sophisticated selection. As messages from the past, they carry meaning. Our task is to discover how to tap that meaning—but this is not easily accomplished.

E. McClung Fleming's now-classic "Artifact Study: A Proposed Model" uses a seventeenth-century court cupboard to suggest the different levels of information and interpretation that are possible with objects. Fleming's model grew out of his close working relationship with furniture historian Benno M. Forman, whose intensive examination of seventeenth-century New England furniture and pertinent local records enabled him to identify and reconstruct the web of relationships among furniture craftsmen and provide new knowledge of craft practices and local and regional preferences.[2]

Early American silver is particularly amenable to material culture analysis in that, as a class of objects, it is often better documented than most other three-dimensional artifacts. Not only does it bear makers' or sellers' stamps that are relatively easy to identify, but it is often engraved with coats of arms, crests, initials, or inscriptions that relate it to specific persons or families. Silver was often enumerated in estate inventories, and sometimes it is possible to correlate the items listed with surviving examples. Silver, then, has a collective provenance that makes it useful for studying social history through patterns of patronage, kinship, status, and other avenues of historical inquiry.[3]

A case in point is the great sugar box made by Edward Winslow (no. 140) and presented to Daniel and Elizabeth Oliver by William Partridge in 1702. Not only is it rich in iconographic allusions to Renaissance literary ideals and folk beliefs (themes of courtly love and chivalry combined with the notion that sugar, when it was newly introduced in Europe, was thought to increase fertility), the box also embodies a network of relationships that maintained and perpetuated a privileged class.[4] Although he was regarded with near awe as a "Puritan saint," Daniel Oliver was rich by American standards of the time. His insistence on a hard currency in the 1720s was consistent with the views of his peers. Oliver shared with his peers a belief in hierarchy and privilege. He expected his social inferiors to be deferential in all things, especially when it came to making decisions affecting the common welfare. The social and political tensions of the 1720s grew to explosive dimensions by the time his two sons gained positions of prominence in the administration of Gov. Thomas Hutchinson. The attitudes of the father lived on in the sons, who, unable or unwilling to adapt to social and political changes, found themselves increasingly at odds with anti-crown and anti-elite sentiments.

As chief justice of Massachusetts Bay Colony, Daniel's son Peter was second only to the governor in importance. When Peter traveled from Boston to his house in Middleborough, he rode in a coach flanked by scarlet-clad outriders.[5] This, after all, was how the judges of the highest English courts comported themselves, and he felt it only fitting that he respect the dignity of his office in a similar fashion. His brother Andrew died a year before Lexington and Concord, prior to the time when like-minded people faced the crucial decision of whether to stay, thereby accepting the uncertain world of potential republican rule, or leave, thereby possibly renouncing the land of their birth and most of their property forever. When the crisis came, Peter had no recourse but to abandon his homeland and flee with the British garrison to Halifax and, eventually, to England—but not before making a frantic visit to Oliver Hall in Middleborough to retrieve some cherished possessions, among them the sugar box once owned by his parents.

Today it takes some effort to recreate the mentalité of the world of Daniel Oliver and his sons, but this is the necessary context for understanding this object. That in 1776—seventy-four years after it was given to his parents—the box commanded the attention of its owner to such an extent that he retrieved it at considerable risk is remarkable testimony to its power. Surely, more than mere sentiment was at work here. The box was charged with more than parental associations, dear though they certainly were. In all likelihood, it signified Peter Oliver's world in microcosm, the last part of it that remained whole. If this is all he could retain of that world, then its retrieval was worth the risk. The box preserved symbolically the network of kin and friends that had nurtured Oliver from his earliest days. The beloved child of a loving family, both immediate and extended, and beneficiary of the many perquisites of his class, Oliver cherished the box as an icon of all he had lost to a hostile world.

Like the Tory families of colonial Boston, the sugar box harked back to an earlier time. Its amatory and martial allusions suggest the world of courtly love and chivalry that found expression in such sixteenth-century works as Edmund Spenser's *Faery Queene* (ca. 1590) and Torquato Tasso's *Gerusalemme Liberta* (1581) and in Henry Peacham's *Complete Gentleman* (1622), a guide for manners and behavior that was profoundly influential during the seventeenth and eighteenth centuries. The vocabulary and manners embodied in these works were, however, not intended for everyone— only for the privileged. Implicit in the sugar box is the assumption that only those with appropriate education would understand its iconography or know that its form was derived from Italian *cassone* of the Renaissance.[6]

The houses built by many of these Loyalist gentlemen also looked to older English prototypes. Oliver Hall was characteristic of this now-vanished species of early American architecture. Based on an English manor house, "with a steep roof and deep, jutting eaves, with walls of white plaster and portico of oak," it was famous for its size and elegance. The wainscoting and wall hangings, along with many other appurtenances, were imported from England. The library occupied a separate wing, and "pleasure houses" dotted the gardens. The hall furnishings are said to have included "high crownback tapestry cushioned chairs," which sound like chairs in the William and Mary style—one more indication of an owner looking toward a glorious past. Following the Olivers' departure, the house, a hated reminder of Tory splendor and British power, was sacked and burned. It is said that for years after, local women wore sprigs of gold leaf in their hair from the wallpaper torn out of Oliver Hall.[7]

More accessible to a present-day audience is the exquisite workmanship of the sugar box, which challenges the plasticity of the metal to its very limits. (So thin is the metal that the combination of stresses introduced by the chasing process and wear from years of polishing have caused fissures to open along fold lines.) It has been proposed that the sophisticated chasing must have been the work of a highly skilled European craftsman recently arrived in Boston, such as Henry Hurst from Sweden. While serving as a journeyman to Richard Conyers, Hurst was charged by Conyers with violating the terms of his agreement. Because Edward Winslow and James Barnes paid his bond, Barbara McLean Ward argues that Hurst must have been making silver for them as well as for Conyers.[8] So little of Hurst's work survives (nothing as sophisticated as the sugar box) that there is little point in attributing the sugar box to his hand instead of Winslow's. The box under discussion is one of four bearing Winslow's stamp. (Only nine American sugar boxes survive: four by Winslow, four by John Coney, and one by Daniel Greenough.) Although Winslow's boxes are more sophisticated than earlier examples by Coney, they embody the same form and many of the same decorative elements. It appears that Winslow (or his workman) improved upon a well-established form by having the technical virtuosity and design skills to create monumental and exciting chased silver hollowware in early eighteenth-century Boston.

That this form is in fact a sugar box is suggested by the listings in estate inventories. The inventory of James Lloyd, Boston, 1693, refers to "2 Sugar boxes" and "a large Sugar box" amid other plate. More to the point, Winslow's own box, now at Yale University Art Gallery, appears in the inventory of his son's estate in 1770. Like the Tory architecture, the sugar box itself refers to an earlier time when sugar was expensive and often kept under lock and key. It is unlikely that by 1702, the date the box was given to the Olivers, the cost of sugar still warranted such an expensive container. By the 1730s the more prosaic sugar bowl had begun to appear. The sugar box was a short-lived phenomenon made over about a twenty-year period, beginning in the 1680s. It coincided, more or less, with a period of great prosperity in the Massachusetts Bay Colony when many fortunes were made in mercantile pursuits and silversmiths enjoyed a relatively high status. The prosperity did not last. By the middle teens, and for the generation following, economic growth slowed, and so did the production of innovative monumental silver in Boston.

This, then, is the context of the Oliver sugar box. As with any great work of art, the search for its meaning takes us far afield. It is the essence of material culture, however, to delve deeply and widely into the meaning of things, ultimately so that we can, in a sense, meet the people associated with them on their own ground and see the world through their eyes. If, as noted earlier, artifacts are events locked in time, they are also lenses that can help us bring into focus "the world we have lost."[9]

NOTES

1. George A. Kubler, *The Shape of Time: Remarks on the History of Things* (New Haven: Yale University Press, 1962), pp. 19–20. Henry Glassie, "Studying Material Culture Today," in *Living in a Material World: Canadian and American Approaches to Material Culture*, ed. Gerald L. Pocius (St. John's: Institute of Social and Economic Research, Memorial University of Newfoundland, 1991), pp. 253–66; Jules David Prown, "Mind in Matter: An Introduction to Material Culture Theory and Method," *Winterthur Portfolio* 17, no. 1 (Spring 1982): 1–19.

2. E. McClung Fleming, "Artifact Study: A Proposed Model," in *Winterthur Portfolio 9*, ed. Ian M.G. Quimby (Charlottesville: University Press of Virginia for the Henry Francis du Pont Winterthur Museum, 1974), pp. 153–73; Benno M. Forman, *American Seating Furniture, 1630–1730* (New York: W. W. Norton, 1988).

3. For an early attempt to link a common silver form to cultural beliefs, see Anthony N. B. Garvan, "The New England Porringer: An Index of Custom, in *Annual Report of the Smithsonian Institution* (Washington, D.C.: Government Printing Office, 1958), pp. 543–52.

4. See catalogue for biography of Winslow; for the Olivers, see no. 140. Edward J. Nygren, "Edward Winslow's Sugar Boxes," *Yale University Art Gallery Bulletin* 33, no. 2 (Autumn 1971): 39–52.

5. Thomas Weston, Jr., "Peter Oliver," *New England Historical and Genealogical Register* 40, no. 3 (July 1886): 241–52; no. 4 (October 1886): 349–59.

6. Nygren, "Edward Winslow's Sugar Boxes," p. 40.

7. Thomas Weston, *History of the Town of Middleboro, Massachusetts* (Boston and New York: Houghton Mifflin Co., 1906), pp. 359–84. While the architectural nature of Oliver Hall is only hinted at, other Tory houses in the area bear out the assertion of backward-looking residences. Col. Francis Brinley of Dorchester (no. 106), also a Loyalist, built an H-plan house that resembled the family seat at Datchet, near Windsor, in England. It is said to have had colonnades, a vestibule with massive mahogany doors studded with silver, and a hall with a "lofty dome of painted glass." Notwithstanding the probable exaggeration in an account written years later, the H plan alone is a key indicator, for it harks back to English building modes of the sixteenth century. This and other houses no longer extant suggest the need for further study to define more clearly the character of Tory material life. For the Brinley house, see Francis S. Drake, *The Town of Roxbury: Its Memorable Persons and Places* (Roxbury, 1878), pp. 327–28.

8. Barbara McLean Ward, "The Craftsman in a Changing Society: Boston Goldsmiths, 1690–1730" (Ph.D. diss., Boston University, 1983), p. 162.

9. Peter Laslett, *The World We Have Lost: England before the Industrial Age* (3d ed.; New York: Charles Scribner's Sons, 1984).

The Question of Authorship

Unlike most other decorative artifacts, silver usually bears one or more stamps that allegedly indicate who made it. Knowing who made the silver and where the silversmith worked helps to establish provenance. If a maker is early and well known, then his silver generally will command a higher price. As a result, much attention has been lavished on identifying and documenting silversmiths, creating a rather extensive literature on American, British, and Continental practitioners. This research was undertaken with the assumption that the silversmith whose name or initials appear on a piece actually made it. Collectors delight in the knowledge that they can put a name, sometimes a face, and occasionally even a personality to the identifying marks on their antique silver. Many carry in their minds an idealized concept of the craftsman: a figure who labored, usually alone, to produce the finest quality work at low, nonunion prices. This romantic notion, which was a tenet of the arts and crafts movement, does not recognize that silversmiths and other preindustrial craftsmen were also entrepreneurs who often ran large shops employing many people, bought and sold a variety of goods, and, if they were really successful, ceased to be known as silversmiths at all. Purveyors of the myth of the noble craftsman have managed to ignore any such evidence.

As collectors in and out of museums began acquiring post-1830 American silver, they inevitably encountered large manufacturers like the Tiffany and Gorham companies. They also found earlier firms that ran virtual factory operations, albeit on a smaller scale, like that of Robert and William Wilson at their Philadelphia Silver Spoon and Fork Manufactory and the firm of Curry & Preston, also in Philadelphia. Most collectors realized that the nature of the silvermaking business had changed dramatically in the nineteenth century as it became more capital intensive and as silver was made in much greater quantities and sold in a national, rather than just a local, market. The focus necessarily shifted from makers (there were now thousands of anonymous makers) to designers. Thus, for example, any discussion of Tiffany silver is incomplete without reference to Edward C. Moore, who is generally regarded as the creative genius behind much of the Tiffany line during the 1860s, 1870s, and 1880s.

Increasing interest in nineteenth- and early twentieth-century silver corrected to some degree the oversights and prejudices of an earlier generation. Expansion of the canon, however, did little to correct the myth of the noble craftsman. Artisans like Paul Revere in Boston, Paul de Lamerie in London, and Thomas Germain in Paris continued to be revered for the quality of their work and for the implicit notion that they made everything bearing their stamps. Gradually, as silver scholars have studied the scant surviving records of the seventeenth and eighteenth centuries, new light has been shed on the question of authorship and of business practices in general.

What does it mean to have a "maker's" stamp on silver? The question arose early in London. By 1675, according to one authority, the maker was often distinct from the retailer, a state of affairs later recognized by the Plate Offenses Act of 1739, which required registry not only of the plate worker's stamp but also that of the merchant or shopkeeper who commissioned the object. With time and increasing specialization, the question of authorship became murkier. Reflecting on these historical developments, Walter T. Prideaux, clerk of the Goldsmiths' Company, told J. Paul De Castro in 1926:

The retailer who causes the wares to be made, the designer, the master manufacturer, the manufacturer's workmen who put the metal into shape, and (in some cases) the chaser who adds his skill have all claims to be registered as the maker. Even with the fullest knowledge of the different stages through which a ware has passed, it must often be difficult to say who has provided the master mind and been the real maker; and the retailer who has caused the ware to be made and adopted it as his own comes in most cases to be regarded as the person whose mark the ware should bear.[1]

By the twentieth century this was certainly the case, but, as noted, the question of authorship had been around for at least 250 years.

In her study of early Boston goldsmiths Barbara McLean Ward distinguishes between merchant-producers, jobbers, and small independent producers.[2] The merchant-producers tended to control the market as a result of their connections to wealthy patrons, connections often based on extensive kinship networks. Their goldsmiths' work helped to support their mercantile ventures. The merchant-producers, while running their own shops, also farmed out extra work to lesser craftsmen whose operations verged on the marginal. Those who lived primarily from such work Ward calls jobbers. Those who combined direct commissions from patrons with farmed-out work she refers to as small independent producers. The financial gap between the merchant-producers and the two dependent groups was often vast.

What all of this indicates is that merchant-goldsmiths did not make all of their own silver. It is quite likely, therefore, that some silver bearing the stamps of, say, John Edwards, John Coney, and Edward Winslow—all of whom ranked in the top 10 percent of the trade—was actually made by the likes of Thomas Savage, Joseph Kneeland, and Daniel Legare, jobbers and small independents. Little of the latter group's work survives—or does it survive under the guise of another's stamp?

A few years ago an eighteenth-century silversmith's account book surfaced and was purchased by Yale University Art Gallery.[3] The volume is rich in transactions among Boston silversmiths. Although it lacks the owner's name, internal evidence suggests that it belonged to Zachariah Brigden, a noted Boston goldsmith who may have trained under Thomas Edwards and who, in any case, married Edwards's daughter. Among Brigden's many patrons were Ebenezer Storer (to whom he was related by marriage through his wife's family), "the Honorable Nathaniel Sparhawk," William Pepperrell, Esq., and Isaac Royall. Among his artisan customers were silversmith Benjamin Hurd (son of Jacob and brother of Nathaniel Hurd) of Boston; Samuel Griffith, goldsmith of Portsmouth, New Hampshire; and Daniel Boyer, goldsmith and jeweler of Boston.

The transactions with the latter group show a different pattern from that found by Ward for the earlier period. In 1773 Brigden sold a cann to Hurd. To Griffith, in 1752, he sold black pots, saltpeter, punches, and sand (for casting)—all silversmiths' supplies. To Boyer, in 1773, he sold large quantities of wrought silver and made repairs to old silver. Boyer paid him mostly in silver by the ounce but sometimes in buttons, earrings, and buckles and once by ten gold beads. It appears that specialization dictated this arrangement, with Brigden providing Boyer with wrought silver for retail and Boyer providing Brigden with some jewelry and the metal for fashioning wrought silver. It is unclear whether Boyer made the buttons, earrings, and buckles that he offered in trade or whether he imported them. Boyer's activities presage the later pattern in which the goldsmith-jeweler became primarily a retailer. The question remains, whose stamp went on the silver made by Brigden and retailed by Boyer?[4]

The best-documented silversmiths in the colonial period are the Richardsons of Philadelphia. Large quantities of silver survive bearing the stamps of Joseph Richardson, Sr., Joseph Richardson, Jr., and the partnership of the latter with his brother Nathaniel. Their business records show that they imported substantial amounts of silver from London, some of which resembles surviving silver bearing their stamps. Take, for example, the fine coffeepot made for Sarah Marshall Morris (no. 457). It is a tall, stately, double-bellied pot, mounted on a pedestal, with a cast S-curve spout. In 1784 the Richardsons ordered from their London supplier "3 Silver Pollished 3 pint Coffee potts double bellied with cast spouts to weigh about 38 oz a piece."[5] The description and weight match the Morris pot. What can be made of this information? Were the Richardsons importing un-marked silver and stamping it with their initials, or were they simply supplementing their own production with these imports? And how were these imports stamped? Did they carry a full set of London marks, or, because they were sold in the colonies, were they unmarked? Spectrographic analysis of the Morris pot shows that three out of the four parts tested meet the sterling standard rather than the characteristic profile for American silver of the period. This does not prove, however, that it is English-made silver since there are a number of documented examples of American-made silver that also meet the sterling standard. In short, there is no way to contradict the claim of authorship by the Richardsons, only circumstantial evidence that causes us to wonder.

We know from newspaper advertisements and other sources that large quantities of English silver were imported into the colonies. In 1761 Gerard Beekman asked Capt. William Davis "once more to bring me some Plate for my Own use. Let it be fashion-able, Genteel and Light, Viz. One Large Salver of about forty Ounces, One Sizeable Coffee Pott with a small salver or stand for the same, One sett of Castors [and] waiter, Two sass boats, and one bread Baskit."[6] Many affluent merchants and all royal gover-nors equipped themselves with English plate. Anglican churches in America were often the recipients of London-made silver communion services presented by the sovereign. This ecclesiastical silver, much of which survives, is now the principal remnant of the once great horde of English silver in America. Some secular English silver was pre-served within families such as the Bowdoins of Massachusetts, the Frankses of Philadel-phia, the Carrolls of Maryland, the Randolphs of Virginia, and the Lenoxes of New York. Still, a far greater amount has lost its provenance and has been dismissed by col-lectors who prefer silver thought to have been made by American craftsmen. The rigid taxonomy of museums has often relegated British and Continental silver (some with American associations) to European decorative arts departments, where it is held in low esteem. Research is needed to rediscover and to place in context this important part of our material history.

Perhaps one of the more intriguing examples of mixed authorship was discovered by Christine Wallace Laidlaw in her study of Teunis D. DuBois. In the 1790s DuBois worked in New York City, where he learned his trade from his brother Joseph and later became his partner. Together the brothers made silver for William G. Forbes as well as for their own retail trade. Laidlaw found that sheaf-of-wheat and eagle stamps, com-monly referred to as pseudohallmarks and thought to be meaningless, were used by the DuBois brothers on silver they made for Forbes and that bore Forbes's stamp. In 1797 Teunis DuBois set up his own shop not far from silversmith John Vernon. He worked as a jobber selling silver to merchants, jewelers, and other silversmiths, such as Vernon, John Targee, Lemuel Wells, and John Schanck. During the depressed economy of 1800, DuBois moved to Freehold Township in Monmouth County, New Jersey. He took up farming but continued to make silver, mostly spoons destined for the wholesale market, a reversal of the usual pattern of distribution in which silver was made in the city and dispersed to the hinterland.[7] Many of DuBois's spoons bear his stamps: "T•D•DuBOIS" or "T•D•D." The spoons sold to John Vernon bear Vernon's stamp plus the double sheaf-of-wheat or eagle and letter *P*, both in a shield, that Laidlaw has clearly demonstrated signify Teunis D. DuBois. Just how representative this practice was is hard to say, but it does serve as a warning that the silversmithing business often involved complex business arrangements that may not always be reflected in the stamps.

The quintessential colonial silversmith, the one who best epitomizes the legendary noble craftsman, was unquestionably Paul Revere, Jr. Even without the aura that gathered about him following the publication of the Henry Wadsworth Longfellow poem "Paul Revere's Ride," his career and persona fit the mold and met our expectations. His portrait by John Singleton Copley tells it all. Here is no bewigged shopkeeper who aspires to merchant status. Here is an honest craftsman, wearing his working clothes, who has paused momentarily to look us in the eye. There is an engaging sense of immediacy in the portrait, a sense that this is reality instead of a painted likeness. How could one not admire such an engaging fellow who projects republican virtue, good citizenship, and technical competence?

The story of Revere's life and work is equally impressive. Son of an immigrant, he learned his craft from his father, worked hard, was active in local affairs, participated in important historical events, was an enterprising businessman and manufacturer, and acquired great wealth. He was perhaps the most prolific silversmith of his day. Because of his fame, Revere's silver sells today for high prices. In other words, he was—and remains—an American success story. Surely the Revere stamp on a silver teapot guarantees that it was made by the hands of the master himself, as portrayed in the Copley portrait. The realistic answer is, well, maybe. Few silversmiths had such long careers, and even fewer successfully bridged the tumultuous years of the Revolution, enjoying marked success in the radically different worlds of before and after.

Revere's early career was not unusual, albeit more blessed than many. He was fortunate in having been trained by his father, who, in turn, had been trained by John Coney. His marriage had the much-sought-after result of providing him with a network of patrons. He was a gregarious soul who commanded the respect of friends and neighbors. His shop, at least in the early years, was probably typical, and even in his middle years had no more than the normal complement of apprentices and journeymen. His business suffered from the time of the Stamp Act until well after the Revolution, but he was enterprising. His business improved to the extent that it provided surplus funds for other business ventures.

Thanks to the survival of so many of his account books, we have a good idea of what came out of his shop and who his customers were. Deborah Anne Federhen's analysis of these accounts shows that operations during the prewar years differed markedly from those of the postwar period. The later period saw not only an increase in the production of silver but great increases in ancillary activities such as the number of engravings and prints produced. During this period Revere also began manufacturing sheet copper and casting cannons and bells. He could no longer afford to work at the bench; he was now a manager and entrepreneur, and his silver shop increasingly came under the direction of his son, Paul Revere III. That there were many different hands employed is evident from the variations in the silver produced in the postwar period. As Federhen points out, "The silver is not hammered to a consistent gauge; covers do not always fit perfectly; and a number of variations in seaming techniques are in evidence."[8] The elder Revere continued to guide stylistic development, for his correspondence shows an avid interest in the trade catalogues for fused plate from Sheffield. Many examples of silver produced in the Revere shop in the 1780s and 1790s rely for their inspiration on patterns illustrated in these catalogues. Overall artistic control remained with the master, but production and quality control were overseen by others. The Revere stamp had come to serve as the imprimatur for the work of others. The craftsman in the Copley portrait had given way to the elderly businessman portrayed by Gilbert Stuart in 1813.

It is fitting to conclude discussions of authorship with the first names in American silver, John Hull and Robert Sanderson. Hull traditionally has been viewed as the father of the silversmiths' craft in America, but there is every reason to believe that Sanderson is more deserving of the title. He was older, had served a proper apprenticeship in England, and had practiced in London before coming to America. Hull, on the other hand, had rudimentary training from his stepbrother Richard Storer, who was not a practicing goldsmith. The one surviving piece bearing only Hull's stamp is a poorly wrought beaker, a performance that reflects his inadequate training. The other works bearing his stamp also bear the stamp of Sanderson, his partner from 1652 on and the probable maker of all such pieces. From Patricia E. Kane's study of the partnership, it appears that Hull was primarily a manager and entrepreneur, and Sanderson was the working craftsman. Hull amassed his wealth through investments in shipping and land. His business affairs were so complex it is unlikely that he would have had time to work at the bench. It is significant that his diary speaks extensively of his business dealings but is virtually silent when it comes to silversmithing.[9] He does record taking apprentices Jeremiah Dummer and Samuel Paddy, and there are references to establishing the mint where he and Sanderson produced coins for Massachusetts Bay Colony. The fact that Hull felt compelled to ask Sanderson to join him in this effort is further proof that Hull was not up to the technical demands of the enterprise.

From the very beginnings of silversmithing in British North America, and extending to its antecedents in England, questions of authorship have arisen. For the most part these questions defy resolution. There is enough evidence to suggest, however, that the so-called maker's stamp should be viewed as a sort of trademark—rather than as an artist's signature—suggesting a certain level of quality and reliability. As with modern products, the name attached to a product does not always signify the manufacturer. Stamps were also there by tradition to assure accountablity and recourse in the event of fraud. Thus, whether the silversmith actually made the piece was less important than the implicit guarantee offered by his stamp. As long as this is understood, we can continue to make guarded attributions based on stamps.

NOTES

1. As quoted in J. Paul De Castro, *The Law and Practice of Hall-Marking Gold and Silver Wares* (London: Crosby Lockwood and Son, 1926), p. 40. See also John Culme, *Attitudes to Old Plate, 1750–1900* (London: Sotheby's, 1985).

2. Barbara McLean Ward, "The Craftsman in a Changing Society: Boston Goldsmiths, 1690–1730" (Ph.D. diss., Boston University, 1983).

3. A photocopy is available in the Winterthur library.

4. Since this writing, Hilary Anderson, a Winterthur Fellow, analyzed the account book in "The Business of Silversmith Zachariah Brigden" (Master's thesis, University of Delaware, forthcoming).

5. Martha Gandy Fales, *Joseph Richardson and Family: Philadelphia Silversmiths* (Middletown, Conn.: Weslyan University Press for the Historical Society of Pennsylvania, 1974).

6. Philip L. White, ed., *The Beekman Mercantile Papers, 1746–1799*, 3 vols. (New York: New-York Historical Society, 1956), 1:370.

7. Christine Wallace Laidlaw, "Silver by the Dozen: The Wholesale Business of Teunis D. DuBois," *Winterthur Portfolio* 23, no. 1 (Spring 1988): 25–50. The DuBois pattern of distribution is paralleled by David Alling of Newark, N.J., who made chairs for the wholesale market in New York City; see Don C. Skemer, "David Alling's Chair Manufactory: Craft Industrialization in Newark, New Jersey, 1801–1854," *Winterthur Portfolio* 22, no. 1 (Spring 1987): 1–21.

8. Deborah A. Federhen, "From Artisan to Entrepreneur: Paul Revere's Silver Shop Operation," in *Paul Revere—Artisan, Businessman, and Patriot: The Man Behind the Myth* (Boston: Paul Revere Memorial Association, 1988), pp. 65–93. Paul Revere's account books are owned by the Massachusetts Historical Society; microfilm copies are at Winterthur.

9. Patricia E. Kane, "John Hull and Robert Sanderson: First Masters of New England Silver" (Ph.D. diss., Yale University, 1987); "The Diaries of John Hull, Mint-Master and Treasurer of the Colony of Massachusetts," *Transactions and Collections of the American Antiquarian Society* 3 (1857): 109–316.

Style in American Silver

Stylistic terminology in American decorative arts has oscillated between antiquarian terms derived from English decorative arts and art historical terms derived from the European fine arts. Thus, in the first case, we have William and Mary, Queen Anne, Georgian, Chippendale, Sheraton, Hepplewhite, and Regency, while in the second we have mannerist, baroque, rococo, and neoclassical. By more-or-less common agreement Americans prefer seventeenth century over James I, Charles I, and Charles II (both Charleses sometimes rendered as Caroline or Carolean), and Charles Montgomery firmly established the term *federal* in place of *Sheraton* and *Hepplewhite*. The French term *empire* has long been accepted for *late classical*. Over the past generation the trend in America has been toward art historical rather than antiquarian usage.

In his pioneering *Old Plate, Ecclesiastical, Decorative, and Domestic: Its Makers and Marks* (1888), J. H. Buck avoided the question of style entirely and was more concerned with establishing chronological sequence. Similarly, E. Alfred Jones, in his landmark work *Old Silver of American Churches* (1913), relied on physical description accompanied by documentation on donors. Francis Hill Bigelow, who encouraged Jones to undertake the tome on church silver, followed the same pattern in his *Historic Silver of the Colonies and Its Makers* (1917). C. Louise Avery, in *Early American Silver* (1930), was reticent about using stylistic categories, going only so far as to say that "Philadelphia silverwork made prior to the Revolution is . . . based rather closely upon English styles," without ever specifying what those styles were. By 1949, however, John Marshall Phillips had adopted hybrid terms combining antiquarian and art historical usage. Some of the chapter titles in his *American Silver*— "The Baroque of the William and Mary Style," "The Exuberance of the Rococo," and "The Classical Reserve of the Federal Style"—suggest the influence of the art historians at Yale, where Phillips struggled for intellectual respectability as he taught a course in American decorative arts popularly known as "pots and pans." The Yale method took root, however, as several chapter titles in Graham Hood's *American Silver: A History of Style, 1650–1900* (1971) show: "Baroque Silver of the William and Mary Period," "Fully Developed Rococo Silver," and "The Classical Taste of the Early Republic." Phillips would have been delighted that his successor at Yale so nearly followed his schema. Martha Gandy Fales's *Early American Silver for the Cautious Collector* (1970) and *Early American Silver* (1973) varied this formula somewhat. Subheads in her chapter on style read as follows: The Lingering Renaissance Tradition (1650–1690), The Advent of the Baroque (1690–1720), The Age of Hogarth (1720–1750), Elaboration of the Rococo (1750–1775), Return to the Classical (1775–1810), and The Reaffirmation of Antiquity (1810–1840). Her classifications correspond, of course, to the accepted terms for American furniture: *seventeenth century, William and Mary, Queen Anne, Chippendale, federal,* and *empire.*

More recent scholarship has tended toward art historical terminology. In *New England Begins: The Seventeenth Century* (1982), Robert F. Trent argues for a strong mannerist influence in seventeenth-century furniture and silver. In her dissertation on Boston goldsmiths, Barbara McLean Ward uses *baroque* and *rococo*, but she also refers to the Queen Anne style for lack of an art historical equivalent.[1] We continue to labor under an inconsistent typology that cannot classify a half dozen or so styles without using a combination of art historical terms, the names of British sovereigns, and the names of designers, centuries, and eras.

Varied as they are, all of these stylistic designations have—or had—some justification. The problem comes when they are removed from their original context. Can we really include the Edward Winslow sugar box (no. 140) in the same stylistic category as the paintings of Caravaggio and the architecture of Bernini? Is not *William and Mary* a more apt stylistic descriptor than *baroque* for this important work of American silver, as suggested by recent scholarship?[2] Although the William and Mary style shares some characteristics of the baroque, as a stylistic term it is more focused and, hence, more useful for our purposes. In an American context, of course, even the most appropriate terms sometimes have to be stretched.

Before discussing the progression of styles, there are two points to keep in mind. One is the relative backwardness of early American society and its remoteness from the style centers of Europe; the other concerns the functional aspect of silver objects and the resistance of certain forms to stylistic change. Before independence, British North America was a colonial culture on the periphery of the Atlantic world, and the center for that world was London. Whether capable of doing so or not, silversmiths repeatedly claimed that their work was as well made and fashionable as that from London. American silver, however, partakes more of the character of silver made in the larger market towns of England. The level of wealth and sophistication among the American silversmith's customers simply did not match that of the English court and aristocracy, notwithstanding Daniel Neal's oft-repeated quote of 1718: "A gentleman from London would almost think himself at home in Boston, when he observes . . . their houses, their furniture . . . their dress, and conversation." Significantly, Neal also adds, "They affect to be as much English as possible."[3]

Just as it was possible for a British officer to have the latest fashion creamware in remote Fort Michilimackinack, in what is now Michigan, so it was even easier for Boston, New York, Philadelphia, or Virginia gentry to have reasonably current fashions from "home."[4] But of course we are speaking of consumer goods that were affordable in the colonies, just like those in English market towns and among affluent London tradesmen.

Given this situation, American silversmiths produced fewer forms, most of which were generally smaller and lighter than their high-fashion English counterparts. As always, cultural, social, and religious conditions dictated the forms produced. Dutch and French émigrés had profound influence, especially on the silver made in the New York area during the late seventeenth and early eighteenth centuries, the tall beaker being the preferred communion vessel in the Dutch and French reformed churches. An extraordinarily large portion of surviving early American silver was made for ecclesiastical use—especially for the Puritan churches (and their successors) in New England. Church silver tended to be stylistically conservative, like the flagon and pair of communion dishes made for Boston's Second Church (nos. 102, 138, 139).

The porringer became even more popular here than in England, where it died out early. In America the porringer remained almost unchanged throughout the eighteenth century, and for the most part it defies classification in conventional stylistic terms. Tankards too were an enduring form. They were somewhat more susceptible to stylistic ebb and flow than porringers, but when they did affect a stylistic identity, it was mostly in superficial ways. They were more likely to reflect regional differences, as any comparison of New York, Boston, and Philadelphia tankards shows. Tradition sometimes played a larger role than style in shaping the appearance of objects. Can we really speak of a baroque porringer or a Queen Anne tankard or a William and Mary beaker? Not really. Although it would be an exaggeration to say that this silver lacks all stylistic identity, it is equally true that it often defies classification by this means.

The concept of style is, fortunately, elastic. As Meyer Schapiro admitted in his seminal essay: "Styles are not usually defined in a strictly logical way. As with languages, the definition indicates the time and place of a style or its author, or the historical relation to other styles, rather than its peculiar features. The characteristics of styles vary continuously and resist a systematic classification into perfectly distinct groups."[5]

Another factor working against a neat series of stylistic classifications over a 200-year time span is the combined impact of the industrial and consumer revolutions, which accelerated the pace of stylistic change as well as the quantity and variety of wares produced. The trend toward specialized forms was well developed by the third quarter of the eighteenth century, but it continued for another hundred years. By the close of the nineteenth century there was a silver implement for almost any conceivable function at table, available in many different "styles." What made this dubious achievement possible was mechanization, organized large-scale production, mass markets, and innovative marketing and distribution techniques. The result was a plethora of mini-styles, or patterns, churned out by company designers, that bore little relation to the concept of style as it had been practiced earlier, that is, a commonly accepted vocabulary of form and ornament distinctive to a cultural group during a given historical era.

Silver and gold artifacts (excluding jewelry), indeed almost all so-called decorative arts, have one thing in common that is unrelated to style. They are usually designed to serve a purpose: for serving tea, coffee, wine, or beer; for holding wineglasses or other serving vessels; for holding various foods and condiments; for cutting and eating; and so forth. The first consideration in their design, therefore, is to make them effective tools. Once the mechanical requirements of a cup are determined, questions of stylistic expression become possible: should the body be circular or octagonal; should it be straight or should it taper; should it have a base, a rim, cast decoration, extra curves in the handle; should it be chased or engraved? Primarily, however, it must be capable of holding a liquid, stable when set down, and easily brought to the mouth. As scholars have concentrated on style, they have tended to neglect one of the accomplishments of Western civilization: the development of a wide range of functional forms, most associated with eating and drinking, over a relatively brief period of time.

Consider the lowly spoon. It is actually a sophisticated artifact that serves its purpose remarkably well. It only assumed its present form during the eighteenth century. For thousands of years people ate with their hands, sometimes assisted by a knife. The first spoons were clumsy affairs with straight handles and shallow wide bowls, and those that survive are without exception unbalanced (no. 77). Starting in the late seventeenth century, handles were flattened and broadened at the end, and bowls were deepened and elongated. During the eighteenth century, handles were formed into a gentle S curve that turned slightly up, or down, at the end. Bowls went from being oval to slightly pointed. Spoons became more delicate and came in different sizes. They were so well designed that they can be balanced when the shank is rested on a finger. All of this happened in a century or less, and there has been no real improvement in spoon design since the eighteenth century.[6] There have been many attempts to alter the shape of spoons, especially in the nineteenth century with decorative and novelty handles, but these innovations tended to remove spoons from their original intended use. Notwithstanding the continued prevalence of patterns nor, even, the influence of modern design, the spoon has retained its basic shape, which was determined by function.

What, then, is the role of style in early American silver, and how do we go about classifying silver in stylistic terms? Although some forms are resistant to classification, others are indeed amenable to this process. As noted earlier, style is expressed through a commonly accepted vocabulary of form and ornament that is distinctive to a cultural group in a given historical era. Silver and other decorative arts in colonial America partook selectively of English, French, and Dutch influences. Most seventeenth-century American silver was based on prototypes made in England prior to 1688 (often prior to 1660) or in the Dutch republic of the early and middle years of that century. Tradition and simplicity are much in evidence, but statements of style surface here and there with boldly chased floral designs and elaborate engraving, as lingering medieval and Renaissance influences were challenged by mannerism.

Originating in Rome in the early sixteenth century, mannerism was carried to northern Europe and then to England. It was greatly modified by the time it reached New England in the seventeenth century. Still, such characteristics as heavy ornamentation, strapwork, exotic human and animal forms, and obscure iconography did turn up there. The cherub growing out of a flower stem engraved on the lid of the John Coney tankard (no. 37) and the caryatid handles on the Robert Sanderson caudle cup (no. 121) are but two examples.

Following the Glorious Revolution of 1688 and the accession of William and Mary to the British throne, craftsmen and designers flocked to England from the Continent. Many of them were French; some had already been in exile in Holland as a result of Louis XIV's revocation of the Edict of Nantes (which had guaranteed Protestants their rights) in 1685, and a few found their way to British North America, especially the New York area. One of the important designers of the period was Daniel Marot—son of Jean Marot, a Parisian architect and designer—who accompanied William of Orange when he left the Netherlands to become William III of England. Marot embodies the international nature of the William and Mary style, so named for the sovereigns whose patronage, protestantism, and acceptance of constitutional government provided a period of relative tranquility and prosperity.[7] There is a clear line of descent as French styles were assimilated and transformed, first in Holland and later in England. As Continental influences were absorbed, the decorative arts of England and America assumed a wholly different character. In silver the metal was manipulated to produce rich and bold chased and repoussé ornament alternating with plain, highly polished surfaces. Repoussé acanthus leaves and bold gadrooning, the latter sometimes swirled, produced rich surfaces that gave off sparkling points of reflected light. Perhaps the two best examples at Winterthur of this style are the sugar box by Edward Winslow (no. 140) and the two-handled covered cup by Jurian Blanck, Jr. (no. 152).

Although this Anglo-Franco-Dutch style incorporates elements of the baroque (the dramatic contrasts between boldly worked and plain surfaces presumably corresponding to the dramatic chiaroscuro of Italian baroque painting, for example), it seems reasonable to let it remain the William and Mary style. Perhaps John Marshall Phillips had it right after all when he referred to "The Baroque of the William and Mary Style."[8]

The greater contribution of the William and Mary style was to infuse Anglo-American decorative arts with a strong dose of classicism. This was not the archaeological variety; that came later. It was, rather, a matter of assimilating the basic principles of classicism, as abstract form finally took precedence over awkward structure and as symmetry and proportion became essential to design. These principles would govern Western design for more than 100 years.

Change is the essence of fashion, and fashion itself had now become a commodity. Anglo-American decorative arts, therefore, entered another phase early in the eighteenth century. Queen Anne reigned briefly, from 1702 to 1714, but it was a memorable time in the history of Britain as constitutional government was consolidated under the last Stuart sovereign, foreign enemies were vanquished, imperial power expanded, and the arts flourished. Anne's name came to be synonymous with a style that, in silver at least, emphasized form over ornament, clean outlines over complexity, and restrained use of moldings and faceting.

According to Charles Oman, the style persisted in England through the reign of George I (1714–27).[9] In American silver the apple-shape teapot by Jacob Hurd (no. 80) and the bulbous-bottom teapot by Daniel Christian Fueter (no. 193) are representative examples. The Fueter teapot, although made after 1754, embodies the ideal shape of the Queen Anne style. Note its low center of gravity and the interplay of concave and convex surfaces topped by a domed lid. The faceted S-curve spout balances the bold S-curve handle. The Hurd teapot is simpler in outline and follows the shape of Chinese ceramic wine pots, there being no precedent for teapots. The development of these and related forms show the importance of tea drinking as a social ritual. It is a classic case of artifacts reflecting a new element in human behavior.

Aside perhaps from its handles, the large two-handled cup by Bartholomew Le Roux II (no. 225) embodies the Queen Anne ideal of bold outlines and plain surfaces enriched by moldings. In contrast with the two-handled cup by Blanck, this example is larger; it is elevated on a stepped base and pedestal, and it has a stepped-and-domed cover with a finial. The midband is the only break in the smoothness of the body. The simplicity of this cup is further enhanced by its lack of an engraved armorial or inscription—unusual because these large cups were almost always presentation pieces. Its handles, with their back-to-back C scrolls, suggest, in a typically restrained American manner, a touch of the coming rococo style.

Rococo, a term originally meant to be derisive, has fared well, as the 1992 exhibition and catalogue *American Rococo, 1750–1775* demonstrated. There is general agreement about its characteristics: a combination of sinuous S curves and C curves enlivened with scrolls, acanthus leaves, rocks, shells, and cartouches, often arranged asymmetrically and presented with an air of movement and playfulness. It is like icing on cake, usually added as decoration to solid form, although in its more expressive moments, as in the silver designed by Juste-Aurèle Meissonnier, the form is also expressive of the style.[10] For these reasons there is less ambiguity about rococo than about certain other stylistic classifications. We know it when we see it. Very little American silver exhibits strong rococo characteristics. The more obvious rococo elements are usually limited to touches here and there, such as the asymmetrical handle on the Myer Myers creamer (no. 232) or the Schuyler coat of arms engraved on the salver by John Heath (no. 209). The cruet stand by John David (no. 334) is probably the highest expression of the rococo style in silver at Winterthur. Its play of circular forms, its C scrolls, shell feet, and, most of all, the asymmetrical cartouche-shape handle conform to the tenets of the style.

While the rococo style in America was a pallid affair when compared with the work of Paul de Lamerie or Meissonnier, it nevertheless had an underlying presence. We tend to think of asymmetry as its foremost characteristic when, in fact, as Arthur Grimwade has noted, it is movement.[11] If we look at the undulating bodies found on hundreds of pieces of hollowware, the so-called double-bellied form, we see the most common expression of the style in America. The teapot made by Samuel Edwards for the Dudley family (no. 57) stands in sharp contrast to the apple-shape teapot by Jacob Hurd discussed above. The Hurd pot is simple in outline and plain in its decoration; it is, in short, static.

The Edwards teapot, on the other hand, seen in profile, curves out, then in, then out again, then in again. It plays with the light, and the body seems almost alive. The repetition of the undulation in the lid reinforces the effect. The cast S-curve spout, with its naturalistic "beak" and sinuous loops, adds to the sense of its being a living creature.

A tall, double-bellied coffeepot made in Philadelphia by Joseph and Nathaniel Richardson for the Morris family (no. 457) goes a step further. Instead of a horizontal form sitting on a low base with a low center of gravity, the Richardson pot stands high on a pedestal and base; its center of gravity is shifted upward, its neck is elongated, and it is topped by a domed lid with finial—all of which make it a decidedly vertical form. Stretching out the body to achieve height increases the area of undulating body surface and permits a nobler spout and more complex handle. The pot is indeed stately, but there is a suggestion of playfulness, a hint of instability, even a voluptuous quality that reveals its essentially rococo character. That such a form remained popular into the 1790s, even as the vastly different urn style (the first phase of neoclassicism) was coming into vogue, is a cautionary tale on the practice of pigeonholing styles into chronological frameworks.

Robert Rowe observed that "there can have been few such complete revolutions in taste as that which took place between 1760 and 1770" in England. He was speaking of the advent of neoclassicism and its dramatic impact on all the arts. Neoclassicism was, however, more than a revolution in taste; it was a movement to reform society, an attempt to return to first principles. It was a reaction against irrationality, licentiousness, frivolity, and deception. It sought to replace these qualities with truth, nobility, honesty, and rationality—nothing less than total purification of both society and art. It sought "an art of universal significance and eternal validity."[12] Its paradigm was classical antiquity. Although classicism had informed and inspired Western art at least since the Renaissance, neoclassicism chose not simply to borrow but to penetrate to the Platonic ideal behind actual forms.

Neoclassicism rejected the frivolity and fluid grace of the rococo in favor of uncomplicated, well-defined outlines. Greek vase painting and Doric temples were admired for their simplicity, honesty, and masculinity, and they became models of perfection. The linear paintings of Jacques-Louis David and the marmoreal sculptures of Antonio Canova represent the coldest and most rational phase of neoclassicism. John Flaxman's illustrations for the *Iliad* and the *Odyssey* are pure evocations of the neoclassical spirit. These simple line drawings emphasize form and stasis rather than texture and movement. These were the qualities that carried over into neoclassical silver.

In the decorative arts neoclassicism emphasized linearity and geometric forms, such as circles and ovals. The archetypical form for the first phase of neoclassicism was the urn, which was incorporated as the central element in the design of silver hollowwares. Because of its ubiquity and because it preceded the arrival of a more archaeologically based neoclassicism, I have chosen to call this first phase the urn style.

In England the decorative work of the brothers Robert and James Adam came to be synonymous with neoclassicism—although their interpretations lacked the austerity of the neoclassical ideal. Because of the Adams' prominent role in defining this phase of the style, it is little wonder that the term *Adamesque* is often employed. The brothers devoted themselves primarily to remodeling the houses of rich clients, using designs drawn from Roman and Etruscan sources, but Robert Adam also designed furniture and silver. Among his patrons in this activity was the individual most responsible for interpreting and disseminating the urn style in silver, Matthew Boulton, a manufacturer and owner of the Soho Works in Birmingham. Boulton's productive capacity, his ingenious marketing ability, his quality control, his interest in collecting ancient pottery, and his willingness to employ the best design talent combined to make him successful. He also was one of the pioneers in the manufacture and distribution of fused plate, which provided a much less expensive way to make the new urn-shape vessels. By the 1770s fused-plate hollowwares were produced in large quantity and in increasing variety, almost all in the neoclassical or urn style. Engraved catalogues of these wares circulated throughout the Atlantic community and helped to popularize the style. In America such catalogues were not only used by silversmiths to order fused-plate wares for their customers but also served as design books for making up-to-date silver.

Adamesque classicism is best exemplified in American silver by the urn-style tea and coffee services that proliferated in the 1780s and 1790s, such as the one made by Joseph Richardson, Jr. (no. 446). The pierced galleries encircling the lids are a characteristic feature of Philadelphia silver during this period, while beaded circular pedestals on square bases are also common. Bodies have large expanses of plain surfaces set off by minimal moldings. When these surfaces are decorated, it is not with chasing but with simple, light, symmetrical, and unobtrusive engraving that often incorporates small faceted surfaces, called bright-cut work, designed to catch the light.

Perhaps the emphasis on a few simple geometric forms had something to do with the advent of silver made in matched sets, for it was in this period that the idea took hold. It simply did not occur to people earlier that their creamer and sugar bowl had to be exactly like their teapot. Pieces may have been stylistically compatible, as in the coffeepot, sugar bowl, and creamer made by Myer Myers (nos. 230, 231, 232), but they did not have to match in every detail. The growing number of books offering advice on design and manners, increased wealth, and the proliferation of consumer goods contributed to the increased demand for matching goods. Another factor was surely the dramatic departure from previous styles. It could be argued, however, that strict stylistic purity may not have been as important to American consumers of the late eighteenth century as it is today. For example, the first piece of neoclassical silver made in America, the great urn produced by Richard Humphries (Philadelphia Museum of Art) and presented to Charles Thomson by the Continental Congress in 1774, has a thoroughly rococo engraved cartouche around the inscription. Conversely, the Morris coffeepot, described above as an example of rococo silver, has an inscription in the neoclassical style.

The purity of the urn style dissipated during the first decade of the nineteenth century as designers attempted to hew more closely to antique forms, a phenomenon called archaeological classicism. Since a significant part of this impulse was filtered through France, where it became the official style of the Napoleonic state, it is rightly called *le style empire*, or, as we know it, the empire style. It is a good deal less abstract and considerably more complex than the first-phase neoclassicism just discussed, for it adopts and adapts specific forms based on actual objects found in the ruins of Pompeii and other Roman sites. It also incorporates, for decorative effect, plant and animal forms thought to have been used during antiquity. A good example is the covered sugar urn and stand that is part of the coffee and tea service made by Simon Chaudron and Anthony Rasch for the Dallas family (no. 325). The stand, with its long, slender, curved legs with cloven hooves and goat-head terminals, is based on an antique incense burner.

Thomas Fletcher and Sidney Gardiner of Philadelphia received an important commission in 1812, when they were asked to design a piece of hollowware for presentation to

Isaac Hull, one of several American naval commanders to be so honored. They created a flattened urn, set on a pedestal and raised on a square base with an animal-paw foot at each corner. Overall and in several specific details it is clearly based on an engraved design by Charles Percier and Pierre-François Fontaine that was executed in silver by Martin-Guillaume Biennais.[13] The urn, owned by the Naval Historical Foundation, proved very popular and led to many more commissions. No doubt this explains why it is featured on Fletcher & Gardiner's trade card. More important, echoes of this piece turn up in their other work: the same base appears on subsequent presentation pieces, and a similar base appears on the partners' large ewer with a snakelike handle (no. 347).

With increasing acceptance of second-phase neoclassical silver during the late twentieth century came the need for new terminology. (As stated earlier, *urn style* is a term of my coinage for first-phase neoclassicism.) In *Classical America, 1815–1845* (1963), Berry Tracy distinguished between silver reflecting the "refined Adamesque classicism of the Federal Period (1790–1810)" and the heavier and more decorated silver that followed, for which he could not at first find a name but eventually called "late classical." *Empire* is too restrictive a term to cover all late classical silver, particularly since many of the variants produced at that time bore little resemblance to Napoleonic silver. Donald L. Fennimore faced the problem of terminology in his study of the work of Thomas Fletcher and Sidney Gardiner. He found a pragmatic solution to the problem by seeking out the terms used in the correspondence and business papers of his subjects.[14] They employed such mundane but descriptive adjectives as *oblong*, *round*, and *fluted*, which made sense to them and their contemporaries, who had never heard of neoclassical, federal, or empire styles.

The oblong style, so called because bodies and bases were rectangular in plan with rounded corners, replaced the urn style during the first decade of the nineteenth century. An example is the four-piece tea service (no. 217) by Isaac Hutton of Albany. Bodies are squashed, as if a great weight were bearing down on them, forcing the sides to bulge out. The verticality of the urn style is replaced by horizontality, and straight or gently curved bodies are replaced by rounded ones. The surfaces of these pieces remain plain and unadorned.

The so-called round pattern appeared after 1810; the term is meaningful largely for distinguishing it from the oblong style.[15] Fletcher & Gardiner's large ewer (no. 347) suggests the round style, as do the bodies of the Dallas tea service. The fluted style is represented by James Musgrave's three-piece tea service (no. 415) and is distinguished by a series of vertical ridges alternating with concave channels on the bodies.

An important innovation that appeared in the wake of the War of 1812 was the introduction of die-rolled decorative bands integrated structurally into a body, as in the tea service made by William B. Heyer of New York for presentation to the wife of David Hosack (no. 213). The bands, featuring thickly clustered grapes, vines, flowers, or fruit, usually on a pebbled ground, were made by rolling a strip of silver between a pair of cylindrical dies, one of which was engraved with the design. Hollowware bodies were often made in two parts with the upper part joined to the lower by one of these bands, a technique that no doubt hastened the fabrication process and further emphasized the horizontality of the piece.

Perhaps the most popular style of the 1820s was what I choose to call the lobate style. It is exemplified by the sugar bowl and creamer made by John Crawford of New York (no. 170). Forms are circular, as in the round style, but the most pronounced feature is a series of projecting lobes around the lower body. Lobed bodies first appeared in sixteenth- and seventeenth-century Europe and carried over into the work of Jeremiah Dummer and John Coney in Boston. They are revived here in quite a different context; their convex reflectivity provides a visual counterpoint to the richly detailed decorative bands and heavily chased lid of the sugar bowl. While the bodies still echo late classical models, the C-scroll handles with sprigs are decidedly rococo. Similarly, the Samuel Kirk coffee and tea service (no. 370) employs urn-style bodies for the coffee- and teapots but covers them in detailed repoussé designs that are wholly un-neoclassical. The overall chased decoration, with its dripping foliage, recalls the rococo but is conceived differently. It is busier and more expansive, less fanciful, and more suggestive of narrative than playful decoration. We are drawn into studying its details rather than accepting it as an artful conceit.

The tea service by Eoff & Shephard (no. 174) of New York City, made about 1855, is even more boldly rococo in character, with its undulating bodies and lids, asymmetrical cartouches, vertical ribbing, and arborescent spouts. Although the makers employed a rococo vocabulary, the heavy manner of presentation (especially in the naturalistic motifs on the bases) and the sturdy thick-walled construction place the service squarely in its own time. Echoes of a romantic past live on in solid and serious Victorian splendor.

Other pasts and other lands beckoned as designers of the mid nineteenth century outdid one another to come up with increasingly exotic, innovative, and often monumental silver. Renaissance, gothic, Elizabethan, Egyptian, Louis XV, neo-grec, and a host of other periods, places, and styles were evoked. The Tiffany beverage service (no. 272) reflects the Islamic style as interpreted by designer Edward C. Moore. Although two long-necked pots resemble Middle Eastern hollowwares superficially, most of the pieces in the set are thoroughly Western in form. The intricately decorated bands encircling the bodies lend a certain Islamic character and provide a unifying design element but also suggest Renaissance decoration.

This impulse to borrow elements from the past and combine them in new and innovative assemblages might well be called creative eclecticism. It provided a means of expression that was sometimes playful, sometimes pompous, often busy, even fussy, but always glorying in a sense of abundance and know-how. Technical advances made it possible to manipulate materials to suit every taste and nearly every pocketbook. Among the most malleable of materials, silver can be shaped into an infinite variety of forms, and it was. The Bryant vase (1875, owned by the Metropolitan Museum of Art) and the loving cup made to honor Admiral Dewey (1898, owned by the Chicago Historical Society) epitomize the best and the worst that could be accomplished by creative eclecticism and technical virtuosity.[16]

The idea of silver flatware available in dozens—even hundreds—of different patterns, is another aspect of the nineteenth-century need to demonstrate mastery of materials and to create an economy of abundance. Added to this is the huge amount of raw silver available as a result of discoveries of lodes in Colorado, Nevada, and California. The concept of style, as it had been known in the eighteenth century, fell victim to the consumer revolution. There was a political dimension to this change too. William and Mary, Queen Anne, rococo, and neoclassical were, at the outset, styles intended to serve elite groups. The new aesthetic of abundance, on the other hand, sought to reach the broadest possible audience to maximize profits. It democratized the ownership of luxury goods, but it did so at the expense of coherent, strongly defined styles.

Given this free-wheeling, laissez-faire attitude toward design, a reaction was inevitable—but it came in stages. In the late nineteenth century the arts and crafts movement, at least in the beginning, sought to reform society as well as product design—not unlike the early stages of neoclassicism. It proposed to eliminate the impact of the machine by reviving handcraftsmanship and looked especially to the Middle Ages for models. It idealized preindustrial society and espoused a cult of the craftsman. Things should look handmade. Where silversmiths had always worked diligently to achieve a smooth finish, the arts and crafts rubric called for visible hammer marks. Gorham Company responded with its Martelé line of hand-crafted silver hollowware, such as the black-coffee service (no. 69). The service reflects the tenets of art nouveau with its sinuous and flowing lines. Art nouveau lacked the moral component of the arts and crafts movement and was based almost exclusively on aesthetic considerations. It was, however, a distinctive style and among the first not to ransack the past for ideas.[17] Silver inspired by the arts and crafts movement tended to reflect its tenets more in its method of fabrication than in stylistic expression, which remained remarkably eclectic. The return to traditional techniques had its price. Where earlier the value of the metal far outweighed the value of the craftsman's labor, now just the reverse was true. The result was expensive silver hollowware: luxury goods for an elite market.

Proponents of the international style professed more radical design reform, abandoning ornament almost entirely. But it too remained the province of a small elite and had little effect on the mass of consumer goods during the first half of the twentieth century. Following World War II, however, the international style became a strong presence in functional areas like kitchens and offices. To the international style goes the dubious achievement of convincing many consumers that stylish hollowware and flatware need not be made of silver at all—stainless steel is cheaper and requires less care. A silver service is no longer de rigueur for American brides. Still, those who do purchase silver today tend to select the traditional styles or some interpretation thereof. Paul Revere bowls remain popular, and both adaptations and reproductions of museum-owned eighteenth-century American silver abound.

We are left, then, with a mixed typology for the most innovative stylistic movements in Anglo-American decorative arts: William and Mary, Queen Anne, rococo, and neoclassical (both early and late). On balance, and in spite of the inconsistencies, they remain useful terms. The plethora of nineteenth-century mini-styles made no lasting mark on the silver designs of our own time—unless we regard the continuing tendency to reproduce period styles as a legacy of the last century. We should cease to think of *William and Mary* and *Queen Anne* as antiquarian terms—embarrassing and not quite in the same league as *rococo* and *neoclassical*—and instead think of them as marking equally important phases in the formation of the modern interior.

NOTES

1. Robert F. Trent, "The Concept of Mannerism," in Jonathan L. Fairbanks and Robert F. Trent, eds., *New England Begins: The Seventeenth Century*, 3 vols. (Boston: Museum of Fine Arts, 1982), 3:368–79, nos. 383–427; Barbara McLean Ward, "The Craftsman in a Changing Society: Boston Goldsmiths, 1690–1730" (Ph.D. diss., Boston University, 1983).

2. Rainier Baarsen et al., *Courts and Colonies: The William and Mary Style in Holland, England, and America* (New York: Cooper-Hewitt Museum, distributed by University of Washington Press, 1988).

3. As quoted in Graham Hood, *American Silver: A History of Style, 1650–1900* (New York: Praeger Publishers, 1971), p. 58.

4. Ivor Noël Hume, "Material Culture with the Dirt on It: A Virginia Perspective," in *Material Culture and the Study of American Life*, ed. Ian M. G. Quimby (New York: W. W. Norton, 1978), p. 37.

5. Meyer Schapiro, "Style," in *Aesthetics Today*, ed. Morris Philipson (Cleveland and New York: World Publishing, 1961), p. 83.

6. See John Davis, "The Evolution of the Early American Spoon, ca. 1650–ca. 1850" (Master's thesis, University of Delaware, 1962).

7. Baarsen et al., *Courts and Colonies*, esp. pp. 62–79. Philip Johnston selected the great monteith made by John Coney as "the supreme American achievement in the William and Mary style" (p. 121).

8. In his masterwork *Images of American Living: Four Centuries of Architecture and Furniture as Cultural Expression* (Philadelphia: Lippincott, 1964), Alan Gowans labels certain early eighteenth-century American buildings as William and Mary because their relatively tall and narrow proportions resemble those found in side chairs of the period.

9. Charles Oman, *English Domestic Silver* (1934; rev. and exp. ed., London: Adam and Charles Black, 1968), pp. 89–90; see also Michael Clayton, *Christie's Pictorial History of English and American Silver* (Oxford, Eng.: Phaidon, 1985), chap. 5.

10. Morrison H. Heckscher and Leslie Greene Bowman, *American Rococo, 1750–1775: Elegance in Ornament* (New York: Metropolitan Museum of Art, distributed by Harry N. Abrams, 1992). For Meissonnier's designs, see *Oeuvre de Juste-Aurèle Meissonnier* (ca. 1750; reprint, New York: Benjamin Bloom, 1969); for a candelabra made from his designs, see Frank Davis, *French Silver, 1450–1825* (New York: Praeger Publishers, 1970), fig. 161.

11. Arthur Grimwade, *Rococo Silver, 1717–1765* (London: Faber and Faber, 1974), p. 1.

12. Robert Rowe, *Adam Silver, 1765–1795* (New York: Taplinger Publishing, 1965), p. 1; Hugh Honour, "Neo-Classicism," in *The Age of Neo-Classicism* ([London]: Arts Council of Great Britain, 1972), pp. xxi–xxix.

13. Elizabeth Ingerman Wood, "Thomas Fletcher: A Philadelphia Entrepreneur of Presentation Silver," in Milo M. Naeve, ed., *Winterthur Portfolio 3* (Winterthur, Del.: Henry Francis du Pont Winterthur Museum, 1967), pp. 136–71.

14. Berry B. Tracy, "Late Classical Styles in American Silver," *Antiques* 86, no. 6 (December 1964): 702–6; see also *Classical America, 1815–1845: An Exhibition at the Newark Museum* (Newark, N.J.: By the museum, 1963). Donald L. Fennimore, "Elegant Patterns of Uncommon Good Taste: Domestic Silver by Thomas Fletcher and Sidney Gardiner" (Master's thesis, University of Delaware, 1971).

15. For the progression of these mini-styles, see Donald L. Fennimore, "Thomas Fletcher and Sidney Gardiner: The Stylistic Development of Their Silver," *Antiques* 102, no. 4 (October 1972): 642–49.

16. David B. Warren, Katherine S. Howe, and Michael K. Brown, *Marks of Achievement: Four Centuries of American Presentation Silver* (New York: Harry N. Abrams in association with the Houston Museum of Fine Arts, 1987), pp. 164–66, 171–73.

17. Winterthur has no arts and crafts silver. For the quintessential American arts and crafts silversmith, see Elenita C. Chickering, "Arthur J. Stone, Silversmith," *Antiques* 129, no. 1 (January 1986): 274–83. Stone was a founding member of the Boston Society of Arts and Crafts.

Building a Collection

When Martha Gandy Fales's *American Silver in the Henry Francis du Pont Winterthur Museum* was published in 1958, it captured the highlights of the collection that had been amassed by H. F. du Pont since the 1920s. Some 142 examples were illustrated in a picture book of fifty-six pages. The present volume contains 517 entries (counting sets as one) and by no means includes all of the museum's silver. This should give pause to those who tend to think of Winterthur's holdings as having remained static since the 1950s. The silver owned by Winterthur today is the product of seventy-one years of continuous collecting, first by H. F. du Pont and later by curators and donors.

The du Pont purchase records for silver begin in 1924. The first acquisition was an eighteenth-century French wine taster *(tâte-vin)* bought in September. According to du Pont's daybook, the first silver identifiable as American (destined to become the nucleus of the museum's silver collection) came to Winterthur in May 1926 through dealer Israel Sack, then located in Boston. The lot consisted of six silver tankards belonging to the First Church of Charlestown, Massachusetts, and included two by Josiah Austin (nos. 3, 4), two by Jeremiah Dummer (nos. 43, 44), and two by Edward Winslow (nos. 136, 137). This was to be the first of several major acquisitions of New England church silver. At a cost of $27,500, it was also a major investment for the time.

Several individual purchases were made over the next year, culminating in the acquisition of the Francis Hill Bigelow collection, sold through Brooks Reed Gallery, Boston, in April 1927. Bigelow, an important early collector and member (along with H. F. du Pont) of the Walpole Society, had suggested the exhibition "American Silver," held at the Museum of Fine Arts, Boston, in 1906. Bigelow's *Historic Silver of the Colonies and Its Makers* was published in 1917; his collection included tankards by Richard Conyers (no. 39), Dummer (no. 45), and David Jesse (no. 95); a chafing dish by John Potwine (no. 106); two caudle cups by Dummer (nos. 46, 47) and one by Robert Sanderson (no. 121); a Jacob Hurd coffeepot (no. 79); Knight Leverett candle branches (no. 97); and a number of other pieces. Bigelow had organized his research on this silver in a scrapbook, which he also passed on to du Pont, who by this time was well on his way to amassing a major collection of American silver, albeit heavily weighted toward New England.

In October 1927 a significant portion of du Pont's silver, forty-four pieces, was deposited with the Metropolitan Museum of Art. These were augmented over the next two years by additional pieces. Some of the du Pont silver was exhibited in the museum's American Wing, which, in 1927, was only three years old. The *Bulletin of the Metropolitan Museum of Art* commented on the addition of three new alcoves in the wing, one on each floor. The third floor alcove had "a few pieces of furniture . . . arranged against the walls, a painted chest on frame affording a setting for a case of very fine silver of the late seventeenth and early eighteenth century, lent by Henry F. du Pont. This group of silver has not been shown before. It includes three caudle cups of high quality, two by Jeremiah Dummer, and one by Robert Sanderson, tankards by John Noyes and Edward Winslow, and a trencher salt by J. Ten Eyck."[1]

Most of the silver remained at the Metropolitan Museum until, at du Pont's request, it was returned to Winterthur in April 1931. The loan had served two purposes. It showed the world an important new collection in the making, and it put the silver into safe hands during the building campaign of 1928–31, when the Winterthur house was greatly enlarged.

One of du Pont's greatest silver acquisitions came in 1928 when Frank McCarthy, an antiques dealer in Longmeadow, Massachusetts, offered for sale the set of six matched communion tankards by Paul Revere (no. 111). Made in 1772 as a result of a bequest to a church in Brookfield, Massachusetts, the tankards had remained in Brookfield until their purchase by the dealer. They had been mentioned by Alfred Jones in his *Old Silver of American Churches* but not illustrated. As the only set of six matching tankards known (and documented in Revere's accounts), this purchase was a collecting coup for du Pont.

Du Pont's regional bias in favor of New England was partially offset by the purchase of the Helen Seabrease collection in the summer of 1929 through Robert Ensko, Inc. Mr. and Mrs. N. McLean Seabrease lived in Germantown, Pennsylvania. Their collection included tankards by Daniel Russell (no. 118) and Simeon Soumaine (no. 257); a sugar bowl by Myer Myers (no. 231); snuffers and tray by Daniel Carrell (no. 324); a cann by Francis Richardson (no. 436); and about twenty-five other items. With this acquisition du Pont began a long and fruitful relationship with Ensko, from whom he ultimately bought 45 percent of his collection. Throughout the 1930s most additions to the du Pont collection were individual items ranging from spoons to such major pieces as a John Heath salver (no. 209), purchased from Ensko in 1932, and an Irish silver chandelier acquired in 1934 from the American Art Association (not included in this catalogue but on display in Winterthur's Readbourne Parlor).

The 1940s opened on an optimistic note. Du Pont bought a Daniel Christian Fueter teapot (no. 193) in May 1940 from Edmund Bury and a whistle-coral-bells by Joseph Richardson, Sr. (no. 438) in 1942 from J. A. Lloyd Hyde. Purchases slowed during World War II but picked up after 1945. In 1946 du Pont acquired a Hull & Sanderson porringer (no. 76) and Nathaniel Morse candlesticks once owned by Peter Fanueil—both through Ensko. Holdings in New York silver were strengthened in 1947 by the purchase of a Jacobus Van der Spiegel footed salver (no. 278) and a rare Jurian Blanck, Jr., two-handled covered cup engraved with the Philipse arms (no. 152), both from Ensko.

The last purchase from Ensko recorded in the daybook was on December 29, 1948, when du Pont bought a hot water kettle and stand allegedly made by Nicholas Roosevelt and bearing the arms of the Roosevelt family. Questions concerning its authenticity arose over the next few years. In early 1951 du Pont wrote to Stephen Ensko (son of Robert Ensko, who founded Robert Ensko, Inc.) casting doubt on the history of the object. There is no record of Ensko's response. Apparently the kettle and stand were sent to Gebelein Silversmiths in Boston for examination. J. Herbert Gebelein's response in a letter dated March 31, 1951, was devastating. He found traces of English hallmarks, considerable reworking, and evidence that the Roosevelt coat of arms had been inserted into the body. The kettle and stand disappeared from Winterthur, and the long-standing relationship with Ensko cooled but did not end. Not recorded in the daybook, but discussed in correspondence, is the purchase of an Edward Winslow sugar box (no. 140) during the spring of 1951. Ensko had owned the box since 1937, after finding it in England. He offered it to du Pont in 1937, but they did not come to terms until 1951. In a letter to Ensko giving shipping instructions for the box, du Pont regretted "the inconvenience that Mr. Nicholas Roosevelt has caused us both." This allusion to the awkward situation with the kettle and stand is the last known letter to Ensko. Apparently, one of the great dealer-collector relationships had ended.

H. F. du Pont was offered far more silver than he purchased. He was a discriminating collector who constantly questioned attributions and histories and requested additional information on makers and owners. He frequently sought counsel from experts such as John Marshall Phillips, curator of the Garvan collection at Yale University Art Gallery. As a wealthy collector du Pont was well aware that there were people ready to take his money for spurious goods. The records show several major purchases that were later deaccessioned—probably because of doubts about their authenticity. In addition to the Roosevelt kettle and stand, one might ask what happened to the "collection plate" supposed to have been made for Christ Church, Philadelphia, in 1698. Still, considering the amount of silver collected, these were rare exceptions.

Du Pont's greatest perceived competitor was Francis P. Garvan, who was building an enormous collection of American silver for Yale. Garvan wrote to du Pont in June 1931 during the depths of the Great Depression:

Apparently we are the only two purchasers of American antiques left in America, and I am a purchaser only to the most limited extent, and I feel that we are being used to our mutual disinterest. I am not interested in anything except prints and silver, and very little in prints. Practically, I am only interested in completing the educational exhibit of silver at Yale. It is most comprehensive and I would like to complete that one job so that art be secured for historical preservation and study. However, whenever I want a piece I am threatened with it being sold to Mr. du Pont if I do not pay an extravagant price for it, and undoubtedly the same thing is being said to you. Can we not come to some understanding? . . . There is much stuff in the market and here we do not bid each other up, each one can get what he wants at a proper and reasonable price.

Having seen and been impressed by the Garvan silver, du Pont responded that he had no intention of competing with him: "As a matter of fact, I really buy very little silver and have gotten only what I needed for decorative purposes in my house. I am still looking for some seventeenth century pieces, possibly two more tankards and some pieces that might look well on a gateleg table." Du Pont noted that his collection was nearly complete. When it came to furniture, he needed only "two small early pine tables with two legs and stretcher between, a small size Chippendale bed, and a very small ball and claw foot table."[2] Although this may sound disingenuous in light of his subsequent collecting activities, du Pont's silver purchases throughout the 1930s were very selective and, by Garvan's standards, modest indeed. It is doubtful that their gentlemen's agreement had any effect on the silver market.

The differences between these two collectors could not have been greater. Garvan strove for depth and breadth in order to create a didactic collection. As he said in an earlier letter to du Pont when there was talk of a trade: "My one real ambition is to make my silver collection at Yale a comprehensive, permanent, educational one for all times, and I am quite willing to sacrifice any of my other Americana in exchange for anything that will strengthen my [silver] collection. So, we might in the future do some trading." As one might expect of a collector who created aesthetic room settings wherein furniture played a larger role than silver, du Pont responded: "I would be interested in exchanging some silver for the Goddard secretary desk which you kindly lent to the Girl Scout Loan Exhibition last autumn."[3]

There were no trades, possibly because Garvan's silver collection was already so comprehensive. He had been collecting for at least twenty years and by this time (1930) owned at least forty tankards, while du Pont had ten. The same ratio applied to most other forms as well. Garvan died in 1937, cutting short a distinguished career as a collector and philanthropist.

Du Pont, of course, continued his collecting and gradually moved toward his goal of turning his house into a museum. The opening of Winterthur Museum in October 1951 marked the beginning of a new era. For one thing, the silver collection would now be augmented by gifts. Actually, the first gift came about a year before the opening, when Mrs. Francis Woodbridge of Falmouth, Maine, gave du Pont a teapot made by Nathaniel Hurd (no. 91). It was a token of appreciation for a weekend she had spent as a guest at Winterthur. So enthralled was she by the experience that she wrote a fictional account of Winterthur called "The Enchanted Castle."[4] The teapot had remained in Maine since its presentation in 1766 to Samuel and Sarah (Lithgow) Howard at Fort Western (now Augusta).

One of the most important gifts of the 1950s was the large two-handled bowl made by Jacob C. Ten Eyck for the Wendell family (no. 265). It was presented to the museum by Charles K. Davis of Fairfield, Connecticut, a friend of H. F. du Pont and a collector in his own right. When he died in the 1960s, Davis bequeathed to du Pont a superb pair of candlesticks accompanied by snuffers and a tray (nos. 20, 21) made by John Burt for the Warner family of Portsmouth, New Hampshire. Harold Sack, in his *American Treasure Hunt*, recalls how he became the intermediary in the original sale of this silver to Davis.[5] After spotting the silver at the Museum of Fine Arts, Boston in 1935 and noting that it was on loan from Hermann F. Clarke, Sack called Clarke and was encouraged to come to his house on Beacon Hill. When Sack appeared, Clarke handed him, through the door, a picture of the silver and said that he wanted $3,000 for it. Sack was not invited inside nor was he extended any social amenities. On his way back to New York, Sack stopped in Bridgeport to see Davis (who worked at the Remington Arms Company) to tell him about the silver. Davis was impressed when he saw the picture and decided to buy the lot. Following Davis's death, the Burt silver came to Winterthur, where it was immediately put on display.

In 1962 Mr. and Mrs. Alfred E. Bissell of Wilmington, Delaware, presented Winterthur with a large collection of flatware, some 1,700 examples. They had purchased the silver from New York collector Stanley B. Ineson at the suggestion of Charles F. Montgomery. The collection had been created to provide an index of American silversmiths' stamps. Nearly all of the stamps from the original gift were later published in Louise Conway Belden's *Marks of American Silversmiths in the Ineson-Bissell Collection*.[6]

The Bissells also provided funds to encourage the purchase of additional flatware. Thanks to their generosity and aggressive collecting by curators, by 1993 the Ineson-Bissell collection had grown to more than 5,000 examples. Most of the additions represent nineteenth-century makers or retailers. This silver horde is a study collection, meaning that it is not on display but is available by appointment for study by historians of American silver.

Although the professional staff at Winterthur had an increasing role in building the collection during the 1950s and 1960s, H. F. du Pont continued to be very much involved. Without his financial backing several major acquisitions would have been impossible. An important tankard by John Coney (no. 37), purchased in 1965, and the communion silver from Boston's Second Church, acquired in 1966, are but two examples of du Pont's continued interest and generosity. The church silver, consisting of two large dishes by Edward Winslow (nos. 138, 139) and a flagon by Peter Oliver (no. 102), was obtained with difficulty. When church officers authorized the sale, an opposing faction brought suit to stop the transaction. The litigation went on for several years before the court finally determined to permit the sale in 1966.[7]

Gifts from private owners came with increasing frequency. In 1968 Lammot du Pont Copeland donated a gold buckle by Philip Syng, Jr. (no. 475). Exquisitely formed and elaborately chased, it may well be the finest specimen of American gold from the colonial period. Among its many owners was Elizabeth Drinker (1735–1807) of Philadelphia.[8] The largest gift of hollowware in the history of Winterthur was received in the late 1970s from New York collector Marshall P. Blankarn, who, during a four-year period, presented more than 200 objects. The Blankarn gift added the work of many silversmiths previously unrepresented. Among its many treasures is a tumbler cup made by Joseph & Nathaniel Richardson and engraved with a death's head and other memento mori (no. 460). Although the cup was made during the 1780s, the character of the engraving resembles the iconography of death found in earlier centuries.

In 1991 Carl Kossack, a collector from North Haven, Connecticut, gave the museum about thirty examples of hollowware made in New York City from 1820 to 1850. At one time silver of this vintage would not have been welcome, but interest in the nineteenth century had been increasing dramatically since the innovative exhibition "Nineteenth-Century America: Furniture and Other Decorative Arts," held at the Metropolitan Museum of Art in 1970. Even prior to that event Winterthur's curators had been acquiring silver in the late neoclassical style. One of the first major purchases was a large ewer by Fletcher & Gardiner (no. 347) in 1969. From its dolphin finial to the snakelike handle to its paw feet, the piece is a bold restatement of the neoclassical style and offers a sharp contrast to the ubiquitous and sometimes insipid urn style. The newly installed Georgia Dining Room proved to be an appropriate area to display the Samuel Kirk coffee and tea service (no. 370) presented in 1972 by Dr. and Mrs. W. Tyler Haynes. The Kirk repoussé style, with its overall chinoiserie designs, is unique in American silver. Neo-rococo is combined with nineteenth-century romanticism to create an unusual but pleasing effect.

Interest in silver of this vintage accelerated with the appointment of Donald L. Fennimore to the curatorial staff in 1971. Fennimore has been instrumental in strengthening the museum's silver collection, especially in the empire and other late classical styles. The coffee and tea service by Simon Chaudron and Anthony Rasch (no. 325), made for the Dallas family and acquired by gift in 1975 from Mr. and Mrs. Henry Pleasants, is a stunningly executed example of archaeological classicism. In 1987 Fennimore arranged the purchase of a dish warmer made in Boston about 1840, presumably by Obadiah Rich (no. 116). It resembles an empire center table; its supports terminate in cast dog's heads. Fennimore also presided over the acquisition of two beverage services that are beyond Winterthur's period but are of great value for teaching purposes. A Tiffany service made about 1861 in a revival version of the neoclassical urn style was given by Mr. and Mrs. T. Truxton Hare, Jr., in 1983 (no. 274). In the same year Mrs. James H. Knowles donated a four-piece black-coffee service made by Gorham Company about 1902 (no. 69). It is a fine example of the company's hand-wrought line called Martelé. Distinctly art nouveau in style, the set brilliantly evokes its period. Fennimore's other silver acquisitions are too numerous to mention here. Suffice it to say that he has put his own stamp on the silver collection at Winterthur, as he has on the furniture collection.

Unlike Garvan, who collected masterpieces in great quantity and probably without a thought to their display, du Pont was always guided by how the presence of a new piece would affect the entire room. This is why Yale's vaults today are filled with American silver in extraordinary quantities—too much to exhibit—while at Winterthur nearly everything acquired by du Pont is on display in the period rooms. Without the need to worry about display, Garvan could purchase without restraint; du Pont was always limited by his abiding concern for the total impression of the ensemble. Still, in a few locations he could not resist the temptation to amass quantities of silver for effect. He filled the Wentworth Room with impressive Boston silver of the late seventeenth and early eighteenth centuries. It is spread out over several tables and atop a William and Mary–period high chest—all dramatic enough—but the visual coup de main is the closet. The key to the closet was hidden in a desk drawer. No doubt du Pont derived great pleasure—as have hundreds of guides—from the ritual of retrieving the key and opening the closet door to reveal shelf after shelf of gleaming Boston silver. This scene took place in a room where it was perpetual dusk. Du Pont thus provided a concentration of objects, as in a gallery setting, but he managed to do it within the context of a period room.

Similarly, in the Queen Anne Dining Room, du Pont spread New York silver about, but the treasures were inside a locked, rather plain Hudson Valley cupboard. Again the ritual. The key was retrieved from a desk drawer, and the cupboard doors were opened to reveal the well-lighted treasure within, while guests, standing in the dim room, gasped. The man who had earlier learned the dramatic impact of massing blooms in his garden put this skill to good use indoors as well.

A different kind of drama is played out in an impressive concentration of silver spread over three sideboards along the north wall of the Du Pont Dining Room, an interior of unyielding symmetry. Regional consistency was sacrificed in the interest of aesthetics and patriotism. On the middle sideboard, under Benjamin West's unfinished portrait of the commissioners to the preliminary negotiations for the Treaty of Paris, sit the six Paul Revere tankards from the Brookfield church. The grouping—founding fathers above, patriot goldsmith's work below—forms a shrine of sorts. The right sideboard on the north wall offers more Revere, tankards by both father and son, while in the corner on a cellaret stand two Liverpool-type silver pitchers, one by Revere, the other by George Carleton—one hand-raised, the other seamed from sheet silver. The left sideboard displays silver, more or less of the revolutionary war generation, made in Philadelphia and Wilmington. On the south wall, directly opposite the West painting and Revere tankards, is a portrait of George Washington by Gilbert Stuart that adds to the patriotic imagery of the room.

In spite of these few areas of concentrated displays, most of the museum's silver is dispersed throughout the rooms. It is displayed in what might be called functional settings: on tea tables or other appropriate surfaces, where in earlier times it might have been used. To the casual observer who sees a few pieces here and there, this method of display can give the impression that the silver collection is smaller than it really is.

Because individual pieces are so small, most of the museum's antique gold is displayed in a glass case located in an alcove outside the Imlay Room. This gallery form of display was born out of necessity rather than choice. It is partly relieved by having some of the gold within a small antique display cabinet within the case.

As the museum acquired ever-greater quantities of silver following du Pont's death, the problem of where to put it had to be addressed. The Blankarn gift of more than 200 pieces forced the issue; there were simply too many items to distribute throughout the period rooms. An alcove on the seventh floor of the museum, which had been used to display Chinese export porcelain, was appropriated, and a new shelved niche was created in the fifth-floor Montmorenci Stair Hall. The rest of the Blankarn gift was then distributed throughout the period rooms.

With the completion in 1992 of the Galleries, Winterthur's new exhibition building, opportunities opened up for displaying silver. The permanent exhibition on the first floor incorporates silver into a thematic interpretive scheme, which had not been possible previously. The second floor has space for changing exhibitions, allowing for the display of objects in an infinite variety of contexts and juxtapositions. The peculiar richness and documentation of early American silver make it the ideal subject of interpretation. Winterthur is now uniquely positioned to use this great collection in creative ways to reveal to all its audiences fascinating aspects of early American life.

As a result of many years of judicious collecting, Winterthur now owns one of the largest and most important caches of antique American silver. H. F. du Pont created the core, but two generations of curators and generous donors have greatly enlarged it. Nevertheless, there is no such thing as a complete collection, and there is every reason to hope that this one will continue to grow.

NOTES

1. "Accessions and Notes," *Bulletin of the Metropolitan Museum of Art* 23, no. 5 (May 1928): 173.

2. Francis P. Garvan to H. F. du Pont, June 18, 1931, box 22, Antiques Dealers Correspondence, Winterthur Archives, Winterthur Library (hereafter, Antiques Dealers Correspondence). Du Pont to Garvan, July 2, 1931, Antiques Dealers Correspondence.

3. Garvan to du Pont, February 27, 1930, du Pont to Garvan, April 10, 1930, Antiques Dealers Correspondence.

4. Typescript, Winterthur Archives.

5. Harold Sack with Max Wilk, *American Treasure Hunt: The Legacy of Israel Sack* (Boston: Little, Brown, 1986), pp. 123–29.

6. For Stanley B. Ineson, see Millicent Stow, "Making a Specialty of Early American Spoons," *Avocations* (May 1938): 126–30; Louise Conway Belden, *Marks of American Silversmiths in the Ineson-Bissell Collection* (Charlottesville: University Press of Virginia for the Henry Francis du Pont Winterthur Museum, 1980).

7. John Booth, "Memoirs of a Magician's Ghost," *Linking Ring* (June 1974): 44–46, 93 *(Linking Ring* is published by the International Brotherhood of Magicians). Booth phased out the sacrament of communion at the Second Church for theological reasons that he chose not to explain in "Memoirs." Although this step rendered all the communion silver redundant, he attempted the sale of only 5 out of 24 objects. The court finally allowed for the disposition of 3 pieces.

8. Elaine Forman Crane, ed., *The Diary of Elizabeth Drinker*, 3 vols. (Boston: Northeastern University Press, 1991).

Scientific Analysis of Silver

All silver in the catalogue has been subjected to nondestructive, energy dispersive X-ray fluorescence analysis to determine the principal components and their proportions within the alloy. The results appear within each entry. For hollowware, multiple readings were taken of several parts, such as the body, lid, handle, and foot, and the four principal components of the alloy—silver, copper, gold, lead—are reported. For flatware, a single reading is noted, consisting of only the silver content. In both cases I selected the readings from more extensive data generated and compiled by Winterthur's analytical lab. For example, all spoons were tested obverse and reverse, but to keep the data from overwhelming the catalogue, only the obverse readings are reported.

The purity of the alloy is judged by the amount of copper added. In English silver this amount can be no more than 7.5 percent, whereas in American silver it varies from 5.0 to 15.0 percent. Lacking an enforced sterling standard, American silversmiths had broader latitude—and they exercised it.

Silver is found in nature in the company of other metals, especially lead and copper but also gold, nickel, zinc, and a number of others. Until the mid to late nineteenth century, when improved procedures were developed, traditional refining methods left trace elements of the associated metals.

When Victor Hanson, a retired DuPont Company scientist, set up Winterthur's analytical lab in 1969 and developed the analytical program for silver in the early 1970s, one of his earliest findings was that gold and lead were almost always absent from silver objects made after the middle of the nineteenth century but were usually present in those made earlier. This important fact made it possible to detect bogus silver that was being passed as antique. Indeed, when a large collection of silver bequeathed to another institution was deposited at Winterthur in the 1980s and thoroughly analyzed, the curators' suspicions were confirmed: nearly all pieces bearing the alleged stamps of the best-known early American silversmiths were found to be made of modern silver.

When looking at the Winterthur collection, Hanson used a recently developed X-ray fluorescence spectrometer to examine a wide variety of inorganic materials as well as silver. The process is based on the principle that when the atoms of a given element are subjected to certain types of radiation, they emit energy of a characteristic wavelength. By detecting and processing these emissions and comparing them with those of known elements, the unknown element can be identified—almost instantly.[1] The radiation source used for the early experiments was cadmium 109, a man-made isotope. More recently, the lab has been using an X-ray tube with a silver secondary source. The secondary target is irradiated by the X-ray tube, and it is the emissions from the secondary that excite the atoms of the object under examination. To evaluate the results of analyses it is important to have some basic information about the process of analysis and about antique silver itself. First, the process reads only the surface of the metal; there is no penetration beyond a few microns. Even the thinnest metallic coating will prevent access to the body beneath, or at best skew the reading in favor of the surface material. Thus, an electroplated base-metal object will read as nearly pure silver.

Second, the keen observer will note in the analyses presented in the catalogue that the undersides of hollowware often show an alloy richer in silver than other parts of the body. This phenomenon is thought to be a result of the pickling process used by silversmiths. At the end of fabrication, a silversmith dipped the piece into an acidic solution to remove discoloration and give a whiter and more uniform color. The acid actually dissolved a portion of the copper in the alloy, leaving a silver-rich surface. Repeated polishing, however, gradually wore away this surface—but not all areas were polished with equal frequency. Undersides were more protected from handprints and tarnishing and far less likely to be polished; hence, they tend to retain their silver-rich surfaces.

Yet another peculiarity of antique silver investigated by Hanson is the problem of element segregation. Alloys were created in the melting pot by mixing measured amounts of silver and copper, or materials already mixed whose proportions were known. Obviously, the desired result was a thorough blending of the elements. In fact, however, after the molten silver alloy was poured into billets or molds and began to cool, elements tended to segregate according to melting point. This segregation was carried over in the metal even after it was subjected to hammering, rolling, drawing, or spinning. As a consequence, we routinely find different readings from different parts of the same piece of metal. Hanson found as much as a 6.0 percent difference between the two sides of a silver 50¢ piece. This idiosyncratic behavior of the alloy was known in the nineteenth century, if not before. An English assay master noted before a parliamentary committee that "silver is a metal that is very difficult to get uniform in its combination when alloyed."[2]

Cast parts tend to be richer in silver content than forged, drawn, or raised ones. Lowering the copper content softens the alloy, facilitating the casting process. Since cast parts require hand finishing, filing and the other toolwork is eased by using a softer metal.

Occasionally mercury is detected in silver objects in relatively significant amounts, suggesting that the piece has been mercury gilded. (Salts, goblets, and a few other forms often had gilded interiors.) Gilding was accomplished by using an amalgam of gold and mercury—very hazardous to the workman. When heated, most of the mercury burned off, leaving a thin coating of gold. Gilding is fragile, however, and it often disappeared with wear. Sometimes the only evidence remaining are traces of mercury.

According to analysis, the Hull & Sanderson pine-tree sixpence (no. 78) appears to contain 35.8 percent mercury and 1.3 percent gold, with only 57.9 percent silver and 1.5 percent copper. This is an anomalous but explainable situation. Sometime during its history, someone subjected the coin to mercury gilding, and now most of the gold is gone—at least it is no longer visible.

Recalling that X-ray fluorescence reads only the surface, it is highly probable that a test boring would reveal quite a different ratio of elements: much more silver and copper, much less gold, and no mercury. One of the great advantages of X-ray fluorescence analysis is that it is nondestructive. It was adopted to avoid damaging valuable antiques. Yet in cases like the sixpence, we are denied knowledge of its true composition, which can only be determined by a destructive procedure.

Unlike silver, most early American gold objects consist of three elements present in significant quantities: gold, silver, and copper. The major exception is found in the medals produced by and for the United States government in the early nineteenth century, such as the one made by Moritz Fürst (no. 352) and awarded to Stephen Cassin that is almost pure gold. Still, the more typical formulations for gold objects are found in the following table.

Composition of Representative Gold Objects

OBJECT	SILVERSMITH	GOLD	SILVER	COPPER
Buckle, no. 475	Syng	85.9%	9.8%	4.2%
Clasp, no. 448	Richardson, Jr.	85.3	8.2	6.4
Necklace, no. 28	Casey	87.4	7.6	5.0
Spoon, no. 288	Van Voorhis	80.0	11.5	8.5
Ring, no. 50	Dummer	86.0	10.9	3.1

The gold content of unstamped gold jewelry with an American provenance ranges more widely: from 30.0 to 86.0 percent. Those pieces with lower gold content contain more copper than silver, while those with higher gold content may contain nearly equal amounts of copper and silver. Even spectacle frames by one maker, McAllister of Philadelphia (no. 407), range from 41.8 to 70.5 percent gold. When copper and silver are added in large quantities, the color of the gold is affected; copper reddens it while silver whitens it. If copper and silver are present in nearly equal amounts, the natural color of gold is more likely to remain.

These, then, are some of the characteristics of the process of X-ray fluorescence analysis, as applied to silver, and some of the peculiarities of silver and gold as metals. Generally speaking, the data serves to complement judgments based on solid connoisseurship or documentary evidence. It is nevertheless useful to have the large database that has been assembled as a result of this project. One would hope that out of such a large body of data patterns might emerge, providing further insights into the workings of the craft. That has not proven to be the case, however. Possibly because Winterthur's silver collection ranges broadly in geography and time, patterns are impossible to detect. Perhaps what is needed is a more narrowly focused database, using more objects for specific places and times than any one collection could muster, thus producing a larger sampling within narrower parameters. If, for example, analyses could be assembled for all Boston tankards made between 1700 and 1730, interesting patterns might emerge. Intensive multiple-collection studies such as this have yet to be undertaken, but they could well be a potentially fruitful enterprise.[3]

NOTES

1. For more details, see Victor F. Hanson, "Quantitative Elemental Analysis of Art Objects by Energy-Dispersive X-ray Fluorescence Spectroscopy," *Applied Spectroscopy* 27, no. 5 (September/October 1973): 309–34. Additional information is available in unpublished reports on file in the Winterthur analytical lab.

2. The assay master from the Royal Mint was interviewed by the Select Committee on Silver and Gold Wares, April 17, 1856; see "Report from the Select Comittee on Silver and Gold Wares," in *British Parliamentary Papers: House of Commons Report*, 2 vols. (Shannon: Irish University Press, 1971), 1:103. V. F. Hanson, "Museum Objects," in *X-Ray Spectrometry*, ed. H. K. Herglotz and L. S. Birks, 17 vols. to date (New York: Marcel Delcker, 1978–), 2:413–81.

3. A cross-referenced file of original owners of silver, similar to the files on cabinetmakers and silversmiths in the Visual Resources Collection (formerly DAPC) at Winterthur, would be an invaluable reference tool.

Notes on the Catalogue

The organization of this catalogue differs markedly from that of Kathryn C. Buhler and Graham Hood's *American Silver: Garvan and Other Collections in the Yale University Art Gallery* (1970) and Buhler's *American Silver, 1655–1825, in the Museum of Fine Arts, Boston* (1972), where the silver is arranged chronologically within regions by dates of the makers. Having spent too much time looking for specific silversmiths in these catalogues, I decided that a catalogue arranged alphabetically by maker within region would be easier to use. Hence, the present arrangement. Another potential advantage of this arrangement is the interesting juxtaposition of works from different periods.

I also elected to use only three regional groupings. New England and New York are fairly obvious in their coverage. The third region, Pennsylvania and the South, requires an explanation. It includes not only Philadelphia and the Pennsylvania hinterland but also Wilmington, Baltimore, Annapolis, Washington, and the states of Virginia, South Carolina, Georgia, and Kentucky. Most of the silver from these areas was deeply influenced by Philadelphia, whether in the form of migrating craft skills or through distribution of Philadelphia products to southern markets. New York was also influential in places like Savannah and Charleston, but as far as the Winterthur collection is concerned, the Philadelphia influence was dominant. Hence the seemingly awkward geographical category.

The first half of each entry provides physical and quantitative data that includes the following: dimensions, weights, stamps, engraving, description, and spectrographic analysis. Measurements are given in United States units (to the nearest sixteenth inch) and metric (to the nearest tenth of a centimeter). Weights are given in troy (to the nearest grain) and metric (to the nearest tenth of a gram). Troy weights were derived from metric by a conversion formula. Stamps, whether makers' names and initials, hallmarks, pseudohallmarks, date stamps, or retailers' stamps, are described. The term *stamp* is used, instead of *mark*, to correspond with its usage in eighteenth-century silversmiths' advertisements and probate inventories. The term *mark* in the eighteenth century referred to owners' initials. All identifying engraving is described completely. Scratched numbers and names are also included under engraving.

Object descriptions provide the various methods of fabrication employed by makers (insofar as these methods can be identified). Descriptions are intended to assist the reader in fully comprehending the complexity—or simplicity—of forms that are often perceived as complete units rather than as conglomerations of parts. Spectrographic analyses are provided in some detail to show how the principal constituent elements in early American silver vary in quantity. Data is presented in percentages, with primary elements carried to one decimal place and trace elements carried to two. Further discussion of the interpretation of this data is found elsewhere in this volume.

The second half of each entry provides historical context—to the extent that such information is available. Sometimes it was possible to find extensive histories of early owners, but more often such information has been lost as objects passed from hand to hand. The provenance section usually provides more recent histories of ownership. The record of exhibitions and publications is an important part of the history of every work of art. It tends to reflect the importance granted to objects by curators and collectors of the twentieth century but cannot always be used as an index of the piece's historical importance. (Paul Revere's set of six tankards remained in their original location until the twentieth century; even after they were acquired by H. F. du Pont, they remained relatively unknown until the 1960s and 1970s and were not featured in an exhibition catalogue until 1989.) Not all published references are included. It seemed pointless, for example, to list all instances of an object's appearance in print if nothing of interest was said about it.

Under Exhibitions, a number of pieces are noted to have been on loan to the Metropolitan Museum of Art. Both H. F. du Pont and Stanley B. Ineson had portions of their silver collections on loan there during the late 1920s and 1930s. While not part of any formal exhibition, most of the silver was displayed.

Users of this catalogue may wonder why H. F. du Pont is mentioned so many times as donor, when a covering statement at the beginning might have taken care of the matter. They will find, however, that a significant portion of the silver was acquired through other donors or directly from dealers.

Readers familiar with Louise Conway Belden's *Marks of American Silversmiths* will know that it illustrates some 1,700 stamps from Winterthur's Ineson-Bissell collection. I have included materials from that collection selectively: where a maker is represented by hollowware, I have included, usually without illustrations, pared-down entries of the spoons by that silversmith. By so doing, the full range of a maker's work at Winterthur is presented. Except for some early spoons that have individual entries, I have grouped most into entries based on the type of stamp. Any variation in a silversmith's stamp warranted a new entry.

Style is mentioned only occasionally in the entries. I have chosen instead to deal with this issue in an essay ("Style in American Silver") in order to avoid repetition.

In general I have used the accepted terms for various forms. Some are problematic, however, because names changed over time. For example, milk and cream servers have been known at various times as milk jugs, milk pots, creamers, and creampots; for the most part I refer to them as creamers or milk pots. I have chosen the period term *candle branches* for single candleholders attached to glazed boxes; they have heretofore been called sconces. The term *cup* is so encompassing as to be meaningless without a modifier, and sometimes it is better simply to find another term. Short beakers, such as those produced by Peter L. Krider (no. 375), were called cups by contemporaries, or more specifically cattle cups because of their widespread use as prizes at agricultural fairs. Since they served different functions in other contexts (sets of six or twelve accompanied water pitchers, for example), we could simply call them cups (too general) or tumblers (associated with glassware), but in the end it is easier to settle for the term *beaker*. Similarly problematic, large circular boxes with the American eagle in relief on the cover have been called seal boxes because they contained the wax seal attached to treaties, but the proper term is *skippet*.

The language of heraldry is so esoteric as to be unintelligible to all but a handful of specialists. I decided on a mix of heraldic terms and plain English in the hope that such a compromise would do justice to the complexity of the armorial tradition while remaining understandable to most readers. This solution still requires the reader to be familiar with the tinctures (colors) as expressed in armorial engraving: *azure* (blue) is represented by horizontal parallel lines; *gules* (red) by vertical parallel lines; *sable* (black) by cross-hatching; *vert* (green) by diagonal parallel lines, upper left to lower right; *purpure* (purple) by diagonal parallel lines, upper right to lower left; *argent* (silver) by no lines; *or* (gold) by a dotted field. A wide diagonal band on the shield is called a *bend;* a wide horizontal band is a *fesse.* For descriptive purposes, shields are divided into nine quarters, or fields, grouped as follows: the upper three constitute the *chief;* the middle three the *fesse;* the lower three the *base.* The left three quarters make up the *dexter,* the middle three quarters the *pale,* the right three quarters the *sinister.* These terms indicate the position of other devices on the shield.

Museum accession numbers are listed at the end of each entry, along with the name of the donor or dealer. For objects acquired after 1951 (the year the museum opened), Winterthur follows standard practice by using the last two digits of the year of acquisition as the prefix of the accession number. Thus, the dish warmer by Obadiah Rich (no. 116), acquired by the museum in 1987, is accession number 87.20. Since, however, a large portion of the Winterthur collection was acquired prior to 1951, staff devised a unique system of numbering during the 1950s. Because the date of acquisition was often unknown, they used the current year instead of the year of acquisition as prefix. So as not to confuse these items with current accessions, all of the older pieces were assigned suffixes over 500. Thus 59.2301, the salver by John Heath (no. 209), was catalogued in 1959 but acquired by H. F. du Pont at an earlier date. The tray did not become the property of the museum, however, until 1965, when du Pont included it in a large gift of silver. The foregoing circumstances explain what may appear to be discrepancies among accession numbers and between accession numbers and acquisition dates.

THE CATALOGUE

New England

ℰ *Pygan Adams*

1712–76
New London, Connecticut

The son of the Reverend Eliphalet and Lydia Adams of New London, Pygan Adams was referred to by contemporaries as both a goldsmith and a merchant. He married Ann Richards in 1744. He was active in the local militia, served in the General Assembly from 1753 to 1765, and was a deacon in the First Church of New London in 1758. Additionally, he was colony auditor, an overseer of the Mohegan Indians, and was involved in the building of the New London lighthouse in 1760. It is likely that he abandoned silversmithing midway in his career to pursue other interests. Few examples of his work survive. A tankard at Yale University Art Gallery bears the Lynde arms, and the Lyman Allyn Art Museum, New London, Connecticut, owns a three-tine fork.

References: Bohan and Hammerslough, *Early Connecticut Silver*, p. 219. Flynt and Fales, *Heritage Foundation*, p. 143. Jennifer F. Goldsborough, *An Exhibition of New London Silver, 1700–1835* (New London, Conn.: Lyman Allyn Museum, 1969), pp. 8–9.

ℰ I
PORRINGER, 1735–65

DIAM. bowl 5 ⁷⁄₁₆" (13.8 cm), H. 2" (5.1 cm), W. 7 ¹⁵⁄₁₆" (20.2 cm)
8 oz. 5 dwt. 16 gr. (257.7 g)

Stamps: "PA" (conjoined lower serifs) in roman letters, in a rectangle, struck once on front of handle.

Engraved on front of handle: "L/ RE" in roman letters.

Description: raised circular bowl with bulging sides and slightly angled rim; bottom domed in center; centerpunch inside; cast handle pierced in keyhole pattern with 11 voids.

Spectrographic analysis:

	SILVER	COPPER	LEAD	GOLD
BOWL	91.0	8.4	0.18	0.13
HANDLE	90.0	9.0	0.26	0.20

History: The initials "L/ RE" probably refer to Richard and Elizabeth Lord, who were married in Lyme, Conn., in 1720.

Provenance: Bernice Loring, New Rochelle, N.Y., sold to H. F. du Pont, January 1930.

Exhibitions: "Masterpieces of American Silver," Virginia Museum of Fine Arts, Richmond, 1960.

Comments: A tankard by John Gardner in the Hammerslough collection, Wadsworth Atheneum, bears the same initials plus an inscription identifying "RL" as Richard Lord; see Bohan and Hammerslough, *Early Connecticut Silver*, pl. 63.

References: Fales, *American Silver*, no. 122. Bohan and Hammerslough, *Early Connecticut Silver*, pl. 32. *Masterpieces of American Silver*, no. 143.

55.586 Gift of H. F. du Pont, 1965

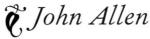 John Allen

1671/72–1760
Boston, Massachusetts

John Allen was the son of the Reverend James Allen of Boston's First Church, whose first wife, Hannah, was silversmith Jeremiah Dummer's sister. Allen's mother, Elizabeth, was the widow of John Endicott II. There is speculation that Allen served his apprenticeship with Dummer, but he more likely served it with John Edwards, his future brother-in-law and partner. He married Elizabeth Edwards in 1697. He enjoyed independent wealth (at least in terms of land ownership), and capital may have been his principal contribution to the partnership with John Edwards in the late 1690s. Later, he followed silversmithing sporadically. In 1710 he referred to himself as a grazier but in subsequent documents again called himself a goldsmith. His output remained small, and he probably devoted most of his time and energy to managing his extensive landholdings. In 1736, "weak in body," Allen drew up his will but lived for another twenty-four years. Few examples of work by Allen alone survive; most were made during the partnership with Edwards. See, for example, the standing salt owned by the Metropolitan Museum of Art and spoon no. 56.

References: Buhler, "John Edwards," pp. 288–92. Kane, *Dictionary*, s.v. "Allen, John." Francis Gruber Safford, *Colonial Silver in the American Wing* (New York: Metropolitan Museum of Art, 1983), no. 24. Ward, "Edwards Family," pp. 66–76.

2
TEAPOT, ca. 1735

H. 6⅜" (16.2 cm), w. 8³⁄₁₆" (20.8 cm)
15 oz. 5 dwt. 11 gr. (475.0 g)

Stamps: "I•A" in roman letters, in a rectangle, struck once in center on underside.

Engraved on body to left of handle: armorial device consisting of a single lion rampant in a shield against a diaper-pattern background, all surrounded by leafy foliage and C scrolls and topped with the crest of a lion's head on a heraldic band. *Scratched on underside:* "Stone" ("Storer"?) in roman letters.

Description: raised circular body with bulbous lower half rising to a narrow, slightly flared neck with molded rim and single-scored line encircling neck just under rim; applied footring; cast S-curve spout paneled on lower half, panels overlap body to form scalloped edge. Raised stepped-and-domed lid with large finial consisting of reel-shape lower section separated from bell-shape upper section by a wooden insulator; finial attached to lid by a silver nut and bolt; lid attached to body by a cast 5-segment hinge. C-shape, boldly curved wooden handle with 1 sprig, attached to body by 2 cylindrical sockets and silver pins.

Spectrographic analysis:

	SILVER	COPPER	LEAD	GOLD
UNDERSIDE	92.8	6.5	0.28	0.16
BODY SIDE	90.4	8.9	0.28	0.16
SPOUT	91.1	8.3	0.24	0.13
LID	91.0	8.4	0.21	0.16

History: According to dealer James Graham, the teapot was owned in the Dudley, Saltonstall, Coolidge, and Toppan families of Boston. There is, however, no documentation until it entered the Toppan family. The arms are those used by the Dudleys of Massachusetts.

Provenance: According to Graham, the teapot was inherited in 1910 by Cushing Toppan and passed to his sister-in-law Mrs. Persus Toppan. Presumably it was acquired from her by James Graham & Sons of New York City, which sold the teapot to H. F. du Pont in 1967. See *References* below for ownership that is not wholly consistent with dealer's history.

Exhibitions: "American Church Silver," Museum of Fine Arts, Boston, 1911 (lent by Mrs. Robert N. Toppan), where it was attributed to Josiah Austin. "Colonial Silversmiths: Masters and Apprentices," Museum of Fine Arts, Boston, 1956.

Comments: This early version of the so-called Queen Anne teapot is a rare attempt on the part of a Boston silversmith to work in this form. The only earlier example is one by John Coney, now owned by the Metropolitan Museum of Art. In Boston the form did not achieve the perfection realized in New York by Peter van Dyck and other craftsmen. Bostonians preferred the apple-shape teapot and the later double-bellied version of this form. In its entirety this teapot may not be an overwhelming design success, but it has a stolid majesty; its spout is a masterpiece. An apple-shape teapot made by John Burt, and bearing the same arms, is owned by Yale University Art Gallery.

References: American Church Silver, no. 28, p. 3. Bigelow, *Historic Silver*, pp. 336–37. Buhler, *Masters and Apprentices*, no. 1, fig. 38, where it is attributed "perhaps John Allen," with the lender identified as Cushing Toppan. Buhler and Hood, *American Silver*, no. 112. Donald L. Fennimore, "John Allen Teapot," *Silver* 16, no. 4 (July/August 1983): 19, 20.

67.1906 Bequest of H. F. du Pont, 1969

℞ *Josiah Austin*

1719–80
Boston and Charlestown, Massachusetts

Josiah Austin's parents were James and Mary (Tufts) Austin of Charlestown. In 1742 Josiah married Mary Phillips, and they had eleven children. A number of silver pieces survive that carry the stamps of Austin and Samuel Minott. Austin also shared a partnership with Daniel Boyer, and some items have appeared with the stamps of Austin and Paul Revere. Austin's nephews James and Nathaniel were also silversmiths. Following the military action and subsequent fire of 1775 in Charlestown, Austin claimed losses amounting to £96.8.0, of which £60 was for damage to buildings. Pieces bearing an "IA" stamp were once attributed to Austin but are now ascribed to John Allen. A fine globular teapot with the coat of arms of the Ware family is owned by the Metropolitan Museum of Art.

References: Flynt and Fales, *Heritage Foundation*, p. 147. James F. Hunnewell, *A Century of Town Life: A History of Charlestown, Massachusetts, 1775–1887* (Boston: Little, Brown, 1888), p. 241. Jones, *Old Silver*, pp. 272, 323, 325, 482, 504.

℞ 3
TANKARD, ca. 1763

H. 8 ⅛" (20.6 cm), DIAM. base 5 1/16" (12.8 cm), W. 7 5/16" (18.6 cm)
25 oz. 7 dwt. 18 gr. (789.6 g)

Stamps: "J•AUSTIN" in roman letters, in a rectangle, struck once on body below rim, left of handle.

Engraved on body opposite handle: "The GIFT of/ Mrs. Abigail Stevens/ to the Church/ in/ Charlestown" in roman letters and script, in an oval medallion with a bright-cut border, with a bowknot and pendant ribbons at top. *Engraved on handle:* "CC/ 1763" in roman letters and arabic numbers.

Description: raised body with straight sides; applied base molding rises from plain lower edge to torus molding followed by cyma-recta molding with double bead above; applied molding around rim; double-scored lines encircle body below rim; centerpunch on bottom. Raised, 4-step, slightly domed lid with overlapping flange; double-scored lines encircle edge; cast flame finial attached by a rivet. Cast thumbpiece, gently S curved in profile, with rudimentary scroll motif across top edge; attached to cast 5-segment hinge with a pendant drop; arabic "3" struck into underside of hinge (lid side) and on side of hinge (handle side). Raised-and-soldered hollow S-curve handle terminating in a convex oval tailpiece; notched vent; lower part of handle attached to body with circular plate; upper part of handle has large rounded drop attached to body.

Spectrographic analysis:

	SILVER	COPPER	LEAD	GOLD
BODY	93.3	6.1	0.17	0.11
BOTTOM	94.7	4.7	0.16	0.10
LID	90.3	9.2	0.13	0.09
BASE MOLDING	94.3	5.3	0.12	0.07

History: Although this tankard was indeed part of the communion service owned by the First Church of Charlestown, its history is not what it would appear to be from the inscription. Abigail Stevens, born in 1700, was the daughter of David and Mabel Jenner. She married Edward Wyer in 1719; following Wyer's death, she married sea captain John Stevens of Boston in 1722. Stevens died in 1748, leaving an estate valued at £6,301. In her will, dated May 13, 1776, Abigail Stevens made the following bequest: "I give to the Church of Christ in Charlestown a large silver Tankard marked S/IG and a large Damask Table cloth marked S/IA." The tankard referred to here is not the subject of this entry.

Abigail Stevens's tankard undoubtedly was among the 3 flagons, 7 tankards, and 4 pewter dishes that, "not having been used for many years, were sold, and the proceeds loaned to the town of Charlestown, to be again invested in plate for the use of the communion table, at the pleasure of the church," according to William Budington in 1845. The Stevens inscription was engraved on another tankard (the subject of this entry) that had been acquired earlier, probably in 1763, and not on the tankard she bequeathed—a warning that inscriptions cannot always be taken at face value. The initials "CC" clearly signify Charlestown Church. Abigail Stevens's bequest is nonetheless memorialized, if on the wrong piece.

Abigail Stevens's will, proved June 12, 1782, reveals that she owned considerable property at the time of her death: at least 3 houses (1 in Boston, the "house I live in," and the house occupied by "Matthew Johnson"), the "pasture near the battery," and the pasture on the "neck." She instructed that her slaves Sambo, Dinah, and Violet be freed and cared for if in distress. There were legacies to ministers and relatives as well as the one to the church. A further legacy was provided to "the ten poorest widows in town, the income of £133, if the town make good my loss by the fire, if not then £40 immediately."

Provenance: In March 1926 the First Church of Charlestown sold 14 pieces of communion plate to Alfred Stainforth of Winthrop, Mass., for $7,500. The lot included this and another tankard by Austin (no. 4) plus 2 tankards by Jeremiah

Dummer (nos. 43, 44) and 2 tankards by Edward Winslow (nos. 136, 137). H. F. du Pont puchased the 6 tankards from Israel Sack, Boston, April 1926.

Exhibitions: "American Church Silver," Museum of Fine Arts, Boston, 1911.

Comments: See companion tankard by Austin, no. 4.

References: American Church Silver, nos. 20, 21, pl. 3. William I. Budington, *The History of the First Church of Charlestown* (Boston: By the author, 1845), pp. 240–41. Jones, *Old Silver*, pp. 121–22. Thomas B. Wyman, *Genealogies and Estates of Charlestown in the County of Middlesex and Commonwealth of Massachusetts, 1629–1818*, 2 vols. (Boston, 1879), 2:900.

61.668 Gift of H. F. du Pont, 1965

ℰ 4
TANKARD, ca. 1763

H. 8 ⅛" (20.6 cm), DIAM. base 5 ⅛" (13.0 cm),
W. 7 ⁵⁄₁₆" (18.6 cm)
25 oz. 7 dwt. 14 gr. (789.4 g)

Stamps: "J•AUSTIN" in roman letters, in a
rectangle, struck once on body below rim, left
of handle.

Engraved on handle: "CC/ 1763" in roman
letters and arabic numbers.

Description: same as Austin tankard no. 3 except
for centerpunch on both inside and outside of
bottom and arabic "5" struck into underside
of hinge on lid side and on outside of hinge on
handle side.

Spectrographic analysis:

	SILVER	COPPER	LEAD	GOLD
BODY	91.8	7.5	0.21	0.13
BOTTOM	94.5	7.5	0.18	0.13
LID	90.4	9.1	0.14	0.14
BASE MOLDING	94.2	5.3	0.12	0.12

History: Part of the communion service of the
First Church of Charlestown. Probably a gift
or bequest to the church in 1763. The initials
"CC" clearly signify Charlestown Church.

Provenance: See no. 3.

Exhibitions: See no. 3.

Comments: See companion tankard by Austin,
no. 3.

References: See no. 3.

61.667 Gift of H. F. du Pont, 1965

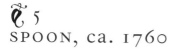

ℰ 5
SPOON, ca. 1760

L. 8" (20.3 cm)
1 oz. 12 dwt. 8 gr. (50.3 g)

Stamps: "I Austin" (with a distinctive long "S")
in roman letters, in a rectangle, struck once on
back of handle.

Engraved on back of handle: "MC" in roman
letters.

Description: elongated oval bowl with swage-
formed shell with 15 lobes and a drop on back;
rounded upturned handle with midrib on front.

Spectrographic analysis: Silver content is 89.8
percent.

Provenance: Mr. and Mrs. Stanley B. Ineson,
New York City; Mr. and Mrs. Alfred E. Bissell,
Wilmington, Del.

References: Belden, *Marks of American Silversmiths*, p. 36 a.

62.240.895 Gift of Mr. and Mrs. Alfred E.
Bissell, 1962–63

Butler Bement

1784–1869
Pittsfield, Massachusetts

Born in Waterbury, Connecticut, Butler Bement spent most of his life in the western Massachusetts town of Pittsfield. He was a business partner of Nathaniel Dexter from 1808 to 1810. His newspaper advertisement of 1816 said that he did gold and silver work and was a watch- and clockmaker. He is represented by a few pieces of flatware and some presentation vases. He died prosperous, which suggests that he had other more lucrative pursuits than silversmithing.

References: Flynt and Fales, *Heritage Foundation*, p. 156.

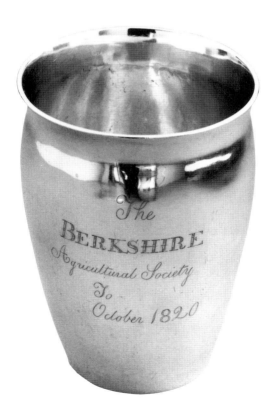

6
VASE, ca. 1820

H. 3 5/16" (10.0 cm), DIAM. rim 3 3/8" (8.6 cm), DIAM. base 1 3/4" (4.5 cm)
4 oz. 11 dwt. 4 gr. (141.8 g)

Stamps: "B.BEMENT" in roman letters, in a rectangle, struck twice on underside.

Engraved on side: "The/ BERKSHIRE/ Agricultural Society/ To [blank]/ October 1820" in script and shaded roman letters.

Description: circular flat-bottomed vessel with gently bulging sides, incurved neck, and flared plain rim; centerpunch on underside.

Spectrographic analysis:

	SILVER	COPPER	LEAD	GOLD
SIDE	88.8	10.9	0.15	0.12
UNDERSIDE	91.1	8.7	0.06	0.15

History: The Berkshire Agricultural Society (BAS), founded in 1811, was the brainchild of Elkannah Watson (1758–1842), an indefatigable merchant, canal promoter, and advocate of scientific farming. In 1807 Watson moved from Albany to Pittsfield, where he purchased a large farm for the purpose of practicing scientific agriculture. He concluded that new and better methods of agriculture could best be introduced through a competitive exhibition of farm products. The Berkshire Plan, as it came to be known, was widely emulated and marked the beginning of the American county fair. Watson recommended that small silver cups be given as prizes at these fairs and even provided a sample illustration. Watson's design is reflected in this vase by Bement.

Watson sold his farm and moved back to Albany in 1816, but the society continued to flourish. Awards took various forms in silver: bowls, sugar bowls, cups, spoons, and medals. By 1817 the small vase form was adopted, and several survive. The history of this particular vase is unknown because it lacks the name of the person to whom it was awarded, an unusual occurence since other surviving BAS vases are engraved with the names of recipients.

Provenance: Purchased in Kentucky by Charles van Ravenswaay.

Comments: The simplicity of this small vase is in keeping with Watson's idea of a democratic agricultural exhibition. The exhibitions and the awards were not for gentlemen farmers only but for all farmers. The sheer number of awards given dictated modest individual prizes.

A similar BAS presentation piece, also made by Bement for the 1820 fair, is in the Hammer-slough collection, Wadsworth Atheneum.

References: DAB, s.v. "Watson, Elkannah." Mary Ellen Hern, "Silver Beaker 69.207 from the Berkshire Agricultural Society," Registration Division, Winterthur. Wayne C. Neely, *The Agricultural Fair* (New York: Columbia University Press, 1935), esp. chap. 5. Warren, Howe, and Brown, *Marks of Achievement*, fig. 82, for illustration of Watson's cup design.

69.207 Gift of Charles van Ravenswaay, 1969

7
SPOON, ca. 1825

L. 5 1/2" (14.0 cm)
8 dwt. 8 gr. (12.9 g)

Stamps: "B.BEMENT" in roman letters, in a rectangle, struck once on back of handle.

Engraved on front of handle: "CH" (sideways) in neoclassical script.

Description: pointed oval bowl with incised pointed drop on back; rounded downturned fiddle-shape handle.

Spectrographic analysis: Silver content is 89.6 percent.

Provenance: Mr. and Mrs. Stanley B. Ineson, New York City; Mr. and Mrs. Alfred E. Bissell, Wilmington, Del.

References: Belden, *Marks of American Silversmiths*, p. 56.

62.240.93 Gift of Mr. and Mrs. Alfred E. Bissell, 1962–63

William Breed

1719–ca. 1761
Boston, Massachusetts

William Breed was the son of Nathaniel and Sarah (Davise) Breed. He married Susannah Burrington in 1743. In January 1762 the court appointed brewer Sampson Salter of Boston as guardian of Breed's son; the papers refer to "William Breed, Goldsmith" and suggest that Breed died in the latter part of 1761. Only a few examples of his work survive. An interesting strainer, owned by Massachusetts Historical Society, has a lengthy inscription in Latin commemorating Jonathan Vryling, who died in 1744.

References: American Silver and Art Treasures (London: Christie's for the English-Speaking Union, 1960), no. 26, for the strainer. Flynt and Fales, *Heritage Foundation*, p. 164. Kane, *Dictionary*, s.v. "Breed, William."

8
PORRINGER, ca. 1750

DIAM. bowl 5 ⁹⁄₁₆" (14.1 cm), H. 1 ¾" (4.5 cm), w. 8" (20.3 cm)
8 oz. 4 dwt. 13 gr. (255.9 g)

Stamps: "WB" (conjoined upper serifs) in italics, in a rectangle with rounded corners, struck once on upper surface of handle; "WBreed" (conjoined "WB") in script, in a rectangle, struck on upper surface of handle.

Engraved on upper surface of handle: "I/ A*E" in roman letters.

Description: raised circular bowl with bulging sides and slightly angled rim; bottom domed in center; centerpunch inside; cast handle in keyhole pattern with 11 voids.

Spectrographic analysis:

	SILVER	COPPER	LEAD	GOLD
BOWL BOTTOM	90.6	8.9	0.14	0.05
HANDLE	94.5	5.1	0.09	0.06

History: Possibly owned by the Johonnot family of Boston; see no. 108.

Provenance: Katrina Kipper, Queen Anne Cottage, Accord, Mass., sold to H. F. du Pont, August 1930.

Exhibitions: None, but an identical porringer with the same initials ("American Church Silver," Museum of Fine Arts, Boston, 1911) was owned by William Beltran de Las Casas.

Comments: Another porringer by Breed, bearing the same engraved inscription and the same stamps, is owned by the Museum of Fine Arts, Boston.

References: Fales, *American Silver*, no. 13. *American Church Silver*, no. 63. Buhler, *American Silver*, no. 244.

59.3355 Gift of H. F. du Pont, 1965

Benjamin Brenton

1710–66
Newport, Rhode Island, w. 1732–47

The son of Benjamin Brenton, mariner, and Sarah (Collins) Brenton and grandson of Arnold Collins (d. 1735), the silversmith who made a seal for the Rhode Island General Assembly in 1689, Benjamin Brenton may have learned the silversmith trade from his grandfather. He apparently combined two careers, for in 1742 he was referred to as "Mariner alias Goldsmith." He retired to his farm in South Kingston, Rhode Island, about 1747. His death was noted in records of the Naragansett Church: "April 1st [1766] Major Benjamin Brenton Died and Three Days After (Which was the 4th of April) Buried On his own Farm: The Burial Service Performed by Mr F[ayerweather] At the Majors Desire Who in his Sickness was Visited by Mr F and Prayed With." Brenton made a pair of flagons for Trinity Church, Newport, in 1733.

References: Margaret Ballard, "Early Silver in Trinity Church, Newport, Rhode Island," *Antiques* 120, no. 4 (October 1981): 922–25. Flynt and Fales, *Heritage Foundation*, pp. 164–65. Wilkins Updike, *A History of the Episcopal Church in Narrangansett, Rhode Island*, 3 vols. (Boston: D. B. Updike, 1907), 2:59, 291, 574–75.

9
BOX, ca. 1730

H. ⅝" (1.6 cm), w. 2 ¹¹⁄₁₆" (6.9 cm), D. 2" (5.1 cm)
1 oz. 1 dwt. 6 gr. (33.1 g)

Stamps: "BB" in roman letters, in a rectangle with rounded corners, struck once on inside bottom of body.

Engraved on underside of body: "I+S/ M+S" in roman letters. *Engraved on top of lid:* central putto head (face-on) under spread-winged phoenix, surrounding space filled with leafy scrolls, all enclosed within border of incised lines and stylized pointed leaves enfilade.

Description: small oval box with friction-fit lid. Sides formed from seamed sheet silver that is soldered to flat base. Lid similarly made. Both top of lid and base of body formed from sheet.

Spectrographic analysis:

	SILVER	COPPER	LEAD	GOLD
UNDERSIDE	93.1	5.9	0.37	0.18
LID	91.4	8.1	0.18	0.14
SIDE	90.1	8.7	0.54	0.12

Provenance: H. F. du Pont.

Comments: The attribution to Brenton remains questionable. In the absence of another American "BB" stamp of this period, however, it seems best to keep the association. An oval box by Samuel Vernon with a nearly identical engraved lid design was offered for sale by Parke-Bernet Galleries in 1971. Oval boxes by William Whittemore and Vernon also employ a border of stylized pointed leaves; see nos. 130, 134.

References: Kenneth Blakemore, *Snuff Boxes* (London: Frederick Muller, 1976), fig. 29. Fales, *American Silver*, no. 17. Kauffman, *Colonial Silversmith*, p. 139. Parke-Bernet Galleries, sale no. 3229 (June 15, 1971), lot 151.

52.290 Gift of H. F. du Pont, 1952

ℰ Zachariah Brigden

1734–87
Boston, Massachusetts

Born in Charlestown, Massachusetts, to blacksmith Michael Brigden and his wife Winifred, Zachariah Brigden served his apprenticeship under Thomas Edwards, whose daughter Sarah became Brigden's first wife in 1756. In 1764 his shop was in Cornhill "opposite the West Door of the Town House." His newspaper advertisement of that year offered:

Coral beads and Stick Coral for Children's Whistle's; Money Scales and Weights; neat Watch Plyers; Sliding Tongs; Shears and hand Vices; coarse and fine Iron Binding Wire; Brass Hollow Stamps and Blow Pipes; and Assortment of Files for the Goldsmith's use; Gravers; Scorpers; Dividers; Sand Paper; Sandever; Black Lead Pot; large and small Crucibles; Wood and Bone Polishing Brushes; Borax; Salt Petre; Rotten and Pumice Stone; Molding Sand by the Cask or Retail. Also Shoe, Knee and Stock Stone Buckles; Buttons; Christal and Cornelian Seals; Neat Stone Bosom Broaches; Garnet; Hoop Rings. A few Pair of neat Stone Earings set in Clusters, in Shagreen Cases, Cheap for Cash.

It is notable that this advertisement is directed primarily toward other goldsmiths; merchandise for the retail trade is almost an afterthought. Brigden worked in both the rococo and neoclassical styles. E. Alfred Jones found Brigden's silver in churches in Duxbury, Northborough, Salem, Springfield, and Stoneham, Massachusetts; Kittery, Maine; and Hartford, Connecticut. More than 100 examples of his work survive.

Brigden's estate inventory shows that he had in his parlor a "Parlour eight Day Clock," one small and one large carpet, a spinnet, a large dining table, two mahogany tea tables, one painted tea table, eight mahogany frame chairs, and a stove and funnel. His shop included several glass display cases. His goldsmith's tools were sold to Benjamin Burt, one of the appraisers of his estate.

An account book surfaced in the 1980s that is thought, on the basis of internal evidence, to have been used by Brigden. Purchased by Yale University Art Gallery, the volume shows a broad range of transactions with other silversmiths. (See essay "Authorship.")

References: Hilary Anderson, "The Business of Silversmith Zachariah Brigden" (Master's thesis, University of Delaware, forthcoming). Dow, *Arts and Crafts,* p. 42. Flynt and Fales, *Heritage Foundation,* p. 166. SCPR book 86, pp. 220–22. Kane, *Dictionary,* s.v. "Brigden, Zachariah."

ℰ 10
CASTER, 1765–87

H. 5 ¹¹⁄₁₆" (14.5 cm), DIAM. 2 ¹⁄₁₆" (5.2 cm)
3 oz. 13 dwt. 7 gr. (114.0 g)

Stamps: "Z•B" in roman letters, in a rectangle, struck once on underside.

Engraved on side of body: "WA" in foliate script, in a bright-cut circle. *Engraved on underside:* "A/ WP" in roman letters. *Scratched on underside of foot and on bezel of lid:* "M 6811". *Engraved on lid:* rectilinear borders for 6 panels with cross-hatching within panels.

Description: consists of body, foot, and friction-fit lid. Double-bellied lower body with tall inward-tapering neck and molded rim; center-punch on underside. Circular stepped foot applied to body. High-dome lid with cast pine-applelike finial and molded flange; sides divided into 6 vertical panels with about 29 drilled perforations per panel. Lower body raised; upper body seamed; rim drawn; foot cast; dome and finial cast; remainder of lid raised.

Spectrographic analysis:

	SILVER	COPPER	GOLD	LEAD
BODY	90.0	9.7	0.21	0.11
LID	88.8	10.9	0.14	0.21

Provenance: Marshall P. Blankarn, New York City.

Comments: Two other nearly identical casters by Brigden exist: 1 is in the Minneapolis Institute of Art; the other was advertised by William Core Duffy in *Maine Antique Digest* (April 1986).

79.200 Gift of Marshall P. Blankarn, 1979

🜸 11 a, b
SPOONS, 1755–87

(a) L. 8 15/16" (22.7 cm)
1 oz. 15 dwt. 7 gr. (54.9 g)
(b) L. 8 ⅜" (21.3 cm)
2 oz. 3 dwt. (66.9 g)

Stamps: "Z•B" in roman letters, in a rectangle, struck once on the back of each handle.

Engraved on front of handle: (a) "M∗C" in roman letters. *Engraved on back of handle:* (b) "SS" in roman letters.

Description: (a) oval bowl with swage-formed triangular drop on back; pointed downturned handle with no midrib; (b) oval bowl with swage-formed drop and 13-lobe shell on back; rounded upturned handle with midrib on front.

Spectrographic analysis: Silver content ranges from 85.4 to 91.5 percent.

Provenance: (a) Mr. and Mrs. Stanley B. Ineson, New York City; Mr. and Mrs. Alfred E. Bissell, Wilmington, Del.; (b) Mr. and Mrs. Dean A. Fales, Wilmington, Del.

References: (a) Belden, *Marks of American Silversmiths*, p. 75 c.

(a) 62.240.985 Gift of Mr. and Mrs. Alfred E. Bissell, 1962–63; (b) 57.123 Gift of Mr. and Mrs. Dean A. Fales, Jr., 1957

🜸 12 a, b
SPOONS, 1765–87

(a) L. 8" (20.3 cm)
1 oz. 17 dwt. (57.5 g)
(b) L. 8 9/16" (21.8 cm)
2 oz. 3 dwt. (66.9 g)

Stamps: "Z•Brigden" in roman letters and script, in a conforming cartouche, struck once on back of each handle.

Engraved on back of handle: (a) "D/ JM" in roman letters. *Engraved on front of handle:* (b) "ARB" in neoclassical script.

Description: (a) elongated oval bowl with swage-formed square drop and an 11-lobe shell on back; rounded upturned handle with midrib on front; (b) oval bowl with swage-formed rounded drop and elaborate 8-lobe webbed shell on back; downturned handle with midrib on back and bright-cut featheredge on front.

Spectrographic analysis: Silver content ranges from 88.5 to 93.8 percent.

Provenance: Mr. and Mrs. Stanley B. Ineson, New York City; Mr. and Mrs. Alfred E. Bissell, Wilmington, Del.

References: Belden, *Marks of American Silversmiths*, p. 75 a.

(a) 62.240.927, (b) 62.240.928 Gift of Mr. and Mrs. Alfred E. Bissell, 1962–63

ℰ Samuel Burrill

1704–before 1740
Boston, Massachusetts,
w. ca. 1725–ca. 1740

Samuel Burrill was the son of Samuel Burrill, sailmaker, and his wife Martha. At age eighteen Burrill witnessed a deed for silversmith Andrew Tyler, which may indicate that he served his apprenticeship with Tyler. There is no record that Burrill married. The *Boston Weekly News-Letter* of April 15/22, 1731, noted the removal of one Joseph Goldthwait, goldsmith, from "Mr. Burril's shop." His father's will, drawn up in 1740, does not mention him. Two pieces of church silver by Burrill—a tankard in the First Church of Watertown and a flagon in Boston's Second Church—are recorded by E. Alfred Jones, and an elegant pair of chafing dishes is owned by the Heritage Foundation at Historic Deerfield. Otherwise, few examples of his work survive.

References: Dow, *Arts and Crafts*, p. 46. Flynt and Fales, *Heritage Foundation*, p. 173. Jones, *Old Silver*, pp. 39, 482. Kane, *Dictionary*, s.v. "Burrill, Samuel."

ℰ 13
MILK POT, ca. 1735

H. 4" (10.2 cm), w. 3 ¹¹/₁₆" (9.4 cm)
3 oz. 13 dwt. 13 gr. (114.4 g)

Stamps: "SB" in roman letters, in a rectangle, struck once on underside.

Engraved on body under pouring lip: "AJC/ 1823" in foliate script and arabic numbers. *Engraved on side of body:* "PFB/ 1864" in script and arabic numbers. *Engraved on bottom of feet:* "R"; "C", both in roman letters; and "1719". *Scratched into underside:* "A.J.C." in crude script.

Description: raised pear-shape body with curvilinear flared rim and prominent curved pouring lip; centerpunch on underside; cast double–C-scroll handle with sprig on upper handle and scroll terminal on the lower; 3 short legs cast as back-to-back C scrolls with trifid feet.

Spectrographic analysis:

	SILVER	COPPER	LEAD	GOLD
BODY SIDE	95.6	4.1	0.18	0.12
HANDLE	93.4	6.0	0.35	0.17

Provenance: Marshall P. Blankarn, New York City.

Comments: All inscriptions are nineteenth century (or later) with the possible exception of those on the feet, which were probably added in the late eighteenth century. The milk pot could not have been made in 1719, as suggested by the inscription. It is an early example of the form.

79.196 Gift of Marshall P. Blankarn, 1979

ℰ 14
SPOON, ca. 1730

L. 6 ¹/₁₆" (12.9 cm)
16 dwt. 5 gr. (25.2 g)

Stamps: "S[?]" (illegible second letter but presumed to be "B") in roman letters, in a rectangle, struck once on back of handle. "[?] Burrill" (illegible first letter but assumed to be "S") in script, in a rectangle with rounded corners, struck once on back of handle.

Description: elongated oval bowl with long rattail on back; rounded upturned handle with midrib on front.

Spectrographic analysis: Silver content is 92.7 percent.

Provenance: Mr. and Mrs. Stanley B. Ineson, New York City; Mr. and Mrs. Alfred E. Bissell, Wilmington, Del.

Comments: It is unfortunate that there are no better impressions of these 2 stamps; they are sufficient, however, to document the "SB" stamp when found alone elsewhere.

References: Belden, *Marks of American Silversmiths*, p. 89.

62.240.949 Gift of Mr. and Mrs. Alfred E. Bissell, 1962–63

Benjamin Burt

1729–1805
Boston, Massachusetts

A son of John Burt, Benjamin Burt, like his brothers Samuel and William before him, became a silversmith. Unlike his brothers, who died at an early age, Benjamin enjoyed a long and prosperous career. In 1800, at age seventy-one, he was chosen to lead Boston silversmiths in the memorial procession honoring George Washington. Burt was also notable for his enormous bulk; he is said to have weighed 380 pounds. He lived on Fish Street, adjoining North Square, near Paul Revere, and he rivaled Revere in craftsmanship and quantity of silver produced. Although he adapted neoclassical decoration—largely engraving—his forms remained those of the rococo style of the third quarter of the eighteenth century. E. Alfred Jones reported finding Burt's silver in churches in Lexington, Marblehead, Medford, Northborough, Romney Marsh, Gloucester, Salem, Lynn, Reading, Woburn, Berkeley, Brookline, Dorchester, and Ipswich. Burt was related to Samuel Shaw, who was supercargo on the *Empress of China* (the first American ship to enter the China trade), through his daughter's marriage to Shaw's brother. Shaw sent Burt two "china" punch bowls from Canton, which he described in his will as his largest and second-largest bowls. Burt bequeathed his tools to silversmith Samuel Waters, and he appointed silversmith Joseph Foster, "my trusty friend," as executor of his estate. (Foster had been one of his apprentices.) His will refers to two silver tumblers "with my name engraven thereon" and "my large Silver Tankard having a coat of arms engraven thereon." Although not itemized in his inventory, in total he owned 207 ounces of silver.

References: Flynt and Fales, *Heritage Foundation*, p. 173. Forbes, *Paul Revere*, pp. 164–65. Kane, *Dictionary*, s.v. "Burt, Benjamin." SCPR book 103, pp. 498–500.

15 a, b
CASTERS, 1760–80

(a) H. 5" (12.7 cm), w. 1 ¹⁵⁄₁₆" (4.9 cm)
2 oz. 17 dwt. 8 gr. (89.2 g)
(b) H. 5 ¹⁄₁₆" (12.9 cm), w. 2" (5.1 cm)
2 oz. 17 dwt. 20 gr. (89.9 g)

Stamps: "B•Burt" in roman letters, in a rounded rectangle, struck once on side of each body.

Engraved on underside of each: "B/ I•A" in roman letters; a cross next to centerpunch.
Engraved on lids: rectilinear borders for 6 panels and cross-hatching within panels.

Description: consists of body, foot, and friction-fit lid. Double-bellied lower body with tall inward-tapering neck and molded rim; center-punch on bottom. Circular stepped foot applied to body. High-dome lid with cast pineapplelike finial and molded flange; sides divided into 6 vertical panels with about 27 drilled perforations per panel, with those on (a) larger than those on (b). Body cast in 2 vertical sections and seamed. Foot and top of lid cast. Main body of lid formed with seamed sheet silver.

Spectrographic analysis:

	SILVER	COPPER	LEAD	GOLD
(a)				
FOOT	92.8	6.3	0.30	0.22
BODY SIDE	89.0	9.9	0.38	0.16
LID	89.2	9.4	0.50	0.21
FINIAL	89.7	8.7	0.42	0.24
(b)				
FOOT	92.8	6.2	0.28	0.25
BODY SIDE	88.7	10.2	0.35	0.18
LID	90.8	8.1	0.31	0.18
FINIAL	93.0	6.6	0.07	0.05

History: Tradition of ownership in the Russell and Middleton families of Bristol, R.I. Since, however, the Browns of Providence are known to have been patrons of Benjamin Burt, there is the possibility of a Brown family provenance.

Provenance: Mr. and Mrs. N. McLean Seabrease, Germantown, Pa.; Robert Ensko, Inc., New York City, sold to H. F. du Pont as part of the Seabrease collection, August 1929.

Comments: The caster with the larger perforations was probably for salt; the one with the smaller perforations was probably for pepper. See spoon by Samuel Vernon also bearing initials "B/I•A" (no. 131 f).

References: Richard G. Baumann, "Peppering the Bostonian Palate: Two Silver Casters by Paul Revere II," *MUSE* (Museum of Art and Archaeology, Univ. of Missouri-Columbia) 10 (1976): 37–47, for a similar pair of casters. Fales, *American Silver*, no. 102. Kauffman, *Colonial Silversmith*, p. 145.

(a) 59.3356, (b) 59.3357 Gift of H. F. du Pont, 1965

16 a, b
SPOONS, 1775–1805

(a) L. 5" (12.7 cm), 8 dwt. 1 gr. (12.5 g)
(b) L. 5 1/16" (12.9 cm), 6 dwt. 8 gr. (9.9g)

Stamps: "B•BURT" in roman letters, in a rectangle.

Engraved on back of handle: (a) "IT" in roman letters; (b) "WT" in roman letters.

Description: (a) oval bowl with swage-formed bird (branch in beak) and a drop on back; rounded downturned handle with midrib on back and bright-cut featheredge decoration on front; (b) oval bowl with swage-formed drop on back; pointed downturned handle with floral pendant in bright-cut oval on front.

Spectrographic analysis: Silver content ranges from 89.4 to 90.9 percent.

Provenance: Mr. and Mrs. Stanley B. Ineson, New York City; Mr. and Mrs. Alfred E. Bissell, Wilmington, Del.

Exhibitions: (a) Metropolitan Museum of Art, New York City, 1935–61.

References: Belden, *Marks of American Silversmiths*, p. 89.

(a) 62.240.129, (b) 62.240.164 Gift of Mr. and Mrs. Alfred E. Bissell, 1962–63

17
SPOON, 1760–1805

L. 4 7/16" (11.3 cm), 4 dwt. 14 gr. (7.2 g)

Stamps: "B•BURT" in roman letters, in a rectangle, struck once on back of handle.

Engraved on back of handle: "MP" in roman letters.

Description: oval bowl with swage-formed shell and drop on back; rounded upturned handle with midrib on front.

Spectrographic analysis: Silver content is 88.8 percent.

Provenance: Mr. and Mrs. Stanley B. Ineson, New York City; Mr. and Mrs. Alfred E. Bissell, Wilmington, Del.

Comments: Appears to be a different stamp from previous spoons; see no. 16.

References: Belden, *Marks of American Silversmiths*, p. 89.

62.240.131 Gift of Mr. and Mrs. Alfred E. Bissell, 1962–63

18 a, b
SPOONS, 1775–1805

(a) L. 5 1/8" (13.0 cm), 8 dwt. 4 gr. (12.8 g)
(b) L. 4 15/16" (12.5 cm), 6 dwt. 14 gr. (10.3 g)

Stamps: "B•BURT" in roman letters, in a rectangle, struck once on back of each handle.

Engraved on front of handle: (a) "IM" in roman letters; (b) "D/ IS" in roman letters, in an oval.

Description: (a) oval bowl with swage-formed shell and drop on back; rounded downturned handle with midrib on back and featheredge decoration on front; (b) oval bowl with swage-formed elongated drop on back; pointed handle with bright-cut floral pendant in oval on front.

Spectrographic analysis: Silver content ranges from 92.0 to 96.0 percent.

Provenance: Mr. and Mrs. Stanley B. Ineson, New York City; Mr. and Mrs. Alfred E. Bissell, Wilmington, Del.

Comments: Stamp is similar to no. 17.

References: Belden, *Marks of American Silversmiths*, p. 89.

(a) 62.240.162, (b) 62.240.163 Gift of Mr. and Mrs. Alfred E. Bissell, 1962–63

19 a, b
SPOONS, 1750–75

(a) L. 7 3/4" (19.7 cm), 1 oz. 15 dwt. 9 gr. (55.0 g)
(b) L. 7 7/16" (18.9 cm), 1 oz. 8 dwt. 14 gr. (44.5 g)

Stamps: "BENJAMIN/ BURT" in slanted roman letters, in a conforming cartouche, struck once on back of each handle.

Engraved on back of handle: (a) "T/ IM"; (b) "H/ IS", both in roman letters.

Description: oval bowls with swage-formed shell and drop on back; rounded upturned handles with midrib on front.

Spectrographic analysis: Silver content ranges from 90.1 to 92.1 percent.

Provenance: Mr. and Mrs. Stanley B. Ineson, New York City; Mr. and Mrs. Alfred E. Bissell, Wilmington, Del.

References: Belden, *Marks of American Silversmiths*, p. 89 b.

(a) 62.240.948, (b) 62.240.1203 Gift of Mr. and Mrs. Alfred E. Bissell, 1962–63

John Burt

1692/93–1746
Boston, Massachusetts

John Burt founded a dynasty. In 1714 he married Abigail Cheever, daughter of the Reverend Thomas Cheever. His sons—Samuel, William, and Benjamin—all became silversmiths. His son and namesake, John Burt (1716–75), graduated from Harvard College and ministered to the flock of the First Church of Bristol. The senior John Burt had many distinguished clients, including Harvard College. He made a considerable number of pieces for presentation by students to Harvard tutor Nicholas Sever (1680–1764), who compiled a list of the gifts in 1728. The list included a two-quart tankard, a quart tankard, a pair of chafing dishes, a pair of candlesticks, two salvers, a pair of canns, two porringers, a teapot, and two salts. Most of this silver survived to be included in a 1934 exhibition at the Fogg Art Museum in Cambridge. The two chafing dishes, made about 1724 and now in the Hammerslough collection, Wadsworth Atheneum, are elegant examples of the form. Burt was a prolific craftsman, and large quantities of his silver survive. E. Alfred Jones recorded many of his pieces in American churches. An impressive lighthouse coffeepot made for David and Mary Grimm of Boston is now in the Detroit Institute of Arts. A hexafoil salver on pedestal is in the Harrington collection at Dartmouth College.

The inventory of Burt's estate includes a lengthy and detailed list of goldsmith's tools, some of which are uncommon in such lists: a touchstone, a thimble stamp, a pair of brass salt punches, and two spoon teastes. One of the appraisers of the estate was goldsmith William Simpkins, who, no doubt, provided the detailed information on the tools. Burt was one of the wealthier silversmiths of his generation, having accumulated an estate of £6,460 by the time of his death.

References: W. Nicholas Dudley, "Nicholas Sever's Plate Returns to Harvard," *American Collector* 2, no. 1 (June 28, 1934): 3, 8. Flynt and Fales, *Heritage Foundation*, pp. 173–74. Richard Walden Hale, *Catalogue of Silver Owned by Nicholas Sever, A.B. 1701, in 1728* (Boston: By the author, 1931). Kane, *Dictionary*, s.v. "Burt, John." SCPR book 39, pp. 160–61.

20 a, b
CANDLESTICKS, ca. 1720

(a) H. 7 ³⁄₁₆" (18.3 cm), w. base 4 ⁷⁄₁₆" (11.3 cm)
14 oz. 16 dwt. 14 gr. (461.3 g)
(b) H. 7 ³⁄₁₆" (18.3 cm), w. base 4 ⁷⁄₁₆" (11.3 cm)
15 oz. 6 dwt. 4 gr. (476.1 g)

Stamps: "J.BURT" in slanted roman letters, in an elongated oval, struck 4 times, once on each inside edge on base of each candlestick.

Engraved on inside of base: "W / D+S" in roman letters.

Description: cast-and-seamed baluster-form candlesticks consisting of the following: square, stepped base with double-scalloped corners and circular drip pan as an integral part of base. The baluster-form shaft has 2 knops and a pedestal; the lower knop is circular in plan and stepped vertically; the upper knop is square in plan with scalloped corners repeating those on base; the upper knop rises out of a hexagonal flaring shaft. Cylindrical socket with double-molded bands around base and rim and single-molded midband.

Spectrographic analysis:

	SILVER	COPPER	LEAD	GOLD
(a)				
BASE	92.5	6.6	0.25	0.18
SOCKET	91.3	8.2	0.26	0.12
(b)				
BASE	93.9	5.2	0.19	0.21
SOCKET	91.4	8.0	0.26	0.14

History: The initals "W / D+S" refer to Daniel and Sarah Warner of Portsmouth, N.H., who were married December 15, 1720. Daniel's parents were Philemon and Abigail (Tuttle) Warner of Ipswich (and later Gloucester), Mass. Sarah's parents were Nathaniel and Sarah (Nutter) Hill. Daniel Warner (1694–1778) was a merchant and active in public life. He was appointed to the New Hampshire Council in 1753 and served until the revolutionary war. He was involved with the building of the first State House. His own house, much modified, still stands on Islington

Street in Portsmouth. Warner died intestate. The inventory of his estate reveals his extensive landholdings in addition to his "Mansion House Gardens and Outhouses" in Portsmouth and includes 21 gold rings and 173 oz. 12 dwt. of "Wrot Plate," the latter regrettably not itemized.

Daniel's son Col. Jonathan Warner (1726–1813) is perhaps better known. He became a member of the New Hampshire Council in 1766. His inventory includes 689 oz. 6 dwt. of "Silver Plate." Among the other children of Daniel and Sarah were Capt. Samuel Warner (1737–71), who, in 1761, married Elizabeth Wentworth (1739–93), the granddaughter of Lt. Gov. John Wentworth; and Sarah Warner (born 1721/2), who married Henry Sherburne (1709–67) in 1740. Because the candlesticks and related pieces were purchased early in the twentieth century from a Sherburne descendant, it is assumed that these objects descended through Sarah (Warner) Sherburne.

Provenance: Daniel Warner (1699–1778) and his wife Sarah (d. 1788); Sarah (Warner) Sherburne (1721/2–?) and her husband Henry (1709–67) of Portsmouth, N.H.; descending eventually to Evelyn Sherburne, who in the early twentieth century sold them to Hermann F. Clarke, Boston; Israel Sack, Inc., New York City, sold to Charles K. Davis (1889–1967), who bequeathed them to H. F. du Pont.

Exhibitions: "Harvard Tercentenary Exhibition," Harvard University, Cambridge, 1936. "Masterpieces of New England Silver," Gallery of Fine Arts, Yale University, New Haven, 1939.

References: Agnes Bartlett, "Portsmouth Families," ca. 1940, manuscript notebooks, State Archives, Concord, N.H. Bigelow, *Historic Silver*, p. 294. *Harvard Tercentenary Exhibition: Furniture and Decorative Arts of the Period 1636–1836* (Cambridge: Harvard University Press, 1936), no. 132. John Mead Howells, *The Architectural Heritage of the Piscataqua* (New York: Architectural Book Publishing, 1937), fig. 131, for illustration of Daniel Warner's house. *Masterpieces of New England Silver, 1650–1800* (New Haven: Gallery of Fine Arts, Yale University, 1939), nos. 19 a, b. Daniel Warner, Rockingham County Probate Records, no. 4496. Harold Sack with Max Wilk, *American Treasure Hunt* (Boston: Little, Brown, 1986), pp. 123–29, for an account of the sale of candlesticks, snuffers, and a tray by Hermann F. Clarke to Charles K. Davis through Israel Sack, Inc. John Wentworth, *The Wentworth Genealogy*, 3 vols. (Boston: Little, Brown, 1878): 1:295, 316–17, 328–29; 3:10.

Comments: The candlesticks are part of a unique set that includes a snuffer and tray, also by Burt; see no. 21 a, b. I am indebted to James L. Garvin for information on Daniel and Sarah Warner and their progeny. A pair of candlesticks of a different design, also made by Burt, is owned by Harvard University. They were presented to tutor Nicholas Sever in 1724.

(a) 67.1443.1, (b) 67.1443.2 Bequest of H. F. du Pont, 1969

21 a, b
SNUFFERS AND TRAY, ca. 1720

(a) L. 5 11/16" (14.5 cm)
2 oz. 16 dwt. 13 gr. (87.8 g)
(b) L. 7 5/16" (18.6 cm), H. 2 5/8" (6.7 cm), w. 3 13/16" (9.7 cm)
8 oz. 11 dwt. 12 gr. (266.1 g)

Stamps: (a) "JOHN/ BURT" in slanted roman letters, in a rectangle with rounded ends, struck once inside pan; (b) same stamp struck once on upper surface near center.

Engraved on underside of pan (a) and on underside of tray (b): "W/ D+S" in roman letters.

Description: (a) cast scissor form with semicircular pan on 1 arm and a quarter-sphere hood and pointed terminal on the other; circular grips with spurs; (b) flat surface, octagonal on ends, with boldly incurved sides; flared edge probably formed as 1 piece with tray; cast handle in the form of an open double-sprig C scroll applied to 1 incurved side; 4 cast-and-applied short cabriole legs with double-pad feet.

Spectrographic analysis:

	SILVER	COPPER	LEAD	GOLD
SNUFFERS	89.4	9.8	0.25	0.17
TRAY BODY	93.3	6.0	0.17	0.14
TRAY FOOT	90.6	8.5	0.22	0.21

For *History, Provenance, Exhibitions,* and *References,* see no. 20.

Comments: The snuffer and tray were made en suite with a pair of candlesticks by the same maker; see no. 20. The Hollis French collection at Cleveland Museum of Art includes a snuffer and tray with the "JOHN/ BURT" stamp, but its authenticity has been questioned.

64.1401a, b Bequest of H. F. du Pont, 1969

ℰ 22
SPOON, ca. 1720

L. 7 11/16" (19.5 cm)
1 oz. 13 dwt. 15 gr. (52.3 g)

Stamps: "I BURT" in slanted roman letters, in a rectangular surround with serrated top and sides and cyma curves on bottom, struck once on back of handle.

Engraved on back of handle: "C+C" in roman letters.

Description: elongated oval bowl with swage-formed rattail on back; rounded upturned handle end with midrib on front.

Spectrographic analysis: Silver content is 92.4 percent.

History: The engraved "C+C" is identical to that found on holloware owned by the First Church of Charlestown. E. Alfred Jones describes it as follows: "The spoon has a rattail on the bowl, and the handle is turned up. On the back are the initials: C + C (for Charlestown Church). Length, 11 ¾ in. Maker's mark: I BURT, for John Burt of Boston (1691–1745)." Everything fits except the length, but there is reason to believe that Jones's sources erred in this respect. The spoon was included in the 1911 exhibition of church silver at the Museum of Fine Arts, Boston and is illustrated in the catalogue. Although dimensions are not given, it is shown with a group of spoons, some with known dimensions. It is clear that the spoon illustrated in that catalogue is in the range of 7" to 8" rather than 11" to 12".

Provenance: First Church, Charlestown, Mass.; H. F. du Pont.

Exhibitions: "American Church Silver," Museum of Fine Arts, Boston, 1911.

Comments: See nos. 3, 4, and 33 for other silver at Winterthur from the First Church of Charlestown.

References: Jones, *Old Silver*, p. 124. *American Church Silver*, no. 152, pl. 14.

59.3358 Gift of H. F. du Pont, 1965

ℰ 23
SPOON, ca. 1720

L. 4 ½" (11.4 cm)
5 dwt. 16 gr. (8.9 g)

Stamps: "J•BURT" in slanted roman letters, in an elongated oval, struck once on back of handle.

Engraved on back of handle: "R+S/ to/ I+C" in crude roman letters.

Description: elongated oval bowl with swage-formed shell and drop on back; rounded upturned handle with midrib on front.

Spectrographic analysis: Silver content is 91.9 percent.

Provenance: Mr. and Mrs. Stanley B. Ineson, New York City; Mr. and Mrs. Alfred E. Bissell, Wilmington, Del.

References: Belden, *Marks of American Silversmiths*, p. 90 a.

62.240.130 Gift of Mr. and Mrs. Alfred E. Bissell, 1962–63

ℰ 24
SPOON, ca. 1730

L. 7 9/16" (19.2 cm)
1 oz. 5 dwt. 16 gr. (39.9 g)

Stamps: "JOHN/ BURT" in slanted roman letters, in a rectangle with rounded ends, struck once on back of handle.

Engraved on back of handle: "M+W" in roman letters.

Description: oval bowl with swage-formed shell and drop on back; rounded upturned handle with midrib on front.

Spectrographic analysis: Silver content is 90.8 percent.

Provenance: Mr. and Mrs. Stanley B. Ineson, New York City; Mr. and Mrs. Alfred E. Bissell, Wilmington, Del.

References: Belden, *Marks of American Silversmiths*, p. 90 b.

62.240.951 Gift of Mr. and Mrs. Alfred E. Bissell, 1962–63

ℰ 25
SPOON, ca. 1710

L. 7 9/16" (19.2 cm)
1 oz. 3 dwt. 20 gr. (37.1 g)

Stamps: "IB" in roman letters, with a crown above and a pellet below, all in a shield, struck once on back of handle.

Engraved on back of handle: "T/ IH" in roman letters.

Description: elongated oval bowl with swage-formed rattail on back; rounded upturned handle with midrib on front.

Spectrographic analysis: Silver content is 92.6 percent.

Provenance: Mr. and Mrs. Stanley B. Ineson, New York City; Mr. and Mrs. Alfred E. Bissell, Wilmington, Del.

References: Belden, *Marks of American Silversmiths*, p. 90 c.

62.240.973 Gift of Mr. and Mrs. Alfred E. Bissell, 1962–63

William Burt

1726–51
Boston, Massachusetts

William Burt was one of the three silversmith sons of John and Abigail (Cheever) Burt. Burt's twin sister, Sarah, married Francis Shaw. Burt married Mary Glidden in 1749 in the New North Church. He died at age twenty-six. Little of his work survives. E. Alfred Jones credits him with a flagon given to Old South Church, Boston, by Nathaniel Cunningham in 1748.

References: Flynt and Fales, *Heritage Foundation*, p. 174. Jones, *Old Silver*, p. 55. Kane, *Dictionary*, s.v. "Burt, William."

26
PORRINGER, 1747–51

DIAM. bowl 5 ⅛" (13.0 cm), H. 2" (5.1 cm), w. 7 ¹³⁄₁₆" (19.8 cm)
7 oz. 6 dwt. 11 gr. (227.8 g)

Stamps: "W. BURT" in roman letters, in a rectangle with rounded corners, struck once on front of handle and once inside bottom near center; 1 of the strikes is a double, giving the impression of an extra letter.

Engraved on front of handle: "M*M" in roman letters.

Description: raised circular bowl with bulging sides and slightly angled rim; bottom domed in center; centerpunch inside and on bottom; cast handle pierced in keyhole pattern with 11 voids.

Spectrographic analysis:

	SILVER	COPPER	LEAD	GOLD
BOWL	90.0	9.2	0.26	0.18
HANDLE	93.0	6.3	0.25	0.20

Provenance: Katrina Kipper, Queen Anne Cottage, Accord, Mass., sold to H. F. du Pont, June 1930.

References: Fennimore, *Silver and Pewter*, no. 96.

65.1382 Gift of H. F. du Pont, 1965

ℰ James Butler

1713–76
Boston, Massachusetts

The son of James Butler, ropemaker, and Abigail (Eustis) Butler, the younger James Butler was apparently orphaned early because he was under the care of his stepmother and then, at age fourteen, under three court-appointed guardians. In 1739 Butler married Elizabeth Davie, who died the following year. In 1744 he married Sarah Wakefield. He served as a captain in the militia. For a brief period he lived in Halifax, Nova Scotia. There are a few objects stamped "J BUTLER" that are clearly attributable to this maker, including a beaker made for the First Congregational Church in Saybrook, Connecticut. Questions arise over the "IB" stamp, which has been associated with Butler (but not conclusively proven to be his) as well as with James Boyer and John Burt.

References: Flynt and Fales, *Heritage Foundation*, p. 174. Buhler and Hood, *American Silver*, pp. 95, 151. Jones, *Old Silver*, p. 443. Kane, *Dictionary*, s.v. "Butler, James."

ℰ 27 a, b
GOLD BUTTONS
(2 PAIRS)

(a) DIAM. ½" (1.3 cm)
1 dwt. 4 gr. (1.8 g)
(b) DIAM. ½" (1.3 cm)
1 dwt. 3 gr. (1.8 g)

Stamps: "IB" in roman letters, in a rectangle, struck twice on back of each unit.

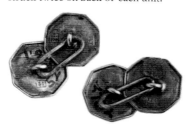

Engraved on front of each unit: stylized plant consisting of a central trunk with scrolls branching out to sides.

Description: each button consists of 2 units connected by an oval link. Each unit consists of a flat piece of metal, hexagonal in shape, with rolled edges; an oval link runs through shank attached to back of each unit.

Spectrographic analysis:

	GOLD	SILVER	COPPER	
(a)	81.4	11.5	7.1	20 karat
(b)	83.0	10.9	6.1	20 karat

Provenance: H. F. du Pont.

Exhibitions: "American Jewelry," National Society of the Colonial Dames of America in the State of Delaware, Wilmington Fine Arts Center, 1962.

Comments: Long referred to as cuff links, these are more properly called buttons since they were used not only on shirt cuffs but also on shirt fronts. In a 1744 commonplace book Joseph Richardson, Sr., listed "73 links of gold buttons." In 1762 Richardson ordered from Thomas Wagstaffe in London "a Pair of Button Stamps to Stamp Gold or Silver Buttons" for the patterns and "Plain Punches to Stamp the Buttons [out] with."

Identical pairs of gold buttons, also stamped "IB," are at Yale University Art Gallery and Colonial Williamsburg. Kathryn C. Buhler and Graham Hood attribute the Yale links to Butler while noting the similarity of the stamp to one used by John Burt.

References: Buhler and Hood, *American Silver*, no. 183. Fales, *American Silver*, no. 65. Martha Gandy Fales, *Joseph Richardson and Family: Philadelphia Silversmiths* (Middletown, Conn.: Wesleyan University Press for the Historical Society of Pennsylvania, 1974), pp. 201, 240.

(a) 52.276.1, (b) 52.276.2 Gift of H. F. du Pont, 1952

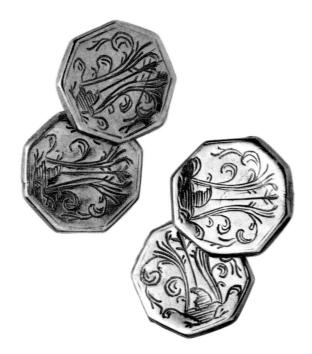

Samuel Casey

ca. 1724–after 1779

Samuel & Gideon Casey, w. 1753–63
Exeter and South Kingston (Little Rest),
Rhode Island

The son of Samuel and Dorcas (Ellis) Casey, Samuel Casey was probably born in Newport, Rhode Island. He may have served his apprenticeship with Jacob Hurd in Boston before setting up shop as a silversmith in Exeter, Rhode Island, where he was admitted as a freeman in 1745. About 1750 he moved to South Kingston, then known as Little Rest. He married Martha Martin about 1753. From 1753 to 1763, his brother Gideon, also a silversmith, was his partner. His home was destroyed in 1764 by a fire that originated in his forge. A newspaper reported that "the very valuable Dwelling-House . . . unhappily took Fire and was entirely consumed with a great Quantity of rich Furniture." He then set up shop in a portion of the James Helme house, where, by 1770, he had become insolvent. No doubt his strained circumstances accounted for his unfortunate decision to make counterfeit coins. He had little success and was soon arrested, tried, convicted, and sentenced to death by hanging. He was released by a mob on the night before he was scheduled to hang. He left the area and, according to the petition for amnesty drawn up by his wife in 1779, "wandered in exile nine years forlorn and forsaken and destitute of every means of support . . . separated from his wife and offspring." The General Assembly agreed to a pardon, but we do not know if he chose to return to his home.

Notwithstanding his later difficulties, Casey was a silversmith of considerable competence, and much of his silver survives. In proportion to his other surviving work, he made an unusually large number of creamers.

References: Kathryn C. Buhler, "Samuel Casey's Apprenticeship," *Bulletin of the Museum of Fine Arts* 38, no. 2 (April 1940): 33–35. Flynt and Fales, *Heritage Foundation*, pp. 178–79. William Davis Miller, *The Silversmiths of Little Rest* (Kingston, R.I.: By the author, 1928), pp. 3–9, 43–45, plus illus. William Davis Miller, "Samuel Casey, Silversmith," *Rhode Island Historical Society Collections (RIHSC)* 21, no. 1 (January 1928): 1–14. William Davis Miller, "Samuel and Gideon Casey, Silversmiths," *RIHSC* 22, no. 4 (October 1929): 103–9. Kenneth Scott, *Counterfeiting in Colonial America* (New York: Oxford University Press, 1957), pp. 210–35. Kenneth Scott, "A Letter and a Porringer by Silver Sam," *Antiques* 68, no. 5 (November 1955): 462.

28
GOLD NECKLACE AND CLASP, ca. 1760

L. necklace and clasp 18 9/16" (47.2 cm),
w. clasp 5/8" (1.6 cm), L. clasp 1 1/8" (2.9 cm)
12 dwt. 17 gr. (19.8 g)

Stamps: "SC" in roman letters, in a rectangle with rounded corners, struck once on reverse of clasp.

Engraved on obverse of clasp: a spread-winged phoenix enclosed by stylized leaf border. *Scratched on tongue:* "60/ 325".

Description: strand of 116 variably sized, hollow, round beads arranged in a pattern of 3 small followed by 2 or 3 large beads. Clasp consists of 2 oval-shape sheets joined by side wall to create hollow interior to receive friction-fit tongue; bottom plate has extension with 3 holes; tongue has 3 holes on right side.

Spectrographic analysis:

	GOLD	SILVER	COPPER	
CLASP	85.7	9.0	5.3	
BEADS	87.4	7.6	5.0	21 karat

History: When acquired by the previous owner, the necklace was accompanied by a handwritten note, old but not eighteenth century, indicating that the necklace had been made for a Prudence Williams, born in 1742. She remains unidentified.

Provenance: Philip H. Hammerslough, West Hartford, Conn.

Exhibitions: "American Gold, 1700–1860," Yale University Art Gallery, New Haven, 1963. "American Jewelry," National Society of the Colonial Dames of America in the State of Delaware, Wilmington Fine Arts Center, 1962. "Colonial Silversmiths, Masters and Apprentices," Museum of Fine Arts, Boston, 1956.

Comments: Each bead was formed by raising 2 hemispheres with a hammer and soldering the halves together. The process is described by Daniel Burnap, Connecticut clockmaker and silversmith, in Penrose R. Hoopes, *Shop Records of Daniel Burnap, Clockmaker* (Hartford: Connecticut Historical Society, 1958), p. 117. The clasp was designed for 3 strands of beads, not 1, thus raising the question of whether the beads and clasp were made for each other or joined at a later date.

References: Hammerslough, *American Silver*, 1:138. Bohan, *American Gold*, no. 44. Buhler, *Masters and Apprentices*, no. 150, fig. 52. Fales, *Early American Silver*, fig. 190.

60.325 Museum purchase from Philip H. Hammerslough, 1960

29
FOOTED BEAKER, ca. 1767

H. 3⅝" (9.2 cm), DIAM. top 3⅜" (8.6 cm)
4 oz. 11 dwt. 22 gr. (142.9 g)

Stamps: "S:C" in roman letters, in a rectangle with rounded corners, struck once on underside of body.

Engraved on underside of body: "ESTER/HELME" in shaded roman letters.

Description: raised body in shape of inverted bell; incised line encircles body at rim; center-punch on underside; cast circular foot; stepped moldings.

Spectrographic analysis:

	SILVER	COPPER	GOLD	LEAD
FOOT	94.5	4.7	0.22	0.17
BODY	88.9	10.1	0.21	0.31

History: One of a set of at least 2 identical beakers, both with the name Ester Helme engraved underneath, made for Ester Helme (1740–1817) of South Kingston, R.I. She was the daughter of Judge James Helme (d. 1777) and Ester (Powell) Helme. Young Ester married Francis Carpenter, son of Joseph Carpenter of Long Island, nephew and heir to Francis Willet of Boston Neck, R.I., whose lands and mansion house he inherited.

Esther Bernon Carpenter (1848–?), author of *South County Studies . . .* , was a great-granddaughter of Ester Helme. She spent her earliest years in the Willet mansion and was familiar with many relics handed down in the family. She mentions a psalm book owned by Gabriel Bernon, one of her Huguenot ancestors; a gold rattle that went from one eldest daughter to the next (usually named Ester); several pieces of needlework made by Ester (Powell) Helme; and various silver canns, porringers, drinking cups, and apostle spoons.

Following a fire in 1764 that destroyed his house in South Kingston, Casey moved into a house owned by James Helme, brother of Ester. It was here that Casey produced the counterfeit money that led to his downfall. Ester's father was one of the justices of the superior court involved in the case.

Provenance: Ester (Helme) Carpenter (1740–1817) and Francis Carpenter; their son Willet Carpenter (1772–1854), who married Elizabeth Case; Willet and Elizabeth's son, the Reverend James Helme Carpenter, who married Mary Hoxie Hazard; their daughter Esther Bernon Carpenter (1848–?). Acquired in the twentieth century by Charles F. Montgomery, Wallingford, Conn., who sold it in 1944 to Charles K. Davis (1889–1967) of Fairfield, Conn.

Exhibitions: The Yale beaker was exhibited at the Rhode Island Tercentenery "Exhibition of Paintings by Gilbert Stuart, Furniture by the Goddards and Townsends, Silver by Rhode Island Silversmiths," Museum of Art, Rhode Island School of Design, Providence, 1936.

Comments: The other beaker in the set is at Yale University Art Gallery; 2 more beakers, also by Casey, are in the Museum of Art, Rhode Island School of Design.

References: Buhler and Hood, *American Silver*, no. 484. Esther Barron Carpenter, *South County Studies of Some Eighteenth-Century Persons, Places and Conditions in the Portion of Rhode Island called Narragansett* (Boston: By the sub-scribers, 1924), esp. pp. 156–74 (note: published posthumously, the book was compiled by Car-olyn Hazard from letters written by Carpenter to Oliver Wendell Holmes starting in 1869, when Carpenter was 21 years old). Fales, *American Silver*, no. 133. *Catalogue of an Exhibition of Paintings by Gilbert Stuart, Furniture by the Goddards and Townsends, Silver by Rhode Island Silversmiths* (Providence: Museum of Art, Rhode Island School of Design, 1936), no. 72.

56.46.3 Gift of Charles K. Davis, 1956

30
SPOON, ca. 1760

L. 4 %₆" (11.6 cm)
6 dwt. 15 gr. (10.4 g)

Stamps: "S:C" in roman letters, in a rectangle with rounded corners, struck once on back of spoon.

Engraved on back of handle: "TT" (with elabo-rate scrolls extending from serifs) in shaded roman letters.

Description: elongated oval bowl with swage-formed 12-lobe shell and rounded drop on back; rounded upturned handle with short midrib on front.

Spectrographic analysis: Silver content is 93.1 percent.

Provenance: Charlotte and Edgar Sittig, Shawnee-on-Delaware, Pa.

Comments: Same swage probably used for bowl of spoon no. 31.

References: Belden, *Marks of American Silversmiths*, p. 101 b.

64.113 Museum purchase from Charlotte and Edgar Sittig, 1964

31
SPOON, ca. 1760

L. 7 ⅝" (19.4 cm)
1 oz. 9 dwt. 13 gr. (45.9 g)

Stamps: "S:CASEY" in roman letters, in a rectangle, struck once on back of handle.

Engraved on back of handle: "I*E" in shaded roman letters.

Description: oval bowl with swage-formed 12-lobe shell and rounded drop on back; rounded upturned handle with midrib on front.

Spectrographic analysis: Silver content is 90.7 percent.

Provenance: Mr. and Mrs. Stanley B. Ineson, New York City; Mr. and Mrs. Alfred E. Bissell, Wilmington, Del.

Comments: Same swage probably used for bowl of spoon no. 30.

References: Belden, *Marks of American Silversmiths*, p. 101 a.

62.240.1012 Gift of Mr. and Mrs. Alfred E. Bissell, 1962–63

Jonathan Clarke

1706–66
Newport, Rhode Island, w. 1734–55
Providence, Rhode Island, w. 1755–66

Regrettably, little is known about Jonathan Clarke other than his dates and places of work. He served in the militia, as an ensign in 1735 and a captain in 1742, and was justice of the peace in Newport in 1750. His name is spelled both with and without a final *e*. He made a remarkably handsome punch strainer for Jabez Bowen that is now at Yale University Art Gallery. The patron's name, place, and date are spelled out in the drilled perforations. His work has been confused with that of Joseph Clark of Boston, especially by E. Alfred Jones, who mistakenly credited Jonathan Clarke with silver at churches in Scituate, Lynn, Plymouth, and Andover, Massachusetts.

References: Buhler and Hood, *American Silver*, no. 471. Ralph E. Carpenter, *The Arts and Crafts of Newport, Rhode Island, 1640–1820* (Newport, R.I.: Preservation Society of Newport County, 1954), pp. 157–58, nos. 105, 122, 131, 139. Flynt and Fales, *Heritage Foundation*, p. 184. Jones, *Old Silver*, pp. 348, 374, 441, 444 (but see comments above).

32
PORRINGER, 1730–66

DIAM. bowl 5 3/16" (13.5 cm), H. 2 3/16" (5.6 cm), W. 7 7/8" (20.0 cm)
8 oz. 8 dwt. 3 gr. (261.5 g)

Stamps: "J•Clarke" in script, in a rectangle with rounded ends, struck once on back of handle.

Engraved on front of handle: "T / W+L" in roman letters.

Description: raised circular bowl with bulging sides and slightly angled rim; bottom domed in center; centerpunch inside and on bottom; cast handle pierced in keyhole pattern with 11 voids.

Spectrographic analysis:

	SILVER	COPPER	LEAD	GOLD
BOWL	92.9	6.5	0.22	0.06
HANDLE	93.4	6.0	0.15	0.11

Provenance: Katrina Kipper, Queen Anne Cottage, Accord, Mass., sold to H. F. du Pont, August 1930.

Exhibitions: Possibly the same porringer loaned by George S. Palmer to the Hudson-Fulton exhibition, Metropolitan Museum of Art, New York City, 1909.

References: Fales, *American Silver*, no. 57. Possibly no. 291 in Henry Watson Kent and Florence N. Levy, *Catalogue of an Exhibition of American Paintings, Furniture, Silver, and Other Objects of Art* (New York: Metropolitan Museum of Art, 1909).

59.3359 Gift of H. F. du Pont, 1965

33
SPOON, 1730–66

L. 7 5/8" (19.4 cm)
1 oz. 11 dwt. 23 gr. (49.7 g)

Stamps: "J•Clarke" in script, in a rectangle with rounded ends, struck once on back of handle.

Engraved on back of handle: "CC" in roman letters.

Description: oval bowl with swage-formed drop and rattail on back; rounded upturned handle with midrib on front.

Spectrographic analysis: Silver content is 89.3 percent.

History: The engraved initials "CC" are similar to those found on silver owned by the First Church of Charlestown, Mass. According to Jones, they stand for Charlestown Church.

Provenance: Mr. and Mrs. Stanley B. Ineson, New York City; Mr. and Mrs. Alfred E. Bissell, Wilmington, Del.

References: Belden, *Marks of American Silversmiths*, p. 112 a.

62.240.1019 Gift of Mr. and Mrs. Alfred E. Bissell, 1962–63

34
SPOON, 1730–66

L. 7 7/8" (20.0 cm)
1 oz. 12 dwt. 9 gr. (50.4 g)

Stamps: "J:CLARKE" in roman letters, in a rectangle, struck once on back of handle.

Engraved on back of handle: "A∗W" in roman letters.

Description: oval bowl with swage-formed rattail on back; rounded upturned handle with midrib on front.

Spectrographic analysis: Silver content is 90.5 percent.

Provenance: Mr. and Mrs. Stanley B. Ineson, New York City; Mr. and Mrs. Alfred E. Bissell, Wilmington, Del.

Exhibitions: Metropolitan Museum of Art, New York City, 1935–61.

References: Belden, *Marks of American Silversmiths*, p. 112 b.

62.240.1018 Gift of Mr. and Mrs. Alfred E. Bissell, 1962–63

John Coburn

1724–1803
Boston, Massachusetts

John Coburn was born in York, Maine, to Ebenezer and Sarah (Storer) Coburn. He may have served his apprenticeship with the Edwards family in Boston. (His uncle Ebenezer married Mary Edwards, the daughter of John Edwards, and his uncle Seth Storer married Mary Coney, the daughter of John Coney.) Coburn was established as a goldsmith in Boston by 1750, when he advertised in the *Boston Weekly News-Letter*. In the same year he married Susanna Greenleaf. He was a sergeant in the Artillery Company in 1752. He left the city during the siege of 1775 but returned in 1776 to set up shop on King Street "opposite the American Coffee-House." Boston directories list him as a boardinghouse owner in 1789 and as a gentleman in 1796. In 1784 Coburn took as his second wife Catharine Vance.

Paul Revere's account books show that Coburn purchased silver and engraving from him on numerous occasions. In 1766 Revere made two silver snuffboxes for Coburn and in 1774 charged him for "Engraving Crest & two letters on 42 Dishes and plates." Coburn bequeathed to his wife Catharine all the household furniture and plate but not his portrait, the portrait of his first wife, or the "Coat of Arms in Philigree"; the last item went to his daughter Susanna Coburn Ingraham. He appointed Catharine and Gen. John Winslow executors. Coburn's silver survives in quantity. E. Alfred Jones recorded his silver in churches in Boston, Springfield, and Wakefield, Massachusetts; Danbury and Glastonbury, Connecticut; and Portland, Maine. The communion dish given by Thomas Hancock to Boston's Brattle Street Church in 1764 (now at the Museum of Fine Arts, Boston) is engraved with the cherub's head more commonly found on the silver and gravestones of sixty years earlier. Coburn also made tea equipage in quantity and in the fashionable styles of the third quarter of the eighteenth century. A superb teapot, caster, and creamer bearing the Welles arms are at Historic Deerfield.

References: Buhler, *American Silver*, p. 302, nos. 257–76. Flynt and Fales, *Heritage Foundation*, pp. 185–86. Jones, *Old Silver*, pp. 69, 135, 185, 378, 456, 476. Kane, *Dictionary*, s.v. "Coburn, John." SCPR book 101, pp. 99–105.

35
CANN, ca. 1765

H. 5 ¼" (13.3 cm), w. 5 ⁷⁄₁₆" (13.8 cm)
12 oz. 1 gr. (403.5 g)

Stamps: "J•COBURN" in roman letters, in a rectangle, struck once on underside of body.

Engraved on body opposite handle: armorial device consisting of 3 lions rampant on a fess azure, 7 ermine tails in chief, and 9 ermine tails in base; all in a cartouche of C scrolls and foliage; swags below; lion couchant crest.
Scratched on bottom: "S Badlam"; "12 03 7"; and "12 17" plus some illegible numbers.

Description: raised circular body; bulbous lower body, incurving neck, flared rim with incised ring; centerpunch inside and outside; cast, circular, stepped foot. Double–C-scroll handle with scroll and sprig on upper and lower parts; hollow handle cast in 2 vertical sections and joined; vents in both upper and lower sections; lower end of handle attached to body by a circular plate.

Spectrographic analysis:

	SILVER	COPPER	LEAD	GOLD
BODY	86.9	12.9	0.18	0.04
FOOT	96.0	3.8	0.14	0.07
HANDLE	90.4	9.4	0.12	0.07

History: The arms, according to Charles Knowles Bolton, are those of the Barrett family. He records them as being on a silver tray owned by Barrett Wendell of Boston in 1920. A tall coffeepot, also by Coburn and bearing the same arms, is owned by the Sterling and Francine Clark Art Institute in Williamstown, Mass. Its original owner is said to have been merchant John Barrett (1708–86) of Boston, who married Sarah Gerrish (1711–98) in 1731. A pair of portraits of John and Sarah (Gerrish) Barrett, by John Singleton Copley, were owned by Mrs. Bar-rett Wendell in 1938. Barrett Wendell had purchased them from his aunt, Miss S. D. Barrett, about 1915. Although John Barrett may also have owned the Coburn cann featured here, there were other Barretts who could have been the first owners.

For much of its history the cann descended in the Badlam family. Just when and how it made its way from the Barretts to the Badlams cannot be determined. The scratched inscription "Stephen Badlam" calls to mind cabinetmaker Stephen Badlam (1751–1815) of Dorchester, Mass. There were, however, several members of the Badlam family named Stephen. The senior Stephen Badlam (1720–58) was the first in the family to take up woodworking, and he is referred to in documents as a carpenter or a joiner. He was the father of Stephen Badlam, the cabinetmaker, who was orphaned when he was 6 years old. Young Stephen lived with his grandfather until age 19, at which time he went to live with his brother Ezra at Dorchester's Lower Mills Village "to learn a Cabinet Makers trade." Although he had little schooling, he gained sufficient mathematical knowledge to become proficient in cabinetmaking, surveying, and gunnery.

Stephen and Ezra Badlam formed a partnership in 1773 that lasted until Ezra's death in 1788. The business was interrupted by Stephen's military service during the Revolution. He served from the initial engagement at Lexington and Concord to the capture of Mount Independence, opposite Fort Ticonderoga, in July 1776. His aptitude for artillery is reflected in a rapid series of promotions in that branch. By May 1776 he was placed in command of artillery in the Northern Department. He left the army in January 1777 because of ill health. After the Revolution he was appointed brigadier general in the Massachusetts Militia, and thereafter he was known as General Badlam. He became active in civic and religious affairs as he continued to pursue his cabinetmaking enterprise.

Wendell B. Cook says that Badlam's "cabinetworking operations and connections were an influential force in the woodworking sector of the manufacturing and merchandising operations centered on the Neponset River at Lower Mills and Milton villages." Surviving examples of his furniture are in the Museum of Fine Arts, Boston and Yale University Art Gallery. The latter owns his masterpiece, a magnificent chest-on-chest with carved figures on top made for Elias Haskett Derby.

Stephen Badlam married Mary Adams in 1775. They had 10 children; 2 died immediately after birth and 1 at age 10. They had 2 sons: Stephen and John. Badlam died August 25, 1815, at age 64 and was interred in his tomb at Dorchester North Burying Ground.

John Badlam (1789–1814) went off to Argentina at age 20. In 1812 he married Maria de las Nieves Moreno. Their son Esteban (Spanish for Stephen) was born in 1813. The following year John, or Juan as he became

known, died. Esteban died in 1835 as a result of terrorism and became a minor martyr in Argentinian history. His grandfather, General Badlam, provided for him in his will.

Stephen Badlam III (1779–1847) is presumed to have inherited the silver cann from his father. He served as jailer for the city of Boston and kept a furniture and looking-glass shop at No. 45 Cornhill. He married Nancy Clark, by whom he had 9 children, including a son who was also named Stephen. It is his son Theodore Henry Badlam (1827–1902) who apparently inherited or was given the Coburn cann. It then passed to his daughter Mary Elizabeth Badlam (1857–1947) and thence into the Nichols family by reason of her marriage to Edward L. Nichols, merchant, in 1884. The subsequent descent of the cann is given under *Provenance*.

Provenance: Barrett family of Boston, possibly John Barrett (1708–86); Stephen Badlam (1751–1815) of Dorchester, Mass.; his son Stephen Badlam (1779–1847) of Boston; his son Theodore Henry Badlam (1827–1902) of Dorchester; his daughter Mary Elizabeth Badlam (1857–1947), who married Edward L. (or Towne) Nichols, Boston merchant; their son Edward Leonard Nichols; his son Edward Lawrence Nichols, whose widow sold it to dealer Robert Lawrence Simms of St. Petersburg, Fla.

Comments: The Boston firm of Firestone & Parson advertised in *Antiques* (November 1982) a teapot with the Barrett arms. Engraved on its base is the name Hepzibah Barrett and the date 1772. Hepzibah does not appear in the Barrett genealogy. An unstamped cann in the collection of the DAR Museum, Washington, D.C., bears the Barrett arms and is said to have been owned by Samuel Barrett (1738–?), the son of John and Sarah Barrett. A pair of sauceboats by Daniel Henchman, exhibited in "Colonial Silversmiths: Masters and Apprentices" (Museum of Fine Arts, Boston, 1956), also have the Barrett coat of arms. Three nearly identical canns made by Coburn are known: 1 in the Museum of Fine Arts, Boston bearing the Gardiner arms; 1 at Hood Museum, Dartmouth College (no arms); and 1 in a private collection as of 1976.

References: Joseph H. Barrett, "Thomas Barrett of Braintree, William Barrett of Cambridge, and Their Early Descendants," *NEH&GR* 42 (July 1888): 257–64. Buhler, *Masters and Apprentices*, no. 76. Wendell B. Cook, "William Badlam, Ship Master of Boston and Weymouth and Some of His Descendants," *NEH&GR* 141 (January 1987): 3–18; (April 1987): 135–49. Fennimore, *Silver and Pewter*, no. 152. David Firestone to Ian Quimby, March 31, 1989. Jean Taylor Frederico, "Two Revolutionary Period Boston Families and Their Silver," *American Antiques* 6, no. 5 (May 1978): 17–20. Barbara Neville Parker and Anne Bolling Wheeler, *John Singleton Copley* (Boston: Museum of Fine Arts, 1938), pp. 32–34, pl. 24. "Great Silver from Three Centuries," *Antiques* 92, no. 3 (September 1967): 335.

72.1 Museum purchase from Robert Lawrence Simms, 1972

36 a, b
SPOONS, ca. 1765

(a) L. 8 5/16" (21.1 cm)
1 oz. 6 dwt. 18 gr. (41.6 g)
(b) L. 8" (20.3 cm)
2 oz. 3 dwt. 12 gr. (67.6 g)

Stamps: "J. COBURN" in roman letters, in a rectangle.

Engraved on back of handle: (a) "M+T"; (b) "CB/ to/ SL". Both in roman letters.

Description: (a) elongated oval bowl with swage-formed 12-lobe shell, double eared, 3 incised lines at base, single rounded drop on back; rounded upturned handle with short midrib on front; (b) oval bowl with swage-formed 13-lobe shell and single rounded drop on back; rounded upturned handle with long midrib.

Spectrographic analysis: Silver content ranges from 88.7 to 92.5 percent.

Provenance: Mr. and Mrs. Stanley B. Ineson, New York City; Mr. and Mrs. Alfred E. Bissell, Wilmington, Del.

References: Belden, *Marks of American Silversmiths*, p. 114 a.

(a) 62.240.1023, (b) 62.240.1024 Gift of Mr. and Mrs. Alfred E. Bissell, 1962–63

John Coney

1655/56–1722
Boston, Massachusetts

John Coney is unquestionably one of the giants of his craft and is regarded by some as the preeminent goldsmith of the colonial era. Certainly in quantity, quality, and variety of forms, his work is unsurpassed. The great monteith in the Garvan collection at Yale University Art Gallery, with its elaborate cast ornament, is a bravura performance that would have been admired on both sides of the Atlantic. A few of his other monumental works include the Stoughton cup at Harvard, the triangular inkstand at the Metropolitan Museum of Art, and his two sugar boxes (not to mention the highly decorated matching fork and spoon) at the Museum of Fine Arts, Boston.

Coney's name surfaces frequently in the literature of his time. Diarist Samuel Sewall mentions him in connection with his appearances as a bearer at funerals and as the maker or seller of various gold and silver items. On January 17, 1719, for example, Sewall paid his respects to Gov. Samuel Shute and gave him a "Gold Ring wt 4 Pennys wanting one Grain, with this Poesy fairly engraven by Mr. Cony, *AEternitati pingo Jan. 1719.* Govr accepted it kindly." A year later, on January 18, 1720, when Sewall was a bearer at the funeral of Eunice Willard, the wife of the Reverend Samuel Willard, he noted, "Bought my [funeral] ring of Mr. Coney 19.3."

A direct historical reference to a particular silver object that survives to this day is rare. In 1701 Massachusetts Lt. Gov. William Stoughton, unable to make the presentation of a great two-handled cup made by Coney for Harvard College, asked Sewall to do it for him. Stoughton was ill and had only a few days to live. On

Wednesday, July 2, Sewall presented the cup at the commencement ceremonies: "After dinner and singing, I took it, had it fill'd up, and drank to the president, saying that by reason of the absence of him who was the Firmament and Ornament of the Province, and that Society, I presented that Grace-cup *pro more Academiarium in Anglia.* The Providence of our Sovereign Lord is very investigable in that our Grace Cups, brim full, are passing round; when our Brethren in France are petitioning for their Coup de Grace." Sewall was obviously pleased with himself, and Coney's handiwork was thus immortalized.

Coney has been written about at length, largely in the many catalogues that featured representative samples of his work but also in a monograph (1932) by Hermann Frederick Clarke, the first such book-length treatment of an early American silversmith. (Books about Paul Revere do not count under this rubric.) Clarke's checklist has 112 items, and today many additional pieces are known, including the tankard and spoon in the entries that follow. An exhibition devoted solely to John Coney was held in 1932 at the Museum of Fine Arts, Boston. This was probably the first exhibition to concentrate on one American silversmith; it featured 88 examples of his work, a substantial portion of the known Coney oeuvre at that time.

The inventory of Coney's estate is notable on several counts. It lists an enormous number of goldsmith's tools. One entry alone mentions "112 Hammers for Raising, Pibling (?), Swelling, Hollowing, Creasing, Planishing &c." There were 9 spoon punches, 2 pepperbox punches, 6 caster punches, and swages of several kinds, including 2 ring swages. There was 1 "Brass Salt Stamp" weighing 11 ½ pounds and 4 "Brass Caster Stamps," weighing together 19 pounds. He had 26 anvils of various sizes, of which the largest was the forging anvil that weighed 161 pounds. Among the precious metals owned at the time of

his death were 8 oz. 12 dwt. of gold; 28 ¾ oz. in pieces of eight; 515 oz. of wrought plate; 6 oz. of "Burnt Silver & Ingot Silver"; and 8 oz. 2 dwt. of "Refined Siver." He also owned "An Engine for Coining with all Utensils belonging thereto." This has lead to speculation that Coney served his apprenticeship with John Hull, the mint master. Of course, Coney could have acquired the device under other circumstances. Lastly, the inventory lists the credit for the unexpired time of his apprentice, "Paul Rivoire" (the senior Paul Revere), which the appraisers valued at £30 but which, when sold, yielded £40. The valuation for the entire estate was £3,714.2.11 ¼, which included £2,516 in real property. One of the appraisers was silversmith Andrew Tyler.

Coney's father was the cooper John Coney. Young Coney would have started his apprenticeship around 1670, and although it has been suggested that he served under John Hull, Patricia E. Kane has shown that he learned the craft under Jeremiah Dummer. On January 5, 1669/70, he was listed as one of Dummer's servants. He probably finished his apprenticeship in 1676 or 1677. Shortly afterward he married Sarah Blakeman. In 1694 Coney married Mary Atwater Clark. The complications resulting from multiple marriages and the tangled web of ensuing relationships are touched upon by Sewall, who patiently tried to sort it all out in a letter to Governor Shute on February 19, 1716/17:

My answers to your Enquiries yesterday were so confused, That, with your Excellency's Indulgence, I will a little set them right. Mr. Atwater a principal Shop-keeper in Boston had (besides other Children) Two Daughters, Anna and Mary. Mr. Jeremiah Dumer Goldsmith, now under indisposition, Married Mrs. Anna: The Lt. Govr. and Mr. Agent Dumer are their Sons. Mr. John Clark Ship-master Son of Capt. Christopher Clark, Married Mrs. Mary

Atwater, and by her had Mrs. Mary Clark (now Pemberton) and died. Mr. John Coney Goldsmith, being a widower, married Mrs. Mary Clark the widow, and by her had divers Daughters, who are the gentle-women your Excellency saw in the Coach accompanying their Mother not well able to goe a-foot: They are half-Sister to Madam Pemberton; and the widow Taylor to be heard this day, is her Aunt.

If this is clarification, one can only wonder at the nature of his first communication with Shute.

William Dunlap and Mantle Fielding list Coney as an engraver because he made the plates for bills of credit issued by Massachusetts Bay Colony. The documentation refers to the bills issued in 1702/3, but since they so closely resemble the bills issued in 1690, it has been assumed that Coney did the engraving for these too. If that assumption is correct, Coney is the first American engraver on copper of whom there is any record. No other engraved print from his hand is known; most of his engraving was confined to his silver.

During his early years Coney saw to his spiritual needs at the Second Church of Boston, but he later became one of the original subscribers to King's Chapel in 1689. He held only minor public offices, such as constable and hog reeve. He served in the militia in the company of Capt. Penn Townsend. Unlike most of his peers, he was not active in real estate transactions. He had twelve children, but only five daughters lived to adulthood, so he left no male heirs. His son-in-law, the Reverend Thomas Foxcroft, married to his daughter Anna, preached his funeral sermon, "A Lamentation and Complaint at the Righteous Man's Funeral." In the manner of the day, it was wholly laudatory. Clarke reproduced portions of it in his monograph.

References: Buhler, *American Silver*, pp. 39–75. Buhler and Hood, *American Silver*, pp. 28–47. *DAB*, s.v. "Coney, John." Dunlap, *Arts of Design*, pp. 291–92. Ensko, *American Silversmiths III*, pp. 40, 191, 263. *Exhibition of Silversmithing by John Coney, 1655–1722* (Boston: Museum of Fine Arts, 1932). Fielding, *American Engravers*, pp. 10–11. Hermann Frederick Clarke, *John Coney, Silversmith, 1655–1722* (1932; reprint, New York: Da Capo, 1971), p. 939. Jones, *Old Silver*, lists 45 items in various churches. Kane, *Dictionary*, s.v. "Coney, John." Kane, "John Hull and Robert Sanderson," p. 113. "Letter-Book of Samuel Sewall," *Collections of the Massachusetts Historical Society*, 6th ser., 1 (1886): 67. Sewall, *Diary*, pp. 449–50, 914, 938. Ward, "Boston Goldsmiths," p. 350.

℮ 37
TANKARD, ca. 1690

H. 7 3/16" (18.3 cm), DIAM. base 5 3/4" (14.6 cm),
w. 8 9/16" (21.8 cm)
31 oz. 2 dwt. 20 gr. (968.6 g)

Stamps: "IC" in roman letters, over a fleur-de-lis, all in a heart, struck on body, left of handle, on top of lid, and on outside of bottom.

Engraved on front of body opposite handle: "B/ MS" in shaded roman letters, in a leafy cartouche. *Engraved on lid:* flowering vine with fat cherub emerging from 1 of the blossoms. *Engraved on handle near hinge:* a fleur-de-lis.

 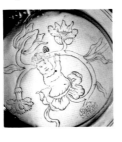

Description: raised body with straight sides; applied base molding consists of an ogee topped by 2 beads; double-scored lines encircle upper body below rim. Raised bottom with no centerpunch. Raised 2-step lid with centerpunch on top; crenate lip; double-scored lines encircle lid at edge. Cast ram's horn thumbpiece. Cast 5-segment hinge with meander wire on each side that terminates in wavy drop over handle. Raised-and-soldered hollow handle with irregularly shaped tailpiece; notched vent.

Spectrographic analysis:

	SILVER	COPPER	LEAD	GOLD
BASE	95.1	4.3	0.27	0.07
BODY	91.3	8.2	0.25	0.05
LID	89.1	10.4	0.22	0.02
HANDLE BACK	92.7	6.3	0.31	0.24
HINGE	92.1	6.6	0.48	0.27
BASE MOLDING	87.8	11.5	0.25	0.02

History: The initials remain unidentified and the early history unknown. The dealer who sold the tankard believed that it may have come from the Bowditch family of Boston but no Bowditch couple with the appropriate initials could be found.

Provenance: Jerome Kern, Hollywood, Calif.; Peter Guille, New York City; James Graham & Sons, New York City.

Comments: The motif of the fat cherub and the flowering vine appears on 2 of Coney's caudle cups but in embossed, rather than engraved, form. See the cup owned by the Museum of Fine Arts, Boston originally owned by John and Sarah Mico, who were married in 1689, and the Holyoke cup owned by Harvard University. These 2 cups are nearly identical, and their chased decoration is closely related to the engraved decoration on the lid of the Winterthur tankard. Related engraving featuring vines, leaves, flowers, and cherubs' heads (but no torsos) is on a plate by Coney, also at the Museum of Fine Arts, Boston. An engraved cherub without flowering vines but with a similar flared skirt appears on the lid of a tankard made by Jeremiah Dummer. (See Parke-Bernet Galleries, sale no. 2888, Wetmore sale [September 16–18, 1969], lot 850).

References: Not listed in Clarke, *John Coney.* For related pieces, see Fairbanks and Trent, *New England Begins,* no. 383; *American Art at Harvard* (Cambridge: Fogg Art Museum, Harvard University, 1972), no. 172.

65.33 Museum purchase from James Graham & Sons, 1965

ℰ 38
SPOON, ca. 1710

L. 7 ⁷⁄₁₆" (18.9 cm)
1 oz. 11 dwt. 13 gr. (49.1 g)

Stamps: "IC" in roman letters, with a crown above and "coney" below, all in a shield, struck once on back of handle near bowl.

Engraved on back of handle: "IC[?]" in shaded roman letters; the second letter has been altered by the addition of what appears to be "I."

Description: oval bowl with swage-formed plain rattail on back; flat wavy-end upturned handle.

Spectrographic analysis: Silver content is 92.7 percent.

Provenance: Mr. and Mrs. Stanley B. Ineson, New York City; Mr. and Mrs. Alfred E. Bissell, Wilmington, Del.

References: Belden, *Marks of American Silversmiths,* p. 119.

62.240.1001 Gift of Mr. and Mrs. Alfred E. Bissell, 1962–63

Richard Conyers

1666–1709
Boston, Massachusetts, w. 1697–1709

Unlike several of his fellow goldsmiths in turn-of-the-century Boston, Richard Conyers had a short career, and very little of his work survives. Nor does he figure like John Coney, Jeremiah Dummer, and Edward Winslow in accounts of the time. Samuel Sewall does not mention him. Although well prepared by an apprenticeship in London, he was notably unsuccessful in business, so much so that he was once imprisoned for debt. The value of his estate was only £86.16.0 and included no real estate. Most of what we know about Conyers's career in Boston comes from his will and the inventory of his estate. The latter includes a lengthy and detailed list of his tools and supplies, which were appraised by Dummer and Edward Webb for £126.0.2. Conyers left the tools to his wife, Mary, and his son James but specified that Thomas Milner, goldsmith, could have temporary use of them. Because of this clause, it has been assumed that Milner was his apprentice. He also employed Henry Hurst, a "Sweed by birth," as a journeyman.

Thanks to the research of Mrs. G. E. P. How of London and Edinburgh, his early years are now documented. The Goldsmiths' Company's Apprentice Register has the following entry for July 28, 1682: "Memorandum That I Richard Conyers the sonn of Robert Conyers of Holmesly in the County of York Sadler doo put myself Apprentice unto Roger Goring [or Graing] Citizen & Goldsmith of London for the Term of Seven years from this present day."

Neither "Goring" nor "Graing" are listed in Charles James Jackson, *English Goldsmiths and Their Marks* (1921; reprint, New York: Dover Publications, 1964), or Arthur G. Grimwade, *London Goldsmiths, 1697–1837* (London: Faber and Faber, 1976). Conyers became a liveryman in 1694, after which he took three apprentices of his own. In 1693 he married Mary James, and their son James was baptized in Saint Mary, Woolnoth, London, April 30, 1696. His career in Boston ran from about 1697 to his death early in 1709.

References: Kathryn C. Buhler, *Massachusetts Silver in the Frank L. and Louise Harrington Collection*, 2 vols. (New Haven: Yale University Press for Yale University Art Gallery, 1970), 1:20. Mrs. G. E. P. How to Mrs. Gail Belden, April 24, 1974, Registration Division, Winterthur. Kane, *Dictionary*, s.v. "Conyers, Richard." The list of tools in Conyers inventory is reproduced in John Marshall Phillips, *American Silver* (New York: Chanticleer Press, 1949), and in Kauffman, *Colonial Silversmith*. Ward, "Boston Goldsmiths," pp. 56, 161, 239, 350.

39
TANKARD, 1696–1708

H. 8 9/16" (21.8 cm), DIAM. base 6 7/16" (16.4 cm),
w. 9 5/8" (24.5 cm)
42 oz. 1 dwt. 2 gr. (1305.0 g)

Stamps: "RC" in roman letters, with a crown above and a pellet below, all in a shield, struck on upper body, right of handle, and on lid.

Engraved on casting near hinge: "EB" in roman letters.

Description: raised body with straight sides; flared applied base molding consists of a step, a cove, a smaller cove, and a double bead; double-scored lines encircle upper body below rim. Raised bottom with centerpunch outside. Raised 2-step lid with large overhang and centerpunch inside; strong crenate lip; 2 pairs of scored lines encircle lid at edge. Cast ram's horn thumbpiece. Cast 5-segment hinge. Raised-and-soldered hollow handle with tapered drop soldered to body below upper juncture with body; beaded rattail and decorative casting on upper back; cut-card escutcheon on body at lower handle juncture; rectangular tailpiece notched on 4 sides; notched vent.

Spectrographic analysis:

	SILVER	COPPER	LEAD	GOLD
BODY	89.1	10.5	0.29	0.00
BASE	94.2	5.2	0.48	0.06
LID	92.6	7.3	0.23	0.00
HANDLE BACK	89.9	9.4	0.44	0.07
THUMBPIECE	95.0	4.8	0.19	0.01

History: According to Francis Hill Bigelow, the tankard probably originally belonged to Francis Brinley (1632–1719) of Newport, R.I. Brinley directed in his will that "all my Plate & Household Goods" be divided between "my Grand Children Francis Brinley and Elizabeth Hutchinson." Elizabeth Brinley married William Hutchinson, who died in 1721. Bigelow suggests that the initials "EB" refer to her. Col. Francis Brinley of Roxbury, Mass., the grandson, was born in England in 1690. He came to Rhode Island at the invitation of his grandfather in 1710. He married Deborah Lyde in 1718. They built a large house in Roxbury, where they lived until his death in 1766. Their portraits, by John Smibert, are owned by the Metropolitan Museum of Art. Brinley also owned the chafing dish by John Potwine, no. 106.

Provenance: Francis Brinley (1632–1719); Elizabeth Brinley Hutchinson; Col. Francis Brinley of Roxbury (1690–1766); Nathaniel Brinley (1733–1814) of Tyngsborough, Mass.; Robert Brinley of Roxbury, Mass.; Nathaniel and Sarah Elizabeth (Bridge) Brinley. In her will, proved

July 16, 1878, Sarah Brinley appointed Daniel S. Richardson and George Richardson as executors. Miss Rita Abbot, a granddaughter of Daniel S. Richardson, sold the tankard to Francis Hill Bigelow. Brooks Reed Gallery, Boston, sold to H. F. du Pont, June 1927.

Comments: An almost identical tankard by Conyers is in the Harrington collection at Dartmouth College. The only other known Conyers tankard is in a private collection. It is similar in form, but the lid is gadrooned; the handle is ribbed and has a scroll, and the tailpiece is a putto mask.

References: John Osborne Austin, *The Genealogical Dictionary of Rhode Island* (1887; reprint, Baltimore: Genealogical Publishing, 1969), pp. 256–57. Thomas Bridgman, *Memorials of the Dead in Boston, Containing Exact Transcripts of Inscriptions on the Sepulchral Monuments in the Kings Chapel Burying Ground* (Boston: B. D. Mussey, 1853), pp. 44, 45, 219–28. Francis Brinley, "The Craddock Family," *NEH&GR* 8, no. 1 (January 1854): 25–28. Francis S. Drake, *The Town of Roxbury: Its Memorable Persons and Places* (Roxbury, Mass.: By the author, 1878), pp. 326–34. Fales, *American Silver*, no. 11. "Marriages and Deaths," *NEH&GR* 21, no. 3 (July 1867): 286, s.v. "Brinley, Robert." *Sibley's Harvard Graduates*, 5:154–56, for William Hutchinson; 11:366–67, for Thomas Brinley. Will of Francis Brinley, 1719, no. 4234, docket 21, pp. 525–29, SCPR. Henry F. Waters, "Genealogical Gleanings in England," *NEH&GR* 37, no. 4 (October 1883): 376–88, reproduces will of Thomas Brinley, father of the first Francis Brinley and auditor-general to Charles I.

65.1355 Gift of H. F. du Pont, 1965

John Dixwell

1680/81–1725
Boston, Massachusetts

John Dixwell was born in New Haven, Connecticut, March 6, 1680/81. Just when he moved to Boston is uncertain, but by September 1705 he was called on to deface the old province seal, which was to be replaced by a new one. In the words of Samuel Sewall, he "cut it in two in the middle with a Chisel." In 1708 Dixwell married Mary Prout, who bore him four daughters and at least two sons. Basil, also a silversmith, was born in 1711 and died at the assault on Louisburg, as did two sons of silversmith Edward Winslow. Another son, John, was an ironmonger. Mary died in 1721 at age thirty-five. Dixwell married again in 1722 and yet again in 1723. On April 21, 1725, Sewall tersely noted, "Elder Dixwell dies." Most accounts of Dixwell stress that he was the son of John Dixwell, M.P., a member of the High Court of Justice that tried Charles I, who was subsequently executed. Following the Restoration in 1660, the elder Dixwell fled to Germany and later to Connecticut, where he lived out his years as James Davids.

That Dixwell maintained his ties to Connecticut is suggested by the fact that of his 27 pieces of church silver recorded by E. Alfred Jones, 10 were made for Connecticut churches. Of the remaining 17 pieces, 7 were made for New North Church in Boston. The church was founded in 1714 by "17 substantial mechanics [including Dixwell] unassisted by the more wealthy part of the community except by their prayers and good wishes." Dixwell was first a deacon and later a ruling elder of the church. One of the 7 pieces he made for New North was a cup given as his own donation in 1717. The church was later dissolved, and all its silver was transferred to King's Chapel.

One of Dixwell's patrons was Sarah Knight, who commissioned a two-handled cup for the church in Norwich, Connecticut, in 1722. A native of Boston and author of the famous journal of her trip from Boston to New York in 1704, she spent her later years in New London and Norwich with her only daughter, Elizabeth, and her son-in-law, Col. John Livingston.

References: American Church Silver, nos. 309–37. Buhler, *American Silver*, pp. 116–20. Ensko, *American Silversmiths III*, pp. 47, 191. *Harvard Tercentenary Exhibition: Furniture and Decorative Arts of the Period 1636–1836* (Cambridge: Harvard University Press, 1936), pp. 32, 101. Jones, *Old Silver*, pp. 59–66, index. Kane, *Dictionary*, s.v. "Dixwell, John." Sewall, *Diary*, pp. 528, 1029.

40
CAUDLE CUP, ca. 1710

H. 3¾" (9.5 cm), w. 6¹³⁄₁₆" (17.3 cm), DIAM. rim 3½" (8.9 cm)
8 oz. 14 dwt. 12 gr. (271.4 g)

Stamps: "ID" in roman letters, in an oval, struck once on upper body.

Engraved on base: "R*T" in crude shaded roman letters. *Scratched on base:* "oz 8   dwt 13".

Description: raised body with bulbous lower half and concave upper half; bottom is a separate oversize disc soldered to body; centerpunch on underside; 2 cast S-scroll handles with spurs on upper and lower backs of handles.

Spectrographic analysis:

	SILVER	COPPER	LEAD	GOLD
BOTTOM	94.4	5.4	0.24	0.05
BODY	93.7	6.2	0.10	0.08
HANDLE 1	93.9	5.6	0.29	0.13
HANDLE 2	94.1	5.4	0.24	0.13

History: According to the dealer who sold the cup to H. F. du Pont, it descended in the Collins family. Engraved initials remain unidentified.

Provenance: Mrs. N. McLean Seabrease, Germantown, Pa.; Robert Ensko, Inc., New York City, sold it, along with 29 other pieces from the Seabrease collection, to H. F. du Pont, August 1929.

Comments: A similar cup by Dixwell was offered for sale by Bernard & S. Dean Levy, in *Antiques* (December 1978), p. 1116. These are the only 2 caudle cups known to have been made by this craftsman.

References: Fales, *American Silver*, no. 5. Kauffman, *Colonial Silversmith*, p. 82.

65.1350 Gift of H. F. du Pont, 1965

41
SPOUT CUP, 1700–1725

H. 3 ⅞" (9.8 cm), w. 4 ¾" (12.1 cm)
5 oz. 13 dwt. 4 gr. (176.0 g)

Stamps: "ID" in roman letters, in an oval, struck twice on neck, once on each side of handle.

Engraved on base: "C/ NS" in roman letters.

Description: bulbous lower body with straight cylindrical neck; double-scored lines encircle neck near rim; centerpunch on bottom. Applied molded footring; applied S-curve strap handle; applied S-curve seamed spout mounted perpendicular to handle, rises from lowest portion of body to above rim.

Spectrographic analysis:

	SILVER	COPPER	LEAD	GOLD
BODY SIDE	92.5	7.3	0.20	0.06
BODY BOTTOM	95.3	4.5	0.19	0.05
HANDLE	93.5	6.1	0.15	0.25
SPOUT	93.0	6.6	0.16	0.18

History: Engraved initials may refer to Noah and Sarah Champney, who were married by Cotton Mather on August 14, 1701. This attribution was made by Francis Hill Bigelow on the basis that this is the only such set of initials found in Boston records. Noah Champney's will, dated

November 4, 1728, was witnessed by silversmiths John Burt and Pygan Adams. It mentions no silver. Bigelow records that the last private owners were unwilling to discuss its history.

Provenance: Alfred Stainforth, Winthrop, Mass.; Frances Hill Bigelow, Boston; Brooks Reed Gallery, Boston, sold to H. F. du Pont, 1927.

Comments: A similar spout cup made by Dixwell is owned by the Minneapolis Institute of Arts. Together with Winterthur's cup, they constitute the only known surviving examples of the form made by Dixwell.

References: Fales, *American Silver*, no. 12. Will of Noah Champney, 1728, no. 5869, docket 26, pp. 496–97, SCPR. V. Isabelle Miller, "American Silver Spout Cups," *Antiques* 44, no. 2 (August 1943): 73–75.

65.1357 Gift of H. F. du Pont, 1965

42
SPOON, ca. 1710

L. 8 ⅛" (20.6 cm)
1 oz. 9 dwt. 17 gr. (46.2 g)

Stamps: "ID" in roman letters, in an oval, struck once on handle back.

Engraved on back of handle: "B/ IR" in shaded roman letters.

Description: oval bowl with swage-formed plain rattail on back; wavy-end upturned handle.

Spectrographic analysis: Silver content is 91.5 percent.

History: According to the papers of Stanley B. Ineson, the initials refer to Joseph and Ruhamma (Wellington) Brown, who married in 1699. This was the supposed "Deacon" Joseph Brown (1679–1764). This information could not be verified.

Provenance: Mr. and Mrs. Stanley B. Ineson, New York City; Mr. and Mrs. Alfred E. Bissell, Wilmington, Del.

Exhibitions: "Masterpieces of New England Silver," Gallery of Fine Arts, Yale University, New Haven, 1939.

Comments: A similar spoon with the same initials is privately owned.

References: Belden, *Marks of American Silversmiths*, p. 136. *Masterpieces of New England Silver, 1650–1800* (New Haven: Gallery of Fine Arts, Yale University, 1939), no. 63. Stanley B. Ineson Papers, 76x168.2338B, Downs collection, Winterthur.

62.240.1038 Gift of Mr. and Mrs. Alfred E. Bissell, 1962–63

Jeremiah Dummer

1645–1718
Boston, Massachusetts, w. 1667–ca. 1710

To Samuel Sewall, the diarist, Jeremiah Dummer was almost always Cousin Dummer, and references to visiting "Cous. Dummer" or attending funerals with "Cous. Dummer" are frequent. (They were cousins by marriage; Jane Dummer, Jeremiah's aunt, married Henry Sewall, and they became the parents of Samuel.) On May 12, 1696, Dummer and Sewall visited Increase Mather to "acknowledge that his Preaching the Lecture once or twice was very pleasing to us, and that we were thankfull for it, and desired more." On February 5, 1702/3, Dummer and Sewall, joined by four others, rode out to Roxbury, Massachusetts, "to speak to the Governour against having Illuminations, especialy in the Town house; that so the profanation of the Sabbath might be prevented." Dummer owned a sedan chair that was borrowed by others for special occasions. On May 31, 1715, Sewall observed that the governor (Joseph Dudley) was carried "to the Town-House in Cous. Dummer's Sedan: but twas too tall for the Stairs, so [he] was fain to be taken out near the top of them." Dummer was civic-minded as well as pious, and town, county, and provincial records attest to his public service in such roles as justice of the peace, county treasurer, constable, selectman, and member of the Artillery Company. Although the inventory of his estate does not survive, he is thought to have been among the top ten merchant-goldsmiths of Boston in terms of wealth about 1710. He was part owner of at least eleven ships, which suggests a more than passing interest in mercantile pursuits.

Like silversmith John Hull, Dummer appears to have conducted his life as an exemplary puritan. It is all the more bizarre, therefore, to read of his role in the Captain Kidd affair. When Kidd was seized by order of the Earl of Bellomont in 1699, Dummer, along with Sewall, Nathaniel Byfield, and Andrew Belcher, was appointed "to receive into their custody all the Goods, Merchandizes and Treasures imported in the Sloop Antonio by Captn William Kidd." Keeping in mind that a large part of the Kidd treasure had been stashed in Hispaniola prior to his voyage north, the inventory produced by Dummer and his colleagues reveals that the *Antonio* carried a treasure of impressive dimensions. The gold amounted to 1,111 ounces and the silver 2,353. Most of the silver was in the form of bars, although Kidd's own chest included two silver basins, two silver candlesticks, and one silver porringer. The treasure also included numerous precious stones, such as 67 "Rubies small and great." Much, but not all, of the treasure was forfeited to the crown, which realized £6,471. Queen Anne used the proceeds to establish Greenwich Hospital.

Jeremiah Dummer was born in Newbury, Massachusetts, September 14, 1645, the son of Richard Dummer and Frances Burr. In 1659 he began an eight-year apprenticeship under the tutelage of John Hull, who noted in his diary: "I received into my house Jeremie Dummer and Samuel Paddy, to serve me as apprentices eight years. The Lord make me faithful in discharge of this new trust committed to me, and let his blessing be to me and them." Dummer married Anna Atwater in 1672, around the time of his twenty-seventh birthday. (Anna's sister Mary later married John Coney, who was probably trained by Dummer.) He took the oath of allegiance in 1679 before Gov. Simon Bradstreet, thereby becoming a freeman. By this time he had entered several positions of public service.

It is tempting to see in Dummer's career a rise from humble origins, but such is not the case. His father was a gentleman and, hence, was entitled to all the respect implied by the term in the Anglo-American world of the seventeenth century. Dummer himself hobnobbed with the rich and powerful alongside his cousin Sewall. Two of his sons, William and Jeremiah, became well-known figures in their own right. William Dummer, born in 1677, served as lieutenant governor of Massachusetts from 1723 to 1728 and from 1729 to 1730. He inherited the ancestral home in Newbury, where Governor Dummer Academy is now located. Jeremiah was the family intellectual. Following graduation from Harvard in 1699, he went on to receive a Ph.D. at Utrecht. He became the London agent for the colonies of Massachusetts and Connecticut.

On May 24, 1718, Sewall noted laconically in his diary: "This day Capt. Dummer dies." With equal brevity, but with his usual eye for funereal details, he noted: "Capt. Dummer buried: Bearers, Sewall, Townsend, Bromfield, Stoddard, Belcher, Dudley, Scarvs and Gloves." The respectful obituary published in the *Boston News-Letter* (June 2, 1718) said he died "in the 73d year of his Age, after a long retirement, under great infirmities of Age and Sickness." What constituted a long retirement is of interest when it comes to dating his silver. Certainly when Sewall wrote to Gov. Samuel Shute on February 19, 1716/17, and referred to "Mr. Jeremiah Dummer Goldsmith, now under indisposition," Dummer's productive years were over. Because of his varied activities that led to his designation as "merchant" or "esquire," it is tempting to say that he left his craft by his middle years. But Sewall's letter to Sir William Ashhurst of March 19, 1704/5, states: "Mr. Jeremiah Dummer is a Justice of Peace and one of the Judges of the Inferior Court, and servicable as a Goldsmith." Dummer was sixty years old at the time. This evidence suggests that he remained active as a goldsmith throughout most of his adult life. His working dates span the years from 1667 to roughly 1710.

Although published in 1935, the monograph by Hermann Frederick Clarke and Henry Wilder Foote entitled *Jeremiah Dummer, Colonial Craftsman and Merchant, 1645–1718* is still useful. The biographical information is generally correct, and the checklist of some ninety-four pieces of silver is a convenient tool. In the years since it was published, the total number of pieces attributed to Dummer has grown by nearly a dozen, but there are no surprises. The section on portraits (pp. 159–205) should be ignored; the inscriptions that led to the idea that Dummer was a portrait artist are spurious.

References: Buhler, *American Silver*, pp. 10–27. Buhler and Hood, *American Silver*, pp. 12–26. Kathryn C. Buhler, *Massachusetts Silver in the Frank L. and Louise Harrington Collection*, 2 vols. (New Haven: Yale University Press for Yale University Art Gallery, 1970), 1:11–20. Hermann F. Clarke, "Jeremiah Dummer, Silversmith (1645–1718)," *Antiques* 28, no. 4 (October 1935): 142–45. Hermann Frederick Clarke and Henry Wilder Foote, *Jeremiah Dummer: Colonial Craftsman and Merchant, 1645–1718* (1935; reprint, New York: Da Capo, 1970). John J. Currier, *History of Newbury, Massachusetts, 1635–1902* (Boston: Damrell and Upham, 1902), esp. chap. 4. *DAB*, s.v. "Dummer, Jeremiah," "Dummer, William." Sewall, *Diary*, for numerous references; pp. 1093–95, for a genealogy of the Dummer family. Ensko, *American Silversmiths III*, pp. 48, 192, 264. Flynt and Fales, *Heritage Foundation*, pp. 207–8. Jones, *Old Silver*. Morton Pennypacker, "Captain Kidd: Hung Not for Piracy but for Causing the Death of a Rebellious Seaman Hit with a Toy Bucket," *New York History* 25, no. 4 (October 1944): 482–531, esp. app. 2. Richard D. Pierce, ed., *Records of the First Church in Boston, 1630–1868*, 3 vols. (Boston: Colonial Society, 1961). Roberts, *Artillery Company*, 1:213. Samuel Sewall to Sir William Ashhurst, March 19, 1704/5, in "Letter-book of Samuel Sewall," in *Collections of the Massachusetts Historical Society*, 6th ser., 1 (1886), p. 311.

43
TANKARD, ca. 1676

H. 6 1/16" (15.4 cm), DIAM. base 5 1/16" (12.9 cm), W. 7 3/16" (18.3 cm)
24 oz. 9 dwt. (760.5 g)

Stamps: "I•D" in roman letters, over a fleur-de-lis, all in a heart, struck on body, right of handle, and on top of lid.

Engraved on handle: "R∗R/ to/ CC" in script.

Description: raised body with straight sides and narrow applied base molding, double-scored line around upper body below rim; raised bottom with no centerpunch. Raised 3-step lid with centerpunch on top; scored circle around edge; crenate lip. Cast 2-cusp thumbpiece. Cast hinge with double meander wire on body side, incuse "7" struck on hinge, once on handle section (left), and once on lid section (underneath). Raised-and-soldered hollow handle with plain tailpiece; circular vent.

Spectrographic analysis:

	SILVER	COPPER	LEAD	GOLD
BODY	90.8	8.2	0.35	0.26
BOTTOM	92.2	6.8	0.43	0.24
LID	93.3	6.3	0.17	0.11
HANDLE	92.1	6.7	0.36	0.30
THUMBPIECE	94.7	4.7	0.28	0.19
BASE MOLDING	94.8	4.4	0.23	0.28

History: "RR" refers to Richard Russell (1611–76), who came from Hereford, Eng., in 1640 and settled in Charlestown, Mass. "CC" refers to Charlestown Church, the First Parish Church, which Russell joined in 1641. Russell was a merchant who held many public offices, from selectman to representative to the General Court, where he was speaker from 1648 to 1658. He was treasurer of the colony for 20 years. His will, dated May 29, 1674, and proved March 18, 1676, provided the following legacy to the church: "To the Church of Ch^t in Charlestown with whom I have been in sweet Christian fellowship for many years, I do give and bequeath one hundred pounds to be pd by Ex^r to the Deacons for the use of the Church." This tankard and one other (no. 43) were presumably purchased from the bequest. Russell also bequeathed £200 for the poor and £100 to Harvard College and provided legacies for the Reverend Thomas Shepard, the Reverend Samuel Whitney, and other pastors. His second wife, Mary Chester (d. November 30, 1688, at age 80), left £5 to son-in-law Richard Sprague and a silver cup marked "M.I.D" and other silver with the Chester arms to John Coultman of Wethersfield, Conn. Mary's first husband was Leonard Chester of Hartford, Conn. (See no. 136 for tankard by Edward Winslow with Chester arms purchased by the First Church with funds bequeathed by Sprague.)

In his history of the First Church, William Budington indicates that in 1800 the "sacramental furniture" belonging to the church consisted of 4 flagons, 14 tankards, 1 cup, 1 basin, and 1 spoon, all in silver; 8 pewter dishes; and 2 tablecloths. Three flagons, 7 tankards, and 4 pewter dishes, "not having been used for many years, were sold, and the proceeds loaned to the town of Charlestown, to be again invested in plate for the use of the communion table, at the pleasure of the church."

Provenance: In March 1926 the First Church of Charlestown, Mass., sold 14 pieces of communion plate to Alfred Stainforth of Winthrop, Mass., for $7,500. The lot included this and another tankard by Dummer (no. 44) plus 2 tankards by Austin (nos. 3, 4) and 2 by Edward Winslow (nos. 136, 137). H. F. du Pont purchased the 6 tankards from Israel Sack, April 1926.

Exhibitions: "American Church Silver," Museum of Fine Arts, Boston, 1911.

Comments: See no. 44 for similar tankard by same maker.

References: American Church Silver, no. 368 or 369. William I. Budington, *The History of the First Church of Charlestown* (Boston: By the author, 1845), pp. 159, 240–42. Thomas B. Wyman, *Genealogies and Estates of Charlestown in the County of Middlesex and Commonwealth of Massachusetts, 1629–1818*, 2 vols. (Boston, 1879), pp. 829–31. Henry R. Stiles, *History of Ancient Wethersfield, Connecticut*, 2 vols. (New York: Grafton Press, 1904), pp. 209–11. Jones, *Old Silver*, pp. 119–25, pl. 48. Clarke and Foote, *Jeremiah Dummer*, no. 78.

64.679 Gift of H. F. du Pont, 1965

44
TANKARD, ca. 1676

H. 6 1/16" (15.4 cm), DIAM. base 5 1/8" (13.0 cm),
W. 7 3/16" (18.3 cm)
20 oz. 18 dwt. 13 gr. (650.9 g)

Stamps: "I•D" in roman letters, over a fleur-de-lis, all in a heart, struck on body, left of handle, and on top of lid.

Engraved on handle: "CC" in shaded roman letters.

Description: raised body with straight sides and narrow applied base molding; single-scored line encircles upper body below rim; raised bottom with centerpunch outside. Raised 3-step lid with centerpunch inside; crenate lip; scored line encircles lid at edge. Cast 2-cusp thumbpiece. Cast hinge, incuse "2" struck on hinge, once on handle section (left) and once on lid section (underneath). Raised-and-soldered hollow handle with shield-shape tailpiece with serrated edge; circular vent; triangular decorative casting with punchwork on handle next to hinge. Tapered drop (raised) applied to body below upper juncture of handle.

Spectrographic analysis:

	SILVER	COPPER	LEAD	GOLD
BODY	92.4	7.1	0.33	0.09
BOTTOM	94.8	4.8	0.28	0.14
LID	93.0	6.5	0.19	0.08
HANDLE	93.1	6.7	0.15	0.09
THUMBPIECE	93.2	6.1	0.24	0.23
BASE MOLDING	93.8	6.0	0.14	0.04

History: Part of communion service owned by the First Church of Charlestown, Mass.; see no. 43.

Provenance: See no. 43.

Exhibitions: "American Church Silver," Museum of Fine Arts, Boston, 1911. "New England Begins: The Seventeenth Century," Museum of Fine Arts, Boston, 1982.

Comments: See no. 43 for similar tankard by same maker.

References: Fales, *American Silver*, no. 8. Hood, *American Silver*, pp. 27–28, fig. 4. Fairbanks and Trent, *New England Begins*, no. 259. See no. 43.

64.678 Gift of H. F. du Pont, 1965

ℭ 45
TANKARD, ca. 1693

H. 6 5/16" (16.0 cm), DIAM. base 5" (12.7 cm),
W. 7 ½" (19.1 cm)
25 oz. 6 dwt. 17 gr. (788.0 g)

Stamps: "ID" in roman letters, over a fleur-de-lis, all in a heart, struck on body, left of handle, and on top of lid.

Engraved on base: "R/ D•S" in roman letters.
Engraved on front of body: "SP/ to/ MR" in script.

Description: raised body with straight sides; applied base molding consists of an ogee topped by 3 beads; double-scored line encircles upper body below rim; raised bottom with centerpunch outside. Raised 2-step lid with no centerpunch; crenate lip; scored lines encircle lid edge; cut-card escutcheon applied to lid next to thumbpiece. Cast double-spiral thumbpiece. Cast hinge with meander wire on each side. Raised-and-soldered hollow handle with vertical ribbed design and scroll on back; notched vent; cast cherub's-head tailpiece. Rattail drop (raised) applied to body below upper juncture of handle.

Spectrographic analysis:

	SILVER	COPPER	GOLD	LEAD
BODY	93.8	5.7	0.27	0.18
BOTTOM	95.9	3.7	0.26	0.16
LID	94.2	5.1	0.31	0.20
BASE MOLDING	95.2	4.4	0.27	0.14

History: The initials "R/ D•S" refer to Daniel Rogers (1667–1722) and Sarah Appleton (1671–1775), who were married about 1693. Daniel Rogers was the son of John Rogers (ca. 1630–84), president of Harvard College. Sarah was the daughter of Capt. John Appleton of Ipswich. "SP" refers to their granddaughter Sarah (Rogers) Parkman, and "MR" refers to Sarah Parkman's niece Mary Rogers. Shortly after graduating from Harvard College in 1686, Daniel Rogers taught grammar school in Ipswich until 1716. During his tenure, 15 people entered Harvard from Ipswich. He was justice of the Court of Sessions, register of probate, and town clerk for Ipswich. Abraham Hammatt, historian of Ipswich, writing in 1852, could not resist commenting on Rogers's sloppy recordkeeping: "Mr. Rogers was, without doubt, an estimable man. . . . but, regard for the truth of history obliges me to add he is entitled to the unenviable distinction of being the worst scribe that ever had the custody of our records. He was careless, incorrect, and his handwriting is frequently illegible." On December 1, 1722, returning from a visit to Hampton, N.H., Rogers died during a violent snowstorm after losing his way.

Provenance: Daniel and Sarah Rogers; their son Rev. Daniel Rogers (1706–82) of Littleton, Mass.; his daughter Sarah (1755–1835), who married Samuel Parkman in 1784; her niece Mary Rogers, Milford, Mass.; her niece Susannah Dalton Rogers; her nephew James Rogers Rich; his brother Thomas Phillips Rich; his widow, from whom it was purchased in 1920 by Francis Hill Bigelow; Brooks Reed Gallery, Boston, sold to H. F. du Pont, 1927.

Comments: Other tankards by Dummer incorporating the cut-card escutcheon on the lid and ribbed handle with scroll are owned by the Metropolitan Museum of Art and Addison Gallery of American Art, Andover, Mass. A third example is reproduced in Clarke and Foote, *Jeremiah Dummer*, pl. 17.

References: Abraham Hammatt, "Ipswich Grammar School," *NEH&GR* 6, no. 1 (January 1852): 64–71. *Sibley's Harvard Graduates*, 3:358–60. Clarke and Foote, *Jeremiah Dummer*, no. 89. Fales, *American Silver*, no. 10.

65.1362 Gift of H. F. du Pont, 1965

ℭ 46
CAUDLE CUP, ca. 1690

H. 3 ⅛" (7.9 cm), DIAM. rim 4 ½" (11.4 cm),
W. 6 ⅞" (17.5 cm)
6 oz. 16 dwt. 20 gr. (212.8 g)

Stamps: "I•D" in roman letters, over a fleur-de-lis, all in a heart, struck once on side of body.

Engraved on bottom: "Benjamin Coffin/ to/ RG [or RC]" in script and roman letters.

Description: raised cup form with flared lip, flat bottom, and spiral gadrooning chased on lower third of body all around; 2 cast double–C-scroll handles, 1 on each side, featuring foliation and rows of beads.

Spectrographic analysis:

	SILVER	COPPER	LEAD	GOLD
BODY SIDE	92.4	7.2	0.20	0.17
BODY BOTTOM	93.9	5.8	0.13	0.16
HANDLE (LEFT OF STAMP)	93.1	6.4	0.19	0.19
HANDLE (RIGHT OF STAMP)	93.3	6.2	0.11	0.11

History: According to the history that came with this piece, "RG" stands for Ruth Gardner, daughter of John Gardner of Nantucket. She married James Coffin, Jr., in 1692. It was alleged that Benjamin Coffin was probably an uncle of James. There are serious obstacles to this history, the most important of which is the lack of a Benjamin Coffin of the right age and generation. According to the Coffin family genealogy, the first Benjamin Coffin (son of James, 1640–1720) was born in 1683 but died young. It is not until the fifth generation (the first starting with Peter Coffin, who died in 1628) that another Benjamin Coffin appears, and then there are 4: Benjamin (1710–84), son of Stephen; Benjamin (1718–93), son of James, Jr., and Ruth Gardner (married in 1692); Benjamin (1705–80), son of Nathaniel; and Benjamin (1718–93), son of Enoch. Since Dummer died in 1718, it is unlikely that any of them is the donor—unless, of course, the inscription was added later. Further complications arise upon close examination of the engraved initials. It appears that someone may have changed the *C* to a *G*, although the crudeness of the engraving makes it difficult to be certain. In the fifth generation, Benjamin, son of James, Jr., married Rebecca Coffin, and his sister Ruth (1716–1801) married Cromwell Coffin (1709–83). Here, then, are 2 candidates if the initials were originally "RC."

Provenance: Purchased in 1917 from George H. Gardner by Francis Hill Bigelow. (Note: James and Ruth [Gardner] Coffin had a son named George [1693–1727] who married Ruth Swain. They had 3 daughters and no sons.) Brooks Reed Gallery, Boston, sold to H. F. du Pont, 1927.

Comments: E. Alfred Jones recorded a nearly identical caudle cup by Dummer that was owned by the First Congregational Society of Chelmsford, Mass. It is engraved with the initials "F/ IL," which refer to John and Lydia Fiske, who were married in 1666. The cup is illustrated in Jones, *Old Silver*, pl. 49. Another nearly identical caudle cup is owned by Historic Deerfield. It should be noted that Dummer used this same form for the cup portion of his standing church cups. See, for example, Bigelow, *Historic Silver*, fig. 8.

References: Charles H. Carpenter, Jr., and Mary Grace Carpenter, *Decorative Arts and Crafts of Nantucket* (New York: Dodd, Mead, 1987), fig. 7. "The Coffin Family," *NEH&GR* 24, no. 2 (1870): 149–54, 305–15. Francis Hill Bigelow, "Early New England Silver," *Antiques* 8, no. 3 (September 1925): fig. 3. Clarke and Foote, *Jeremiah Dummer*, no. 18. Fales, *American Silver*, no. 4. Kauffman, *Colonial Silversmith*, p. 84.

60.1053 Gift of H. F. du Pont, 1965

47
CAUDLE CUP, ca. 1690

H. 3 ¼" (8.3 cm), w. 6 ½" (16.5 cm),
DIAM. rim 3 ⁹⁄₁₆" (9.1 cm)
7 oz. 14 dwt. 19 gr. (240.2 g)

Stamps: "I•D" in roman letters, in a rectangle, struck near center on bottom; "I•D" in roman letters, over a fleur-de-lis, all in a heart, struck on outside of body between handles.

Engraved on underside: "The gift of M•C" and "B/ I•H" in script and shaded roman letters.

Description: raised 1-piece body with bulbous lower half and concave upper half, no center-punch visible; hammer marks still clearly visible on outside of body; cast C-scroll handles with spurs at top and double scrolls at bottom.

Spectrographic anlysis:

	SILVER	COPPER	LEAD	GOLD
BODY BOTTOM	91.7	7.9	0.33	0.05
BODY SIDE	90.6	9.1	0.26	0.02
HANDLE (RIGHT OF STAMP)	89.2	9.2	0.42	0.32
HANDLE (LEFT OF STAMP)	90.3	8.0	0.38	0.32

History: According to the history that came with the piece, it descended in the Bird, Topliff, and Farrar families and was said to be traceable back to Samuel Topliff Bird (1820–98). Francis Hill Bigelow speculated that the initials "MC" referred to Mary Clap, who married Thomas Bird in 1718. The initials "B/ IH" he suggested referred to James and Hannah Bird, who were married in 1727/28. Matching initials and names on silver with historical personages is risky in the absence of clear documentation. A perusal of the Bird family genealogy (*NEH&GR*) provides the following information: The founder of the Bird family in America was Thomas Bird (d. 1667) of Dorchester, Mass. His son James (1647–1723) was married twice, creating 2 lines of descent. James's

grandson, also named James Bird (1703–57), married Hannah Wales in 1727/28. James and Hannah Bird, therefore, are probably the "B/ IH" on this cup. By his second wife, the first James Bird had a son named Thomas Bird (1692/93–1770), who, in 1718, married Mary Clap. Their son, Thomas Bird (1722–72), in 1749, also married a Mary Clap.

Although Bigelow assumed that the initials "MC" referred to the first Mary Clap, they could also refer to the second. The second Thomas and Mary Clap became the parents of Thomas Bird (1754–93), who married Hannah Topliff in 1777. The published genealogy ends here. Family tradition picks up with the Samuel Topliff Bird noted earlier, whose dates rule him out as the son of Thomas and Hannah Bird but who could have been a grandson. See *Provenance* for remaining line of descent.

Provenance: Probably Mary Clap (d. 1761), who married Thomas Bird (1692/93–1770) in 1718; James (1703–57) and Hannah Wales (d. 1775) Bird; Thomas (1754–93) and Hannah Topliff Bird (1755–1815); descending to Samuel Topliff Bird (1820–98), who married Caroline Elizabeth Farrar (d. 1918) in 1875; her nephew George Otis Farrar (1906–?), from whom it was purchased in 1925 by Francis Hill Bigelow; Brooks Reed Gallery, Boston, sold to H. F. du Pont, 1927.

Comments: Similarly shaped cups with identical handles are in the Henry Ford Museum, Minneapolis Institute of Art, Art Institute of Chicago, and Yale University Art Gallery. Cups of similar shape but with different handles are in the Museum of Fine Arts, Boston; the Old Colony Historical Society, Taunton, Mass.; and the Department of State Diplomatic Reception Rooms (on loan from the Bortman-Larus collection). See Jones, *Old Silver*, for additional examples.

References: "Thomas Bird, of Dorchester, Massachusetts, and Some of His Descendants," *NEH&GR* 25, no. 1 (1871): 21–30. Clarke and Foote, *Jeremiah Dummer*, p. 77, no. 33. Fales, *American Silver*, no. 21.

65.1349 Gift of H. F. du Pont, 1965

ℰ 48
SPOON, ca. 1685

L. 7 5/16" (18.6 cm)
1 oz. 6 dwt. 10 gr. (41.1 g)

Stamps: "I•D" in roman letters, over a fleur-de-lis, all in a heart, struck on back of handle and inside bowl.

Engraved on back of handle: "EB" in roman letters.

Description: raised oval bowl with swage-formed rattail and leafy scrolls on back; wavy-end handle cut from sheet silver and soldered to bowl.

Spectrograph analysis: Silver content of bowl is 92.5 percent; silver content of handle is 91.7 percent.

History: According to Hermann F. Clarke and Henry Foote, the initials "EB" refer to either Eleazer Bellows, his wife Esther Barrett, or their son Eleazer Bellows.

Provenance: Francis Hill Bigelow, Boston; H. F. du Pont.

Comments: For other spoons by Dummer with "floral design and rat-tail" on the underside of the bowl, see Clarke and Foote, *Jeremiah Dummer*, nos. 64–70, 75; examples also in the Cleveland Museum of Art (Hollis French collection); Museum of Fine Arts, Boston; and Yale University Art Gallery. Similarly decorated spoons were made by John Coney, Edward Winslow, and John Edwards.

References: Clarke and Foote, *Jeremiah Dummer*, no. 73.

60.1052 Gift of H. F. du Pont, 1965

ℰ 49
SPOON, ca. 1685

L. 7 5/8" (19.4 cm)
1 oz. 11 dwt. 7 gr. (48.7 g)

Stamps: "I•D" in roman letters, over a fleur-de-lis, all in a heart, struck on back of handle and inside bowl.

Engraved on back of handle: "C/ IM" in roman letters.

Description: raised oval bowl with swage-formed rattail and leafy scrolls on back. Handle cut from sheet silver and soldered to bowl; trifid-end handle with swage-formed heart and scroll on front.

Spectrographic analysis: Silver content of bowl is 94.2 percent; silver content of handle is 94.8 percent.

Provenance: Mr. and Mrs. Stanley B. Ineson, New York City; Mr. and Mrs. Alfred E. Bissell, Wilmington, Del.

Exhibitions: Metropolitan Museum of Art, New York City, 1938–61.

Comments: Foliate-decorated trifid handles are rare. There is 1 by Dummer and 1 by John Coney at Yale University Art Gallery.

References: Belden, *Marks of American Silversmiths*, p. 144.

62.240.1040 Gift of Mr. and Mrs. Alfred E. Bissell, 1962–63

50
GOLD RING, dated 1693

Outside DIAM. ¾" (1.9 cm)
2 dwt. (3.1 g)

Stamps: "ID" in roman letters, in a rectangle, struck once inside band.

Engraved on inside of band: "Iames Lloyd. Obyt.21.Augt 1693" in roman letters and script.

Description: circular band, convex on outside and flat on inside, with diaper pattern impressed on outside. Outer surface probably formed with ring swage before metal was bent into a ring; soldered joint is visible. Vestiges of black enamel remain in crevices of pattern.

Spectrographic analysis:

	GOLD	COPPER	SILVER	
OUTSIDE SURFACE	86.0	10.9	3.1	21 karat

History: The ring commemorates the death of James Lloyd (ca. 1653–93), Boston merchant and founder of the Lloyd family in America. The son of Sir John Lloyd of Bristol, James emigrated from England to America as a young man. He settled in Boston about 1673 and in 1676 married Grizzell Sylvester. Following her death, he married Rebecca Leverett, daughter of Gov. Sir John Leverett. The Lloyds of Long Island are descended from his son, Henry Lloyd. Both the will and inventory of James Lloyd were published in *The Papers of the Lloyd Family of the Manor of Queens Village, Lloyd's Neck, Long Island, New York, 1654–1826.* The inventory of his household effects is extensive, and the inventory of his warehouse is a treasure trove of seventeenth-century textiles. Also in the Lloyd papers are the accounts of Francis Brinley, of Newport, R.I., executor of James Lloyd's estate, in which he records paying "Mr. Dummer" five shillings for "a bodkin for Grizzell" (November 2, 1695) and 1 shilling and 1 pence "for exchange of a thimble for Grizzell" (June 1697). (The Grizzell referred to here was the daughter of James and Grizzell Lloyd.) Unfortunately, there is no reference in the Lloyd papers to purchasing the mourning ring.

Provenance: Lloyd family, descending through Vassell and Borland families to Mrs. George L. Batchelder, Beverly, Mass.

Exhibitions: "New England Begins: The Seventeenth Century," Museum of Fine Arts, Boston, 1982.

Comments: Although the maker's stamp is similar to the "ID" in a rectangle found on caudle cup no. 47, it is not identical, and it is not found on any other work attributed to Dummer. Still, the circumstantial evidence points to Dummer as the maker. In addition to the purchases noted above, Dummer also served the family when, in 1710, as justice of the peace for Suffolk County, Mass., he recorded releases to Henry Lloyd and Rebecca (Leverett) Lloyd for claims against the manor of Queens Village. While no other rings by Dummer are known, Samuel Sewall noted in his diary for April 21, 1702, "I gave Madame Cooke a Ring cost 19s of Cous. Dumer in Remembrance of my dear Sister Moodey." Because of their small size, rings required a smaller die for stamping the maker's initials.

References: Fairbanks and Trent, *New England Begins*, no. 322, which mistakenly states that the ring is marked on the outside with the maker's stamp "ID" over a fleur-de-lis, all in a heart. *NYHS Collections:* vols. 59, 60: *The Papers of the Lloyd Family of the Manor of Queens Village, Lloyd's Neck, Long Island, New York, 1654–1826,* 2 vols. (New York: New-York Historical Society, 1926, 1927), 1:117–28, for will and inventory; 2:880 ff, for genealogical data; 1:140, 142, for purchases from Dummer.

72.60 Gift of Mrs. George L. Batchelder, 1972

John Edwards

1671–1746

Edwards & Allen, w. ca. 1694–99
Boston, Massachusetts

In the early 1680s John Edwards arrived in Boston with his father, John, a surgeon from Middlesex, England, and his mother and two sisters. His father must have secured a good apprenticeship for him—possibly with Jeremiah Dummer—for by 1694 he was married and shortly thereafter became the partner of John Allen. Although the partnership did not last past 1699, Edwards was launched on a successful career as a silversmith. As always, kinship networks eased the road to prosperity. Edwards's wife Sibella was a grandchild of the younger Gov. John Winthrop and step-daughter of Zerubbabel Endicott. His partner, John Allen, was nephew to Dummer, who, in turn, married Edwards's sister Elizabeth. Daughter Mary married Ebenezer Storer, who heavily patronized Edwards's silversmith sons, Thomas and Samuel. Active in local affairs, Edwards was tithingman, constable, and assessor and served in the Boston militia and the Artillery Company. He is often referred to in the records as "Mr. Edwards," an honorific not easily bestowed on craftsmen in those days.

Edwards served as a middleman in the transmission of precious metals from Governor Talcott of Connecticut to that colony's agent in England, one Francis Wilks. In 1732 Massachusetts Gov. Jonathan Belcher assured Talcott that "Mr. Edwards, who you say has the care of your Packets, is an honest, careful man." Samuel Sewall, the diarist, purchased three silver spoons from Edwards for his "Cousin Moodey" (the Reverend Samuel Moody of York, Maine) that bore the inscription "S. L. 1711" and cost 41s.

At his death, in 1746, Edwards was a man of substance. His total estate was valued at £4,840.8.0, of which £2,866.1.4 was in personal property. His shop tools must have been numerous because they were valued at £336.5.9. Goods in his shop totaled £1,042.10.5 and apparently did not include the £2,305.6.4 in silver and gold listed elsewhere in his inventory. He bequeathed to his son Thomas Edwards £200 and the "house and land in Cornhill, Boston, where I dwell." Son Samuel received the house and land in Hanover Street plus £520. He bequeathed his pew in the Brattle Street Church to sons Samuel and Joseph and daughter Anne.

His work is usually conservative; it includes many seventeenth-century forms and is not given to the baroque flourishes found in the work of Edward Winslow and others. He was a major supplier of church silver and made one of the four identical flagons owned by the Brattle Street Church; the other three were made by Winslow, Nathaniel Morse, and John Noyes.

References: Buhler, "John Edwards," pp. 288–92. Jones, *Old Silver,* index. Kane, *Dictionary,* s.v. "Edwards, John." "The Talcott Papers," in Mary Kingsbury Talcott, ed., vols. 4, 5 of *Collections of the Connecticut Historical Society* (Hartford: By the society, 1892, 1896), 4:257–59, 267–68, 284–87, 293, 303, 309, 310–12, 317–18, 372–75. SCPR book 38, pp. 514–18. Ward, "Edwards Family," pp. 66–76.

51
SPOUT CUP WITH LID, ca. 1700

H. 4 ¾" (12.1 cm), w. 3 ¾" (9.5 cm)
5 oz. 8 gr. (156.0 g)

Stamps: "IE" in roman letters, with a crown above and a fleur-de-lis below, all in a shield of conforming shape, struck once on upper body between spout and handle.

Engraved on base: "SM" in roman letters. *Engraved on side:* "MC" in late eighteenth-century script. *Scratched on base:* "5 oz/ hwt" and "$5.60".

Description: pear-shape body with centerpunch on bottom; applied S-curve seamed spout mounted perpendicular to handle rises from lowest portion of body to above rim; S-curve cast handle with beaded rattail, sprigs, and bud terminals. Applied molded footring. Circular, stepped, domed lid with cast globular finial.

Spectrographic analysis:

	SILVER	COPPER	GOLD	LEAD
BODY SIDE	92.4	6.9	0.34	0.30
HANDLE	92.3	7.2	0.22	0.25
SPOUT	91.2	8.2	0.28	0.29
LID	88.9	10.3	0.28	0.39

History: According to Francis Hill Bigelow, the initials "SM" may refer to Sarah Marshall of Boston. A Sarah Webb married John Marshall, May 26, 1699. Their daughter, Sarah Marshall, was born April 5, 1700. On January 3, 1721, she married Samuel Thaxter of Hingham. She died in 1727. The cup descended in the Thaxter-Cushing family. The initials "MC" are said to refer to Mary (Thaxter) Cushing (1784–1867), who married Jerome Cushing in 1813.

Provenance: Sarah (Webb) Marshall (m. 1699); Sarah (Marshall) Thaxter (1700–1727); Samuel Thaxter, Jr. (1723–71), who in 1743 married Abigail Smith (1722–1807) of Sandwich;

Thomas Thaxter (1748–1813), who in 1775 married Mary Barker; Mary Thaxter (1784–1895), who in 1813 married Jerome Cushing; Benjamin Cushing (1822–95), who in 1848 married Anna Quincy Thaxter (1825–1900); Susan Thaxter Cushing sold the cup in 1920 to Francis Hill Bigelow; Brooks Reed Gallery, Boston, sold to H. F. du Pont, June 1927.

References: Fales, *American Silver*, no. 20. Fennimore, *Silver and Pewter*, no. 130. Kauffman, *Colonial Silversmith*, p. 163, where it is mistakenly attributed to John Dixwell. For discussion of the form, see V. Isabelle Miller, "American Silver Spout Cups," *Antiques* 44, no. 2 (August 1943): 73–75.

65.1358 Gift of H. F. du Pont, 1965

ℰ 52
PORRINGER, ca. 1700

DIAM. bowl 5 ⅛" (13.0 cm), H. 2 ⅛" (5.4 cm), W. 7 ½" (19.1 cm)
5 oz. 19 dwt. 18 gr. (186.3 g)

Stamps: "IE" (lower part of stamp illegible) in roman letters, with a crown above, all enclosed in what appears to be a shield, struck once on body, right of handle.

Engraved on top of handle: "W / I+S" in roman letters. *Scratched into bottom of body:* a crude heart.

Description: raised circular form with bulging sides and straight rim; bottom domed in center; centerpunch inside and on bottom; cast handle pierced in keyhole pattern with 13 voids.

Spectrographic analysis:

	SILVER	COPPER	LEAD	GOLD
BODY SIDE	93.8	5.6	0.32	0.15
BODY BOTTOM	94.1	5.3	0.32	0.16
HANDLE	93.1	6.4	0.22	0.14

Provenance: Israel Sack, Boston, sold to H. F. du Pont, November 1926; or American Antique Shop, A. J. Pennypacker, proprietor, Pennsburg, Pa., sold to H. F. du Pont, February 1929. There are 2 porringers by John Edwards at Winterthur, and the original bills of sale do not identify them sufficiently to distinguish between them. See no. 53.

65.1353 Gift of H. F. du Pont, 1965

🕊 53
PORRINGER, ca. 1700

DIAM. bowl 5 ⁷/₁₆" (13.8 cm), H. 2" (5.1 cm),
W. 7 ¹³/₁₆" (19.8 cm)
6 oz. 11 dwt. 8 gr. (204.3 g)

Stamps: "IE" (lower part of stamp illegible) in
roman letters, with a crown above, all enclosed
in what appears to be a shield, struck once on
body, right of handle.

Engraved on handle: "LBS[?]" (in a cypher).
Engraved on bowl: "From Agnes McKean" in
late script.

Description: raised circular form with bulging
sides and straight rim; bottom domed in center;
centerpunch inside and on bottom; cast handle
pierced in keyhole pattern with 13 voids.

Spectrographic analysis:

	SILVER	COPPER	GOLD	LEAD
BODY SIDE	91.2	7.5	0.21	0.19
BODY BOTTOM	93.1	6.5	0.15	0.15
HANDLE	93.5	6.0	0.13	0.27

Provenance: Israel Sack, Boston, sold to H. F.
du Pont, November 1926; or American Antique
Shop, A. J. Pennypacker, proprietor, Pennsburg, Pa., sold to H. F. du Pont, February 1929.
There are 2 porringers by John Edwards at
Winterthur, and the original bills of sale do
not identify them sufficiently to distinguish
between them. See no. 52.

Exhibitions: "American Silver," Museum of
Fine Arts, Boston, 1906.

References: American Silver, MFA, no. 104.

65.1377 Gift of H. F. du Pont, 1965

🕊 54
SPOON, ca. 1690

L. 7 ⅜" (18.7 cm)
1 oz. 6 dwt. 3 gr. (40.6 g)

Stamps: "IE" in roman letters, in a quatrefoil
surround, struck once on back of handle near
bowl.

Engraved on back of handle: "G / IM" in shaded
roman letters.

Description: elongated oval bowl with swage-
formed rattail flanked by dotted scrolls in relief;
trifid-end upturned handle cut from sheet and
soldered to bowl.

Spectrographic analysis: Silver content of bowl
is 92.4 percent; silver content of handle is 92.6
percent.

Provenance: Francis Hill Bigelow, Boston; Brooks Reed Gallery, Boston, sold to H. F. du Pont, June 1927.

Comments: The "G" in the owner's initials is very crude and not of the same character as the other initials.

References: Fales, *American Silver*, nos. 72, 73. Fales, *Early American Silver*, no. 53. Kauffman, *Colonial Silversmith*, p. 58.

65.1369 Gift of H. F. du Pont, 1965

ℭ 55
SPOON, ca. 1700

L. 8 ⅛" (20.6 cm)
2 oz. 1 dwt. 2 gr. (63.9 g)

Stamps: "IE" in roman letters, with a crown above and rudimentary fleur-de-lis below, all in a conforming shield, struck once on handle back near bowl. Superb impression.

Engraved on handle back: "G/ GE" in roman letters; "Nantucket/ 1694" in script (the latter inscription is clearly of a much later date than the spoon itself). *Engraved on handle front:* "W. W. L. TO Mrs. D. B./ July 7th 1869" in script.

Description: elongated oval bowl with plain swage-formed rattail on back; rounded up-turned handle end with midrib running part-way down handle.

Spectrographic analysis: Silver content is 92.4 percent.

Provenance: Mr. and Mrs. Stanley B. Ineson, New York City; Mr. and Mrs. Alfred E. Bissell, Wilmington, Del.

Comments: In the Cornelius C. Moore collection, Providence College, there is a tankard, also by Edwards, with the initials "G/ GE" (*American Silver, 1670–1830: The Cornelius C. Moore Collection at Providence College* [Providence: Rhode Island Bicentennial Foundation and Providence College, 1980], no. 94). If indeed there really is an early Nantucket connection, the owners might have been George and Eunice Gardner (James Savage, *A Genealogical Dictionary of the First Settlers of New England* [1860–62; reprint, Baltimore: Genealogical Publishing, 1965], 2:227).

References: Belden, *Marks of American Silversmiths*, p. 151 a.

62.240.1077 Gift of Mr. and Mrs. Alfred E. Bissell, 1962–63

ℭ 56
SPOON, ca. 1695

L. 6 ¹⁵⁄₁₆" (17.6 cm)
1 oz. 2 dwt. 2 gr. (34.3 g)

Stamps: "IA" in roman letters, in quatrefoil surround, struck once on back of handle; "IE" in roman letters, in quatrefoil surround, struck once on handle back near bowl.

Engraved on handle back: "MB" in roman letters.

Description: elongated oval bowl with swage-formed rattail flanked by flowery scrolls in relief; trifid-end upturned handle end; handle cut from sheet and soldered to bowl.

Spectrographic analysis: Silver content of bowl is 92.5 percent; silver content of handle is 94.0 percent.

Provenance: Mr. and Mrs. Stanley B. Ineson, New York City; Mr. and Mrs. Alfred E. Bissell, Wilmington, Del.

Exhibitions: On loan to the Metropolitan Museum of Art, New York City, 1939–42.

Comments: This spoon is a product of the partnership with John Allen and therefore was made during the 1690s.

References: Belden, *Marks of American Silversmiths*, p. 151 b.

62.240.867 Gift of Mr. and Mrs. Alfred E. Bissell, 1962–63

Samuel Edwards

1705–62
Boston, Massachusetts
See partnership of Samuel & Thomas Edwards

One of the two silversmithing sons of John Edwards, Samuel, as well as his brother Thomas, was probably trained by his father. Although Samuel went on to become one of the three leading merchant-artisans of Boston—brother Thomas and Jacob Hurd were the other two—relatively little is known about his life. In 1733 he married Sarah Smith, whose mother later became his father's second wife. Samuel's nephew Joseph

Edwards, Jr., son of Samuel's deceased brother John, Jr., also became a silversmith, probably under Samuel's tutelage. In his will Samuel bequeathed a spoon swage and a thimble stamp to young Joseph. Samuel's estate was valued at £2,134.12.1 ½. On hand when he died was wrought plate to the value of £775.3.3½ and goldsmith's tools valued at £98.12.7½. Two of the three appraisers of his estate were silversmiths William Simpkins and John Coburn. Edwards had a substantial library for the time—200 titles—that included *Artists Vade Mecum, New Touchstone for Silver,* and *Quarles's Emblems,* all useful for a silversmith.

Edwards benefited from his sister Mary's marriage to Ebenezer Storer in 1723, for in subsequent years the Storer family purchased quantities of silver from him. Much of his work reflects a conservative strain with a strong persistence of seventeenth-century forms. See especially the communion cups made for the West Church on Lynde Street, one of which is now at the Metropolitan Museum of Art. The teapot discussed in the following entry is a stylistically up-to-date example of his work.

References: Buhler, "John Edwards," pp. 288–92. Jones, *Old Silver,* p. 87, pl. 33. SCPR book 63, pp. 37–38. Kane, *Dictionary,* s.v. "Edwards, Samuel." Ward, "Edwards Family," pp. 66–76. Barbara McLean Ward, "Hierarchy and Wealth Distribution in the Boston Goldsmithing Trade, 1690–1760," *Essex Institute Historical Collections* 126, no. 3 (July 1990): 129–47.

ℰ 57
TEAPOT, ca. 1757

H. 5 ¾" (14.6 cm), w. 9 ⅛" (23.2 cm)
16 oz. 18 dwt. 15 gr. (525.4 g)

Stamps: "S•E" in roman letters, with a crown above and fleur-de-lis below, all in a shaped shield, struck once on base.

Engraved on base: "L*D to E*R/ 1757" in roman letters. *Engraved on underside of lid:* "ES/ to/ ER" in roman letters. *Engraved on both sides of body:* "ER" in neoclassical script. *Scratched on base:* "oz 16 dwt 1".

Description: circular bulbous body with lower extension; flat chased decorative border encircles rim. Applied step-molded footring. Cast S-curve spout with decorative moldings at lower end and upper tip. C-curve sprigged wooden handle attached by silver pins in silver sockets soldered to body; upper socket has cast hood similar to that on upper end of spout. Circular 1-step lid with 8-point flat-chased decoration continued from body; cast cone finial.

Spectrographic analysis:

	SILVER	COPPER	LEAD	GOLD
BODY SIDE	88.3	11.2	0.20	0.08
BODY BOTTOM	95.3	4.7	0.09	0.06
FOOTRING	94.8	5.2	0.09	0.09
SPOUT	94.1	5.8	0.08	0.06
LID	89.3	10.4	0.18	0.08

History: According to Francis Hill Bigelow, "LD to ER" refers to Lucy Dudley and her niece Elizabeth Richards. In 1703 Lucy Wainwright (d. 1756) married Paul Dudley (1675–1751), son of Massachusetts Gov. Joseph Dudley, chief justice of Massachusetts and fellow of the Royal Society (for contributing a paper on the manufacture of maple syrup). Famed for his aristocratic manner, Dudley was instrumental—along with John Read (see no. 97)—in modernizing court procedures and documents. In 1721 he suffered the theft of "a pair of Silver Candlesticks of Mr. Dummer's make, a Silver-hilted Sword, Silver Spurs, and Silver Buckles, Three or Four Small Silver Tea Spoons, a Beaver Hat, a light Periwig ty'd up, almost new; a gray broad Cloth Coat, trim'd and fac'd with black, half worn, half a dozen Holland Shirts, Three Shifts, Four Muslin Neckcloths, and a pair of Mens English Shoes rosted soles." Portraits of Dudley hang in the Boston Athenaeum and the Massachusetts Supreme Court.

One of Dudley's love letters to Lucy, sent to Lucy's sister, Mrs. Davenport, prior to their marriage, is a model of indirect address to the beloved. References abound to "my Sweetest, fairest, Deerest Lucy," "my Divine Mistress," and "My Charming Nymph." The Dudleys had 6 children, but they all died young.

The "ER" of the inscription on the base refers to Elizabeth (Dudley) Richards (1724–1805), daughter of Elizabeth Davenport (d. 1750) and Col. William Dudley (1686–1747), a brother of Paul Dudley. Although Lucy Dudley's will, proved in 1756, shows only a bequest of £6.13.4 "to the six daughters of my late brother-in-law William Dudley," it is reasonable to suppose that the teapot owned by the aunt came into the possession of the niece. The inscribed date of 1757 is crudely done and may well have been added later.

In light of the later owners, the "ES" on the underside of the lid in all likelihood also refers to Elizabeth Richards following the death of her first husband and her subsequent marriage to Samuel Scarboro. "ER" in this inscription refers to Elizabeth Richards (1781–1878), the senior Elizabeth's granddaughter. This Elizabeth Richards married Boston merchant Richard Child. The teapot descended in the Child family. The script initials "ER" on the side of the body undoubtedly refer to the second Elizabeth Richards.

Provenance: Lucy Dudley (d. 1756); Elizabeth (Dudley) Richards Scarboro (1724–1805); Elizabeth (Richards) Child (1781–1878); Henry Richards Child (1816–47); Dudley Richards Child (1845–83); Dudley Richards Child (b. 1867); Francis Hill Bigelow (purchased 1917); Brooks Reed Gallery, Boston, sold to H. F. du Pont, June 1927.

Exhibitions: "American Church Silver," Museum of Fine Arts, Boston, 1911 (lent by "Miss Edith and Rev. Dudley R. Child"). "Selections from Winterthur Museum: Change and Choice in Early American Decorative Arts," IBM Gallery of Science and Art, New York City, 1989–90.

Comments: This is an extraordinarily fine and fashionable example of Edwards's work. The flat chasing on the shoulders creates an attractive design especially when viewed from overhead.

References: Dean Dudley, *History of the Dudley Family* (Wakefield, Mass., 1886–89, published in sections without an index), pp. 521–34, for sketch of Paul Dudley and wills of Paul and Lucy Dudley; pp. 534–42, for sketch of William Dudley and inventory of his estate (which included 365 oz. of wrought plate and "52 chairs with leather bottoms," the latter in the hall only); pp. 685–86, for Elizabeth (Richards) Child; p. 833, for Elizabeth (Dudley) Richards Scarboro; p. 16 of enclosed "Memorial of the Dudley Reunion," for a reference to an oil portrait of Lucy (Wainwright) Dudley owned at that point by Dudley Richards Child. *Sibley's Harvard Graduates,* 4:42–54, for biography of Paul Dudley. *American Church Silver,* no. 465. Fales, *American Silver,* no. 27. Fennimore, *Silver and Pewter,* no. 142. Quimby, "Silver," p. 79. SCPR book 51, pp. 751–52.

65.1363 Gift of H. F. du Pont, 1965

58
LADLE, ca. 1755

L. 13 ¼" (33.7 cm), w. bowl 4 ⁵⁄₁₆" (11.0 cm)
3 oz. 3 dwt. 5 gr. (98.3 g)

Stamps: "SE" in roman letters, in a rectangle with rounded corners, struck once on inside center of bowl.

Description: raised fluted oval bowl with flared pouring lips on each side; no centerpunch visible (may be obscured by maker's stamp). Silver portion of handle consists of cast forked section, cast C scroll, and cast tapered shaft, circular in section. A turned hardwood handle is secured to the silver portion of shaft by a silver pin.

Spectrographic analysis:

	SILVER	COPPER	LEAD	GOLD
BOWL	88.8	10.5	0.26	0.17
HANDLE	94.1	5.4	0.31	0.10

History: According to J. Herbert Gebelein: "I asked where I found this [and] did it probably come from one of the local families, and the answer was it came from one of the Bradleys, having relationship with Randolphs of Cambridge. While my thought of [the] occurence of the latter name up here connects the Virginia-Massachusetts tie dating from Thomas Jefferson's daughter and granddaughter . . . I suppose there were already other Randolphs in Massachusetts, perhaps accounting for the naming of the town south of Milton if that were a prior event."

Provenance: J. Herbert Gebelein, Boston, sold to H. F. du Pont, November 1956.

Comments: A pair of nearly identical ladles, made by Paul Revere, was presented to St. Andrew's Masonic Lodge in Boston in 1762 by Samuel Barrett. See also apparently identical ladle made by Elias Pelletreau in Buhler and Hood, *American Silver*, no. 676.

References: Fales, *American Silver*, no. 90. Fennimore, *Silver and Pewter*, no. 16. J. Herbert Gebelein to Charles Montgomery, November 21, 1956, Registration Division, Winterthur. Warren, Howe, and Brown, *Marks of Achievement*, no. 54.

56.100 Gift of H. F. du Pont, 1956

59
SCISSOR TONGS, ca. 1750

L. 4 ⅜" (11.1 cm.)
17 dwt. 2 gr. (26.6 g)

Stamps: "SE" in roman letters, in a rectangle with rounded corners, struck once on underside of right grip.

Engraved on handles: "M" on 1 handle; "H" on the other, both in roman letters. *Engraved on both sides of circular pivot:* a rose blossom.

Description: scissors made in 2 identical but reversed pieces, joined at circular pivot. Each piece consists of a cast shell grip; shaft; cast C scroll; circular pivot; and cast sprigged C-scroll handle with cast ringlike grip.

Spectrographic analysis:

	SILVER	COPPER	LEAD	GOLD
ARM 1	93.5	6.2	0.22	0.07
ARM 2	92.5	7.2	0.25	0.12

Provenance: Mr. and Mrs. Stanley B. Ineson, New York City; Mr. and Mrs. Alfred E. Bissell, Wilmington, Del.

References: Belden, *Marks of American Silversmiths*, p. 153 e.

62.240.780 Gift of Mr. and Mrs. Alfred E. Bissell, 1962–63

ℰ 60 a–e
SPOONS, ca. 1750

(a) L. 7 ⅞" (20.0 cm)
1 oz. 18 dwt. (59.1 g)
(b) L. 7 ¹⁵⁄₁₆" (20.2 cm)
1 oz. 17 dwt. 6 gr. (57.4 g)
(c) L. 7 ⅝" (19.4 cm)
1 oz. 9 dwt. 8 gr. (45.6 g)
(d) L. 7 ¹³⁄₁₆" (19.8 cm)
1 oz. 14 dwt. 16 gr. (53.9 g)
(e) L. 7 ⁷⁄₁₆" (18.9 cm)
1 oz. 1 dwt. 19 gr. (33.9 g)

Stamps: "S•E" in roman letters, with a crown above and fleur-de-lis below, all in a conforming shield.

Engraved on back of handle: (a) "S/ I∗E"; (b) "S/ I∗H"; (c) "M∗P"; (d) "G/ E+M" and (added later) a bird standing next to a tree with cut-off limbs; (e) "M+H". All in shaded roman letters.

Description: all spoons have rounded upturned handles with midribs; (a) and (b) have long oval bowls with swage-formed drops on back; (c) and (d) have long oval bowls with swage-formed shells on back; (e) has an oval bowl with a swage-formed rattail on back.

Spectrographic analysis: Silver content ranges from 88.8 to 91.4 percent.

History: (a) Initials "S/ I∗E" probably refer to Isaac and Elizabeth (Storer) Smith, who were married in 1746. Elizabeth Storer was Edwards's niece. (d) Initials "G/ EM" with identical engraved crest are on a pair of spoons by Edwards at the Museum of Fine Arts, Boston. They were owned by Edward and Mary (Storer) Green, who were married in 1757 in the Brattle Street Church, Boston.

Provenance: Mr. and Mrs. Stanley B. Ineson, New York City; Mr. and Mrs. Alfred E. Bissell, Wilmington, Del.

Exhibitions: Metropolitan Museum of Art, New York City, 1935–61 (1 of the 5 spoons).

References: Belden, *Marks of American Silversmiths*, p. 153. Buhler, *American Silver*, no. 206; see also no. 166 for a spoon by Jacob Hurd with a similar armorial device.

62.240.1080, .1081, .1083–.1085 Gift of Mr. and Mrs. Alfred E. Bissell, 1962–63

ℰ 61 a, b
SPOONS, ca. 1750

(a) L. 4 ⁷⁄₁₆" (11.3 cm)
5 dwt. 8 gr. (8.3 g)
(b) L. 4 ¹³⁄₁₆" (12.2 cm)
5 dwt. 2 gr. (8.1 g)

Stamps: "SE" in roman letters, in a rectangle with rounded corners, struck once on back of handle.

Engraved on back of handle: (a) "H+S" in roman letters; (b) "RW" in roman letters.

Description: both spoons have rounded upturned handles with midribs; (a) has a long oval bowl with swage-formed shell and drop on back; (b) has a long oval bowl with swage-formed rattail on back.

Spectrographic analysis: Silver content ranges from 90.2 to 91.6 percent.

Provenance: Mr. and Mrs. Stanley B. Ineson, New York City; Mr. and Mrs. Alfred E. Bissell, Wilmington, Del.

References: Belden, *Marks of American Silversmiths*, p. 153.

(a) 62.240.227, (b) 62.240.705 Gift of Mr. and Mrs. Alfred E. Bissell, 1962–63

Samuel & Thomas Edwards

Boston, Massachusetts
See individual biographies

62
STRAINER, ca. 1750

W. 10⅝" (27.0 cm), DIAM. bowl 4⅛" (10.5 cm)
3 OZ. 15 dwt. 12 gr. (117.5 g)

Stamps: "SE" in roman letters, in a rectangle with rounded corners, struck once on upper surface of 1 handle; "TE" in roman letters, in a rectangle, struck twice on underside of handle opposite handle with "SE" stamp and once on underside of other handle; 2 other unidentifiable strikes on handles.

Description: shallow circular bowl with flattened rim; bowl pierced with small drilled holes to serve as strainer; holes pierced on a grid pattern except around edge, which forms a 6-point star. Cast U-shape handles with circular terminals applied opposite each other to each side of bowl.

Spectrographic analysis:

	SILVER	COPPER	LEAD	GOLD
BOWL	90.5	8.8	0.27	0.22
HANDLE	97.6	1.6	0.13	0.28

Provenance: Philip H. Hammerslough, West Hartford, Conn.

Comments: For similar strainers by Samuel Edwards, see Buhler, *American Silver*, nos. 201, 202. The 2 strainers differ from the Winterthur example only in having more elaborate piercing. The second of the 2 Museum of Fine Arts, Boston strainers is dated 1746 and was made for Isaac and Elizabeth (Storer) Smith. Elizabeth Storer was Samuel Edwards's niece. Both Samuel and Thomas Edwards made silver for members of the Storer family. The Winterthur strainer may be the only known work combining the stamps of the 2 brothers.

References: Hammerslough, *American Silver*, 1:102.

60.82 Museum purchase from Philip H. Hammerslough, 1960

Thomas Edwards

1701/2–55
Boston, Massachusetts
See partnership of Samuel & Thomas
Edwards

Son of silversmith John Edwards, from whom he most likely learned the craft, and older brother of Samuel, Thomas Edwards took over his father's business upon John's death in 1746. Although he was one of the three most important artisan-merchants of the period, Thomas's career was cut short by an early death. It is possible that he trained Zachariah Brigden, who married Edwards's daughter Sarah in 1756, shortly after Brigden would have completed his apprenticeship. Edwards employed two journeymen, John Le Roux and Thomas Townsend, whose wages were pitifully low and often paid in kind. Townsend sued him in 1751. Edwards also used the services of other goldsmiths, several of whom sued him for not paying his debts. Edwards gave more attention to merchandising than did his brother Samuel and less attention to working at his bench. A Thomas Edwards became a freeman in New York City, May 25, 1731. Edwards may have worked in that city temporarily before returning to his father's shop in Boston. That he had connections in New York is further suggested by the presence of Le Roux in his shop. There were several silversmiths of this name in New York City.

Edwards was a member of the Artillery Company, serving as sergeant, ensign, lieutenant, and finally, in 1753, captain. He was clerk of the market in 1729 and 1747. In 1723 he married Sarah Burr of Charlestown; following her death some years later, he married a woman named Eleanor (last name unknown).

In his will he divided his estate, after several minor bequests of cash to other relatives, between his wife Eleanor and daughter Sarah. The total value was £1,780.12.1, of which £600 was for his house in Cornhill. Precious metals included 532 ounces of wrought silver and 365 ounces of "wrought and unwrought Gold." The inventory also includes "Burnt Silver, Bullion, Lace, & Fringe" worth £20.6.6, 122 books of gold leaf, and "A Chaise, Harness & Runners."

References: Buhler, "John Edwards," pp. 288–92. Roberts, *Artillery Company*, 1:416. Kane, *Dictionary*, s.v. "Edwards, Thomas." SCPR book 50, pp. 544–46; book 51, pp. 52–53. Ward, "Edwards Family," pp. 66–76. Ward, "Boston Goldsmiths," pp. 82–87. Barbara McLean Ward, "Hierarchy and Wealth Distribution in the Boston Goldsmithing Trade, 1690–1760," *Essex Institute Historical Collections* 126, no. 3 (July 1990): 129–47.

63
SALVER, ca. 1750

DIAM. 12 ⁷⁄₁₆" (31.6 cm), H. ½" (1.3 cm)
25 oz. 9 dwt. 12 gr. (792.4 g)

Stamps: "T.Edwards" in roman letters and italics, struck once on upper surface.

Engraved on underside: "B∗P/ to/ S∗H" in roman letters and script. See *Description* for engraved border.

Description: octagonal sheet silver with applied curvilinear molded edge. Border consists of wide C scrolls at the 4 main compass points with boldly pointed and curved elements in the corners. Engraved border, just inside molded edge, consists of asymmetrical shells over diaper-pattern border at the 4 main compass points and Tudor roses over diaper-pattern border at the corners, with a fleur-de-lis between each of the 8 border segments.

Spectrographic analysis:

	SILVER	COPPER	LEAD	GOLD
UPPER SURFACE	90.2	9.2	0.20	0.19
LOWER SURFACE	96.1	3.4	0.14	0.24
APPLIED EDGE	93.0	6.4	0.14	0.22

Provenance: Purchased by Mrs. Francis B. Crowninshield of Salem, Mass., and Wilmington, Del., "from the children of Mrs. Haskett Derby in Boston," ca. 1933.

References: Fales, *American Silver*, no. 114. Robert Bishop and Patricia Coblentz, *American Decorative Arts: 360 Years of Creative Design* (New York: Harry N. Abrams, 1982), p. 91.

53.2 Gift of Mrs. Francis B. Crowninshield, 1953

64
SALVER, ca. 1750

DIAM. 11 ⅝" (29.5 cm), H. 1 ⅞" (4.8 cm)
26 oz. 8 dwt. 21 gr. (822.5 g)

Stamps: "T.Edwards" in roman letters and italics, struck once on upper surface.

Engraved on upper side: circular medallion with split shield in the center containing (left) 2 lion heads erased, chevron, 7 ermine tails and (right) 2 lion faces, chevron or, 1 lion face; surrounded by dotted diaper pattern sprouting elaborate leafy scrolls; crest of lion's head erased at upper center; scallop shell at bottom; enclosed border of leaves.

Description: circular sheet silver with applied molded edge consisting of a series of cyma-recta cyma-reversa curves, 6 equidistant cast shells, and 6 equidistant C scrolls; 3 short cast cabriole legs with pad feet.

Spectrographic analysis:

	SILVER	COPPER	LEAD	GOLD
UPPER SURFACE	91.6	8.1	0.31	0.00
LOWER SURFACE	91.4	8.2	0.25	0.03
APPLIED EDGE	91.2	8.3	0.18	0.13

History: Charles Knowles Bolton identified the arms on the left as being those of the Allen family and those on the right as being, possibly, those of the Parkers. According to Francis Hill Bigelow, the salver descended in the Hayward family, starting with James Hayward (1764–1866) of Concord, Mass., to Katherine (Hayward) Sturtevant, whose daughter, Mrs. Charles F. Dutch, sold it to Bigelow in 1926. The only apparent connection between the arms and the Hayward family is that James Hayward, Jr., married Mary Parker as his second wife.

Provenance: James Hayward (1764–1866); James Hayward, Jr. (m. Katharine Saltonstall; Mary Parker), who bequeathed the salver to his grandniece Katharine (Hayward) Sturtevant, whose daughter married Charles F. Dutch. Sold by Mrs. Charles F. Dutch in 1926 to Francis Hill Bigelow; Brooks Reed Gallery, Boston, sold to H. F. du Pont, July 1927.

Exhibitions: "The American Craftsman and the European Tradition, 1620–1820," Minneapolis Institute of Arts, 1989.

Comments: According to Bigelow, the Reverend James Allen (1692–1747) used this combination of Allen and Parker arms. Similar arms were also used by Thomas Alleyne, whose bookplate was engraved by Nathaniel Hurd. According to John Guillim, the arms on the right are "Or, a Chevron between three Leopards heads Sable" as the "Coat-Armour of Sir Charles Wheeler of Burbury in Warwickshire."

References: Bolton, *Bolton's American Armory*, pp. 3, 126. Fales, *American Silver*, nos. 30, 49. French, *Jacob Hurd and His Sons*, p. 92. Guillim, *Display of Heraldry*, p. 260. Francis J. Puig and Michael Conforti, *The American Craftsman and the European Tradition, 1620–1820* (Minneapolis: Minneapolis Institute of Arts, 1989), no. 25. Walter Muir Whitehill and Norman Kotker, *Massachusetts: A Pictorial History* (New York: Charles Scribner's Sons, 1976), p. 63.

61.938 Gift of H. F. du Pont, 1965

65
SPOON, ca. 1750

L. 7 15/16" (20.2 cm)
1 oz. 12 dwt. 9 gr. (50.2 g)

Stamps: "T.Edwards" in roman letters and italics, struck once on back of handle.

Engraved on back of handle: "Hannah Stor[?]/ Jan 1 1755" in script, over a long-necked animal, head facing left.

Description: oval bowl with swage-formed shell and drop on back; rounded upturned handle end with midrib on front.

Spectrographic analysis: Silver content is 87.0 percent.

History: Sold by Carl Jacobs and catalogued for many years as the original property of Hannah Stone, the inscription actually refers to Hannah Storer. A similar spoon by Edwards is in the Museum of Fine Arts, Boston. It bears the inscription "Mary Storer/ Jan 1 1755" over the same crest used by Ebenezer Storer. Mary Storer was born in 1725 and married Edward Green in 1757.

Provenance: Carl Jacobs, Southwick, Mass.

References: Buhler, *American Silver*, no. 143. For family connections, see Margi Hofer, "A Spoon by Thomas Edwards," Registration Division, Winterthur.

59.33.1 Museum purchase from Carl Jacobs, 1959

66
SPOON, ca. 1750

L. 4 1/8" (10.5 cm)
4 dwt. 12 gr. (7.0 g)

Stamps: "T.EDWARDS" in uneven roman letters, in a rectangle with rounded corners.

Description: long oval bowl with swage-formed shell and drop on back; rounded upturned handle end with midrib on front.

Spectrographic analysis: Silver content is 93.4 percent.

Provenance: Mr. and Mrs. Stanley B. Ineson, New York City; Mr. and Mrs. Alfred E. Bissell, Wilmington, Del.

References: Belden, *Marks of American Silversmiths*, p. 154.

62.240.226 Gift of Mr. and Mrs. Alfred E. Bissell, 1962–63

Joseph Foster

1760–1839
Boston, Massachusetts

Joseph Foster served his apprenticeship under Benjamin Burt, who later referred to him in his will as "my trusty friend Joseph Foster of Boston Goldsmith" and also named him executor. Foster advertised at 171 Ann Street in 1789 and on Fish Street in 1798, but this may be the same street. Esther Forbes, in her biography of Paul Revere, quotes Henry Lee, who wrote in 1881 of the North End neighborhood of his youth. He talked of "Honest Foster, the silversmith who in his long coat, knee-breeches and shoe buckles, dwelt with his spinster sister in an impractically low jettied house on Anne Street, one step below the narrow sidewalk." In spite of a long career, few examples of Foster's work are known, perhaps because he made silver for other silversmiths and retailers, silver that did not carry his own stamp. Foster did, however, make communion plate for at least six different churches. One of these, the First Church of Lancaster, Massachusetts, commissioned him to make eight silver cups in 1810. The details of the transaction and a letter and invoice from Foster are reproduced in Jones, *Old Silver*.

References: Buhler, *American Silver*, p. 505. Buhler and Hood, *American Silver*, no. 295. Forbes, *Paul Revere*, p. 455. Jones, *Old Silver*, pp. 57, 67, 79, 88, 227, 238–40.

67 a, b
CONDIMENT POT AND LID, ca. 1826

(a) H. body 2 ⅞" (7.3 cm), DIAM. rim 3 ⅜" (8.6 cm), overall w. 4 ¾" (12.1 cm)
5 oz. 4 dwt. 21 gr. (163.1 g)
(b) DIAM. lid 3 ½" (8.9 cm), H. lid 1 ⅛" (2.9 cm)
1 oz. 17 dwt. 20 gr. (58.7 g)

Stamps: "FOSTER" in roman letters, in a rectangle, struck once on underside of body; no stamp on lid.

Engraved on body opposite handle: "EF" in foliate script. *Engraved on underside:* "Feb.ʸ 14th 1826" in script. *Engraved on upper surface of lid:* "EF" in foliate script; "Feb.ʸ 14, 1826" in script.

Description: (a) raised cylindrical body with slightly flared rim; scored line encircles body just below rim; applied reeded base band; centerpunch on underside; C-curve strap handle with converging incised lines on back; (b) low-dome circular lid with flat rim; 1 notch on edge for spoon; cast spherical finial attached by solder through top of lid.

Spectrographic analysis:

	SILVER	COPPER	GOLD	LEAD
BOTTOM	94.8	5.1	0.09	0.05
SIDE	91.1	8.8	0.10	0.05
LID	91.7	8.1	0.13	0.04

Provenance: William Core Duffy, Kittery, Maine.

Comments: The body is the traditional cup form. The lid, making it a condiment pot, may be a later addition.

88.69 Museum purchase from William Core Duffy, 1988

68
SPOON, ca. 1800

L. 5 ⅛" (13.0 cm)
8 dwt. 19 gr. (13.7 g)

Stamps: "FOSTER" in roman letters, in a rectangle, struck once on back of handle.

Engraved on front of handle: "JSJ" (or "JPJ") in foliate script, in a bright-cut oval with pendant bellflowers.

Description: pointed oval bowl with swage-formed asymmetrical foliage and single rounded drop on back; pointed downturned handle.

Spectrographic analysis: Silver content is 88.0 percent.

Provenance: Mr. and Mrs. Stanley B. Ineson, New York City; Mr. and Mrs. Alfred E. Bissell, Wilmington, Del.

Comments: Very fine foliate decoration on bowl.

References: Belden, *Marks of American Silversmiths*, p. 176.

62.240.256 Gift of Mr. and Mrs. Alfred E. Bissell, 1962–63

ℭ Gorham Company

1831–
(Gorham Manufacturing Company)
Providence, Rhode Island

Jabez Gorham (1792–1869) served his apprenticeship under Providence silversmith Nehemiah Dodge from 1806 to 1813. In 1813 Gorham set up in business as a manufacturing jeweler with four partners. When business turned bad, the partnership was dissolved, but the firm continued with Gorham as sole owner. During the 1820s the company prospered from the sales of gold beads, earrings, finger rings, "French filigree," and the like. More spacious quarters, about half a dozen employees, an improved distribution network, and tedious selling trips around New England contributed to its success. Silver manufacturing began in 1831 when Gorham added spoons to the line of jewelry. The Gorham company may be said to date from this decision. Henry Webster of Boston, brought in as a partner, was in charge of silver production. In 1840–41 Gorham sold his interest in the business and retired but then repurchased the silver branch of the firm with his son John. The company became J. Gorham & Son. During the 1840s, as sales increased, the need for larger quarters and a power source grew. A new four-story brick building was constructed using mostly borrowed money. Uneasy about the debt, Jabez sold his interest in the business to son John in 1848. John was ambitious and planned on a grand scale. He envisioned and implemented plans to transform the small company with a limited line into a large manufacturer using sophisticated techniques for the quantity production of a full line of silver flatware and hollowware. The marketing of goods through peddlers, which had been standard practice, was replaced by the company's own sales force. The change was dramatic. Sales rose from $29,000 in 1850 to $397,000 in 1859, and the number of employees grew from 14 to 200. During the 1860s sales approached $1 million a year. The expansion had required an influx of capital, which was achieved in 1850 when John brought in a partner, his cousin Gorham Thurber. The firm then became Gorham & Thurber.

In 1852 another partner joined the firm, and the name became Gorham & Company. John Gorham sought to produce high-quality silver using labor-saving machinery. He went to England in the 1850s to buy equipment, entice experienced craftsmen to America, and seek the best examples of English and French silver to use as models. Perhaps one of his great accomplishments was the purchase of a steam-powered drop press. In 1863 the firm was incorporated, with John Gorham and Gorham Thurber owning a controlling interest. George Wilkinson, chief designer from 1860 to 1891, was the first of several foreign designers to work for the company. He was succeeded by William C. Codman (1839–1921), who served until 1914. John Gorham, who had done so much to create the great enterprise, ignominiously left the company in 1878 following disastrous private investments that caused him to lose all his Gorham company stock. The dominant figure at the turn of the century was Edward Holbrook, an ambitious entrepreneur who, soon after 1900, gained control of the company. Through a holding company, he also controlled several other silver companies. Because of his efforts, a new and much larger manufacturing plant was built in the Elmwood section of Providence in 1890. A showcase office building designed by Stanford White was erected in New York City in 1905. The company went through another period of expansion during the 1950s and 1960s when it acquired more silver firms and diversified by acquiring a paper company and an electronic research and development firm. Finally, in 1966, Gorham & Company was acquired by Textron, a conglomerate based in Providence.

Over the years Gorham produced vast quantities of silver and silver plate. The company catered to a wide range of tastes and incomes, and its products mirrored multitudinous changes in fashion. Although committed to machine production, during the 1890s the company responded to the revival of interest in handcrafted metals by introducing Martelé, handwrought silver with a hammered finish. This line was developed under the direction of William C. Codman, who, in effect, brought the arts and crafts aesthetic to Gorham. Some of the most striking products in this line reflected an art nouveau aesthetic. Unlike most of the silversmiths discussed in this catalogue, the Gorham company has had a long, complicated history and an incredibly varied output. Many documents and records survive. To his credit, Charles Carpenter mastered the vast quantity of data available and produced a useful book on Gorham and its products. No short sketch can hope to capture the story, and so the reader is referred to Carpenter's book.

References: Charles H. Carpenter, Jr., *Gorham Silver, 1831–1981* (New York: Dodd, Mead, 1982). Company records are at the John Hay Library, Brown University, while the company collection of silver is at the Museum of the Rhode Island School of Design, both in Providence.

69 a–d
BLACK COFFEE SERVICE, 1900–1904

(a) Tray: L. 15" (38.1 cm), w. 12 ⅝" (32.1 cm), H. 1 1/16" (2.7 cm)
43 oz. 13 dwt. 21 gr. (1359.0 g)
(b) Coffeepot: H. 11" (27.9 cm), w. 7 5/16" (18.6 cm)
26 oz. 3 dwt. 4 gr. (813.7 g)
(c) Creamer: H. 4 ⅝" (11.8 cm), w. 4 9/16" (11.6 cm)
9 oz. 8 dwt. 1 gr. (292.4 g)
(d) Sugar bowl: H. 3 ½" (8.9 cm), w. 6 ⅛" (15.6 cm)
11 oz. 9 gr. (342.7 g)

Stamps: "Martelé" in gothic letters, over a spread-winged eagle; directly beneath are the following stamps: a lion passant facing right in an octagon, an anchor in a shield, and a gothic "G" in an octagon; directly beneath these: "950-1000 FINE" in sans serif letters; directly beneath these: "14 IN"; all the foregoing stamps are struck once intaglio on the underside of each piece in the set. "CIV" in roman letters, struck intaglio under rim of tray; "CIU" in roman letters, struck itaglio on base rims of other pieces.

Scratched on underside of all pieces: "188-36-5215" and "79117". *Scratched on underside of coffeepot:* "87".

Description: (a) tray: rectangular in plan but with bowed sides and rounded corners; convex rim continuous with body with undulating edge and decorated with chased and repoussé floral design that continues onto body as incised lines in the surface; (b) coffeepot: raised circular form with low bulbous body and very high, slightly bulbous neck with flared undulating rim. Circular raised onion-dome lid with a top-like cast finial; 1-piece flange-bezel; cast 5-segment hinge. Applied base ring divided into 8 equal lobes. High S-curve seamed spout, circular in cross section; lower end broadens to blend into body. High C-curve seamed handle, circular in cross section, with 2 ivory insulators and 4 silver pins; handle attachments broaden from tubular to lotus leaf pattern on body. Chased and repoussé design of undulating leaves and 5-petal flowers covers body, lid, handle, spout,

and base; flowers on neck have long stems; (c) creamer: circular raised body with bulbous lower body, narrow incurving waist, slightly bulbous neck, and flared undulating rim; rim extended for pouring lip. Applied base ring as on coffeepot. Handle same as on coffeepot but is made as 1 piece without insulators; (d) sugar bowl: circular raised body with bulbous lower body, incurving neck, and flared undulating rim. Applied base ring as on coffeepot; 2 C-curve seamed handles, circular in cross section, with circular vents inside each handle; lower handle ends broaden from tubular to lotus leaf pattern on body. Chased and repoussé design as on coffeepot.

Spectrographic analysis:

	SILVER	COPPER	LEAD	GOLD
(a) Tray				
TOP	95.5	4.6	0.03	0.00
UNDERSIDE	95.5	4.4	0.05	0.00
(b) Coffeepot				
BODY SIDE	95.4	4.3	0.09	0.00
SPOUT	95.6	4.3	0.02	0.00
FOOTRING	95.0	4.7	0.09	0.02
LID	96.2	3.7	0.02	0.00
(c) Creamer				
BODY SIDE	95.3	4.5	0.04	0.02
FOOTRING	95.5	4.3	0.04	0.00
HANDLE	95.3	4.6	0.03	0.00
(d) Sugar bowl				
BODY SIDE	95.5	4.3	0.01	0.00
FOOTRING	96.6	3.3	0.01	0.00
HANDLE 1	95.3	4.5	0.10	0.00
HANDLE 2	94.9	5.0	0.09	0.00

History: According to the donor, the service was a wedding gift to Helen Bowman Mason, who married George Reed, October 28, 1903, in Pittsburgh. Helen Reed was the donor's mother-in-law.

Provenance: Helen Bowman (Mason) Reed, Pittsburgh; Elizabeth McC. Knowles, Ligonier, Pa.

Comments: Martelé was Gorham's line of hand-wrought silver with traces of hammer marks deliberately left to show the process. The overall finish was not highly reflective but was described in company literature as "soft mist texture." The line is characterized by generous use of silver, resulting in heavy walls that permitted deep chased and repoussé decoration, sometimes to the point of being 3 dimensional. Small fractures in the metal, where it has been bent, show the stresses it was subjected to during fabrication and suggest insufficient annealing. This particular set is decorated in an undulating art nouveau style; with the exception of the coffeepot, however, all forms are also typical of nineteenth-century rococo revival.

References: Carpenter, *Gorham Silver*, pp. 221–52, for discussion of Martelé; pp. 290–91, for stamps. Charles H. Carpenter, Jr., "Gorham's Martelé Silver," *Antiques* 122, no. 6 (December 1982): 1256–65.

83.108.1–.4 Gift of Elizabeth McC. Knowles, 1983

Rufus Greene

1707–77
Boston, Massachusetts

Son of Nathaniel and Anne (Gould) Greene, shopkeepers, and brother of silversmith Benjamin Greene, Rufus Greene served his apprenticeship under William Cowell. In 1728 he married Katharine Stanbridge, and together they had ten children. He made a pair of flagons for Christ Church about 1729. Greene made the transition to successful merchant early in his career, which is why few examples of his work survive. His rising status is suggested by the fact that his portrait was painted by John Singleton Copley. A recently discovered heraldic embroidery has the Greene arms and the inscription "RUF[S] GREENE/ KATH GREENE/ 1745." A later inscription says it is "the work of Mrs. Catherine Amory daughter of Mr. Rufus Greene done at the age of 14, 1745." (Katharine Greene married John Amory in 1751.) A silver tankard made by David Jesse and owned by Rufus and Katharine Greene is in the Museum of Fine Arts, Boston. The inventory of Greene's estate is rich in household objects, especially ceramics, glass, and furniture. Sample entries include: "1 Baskett with 4 Glass Decanters 2 Beer and 8 Wine Glasses," "1 Basket with 18 Figu'd Wine Glasses," "23 Wine & 5 Gelley Glasses," "1 Vinegar Cruet & 4 Green Pickel Leaves," "1 pr cut Salts & orange Glass," "1 White Spitting Pott & 4 Pattey Pans," "5 Tea potts & 1 yellow Sugar Dish," "4 Decanters & 5 Glass Candlesticks," "8 Chairs Work'd Bottoms," "34 Pictures framed & Glassed [in the front chamber alone]," and "6 Leather bottom Chairs & 1 Round About."

References: Flynt and Fales, *Heritage Foundation,* p. 233. Buhler, *American Silver,* pp. 90, 91, 255. Buhler, *Masters and Apprentices,* pp. 33, 34. Kane, *Dictionary,* s.v. "Greene, Rufus." Betty Ring, "Heraldic Embroidery in Eighteenth-Century Boston," *Antiques* 141, no. 4 (April 1992): 622–23. SCPR book 77, pp. 16–21; book 89, pp. 372–78, 700–703.

70
CANN, ca. 1760

H. 4 1/16" (10.3 cm), W. 4 5/16" (11.0 cm), DIAM. 3 1/16" (7.8 cm)
7 oz. 7 dwt. 22 gr. (230.0 g)

Stamps: "RG" in roman letters, in a rectangular enclosure with double cyma curves above and below, struck once on underside.

Scratched on underside: "X17937".

Description: raised circular body with somewhat bulbous lower section, slightly incurving neck, and short flared rim with single-incised line above double-incised lines encircling body just below rim; centerpunch probably covered by stamp. Cast S-curve hollow handle with leaf on upper side and ball tailpiece; scroll and double drop at upper handle attachment; slit vent. Cast stepped footring.

Spectrographic analysis:

	SILVER	COPPER	LEAD	GOLD
BODY SIDE	89.1	10.6	0.24	0.15
HANDLE	91.1	8.4	0.21	0.23

Provenance: Marshall P. Blankarn, New York City.

80.181 Gift of Marshall P. Blankarn, 1981

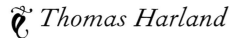

Thomas Harland

1735–1807
Norwich, Connecticut

Henry Harland

1789–1841
Norwich, Connecticut, and
New Orleans, Louisiana

Thomas Harland was born in England in 1735. He arrived in Boston during December 1773 and settled in Norwich, Connecticut, where he married Hannah Clark, daughter of Elisha and Hannah (Leffingwell) Clark. In December 1773 he advertised as a "Watch and Clockmaker from London," announcing that he had "opened a shop near the store of Christopher Leffingwell in Norwich where he makes in the neatest manner . . . horizontal, repeating and plain watches in gold, silver, metal or covered cases. Spring, musical and plain clocks; church clocks; regulators, &c." By 1790 his watch and clock business was thriving, and he employed ten to twelve regular employees who made 200 watches and 40 clocks a year. In 1795 he lost everything in a disastrous fire. (Ironically, in 1788 he had made a fire engine for the town.) He reestablished his business and in 1796 advertised "Warranted Watches, of most of the various kinds in use and of the newest fashion; Gold Beads; Cypher & Brilliant Gold Ear Rings; Plain Gold Rings; Bosom Broaches; Twist Rings, with double and single Heart Stones; Silver Table Spoons; Carved and Plain Tea Spoons; Sugar Tongs; Watch Chains, Seals, Keys, &c." He is also known to have made silver hollowware.

His obituary designated him a goldsmith, adding, however, that he made the first watch ever manufactured in America. It is unclear how many watches were made in his shop and how many were imported.

Harland was a highly skilled and unusually talented craftsman. After serving his apprenticeship in England, he is said to have traveled extensively on the Continent. His personal library included books in French, which suggests a reading knowledge of that language. He owned gear- and fusee-cutting machines (used for making clock and watch parts) that he probably brought with him from England, as they were not readily available in America. His work reveals a sophistication that warrants the designation "a mechanician of great skill and efficiency."

Prominent clockmaker Daniel Burnap served his apprenticeship with Harland, as, probably, did Harland's sons Thomas and Henry. Thomas, Jr., died in 1806, only a few months before his father, at age twenty-six. A Thomas Harland was listed in New York City directories for 1805–6 as a watch- and clockmaker at 2 Wall Street. It seems likely that this is Thomas, Jr., rather than Thomas, Sr.

By 1815 Henry Harland, Thomas's younger son, was on Conti Street in New Orleans, where he ran a watch repairing and jewelry business and displayed and sold the products of New York City watchmakers Hemsted & Wallach. In 1819 he moved to 25 Chartres Street, then back to Conti Street, and in 1823 back to Chartres Street.

About 1830 Henry Harland formed a partnership with H. Bliss, who died later that same year. From December 1830 until 1834, he was a business partner with Daniel Blair, who had come from St. Louis. Harland appears to have shuttled between New Orleans and Norwich before finally returning to Norwich, where he died in 1841. He married Abigail Leffingwell Hyde in Norwich in 1822, and all their children were born there. His portrait, painted by John Wesley Jarvis, is owned by Yale University Art Gallery.

The most impressive example of Henry Harland's work as a silversmith is an urn, now owned by Yale University Art Gallery, that was made for presentation in 1831 to Henry M. Dobbs, Sr. Following a career in New York City as a watchmaker, Dobbs moved to New Orleans about 1805. He was a founder of the New Orleans Mechanic Society in 1806, of which Harland was also a member.

Henry Harland's stamp usually consisted of his surname in a banner, accompanied by pseudohallmarks. It is said, however, that on occasion he used his father's old silver stamp: "HARLAND" in roman letters, in a rectangle. As the following entries show, distinguishing between the work of father and son is not always easy.

A covered porringer in the Hammerslough collection at Wadsworth Atheneum bears the engraved initials "ALH" for Anna Leffingwell Hyde of Norwich. The stamp is "HARLAND" in a rectangle, accompanied by stamps of an eagle and a profile head. This piece has been attributed to Thomas, Sr., but it could be the work of Henry Harland.

References: Christopher H. Bailey, *Two Hundred Years of American Clocks and Watches* (New York: Prentice-Hall, 1975), pp. 65–67, fig. 242. Bohan and Hammerslough, *Early Connecticut Silver*, p. 156, for porringer. Francis Manwaring Caulkins, *History of Norwich* (1866; Norwich, 1874), pp. 372, 608. *Crescent City Silver* (New Orleans: Historic New Orleans Collection, 1980), pp. 82–84, 121, 126. George Munson Curtis, *Early Silver of Connecticut and Its Makers* (Meriden, Conn.: International Silver Co., 1913), pp. 70–71, 99–100. Flynt and Fales, *Heritage Foundation*, pp. 242–43. Penrose R. Hoopes, *Shop Records of Daniel Burnap, Clockmaker* (Hartford: Connecticut Historical Society, 1958), for numerous references to Thomas Harland, Sr. Warren, Howe, and Brown, *Marks of Achievement*, no. 154. George S. Porter, *Inscriptions from Gravestones in the Old Burying Ground, Norwich Town, Connecticut* (Norwich: Society of Founders, 1933), p. 116. Von Khrum, *Silversmiths*, p. 62. Prime cards, Winterthur, for advertisement by Thomas Harland, March 30, 1796.

71 a–l
FORKS, ca. 1800 or ca. 1832

average L. 8 5/16" (21.1 cm)
(a) 2 oz. 9 dwt. 8 gr. (76.8 g)
(b) 2 oz. 7 dwt. 12 gr. (73.9 g)
(c) 2 oz. 9 dwt. (76.3 g)
(d) 2 oz. 10 dwt. 10 gr. (78.4 g)
(e) 2 oz. 7 dwt. 13 gr. (74.0 g)
(f) 2 oz. 10 dwt. 13 gr. (78.7 g)
(g) 2 oz. 13 dwt. 22 gr. (83.8 g)
(h) 2 oz. 8 dwt. 20 gr. (75.9 g)
(i) 2 oz. 12 dwt. 1 gr. (81.0 g)
(j) 2 oz. 9 dwt. 8 gr. (76.7 g)
(k) 2 oz. 11 dwt. 15 gr. (80.3 g)
(l) 2 oz. 8 dwt. 15 gr. (75.6 g)

Stamps: "HARLAND" in roman letters, in a rectangle, struck once on back of each handle.

Description: 4 tines with middle 2 generally longer than outside tines; downturned fiddle-shape handle with rounded shoulders at lower end; swage-formed design on upper front: profile of male head facing right under relief inscription "WASHINGTON" in roman letters; double-thread conforming border, upper section of which has a stylized leaf border, lower sections meet at central 6-petal floret flanked by anthemia; plain back.

Spectrographic analysis:

	SILVER	COPPER	GOLD	LEAD
(a)	90.0	9.8	0.11	0.06
(b)	90.2	9.7	0.08	0.06
(c)	89.5	10.4	0.11	0.06
(d)	91.3	8.5	0.13	0.06
(e)	89.6	10.2	0.15	0.06
(f)	89.2	10.6	0.11	0.08
(g)	89.5	10.3	0.12	0.06
(h)	90.6	9.3	0.12	0.05
(i)	89.4	10.5	0.11	0.06
(j)	91.3	8.6	0.07	0.04
(k)	91.5	8.3	0.12	0.07
(l)	91.0	8.9	0.05	0.05

History: Original owner was possibly Col. Edward Leverich of Newtown (now Elmhurst), Long Island, N.Y.

Provenance: Inherited by Daisy Warden of Jamaica, Long Island, N.Y., through her aunt Sarah A. Cox from her grandmother Sarah A. Leverich. Because of the line of descent, Daisy Warden thinks it likely the forks were once owned by her great-grandfather Col. Edward Leverich of Newtown. Sold by Warden to H. F. du Pont, 1930.

Exhibitions: (a) Leffingwell Inn, Norwich, Conn., sponsored by Society of Founders, 1960; Winter Antiques Show, New York City, 1982.

Comments: Controversy surrounds the dating of these forks and related spoons (no. 72). Stylistically, double-thread flatware should not have appeared in America until about 1825. For this reason John Marshall Phillips thought they must have been made for the centennial of George Washington's birth in 1832. The double-thread design, known as the king's pattern, was a French innovation of the late eighteenth century that presumably came to America via

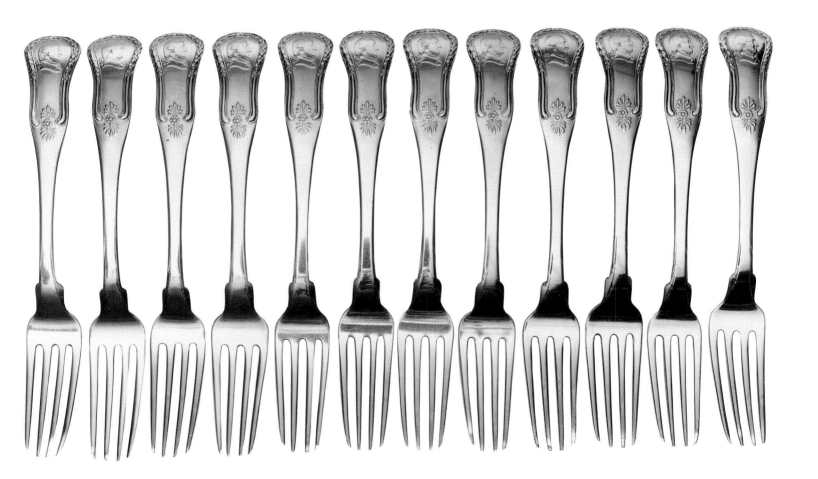

England in the second or third decade of the nineteenth century. Skeptics have reasoned that Thomas Harland, Sr., who died in 1807, could not possibly have made this flatware. Was the maker his son Henry or, as has been suggested privately, Maltby Pelletreau, whose "MP" appears on a ladle with a Washington's head of markedly different character? Did Henry Harland serve merely as retailer? Thomas Harland was not a run-of-the-mill provincial craftsman. He had exceptional technical skills as well as the familiarity with high-style French silver to produce flatware requiring sophisticated die cutting a generation before such products appeared elsewhere in this country.

There is an alternative scenario. It is possible that Henry Harland made the flatware but used his father's stamp (see *Crescent City Silver*), in which case the flatware could indeed have been created for the centennial of Washington's birth. Harland's wife Abigail was related to both James Nevins Hyde and Charles Wooding Goodrich, who ran a successful jewelry and fancy hardware store in New York City and who routinely purchased the products of silversmiths. They may have commissioned the forks. Possibly, the stamp traditionally attributed to Thomas Harland, Sr. ("HARLAND" in a rectangle) was actually that of his son Henry.

Stylistic evidence favors Henry as the author of the Washington-head flatware, but the unusual knowledge, experience, and technical skills of his father should not be ignored. Given his training, work experience, and travels, the senior Harland no doubt had contacts through whom he could have ordered custom-made dies following Washington's death in 1799—if, indeed, he did not cut them himself. We may never know the answer.

Also see the 4 spoons made by Harland (no. 72) with the same swage-formed decoration. A ladle in a private collection and a spoon in the Metropolitan Museum of Art have the same decoration.

References: Bohan and Hammerslough, *Early Connecticut Silver*, no. 131. Fales, *American Silver*, no. 83. Fales, *Early American Silver*, fig. 178c. Fennimore, *Silver and Pewter*, no. 25. Buhler and Hood, *American Silver*, no. 367.

60.753.1–.12 Gift of H. F. du Pont, 1965

72 a–d
SPOONS, ca. 1805 or ca. 1832

average L. 8 ⅝" (21.9 cm)
(a) 1 oz. 19 dwt. (60.7 g)
(b) 1 oz. 17 dwt. 16 gr. (58.6 g)
(c) 1 oz. 19 dwt. 12 gr. (61.5 g)
(d) 2 oz. 7 dwt. 2 gr. (73.3 g)

Stamps: "HARLAND" in roman letters, in a rectangle, struck once on back of each handle.

Engraved on upper handle front: "DCY" (sideways) in script.

Description: pointed oval bowl with swage-formed 12-lobe shell on back; downturned fiddle-shape handle rounded at lower end; swage-formed design on upper front: profile of male head facing right under relief inscription "WASHINGTON" in roman letters; double-thread conforming border, upper section with stylized leaf border, lower sections meet at central 6-petal floret flanked by anthemia; plain back.

Spectrographic analysis:

	SILVER	COPPER	LEAD	GOLD
(a)	87.1	12.0	0.30	0.23
(b)	89.1	10.2	0.26	0.16
(c)	89.3	9.9	0.26	0.23
(d)	90.0	9.1	0.30	0.22

History: Possibly owned by Daniel Yeomans of Norwich, Conn.

Exhibitions: (a) Leffingwell Inn, Norwich, Conn., sponsored by Society of Founders, 1960. "Man and the Myth: George Washington," Peale Museum, Baltimore, 1981.

Comments: See forks no. 71 a–l.

References: Bohan and Hammerslough, *Early Connecticut Silver*, no. 130. Fales, *American Silver*, no. 85. Mary E. Perkins, *Old Houses of the Ancient Town of Norwich, 1660–1800* (Norwich, Conn., 1895), p. 35. Buhler and Hood, *American Silver*, no. 367.

60.752.1–.4 Gift of H. F. du Pont, 1965

₡ 73
WATCH, ca. 1800

DIAM. 2" (5.1 cm), H. 2 ⅜" (6.0 cm)
3 oz. 6 dwt. 18 gr. (103.8 g) (includes works)

Stamps: see engraving.

Engraved on backplate of works: "Thos Harland/ N° 481" in script. *Engraved on outside of back cover:* "EL" in large floriate script. *Scratched on inside of back cover:* "WA[?]L" in roman letters.

Description: circular silver case (solid back, open front) with works hinged at 12 o'clock; circular hole in back for watch key. Circular silver back cover hinged at 9 o'clock; circular front cover mounted at 9 o'clock consists of silver ring mounted with circular domed crystal. Stem with ring handle at 12 o'clock. Works: key-wound verge escapement; gilded brass balance bridge in openwork pattern of urn, central flower, vines, and smaller flowers. Face: white enamel dial with black figures for hours (I to XII), minutes (5–60), days of month (1–31). Brass and steel key consists of hollow shaft attached to large ring, in turn hinged to small ring.

Spectrographic analysis:

	SILVER	COPPER	GOLD	LEAD
BACK OF CASE	90.6	8.8	0.42	0.29

Also significant mercury.

Provenance: John S. Walton, Inc., New York City.

Comments: Although it is well established that Thomas Harland, Sr., made clocks and watches and is credited with manufacturing the first American watches, he also imported foreign ones. Analysis of the case, however, suggests that it is of American manufacture.

References: Chris H. Bailey, *Two Hundred Years of American Clocks and Watches* (New York: Prentice-Hall, 1975), fig. 236.

61.104 Museum purchase from John S. Walton, Inc., 1961

Benjamin Hiller

1687/88–ca. 1745
Boston, Massachusetts

Benjamin Hiller was the son of Joseph Hiller, tinplate worker, and Susanna Dennis. Benjamin was possibly apprenticed to John Coney because he, along with Nathaniel Morse, witnessed a deed for Coney in 1708. Hiller and Elizabeth Russell were married by Cotton Mather in 1714. Elizabeth's grandfather had been a minister at the First Baptist Church, and her parents, Joseph and Mary Russell, presented communion silver made by Hiller to the same church in 1714. Five years later Hiller became a deacon of this church. He was clerk of the Artillery Company in 1716–17 and fourth sergeant in 1717. His son Joseph became a jeweler.

References: Buhler, *American Silver*, p. 134. Flynt and Fales, *Heritage Foundation*, p. 247. Jones, *Old Silver*, pp. 29, 45, 46. Kane, *Dictionary*, s.v. "Hiller, Benjamin." Roberts, *Artillery Company*, 1:389.

74
TANKARD, ca. 1720

H. 10 ¼" (26.0 cm), DIAM. base 7 ⅛" (18.1 cm), W. 10 ⅝" (27.0 cm)
59 oz. 4 dwt. 11 gr. (1842.0 g)

Stamps: "BH" in roman letters, over addorsed crescents, all in a shield with double–cyma-curve top and small projections from the 3 lower corners of the shield, struck on underside of base and on upper body, left of handle.

Engraved on back of handle: "E∗I/ to/ A∗E∗C" in roman letters.

Description: raised oversize body with straight sides; applied base molding consists (from the bottom up) of a torus molding, cyma-recta molding, and small torus molding; applied molding at rim over double-scored lines encircling upper body; no centerpunch (probably covered by maker's stamp). Raised 3-step lid domed in center, broad flat rim with crenate lip and double-incised lines, small cast finial; spurs project from lid on each side of thumbpiece. Cast thumbpiece, gently S curved in profile, with rudimentary scroll motif across top edge; attached to a cast 5-segment hinge with pendant drop. Raised-and-soldered hollow S-curve handle terminating in a cast cherub mask; lower part of handle attached to body by an oval plate secured by 4 silver rivets; upper part of handle has 2 bulbous projections and a long rattail where it attaches to body.

Spectrographic analysis:

	SILVER	COPPER	LEAD	GOLD
BODY	92.1	7.2	0.41	0.11
BOTTOM	94.3	5.1	0.32	0.13
LID	91.7	6.2	1.8	0.12
HANDLE SIDE	95.3	3.9	0.52	0.13
THUMBPIECE	94.0	3.9	0.54	0.15

Provenance: Charles F. Montgomery, Wallingford, Conn., sold to H. F. du Pont, March 1947.

Comments: This is an extraordinary tankard because of its unusual size and capacity. When filled, it would be virtually impossible to lift. It is early in form, if not in proportions, and the mask tailpiece resembles those on the Edward Winslow tankards. Most peculiar of all, perhaps, is the tiny finial, which is out of proportion with the body. The crenate lip is extraordinarily fine. In 1710 the estate of Mercy Oliver of Cambridge included "1 great tankard 43 ounces."

References: Fales, *American Silver*, no. 97. Kauffman, *Colonial Silversmith*, p. 111. Robert Trent, "Silver Abstracts from Middlesex Probate," author's collection (a copy of this 1974 compilation was generously provided by Trent).

59.2902 Bequest of H. F. du Pont, 1969

𝒞 75
CUP, ca. 1720

H. 3" (7.6 cm), w. 4 7/16" (11.3 cm)
4 oz. 13 dwt. 12 gr. (145.4 g)

Stamps: "BH" in roman letters, over addorsed crescents, all in a shield with double–cyma-curve top and small projections from the 3 lower corners of the shield, struck on underside of base and on upper body, left of handle.

Engraved on body opposite handle: "P/ IH" in roman letters. *Engraved on underside of base:* "HE" in roman letters.

Description: raised cylindrical body with straight sides and slightly flared rim; single-scored line encircles body just below rim; applied base molding consists of an ogee topped by 2 beads. Cast S-shape handle with beaded rattail on upper back and single sprig on lower back.

Spectrographic analysis:

	SILVER	COPPER	LEAD	GOLD
BODY SIDE	92.7	6.8	0.25	0.11
BASE	94.1	5.4	0.23	0.14
HANDLE	94.2	5.3	0.27	0.15

History: The initials "P/ IH" are also on a porringer, made by Hiller and now at Yale University Art Gallery, that has a later inscription: "James and Hanah Pitson/ to/ their daughter Elizabeth/ 1716/ who married Capt. John North/ 1746." James and Hannah Pitson were married in 1716.

Provenance: Purchased from the J. Duke Smith collection in 1921 by Francis Hill Bigelow; Brooks Reed Gallery, Boston, sold to H. F. du Pont, June 1927.

Comments: A similar cup by Hiller is owned by the Currier Gallery of Art, Manchester, N.H.

References: Buhler and Hood, *American Silver*, no. 99. Fales, *American Silver*, no. 13. Kauffman, *Colonial Silversmith*, p. 76. Marvin D. Schwartz, *Collector's Guide to American Antique Silver* (New York: Doubleday, 1975), fig. 51.

65.1360 Gift of H. F. du Pont, 1965

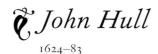
John Hull
1624–83

Hull & Sanderson, w. 1652–83
Boston, Massachusetts

John Hull is considered the patriarch of American silversmiths and the epitome of Puritan orthodoxy. Born in Leicestershire, England, the son of blacksmith Robert Hull, he came to America with his father and stepmother, Elizabeth Storer, in 1635. After seven years of schooling he undertook a curious apprenticeship with his stepbrother Richard Storer. As Hull put it in his diary, "And then by God's good hand I fell to learning (by the help of my brother) and to practicing the trade of a goldsmith; and through God's help obtained that ability in it, as I was able to get my living by it." Storer had been apprenticed to James Fearne, a London goldsmith, but had completed only six of the ten years stipulated in his indenture. Since Storer was not a practicing goldsmith, we can only wonder how much shop training Hull could have had. In 1647 Hull married Judith Quincy, daughter of Edward Quincy, a founder of Braintree, Massachusetts. A house and substantial landholdings were bestowed on the young couple by Hull's father. In the following year Hull became a member of the First Church, whose minister, John Wilson, predicted a promising future for him: "God will certainly bless that young man; John Hull shall grow rich and live to do God good service in his generation." And so he did.

In 1652, when the General Court of Massachusetts Bay Colony passed the act establishing a mint for coining money, it also appointed John Hull as mintmaster. With the court's consent, Hull immediately asked Robert Sanderson to become his partner. Sanderson had served a full apprenticeship under an English goldsmith and, therefore, was fully proficient in technical skills. The sixteen-foot-square house erected for the mint also served as the workshop where wrought silver was made for their private customers. Under the act, Hull was permitted to keep 1 shilling and sixpence for every 20 shillings coined, a lucrative commission that helped to make him a rich man. From the start, he engaged in overseas trade, the surest route to wealth, and became one of the great merchants of seventeenth-century Boston.

Of his many apprentices, the most important for the development of the silversmith's craft in New England was Jeremiah Dummer, who entered Hull's service in 1659 along with Samuel Paddy. Hull noted the event in his diary, commenting, "The lord make me faithfull in discharge of this new trust Committed to me & let his blessing be to me & them." Dummer prospered; Paddy went to Jamaica, where he failed to achieve the success of his fellow apprentice.

Hull's record of public service is exemplary. He was a selectman and treasurer of the town of Boston. He was elected deputy to the General Court, representing the towns of Wenham, Westfield, Concord, and Salisbury, all the while remaining in Boston. He served much of his life in the Artillery Company and rose to the rank of captain. (In his later years he was commonly referred to as Captain Hull.) He served on innumerable commissions and committees. He functioned as banker for the colony, and when it appeared to be in fiscal danger, he advanced his own money. Hull died in 1683 in his fifty-ninth year and was interred in the Granary Burying Ground. His widow, Judith, stayed on in their house with their daughter Hannah, who had married Samuel Sewall, the diarist. There are many references in Sewall's diary to "Mother Hull." Hull died intestate, and no inventory survives. There are, however, numerous extant documents, including a lengthy diary owned by the American Antiquarian Society. The diary deals mostly with Hull's business affairs, current events, and religious preoccupations. It is regrettably terse on silversmithing.

In her monumental study of Hull and Sanderson, Patricia E. Kane found fifty-one examples of their wrought work and hundreds of their coins. Through careful analysis of their stamps, she has established a chronology of their work.

References: Clarke, *John Hull.* "The Diaries of John Hull, Mint-Master and Treasurer of the Colony of Massachusetts Bay," in *Transactions and Collections of the American Antiquarian Society,* vol. 3 (Boston: John Wilson and Son, 1857), pp. 109–316. *DAB,* s.v. "Hull, John." Jones, *Old Silver.* Kane, *Dictionary,* s.v. "Hull, John." Kane, "John Hull and Robert Sanderson." Edmund S. Morgan, "Light on the Puritans from John Hull's Notebooks," *New England Quarterly* 15, no. 1 (1942): 95–101. Samuel Eliot Morison, *Builders of the Bay Colony* (Boston and New York: Houghton Mifflin Co., 1930), pp. 134–82.

ℰ 76
PORRINGER, 1675–83

DIAM. bowl 4 7/16" (11.3 cm), H. 1 9/16" (4.0 cm),
W. 6 3/16" (15.7 cm)
3 oz. 14 dwt. (115.1 g)

Stamps: "IH" in roman letters, in a heart, struck once on body, left of handle; "RS" in roman letters, under a stylized sun, in a conforming shape, struck once on body, right of handle.

Engraved on front of handle: "WF" in roman letters, in a cabochon. *Pricked on body opposite handle:* "V / IM" in roman letters, flanked by scrolls.

Description: raised circular bowl with straight sides; slightly domed in center; centerpunch inside. Cast handle in pattern of 2 full-length human figures facing each other and clasping hands; cabochon in center; handle attached ¼" below rim of bowl.

Spectrographic analysis:

	SILVER	COPPER	GOLD	LEAD
BOWL	90.4	8.3	0.42	0.38
HANDLE	90.1	8.8	0.24	0.29

History: The initials "V / IM" refer to Isaac Vergoose (1637–1710) and his wife Mary (1648–90) of Boston. They were married in 1668 and, presumably, attended the Third Church, where both were baptized as adults. They had at least 10 children. Following Mary's death, Isaac married Elizabeth Foster, by whom he had at least 6 more children. Elizabeth Vergoose, daughter of Isaac and Elizabeth, inherited the porringer. She married Thomas Fleet (1685–1758), a printer who arrived in Boston in 1712. It is their son William Fleet (1720–87), mariner, whose initials are on the handle of the porringer. The inventory of his estate includes 1 small porringer weighing 3 oz. 16 dwt.

Samuel Sewall mentions Isaac Vergoose several times in his diary. (Because the surname was Dutch, it was often shortened to Goose, which is how Sewall used it.) Isaac accompanied Sewall on a number of occasions, and the latter recorded the death of Isaac's first wife, Mary, on October 19, 1690: "Mrs. Goose dies of an Apoplexy." On July 15, 1693, the second Mrs. Goose was the subject of a diary entry: "I went to Mr. Goose and told him his wife could not conveniently sit any longer in my wives Pue, and therefore desired her to look out another place."

This is 1 of only 2 porringers bearing the stamps of Hull and Sanderson. The other, owned by the Museum of Fine Arts, Boston has a similarly shaped body but a simplified handle consisting of 3 loops and a shield-shape reserve. Patricia E. Kane dates it to 1667–70 based on the chronology of the stamps. Her dating is also used for the Winterthur porringer.

Provenance: The last private owner was Catharine Scott of Washington, D.C., who claimed that the porringer came into her family in 1896 upon the marriage of her aunt to Edward Perry Fisk, "in whose family it had been for many years." Fisk predeceased his wife, Josephine, who passed the porringer on to her sister, Catharine Scott's mother. It then passed to Catharine Scott, who sold it in 1930 to Alvin Detwiler, acting as agent for Julia D. Cordley, a Washington, D.C., antiques dealer. Sold in 1931 to Howard P. Okie, Okie Galleries, Washington, D.C. Acquired at some point by Robert Ensko, Inc., New York City, who sold it to H. F. du Pont, 1946.

Comments: During 1930 and 1931, when the porringer first came on the market, it was greeted with intense skepticism. The unusual handle, not to mention its unorthodox placement, frightened off potential buyers. The Museum of Fine Arts, Boston declined to purchase it after protracted negotiations. It is said that Francis P. Garvan went into a rage upon being offered the piece by a dealer, and H. F. du Pont also initially declined to have anything to do with it. Odd though it may be, no one has been able to find any compelling reason to declare it "not right." (It has been examined and tested in the laboratories of 2 major museums.)

Its early history is inferred on the basis of the initials. Support is lent to this history by the same initials found on the Sanderson tankard described in Kathryn C. Buhler, "The Robert Sanderson Tankard." The later history tends to cast doubt on the identity of "WF." If Catharine Scott's story—that it descended in the Fisk family—is true, then the "WF" may refer to a member of the Fisk family. Until and unless this can be documented, the Fleet association remains the more plausible alternative.

Concerning the cast handle with its 2 cherubs leaning toward each other, Kane noted in her dissertation that this was one of the most innovative and up-to-date designs by Hull & Sanderson. Although no English precedents in silver have been located, Kane observes that similar designs were used in clock spandrels; the inspiration for this handle may have come from one of the several clocks imported by Hull in his role as merchant. An alternative theory for the design of this handle, put forth by Mrs. Russell Hastings, is that Vergoose may have salvaged the handle from a family-owned Dutch brandy bowl or a French *équelle* that came originally from the Low Countries. Hastings also suggests that the porringer was actually a cover for a skillet. Note: There is no truth to the story that Mary or Elizabeth Vergoose was the original Mother Goose of legend, as has been alleged in some of the antiquarian literature.

References: Kathryn C. Buhler, "The Robert Sanderson Tankard," *Bulletin of the Museum of Fine Arts* 35, no. 209 (June 1937): 33–35, for a piece with the same initials. Buhler and Hood, *American Silver*, no. 7, for a spoon possibly owned by Mary Vergoose. Clarke, *John Hull*, pp. 125, 126, no. 22. Sewall, *Diary*. Fales, *American Silver*, no. 14. Mrs. Russell Hastings, "Verifying a Hull and Sanderson Porringer," *Antiques* 32, no. 3 (September 1937): 116–18. Kane, "John Hull and Robert Sanderson," pp. 150–51, no. 56.

57.544 Gift of H. F. du Pont, 1965

77
SPOON, 1652–ca. 1655

L. 6⅝" (16.8 cm), w. bowl 1⅞" (4.8 cm)
1 oz. 7 dwt. 1 gr. (42.1 g)

Stamps: "IH" (upper part of stamp illegible) in sans serif letters, in an oval, struck once on inside of bowl; "R[S]" (upper part of stamp illegible) in roman letters, in an oval, struck once on back of handle.

Engraved on tip of handle: "P/ BM" in roman letters.

Description: wide oval bowl with incised triangular drop on back; straight handle, rectangular in section, with so-called slip end; probably cast in 1 piece.

Spectrographic analysis:

	SILVER	COPPER	LEAD	GOLD
BOWL	93.0	6.8	0.09	0.07
HANDLE	94.9	5.0	0.08	0.07

Provenance: Purchased by H. F. du Pont from "Boney," who remains unidentified.

Comments: According to Kane this is one of the earliest products of the partnership because it is the only object to bear Sanderson's London stamp and Hull's stamp. It is unquestionably the earliest piece of American silver in the Winterthur collection. A similar spoon is owned by the Essex Institute, Salem; it was made for William and Hannah Brown of Salem, who were married in 1664.

References: Not in Clarke, *John Hull.* Marshall B. Davidson, "John Hull of Boston, Goldsmith," *American Art and Antiques* 1, no. 1 (July/August 1978): 86. Davidson, *Colonial Antiques*, p. 35. Fales, *American Silver*, no. 68. Fennimore, *Silver and Pewter*, no. 29. Kane, "John Hull and Robert Sanderson," pp. 53, 54, no. 9. Susan Burrows Swan, "Collecting American Silver Spoons," *Early American Life* 11, no. 6 (December 1980): 33, fig. 2.

53.7 Gift of H. F. du Pont, 1958

78 a
OAK-TREE SHILLING, 1657–67

DIAM. 1 1/16" (2.7 cm), precise measurement difficult because of irregular outline
3 dwt. (4.7 g)

Description: circular die-stamped coin with design in relief. Obverse: oak tree in center surrounded by circular beaded border, in turn encircled by inscription "MASATHVSETS•IN•", in turn encircled by outer circular beaded border. Reverse: "1652/ XII" in center surrounded by circular beaded border, in turn encircled by inscription "NEWENGLAND•ANDOM•", in turn encircled by outer circular beaded border.

Spectrographic analysis:

SILVER	COPPER	LEAD	GOLD
95.2	4.4	0.26	0.02

64.1093 Bequest of H. F. du Pont, 1969

ℰ 78 b
PINE-TREE SHILLING, 1667–75

DIAM. 1 1/16" (2.7 cm), precise measurement difficult because of irregular outline
2 dwt. 22 gr. (4.6 g)

Description: circular die-stamped coin with design in relief. Obverse: pine tree in center surrounded by circular beaded border, in turn encircled by inscription "MASATVSETS•IN•", in turn surrounded by outer circular beaded border. Reverse: "1652/ XII" in center surrounded by circular beaded border, in turn surrounded by inscription "NEWENGLAND•ANDOM•", in turn surrounded by an outer circular beaded border. All *N*'s are backwards.

Spectrographic analysis:

SILVER	COPPER	LEAD	GOLD	MERCURY
96.7	2.9	0.16	0.08	0.03

64.1094 Bequest of H. F. du Pont, 1969

ℰ 78 c
PINE-TREE SIXPENCE, 1667–75

DIAM.. 3/4" (1.9 cm), precise measurement difficult because of irregular outline
1 dwt. 11 gr. (2.3 g)

Description: circular die-stamped coin with design in relief. Obverse: pine tree in center surrounded by circular beaded border, in turn encircled by inscription "MA[SATHVS]ETS•IN•", in turn encircled by an outer circular beaded border. Reverse: "1652/ VI" in center surrounded by circular beaded border, in turn surrounded by inscription "NEWENGLAND•ANO•", in turn surrounded by outer circular beaded border.

Spectrographic analysis:

SILVER	MERCURY	COPPER	GOLD	LEAD
57.9	35.8	1.5	1.3	0.25

History: Twenty-two years after the founding of the colony, Massachusetts Bay found itself chronically short of specie. In May 1652 the General Court passed legislation authorizing the establishment of a mint. Since the minting of money was a prerogative of the Crown, this would not have been possible but for the unsettled conditions in England. Charles I had been executed in 1649, and Charles II had been defeated in 1651 at Worcester. Cromwell and Parliament were sympathetic to the doctrines of New England Puritans but were much too involved in internal affairs to extend the power of the Commonwealth to the New World.

As John Hull explains in his diary: "Also upon occasion of much counterfeit coin brought in the country, and much loss accruing in that respect (and that did occasion a stoppage of trade), the General Court ordered a mint to be set up, and to coin it, bringing it to the sterling standard for fineness. . . . And they made choice of me for that employment; and I chose my friend, Robert Sanderson, to be my partner, to which the Court consented."

The earliest coins were plain with "NE" on one side and the denomination on the other. These were followed by the willow-tree, oak-tree, and pine-tree coins. It should be noted that tree designs were substituted for the sovereign's head. The date is always 1652, the date of the act establishing the mint, although most surviving coins were made later. The denomination is expressed in roman numerals, which refer to pence. The Massachusetts mint remained active until 1682. Not until the early 1680s did the minting of coinage threaten the colony's charter.

The early history of these particular coins is unknown. Numerous examples of these and others struck by Hull & Sanderson are extant.

Provenance: William C. Baldwin, West Chester, Pa., sold to H. F. du Pont, 1948.

Comments: Sylvester S. Crosby and Sydney P. Noe examined many examples of Hull & Sanderson coinage and established which dies were used and the order of their use. Every product of the mint can be keyed into their systems of die identification.

	Crosby	Noe
(a) Oak-tree shilling	2b-D	no. 7, pl. II D
(b) Pine-tree shilling	2a-A1	no. 11
(c) Pine-tree sixpence	A-1	no. 33

Crosby also reprints many of the documents connected with the Massachusetts mint.

References: Clarke, *John Hull*, chap. 7. Hermann Frederick Clarke, "John Hull: Mintmaster," *New England Quarterly* 10, no. 4 (December 1937): 668–84. Sylvester S. Crosby, *The Coins of America and the Laws Governing Their Issue* (1875; reprint, El Cajon, Calif.: Token and Medal Society, 1965). "Diaries of John Hull," pp. 145–46. Fales, *American Silver*, no. 15. Sydney P. Noe, *The Oak Tree Coinage of Massachusetts*, Numismatic Notes and Monographs No. 110 (New York: American Numismatic Society, 1947). Sydney P. Noe, *The Pine Tree Coinage of Massachusetts*, Numismatic Notes and Monographs No. 125 (New York: American Numismatic Society, 1952).

64.1095 Bequest of H. F. du Pont, 1969

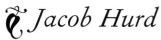

Jacob Hurd

1702/3–58
Boston, Massachusetts

Jacob Hurd was the fourth generation of his family in Boston, the earliest having arrived about 1639. His father, also called Jacob, was a joiner who resided first in Boston and later in Charlestown. Although Kathyrn C. Buhler opined that young Hurd had been apprenticed to John Edwards because of the similarities between Hurd's work and that of Edwards's sons Samuel and Thomas, no supporting record has been found. Hurd was married in 1725 to Elizabeth Mason, by whom he had fourteen children. Not one of their four daughters named Prudence survived childhood. Daughter Elizabeth married silversmith Daniel Henchman, who served his apprenticeship with Hurd. Sons Nathaniel and Benjamin became silversmiths. Hurd's eldest son, also named Jacob, moved to Halifax, Nova Scotia, in the 1750s and has caused consternation among historians of early Canadian silver who have confused him with his father.

Hurd became first sergeant of the Artillery Company and served as captain of the Boston Regiment until his death. His new house on Atkinson Street was struck by lightning in 1738 and severely damaged. Hurd moved to Roxbury following his bankruptcy in 1755. Three years later he died of a stroke while visiting a relative in Boston. As one news account put it, "Last Wednesday in the Afternoon Capt. Jacob Hurd . . . a noted Goldsmith, was seized with a Lethargy, in which he continued till Friday Evening, and then expired, much lamented" (*Boston Gazette*, February 20, 1758).

For so prolific a silversmith, Hurd did not accumulate a substantial estate. When he died, he was heavily in debt, owing £743.6.5 ½. The largest single creditor was William Sitwell & Company—for what we do not know. The inventory of his estate is pathetically meager, amounting to £72.13.0, which included a house valued at £50. Two of the three appraisers were silversmiths Samuel Edwards and William Simpkins.

Large quantities of Hurd's silver survive, indicating that he was well patronized. In his monograph on the Hurds, Hollis French records about 300 pieces, and dozens more have turned up since. In 1725 Samuel Sewall, the diarist, noted that he gave his daughter-in-law a spoon for her infant son that had an inscription engraved by Hurd. Hurd is well represented by many examples of church silver, as recorded by E. Alfred Jones, and by many high-style pieces made for Boston's elite, such as the large two-handled covered cups memorializing John Rowe and Edward Tyng. A silver mace in the form of an oar was made for the provincial admiralty court; it is now at the Massachusetts Historical Society.

References: Sewall, *Diary*, p. 1034. French, *Jacob Hurd and His Sons.* Edward W. Hanson, "The Hurds of Boston," *NEH&GR* 132, no. 2 (April 1978): 83–96. Jones, *Old Silver*, index. Kane, *Dictionary*, s.v. "Hurd, Jacob." SCPR book 54, pp. 58–59, 181–82; book 53, pp. 580–81. Ward, "Boston Goldsmiths." Barbara McLean Ward, "Hierarchy and Wealth Distribution in the Boston Goldsmithing Trade, 1690–1760," *Essex Institute Historical Collections* 126, no. 3 (July 1990): 129–47.

79
COFFEEPOT, ca. 1740

H. 9 ¾" (24.8 cm), W. 8 ⁹⁄₁₆" (21.8 cm), DIAM. base 5 ¼" (13.3 cm)
29 oz. 14 dwt. 2 gr. (923.9 g)

Stamps: "HURD" in roman letters, in a rectangle, struck twice on body below rim, left and right of handle.

Engraved on body: asymmetrical cartouche containing 3 swords, side-by-side, pointing down; cartouche surrounded by asymmetrical leafage and C scrolls; crest of a single sword, pointing down. *Scratched on base:* "EP" in crude roman letters; "oz dwt/ 28 15". *Painted on base in red enamel:* "[?] 1929.8".

Description: raised form with straight sides in the so-called lighthouse shape; applied molded base; double-scored lines encircle body below applied molded rim; centerpunch on bottom. Cast S-curve spout with pendant bellflower drops; 2 cylindrical handle sockets applied to body with symmetrical cut-card drops echoing cast drops below spout. C-curve sprigged fruitwood handle. Stepped-and-domed raised lid with double-scored lines around top of flange; centerpunch inside; cast-and-turned finial with central knop. Minimal C-curve thumbpiece applied to edge of lid is part of a 5-segment hinge mounted on upper handle socket.

Spectrographic analysis:

	SILVER	COPPER	LEAD	GOLD
BODY SIDE	91.1	8.3	0.17	0.06
BASE	92.3	7.1	0.16	0.08
LID	92.7	6.6	0.14	0.14
SPOUT	92.7	6.7	0.12	0.17
BASE MOLDING	92.5	6.9	0.12	0.12

History: According to Francis Hill Bigelow, the family from whom he purchased the coffeepot said the arms are those of the Gallisons. Both Charles Knowles Bolton and French, however, refer to this as the Clarke arms because they closely resemble the arms on a baptismal basin bequeathed to the Old South Church by Mary Saltonstall (d. 1729/30), whose first husband, and first owner of the basin, was William Clarke (d. 1710). Yale University Art Gallery owns a salver, also by Hurd, with the same arms as those on the baptismal basin. Its first owner was Maj. William Clarke, who was born

in 1728. On both of these pieces, however, the swords point up, whereas on the coffeepot the point down. We are thus left with a possible but inconclusive connection to the Clarke family of Boston. It is important to note that a variant of this coat of arms appears in *Display of Heraldry*, by John Guillim, who describes it: "The field is gules, three Swords in Pale, Argent, an Inescutcheon of the Second, charged with a sinister Hand couped at the Wrist as the First. This was the paternal Coat-Armour of Sir Symon Clark of Safford, in the County of Warwick . . . sometime Cofferer to King James."

The initials "EP" scratched on the bottom remain unidentified.

Provenance: Purchased from the estate of Mrs. Francis Alexander by Francis Hill Bigelow; Brooks Reed Gallery, Boston, sold to H. F. du Pont, June 1927.

Exhibitions: The painted enamel number on the base—"[?] 1929.8"—suggests that the coffeepot was placed on loan to a museum shortly after its acquisition by H. F. du Pont. It may have been part of the lot lent by du Pont to the Metropolitan Museum of Art in 1928.

Comments: French listed 3 coffeepots of the lighthouse type. In addition to the one owned by du Pont, 1 was engraved with a unicorn's head, and the other was engraved with the arms of Alleyne. Both were said to belong to Francis P. Garvan, although the last was also said to be in another private collection. The coffeepot with the unicorn's head was in the 1937 exhibition held at Yale University Art Gallery, "Masterpieces of New England Silver," but it is not in Buhler and Hood's 1970 catalogue. A lighthouse coffeepot by Hurd, said to bear the Trail arms, was advertised by J. Herbert Gebelein in the December 1972 issue of *Antiques*. It was sold to a private collection. English models for this form do exist. Christie's advertised a similar coffeepot, made by Paul de Lamerie in 1734, in the April 1985 issue of *Antiques*.

References: Bolton, *Bolton's American Armory*, p. 35. Fales, *American Silver*, no. 98. Davidson, *Colonial Antiques*, p. 179. Fennimore, *Silver and Pewter*, no. 147. French, *Jacob Hurd and His Sons*, checklist no. 110, pl. 17. Guillim, *Display of Heraldry*, p. 337. For the Clarke arms on the baptismal basin in the Old South Church, see Jones, *Old Silver*, p. 58. Kauffman, *Colonial Silversmith*, p. 130.

60.1048 Gift of H. F. du Pont, 1965

ℰ 80
TEAPOT, ca. 1750

H. 6 ⅛" (15.6 cm), w. 9 ⁵⁄₁₆" (23.7 cm)
17 oz. 15 dwt. 19 gr. (553.3 g)

Stamps: "IHURD" in roman letters, in a cartouche with wavy top and a bottom of double cyma curves forming a point in the center, struck twice on bottom.

Engraved on bottom: "G / DR" in roman letters.

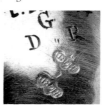

Engraved on side at a later date: "M. Perit/ Maria Perit Gilman" in script. *Engraved on lid and adjoining top of body:* elaborate leafy forms with shells at the handle-spout axis; a basket of fruit and a winged cherub's head at the perpendicular axis.

Description: raised apple-shape body with a nearly flat top; centerpunch on bottom (which is soldered, a common feature on this form of New England teapot). Applied molded base. Applied cast S-shape spout with decorative drop below. C-shape fruitwood handle with spur is attached to body by 2 cylindrical silver sockets soldered to body. Raised circular lid, attached to body by a 3-segment hinge, has a finial composed of cast turned elements consisting of a spool separated from a pointed cone by a flattened wooden ball.

Spectrographic analysis:

	SILVER	COPPER	LEAD	GOLD
BASE	96.5	2.9	0.15	0.11
BODY SIDE	93.0	6.6	0.20	0.11
SPOUT	92.8	6.7	0.16	0.07
FOOT	93.9	5.5	0.16	0.09
LID	93.8	5.5	0.21	0.15
FINIAL	85.3	6.0	0.19	0.05

History: This is 1 of at least 3 pieces of silver owned by Winterthur that came from Norwich, Conn., and were owned in the Gilman, Lathrop, Coit, and Perit families, all of whom were related to one another. The initials "G / DR"

refer to an as yet unidentified member of the Gilman family in Exeter, N.H. A William C. Gilman from Exeter, after a successful sojourn as a merchant in Boston, moved to Norwich in the early nineteenth century. He married Eliza Coit, daughter of Daniel Lathrop Coit and Elizabeth Bull. Their son Daniel Coit Gilman (1831–1908) became a famous scholar and educator and was founding president of Johns Hopkins University.

The Perit family was French Huguenot in origin and settled in the New Rochelle and New York City area early in the eighteenth century. Pelatiah Perit (1785–1865) married Jerusha Lathrop in 1809 and Maria Coit in 1823. Maria was Eliza Coit Gilman's sister. It is likely that the Maria Perit of the inscription is the daughter of Pelatiah and Maria. Around the turn of the twentieth century there were 3 Gilman sisters living in Norwich; 1 was a Maria Gilman.

Norwich directories for 1875 and 1878 list a Maria Gilman, teacher, living on E. Town St., but whether this is the Maria of the inscription and whether her middle name was Perit is uncertain.

Provenance: Sale of this teapot and "1 chest, 1 mirror, 1 table" to H. F. du Pont was arranged by George H. Gilman, counselor at law, Norwich, Conn., 1925. It is unclear on whose behalf he was acting.

Exhibitions: "Tea: A Revolutionary Tradition," Fraunces Tavern Museum, New York City, 1980–81.

Comments: Hollis French records 17 teapots of this shape made by Hurd. Contrary to most holloware, this form was made so that the bottom, following the raising process, became the top, and the lid was cut out of it. The narrow end became the bottom, and it became necessary to cut an appropriately shaped piece of silver for the bottom—hence the circular line of solder around the interior of the inside bottom. See milk pot by Nathaniel Hurd, no. 92, with a similar family history.

References: Fales, *American Silver*, no. 106. French, *Jacob Hurd and His Sons*, checklist no. 273. Kauffman, *Colonial Silversmiths*, p. 123. Mary E. Perkins, *Old Houses of the Antient Town of Norwich, 1660–1800* (Norwich, Conn., 1895), pp. 319–23, 549–59. *Stedman's Directory of the City and Town of Norwich* (Norwich, Conn., 1875), p. 82; (Norwich, Conn., 1878), p. 81.

61.937 Gift of H. F. du Pont, 1965

81 a, b
CANDLE BRANCHES, ca. 1735

(a) H. 3 ⅜" (8.6 cm), D. 5 ¹⁵⁄₁₆" (15.1 cm),
DIAM. pan 3 ¹⁄₁₆" (7.8 cm)
3 oz. 4 dwt. 19 gr. (100.8 g) (without wall plate)
(b) H. 3 ½" (8.9 cm), D. 5 ¹⁵⁄₁₆" (15.1 cm),
DIAM. pan 3 ¹⁄₁₆" (7.8 cm)
3 oz. 4 dwt. (99.5 g) (without wall plate)
Note: depth includes wall plate.

Stamps: "Hurd" in slanted roman letters and script, struck once on top of each drip pan.

Description: cast S-curve branch, diamond shape in cross section, with William and Mary–type triple turnings in the vertical section, sprigged decoration and bud finial on wall end, and turned finial under a small horizontal oval plate at candle end. Urn-shape socket with midband and rim; socket cast in halves vertically and seamed. Raised dished circular drip pan with applied molded rim with double-scored lines around inside edge. Drip pan is drilled in center to permit passage of silver screw from socket to plate below. Attached to wall end of the branch is a vertical pin with cast finial; pin rests in a vertical silver cylinder soldered to wall plate in the shape of a symmetrical cartouche.

Spectrographic analysis:

	SILVER	COPPER	GOLD	LEAD
(a)				
DRIP PAN	92.4	6.7	0.24	0.23
SOCKET	91.1	7.7	0.27	0.25
BRANCH	91.0	7.7	0.20	0.32
(b)				
DRIP PAN	93.2	6.0	0.23	0.21
SOCKET	90.2	8.4	0.25	0.26
BRANCH	89.9	8.7	0.20	0.29

History: Although there are no engraved initials or names on these branches, there is a strong family history that appears to be accurate. The branches descended in the Smith family to the last private owner, who sold them to H. F. du Pont. Family tradition holds that they came into the family upon the marriage of Thomas Smith to his third wife, Elizabeth (Hunt) Wendell of Boston.

Thomas Smith (1702–95), son of a Boston shopkeeper, entered Harvard at age 14, where he proceeded to get into one scrape after another. He graduated in 1720—at age 18—and then went on to graduate study and teaching. After a brief sojourn in Falmouth (now Portland), Maine, he was called formally in 1726 to minister to this frontier community. He pursued his calling with great vigor despite Indian wars, doctrinal disputes, raising a large family, and the death of his first 2 wives. He was sole pastor of the First Church for 38 years and continued to preach regularly for another 20 years—until he was 82. He was a powerful personality who merited the informal title given to him by his contemporaries—Bishop Smith. For many years his house was the finest in town, but it was destroyed during the conflagration resulting from the British raid in 1775.

Smith's son Peter Thacher Smith (1731–1826), also a Harvard graduate (1753), was called to the church at New Marblehead (later Windham), Maine, in 1762. Three years later he married Elizabeth Wendell, daughter of Jacob Wendell (1715–53) and Elizabeth Hunt of Boston. (Jacob Wendell, whose father had come from Albany, was a merchant who had led a quiet life. He gained public notice only

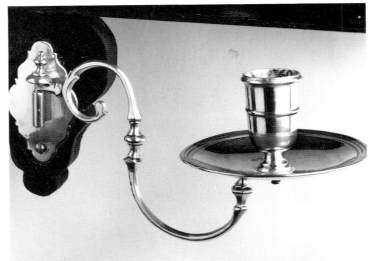

when lightning struck his house in 1745 and melted his pewter plates.) After Jacob's death his widow joined her daughter and son-in-law in Maine. Thomas Smith's second wife had died in 1763; presumably during visits with his son he became acquainted with Elizabeth (Hunt) Wendell. Elizabeth Wendell was described by William Willis as "a lady of fine manners, good education, and dignified deportment. One of our aged citizens has told me that he was present with her at a wedding at which her husband officiated, where she gratified the company by dancing a minuet with all the ease and grace of an accomplished young lady, to the admiration of the company, many of whom had never seen that graceful and at that time very fashionable dance." In August 1766 Thomas Smith and

Elizabeth Wendell were married by Peter Thacher Smith. It is this union that presumably brought the candle branches to Maine and into the Smith family, although the daughter's marriage to Peter could also have occasioned the transfer. In any case, several Wendell family pieces came down in the Smith family to twentieth-century descendants.

According to French, the stamp Hurd used on the branches was one he employed between 1729 and 1740; if true, this means that the branches were probably made before the younger Elizabeth was born. For this reason as well as from stylistic evidence, they probably date from the middle of the 1730s. Elizabeth Hunt had married Jacob Wendell in 1736, and perhaps they were a wedding present. The branches are attached to shadow boxes containing elaborate quillwork that, according to family tradition, was made by 1 of the 2 Elizabeths, most likely the first. For many years the branches remained at the Parson Smith Homestead in Windham, the home of Peter Thacher and Elizabeth (Wendell) Smith. The house still stands and in the 1930s was bequeathed to the Society for the Preservation of New England Antiquities (SPNEA). In 1992 SPNEA put the house up for sale.

Provenance: Elizabeth (Hunt) Wendell Smith (d. 1799); Elizabeth (Wendell) Smith (d. 1799) and Peter Thacher Smith (d. 1826); John Tyng Smith (1772–1856) and his wife Mary (Duguid) Smith (d. 1855); Edward Tyng Smith (1807–85) and his wife Margaret (Foster) Smith (d. 1897); Edward H. Foster Smith (1844–1905); Ethel Smith, who married Chase Boothby; Margaret Boothby, who married Elliott Freeman; H. F. du Pont purchased from Mrs. Elliott Freeman, December 1949.

Comments: Not included in French, *Jacob Hurd and His Sons.*

References: Fales, *American Silver*, no. 1, where they are given an erroneous history. Susan Burrows Swan, *Plain and Fancy: American Women and Their Needlework, 1700–1850* (New York: Holt, Rinehart, and Winston, 1977), fig. 37. John A. H. Sweeney, *Winterthur Illustrated* (Winterthur, Del.: Winterthur Museum, 1963), p. 45. *Sibley's Harvard Graduates*, 6:400–410, for Thomas Smith; 13:355–59, for Peter Thacher Smith; 9:365–67, for Jacob Wendell. Nellie D. Spiller, "The Parson Smith Homestead, South Windham, Maine," *Old-Time New England* 48, no. 2 (Fall 1957): 48–56. William Willis, *Journals of the Rev. Thomas Smith and the Rev. Samuel Deane* (Portland, Maine, 1849), p. 22. Advertisement for sale of Parson Smith House, *Down East* 38, no. 12 (July 1992): 69.

60.588, 60.589 Bequest of H. F. du Pont, 1969

82
SALVER, ca. 1750

DIAM. 6 15⁄16" (17.6 cm), H. 1 5⁄16" (3.3 cm)
8 oz. 16 dwt. 19 gr. (275.0 g)

Stamps: "HURD" in roman letters, in a rectangle, struck once on upper surface.

Engraved on upper surface: apple-shape shield, gules with a bend or containing 3 lions passant, all in a shell-like surround, encircled by C scrolls, cross-hatching, and leafage. 8 bell-flowers equidistant around edge next to rim. *Scratched on underside:* "oz/8-19".

Description: octagonal sheet silver with applied molded edge consisting of 8 bracketlike segments that form points at the joins; 4 equally spaced, short cabriole legs with pad feet (cast). No centerpunch.

Spectrographic analysis:

	SILVER	COPPER	GOLD	LEAD
UNDERSIDE OF TRAY	93.2	5.9	0.18	0.10
BOTTOM OF FOOT	92.0	6.9	0.36	0.28

Provenance: C. W. Lyon, Inc., New York City, sold to H. F. du Pont, January 1935.

Exhibitions: "Technological Innovation and the Decorative Arts," Hagley Museum, Wilmington, Del., March–December 1973.

Comments: John Guillim illustrates and describes similar arms: "He beareth Or, on a Bend, Sable, three Lyons passant, Argent, by the name of Hagar. This Coat belong'd to Thomas Hagar of Bourne, Esquire." Various members of the Hagar family lived in Waltham and Watertown, Mass., during the seventeenth and eighteenth centuries.

References: Fales, *American Silver*, no. 110. French, *Jacob Hurd and His Sons*, no. 292. Guillim, *Display of Heraldry*, p. 173. *Technological Innovation and the Decorative Arts* (Wilmington, Del.: Eleutherian Mills–Hagley Foundation, 1973), p. 75.

61.520 Gift of H. F. du Pont, 1965

83
PEPPER BOX, ca. 1750

H. 3 13⁄16" (9.7 cm), W. 2 ¾" (7.0 cm)
2 oz. 18 dwt. (90.2 g)

Stamps: "HURD" in roman letters, in a rectangle, struck once on bottom.

Engraved on bottom: "L/ DI" in roman letters.

Description: octagonal body formed from sheet silver with applied moldings top and bottom; cast S-curve handle with scrolls at each end and sprigged in 2 places; octagonal applied base. Raised octagonal domed lid with numerous punched holes; cast applied finial.

Spectrographic analysis:

	SILVER	COPPER	LEAD	GOLD
BOTTOM	94.0	5.2	0.25	0.09
SIDE	92.7	6.5	0.26	0.11
HANDLE	90.9	6.7	0.29	0.28

History: In spite of a tradition of ownership in the Lane family and, later, the Huntington and Gardiner families of Norwich, Conn., there is reason to believe that the pepper box was owned by another prominent Norwich family. Yale University Art Gallery owns a porringer made by Daniel Boyer of Boston that bears the same initials. In this instance the "L/ DI" is thought to refer to Daniel and Jerusha Lathrop because the porringer descended through Daniel's sister Lydia Lathrop Coit. Dr. Daniel Lathrop (1712–82), founder of what may have been the first drugstore in Connecticut, married Jerusha Talcott (1717–1805), daughter of Gov. Joseph and Abigail Talcott of Connecticut, in 1744.

Provenance: Daniel and Jerusha Lathrop until 1805; Mr. and Mrs. N. McLean Seabrease, Germantown, Pa., early twentieth century; Robert Ensko, Inc., New York City, sold to H. F. du Pont as part of the Seabrease collection, August 1929.

References: Buhler and Hood, *American Silver*, nos. 197, 350, for pieces with similar histories. Fales, *American Silver*, no. 24. French, *Jacob Hurd and His Sons*, no. 93, where the engraved initials are mistakenly given as "I/ DL".

60.1047 Gift of H. F. du Pont, 1965

84
SAUCEBOAT, ca. 1750

H. (to top of handle) 4 ³⁄₁₆" (10.6 cm), w. 7 ⅛" (18.1 cm)
9 oz. 11 dwt. (297.1 g)

Stamps: "HURD" in roman letters, in a rectangle, struck once on bottom.

Engraved on side: armorial device consisting of an asymmetrical cartouche containing an or fess dancette with 2 eaglets above and 1 below in an azure field; flanking C scrolls with leafage beneath; eagle-head crest.

Description: oval bulbous raised form with flaring cyma-curve rim and large, wide pouring lip. Cast double–C-curve handle, sprigged and terminating in scrolls; 3 applied cast cabriole legs terminating in circular pad feet.

Spectrographic analysis:

	SILVER	COPPER	GOLD	LEAD
BOTTOM	91.4	8.1	0.09	0.09
FOOT	95.3	4.1	0.18	0.08
HANDLE	93.8	5.7	0.16	0.12

Provenance: Judge Robert Walcott, Cambridge.

Exhibitions: Said in sale catalogue to have been on exhibition at the Museum of Fine Arts, Boston prior to sale in 1957.

References: Fales, *American Silver*, no. 52. French, *Jacob Hurd and His Sons*, no. 181, where the arms are said to be those of the Walcotts. Parke-Bernet Galleries, sale no. 1776 (October 26, 1957), lot 31, p. 6.

57.91.4 Museum purchase, funds of C. K. Davis, from Philip H. Hammerslough, 1957

🦢 85
SWORD, ca. 1740

L. 34 ¼" (87.0 cm)
12 oz. 1 dwt. 12 gr. (375.6 g)

Stamps: "IHURD" in roman letters, in a cartouche with wavy top and bottom of double cyma curves forming a point in the center, struck once on counterguard.

Description: forged steel blade, straight and pointed, triangular in cross section, joined to silver hilt. From steel blade up, parts of hilt consist of the counterguard, *pas-d'âne*, grip, pommel, knuckle bow, and quillon. Each half of the counterguard is formed in an oval with a slight rim. The *pas-d'âne* consists of 2 cast circular loops above the counterguard and are integral to the body of the hilt. Wire-wrapped grip. The knuckle bow is a C-shape form cast as an integral part of the hilt and is designed to be the principal protection for the fingers. The quillon is a short, cast, curved form extending out from the other side of the lower grip. The pommel is cast in a ball shape and, together with its small finial, terminates the upper end of the hilt.

Spectrographic analysis:

	SILVER	COPPER	LEAD	GOLD
POMMEL	92.6	6.8	0.28	0.08
HANDLE	94.5	4.7	0.31	0.11
WIRE GRIP	94.1	5.3	0.24	0.12
KNUCKLE BOW	93.9	5.3	0.33	0.08
COUNTERGUARD	95.5	2.9	0.21	0.06

Provenance: Firestone & Parson, Boston.

Comments: This is 1 of 6 smallswords known to have been made by Hurd.

References: Harold L. Peterson, *The American Sword, 1775–1945* (Philadelphia: Ray Riling Arms Books, 1965), for general background.

74.123 Museum purchase from Firestone & Parson, 1974

86
CANN, ca. 1735

H. 5 ¾" (14.6 cm), w. 5 ½" (14.0 cm)
11 oz. 8 dwt. 3 gr. (354.8 g)

Stamps: "Hurd" in slanted roman letters and script, in an oval, struck once on body near rim next to handle.

Engraved on outside of handle: "E-W" in roman letters. *Scratched on underside:* "11-12".

Description: circular drinking vessel with bulbous lower body, centerpunch on bottom, applied molded rim; triple-stepped raised circular foot applied to body. Cast S-curve handle with bud terminal at bottom, spring on upper handle, lower end of handle attached to body by an oval cutout plate; upper end of handle soldered directly to body.

Spectrographic analysis:

	SILVER	COPPER	LEAD	GOLD
BODY SIDE	92.1	7.0	0.42	0.08
FOOT	93.1	5.4	0.31	0.17
HANDLE	91.2	7.2	0.39	0.17

Provenance: Marshall P. Blankarn, New York City.

References: Not in French, *Jacob Hurd and His Sons.*

77.72 Gift of Marshall P. Blankarn, 1977

87 a, b
SPOONS, ca. 1735

(a) L. 7 ¾" (19.7 cm)
1 oz. 6 dwt. 23 gr. (41.9 g)
(b) L. 8 ⅛" (20.6 cm)
1 oz. 15 dwt. 11 gr. (55.1 g)

Stamps: "IHURD" in roman letters, in a cartouche with wavy top and bottom of double cyma curves forming a point in the center, struck once on back of each handle.

Engraved on back of handle: (a) "PC" in roman letters; (b) "AC" in roman letters.

Description: both spoons have rounded upturned handles with midribs on front; (a) has an elongated oval bowl with swage-formed rattail on back; (b) has an elongated oval bowl with swage-formed double drop on back.

Spectrographic analysis: Silver content ranges from 91.5 to 92.3 percent.

Provenance: Mr. and Mrs. Stanley B. Ineson, New York City; Mr. and Mrs. Alfred E. Bissell, Wilmington, Del.

Exhibitions: (b) Metropolitan Museum of Art, New York City, 1935–61.

References: Belden, *Marks of American Silversmiths*, p. 242 e. French, *Jacob Hurd and His Sons*, no. 215.

62.240.1204, 62.240.1206 Gift of Mr. and Mrs. Alfred E. Bissell, 1962–63

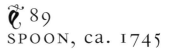

ℰ 88 a–d
SPOONS, ca. 1750

(a) L. 4 9/16" (11.6 cm)
6 dwt. 16 gr. (10.4 g)
(b) L. 4 5/8" (11.8 cm)
7 dwt. 14 gr. (11.8 g)
(c) L. 4" (10.2 cm)
4 dwt. (6.2 g)
(d) L. 4 3/8" (11.1 cm)
4 dwt. 22 gr. (7.7 g)

Stamps: "HURD" in roman letters, in a rectangle, struck once on back of each handle.

Engraved on back of handle: (a) "Ex Don/ Pup:/ -1744" in script; (b) "MM" in roman letters; (c) "MB" in roman letters; (d) "EH" in roman letters.

Description: all spoons have rounded upturned handles with midribs on front; all have elongated oval bowls with swage-formed shell and drop on the back.

Spectrographic analysis: Silver content ranges from 91.2 to 92.8 percent.

Provenance: Mr. and Mrs. Stanley B. Ineson, New York City; Mr. and Mrs. Alfred E. Bissell, Wilmington, Del.

Comments: (a) was clearly a gift from a student to his teacher, perhaps at Harvard College.

References: Belden, *Marks of American Silversmiths*, p. 242 b.

62.240.344, .345, .346, .347 Gift of Mr. and Mrs. Alfred E. Bissell, 1962–63

ℰ 89
SPOON, ca. 1745

L. 4 5/8" (11.8 cm)
5 dwt. 7 gr. (8.3 g)

Stamps: "Hurd" in roman letters, in a surround of cyma curves and double points top and bottom, struck once on back of handle.

Engraved on back of handle: "SI" in roman letters.

Description: elongated oval bowl with swage-formed shell and drop on back; rounded upturned handle with midrib on front.

Spectrographic analysis: Silver content is 91.6 percent.

Provenance: Mr. and Mrs. Stanley B. Ineson, New York City; Mr. and Mrs. Alfred E. Bissell, Wilmington, Del.

References: Belden, *Marks of American Silversmiths*, p. 242 d.

62.240.342 Gift of Mr. and Mrs. Alfred E. Bissell, 1962–63

ℰ 90
SPOON, ca. 1735

L. 4 1/8" (10.5 cm)
4 dwt. 11 gr. (7.0 g)

Stamps: "Hurd" in slanted letters and script, struck once on back of handle.

Engraved on back of handle: "ST" in roman letters.

Description: elongated oval bowl with swage-formed double drop on back; rounded upturned handle with midrib on front.

Spectrographic analysis: Silver content is 94.1 percent.

Provenance: Mr. and Mrs. Stanley B. Ineson, New York City; Mr. and Mrs. Alfred E. Bissell, Wilmington, Del.

References: Belden, *Marks of American Silversmiths*, p. 242 c.

62.240.343 Gift of Mr. and Mrs. Alfred E. Bissell, 1962–63

Nathaniel Hurd

1730–78
Boston, Massachusetts

Nathaniel Hurd was the fourth child of silversmith Jacob Hurd and Elizabeth (Mason) Hurd and older brother of silversmith Benjamin Hurd. Probably trained in his father's shop, Nathaniel may have made some of the silver bearing Jacob's stamp. In his will, he styled himself "goldsmith and engraver," and, indeed, he is better known for his prints than for his silver. His group portrait of George III, General Wolfe, and William Pitt; his caricature of Seth Hudson; and a sheet of Massachusetts currency are all owned by Winterthur, as are several of his bookplates. Bookplates made by Hurd survive for some fifty-five different families. In contrast to his own compositions, which tend to be crude, the armorial bookplates have an elegant, finished quality that derives no doubt from their being copied from a published source. The portrait of Nathaniel Hurd painted by John Singleton Copley, now at the Cleveland Museum of Art, depicts him as a burly craftsman with one arm resting on two books. One of the books is easily identified as John Guillim's *Display of Heraldry*, a major source of designs for coats of arms.

Based on the number of surviving pieces, Hurd's silver production is slight, especially when compared with his father's. Hollis French found only twenty-four examples. That Hurd worked cooperatively with other goldsmiths is suggested by the large monteith, now at Dartmouth College, that was presented to founder Eleaza Wheelock by Gov. John Wentworth and friends. It was made by Daniel Henchman, an apprentice of Jacob Hurd who married Nathaniel's sister Elizabeth. Nathaniel Hurd engraved the inscription on the monteith. Hurd's silver is comparable in quality to that of his father. Hurd never married, and he died relatively early. He left most of his estate to his brothers and sisters. For two brothers and two sisters, he left specific sums "for Silver Spoons or other piece of Plate." For two other sisters, he left specific sums "in Furniture and Money as She chuses." To nephew John Furnass, he left "my large Printing Press & some Tools in consideration for the Love I bear to him & the Genius he discovers for the same Business which I have followed & to which I intended to have brought him up." To Nathaniel Hurd Furnass, John Furnass's brother, he left "Thirteen Pounds as a Legacy for bearing myname." Witnesses to the will included silversmith Zachariah Brigden and printer Thomas Fleet, the latter a legatee.

References: French, *Jacob Hurd and His Sons.* Kane, *Dictionary,* s.v. "Hurd, Nathaniel." SCPR book 17, pp. 13–16. Fielding, *American Engravers,* nos. 739–41. David McNeely Stauffer, *American Engravers upon Copper and Steel,* 2 vols. (New York: Grolier Club, 1907), nos. 1475–79.

91
TEAPOT, 1766

H. 5 ¾" (14.6 cm), w. 9 ¼" (23.5 cm)
19 oz. 2 dwt. 13 gr. (595.0 g)

Stamps: "N. Hurd" in roman letters and script, in a rectangle, struck once on bottom.

Engraved on side: armorial device consisting of an asymmetrical cartouche with a bend between 6 crosslets (3 each side); crest of a lion passant-gardant; cartouche encircled with leafage. *Engraved on other side:* "1766". *Engraved on shoulders of body:* leafage and C scrolls with a smiling mask on spout side and a cartouche with cross-hatching on handle side. *Engraved on lid:* scalloped border and zigzag; floral border on lid around finial. *Engraved around handle sockets and spout:* floral borders.

Description: raised apple-shape body; center-punch on bottom; bottom is soldered, a common feature on this shape of teapot. Applied molded base. Applied cast S-curve spout with decorative drops below a collar and a molded tip. C-shape silver handle with ivory insulators; bottom handle socket, curved and tapered, is soldered to body in middle. Lid is flush with top of body but domed in center with pineapplelike cast finial.

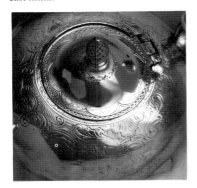

Spectrographic analysis:

	SILVER	COPPER	LEAD	GOLD
BODY SIDE	93.5	6.2	0.14	0.08
BASE	93.5	6.2	0.14	0.08
HANDLE	90.7	7.9	0.55	0.18
SPOUT	91.9	7.1	0.18	0.22
LID	94.6	4.5	0.21	0.17
FINIAL	94.5	5.1	0.18	0.04

History: The teapot has a history of ownership in the Lithgow and Howard families of Maine, both prominent in the settlement and growth of Augusta and surrounding communities. The teapot bears the Howard arms and the date 1766, the year Capt. Samuel Howard (1735–99) married Sarah Lithgow. Samuel's father, James Howard (1702–87), who solemnized the marriage, was a Scots Presbyterian from the north of Ireland. He was one of the first settlers in the Augusta area in 1754, when he was appointed military commander of Fort Western. Previously he had been on the muster roll at Fort Richmond. Together with his sons Samuel and William, he controlled the lumber trade on the upper Kennebec River. Samuel was a master mariner who purchased goods in Boston and brought them to Fort Western, where brother William sold them to settlers. Samuel is said to have made his residence in Boston a few years prior to the Revolution. Sarah and Samuel had two sons, William and Robert, and a daughter, Sarah (d. 1849), who married Thomas Bowman (d. 1837), an Augusta lawyer.

Sarah Lithgow, said to be a "woman of preeminent personal beauty," was the daughter of Col. William (d. 1798) and Sarah (Noble) Lithgow (d. 1807). Colonel Lithgow's father, Robert, was also a Scots Presbyterian who came to America from northern Ireland. William started life as a gunsmith but was active in the militia during the Indian wars and commanded both Fort Richmond and Fort Halifax. He became a large landowner and in about 1767 moved to Georgetown, Maine, near present-day Bath, where he purchased a farm and erected a "conspicuous house." He became a magistrate and judge of the Court of Common Pleas of Lincoln County, which then consisted of all of Maine east of the Androscoggin River.

Provenance: Samuel and Sarah (Lithgow) Howard; Thomas and Sarah (Howard) Bowman; Sarah (Bowman) Sherman Baker; Lydia Bowman Baker; Lydia Bowman Taft of Milton, Mass., 1917; her daughter, Mrs. Francis Woodbridge, of Falmouth, Maine, 1939.

Exhibitions: "American Church Silver," Museum of Fine Arts, Boston, 1911. Also on exhibition at the Museum of Fine Arts, Boston prior to acquisition by Winterthur.

Comments: Thomas Bowman's inventory (1837) lists "1 silver teapot and cream pitcher $25.00." See French, *Jacob Hurd and His Sons*, no. 304, for cream jug also bearing the date 1766 and engraved with the Howard arms (owned by Ray Baker Taft of Hingham, Mass.). A creamer by Nathaniel Hurd bearing the same arms, quite possibly the same one referred to by French, was advertised by Firestone & Parson in the July 1990 issue of *Antiques*. The Howard arms are also on a cann made by Peter Oliver, now in the Bayou Bend collection of the Museum of Fine Arts, Houston, and on a sugar bowl made by Jacob Hurd, now at the Minneapolis Institute of Arts. The arms may be found in Guillim, *Display of Heraldry*.

The donor was inspired to present the teapot to Winterthur following a weekend visit to the museum in 1950. Her account of the event is recorded in a letter to her mother-in-law (November 27, 1950) and in a manuscript entitled "The Enchanted Castle," a fairy tale that is clearly based on the same event. Copies of both manuscripts are in the Winterthur Archives.

References: Jay Adams (curator, Fort Western Museum, Augusta, Maine) to author, August 14, 1991. *American Church Silver*, no. 678. Bigelow, *Historic Silver*, pp. 340–41. Bolton, *Bolton's American Armory*, p. 85. Fales, *American Silver*, no. 28. French, *Jacob Hurd and His Sons*, no. 321. Guillim, *Display of Heraldry*, p. 433. James W. North, *The History of Augusta* (Augusta, Maine: Clapp & North, 1870), pp. 86–90, 96, 97, 223–24, 809, 883, 901.

60.1045 Gift of Mrs. Francis Woodbridge, 1951

𝒞 92
MILK POT, ca. 1760

H. 4 5/16" (11.0 cm), w. 4 3/16" (10.6 cm)
3 oz. 19 dwt. 16 gr. (123.9 g)

Stamps: "N. Hurd" in roman letters and script, in a rectangle, struck once on body, left of handle.

Engraved on bottom: "L/ DI" and "C/ DE" in roman letters. *Engraved on 1 side at a later date:* "M.Perit" in script. *Engraved on other side at a later date:* "E.L.G." in script.

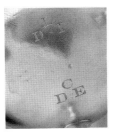

Description: raised pear-shape body with curvilinear flared rim and prominent curved pouring lip; cast C-curve handle with double reverse curves where lower handle attaches to body, scrolls at both ends, and a single sprig; 3 cast pad feet on cabriolelike stumpy legs.

Spectrographic analysis:

	SILVER	COPPER	GOLD	LEAD
BODY SIDE (BELOW INITIALS)	92.5	7.1	0.15	0.11
BODY SIDE (BELOW "M. PERIT")	92.7	6.8	0.16	0.13

History: See no. 83 for discussion of initials "L/ DI." The initials "C/ DE" may refer to Daniel (1754–?) and Elizabeth Coit. Daniel was related to the Lathrops on his mother's side. Their daughter Eliza married William C. Gilman, which may account for the initials "E.L.G." Their son Daniel Coit Gilman (1831–1908) became the founding president of Johns Hopkins University. For the inscription "M.Perit," see no. 80.

Comments: French records 2 cream jugs but not this one. One is the example with the Hickling arms in the Garvan collection at Yale University Art Gallery and the other was owned at the time by Ray Baker Taft of Hingham, Mass.

References: Buhler and Hood, *American Silver*, nos. 197, 350, for pieces with similar early histories. Fales, *American Silver*, no. 26. French, *Jacob Hurd and His Sons*. Mary E. Perkins, *Old Houses of the Antient Town of Norwich, 1660–1800* (Norwich, Conn., 1895), pp. 72, 163–64. Correspondence and research notes in object folder, Registration Division, Winterthur.

60.1046 Gift of H. F. du Pont, 1965

𝒞 93 a–c
SPOONS, ca. 1760

average L. 8 7/16" (21.4 cm)
(a) 2 oz. 3 dwt. 8 gr. (67.4 g)
(b) 2 oz. 3 dwt. 16 gr. (67.9 g)
(c) 2 oz. 1 dwt. 14 gr. (64.7 g)

Stamps: "NHurd" in slanted roman letters and script, in a surround of cyma curves and double points on top, plain on bottom, struck once on back of each handle.

Engraved on back of handle: armorial device consisting of a lion rampant standing on a heraldic wreath.

Description: elongated oval bowl with shell drop on back; rounded upturned handle with midrib on front.

Spectrographic analysis: Silver content ranges from 89.9 to 91.2 percent.

Provenance: Marshall P. Blankarn, New York City.

References: Not in French, *Jacob Hurd and His Sons*.

79.214.1–.3 Gift of Marshall P. Blankarn, 1977

𝒞 94
SPOON, ca. 1765

L. 8 3/8" (21.3 cm)
2 oz. 8 dwt. 13 gr. (75.5 g)

Stamps: "N•Hurd" in roman letters and script, in a rectangle, struck once on back of handle.

Engraved on back of handle: armorial device consisting of bare arm rising from a heraldic wreath with hand grasping a sprig of holly or oak.

Description: elongated oval bowl with single incised drop on back; rounded upturned handle with midrib on front.

Spectrographic analysis: Silver content is 92.8 percent.

Provenance: Mr. and Mrs. Stanley B. Ineson, New York City; Mr. and Mrs. Alfred E. Bissell, Wilmington, Del.

References: Belden, *Marks of American Silversmiths*, p. 242. Not in French, *Jacob Hurd and His Sons*.

62.240.1205 Gift of Mr. and Mrs. Alfred E. Bissell, 1962–63

David Jesse

ca. 1669–1705/6
Boston, Massachusetts

Like his contemporary Richard Conyers, David Jesse's career was cut short by an untimely death, and little of his work survives. E. Alfred Jones records only two pieces of church plate: a beaker in the First Church of Dorchester, Massachusetts, and a caudle cup in the First Church of Farmington, Connecticut. Boston town records mention him only in 1704, when he was chosen to serve as constable after John Noyes declined.

Most of the literature has assumed that he was born in Hartford, Connecticut, but in a search of the pertinent records, Barbara McLean Ward did not find his name. She did find, in the records of the Goldsmiths' Company in London, one "David Jesse, son of John Jesse, Citizen and Joiner of London" who became the apprentice of Alexander Roode, goldsmith of London, on March 7, 1682. Presumably, this is the same David Jesse of Boston who, like Conyers, enjoyed the advantages of training in a London shop prior to coming to America.

Jesse probably arrived in America in 1697 or 1698. In the year following his arrival he married Mary Wilson of Hartford. They became members of Boston's Brattle Street Church, where the births of five of their children are recorded. Jesse joined the Artillery Company in 1700. By the time of his death he had not acquired real property. His estate was valued at £264.9.2 and consisted of household belongings and his goldsmith's tools. The "working Tools in His Shop & Cellar" included, among other things, "Two Drawing Doggs," perhaps for making moldings for tankards, "1 Clasp Stamp," and "1 Press & 1 Glass case."

References: *Boston Newsletter,* January 13, 1705/6, for death notice. Kathryn C. Buhler, *Massachusetts Silver in the Frank L. and Louise Harrington Collection,* 2 vols. (New Haven: Yale University Press for Yale University Art Gallery, 1970), 1:29–31. Ensko, *American Silversmiths III,* pp. 77, 168. Files, Decorative Arts Photographic Collection, Winterthur Library. SCPR book 16, p. 144. Jones, *Old Silver,* pp. 114, 178. Kane, *Dictionary,* s.v. "Jesse, David." Roberts, *Artillery Company,* p. 325. Ward, "Boston Goldsmiths," pp. 160, 238–39, 353.

95
TANKARD, ca. 1698

H. 7⅝" (19.4 cm), DIAM. base 5 7/16" (13.8 cm), w. 8¾" (22.2 cm)
27 oz. 12 dwt. 18 gr. (859.6 g)

Stamps: "DI" in roman letters, with an annulet above and a pellet below, all in an oval, struck twice on upper body, left of handle, and twice on top of lid.

Engraved on upper part of handle back: "L/ IE" in shaded roman letters. *Engraved on underside of lid:* "ISAAC LOTHROP 1698/ ISAAC LOTHROP 1732/ ISAAC LOTHROP 1750/ ISAAC LOTHROP HEDGE 1808/ THOMAS RUSSELL 1900" in modern roman letters. *Scratched in solder on bottom:* "38" or "58".

Description: raised body with straight sides; applied base molding consists of an ogee topped by 3 beads; double-scored lines encircle upper body below molded rim. Raised bottom with centerpunch outside. Raised 2-step lid with centerpunch inside; crenate lip; 2 sets of double-scored lines encircle lid at edge. Cast dolphin-and-mask thumbpiece. Cast 5-segment hinge with copper pin. Raised-and-soldered hollow handle with plain angular tailpiece; notched vent. Cut-card escutcheon applied to body at juncture of lower part of handle.

Spectrographic analysis:

	SILVER	COPPER	LEAD	GOLD
BODY	95.2	4.2	0.36	0.17
BOTTOM	96.7	3.0	0.24	0.13
LID	94.1	5.2	0.30	0.12
HANDLE	91.3	8.3	0.22	0.09

History: The initials "L/ IE" refer to Isaac and Elizabeth Lothrop of Barnstable and Plymouth, Mass., who were married in 1698. Isaac (1673–1743) was a wealthy merchant and had a mansion on Court St. in Plymouth. He was a judge of the Court of Common Pleas, selectman, and colonel of the Plymouth regiment of militia. In 1732 he was sent to the Province Council. Jones records a footed beaker made by Jacob Hurd and presented by Lothrop to Plymouth Church in 1743.

The second Isaac Lothrop (1707/8–50) is the son of the first Isaac. A graduate of Harvard College (1726), he enjoyed considerable success as a merchant. His fear of an inflated currency led him to support the Silver Bank in 1740. Upon the death of the elder Isaac Lothrop, he inherited the family mansion in Plymouth. Although not as active in public service as his father, he was lieutenant colonel of the militia and in the last 2 years of his life served as a judge of the Court of Common Pleas. That he was well thought of by his contemporaries is indicated by the inscription on his gravestone, composed by Peter Oliver, and by the speeches of Israel Loring and Nicholas Sever published on the occasion of his death. His estate was valued at £23,803.

The third Isaac Lothrop, born in Plymouth in 1735, was one of the earliest Americans to become interested in preserving the history and material culture of his forebears. He was, apparently, instrumental in founding the Old Colony Club in 1769. He was also one of the incorporators of the Massachusetts Historical Society in 1794. In addition, he was representative to the Provincial Congress in 1774–75 and register of probate for Plymouth County from 1778 until his death in 1808/9. There is no record of a marriage or children.

Isaac's brother Nathaniel (1737–1828), a legatee of Isaac, married twice but had no children. A graduate of Harvard in 1756, he had a long career in the study and practice of medi-

cine. Of the several bequests in his will, one was to Isaac Lothrop Hedge, of whom virtually nothing is known except that he was a trustee of the Pilgrim Society in 1847. According to the history provided by Francis Hill Bigelow, Hedge's daughters gave the tankard to Thomas Russell in 1900.

Provenance: Isaac Lothrop (d. 1743); Col. Isaac Lothrop (d. 1750); Isaac Lothrop (1735–1808/9); Isaac Lothrop Hedge; daughters of Isaac Lothrop Hedge, who, in 1900, gave it to Thomas Russell; sold by Russell in 1923 to Francis Hill Bigelow; Brooks Reed Gallery, Boston, sold to H. F. du Pont, 1927.

Exhibitions: "American Silver: The Work of Seventeeth- and Eighteenth-Century Silversmiths," Museum of Fine Arts, Boston, 1906.

Comments: The inscription on the underside of the lid is modern and supposedly records the names of the various owners of the tankard. This is 1 of only 2 tankards known to have been made by Jesse. The other is at the Museum of Fine Arts, Boston; Buhler, *American Silver*, no. 74.

References: American Silver, MFA, no. 169, wherein the weight is given as 27 oz. 15 dwt. William T. Davis, *Ancient Landmarks of Plymouth* (Boston: A. Williams, 1883), pp. 175–77. Fales, *American Silver*, no. 9. E. B. Huntington, *A Genealogical Memoir of the Lo-Lathrop Family* (Ridgefield, Conn.: Mrs. Julia M. Huntington, 1884), pp. 55, 71, 72, 103, 104. "History of the Pilgrim Society," *NEH&GR* 1, no. 2 (April 1847): 114–25. *Sibley's Harvard Graduates*, 8:75–77, for biography of the second Isaac Lothrop.

65.1354 Gift of H. F. du Pont, 1965

Vincent Laforme

1823–93

Laforme & Brother, 1850–54
F. J. Laforme & Co., 1854–57
Boston, Massachusetts

The Laforme family left Germany about 1832 and was established in Boston by the following year. The father, Anthony, a silversmith who presumably trained his sons, was active in the craft until his death in 1846. In 1844, at age twenty-one, Vincent opened his own shop at 5 Water Street, Boston. The following year he married Sarah Fielding. In 1850 he took his brother Francis into the business, which became known as Laforme & Brother. The Census of Manufactures for 1850 indicates that the firm employed an average of five workers, owned only human-powered machinery, used 2,400 ounces of silver, and produced goods valued at $5,500. The brothers parted company in 1854. Francis stayed at 5 Water Street under the name of F. J. Laforme & Co., but by 1857 he went out of business. Vincent tried to revive the company but apparently met with little success. In 1856 he made a brief sojourn to the West, where, it is said, he planned to farm. He quickly returned to Boston and, with financial help from his brother Joseph, once again set up shop as a silversmith. Credit reports judged him a competent craftsman but a poor manager. He lacked the capital to create a profitable business, and he faced increased competition from rural-based factories. The number of independent silversmiths in Boston declined from fifteen in 1850 to four by 1891. Laforme's business consisted of work for retailers plus some bespoke work, but increasingly he turned to gilding and plating. From 1877 until his death he was listed in directories only as a plater.

His shop drawings, presentation drawings, and templates are in the Joseph P. Downs Collection of Manuscripts and Printed Ephemera at Winterthur. Laforme made silver for churches as well as for general table use. A shop drawing of a chalice gives detailed instructions on the weight and fabrication techniques to be used for each part: most were formed by spinning on a lathe. From 1850 to 1854, when Francis was part of the firm, they used the stamp "V.L. & B." Most of the time, however, Vincent stamped his pieces with a gothic "L" that was usually accompanied by a spread-winged eagle and the name of the retailer, sometimes adding "Boston," and "Pure Coin." An invoice of 1910, owned in 1972 by George C. Gebelein, has the following header: "Hallett & Smith/ Successor to V. LAFORME & Co./ Established 1833."

References: Janine Skerry, "Mechanization and Craft Structure in Nineteenth-Century Silversmithing: The Laformes of Boston" (Master's thesis, University of Delaware, 1981), for what is virtually the only source of information on Laforme.

96
BOATSWAIN'S WHISTLE, ca. 1860

L. 5 ⅛" (13.0 cm)
14 dwt. 21 gr. (23.1 g)

Stamps: "L" in script, on plate. Also on plate: "COIN", "BOSTON", and a spread-winged eagle. All stamps incuse.

Description: whistle consists of tube, sphere, and plate. Gently curved tube is rolled at mouthpiece and tapers to smaller end over sphere, with opening in top. The plate is a flat, roughly rectangular piece that is also gently curved, with an applied edge: the tube is attached on 1 side and the ball on the end; a hole in 1 end of the plate has a ring for a braided cotton cord.

Spectrographic analysis:

	SILVER	COPPER	GOLD	LEAD
PLATE	91.4	8.0	0.45	0.16

Provenance: Marshall P. Blankarn, New York City.

Comments: Fales notes that boatswain's whistles were made by Edward Long of Salem in the 1780s. Because the form changed so little over time, they are difficult to date unless they bear a maker's stamp.

References: Fales, *Early American Silver*, p. 103, fig. 101, for illustration of 4 boatswain's whistles owned by the Peabody Museum of Salem, Mass. Fennimore, *Silver and Pewter*, no. 217.

80.184 Gift of Marshall P. Blankarn, 1981

Knight Leverett

1702/3–53
Boston, Massachusetts

Knight Leverett's great-grandfather, John Leverett, was knighted by Charles II, and his uncle, also named John Leverett, was president of Harvard College from 1707 to 1724. Considering his distinguished family, Leverett's own career was mediocre. He may have served his apprenticeship with Andrew Tyler because, along with silversmith Samuel Burrill, he witnessed a deed for him in 1722, when Leverett was nineteen. He served as clerk of the market in 1728 along with silversmith Jacob Hurd, who, upon Leverett's death in 1753, became an appraiser of his estate. Leverett served as third sergeant in the Artillery Company in 1736 and as town scavenger in 1742, 1745, and 1748. Prosperity eluded Leverett, who died intestate, and his estate was declared insolvent. His goldsmith's tools were valued at only £0.26.8. He did, however, own some fishing tackle, which may tell us how he preferred to spend his time. His son John became a prosperous merchant who served in numerous civic offices. Little of Knight Leverett's silver survives. E. Alfred Jones records only one beaker made for the First Church in Bristol, Rhode Island.

References: Buhler, *Masters and Apprentices*, p. 31. Roberts, *Artillery Company*, 2:55, 437. Kane, *Dictionary*, s.v. "Leverett, Knight." Nathaniel B. Shurtleff, "Genealogical Notice of the Family of Elder Thomas Leverett," *NEH&GR* 4, no. 2 (April 1850): 121–36. SCPR book 48, pp. 459–61.

97 a, b
CANDLE BRANCHES, 1720

(a) H. 5 3/16" (13.1 cm), L. 7 1/2" (19.0 cm), W. 1 11/16" (4.3 cm)
5 oz. 14 dwt. 12 gr. (178.1 g)
(b) H. 5 3/16" (13.1 cm), L. 7 3/8" (18.7 cm), W. 1 11/16" (4.3 cm)
5 oz. 17 dwt. 22 gr. (183.4 g)
Note: dimensions include wall plate.

Stamps: "K•Leverett" in script, struck once on upper side of each drip pan and twice on each wall plate.

Engraved on underside of each drip pan: "RR/ 1720" (initials in the form of a cypher) in roman letters.

Description: S-curve candle branches made from seamed sheet silver; wall end terminates in cast fitting with moldings and a drop; cast socket, pedestal, and circular drip pan; circular wall plate with keystone-shape upper extension; loop branch holders bolted on each side to wall plate with roundheaded silver bolts.

Spectrographic analysis:

	SILVER	COPPER	LEAD	GOLD
(a)				
SOCKET	94.5	5.2	0.15	0.12
DRIP PAN	92.9	6.7	0.30	0.10
BRANCH	90.8	8.8	0.16	0.24
WALL PLATE	95.4	4.3	0.24	0.07
(b)				
SOCKET	93.3	6.4	0.16	0.11
DRIP PAN	94.8	5.0	0.17	0.07
BRANCH	94.3	5.5	0.19	0.08
WALL PLATE	95.8	3.9	0.20	0.04

History: According to the history accompanying the branches, "RR" refers to Ruth Read, wife of John Read (1679–1749), an eminent lawyer. Little is known about Ruth, but a good deal is known about her husband. Born in Fairfield, Conn., he graduated from Harvard College in 1697. For a few years he preached at various Connecticut churches but declined to become settled or take orders in any one.

During his sojourn in East Hartford, ca. 1699, Read married Ruth Talcott, a half sister of Gov. Joseph Talcott. Probably as a result of his land speculations, he became interested in the law and in 1708 was admitted to the bar by the Connecticut Court of Assistants. About 1720, the date on the candle branches, he moved to Boston, all the while retaining his country seat, "Lonetown Manor," in New Milford. He held the office of attorney general of the province intermittently for 15 years. Later he

served in the General Court and on the Governor's Council. He simplified and modernized much of the legal language used in contracts and generally is credited, along with Paul Dudley, with making the legal system suitable for a modern, expanding society. James Otis, orator and patriot, said that Read was "perhaps justly esteemed the greatest common lawyer this continent ever saw." His portrait by John Smibert hangs in the Addison Gallery of American Art, Andover, Mass.

"Leather-Jacket John," as Read became known in Boston, was something of a brilliant eccentric. Although greatly admired by many, he was hated with almost equal ferocity by others, especially those who felt they had been outwitted by him in legal proceedings. He had an extensive private practice, but he chose to travel incognito throughout the colonies, offering his services to poor clients and then dazzling the courts with his knowledge.

John and Ruth Read had a daughter, born in 1700, who was also named Ruth. In 1737 she married the Reverend Nathaniel Hunn (1708–49), a graduate of Yale College in 1731 and minister at Redding, Conn. They had no children, but the candle branches did descend in the Read family.

Throughout much of their history, the branches were attached to quillwork pictures said to have been worked by Ruth Read. The original pictures are now owned by the Cooper-Hewitt Museum and on extended loan to the Brooklyn Museum, where they are installed in the hall of the Henry Trippe House with branches simulating the originals at Winterthur. An illustration of the 2 original quillwork pictures, with their marvelous pierced crests and with the Knight Leverett branches, appears in Wallace Nutting's *Furniture of the Pilgrim Century* (p. 493).

Provenance: Ruth Read (d. 17??); various members of the Read family to George B. Read, Boston; his son Thomas Read, who sold them to Francis Hill Bigelow prior to 1911; Brooks Read Gallery, Boston, sold to H. F. du Pont, 1927. The quillwork pictures were apparently sold by Bigelow, probably through the Brooks Reed Gallery, to Natalie Blair, who bequeathed them to the Cooper-Hewitt Museum, New York City, 1952.

Exhibitions: "American Silver," Museum of Fine Arts, Boston, 1906. "American Church Silver," Museum of Fine Arts, Boston, 1911. "Courts and Colonies: The William and Mary Style in Holland, England, and America," Cooper-Hewitt Museum, New York City, 1988.

Comments: The engraved date of 1720 reminds us once again of how problematic it is to assume that such inscriptions accurately represent the year of fabrication. Knight Leverett was only 17 years old in 1720 and, most likely, would have still been serving his apprenticeship. Both candle branches are currently mounted on a single, glazed quillwork shadow box of undetermined origin. I am indebted to David McFadden for information on their twentieth-century history.

References: American Silver, MFA, nos. 171, 172, pl. 5. *American Church Silver,* nos. 704, 705, pl. 24. Reinier Baarsen et al., *Courts and Colonies: The William and Mary Style in Holland, England, and America* (New York: Cooper-Hewitt Museum, 1988), no. 132. Bigelow, *Historic Silver,* pp. 295–96, 197. Franklin B. Dexter, *Biographical Sketches of the Graduates of Yale College with Annals of the College History,* 6 vols. (New York: Henry Holt, 1885–1912), 2:429–30. Fales, *American Silver,* no. 33. Fennimore, *Silver and Pewter,* no. 186. Wallace Nutting, *Furniture of the Pilgrim Century, 1620–1720* (Framingham and Boston: Old America Co., 1921), pp. 492–93, illus. Donald C. Pierce and Hope Alswang, *American Interiors: Period Rooms at the Brooklyn Museum* (New York: Brooklyn Museum, 1983), p. 36. *Sibley's Harvard Graduates,* 4:369–78.

59.3380b, c Bequest of H. F. du Pont, 1969

Thomas Milner

ca. 1682–ca. 1745
Boston, Massachusetts

Little is known about Thomas Milner. Richard Conyers specified in his will that Milner was to have temporary use of his extensive collection of goldsmith's tools. This has led to the conclusion that Milner worked for Conyers. Milner married Mary Thwing in 1703 and Mary Reed in 1715. Goldsmith Edward Webb, in his will of 1718, refers to "my kind and trusty friend Thomas Miller of Boston Gold-smith," to whom he bequeathed £20. E. Alfred Jones found a tankard by Milner at the First Church of Chelmsford, Massachusetts. Two footed cups with a similar stamp are in private collections. All of these pieces have stamps similar to the one on the Winterthur two-handled cup. There is, however, a small one-handled cup at Yale University Art Gallery that is attributed to Milner; it has a stamp consisting of a "TM" in a shield with a crowned fleur-de-lis. Since none of the foregoing examples can be documented, all attributions to this maker should be regarded as tentative. The Museum of Fine Arts, Boston has no silver attributed to Milner, although the Metropolitan Museum of Art has a tankard with a "TM" stamp. Barbara McLean Ward, Kathryn C. Buhler, and Graham Hood note that there was a goldsmith named Thomas Mullins working in Boston from about 1708 to 1752 for whom no silver has been identified.

References: Buhler and Hood, *American Silver,* no. 98. Flynt and Fales, *Heritage Foundation,* p. 276. Jones, *Old Silver,* p. 126. Kane, *Dictionary,* s.v. "Milner, Thomas." SCPR book 21, pp. 261–62. Ward, "Boston Goldsmiths," p. 366.

98
TWO-HANDLED CUP, ca. 1740

H. 4 11/16" (11.9 cm), w. 7 9/16" (19.2 cm),
DIAM. rim 4 11/16" (11.9 cm)
13 oz. 17 dwt. 6 gr. (431.2 g)

Stamps: "TM" in roman letters, in a close fitting surround, left end round, right end indistinct, struck once on underside of body.

Engraved on side of body: "JW" in neoclassical script, with floral ornament above and below. *Engraved on underside of body:* "ILB" in shaded roman letters. *Engraved on underside of base:* "EM" in crude roman letters. *Scratched twice on underside of body:* "P83.70" (or "P33.70"). *Scratched once on underside of body:* "1781".

Description: raised circular vase form, slightly bulbous lower body, gently incurved upper body, flared rim with single-scored line defining lip; applied molded midband; centerpunch on underside. Cast, circular, stepped base; 2 cast double–C-scroll handles with sprig on upper section and scroll on lower terminal.

Spectrographic analysis:

	SILVER	COPPER	LEAD	GOLD
BASE	92.7	6.5	0.25	0.11
BODY SIDE	92.7	6.4	0.33	0.20
HANDLE 1	90.6	8.4	0.48	0.17
HANDLE 2	91.1	8.0	0.33	0.18

Provenance: Marshall P. Blankarn, New York City.

Comments: If this cup is by Milner, it would be the largest and most elegant example of his work to surface to date. With its double–C-scroll handles, it is stylistically advanced even for Milner's later years.

77.81 Gift of Marshall P. Blankarn, 1977

℘ Nathaniel Morse

ca. 1685–1748
Boston, Massachusetts

The origins of Nathaniel Morse (often spelled Mors) are unknown. He is said to have served his apprenticeship under John Coney, but the only evidence for this is a deed that Morse witnessed for Coney. He married Sarah Draper in 1710, by whom he had ten children in seventeen years. He married again in 1740. That he achieved more eminence as an engraver than as a silversmith is suggested by the *Boston Gazette,* which on his death in 1748 referred to him as "Nathaniel Morse, an ingenious Engraver." He engraved the portrait of Matthew Henry, a prominent divine, and paper money for the colony. He is called a goldsmith in the inventory of his estate. Morse made one of four flagons for the Brattle Street Church, of which he was a member, and a tankard for the North Parish of Andover, Massachusetts. A caster, chafing dish, and spout cup are at Yale University Art Gallery. Only a few other pieces are known. He died intestate with an estate valued at £688.12.0. Silversmith Samuel Edwards was one of the three appraisers.

References: Buhler, *American Silver,* pp. 131–33. Flynt and Fales, *Heritage Foundation,* p. 278. Jones, *Old Silver,* pp. 68, 347. Kane, *Dictionary,* s.v. "Morse, Nathaniel." SCPR book 41, pp. 398–400. Ward, "Boston Goldsmiths," p. 366.

℘ 99 a, b
CANDLESTICKS, ca. 1730

(a) H. 6 1/16" (15.4 cm), w. base 4" (10.2 cm)
10 oz. 12 dwt. 5 gr. (330.0 g)
(b) H. 6 1/4" (15.9 cm), w. base 3 7/8" (10.0 cm)
10 oz. 1 dwt. 14 gr. (313.5 g)

Stamps: "NM" in roman letters, in a rectangle, struck once on the side of each base.

Engraved on drip pan: armorial device consisting of a central heart, 6-point stars (3 in a column to the left and 4 across the top), and a small cross in an annulet at the lower left, all surrounded by scrolls and leaves. *Also engraved on drip pan (opposite side):* armorial device consisting of a dragon's head rising from a heraldic wreath with motto in ribbon "DEO DUCE FERRO COMITANTE" in roman letters. *Scratched on bottom:* (a) "Will [?] ghby" in script; (b) "93".

Description: octagonal stepped base with circular drip pan. Shaft rises from base with an inverted trumpetlike section, circular knop, octagonal baluster, and octagonal ring. Circular socket mounted on stepped base. Incised line encircles underside of ring and lower part of socket on (a). Shafts cast in 2 vertical sections and joined. Base cast in 1 piece and joined to shaft in trumpetlike section (seam visible).

Spectrographic analysis:

	SILVER	COPPER	LEAD	GOLD
(a)				
BASE	96.6	7.1	0.24	0.09
SOCKET	92.1	7.5	0.35	0.07
(b)				
BASE	93.0	6.7	0.22	0.13
SOCKET	92.5	7.1	0.29	0.12

History: The first armorial device described is the arms of Peter Faneuil (1700–1743), the wealthy (by American standards for the time) merchant and philanthropist of Boston. They are found on his box tomb in the Old Granary Burying Ground. Peter was not exactly a self-made man. He inherited much of his wealth from his uncle Andrew Faneuil, a merchant and one of the wealthier members of Boston's French Huguenot community. (Andrew owned 8,000 oz. of plate.) Peter and his sister Mary lived in Andrew's mansion, which they decorated with fashionable household furnishings. Among other things, Peter ordered glass, china, napkins, tablecloths, and silver made to his order. He asked for silver spoons and 3-pronged forks engraved with the Faneuil arms, saying, "Let them be very neat and handsome." He sent a portion of a candle and asked for candlesticks to be of a size that would fit, adding, "Let them be very neatly made and by the best workmen: let my arms be engraved on each of them." The orders for silver were placed in London. According to Robert Ensko, the second armorial device represents the Caulfield family, although this has yet to be verified. The motto translates as "God my leader, my sword, and my companion."

Peter Faneuil is best known today for Faneuil Hall in Boston, which he constructed at his own expense in 1742 as a gift to the town for use as a market and a meeting hall. The architect, John Smibert, also painted his portrait, which is now owned by the Massachusetts Historical Society. Faneuil's geniality and reputation for being the "jolly bachelor" belie his physical appearance. He died at age 42 and was described by the attending physician as "a fat, squat, lame (man), hip short, [who] went with high heeled shoe" but who also "in my opinion [was] a great loss to this Town . . . I think by what I have heard has done more charitable deeds than any man yet ever lived in this town." Town officials voted that "a hatchment with the arms of Peter Faneuil Esq. be placed at the west end of Faneuil Hall at the towns expence and that the bell on the said house be tolled from one o'clock until the funeral is over."

Faneuil's estate was valued at £44,451, not counting his extensive investments abroad. His inventory is a veritable shopping list for the best household furnishings of the day. It includes 6 "Lignumvitae chocolate cupps lined with silver," "12 carved vineered chairs and a couch," a pier glass valued at £100, "1 copper tea table, cups, saucers, tea-pot-stand, bowl, and sugar dish," "3 alabaster bowls and stand," "3 sconces with arms," "a parcell of Jewells £1,490," and 1,400 oz. of plate valued at £2,122, which

included a "large handsome chamber pot." Faneuil also owned "2 Houses in Occupation of Jacob Hurd" valued at £3,000 plus houses occupied by Daniel Henchman and Joseph Webb valued at £2,000.

Provenance: Peter Faneuil (d. 1743); Dorothy Draper Hamlen through Parke-Bernet Galleries, November 30, 1946, to Robert Ensko, Inc., New York City; sold to H. F. du Pont, December 1946.

Comments: There are distinct differences between these 2 sticks. Details on the shaft and socket of (b) are coarser than those on (a), as if (b) had been cast from a mold made from (a). See especially the undersides of the octagonal rings as well as profiles of the 2 sockets. Several obvious pits on (b).

References: Robert Ensko to H. F. du Pont, December 2, 1946, dealer correspondence, Winterthur Archives. Fales, *American Silver,* no. 115. Fennimore, *Silver and Pewter,* no. 181. Edward Wenham, "The Silversmiths of Early Boston," *Antiquarian* 17, no. 1 (July 1931): 31–34. Abram English Brown, *Faneuil Hall and Faneuil Hall Market; or, Peter Faneuil and His Gift* (Boston: Lee and Shepard, 1901).

61.801.1, 61.801.2 Bequest of H. F. du Pont, 1969

Ebenezer Moulton

1768–1824
Boston and Newburyport, Massachusetts

The Moulton family of Newburyport produced many silversmiths, starting with Ebenezer's grandfather William (1720–ca. 1793); his granduncle Joseph (1724–95); his father, Joseph (1744–1816); his three brothers, William (1772–1861), Enoch (1780–1820), and Abel (1784–1840); and his nephew Joseph (1814–1903). Joseph sold the firm in 1860 to Towle & Jones, which later became Towle Silversmiths. With the repetition of given names among the Moultons and the frequent omission of a first initial in the stamps, considerable confusion has arisen in the identification of stamps.

Ebenezer worked for much of his career in Boston before returning to Newburyport about 1820. While in Boston he advertised "an extensive assortment of English made Silver Plate . . . Jeweler's Tools, Flatting Mills." Even in Newburyport his shop was equipped with six counter cases plus eight other cases for the display of goods, which included 1,027 ounces of wrought silver. The Museum of Fine Arts, Boston owns a pitcher that is documented in the records of Old South Church as having been made by Moulton. It was presented to Isaac Harris for helping to save the church during a fire in 1810.

References: Buhler, *American Silver*, no. 462. *Columbian Sentinel* (Boston): December 5, 1798; January 8, 1800; July 2, 1800. Stephen Decatur, "The Moulton Silversmiths," *Antiques* 39, no. 1 (January 1941): 14–17. Flynt and Fales, *Heritage Foundation*, p. 281.

100
PORRINGER, ca. 1800

H. 2 ⁷⁄₁₆" (6.2 cm), w. 8 ½" (21.6 cm)
8 oz. 18 dwt. 22 gr. (278.3 g)

Stamps: "MOULTON" in roman letters, an incuse stamp with traces of the surround, struck once on back of handle.

Engraved on face of handle: "NLW" in neoclassical script.

Description: raised circular bowl with bulbous sides and flared rim; bottom domed in center; centerpunch on underside; cast handle pierced in keyhole pattern with 11 voids; handle set at rakish angle.

Spectrographic analysis:

	SILVER	COPPER	LEAD	GOLD
BOWL	87.3	12.2	0.27	0.10
HANDLE	86.6	12.9	0.27	0.12

Provenance: Marshall P. Blankarn, New York City.

78.144 Gift of Marshall P. Blankarn, 1978

101 a–f
SPOONS, ca. 1800

(a) L. 5 ¾" (14.6 cm), 9 dwt. 9 gr. (14.6 g)
(b) L. 5 ¹¹⁄₁₆" (14.5 cm), 8 dwt. 12 gr. (13.2 g)
(c) L. 6" (15.2 cm), 9 dwt. 5 gr. (14.3 g)
(d) L. 8 ⁷⁄₁₆" (21.4 cm), 1 oz. 2 dwt. 12 gr. (34.9 g)
(e) L. 7 ⁹⁄₁₆" (19.2 cm), 19 dwt. 9 gr. (30.8 g)
(f) L. 9" (22.9 cm), 1 oz. 16 dwt. 4 gr. (56.1 g)

Stamps: "MOULTON" in roman letters, an incuse stamp with occasional traces of the surround, struck once on back of each handle.

Engraved on front of handle: (a) "P.R" in shaded roman letters, in a bright-cut oval border; (b) "G/ ER" in shaded roman letters, in a bright-cut oval border; (c) "BM" in shaded roman letters; (d) bright-cut oval medallion with no inscription; (e) "MC/ to/ AEG" in foliate script; (f) "LN" in foliate script.

Description: (a) and (b) have pointed oval bowls with incised triangular drops on back; pointed downturned handles; (c) has pointed oval bowl with incised triangular drop on back; coffin-end downturned handle; (d) has pointed oval bowl with incised drop on back; pointed downturned handle; (e) and (f) have pointed oval bowls with swage-formed oval drop on back; coffin-end downturned handles.

Spectrographic analysis: Silver content ranges from 88.2 percent to 92.5 percent.

Provenance: Mr. and Mrs. Stanley B. Ineson, New York City; Mr. and Mrs. Alfred E. Bissell, Wilmington, Del.

References: Belden, *Marks of American Silversmiths*, p. 304.

62.240.428–.430, .1287, .1289, and .1312 Gift of Mr. and Mrs. Alfred E. Bissell, 1962–63

Peter Oliver

1682–1712
Boston, Massachusetts

Peter Oliver was one of a group of capable but unfortunate Boston goldsmiths who died young and whose output is represented by only a few examples. He was a great-grandson of Thomas Oliver, patriarch of the Olivers, who came to Boston in 1632. His father, John Oliver, was a merchant. His brother, also named John, was a cooper. Silversmith John Coney, Peter's "trusty friend," was appointed his guardian upon the death of his mother in 1693. John and Peter both married daughters of Increase Mather; John married Hannah, and Peter married Jerusha. In his will Peter bequeathed £5 each to Increase and Cotton Mather. Jerusha died within two years of their marriage, and Peter then married Hopestill Wensley, daughter of Elizabeth Wensley, donor to the Second Church of the great flagon in the following entry. In his will dated April 24, 1712, Peter bequeathed to Hopestill "All my whole Estate real and personal, whether Debts moneys household stuff plate Goods chattels Shop furniture or whatsoever." The will was witnessed by Sarah Knight, author of the famous journal describing her trip in 1704 from Boston to New York. Peter Oliver died soon after making his will, and Samuel Sewall attended his funeral on April 29, 1712. This is the only mention of him by the diarist. It says something about Oliver's standing in the community that Sewall referred to him as "Mr. Peter Oliver."

References: Kane, *Dictionary*, s.v. "Oliver, Peter." SCPR book 17, pp. 449–50. Ward, "Boston Goldsmiths," pp. 366–67. W. H. Whitmore, "The Oliver Family," *NEH&GR* 19, no. 2 (April 1865): 100–106.

102
FLAGON, 1711

H. 11 ⅞" (30.2 cm), DIAM. base 6 ⁷⁄₁₆" (16.4 cm), w. 8 ¹¹⁄₁₆" (22.1 cm)
47 oz. 5 dwt. 21 gr. (1471.0 g)

Stamps: "PO" in roman letters, in a heart, struck on upper body, left of handle, and in center of bottom.

Engraved on front of body opposite handle: "Mrs. Elizabeth Wensley / To the Second Church / of Christ In / Boston / 1711" in script, all enclosed in a leafy cartouche with tulip blossom at the top.

Description: raised body with straight sides and domed bottom; single bands of convex molding applied to body at rim, about ½" below rim and about 1" above applied foot; no centerpunch in bottom (may be covered by maker's stamp).

Flared molded applied foot. Raised lid consists of cylindrical lower section (to extend height of body) with applied convex moldings above and below; upper section is a 2-step flat-top lid with cast reel finial. Cast 2-cusp thumbpiece. Cast 5-segment hinge. Raised-and-soldered hollow S-curve handle with tapered ends; notched vent.

Spectrographic analysis:

	SILVER	COPPER	LEAD	GOLD
BODY	92.4	7.1	0.30	0.08
BOTTOM	95.1	4.6	0.32	0.05
FOOT	93.9	5.7	0.25	0.15
LID	94.7	5.1	0.21	0.05
THUMBPIECE	94.3	5.3	0.28	0.10
HANDLE	95.2	5.3	0.27	0.07

History: Elizabeth Wensley, born in 1641, was the daughter of William Paddy of Plymouth. She married John Wensley, mariner, and had at least 2 daughters, Mercy and Hopestill, the latter of whom married Peter Oliver, goldsmith. Oliver made this tankard probably as a result of his mother-in-law's bequest. According to the King's Chapel epitaphs, Elizabeth Wensley died February 3, 1710/11.

Elizabeth Wensley lived on property adjoining that of John Foster, whose daughters Lydia and Sarah married Edward and Thomas Hutchinson, respectively. The Hutchinsons presented 2 large communion dishes made by Edward Winslow to the Second Church in 1711 (nos. 138, 139). E. Alfred Jones reproduces a list of plate owned by the Second Church from a document dated March 2, 1729/30. The list includes 11 cups, 3 bowls, 12 tankards, 4 dishes, and 5 flagons. Jones observes that many pieces had disappeared by the time he conducted his survey; this flagon is the only silver by Oliver that he recorded.

Provenance: The Second Church in Boston sold the flagon, along with the 2 dishes donated by the Hutchinsons, to H. F. du Pont in 1966. The sale was attempted earlier but was blocked by a lawsuit on behalf of a disgruntled parishioner.

Exhibitions: "American Church Silver," Museum of Fine Arts, Boston, 1911. "Masterpieces of American Silver," Virginia Museum of Fine Arts, Richmond, 1960.

Comments: Although originally a secular form traditionally used for drinking alcoholic beverages, the flagon became a liturgical vessel for serving communion wine in certain reformed congregations. It does not appear in America as a secular drinking vessel—at least not in silver.

References: American Church Silver, no. 806. John Booth, "Memoirs of a Magician's Ghost," *Linking Ring* (June 1974): 44–46, for an account of the litigation surrounding the sale. Thomas Bridgman, *Memorials of the Dead in Boston, Containing Exact Transcripts of Inscriptions on the Sepulchral Monuments in the Kings Chapel Burying Ground* (Boston: B. D. Mussey, 1853), p. 192. Buck, *Old Plate*, p. 166. *Masterpieces of American Silver*, no. 99. Hood, *American Silver*, pp. 83, 85. Jones, *Old Silver*, p. 38, pl. 16.

66.1052 Bequest of H. F. du Pont, 1969

103
PORRINGER, 1703–12

DIAM. bowl 5 9/16" (14.1 cm), H. 2 1/8" (5.4 cm), W. 8" (20.3 cm)
7 OZ. 8 dwt. 16 gr. (230.7 g)

Stamps: "PO" in roman letters, in a heart, struck once on body, left of handle below rim.

Engraved on front of handle: a talbot's head erased.

Description: raised circular bowl with bulging sides and straight rim; bottom domed in center; centerpunch inside and on bottom; cast handle pierced in geometric pattern with 10 voids.

Spectrographic analysis:

	SILVER	COPPER	LEAD	GOLD
SIDE	88.9	10.8	0.28	0.12
BOTTOM	89.3	10.2	0.29	0.15
HANDLE	89.7	9.6	0.26	0.09

Provenance: Frederick T. Widmer, Boston, sold to H. F. du Pont, April 1930.

Comments: The same armorial device appeared on a "fashionable silver spoon of Mr. Coney's make, crest with Talbotts (or Dog's) head erased" (lost spoon advertisement, *New England Journal* [November 10, 1729], as cited in Dow, *Arts and Crafts*). In a letter to H. F. du Pont, April 23, 1930, Widmer noted that "the porringer is right in every respect, for we know the family well where it has always been." Regrettably, he did not specify the family.

References: Dow, *Arts and Crafts*, p. 43.

65.1352 Gift of H. F. du Pont, 1965

Saunders Pitman

1732–1804
Providence, Rhode Island

Virtually nothing is known about the early years of Saunders Pitman, son of Samuel and Rebecca Pitman. On April 2, 1796, he advertised in the *Providence Gazette* that "he makes and sells, at his Shop, a few Doors North of the State-House, Gold and Silversmith's Ware, amongst which are the following Articles: Gold Necklaces from 7 to 10 Dollars, large and small Silver Spoons, and a Variety of the newest fashioned plated Shoe and Knee Buckles, plated Bridle Bitts in the newest Fashions, warranted to be superior for Service to any imported; also two Sets of elegant plated Mountings for Chaise . . . Wanted, as an apprentice to the above Business, an honest industrious Lad, about 14 Years of Age." Pitman formed partnerships with Nehemiah Dodge (ca. 1790) and Samuel Dorrance (ca. 1795–1800). His daughter Mary married Dorrance in 1803. Pitman served in the elected office of town scavenger from 1777 to 1784.

References: Flynt and Fales, *Heritage Foundation*, p. 300. Prime cards, Winterthur.

104
CREAM POT, ca. 1790

H. 7 ⅜" (20.0 cm), w. 5 ¼" (13.3 cm)
5 oz. 5 dwt. 16 gr. (164.4 g)

Stamps: "PITMAN" in roman letters, in a serrated rectangle, struck once on underside of base.

Engraved on body under pouring lip: "FMR" in foliate script, in a shield. *Engraved on each side of body:* inverted V pattern of leafy strands.

Description: raised helmet-shape body with large pouring lip; applied molded rim; high, looped, fluted handle. Body mounted on tall narrow stem that spreads out to a circular plinth mounted on a square base; bottom edges of base arc slightly. Wheelwork wavy decoration impressed on body below rim and on sides of plinth; dart motif and striations impressed in body below rim; double-scored lines on each side of base.

Spectrographic analysis:

	SILVER	COPPER	LEAD	GOLD
BODY SIDE	90.9	8.7	0.23	0.13
BASE	91.9	7.7	0.29	0.13
HANDLE	92.9	6.8	0.21	0.10

Provenance: Marshall P. Blankarn, New York City.

79.193 Gift of Marshall P. Blankarn, 1979

105 a–d
SPOONS, ca. 1795

(a) L. 7" (17.8 cm) , 19 dwt. 11 gr. (30.3 g)
(b) L. 9 ¼" (23.5 cm), 1 oz. 11 dwt. 8 gr. (48.8 g)
(c) L. 9 ¼" (23.5 cm), 1 oz. 9 dwt. 6 gr. (45.5 g)
(d) L. 9 ¹⁵⁄₁₆" (25.2 cm), 1 oz. 18 dwt. 14 gr. (60.0 g)

Stamps: "PITMAN" in roman letters, in a serrated rectangle, struck once on back of each handle.

Engraved on front of handle: (a) "TAA" (sideways) in foliate script, with a bright-cut border; (b) "HC" in foliate script, in a bright-cut border; (c) "T/ DU" in roman letters; (d) "RW" in roman letters, in a bright-cut border.

Description: pointed oval bowl with swage-formed pointed drop on back; pointed down-turned handle.

Spectrographic analysis: Silver content ranges from 88.6 to 90.7 percent.

Provenance: Mr. and Mrs. Stanley B. Ineson, New York City; Mr. and Mrs. Alfred E. Bissell, Wilmington, Del.

References: Belden, *Marks of American Silversmiths*, p. 338 a.

62.240.1337–.1340 Gift of Mr. and Mrs. Alfred E. Bissell, 1962–63

John Potwine

ca. 1698–1792
Boston, Massachusetts
Hartford, Coventry, and East Windsor,
Connecticut

John Potwine was the son of Huguenot physician John Potwine and his wife Sarah (Hill) Potwine. The elder Potwine was in Boston by 1688. In the next decade he met and married Sarah but died soon after the birth of his son John. The father bequeathed to his son his "silver-headed cane, one gold ring, and my Chirurgeon's Chest." The younger Potwine's master remains unknown, although there is circumstantial evidence to suggest that it was William Cowell. In 1721 Potwine married Mary Jackson. Much of his silver was produced over the next fifteen years, prior to his move to Connecticut. Early in his career, Potwine expanded his business to include fancy textiles and other luxury goods. He moved to Hartford about 1736 and ran a fancy-goods store in partnership with Charles Whiting. Later he moved to Coventry and established a store with an even wider range of goods. It is believed that he stopped making silver as his stores flourished. An account book survives for 1752–53, his last year in Hartford and his first year in Coventry. No silver production is mentioned, but the account book does reveal that he sent Spanish dollars to silversmith Daniel Henchman in Boston. In 1771, five years after the death of his first wife, Potwine married widow Elizabeth Moseley. His son Thomas graduated from Yale and later became pastor of the church in what is now East Windsor.

Potwine spent his later years with Thomas, who described his father as "one who was all Grace." Indeed, Potwine befriended ministers all over Connecticut and even loaned them money. He owned Jonathan Edwards's important book *A Careful and Strict Enquiry into the Modern Prevailing Notions of That Freedom of Will Which Is Supposed to Be Essential to Moral Agency, Vertue and Vice, Reward and Punishment, Praise and Blame* (1754), which was inscribed by the author to "my dear friend John Potwine." It is not surprising, therefore, that he made silver for churches in Boston, Charlestown, and Weston, Massachusetts, as well as for churches in Durham and East Windsor, Connecticut. His tall and elegant flagon, the gift of Mary Lemon to the First Church of Charlestown, is now at Yale University Art Gallery, and a communion dish, given by Capt. Eleazer Dorby to New South Church in Boston, is now at the Museum of Fine Arts, Boston. The Metropolitan Museum of Art owns a lighthouse coffeepot by Potwine. A modest amount of his work survives, much of it of the highest quality.

References: Buhler, *American Silver*, no. 136. Buhler and Hood, *American Silver*, no. 125. Flynt and Fales, *Heritage Foundation*, pp. 303–4. Jones, *Old Silver*, pp. 38, 73, 123, 153, 165, 486. Kane, *Dictionary*, s.v. "Potwine, John." Elizabeth B. Potwine, "John Potwine, Silversmith of Massachusetts and Connecticut," *Antiques* 28, no. 3 (September 1935): 106–9. Ward, "Boston Goldsmiths," p. 367.

106
CHAFING DISH, ca. 1730

H. 3 %6" (9.1 cm), DIAM. bowl 6 1/16" (15.4 cm), w. (incl. handle) 11 ¾" (29.9 cm) 13 oz. 11 dwt. 6 gr. (421.9 g) (without wooden feet)

Stamps: "I:Potwine" in roman letters and script, in a rectangular surround with upper wavy edge, struck once on underside of body.

Description: raised circular body, bowl-like with flat angled rim, double-scored on inner edge, circular depression in center (for coals), small circular hole in center (for shaft of grille); decorative cutouts encircle side of body: symmetrical foliate pattern alternating with groups of 5 arched vertical slots (the latter occur over the supports); decorative cutouts encircle side of depressed center: alternating long and short horizontal rectangles; 3 equidistant cast supports attached to rim and underside, each consisting of a strap with C scroll on lower portion (with an integral silver screw for attaching to wooden-ball feet) and fluted C scroll on upper side attached to rim of body. Handle socket attached to support; boldly turned, hardwood handle with baluster and ball motifs. Cast circular grille set loosely into bottom of body; short capstan finial in center, encircled by cutout swirl pattern; outer ring of small circular and triangular voids; silver screw extends from center of underside; hardwood flattened-ball feet.

Spectrographic analysis:

	SILVER	COPPER	LEAD	GOLD
BODY SIDE	91.8	7.6	0.43	0.06
UNDERSIDE	93.9	5.6	0.39	0.05
HANDLE SOCKET	98.1	1.2	0.08	0.07
GRILLE	81.7	17.5	0.17	0.06

History: According to Francis Hill Bigelow, the chafing dish was probably owned by Col. Francis Brinley (1690–1765) of Roxbury, Mass., who also owned the tankard by Richard Conyers (no. 39). The Brinley house, built on a hill overlooking Boston, was said to resemble the family seat at Datchet, near Windsor, in England. Its plan was H shape, in the manner of many sixteenth-century English manor houses, and it stood, according to one writer, "in the midst of a large domain, of park and wooded hills, and presented a picture of grandeur and stateliness not common in the New World. There were colonnades and a vestibule whose massive mahogany doors, studded with silver, opened into a wide hall, whose tesellated floors sparkled under the light of a lofty dome of richly painted glass." By all accounts Datchet House, as it was called, was a splendid mansion. It passed out of the Brinley family during the 1770s. The Brinleys were Loyalists, and most of the children went into exile rather than adapt to new conditions. The inventory of Col. Francis Brinley's estate lists a pair of "Chaffin dishes" valued at £14. One is at Winterthur; the other is thought to be the one now owned by the Cleveland Museum of Art.

Provenance: Francis Brinley (d. 1765) of Roxbury, Mass.; his son Nathaniel (1733–1814), who married Catherine Braddock; their son Robert (1774–?), who married Elizabeth Pitts; their son Nathaniel (1809–?), who married Sarah Elizabeth Bridge. In her will, proved July 16, 1879, Sarah Elizabeth (Bridge) Brinley appointed Daniel S. Richardson and George F. Richardson as executors. They purchased some of the household furnishings. Mrs. George F. Richardson, Lowell, Mass., sold the chafing dish to Francis Hill Bigelow in 1919. Brooks Reed Gallery, Boston, sold to H. F. du Pont, June 1927.

Exhibitions: "American Church Silver," Museum of Fine Arts, Boston, 1911 (lent by Mrs. George F. Richardson).

Comments: More than 20 chafing dishes survive, most of them made in Boston. The form was more popular in France than in England. The number of French Huguenot families in Boston may account for the large number of chafing dishes commissioned there.

References: American Church Silver, no. 840. Fales, *American Silver,* no. 51. Fennimore, *Silver and Pewter,* no. 74. Mrs. Russell Hastings, "Two Chafing Dishes by Peter Van Dyck," *Antiques* 30, no. 4 (October 1936): 152–55, for chafing dishes. Marvin D. Schwartz, *Collector's Guide to American Antique Silver* (New York: Doubleday, 1975), fig. 21. For references concerning Brinley family, see no. 39.

65.1347 Gift of H. F. du Pont, 1965

107
SPOON, ca. 1730

L. 7 1/16" (17.9 cm)
1 oz. 14 gr. (32.0 g)

Stamps: "I:Potwine" in roman letters and script, in a rectangular surround with upper wavy edge, struck once on back of handle.

Engraved on back of handle: "MS" in shaded roman letters.

Description: oval bowl with swage-formed rat-tail and single rounded drop on back; rounded upturned handle with long midrib on front.

Spectrographic analysis: Silver content is 92.2 percent.

Provenance: Mr. and Mrs. Stanley B. Ineson, New York City; Mr. and Mrs. Alfred E. Bissell, Wilmington, Del.

References: Belden, *Marks of American Silversmiths,* p. 343 a.

62.240.1344 Gift of Mr. and Mrs. Alfred E. Bissell, 1962–63

Jonathan Reed

ca. 1695–1742
Boston, Massachusetts

Little is known about Jonathan Reed. He died intestate with a personal estate valued at £428.10.6. Apparently he owned no real property. The probate records refer to him as a goldsmith, and the inventory of his shop, valued at £171.18.6, included a large glass showcase, one thirty-five-pound spoon teast, and three spoon punches. Silversmith Nathaniel Morse was one of the appraisers.

Only a few pieces are attributed to Reed: two cups made for the New Brick Church, Boston, 1723/24; a pair of spoons at the Museum of Fine Arts, Boston; a spoon at Yale University Art Gallery; a spoon at Deerfield; and the porringer in the following entry.

References: Buhler, *American Silver*, p. 164. Buhler and Hood, *American Silver*, no. 228. Flynt and Fales, *Heritage Foundation*, pp. 308–9. Jones, *Old Silver*, pp. 36–37. Kane, *Dictionary*, s.v. "Reed, Jonathan."

108
PORRINGER, ca. 1730

DIAM. bowl 5 9/16" (14.1 cm), H. 2 1/16" (5.2 cm), W. 8 3/8" (21.3 cm)
8 oz. 8 gr. (249.3 g)

Stamps: "IR" in roman letters, in a shield, struck once on outside of rim.

Engraved on upper surface of handle (facing out): "F+I/ to/ S+I" in roman letters and script. *Engraved on side of body:* "Winthrop Pyemont/ from his Aunt/ Augusta Clinton Winthrop" in later script. *Engraved on underside of body:* "once belonging to the Johannets" in later script. *Scratched on underside of body:* "oz/ 8 [?]/ 4" in script.

Description: raised circular bowl with bulging sides and slightly angled rim; bottom domed in center; centerpunch inside and outside; cast handle pierced in geometric pattern with 10 voids.

Spectrographic analysis:

	SILVER	COPPER	LEAD	GOLD
BODY SIDE	91.3	8.1	0.35	0.16
HANDLE	92.6	6.9	0.38	0.14

History: The Johonnots were one of the many French Protestant families forced to flee their country following the revocation of the Edict of Nantes by Louis XIV in 1685. Daniel Johonnot (1668–1748), who arrived in Boston in 1686, was the founder of the family in America. On his death in 1748, he left an estate valued at £15,478, proving that he had indeed prospered in the New World. His sons Andrew, Zachariah, and Francis also prospered as distillers and merchants. The last 2 belonged to the Sons of Liberty during the troubles with England, brother Andrew having died in 1760. Andrew's son Peter married Katherine Dudley, daughter of Col. William Dudley, which may explain Peter's Loyalist sympathies. Peter went to Halifax with General Gage when Boston was evacuated and later to England, where he lived out his life.

The genealogy of the Johonnot family is complicated by the repetition of the same given names; there are many Francises and Susannahs. Because one inscription suggests the line of descent, we can attribute original ownership with some assurance. It is likely that "F+I/ to/ S+I" refers to Francis Johonnot (1709–75) and his daughter Susannah (1755–1839). The inventory of Francis Johonnot's estate includes, among his other plate, 3 porringers, 1 of which may well be this one.

Provenance: Francis Johonnot (1709–1775); his daughter Susannah (Johonnot) Oliver (d. 1839); her daughter Susan (Oliver) Heard; her daughter Francis Maria, who married Gen. Grenville T. Winthrop; Augusta Clinton Winthrop; her nephew Winthrop Pyemont; purchased by Francis Hill Bigelow from Crichton Brothers, London; Brooks Reed Gallery, Boston, sold to H. F. du Pont, 1927.

Comments: The porringer is accompanied by a cover made by Edward Winslow (no. 142), which also bears the Winthrop/Pyemont inscription and the reference to the Johonnot family. The stamp on the porringer is incomplete. Reed's stamp usually includes a crown over the initials. See also the porringer by William Breed (no. 8) with initials "I/ A✳E." A porringer made by John Burt, now in a private collection, bears eighteenth-century engraved initials "FI/ to/ CI" (see Decorative Arts Photographic Collection files, Winterthur Library). Both the Breed and Burt porringers may have been owned by the Johonnot family.

References: Andrew Johonnot, "The Johonnot Family," *NEH&GR* 6, no. 4 (October 1852): 357–66; 7, no. 2 (April 1853): 141–44.

65.1348 Gift of H. F. du Pont, 1965

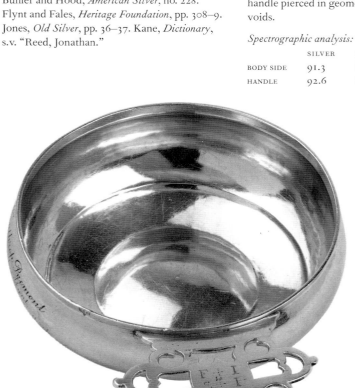

Paul Revere, Sr.

1702–54
Boston, Massachusetts

Born Apollos Rivoire in a small village near Bordeaux, France, the senior Paul Revere was the son of Isaac and Serenne (Lambert) Rivoire, a Protestant family in a nation that had turned increasingly hostile to its Huguenot population throughout the seventeenth century, especially since Louis XIV's revocation of the Edict of Nantes in 1685. At age thirteen Apollos was sent to his uncle Simon Rivoire, on Guernsey in the English Channel. Simon arranged to send him to Boston. Upon arrival in Boston early in 1716, Apollos went to live with silversmith John Coney as his apprentice for a period of ten years. By the time of Coney's death in 1722, Apollos was known as Paul Rivoire and shortly after that as Paul Revere. As he still owed his master more than three years of service, appraisers valued the unexpired time at £30, but the estate actually received £40. Perhaps Revere purchased his freedom himself; in the following year he visited Guernsey, thereby suggesting that he was free. In 1729 Revere married Deborah Hitchborn, whose father was a joiner but whose business holdings included Hitchborn's Wharf. In 1730 Revere advertised "Paul Revere, Goldsmith, is removed from Capt Pitts at the Town Dock to North End over against Col Hutchinson." Revere and his wife were members of the New Brick Church. Their second child, the Paul Revere known to history, was born on January 1, 1735.

A modest number of the senior Revere's works survive, at least half of which are owned by the Museum of Fine Arts, Boston. Among the latter are a teapot bearing the Foster arms, a chafing dish, and a saucepan. Six porringers are attributed to him, as is a lighthouse coffeepot at the National Museum of American History. He used several different stamps, one of which ("P REVERE") was also used by his son.

References: Buhler, *American Silver*, p. 181, nos. 145–54. Forbes, *Paul Revere*, chaps. 1, 2. Kane, *Dictionary*, s.v. "Revere, Paul, Sr." Patrick M. Leehey, "Reconstructing Paul Revere: An Overview of His Ancestry, Life, and Work," in *Paul Revere—Artisan*, pp. 15–39.

109
TANKARD, 1730–50

H. 8 ½" (21.0 cm), w. 7 ⅝" (19.4 cm)
26 oz. 16 dwt. 16 gr. (894.7 g)

Stamps: "PR" in roman letters, in a crowned shield, struck once on upper body, left of handle; once on underside; and once on bezel. Intaglio "WS" on underside of mask tailpiece.

Engraved on back of handle: "C/ J∗N" in shaded roman letters.

Description: raised body with straight sides; applied base molding consists (from bottom up) of a flat vertical section, a broad torus molding, a narrow scotia molding, and a double-bead molding; narrow applied midband; applied rim consisting of a torus molding over 2 narrow step moldings. Centerpunch obscured by stamp on underside. Raised stepped flat-dome lid with cast bell-shape finial soldered to lid; single-scored line encircles edge of rim; edge of lid folds over rim of body. Cast thumbpiece, S curve in profile, with ram's horn scrolls attaches to a cast 5-segment hinge with pendant drop. Raised-and-soldered hollow S-curve handle with a broad oval drop on body below upper handle attachment; oval plate on body at lower handle attachment; tailpiece cast in a lion mask; circular vent.

Spectrographic analysis:

	SILVER	COPPER	LEAD	GOLD
BODY SIDE	91.7	7.8	0.29	0.09
UNDERSIDE	92.1	7.4	0.28	0.10
LID	91.8	8.0	0.08	0.16
BASE MOLDING	93.4	6.9	0.10	0.24
THUMBPIECE	92.8	6.4	0.17	0.23

Provenance: Robert Ensko, Inc., New York City, sold to H. F. du Pont, January 1931.

Exhibitions: "Paul Revere—Artisan, Businessman, and Patriot: The Man Behind the Myth," Museum of Our National Heritage, Lexington, Mass., 1988–89.

Comments: Initials "WS," cast into back of tailpiece, are also found on an identical mask on a tankard made by Boston silversmith William Simpkins for Thomas Cutts (Moore collection, Providence College). This suggests that Simpkins may have supplied tankard tailpieces to other Boston silversmiths.

References: Fales, *American Silver*, no. 36. *Paul Revere—Artisan*, p. 148.

61.616 Gift of H. F. du Pont, 1965

110
SPOON, 1730–50

L. 7 9/16" (19.2 cm)
1 oz. 12 dwt. 1 gr. (49.8 g)

Stamps: "PR" in roman letters, in a crowned shield, struck once on back of spoon.

Engraved on back of handle: "S:B" in shaded roman letters.

Description: elongated oval bowl with swage-formed plain rattail on back; rounded upturned handle with pronounced midrib on front.

Spectrographic analysis: Silver content is 92.0 percent.

Provenance: Mr. and Mrs. Stanley B. Ineson, New York City; Mr. and Mrs. Alfred E. Bissell, Wilmington, Del.

References: Belden, *Marks of American Silversmiths*, p. 352 a.

62.240.1400 Gift of Mr. and Mrs. Alfred E. Bissell, 1962–63

Paul Revere, Jr.

1734–1818
Boston, Massachusetts

Son of the immigrant silversmith of the same name, the younger Paul Revere had a remarkable career by any measure. He not only became a successful artisan who left the largest single body of work of any eighteenth-century American silversmith but also responded to the great changes occurring in his world by participating in events and enterprises that profoundly changed American society. His life is the prototypical American success story. Trained in a traditional craft by his father, he started his career in the accepted manner of preindustrial times and rose to the top of his craft, not just by his bench skills but by his business acumen and a willingness to try anything that might turn a profit.

Although not a skilled draftsman, Revere entered the business of making copperplate prints, several of which have become rare examples of reportage on important events of the time. Two of his most important prints, *A View of Part of the Town of Boston in New England and British Ships of War Landing Their Troops, 1768* and *The Bloody Massacre*, are at Winterthur. Like silversmith Nathaniel Hurd, he had greater aesthetic success with his bookplates, which were adapted from John Guillim's *Display of Heraldry* and similar works.

Revere also practiced a form of dentistry. Commentators remarked on the early loss of teeth among colonial Americans, ascribing the condition to poor air or the consumption of fruit. Artificial teeth made of ivory or other materials were inserted into the mouth to enable the wearer to chew and, in one claim, to smile. These implants had a way of coming loose with some frequency. Having entered dentistry as a sideline, Revere cleaned teeth and made and reset artificial teeth. He noted in an advertisement that "he fixes them in such a Manner that they are not only an Ornament but of real use in Speaking and Eating."

Diversification took other, more profitable forms. In the postwar period he sold imported hardware, a venture that provided capital for what would become an even more important activity. In 1787 he set up a small foundry in Boston's North End to make metal fittings for ships, first in iron and later in copper and bronze. Copper fittings for ships (bolts, spikes, staples, nails, etc.) became his mainstay, and his bill for outfitting the frigate *Constitution* in 1790 came to $3,820.33. By 1792 he was casting bronze bells for churches and public buildings; many of these bells survive. Revere's greatest business venture began in 1800, when he was sixty-five years old. He built a mill in Canton, Massachusetts, for rolling sheet copper, the first such enterprise in the United States. (Heretofore Americans had been dependent on England for imported sheet copper.) Although sheet copper had other uses, its primary use at the time was as plating for wooden hulls of ships. Copper retarded marine growths that damaged or slowed vessels. Ironically, however, Revere's first order was for 6,000 feet of copper sheathing for the dome of the new state house (only later gilded). His son Joseph Warren Revere assisted in the enterprise and in 1811 took over its management when the elder Revere, then seventy-six, retired.

Revere was active in public life through his military service and his membership in various organizations. He was a prominent Mason, a member of the North End Caucus, the Long Room Club, and the Sons of Liberty (for which Revere made a medal). He was useful to Joseph Warren, Samuel Adams, and other Whig leaders because he was highly regarded in the artisan community. He served as courier for the Boston Whigs, traveling to New York, Philadelphia, and, of course, Lexington and Concord for his fateful night ride immortalized in Henry Wadsworth Longfellow's poem. A contemporary observer noted acerbically, "*O tempora, O mores,* is at present the universal cant. Paul Revere haranguing in town meeting, the commandant of every particular company, the gentleman in his domestic circle, & every dishclout politician, however various have their opinions to make upon the times" (John Eliot to Jeremy Belknap, May 9, 1777). Here, then, is an insight into Paul Revere, the public man.

His military service began with the expedition to Crown Point in 1756, a short-lived, if harrowing, affair. His revolutionary war service was spread over five years, 1775–80, a large part of it served as commander of Castle Island in Boston Harbor. In 1779, following British occupation of Castine, on Penobscot Bay, in what is now Maine but was then part of Massachusetts, provincial officials sent an expedition to dislodge the enemy. What should have been easily accomplished was not, and the expedition turned into a fiasco. When supporting privateers failed to attack British forces, American troops delayed their own attack. With the arrival of British reinforcements, the Americans, fearing that they were now outnumbered, scattered in panic.

Colonel Revere's men disappeared into the wilderness. Revere was court martialed, probably unfairly, and it was 1782 before he cleared his name. He was more effective in civilian life. As Boston's preeminent merchant-craftsman, in 1794 he became founding president of the Massachusetts Charitable Mechanics Association, an organization of masters who insisted that apprentices fulfill the terms of their indentures.

In 1757 Revere married Sarah Orne, who bore him eight children. One, the third Paul Revere, also became a silversmith. Following Sarah's death in 1773, Revere married Rachel Walker, by whom he had eight more children. It is interesting to note that the daughters of the first marriage married men who were carpenters or masons, while the daughters of the second marriage married into the merchant class. The sons of the second marriage also did well. Joseph Warren Revere (1777–1868) succeeded his father in the copper manufactory. John Revere (1787–1847) graduated from Harvard in 1807 and became a physician. Thus Paul Revere insured the upward mobility of his second family, if not his first.

Revere produced an enormous amount of silver during his long career. Kathryn C. Buhler's catalogue *American Silver, 1655–1825, in the Museum of Fine Arts, Boston* contains eighty-eight Revere entries. Revere's work is found in almost every collection of early American silver. It is generally of high quality and includes a wide variety of forms. Revere's Sons of Liberty bowl, owned by the Museum of Fine Arts, Boston, rivals in historic importance Philip Syng's inkstand used for the signing of the Declaration of Independence. The engraved inscription on the bowl commemorates the ninety-two members of the Massachusetts Bay House of Representatives who refused to rescind a circular letter sent to other colonial legislatures urging resistance to British taxation. One of the Sons of Liberty commissioned the piece, which is based on a Chinese ceramic model. Silver bowls in this form remain popular in the twentieth century and today are usually referred to as Revere bowls.

Revere's silver may be divided into two stylistic groups. The first employs restrained versions of baroque and rococo elements of design found in most other American silver of the third quarter of the eighteenth century. The second, which appears in the 1780s, is severely neoclassical and is based on imported English fused plate and associated trade catalogues. Perhaps the best example is Revere's fluted tea service made for John Templeman in 1792 and now owned by the Minneapolis Institute of Arts. By this time Revere was involved in his other business enterprises and probably made little, if any, silver himself. His shop was run by his son Paul and was probably well staffed with apprentices and journeymen, which may be deduced from the huge output of silver during the postrevolutionary war years. Efficiency was increased by a degree of standardization. Revere had ceased to be a working craftsman and had become an entrepreneur. The change is reflected in his two portraits. John Singleton Copley showed him as a vigorous working craftsman (ca. 1768); Gilbert Stuart showed him as an aging gentleman (1813). Revere had achieved what would later be known as the American dream.

The Revere family papers at the Massachusetts Historical Society (available on microfilm) include extensive records on the silversmith and his businesses. Daybooks from 1761 to 1797, although incomplete, contain enormous amounts of information, permitting a detailed analysis of his operations and the documentation of many surviving silver objects.

References: "The Belknap Papers, Part 3," *Collections of the Massachusetts Historical Society*, 6th ser., vol. 4 (1891): 109. Buhler, *American Silver*, pp. 384–472. Daniel J. Boorstin, "The Transforming of Paul Revere," *Hidden History*, ed. Daniel J. Boorstin and Ruth F. Boorstin (New York: Harper and Row, 1987), pp. 24–28. *Catalogue Guide to the Microfilm Edition of the Revere Family Papers, 1746–1964* (Boston: Massachusetts Historical Society, 1979; reprint, 1986, distributed by University Microfilms International). *DAB*, s.v. "Revere, Paul." Renee L. Ernay, "The Revere Furnace, 1787–1800" (Master's thesis, University of Delaware, 1989). Deborah A. Federhen, "Paul Revere, Silversmith: A Study of His Shop Operation and His Objects" (Master's thesis, University of Delaware, 1988). Forbes, *Paul Revere*, for popular but generally reliable accounts of Revere and the period. Jones, *Old Silver*, index. Kane, *Dictionary*, s.v. "Revere, Paul, Jr." *Paul Revere—Artisan*, which accompanied an exhibition at the Museum of Our National Heritage, Lexington, Mass., 1988–89. Ian M. G. Quimby, "Introduction," in *The Craftsman in Early America* (New York: W. W. Norton, 1984), p. 7. SCPR book 116, pp. 245–50, 315–17. The literature on Revere is too extensive to list here, but much of it will be found in Forbes, *Paul Revere*, and *Paul Revere—Artisan*. See also Elbridge H. Goss, *Life of Colonel Paul Revere*, 2 vols. (Boston, 1891).

ℰ 111 a–f
TANKARDS, 1772

(a) H. 8 ¼" (21.0 cm), W. 6 ¹¹⁄₁₆" (17.0 cm),
DIAM. base 4 ⅞" (12.4 cm)
24 oz. 10 dwt. 1 gr. (745.6 g)
(b) H. 8 ³⁄₁₆" (20.8 cm), W. 6 ¾" (17.2 cm),
DIAM. base 4 ⅞" (12.4 cm)
24 oz. 19 dwt. 7 gr. (776.5 g)
(c) H. 8 ¼" (21.0 cm), W. 6 ⅞" (17.5 cm),
DIAM. base 4 ¹³⁄₁₆" (12.2 cm)
24 oz. 16 dwt. 6 gr. (771.8 g)
(d) H. 8 ⅛" (20.6 cm), W. 6 ¾" (17.2 cm),
DIAM. base 4 ⅞" (12.4 cm)
24 oz. 18 dwt. 9 gr. (775.0 g)
(e) H. 8 ¼" (21.0 cm), W. 6 ¾" (17.2 cm),
DIAM. base 4 ¹³⁄₁₆" (12.2 cm)
24 oz. 13 dwt. 23 gr. (768.2 g)
(f) H. 8 ¼" (21.0 cm), W. 6 ¾" (17.2 cm),
DIAM. base 4 ¹³⁄₁₆" (12.2 cm)
24 oz. 10 dwt. 3 gr. (762.3 g)

Stamps: "•REVERE" in roman letters, in a
rectangle, struck once on upper body, left of
handle, on each tankard.

Engraved on body opposite handle: "The Gift
of/ Mary Bartlett Widow of Eph^m Bartlett,/
to the third Church in Brookfeild./ 1768" in
script. Punctuation varies slightly on each
tankard. *Scratched on underside:* (a) "oz/ 24
5 = 12"; (b) "oz / 25 3"; "Returned/ Oct 1
1831" in script; and "56 ECB[?]" in script; (c)
"oz/ 25 1"; (d) "oz/ 25 = 1 = 12"; (e) "oz/ 24
19"; (f) "oz/ 24 13".

Description: raised body with straight sides; applied base molding consists (from the bottom up) of a flat vertical section, broad cyma-recta molding, and double-bead molding; applied midband (height varies from tankard to tankard); applied flared rim with single-scored line encircling body just below rim; centerpunch on underside. Raised stepped-and-domed lid with cast flame finial secured by silver rivet through lid; double-scored lines encircle rim of lid; lid folds over rim of body. Cast thumbpiece, S curve in profile, with rudimentary scroll across top edge, attached to cast 5-segment hinge with pendant drop. Raised-and-soldered hollow S-curve handle with oval drop below upper handle attachment; circular plate on body at lower handle attachment; cast tailpiece featuring mask of fierce male face surrounded by decorative border; notched vent.

Spectrographic analysis:

	SILVER	COPPER	LEAD	GOLD
(a)				
BODY SIDE	94.0	5.5	0.22	0.15
UNDERSIDE	93.8	5.4	0.26	0.19
LID	94.6	4.5	0.28	0.13
HANDLE	93.4	6.1	0.20	0.15
FINIAL	94.2	5.2	0.29	0.16
(b)				
BODY SIDE	92.9	6.0	0.31	0.04
UNDERSIDE	93.6	5.4	0.26	0.04
LID	90.7	8.8	0.31	0.15
HANDLE	94.3	5.2	0.29	0.16
FINIAL	92.1	6.5	0.35	0.32
(c)				
BODY SIDE	86.5	12.7	0.30	0.12
UNDERSIDE	93.3	7.0	0.33	0.18
LID	93.4	6.1	0.22	0.14
HANDLE	91.2	7.4	0.21	0.13
FINIAL	94.5	4.9	0.10	0.13
(d)				
BODY SIDE	92.9	6.6	0.17	0.09
UNDERSIDE	93.9	5.4	0.20	0.08
LID	94.3	3.8	0.20	0.16
HANDLE	94.1	5.4	0.19	0.19
FINIAL	93.8	5.7	0.24	0.19

	SILVER	COPPER	LEAD	GOLD
(e)				
BODY SIDE	91.4	8.0	0.24	0.17
UNDERSIDE	93.4	6.0	0.22	0.13
LID	94.0	5.4	0.23	0.16
HANDLE	93.1	6.4	0.17	0.18
FINIAL	93.9	5.7	0.11	0.15
(f)				
BODY SIDE	88.7	10.5	0.37	0.10
UNDERSIDE	93.1	6.4	0.32	0.14
LID	93.8	5.6	0.27	0.17
HANDLE	94.4	5.2	0.21	0.16
FINIAL	91.3	7.0	0.35	0.28

History: Mary Pape married Ephraim Bartlett, tanner, on November 22, 1732. In 1745 Ephraim, "Designing to go in the Expedition against Cape Breton & calling to mind the many Dangers I shall be exposed unto," drew up his will bequeathing all his worldly possessions to his wife. Ephraim survived to enjoy the victory at Louisburg, but in 1761 he died of unknown causes. In the following year, his widow drew up her last will and testament, wherein she bequeathed "two third parts of my Estate Remaining to ye Church in the third Precinct in the Town of Brookfield to be Laid out in Silver vessells for ye Communion Table and the Vessells to be Engraven with my name and when ye vessells are made to be Delivered by my Executor to such person or Persons as Said Church shall appoint to receive ye same and my will is that my Late Husband's name Shall be Engraven on ye vessells with my own." The other third of her estate she bequeathed to the Reverend Nathan Fiske, "minister of the said Church and Congregation." She appointed Jedidiah Foster of Brookfield as executor.

Mary Bartlett died in late 1768 or early 1769. That the date engraved on the tankards, 1768, is not the date of manufacture is known from surviving accounts of Paul Revere, who sold them to Jonathan Trott in early 1772 for an unspecified sum. His entry reads:

Jonathan Trott D^r

To a Silver wine Qt tank^d	*24*	*13*	
To an Dito weight	*25*	*1*	*12*
To one Dito	*25*	*3*	
To one Dito	*24*	*5*	*12*
To one Dito	*25*	*1*	*0*
To one DitO	*24*	*19*	*0*
	149 [oz.]	*3 [dwt.]*	*0 [gr.]*

The weights given here match those scratched on the undersides of the tankards. Unfortunately, and unlike most other entries, no cost is given. This is the only transaction in Revere's records for the sale of a set of 6 tankards. Indeed, it is unique in the annals of early American silver.

Jonathan Trott (1730–1815) was a jeweler and silversmith in Boston prior to moving to Norwich, Conn., in 1772. An advertisement of 1758 put him next door to the White Horse Tavern in Boston's South End. Trott must have been the prime contact of Jedidiah Foster, the executor of the Bartlett estate. In his summary of expenses incurred in settling the estate, dated April 6, 1772, Foster noted, "1 Journey to Boston to Engage the Silver Vessells" and "1 Journey to Boston to Receive the Vessells." He then recorded, "Six Silver Tankards D^d to the third Chh in Brookf^d agreeable to the will as per their Receipt appears 66.18.1." The total value of the estate was £141.16.0. Foster's expenses as executor were £41.9.0, leaving £100.7.1, of which the tankards represented two thirds and the legacy to Nathan Fiske of £33.9.0 ⅓.

Jedidiah Foster (1726–79) graduated from Harvard College in 1744 and then moved to Brookfield to look after the considerable business interests of Col. Joseph Dwight. He was a justice of the peace, a colonel in the militia, and in 1761 was sent to the House of Representatives. During the stormy years prior to the Revolution, he was active in provincial politics, siding with John Adams and John Hancock. His real strength was at the local level, where, it is said, he "became the most beloved man who ever lived in Brookfield because of his cheerful willingness to accept every task which town, parish, and church laid upon him, and to serve his individual neighbors as well as the whole." He was a deacon in the church.

Nathan Fiske (1733–99), minister of the Third Church in Brookfield, graduated from Harvard College in 1754 and taught briefly in the towns of Harvard and Weston before being called to Brookfield. He too was universally loved by his contemporaries. Unlike many in his profession, he avoided controversy and doctrinal disputes. His sermons, which were highly regarded by many, held none of the fire and brimstone so popular with the followers of Jonathan Edwards and George Whitefield. He felt no compulsion to save souls and was relaxed on doctrinal matters. He liked people, and his kindliness brought him the affection and respect of parishioners and townspeople. He read everything he could get his hands on, from Locke, Dryden, and Rousseau to great quantities of trivial fiction. His diary notes 5 consecutive days spent reading London magazines. He was an essayist on such diverse topics as music, debauchery, winter, money, polygamy, watermelon stealing, female delicacy, gaming, wit, agriculture, and religious toleration. First published in the Worcester *Spy* and the *Massachusetts Magazine*, 151 of the essays were later published in 2 volumes entitled *Moral Monitor* (1801).

The diary is a prosaic document penned in tiny script with short daily entries, few of which concern his vocation. Most cover weather conditions and his current reading. A good many refer to his garden or visits to the college. Only once does he mention visiting "the Widow Bartlett" (October 29, 1762). That Mary Bartlett bequeathed him a third of her modest estate may be partially explained by a notation on the cover of the 1767 diary: "The whole of Bartlets Note is now due." Fiske preached the funeral sermon for Jedidiah Foster as, no doubt, he did for Mary Bartlett. The American Antiquarian Society, Worcester, Mass., owns many of his manuscripts, including his diary.

As a postscript to the early history of the tankards, E. Alfred Jones notes that they became the subject of a lawsuit in the 1820s:

In 1827, the parish dismissed its minister because of his too orthodox views. Several members of this church, including two of the three deacons, joined him and forthwith formed "The First Evangelical Society in Brookfield." These vessels were taken by this new body, and no objection was then made. When in 1827 this church became Unitarian, the observance of the Communion was desired, and deacon Heman Stebbins, a lawyer, asked his former colleagues for the loan of these tankards. The request was refused. Deacon Stebbins there-upon called a meeting of the parish, and declared that the vessels belonged legally to the old church—a view which was upheld in the law-suit tried before chief-justice Lemuel Shaw in the supreme court of Massachusetts.

In all likelihood the inscription on the underside of (b) refers to the return of the tankards to the parent church.

Provenance: The tankards remained in the possession of the church, in 1928 known as the First Congregational Unitarian Society of Brookfield, until their sale in December of that year to Frank McCarthy, a dealer in Longmeadow, Mass. On November 18, 1928, McCarthy wrote to H. F. du Pont: "Would you be interested in a complete set of 6 silver tankards by Paul Revere which is owned by a church in an historic Massachusetts town?" In light of the controversy over the ownership of the tankards in the 1820s, McCarthy reveals that the deacons "principally were interested to know . . . whether the potential purchaser I represented [H. F. du Pont] was planning to present the set to the other church in Brookfield." The tankards were purchased by McCarthy on behalf of H. F. du Pont.

Exhibitions: (a) "Paul Revere—Artisan, Businessman, and Patriot: The Man Behind the Myth," Museum of Our National Heritage, Lexington, Mass., 1988–89.

Comments: The set is unique because it is the only set of 6 made-to-match tankards known. Revere achieved a purity of form, balance, and proportion that is quite remarkable. If we can speak of platonic perfection in the universe of tankards, it is found here. It is ironic that they remained virtually unknown—not even illustrated in Jones, *Old Silver*—until acquired by H. F. du Pont. Even then their existence was known to relatively few until the 1950s. The 1768 inscription is one more reminder of the problem of inscribed dates on presentation silver.

References: Fales, *American Silver*, no. 117. Fales, *Early American Silver*, fig. 141. Donald L. Fennimore, "Religion in America: Metal Objects in Service of Ritual," *American Art Journal* 10, no. 2 (November 1978): 26. Fennimore, *Silver and Pewter*, no. 160. Victor F. Hanson, "Quantitative Elemental Analysis of Art Objects by Energy-Dispersive X-ray Fluoresence Spectroscopy," *Applied Spectroscopy* 27, no. 5 (September/October 1973): 309–34. Jones, *Old Silver*, pp. 98, 99. Kauffman, *Colonial Silversmith*, p. 113. *Paul Revere—Artisan*, no. 93. *Heman Stebbins v. Calvin Jennings*, in Octavius Pickering, *Reports of Cases Argued and Determined in the Supreme Judicial Court of Massachusetts*, 24 vols. (Boston: Hilliard, Gray, 1833), 10:172–95. Quimby, "Silver," p. 68. Revere Papers, silver shop ledger, 1761–88, Massachusetts Historical Society. *Sibley's Harvard Graduates*, 11:395–98, for Jedidiah Foster; 13:400–407, for Nathan Fiske. *Vital Records of Brookfield, Massachusetts, to the Year 1849* (Boston and Worcester, Mass., 1909), p. 267, for marriage of Bartletts, but neither their births nor their deaths are recorded here. Ephraim Bartlett, Worcester County Probate Records (WCPR), no. 3970; Mary Bartlett, WCPR, no. 4036. For Jonathan Trott, see George Munson Curtis, *Early Silver of Connecticut and Its Makers* (Meriden, Conn.: International Silver Co., 1913), pp. 75, 113; Flynt and Fales, *Heritage Foundation*, p. 343; Jennifer F. Goldsborough, *An Exhibition of New London Silver, 1700–1835* (New London, Conn.: Lyman Allyn Museum, 1969), pp. 33, 34.

57.859.1–.6 Gift of H. F. du Pont, 1965

112
PITCHER, ca. 1804

H. 6 %₁₆" (16.7 cm), DIAM. base 3 ⅞" (9.8 cm),
W. 7 ¹³⁄₁₆" (19.8 cm)
18 oz. 9 dwt. 5 gr. (572.3 g)

Stamps: "REVERE" in roman letters, in a
rectangle, struck twice on underside; 1 stamp
chattered.

Engraved on body opposite handle: "PRESENTED/
to the/ Rev.ᵈ Joseph McKean,/ by a number
of his Friends/ &/ late Parishioners of/ MIL-
TON,/ as a testimonial, of their affection,/ and
to hold in remembrance how deeply/ they
regret his seperation/ from them./ 1804" in
roman letters and script.

Description: raised body in shape of so-called
Liverpool jug. Cylindrical in upper and lower
extremeties, bulbous in the middle; plain rim;
inset V-shape spout; flat bottom; no centerpunch. Cast C-shape plain handle.

Spectrographic analysis:

	SILVER	COPPER	LEAD	GOLD
BODY SIDE	87.4	12.1	0.13	0.09
UNDERSIDE	94.4	5.2	0.15	0.12
HANDLE	86.6	12.9	0.19	0.15

History: Joseph McKean (1776–1818) was
born in Ipswich, Mass., the son of William M.
McKean, a native of Glasgow. Following graduation from Harvard College in 1794, he taught
school in Ipswich and later in Berwick, Mass. In
1797 he was ordained minister of the church in
Milton, Mass. He gave up the ministry in 1804
due to bad health. A period of residence in the
West Indies improved his health, and in 1809 he
became professor of oratory at Harvard, succeeding John Quincy Adams. Once again his
health failed, and he went to Cuba to recover. He
died on March 17, 1818, in Havana. Revere himself died only a few weeks later (May 10, 1818).

Provenance: Joseph McKean (1804–18); Israel
Sack, Boston, sold to H. F. du Pont, December
1930.

Exhibitions: "Marks of Achievement: Four
Centuries of American Presentation Silver,"
Museum of Fine Arts, Houston, 1987.

Comments: This is 1 of several silver forms borrowed directly from ceramics. This shape is
based on the so-called Liverpool jugs that were
imported from England at that time. Many were
decorated with transfer-printed designs commemorating George Washington, who died in
1799. The jugs were thus at their height of pop-
ularity in 1804. Similar pitchers by Revere are
owned by the Museum of Fine Arts, Boston
and the Paul Revere Insurance Company.
Eleven pitchers in this form survive.

References: Fales, *American Silver*, no. 138. Fen-
nimore, *Silver and Pewter*, no. 128. Kauffman,
Colonial Silversmith, p. 158. Warren, Howe, and
Brown, *Marks of Achievement*, no. 146.

57.858 Gift of H. F. du Pont, 1965

113 a–d
SPOONS, ca. 1790

(a) L. 5 ⅝" (14.3 cm)
10 dwt. 11 gr. (16.3 g)
(b) L. 5 ⅜" (13.7 cm)
8 dwt. 20 gr. (13.8 g)
(c) L. 4 ¹³⁄₁₆" (12.2 cm)
6 dwt. 14 gr. (10.3 g)
(d) L. 6 %₁₆" (16.7 cm)
18 dwt. 5 gr. (28.4 g)

Stamps: "PR" in script, in a rectangle, struck
once on back of each handle.

Engraved on front of handle: (a) "JMT" in foliate script, surrounded by a bright-cut medallion
with floral pendant; (b) crest of a leaping dolphin over a heraldic band; (c) "I=D" in roman
letters; (d) "AJK" in foliate script, in a bright-
cut medallion with floral pendant.

Description: (a) oval bowl with shell-like fluting
with rounded drop on back (drop created by die
from front); pointed downturned handle with
slight midrib on back; (b) oval bowl with

swage-formed single drop and asymmetrical leafage in relief on back; rounded downturned handle with shoulders on lower end, feather edge, and swage-formed asymmetrical cartouche on front; (c) oval bowl with swage-formed rounded drop on back; rounded downturned handle with slight midrib on back; (d) oval bowl with swage-formed rounded drop on back; rounded downturned handle with slight midrib on back.

Spectrographic analysis: Silver content ranges from 87.9 to 93.1 percent.

History: (a) "JMT" refers to John and Mehitable Templeman, who were married in Boston in 1783. In April 1792 John Templeman purchased from Revere the silver tea service now owned by the Minneapolis Institute of Arts. This spoon may well have been part of that set. (See salt spoon with same initials owned by the Museum of Fine Arts, Boston.) (b) The dolphin crest was used by the Sargent family of Boston. Collections at Yale University Art Gallery and the Metropolitan Museum of Art have tablespoons, which are also by Revere, with the same crest. (c, d) Unknown.

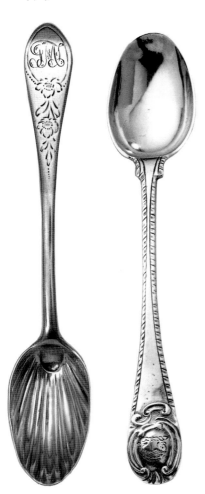

Provenance: Mr. and Mrs. Stanley B. Ineson, New York City; Mr. and Mrs. Alfred E. Bissell, Wilmington, Del.

Exhibitions: (a) Metropolitan Museum of Art, New York City, 1938–61. (b) "Paul Revere—Artisan, Businessman, and Patriot: The Man Behind the Myth," Museum of Our National Heritage, Lexington, Mass., 1988–89.

Comments: (b) See Buhler, *American Silver,* no. 360, for a spoon, made by Revere for a different owner, that has a similar swaged-formed asymmetrical cartouche on the handle. For Sargent crest, see no. 115 a.

References: Belden, *Marks of American Silversmiths,* p. 352 a. (a) Kathryn C. Buhler, "Toward a Tea Set by Paul Revere," *Minneapolis Institute of Arts Bulletin* 50, no. 2 (June 1961): 5–24. Buhler, *American Silver,* no. 390. (b) Buhler and Hood, *American Silver,* no. 245. "Notes," *Metropolitan Museum of Art Bulletin* 33, no. 10 (October 1938): 229. *Paul Revere—Artisan,* no. 90 and related Sargent items. Michael Snodin and Gail Belden, *Collecting for Tomorrow: Spoons* (London: Pitman Publishing, 1976), p. 41.

62.240.560, .561, .564, and .1401 Gift of Mr. and Mrs. Alfred E. Bissell, 1962–63

𝓔 114
SPOON, ca. 1790

L. 7 ⁵⁄₁₆" (18.6 cm)
1 oz. 4 dwt. 2 gr. (37.5 g)

Stamps: "REVERE" (letters not conjoined) in roman letters, in a rectangle, possibly with a serrated lower edge, struck once on back of handle.

Engraved on front of handle: "L" in foliate script.

Description: oval bowl with swage-formed rounded drop on back; rounded downturned handle with slight midrib on back.

Spectrographic analysis: Silver content is 87.1 percent.

Provenance: Mr. and Mrs. Stanley B. Ineson, New York City; Mr. and Mrs. Alfred E. Bissell, Wilmington, Del.

62.240.1402 Gift of Mr. and Mrs. Alfred E. Bissell, 1962–63

𝓔 115 a, b
SPOONS, ca. 1790

(a) L. 8 ¹⁵⁄₁₆" (22.7 cm)
2 oz. 7 dwt. 21 gr. (74.2 g)
(b) L. 8 ½" (21.6 cm)
1 oz. 12 dwt. 14 gr. (50.7 g)

Stamps: "•REVERE" in roman letters, in a rectangle, struck once on back of each handle.

Engraved on front of each handle: (a) crest of a leaping dolphin over a heraldic band; (b) "EP/ to/ EN" in roman letters.

Description: (a) oval bowl with swage-formed drop and asymmetrical leafage in relief on back; rounded downturned handle with shoulders on lower end; featheredge and swage-formed asymmetrical cartouche on front; (b) oval bowl with swage-formed single drop and asymmetrical leafage in relief on back; rounded downturned handle with midrib on back.

Spectrographic analysis: Silver content ranges from 92.1 to 92.6 percent.

History: (a) The dolphin crest was used by the Sargent family of Boston. Collections at Yale University Art Gallery and the Metropolitan Museum of Art have tablespoons, also by Revere, with the same crest.

Provenance: Mr. and Mrs. Stanley B. Ineson, New York City; Mr. and Mrs. Alfred E. Bissell, Wilmington, Del.

Exhibitions: (a) "Paul Revere—Artisan, Businessman, and Patriot: The Man Behind the Myth," Museum of Our National Heritage, Lexington, Mass., 1988–89.

Comments: For Sargent crest, see no. 113 b.

References: Belden, *Marks of American Silversmiths,* p. 352 b. (a) Buhler and Hood, *American Silver,* no. 245. "Notes," *Metropolitan Museum of Art Bulletin* 33, no. 10 (October 1938): 229. *Paul Revere—Artisan,* no. 89. Michael Snodin and Gail Belden, *Collecting for Tomorrow: Spoons* (London: Pitman Publishing, 1976), p. 41.

62.240.1403, .1404 Gift of Mr. and Mrs. Alfred E. Bissell, 1962–63

ℰ Obadiah Rich

1809–88

Rich & Ward, w. 1832–35
Boston, Massachusetts

Born in Charlestown, Massachusetts, to Capt. Aquila Rich and his wife Hannah (Thomas) Rich, Obadiah Rich served his apprenticeship with Moses Morse, a Boston silversmith. By 1830 Rich had opened his own shop at 69 Washington Street. From 1832 to 1835, he worked in partnership with Samuel L. Ward. During the middle 1830s, his shop was at Williams Court, and during much of the 1840s, he was at Court Avenue (perhaps only a name change). In 1834 Rich married Marianne Holden; they had three sons and four daughters. Around 1850 Rich went blind, but this did not prevent him from becoming a partner in the firm of Brackett & Crosby for another fifteen years. In the final year of his life he moved to South Carolina to be with his daughter; he died there.

Rich made silver for Jones, Lows & Ball, the major Boston retailer whose stamp is found on much mid nineteenth-century silver. There is, therefore, a body of silver attributed to him that does not bear his stamp, such as the dish warmer in the following entry. One of Rich's most important commissions was the elaborate vase made for presentation to Daniel Webster in 1835. Modeled on the Warwick Vase, it is inscribed "Made by Ward & Rich Boston, 1835" but stamped "Jones, Lows and Ball." It is now owned by the Boston Public Library. Other highly accomplished pieces by Rich include two beautifully modeled empire-style inkstands, one at Yale University Art Gallery and one at Harvard's Fogg Art Museum. Rich also worked in the rococo revival style as evidenced by a pair of pitchers and salvers made for presentation by the Massachusetts Charitable Mechanics Association to Uriel Crocker in 1842.

References: *American Art at Harvard* (Cambridge: Fogg Art Museum, Harvard University, 1972), no. 176. Buhler and Hood, *American Silver*, no. 326. Martha Gandy Fales, "Obadiah Rich, Boston Silversmith," *Antiques* 94, no. 4 (October 1968): 565–69.

ℰ 116
DISH WARMER, 1838–47

H. 3 ¼" (8.3 cm), DIAM. top 6 ⁹⁄₁₆" (16.7 cm), w. 6 ⅝" (16.8 cm)
17 oz. 9 dwt. 9 gr. (543.4 g)

Stamps: "JONES, BALL & POOR."; "BOSTON"; "PURE COIN". All in roman letters, in rectangular surrounds, struck once on underside of lower shelf.

Engraved on top shelf: armorial device consisting of a lion rampant on gules in fess and base, in chief checkerboard pattern in or and azure. Crest of a dragon's head erased on a heraldic band.

Description: form similar to an empire center table: circular upper surface, circular lower shelf, all joined by 3 supports equidistant around the circumference. Circular upper surface with hole in center and raised rims on outside and inside; molded skirt attached at edges and stepped backward toward center; both portions of upper sections probably spun. Circular bottom shelf stepped around outside, depressed in center (to hold spirit lamp); raised. Each support is cast in a C-curve form with a dog's head emerging from acanthus leaves at the top; lower end of "C" supported on a banded acanthus leaf terminating in a scroll; dogs cast in 2 parts and soldered. Spirit lamp is circular, has a short neck for opening and a recessed base; seamed lower section; both halves probably spun; cast C-scroll handle. Wick holder is a circular plate with vertical tube inserted; small diameter vent hole in plate next to wick holder.

Spectrographic analysis:

	SILVER	COPPER	LEAD	GOLD
CUP BOTTOM	95.5	4.2	0.23	0.14
CUP SIDE	91.0	8.7	0.19	0.07
WARMER TOP	91.1	8.8	0.17	0.03
WARMER BOTTOM	94.8	5.0	0.22	0.08
FOOT	93.2	6.5	0.15	0.15

History: The arms on the warmer were used by the Warren family of Boston. The dish was probably owned by Dr. John Collins Warren (1778–1854), Harvard College, 1797. A coffeepot in the Museum of Fine Arts, Boston has the same arms and was sold by Paul Revere to Dr. John Warren in 1791. This Dr. Warren married Abigail Collins in 1771; they are the parents of Dr. John Collins Warren.

Dr. John Collins Warren was a renowned physician and surgeon. He began learning the profession under his father but soon went abroad for extended study in London, Edinburgh, and Paris. He returned in 1802 and almost immediately assumed his father's practice. In 1806 he was appointed adjunct professor of anatomy and surgery at Harvard, and for most of the rest of his life divided his time between private practice and teaching. His fame spread rapidly, and he refused attractive offers from Philadelphia and New York. He was one of the founders and editors of the *New England Journal of Medicine* and a zealous advocate of temperance. He fought for improved public

water supply for the City of Boston, and he performed the first surgery on a patient anesthetized by ether.

In cultural affairs he bought the land and chaired the building committee for the Bunker Hill monument, was one of the founders of the Boston Athenaeum, and was president of the Boston Society of Natural History. In the last capacity he purchased for the society "the most perfect Mastadon skeleton yet discovered." He also purchased a skeleton from the Peale Museum in Baltimore.

Provenance: William Core Duffy, Kittery, Maine.

Comments: The attribution to Obadiah Rich is based on 2 closely related pieces of silver bearing the stamps "O. Rich" and "Boston." They are the elaborate inkstands owned by Yale University Art Gallery and the Fogg Art Museum at Harvard. Both incorporate the dog's head, C scroll, and acanthus supports that are on the dish warmer. It is unlikely that these complex

castings would have been made by different makers. The Fogg Art Museum attributes the design of their inkstand to Horatio Greenough (1805–52), the sculptor. The dog's head is thought to be derived from Greenough's popular sculpture, dating from about 1838, of his greyhound "Arno" that was reproduced and sold widely. Whether the design of the inkstands and the dish warmer be attributed to Greenough remains in doubt.

References: American Art at Harvard (Cambridge: Fogg Art Museum, Harvard University, 1972), no. 176. Buhler and Hood, *American Silver*, no. 326. Fales, "Obadiah Rich, Boston Silversmith," *Antiques* 44, no. 4 (October 1968), figs. 2, 3, for related pieces. "Memoir of John Collins Warren, M.D.," *NEH&GR* 19, no. 1 (January 1865): 1–12. Margaret M. Honda, "The Obadiah Rich Dish Warmer," and Amanda E. Lange, "Obadiah Rich's Dish Warmer," Registration Division, Winterthur.

87.20 Museum purchase (with Collectors Circle funds) from William Core Duffy, 1987

William Rouse

ca. 1640–1704/5
Boston, Massachusetts

William Rouse was one of a group of immigrant craftsmen who came to Boston during the late seventeenth century; he is the earliest Boston goldsmith to have been trained on the Continent. Jaspar Danckaerts, the Dutch Labadist who was in Boston in 1680, sought him out: "We also found the silversmith, who bade us welcome. His name was Willem Ros, from Wesel. He had married an Englishwoman, and carried on his business here." After lodging with Rouse, Danckaerts observed: "Although his wife was an Englishwoman, she was quite a good housekeeper." Rouse appears in the public record in 1676 when he was taken to court by one Richard Rogers for a debt of "Four pounds in money . . . for two ounces & three quarters of bad gold." Along with silversmiths Jeremiah Dummer, Thomas Savage, and Robert Sanderson, Rouse was one of the bearers at the funeral of goldsmith Timothy Dwight in 1692. He was active in local affairs, having been elected selectman, surveyor, overseer of chimneys, and constable.

Little of his work survives, but what is extant is of more than passing interest. Unique in American silver is a covered skillet with the Foster arms, now at Yale University Art Gallery. It has scroll feet and a hollow handle like those found on tankards. Of the roughly eleven extant pieces of Rouse silver, four of them were made for the Foster family. A tankard now owned by the Los Angeles County Museum of Art exhibits engraving of such extraordinary quality that Barbara McLean Ward felt it was not only derived from a printed source but reflected Rouse's training in a Continental shop.

Rouse is also credited with a pair of sucket forks. E. Alfred Jones records silver in the churches at Dorchester, Massachusetts, and Guilford, Connecticut. Rouse died intestate. His estate was valued at £575.11.6. His tools were appraised by silversmith John Coney at £12.5.0.

References: Graham Hood, "A New Form in American Seventeenth-Century Silver," *Antiques* 94, no. 6 (December 1968): 879–81. Jones, *Old Silver*, pp. 144, 193. Bartlett B. James and J. Franklin Jameson, eds., *Journal of Jasper Danckaerts, 1679–1680* (New York: Barnes and Noble, 1913), p. 260. Kane, *Dictionary*, s.v. "Rouse, William." *Records of the Suffolk County Court, 1671–1680*, pt. 1, vol. 30, of *Publications of the Colonial Society of Massachusetts* (Boston, 1933), p. 689. SCPR book 16, pp. 40–41, 86–87, 236–37. Ward, "Boston Goldsmiths," pp. 158–59.

117
CUP, ca. 1690

H. 2 15/16" (7.5 cm), DIAM. rim 3 15/16" (10.0 cm), W. 4 9/16" (11.6 cm)
5 oz. 9 gr. (156.1 g)

Stamps: "W•R" in roman letters, with a star flanked by 2 pellets above and a pellet below, all in a shield of conforming shape, struck twice on underside.

Engraved on underside: "+T+/ +I∗R+" in shaded roman letters.

Description: raised cylindrical body with slightly flared rim; applied base band with 1 large and 2 small moldings; centerpunch on underside. S-curve strap handle with double-scroll ram's horn upper terminal and trifid lower terminal.

Spectrographic analysis:

	SILVER	COPPER	GOLD	LEAD
BODY SIDE	93.3	6.4	0.18	0.14
BODY BOTTOM	93.1	6.6	0.16	0.12
HANDLE	93.0	6.8	0.06	0.14

Provenance: "From a family in Lebanon, N.H.," to David McCoy (a descendant of William Rouse), Lyme, Conn.; Dr. Harlan Angier, Brookfield, Mass., to Bernard & S. Dean Levy, New York City.

Comments: The Detroit Institute of Arts owns the only other known cup by Rouse.

References: Fennimore, *Silver and Pewter*, no. 155.

74.4 Museum purchase from Bernard & S. Dean Levy, 1974

Daniel Russell, Sr.

ca. 1698–1750

Daniel Russell, Jr.

1726–78
Newport, Rhode Island

It appears that there was more than one silversmith with the name of Daniel Russell and that the biographical information previously published is incorrect. The approximate dates of 1698–1771 are given by Ralph Carpenter, who also has Russell marrying Mary Rumrell in 1722 and Mary Mumford in 1754. Russell is accorded long life based on a 1772 reference to "Mr. Daniel Russell's Garden." More recent research by Charlotte Smith tells a different story. Cemetery records at the Newport Historical Society show that Russell married Mumford in 1722 and that she died in 1745. Other genealogical sources say Russell married Rumrell (Rumreill) in 1754. The story is further complicated by Margaret Ballard's discovery that a Daniel Russell was declared *non compos mentis* in 1750, and Daniel Russell, Jr., was appointed his guardian. No doubt it was the younger Daniel Russell who advertised as a goldsmith in the *Newport Mercury* in 1769. There are, thus, two Daniel Russells, each of whom was a goldsmith in Newport. From this we can deduce that it was the father who married Mary Mumford in 1722 and the son who married Mary Rumrell (Rumreill) in 1754.

Daniel Russell, Sr., was born in Branford, Connecticut, the son of the Reverend Samuel Russell and Abigail Whiting. He was apprenticed to John Dixwell of Boston, for whom he may also have served as a journeyman. By 1722 he was working in Newport.

Foremost among the works of the elder Daniel Russell are two baptismal basins made for presentation to Trinity Church in Newport in 1718 and 1734. (They are still owned by the church.) The latter basin is unique in design with its straight sides and two bail handles. Other works are not so easily dated or sufficiently distinct on the basis of style for us to attribute them with any certainty to father or son.

References: Margaret Ballard, "Early Silver in Trinity Church, Newport, Rhode Island," *Antiques* 120, no. 4 (October 1981): 922–25, figs. 4, 5. Ralph E. Carpenter, *The Arts and Crafts of Newport, Rhode Island, 1640–1820* (Newport, R.I.: Preservation Society of Newport County, 1954), p. 157, nos. 102, 124. Jones, *Old Silver*, pp. 251, 318–19. Charlotte E. Smith, "An Examination of an Eighteenth-Century American Creampot," Registration Division, Winterthur.

118
TANKARD, ca. 1735

H. 8 ⅛" (20.6 cm), DIAM. base 5 ⅝" (14.3 cm), w. 7 ¾" (19.7 cm)
29 oz. 19 dwt. 5 gr. (931.9 g)

Stamps: "DR" in roman letters, in a rectangle with a single foil extending above frame, struck on upper body, left of handle, and on lid.

Engraved on back of handle: "IHM" (or "THM") in floriate neoclassical script.

Description: raised body with straight sides; applied base molding consists (from bottom up) of a torus molding, cyma-recta molding, double-bead molding, torus molding, and double-bead molding; applied molding at rim over double-scored line encircling upper body; centerpunch on underside. Raised 4-step lid rises to flat dome in center with small cast capstan-type finial secured by solder inside; lid folds over rim of body. Cast thumbpiece, S curve in profile, with rudimentary scroll motif across top edge; attached to a cast 5-segment hinge with pendant drop. Raised-and-soldered hollow S-curve handle with bulbous drop below upper handle attachment; circular plate at lower handle attachment; oval-dome tailpiece; notched vent.

Spectrographic analysis:

	SILVER	COPPER	LEAD	GOLD
BODY SIDE	90.7	8.5	0.30	0.13
UNDERSIDE	92.5	6.7	0.29	0.14
BASE MOLDING	91.9	7.3	0.27	0.13
HANDLE	90.1	8.9	0.23	0.12
LID	91.1	8.1	0.27	0.13

History: Tradition of ownership in the Mumford family. Daniel Russell, Sr., married Mary Mumford in 1722. She died in 1745. As was so often the case during the eighteenth century, the bride's family became patrons of the silversmith husband.

Provenance: Mr. and Mrs. N. McLean Seabrease, Germantown, Pa.; Robert Ensko, Inc., New York City, sold to H. F. du Pont as part of the Seabrease collection, August 1929.

Comments: The stamp on the body appears to have been struck over another stamp. In design quality this tankard leaves a lot to be desired; the proportions are particularly awkward.

61.617 Gift of H. F. du Pont, 1965

119
CREAM POT, ca. 1755

H. 3 15/16" (10.0 cm), w. 3 13/16" (9.7 cm)
4 oz. 3 dwt. 17 gr. (130.2 g)

Stamps: "DR" (or "IDR") in roman letters, in an oval, struck once on upper body, left of handle.

Engraved on underside: "S*R/ to/ Mary Rumreill/ 1754" in script.

Description: raised pear-shape body with curvilinear flared rim and prominent curved pouring lip; centerpunch on underside. Cast double–C-scroll handle with acanthus leaf decoration on upper handle and a bud terminal on lower handle; 3 short legs cast as back-to-back C scrolls with pad feet.

Spectrographic analysis:

	SILVER	COPPER	LEAD	GOLD
BODY	94.4	5.2	0.22	0.20
HANDLE	95.4	4.2	0.13	0.13

History: Given the new biographical information on Daniel Russell and his son, it is possible that this creamer was the work of the younger Russell. This idea gains credence from the inscription. A Daniel Russell, probably the younger of 2 silversmiths of that name, married a Mary Rumreill in 1754. The "SR" may refer to Sarah Rumreill, married in 1758, who could have been a sister or a cousin of Mary and who gave the creamer as a wedding gift. Stylistically, the creamer is appropriate for the 1750s.

Provenance: Marshall P. Blankarn, New York City.

Comments: The stamp is difficult to read, and what appears to be "IDR" may be the result of a double strike with a "DR" die. The stamp differs from those usually associated with Daniel Russell, which consist of initials "DR" in a rectangle with a single foil above or the "DR" in conjoined circles—another reason for assigning it to the son.

References: Charlotte E. Smith, "An Examination of an Eighteenth-Century Creampot," Registration Division, Winterthur.

80.189 Gift of Marshall P. Blankarn, 1981

120
SPOON, ca. 1740

L. 7 15/16" (20.2 cm)
1 oz. 17 dwt. 16 gr. (58.6 g)

Stamps: "DR" in roman letters, in a rectangle with a single foil extending above frame, struck once on back of handle.

Engraved on back of handle: "H/ GH" in roman letters; each "H" is shaded, and the "G" is a single line and oddly spaced.

Description: oval bowl with swage-formed rattail and rounded drop on back of bowl; rounded upturned handle with prominent midrib on front.

Spectrographic analysis: Silver content is 91.9 percent.

Provenance: Mr. and Mrs. Stanley B. Ineson, New York City; Mr. and Mrs. Alfred E. Bissell, Wilmington, Del.

References: Belden, *Marks of American Silversmiths*, p. 367 a.

62.240.1369 Gift of Mr. and Mrs. Alfred E. Bissell, 1962–63

Robert Sanderson, Sr.

ca. 1608–93

Robert Sanderson, Jr.

1652–1714
Boston, Massachusetts
For Hull & Sanderson (w. 1652–83), see
John Hull

There is a tendency to think of John Hull, Sanderson's longtime partner, as the father of American silversmithing. This assumption derives, in part, from the line of succession begun when Hull took Jeremiah Dummer as an apprentice. If we are to bestow the title on anyone, however, it more properly belongs to Robert Sanderson, who was the first fully trained and experienced silversmith to bring his talent to Britain's North American colonies. Born in the English provincial parish of Higham (probably near Norwich in Norfolk), he placed himself in 1623 as an apprentice with William Rawlings, goldsmith, of London, for a period of nine years. In July 1632 he was admitted as a freeman of the Goldsmiths' Company. Around this same time he married, and his first child was born the following year. Sanderson, in turn, took his master's son as an apprentice in 1634. Probably impelled by religious convictions, Robert and Lydia Sanderson immigrated to America, settling briefly in Hampton, New Hampshire, in 1638. About 1642, following Lydia's death and Robert's marriage to Mary Cross, he moved to Watertown, Massachusetts, where his brother Edward had settled in 1635. For the next ten years he was apparently engaged in farming, trading,

and, possibly, mining. In any case, he does not appear to have practiced his craft from 1638 until 1652. In 1652 John Hull selected Sanderson to be his partner in the first mint in Britain's North American colonies. Although Hull had received some training as a silversmith, he lacked the long formal training and shop experience of Sanderson. It is probable, therefore, that Hull engaged Sanderson for his technical skills. Hull himself was increasingly involved with mercantile activities and served as business manager in the partnership. Sanderson's son Joseph worked for the partners but died prematurely in 1667. Younger brothers Benjamin and Robert, Jr., also received their training in the Hull & Sanderson shop.

At the time of Hull's death in 1683, Robert Sanderson was seventy-five. Patricia E. Kane feels that he remained active with the assistance of his son Robert Sanderson, Jr. Silver from this period is stamped twice with the "RS" stamp, perhaps signifying joint authorship of father and son. The business continued with Hull's son-in-law Samuel Sewall overseeing the operation and keeping the books. Sewall admired the elder Sanderson and in 1691 took his four children to be blessed by the old man, who was then eighty-three. Following Sanderson's death in 1693, his son Robert, Jr., appears to have ceased work as a silversmith.

Sanderson gave meticulous instructions in his will for the disposition of his property. He provided for his third wife, Elizabeth, "my Cow and three small pieces of plate marked with the Letters of her name, that is to say one small Salt, one Spoon, and Dram Cup. Also Six of my great Bookes . . . and any else of my small Bookes that she pleases to make choices of Together with one halfe part of all my Household Goods and Furniture." The books included *Calvin's Workes*, *My Concordance*, and *Wilson's Compleat Dictionary*. Son Robert received only four books, but one of these was "my Great Bible." Most of the estate,

which included a good deal of real estate, was divided between Robert, Jr., and his sister, Anna West.

Kane's study of Hull and Sanderson is the definitive work on these two important figures. It not only contains copious new information but also redresses the balance in assessing the roles of the two men. Sanderson has finally received the recognition long due him. If John Hull epitomized the Puritan saint, so in a less-public way did Sanderson, which probably explains their compatibility. Sanderson was admitted to the First Church in 1665 and later became deacon. When the congregation splintered over the half-way covenant in 1669, Hull joined the breakaway group that favored it, while Sanderson remained with conservatives who opposed it. This unusual event failed to disrupt the partners' close association.

References: DAB, s.v. "Sanderson, Robert." Kane, *Dictionary*, s.v. "Sanderson, Robert, Sr.," and "Sanderson, Robert, Jr." Kane, "John Hull and Robert Sanderson." Albert S. Roe and Robert F. Trent, "Robert Sanderson and the Founding of the Boston Silversmiths' Trade," in Fairbanks and Trent, *New England Begins*, 3:480–89. SCPR book 13, pp. 264–67, 313–15.

ℰ 121
CAUDLE CUP, ca. 1675

H. 4⅞" (12.4 cm), W. 7¾" (19.7 cm),
DIAM. rim 4¾" (12.1 cm)
11 oz. 18 dwt. 2 gr. (370.3 g)

Stamps: "RS" in roman letters, under a stylized sun, in a conforming shape, struck twice on underside.

Engraved on underside: "S/ TA" in roman letters.

Description: raised circular 1-piece body with bulbous lower half and concave upper half; centerpunch on underside; continuous design on lower half of body formed by chasing, repoussé, and engraving depicting a turkey on 1 side and a rooster on the other, all amid vines terminating in flowers; 2 cast caryatid handles, upper ends terminate in small scrolls, lower ends forked with outside section terminating in small scrolls.

Spectrographic analysis:

	SILVER	COPPER	LEAD	GOLD
SIDE	94.3	5.4	0.21	0.09
BOTTOM	96.6	3.0	0.15	0.10
HANDLE	95.0	4.2	0.23	0.09

History: According to Francis Hill Bigelow, the engraved initials "S/ TA" refer to Thomas Shepard (1635–77) and his wife Ann (Tyng) Shepard (d. 1709), who were married in 1656. Born in England but brought to the New World by his parents during his first year of life, Shepard graduated from Harvard College in 1653 and went on to become one of the ministers of the Charlestown Church. During the smallpox epidemic of 1677, he contracted the disease while visiting one of his sick parishioners and died. Simon Bradstreet wrote: "His death was much lamented and great reason there was for it. He has left few in that colony . . . that did exceed him in respect of his Piety, meekness (eminent charity) Learning and ministeriall gifts." Among Shepard's several bequests was one to the church in Charlestown for plate. The inventory of his estate mentions only "plate to the value of 47 pounds," leaving no way to tell if the cup was included in the

total. This history is questioned by Kane, Albert S. Roe, and Robert F. Trent. Roe and Trent concluded that on stylistic grounds the cup could not have been made before 1670. Kane, who established a chronology of stamps, dates it to between 1685 and 1690. She suggests that the cup belonged to either a Thomas Shepard who married Hannah Ensign in 1658 or his son Thomas Shepard, Jr., who married Hannah Blanchard in 1682. Both were residents of Charlestown in their early years. (This theory presumes that Hannah and Anna were used interchangeably.) Another possibility is that the cup was a memorial for the Reverend Thomas Shepard.

Provenance: The cup descended in the Cary family, whose early members lived in Charlestown and attended the Charlestown Church. How the cup made its way from its original owners to that family is unknown. What is sure is that the cup was owned by Mary Louisa Cary, who in 1846 married Cornelius Conway Felton, president of Harvard College from 1860 to 1862. In 1916 Mrs. Cornelius Conway Felton, Jr., daughter-in-law of Mary Louisa, lent the cup to the Museum of Fine Arts, Boston, whose records describe it as having come from the "Old Cary House in Chelsea." It remained in the museum until late 1921, when it was acquired by Francis Hill Bigelow. He sold it to H. F. du Pont, through Brooks Reed Gallery, Boston, in June 1927.

Exhibitions: "New England Begins: The Seventeenth Century," Museum of Fine Arts, Boston, 1982.

Comments: Roe's "Robert Sanderson's Silver Caudle Cup" is a masterpiece of explication that thoroughly explores the history, design sources, and iconography of this piece and its maker. While this is probably the first American representation of the turkey, the fowl was hardly unknown in the decorative arts of sixteenth- and seventeenth-century Europe, and Roe found several examples of its use. Both Roe and Trent regard this caudle cup as a perfect expression of mannerist design and very up-to-date when it was made.

An English caudle cup with identical turkey repoussé design and the same caryatid handles was made in London in 1663. It is illustrated in the catalogue for the London Antiques Dealers Fair, 1968 (p. 97); it was owned at that time by W. H. Wilson, Ltd., London.

References: Clarke, *John Hull*, p. 215, checklist no. 27. Davidson, *Colonial Antiques*, p. 37. Fales, *American Silver*, no. 2. Donald L. Fennimore, "Robert Sanderson's Caudle Cup," *Silver* 16, no. 1 (January/February 1983): pp. 22, 23. ennimore, *Silver and Pewter*, no. 166. Kane, "John Hull and Robert Sanderson," pp. 461–63. Albert S. Roe, "Robert Sanderson's Silver Caudle Cup in the Winterthur Collection: The Turkey Motif in Seventeenth-Century Design," *American Art Journal* 9, no. 1 (May 1977): 61–77. Albert S. Roe and Robert F. Trent, "Robert Sanderson and the Founding of the Boston Silversmiths' Trade," in Fairbanks and Trent, *New England Begins*, pp. 480–500, no. 463. *Sibley's Harvard Graduates*, 1:327–35.

61.504 Gift of H. F. du Pont, 1965

William Swan

1715–74
Boston and Worcester, Massachusetts

William Swan was the son of mariner Ebenezer Swan of Roxbury, Massachusetts, and Prudence (Foster) Swan. There is no record of his apprenticeship. In 1744 he married Lavinia Keyes in Boston's King's Chapel. He practiced his craft first in Boston and, after about 1754, in Worcester. Although the number of his pieces that survives is small, one of his commissions is significant. He made a large two-handled covered cup presented in 1749 by the Province of Massachusetts Bay to Benjamin Pickman of Salem to honor Pickman's contributions to the Louisburg expedition. The cup is now owned by the Peabody-Essex Institute. In Worcester, Swan became clerk of the market in 1772 and sealer of weights and measures in 1773. Evidently his shop was in his house for, in May 1773, a thief entered his house and stole "5 Pair Stone Earings; ½ Doz. Tea spoons partly finished; 5 Pair Stone Sleeve Buttons; 1 Gold Necklace; Sundry Pair Silver Shoe Buckles, one Pair partly finished; together with Twelve Pounds in Cash, viz. 1 Johanna, 1 Guinea, 6 Crowns, the Remainder in Dollars." The notice gives not only an enumeration of Swan's goods, but it also reveals what he was actually making. E. Alfred Jones records a pair of tall cups by Swan in the First Church of Northborough.

References: Flynt and Fales, *Heritage Foundation*, p. 334. Jones, *Old Silver*, p. 351. Kane, *Dictionary*, s.v. "Swan, William." *Boston News-Letter*, May 27, 1773, as quoted in Dow, *Arts and Crafts*, pp. 55–56.

122
PORRINGER, 1740–70

DIAM. bowl 5 ¾" (14.6 cm), H. 1 ⅞" (4.8 cm), W. 8 ⅛" (20.6 cm)
7 oz. 6 dwt. 8 gr. (227.7 g)

Stamps: "Swan" in script, in a cartouche, struck once on back of handle. Also an illegible strike, possibly "WS".

Engraved on front of handle: "V/ EL/ OL to PL" in roman letters and script.

Description: raised circular bowl with bulging sides and angled rim; bottom domed in center; centerpunch inside and on bottom; cast handle pierced in keyhole pattern with 11 voids.

Spectrographic analysis:

	SILVER	COPPER	LEAD	GOLD
BOWL	91.0	8.4	0.46	0.13
HANDLE	91.2	8.0	0.33	0.15

Provenance: Marshall P. Blankarn, New York City.

77.73 Gift of Marshall P. Blankarn, 1977

123
SPOON, 1740–70

L. 7 ⅞" (20.0 cm)
2 oz. 10 gr. (62.9 g)

Stamps: "W SWAN" in roman letters, in a cartouche, struck once on back of handle.

Engraved on back of handle: "T/ FH" in roman letters. *Engraved on front of handle:* "AH" in script.

Description: elongated oval bowl with swage-formed shell and drop on back; rounded upturned handle with midrib on front.

Spectrographic analysis: Silver content is 92.2 percent.

Provenance: Edna H. Greenwood, Marlborough, Mass.

73.299 Museum purchase from the estate of Edna H. Greenwood, 1973

Thomas Townsend

1703/4–after 1757
Boston, Massachusetts

Little had been known about Thomas Townsend until Barbara McLean Ward completed her work on him for Patricia E. Kane's *Dictionary of Massachusetts Silversmiths*. She has sorted out the several Thomas Townsends in Boston records to settle on the son of Thomas and Sarah (Brown) Townsend, who was born in Boston in January 1703/4 and baptized in the Second Church. Court records reveal that this Townsend was making silver objects. In one instance a Joseph Bradford sued him for failing to deliver 19 ½ ounces of silver within the stipulated three weeks. Townsend was the target of a number of other lawsuits and in one case was codefendant with silversmith Knight Leverett. He was plaintiff in only one suit, this one against silversmith Thomas Edwards for failure to pay for a number of silver objects made by Townsend for Edwards.

Little of Townsend's work survives. There is nothing in Buhler, *American Silver*, and only a spoon in Buhler and Hood, *American Silver*. An elegant caster in the Moore collection at Providence College resembles those by Zachariah Brigden and Benjamin Burt. Two other porringers by Townsend are known, one in the Harrington collection at Dartmouth and one in the Hammerslough collection at Wadsworth Atheneum.

References: Jones, *Old Silver*, pp. 84, 486. Kane, *Dictionary*, s.v. "Townsend, Thomas."

124
PORRINGER, 1740–55

DIAM. bowl 5" (12.7 cm), H. 1 ¾" (4.5 cm), W. 7 ⅝" (19.4 cm)
6 oz. 11 dwt. 16 gr. (204.8 g)

Stamps: "T•T" in roman letters, with a crown above, all in a square, struck once on back of handle.

Engraved on front of handle: "HJ/ to/ HJT/ to / HJB/ 1864" in roman letters and script. The first 3 lines probably date to the eighteenth century; the last 3 lines are clearly later.

Description: raised circular bowl with bulging sides and angled rim; bottom domed in center; centerpunch inside and on bottom; cast handle pierced in keyhole pattern with 11 voids.

Spectrographic analysis:

	SILVER	COPPER	LEAD	GOLD
BOWL	92.4	7.3	0.14	0.13
HANDLE	90.3	9.4	0.22	0.09

Provenance: Marshall P. Blankarn, New York City.

80.188 Gift of Marshall P. Blankarn, 1981

125
SPOON, ca. 1750

L. 7 ¹¹⁄₁₆" (19.5 cm)
1 oz. 7 dwt. 15 gr. (43.0 g)

Stamps: "T·T" in roman letters, with a crown above, all in a square, struck once on back of handle.

Engraved on back of handle: lion's gamb over a heraldic wreath; possibly the crest of the Poole family. *Engraved on front of handle:* "SP"(?) in script.

Description: elongated oval bowl with swage-formed drop on back; rounded upturned handle with midrib on front.

Spectrographic analysis: Silver content is 90.7 percent.

History: Possibly owned by the Poole family.

Provenance: Mr. and Mrs. Stanley B. Ineson, New York City; Mr. and Mrs. Alfred E. Bissell, Wilmington, Del.

References: Belden, *Marks of American Silversmiths*, p. 411.

62.240.1511 Gift of Mr. and Mrs. Alfred E. Bissell, 1962–63

Samuel Vernon

1683–1737
Newport, Rhode Island

Samuel Vernon's parents were Daniel Vernon, who arrived from London in 1666, and Ann (Dyer) Vernon, whose sister, Elizabeth Hutchinson, was silversmith Edward Winslow's mother. In other words, Vernon and the great Boston silversmith were second cousins. No record of Vernon's apprenticeship has been found. He became a freeman in 1714. In 1707 he married Elizabeth Fleet of Long Island, who died in 1722. In 1725 he married Elizabeth Paine of Bristol, who survived him. Daniel, a child from his first marriage, also became a silversmith. Vernon was active in public service. In 1730 he was appointed by the General Assembly to a commission charged with settling claims to Narragansett Indian land. In the same year he helped oversee the movement of people and goods from Boston, where there was a smallpox epidemic. He also served on a committee to settle the boundary dispute between Massachusetts and New Hampshire. He was an assistant in the General Assembly from 1729 to 1737. He was heavily engaged in mercantile activities and was a prolific silversmith who made many tankards and porringers. E. Alfred Jones credits him with two tankards, a beaker, and a cup in the Newport Congregational Church, plus beakers in the Bristol, Rhode Island, and Groton, Connecticut, churches. A pair of spurs bearing his stamp is in the Hammerslough collection at Wadsworth Atheneum. Although his tankards differ in proportion and fittings from those by Winslow, he frequently used the double-dolphin cast thumbpiece favored by Winslow.

References: John O. Austin, *Genealogical Dictionary of Rhode Island* (1887; reprint, Baltimore: Genealogical Publishing Co., 1969), p. 402. Ralph E. Carpenter, *The Arts and Crafts of Newport, Rhode Island, 1640–1820* (Newport, R.I.: Preservation Society of Newport County, 1954), pp. 166–67, nos. 110, 112, 119–21, 126, 130, 138. Flynt and Fales, *Heritage Foundation*, p. 347. Jones, *Old Silver*, pp. 96, 189, 318–20.

126
PORRINGER, ca. 1725

DIAM. bowl 5 ⅜" (12.7 cm), H. 2" (5.1 cm), W. 7 ¾" (19.7 cm)
8 oz. 13 dwt. (269.0 g)

Stamps: "SV" in roman letters, over a fleur-de-lis, all in a heart, struck on back of handle and inside bottom.

Engraved on front of handle: "CN" in later script.

Description: raised circular bowl with bulging sides and flared rim; bottom domed in center; centerpunch inside and on bottom; cast handle pierced in geometric pattern with 12 voids.

Spectrographic analysis:

	SILVER	COPPER	LEAD	GOLD
BOWL SIDE	91.3	7.9	0.34	0.11
HANDLE	90.2	7.2	0.22	0.06

History: According to Benjamin Jackson, the dealer who sold it to H. F. du Pont, the porringer descended in the following Newport, R.I., families: Brown, Norris, Freebody, Potter, Lake, and Spencer.

Provenance: Miss Spencer of Newport, from whom it was acquired by Benjamin A. Jackson, Wickford Hill Antique Shop, Wickford, R.I., who sold it to H. F. du Pont, July 1929.

References: Fales, *American Silver*, no. 55.

65.1383 Gift of H. F. du Pont, 1965

ᾧ 127
PORRINGER, ca. 1725

DIAM. bowl 5 ³/₁₆" (13.2 cm), H. 2 ¼" (5.7 cm),
W. 7 ⁷/₁₆" (18.9 cm)
8 oz. 4 dwt. 22 gr. (256.5 g)

Stamps: "SV" in roman letters, over a fleur-de-lis, all in a heart, struck on back of handle and inside bottom.

Engraved on front of handle: "C/ I∗I" in roman letters.

Description: raised circular bowl with bulging sides and slightly angled rim; bottom domed in center; centerpunch inside and on bottom; cast handle pierced in geometric pattern with 12 voids.

Spectrographic analysis:

	SILVER	COPPER	LEAD	GOLD
BOWL BOTTOM	91.2	7.9	0.36	0.07
HANDLE	93.5	6.0	0.13	0.14

Provenance: H. F. du Pont purchased 4 porringers by Samuel Vernon from 4 different sources; only 1 can be related to its source. This porringer was purchased from 1 of the following: Israel Sack, Boston, February 1929; Clapp & Graham, New York City, May 1930; or A. L. Lusty, Troy, N.Y., November 1930.

References: Fales, *American Silver*, no. 58.

65.1361 Gift of H. F. du Pont, 1965

ᾧ 128
PORRINGER, ca. 1730

DIAM. bowl 5 ¼" (13.3 cm), H. 1 ⅞" (4.8 cm),
W. 7 ¹¹/₁₆" (19.5 cm)
7 oz. 16 dwt. 14 gr. (243.5 g)

Stamps: "SV" in roman letters, over a fleur-de-lis, all in a heart, struck on back of handle and inside bottom.

Engraved on front of handle: "G/ R∗E/ E∗G" in roman letters.

Description: raised circular bowl with bulging sides and slightly angled rim; bottom domed in center; centerpunch inside only; cast handle pierced in keyhole pattern with 13 voids.

Spectrographic analysis:

	SILVER	COPPER	LEAD	GOLD
BOWL INSIDE	90.9	8.7	0.32	0.05
HANDLE	93.1	6.1	0.28	0.08

Provenance: See no. 127.

65.1378 Gift of H. F. du Pont, 1965

ᾧ 129
PORRINGER, ca. 1730

DIAM. bowl 5 ⅝" (14.3 cm), H. 2 ¹¹/₁₆" (6.8 cm),
W. 7 ⅞" (20.0 cm)
8 oz. 14 dwt. 22 gr. (272.0 g)

Stamps: "SV" in roman letters, over a fleur-de-lis, all in a heart, struck on back of handle and inside bottom.

Engraved on front of handle: "E•W/ S•W" in roman letters.

Description: raised circular bowl with bulging sides and slightly angled rim; bottom domed in center; centerpunch inside and on bottom; cast handle pierced in keyhole pattern with 13 voids.

Spectrographic analysis:

	SILVER	COPPER	LEAD	GOLD
BOWL SIDE	87.5	11.0	0.32	0.05
HANDLE	93.4	5.2	0.22	0.09

Provenance: See no. 127.

65.1371 Gift of H. F. du Pont, 1965

℞ 130
BOX, 1704–37

H. ½" (1.3 cm), L. 1 ⅞" (4.8 cm), w. 1 ⅜" (3.5 cm)
9 dwt. 23 gr. (15.5 g)

Stamps: "SV" in roman letters, in a heart with a device below (probably a fleur-de-lis), struck inside on bottom of body and inside lid.

Engraved on underside of body: "N∗V" (or "A∗N" without a crossbar on the "A") in shaded roman letters. *Engraved on top of lid:* leafy scrolls enclosed within a border consisting of double-incised lines and stylized pointed leaves enfilade. Cross-hatching on sides.

Description: small oval box with friction-fit lid. Sides formed from seamed sheet silver, which is in turn soldered to flat base. Lid similarly made. Both top of lid and base of body formed from sheet and rolled at edges.

Spectrographic analysis:

	SILVER	COPPER	LEAD	GOLD
UNDERSIDE	93.7	5.8	0.20	0.16
BODY SIDE	92.8	6.4	0.25	0.17
LID	91.5	7.8	0.33	0.21

History: According to Francis Hill Bigelow, the initials are those of Abigail Northey. Bigelow claims to have purchased the box from a descendant.

Provenance: Abigail Northey; descended to Mrs. Abram Marland, Andover, Mass., who sold it to Francis Hill Bigelow; Brooks Reed Gallery, Boston, sold to H. F. du Pont, 1927.

Exhibitions: Museum of Fine Arts, Boston, when owned by Francis Hill Bigelow.

Comments: At one point a label was attached to the inside of the box: "M.F.A./ 580.12." Oval boxes by William Whittemore and Benjamin Brenton also employ the border of stylized pointed leaves.

65.1366 Gift of H. F. du Pont, 1965

℞ 131 a–f
SPOONS, 1704–37

(a) L. 7 ⁷⁄₁₆" (18.9 cm)
1 oz. 4 dwt. 6 gr. (37.9 g)
(b) L. 7 ⅝" (19.37 cm)
1 oz. 4 dwt. 9 gr. (37.9 g)
(c) L. 7 ⁹⁄₁₆" (19.2 cm)
1 oz. 9 dwt. 2 gr. (45.3 g)
(d) L. 7 ¹⁵⁄₁₆" (18.6 cm)
1 oz. 5 dwt. 9 gr. (39.5 g)
(e) L. 7 ⅝" (19.37 cm)
1 oz. 14 dwt. 8 gr. (53.4 g)
(f) L. 7 ¹¹⁄₁₆" (19.5 cm)
1 oz. 6 dwt. 11 gr. (41.2 g)

Stamps: "SV" in roman letters, over a fleur-de-lis, all in a heart, struck once on back of handle.

Engraved on backs of handles: (a, b) "AN"; (c) "BB/ +/EL"; (d) "S/ ND"; (e) "W/ I∗G"; (f) "B/ IA". *Engraved on front of handle:* (c) "RKP". All in roman letters.

Description: oval bowl with swage-formed rat-tail and drop on back; trifid upturned handle with no midrib.

Spectrographic analysis: Silver content ranges from 91.1 to 93.5 percent.

Provenance: (a, b) Israel Sack, Boston, sold to H. F. du Pont, December 1930; (c–f) Mr. and Mrs. Stanley B. Ineson, New York City; Mr. and Mrs. Alfred E. Bissell, Wilmington, Del.

Exhibitions: (a), (b), or (c) Metropolitan Museum of Art, New York City, 1935–61.

Comments: Owner's initials on (f) same as on pair of casters by Benjamin Burt, no. 15.

References: Belden, *Marks of American Silversmiths,* p. 422.

65.1368, .1359 Gift of H. F. du Pont, 1965; 62.240.1528, .1529, .1526, .1527 Gift of Mr. and Mrs. Alfred E. Bissell, 1962–63

Edward Webb

ca. 1666–1718
Boston, Massachusetts

Born in Berkshire, the son of a yeoman, Edward Webb was bound apprentice to William Denny, a prominent London goldsmith, in 1680. He became a freeman of the Goldsmiths' Company in 1687. Webb was definitely in Boston by 1709, but he may have been there as early as 1706. His master's London shop produced some of the most high-style silver of the time; it is, therefore, surprising to see the plainness of the silver Webb produced in Boston. Little is known about his life in Boston beyond what is contained in his will and inventory and the fact that he was an appraiser of the estate of silversmith Richard Conyers. To his "kind friend Thomas Miller [Milner] of Boston, Goldsmith," Webb bequeathed £20. His housekeeper, Hannah Kelinack, received £100, all his wearing apparel and household goods—"my working tools excepted." His most generous bequest was £200 to the poor of Boston to be distributed by "my Trusty Friend Daniel Oliver" (owner of the sugar box made by Edward Winslow). His inventory consists mostly of tools and materials in his shop. The appraisers were silversmiths John Edwards and John Dixwell. The extensive list of tools includes "2 Te[e]sts with plaine and flower'd Spoon Swages," "3 pr Organ Bellowes," and a "parcel of patterns." Also in his shop were £33.12.0 in gold jewelry, £122.6.10 in unwrought gold, £206.17.0 in unwrought silver, and £401.5.0 in coins. With all this wealth in his shop, his household furnishings were sparse, and he owned no real estate. A small amount of his silver survives, mostly porringers and tankards.

References: Kane, *Dictionary*, s.v. "Webb, Edward." Ward, "Boston Goldsmiths," pp. 162–63, 371. SCPR book 21, pp. 141–42, 261–62.

132
PORRINGER, ca. 1710

DIAM. bowl 5 ¼" (13.3 cm), H. 1 ¾" (4.5 cm), W. 7 ¾" (19.7 cm)
7 oz. 17 dwt. 20 gr. (245.5 g)

Stamps: "EW" in roman letters, in a rectangle, struck once inside bottom and once on underside of handle.

Engraved on front of handle: "B/ to/ E.A.C./ Jany 1, 1846" (facing in) in script.

Description: raised circular bowl with bulging sides and flared rim; bottom domed in center; centerpunch inside; cast handle pierced in geometric pattern with 16 voids.

Spectrographic analysis:

	SILVER	COPPER	LEAD	GOLD
BOWL	89.9	8.9	0.57	0.14
HANDLE	88.7	8.9	0.71	0.38

Provenance: Marshall P. Blankarn, New York City.

Comments: At least 7 other porringers by Webb are known; 2 are in the Museum of Fine Arts, Boston.

76.281 Gift of Marshall P. Blankarn, 1976

133
SPOON, ca. 1710

L. 7 ⁹⁄₁₆" (19.2 cm), 1 oz. 7 dwt. 18 gr. (43.2 g)

Stamps: "EW" in roman letters, in a rectangle, struck once on back of handle.

Engraved on back of handle: "M/ IA" in shaded roman letters.

Description: wide oval bowl with swage-formed beaded rattail flanked by converging ridges on back; trifid-end handle cut from sheet.

Spectrographic analysis:

	SILVER	COPPER	LEAD	GOLD
BOWL	93.4	6.1	0.24	0.20
HANDLE	93.7	6.0	0.21	0.14

Provenance: Mr. and Mrs. Stanley B. Ineson, New York City; Mr. and Mrs. Alfred E. Bissell, Wilmington, Del.

Comments: A similar spoon by Webb is owned by the Metropolitan Museum of Art, New York City.

References: Belden, *Marks of American Silversmiths*, p. 435.

62.240.1553 Gift of Mr. and Mrs. Alfred E. Bissell, 1962–63

William Whittemore

1709/10–ca. 1770
Portsmouth, New Hampshire
Kittery, Maine

William Whittemore's father, Pelatiah Whittemore (1680–1730) of Charlestown, Massachusetts, became commissary of Portsmouth in 1703 and in 1706 married Margery Pepperrell, daughter of William Pepperrell (1648–1733/34) of Kittery. Pepperrell was a major landowner and merchant, and his son was the first American to be knighted for leading the expedition that captured Louisburg from the French. The connection between the Whittemores and the Pepperrells proved useful to William Whittemore when he became a silversmith. His grandfather Pepperrell bequeathed to the First Church in Kittery £60 "to be laid out or turned into Plate or Vessels for the use of the said Church at the Discretion of my Executor & Overseers with the Pastor and Deacons of said Church." They commissioned Whittemore to make three two-handled cups in 1734. (The Kittery Church also has communion plate by Samuel Minott, Zachariah Brigden, and John Burt.) Whittemore also made communion silver for Saint John's Church in Portsmouth and the church in Newington, New Hampshire. Whittemore probably served his apprenticeship under his uncle Andrew Tyler of Boston; he witnessed deeds for him in 1727 and 1728. Whittemore had his shop in Portsmouth until about 1754; for the rest of his years he had a shop on Kittery Point, and its location is shown on a map in Everett S. Stackpole's *Old Kittery and Her Families*. William Maybury of Kittery, mariner, esteemed Whittemore by bequeathing his entire estate to him in 1745 "in Consideration of the Love friendship & Respect which I have & do bear to William Whittemore of Portsmouth in the Province of New Hampshire Goldsmith and of the many favours & Services I have Received of him." Although Whittemore's death date has not been found, his widow's death notice in 1774 identified her as "Mrs. Whittemore, Widow of Mr. Whittemore, Goldsmith, deceased." A small quantity of Whittemore's work survives. A gold mourning ring of his make was recently given to Strawbery Banke Museum in Portsmouth.

References: Boston News-Letter, October 13, 1774, for death notice of Mrs. Whittemore. Jones, *Old Silver*, pp. 236, 310, 382. Kane, *Dictionary*, s.v. "Whittemore, William." *New Hampshire Clocks, Silver, and Furniture: A Salute to Charles S. Parsons* (Manchester, N.H.: Currier Gallery of Art, 1988), nos. 108–12. Sybil Noyes, Charles Thornton Libby, and Goodwin Davis, *Genealogical Dictionary of Maine and New Hampshire* (Portland, Maine: Southworth-Anthoensen Press, 1928–39), p. 750. *Probate Records of the Province of New Hampshire*, State Papers series, 9 vols. (Concord: State of New Hampshire, 1907–41), 3: 323–24. Everett S. Stackpole, *Old Kittery and Her Families* (Lewiston, Maine: Press of Lewiston Journal, 1903), pp. 58–59.

134
BOX, ca. 1740

H. ⅜" (1.0 cm), L. 2 ⁷⁄₁₆" (6.2 cm), W. 1 ¾" (4.5 cm)
16 dwt. 5 gr. (25.2 g)

Stamps: "Whittemore" in script, in a rectangle with indented ends, struck once on underside of body.

Engraved on underside of body: "S=Smith" in italics. *Engraved on top of lid:* central stylized thistle over crosshatched lunette, all within a border of double-incised lines and stylized pointed leaves enfilade.

Description: small oval box with friction-fit lid. Sides formed from seamed sheet silver that is soldered to flat base. Lid similarly made. Both top of lid and base of body formed from sheet. Painted in red inside lid: "L.2769.31B".

Spectrographic analysis:

	SILVER	COPPER	LEAD	GOLD
UNDERSIDE	91.1	7.7	0.27	0.24
LID	87.2	12.1	0.34	0.07
SIDE	91.9	7.1	0.32	0.11

Provenance: Purchased from Alfred Stainforth prior to 1912 by Francis Hill Bigelow; Brooks Reed Gallery, Boston, sold to H. F. du Pont, June 1927.

Exhibitions: Museum of Fine Arts, Boston, for indeterminate period while owned by Bigelow.

Comments: A heart-shape box by Whittemore, owned by the Museum of Art, Rhode Island School of Design, has a similar stylized thistle engraved on its lid. Oval boxes by Samuel Vernon and Benjamin Brenton also employ the border of stylized pointed leaves.

References: Bigelow, *Historic Silver*, p. 394. Fales, *American Silver*, no. 66. Charles S. Parsons, *New Hampshire Silver* (Cranbury, N.J.: Adams Brown, 1983), p. 21.

65.1364 Gift of H. F. du Pont, 1965

135 a, b
SPOONS, ca. 1750

(a) L. 4⅜" (11.1 cm)
5 dwt. 22 gr. (9.2 g)
(b) 7¹¹⁄₁₆" (19.5 cm)
1 oz. 14 dwt. 15 gr. (53.9 g)

Stamps: "Whittemore" in script, in a rectangle with indented sides, struck once on back of each handle.

Engraved on back of handle: (a) "ID/ to/ SL" in roman letters and script; (b) "D/ EL" in shaded roman letters above; "A. E Haven" in later script below.

Description: oval bowls with swage-formed rattails and single rounded drops; rounded upturned handles with midribs on front.

Spectrographic analysis: Silver content ranges from 91.5 to 95.2 percent.

History: (a) The initials "ID" may refer to John Downing (1684–1766), who gave a silver beaker to the Congregational Church in Newington, N.H. (b) Possibly owned by Anne Haven of Portsmouth, N.H., whose will was proved in 1849. She left several bequests of silver flatware to children and grandchildren. Her inventory, which is very detailed, contains quantities of sterling and plated wares. The Havens were a prominent family of Portsmouth.

Provenance: Mr. and Mrs. Stanley B. Ineson, New York City; Mr. and Mrs. Alfred E. Bissell, Wilmington, Del.

Exhibitions: (b) Metropolitan Museum of Art, New York City, 1935–61.

References: Belden, *Marks of American Silversmiths*, p. 444. Jones, *Old Silver*, p. 310. Will of Ann Haven of Portsmouth, proved February 21, 1849; inventory, July 11, 1849, Rockingham County Probate Records, Exeter, N.H.

62.240.627, .1593 Gift of Mr. and Mrs. Alfred E. Bissell, 1962–63

Edward Winslow

1669–1753

Edward Winslow does not appear in Samuel Sewall's diary until 1708, by which time Winslow is thirty-nine years of age and Sewall is fifty-six. The references to "Capt. Winslow" are not numerous but sufficient to suggest that by this time Winslow was accepted by the social elite of Boston. Several times Sewall and Winslow were bearers at burials, such as that of Benjamin Pemberton on March 12, 1708/9. (Elizabeth Dixie, Pemberton's widow, later became Winslow's second wife.) That Sewall patronized Winslow is shown by the diary entry for January 30, 1713/14: "I presented my Son and daughter with six silver spoons, cost about 21s a piece, bought of Capt. Winslow this day." Sewall also presented Gov. Samuel Shute with "a Ring wt 3 p. and 3 Grains, cost 35s and 3d with this Motto, *Post tenebras Lucem.* Jany 1721/22: respecting the Darkness of the Small Pocks, and our Divisions; which his Excellency received very graciously in Mr. Sergeant's Counting Room. Capt. Winslow made it." On one occasion (December 1, 1723) the Winslows accompanied Sewall to church at "the New North Brick." Afterwards most of the party dined at Deacon Townsend's, but "Mr. Sherrif Winslow went home."

During his long life Winslow witnessed major historical events while profiting from a growing and extensive network of kinfolk and influential friends. The Boston of his mature years was hardly the same town that it had been during his youth. Winslow himself, although of distinguished ancestry, enjoyed modest success initially. That he moved up socially and economically is suggested by the fact that only his youngest son, Isaac, went to Harvard. Isaac's first term was paid for with two silver spoons and his second with a necklace of gold beads. After graduation and an apprenticeship in the counting house of James Bowdoin, he went into business with his eldest brother, Joshua. They were among the most successful Boston merchants of the middle decades of the eighteenth century. Edward Winslow's daughter Elizabeth married Richard Clarke. Their daughter Susanna married John Singleton Copley, whose pastel portrait of her is owned by Winterthur (Edgar P. Richardson, *American Paintings and Related Pictures in the Henry Francis du Pont Winterthur Museum* [Charlottesville: University Press of Virginia, 1986], no. 28).

Edward Winslow was the grand-nephew of Gov. Edward Winslow of Plymouth. The silversmith's father, also named Edward, married Elizabeth Hutchinson, a granddaughter of Anne Hutchinson. The Edward of this entry first married Hannah Moody, daughter of the Reverend Joshua Moody, who was buried in John Hull's tomb in 1697. (Moody was a combative soul who openly opposed the witchcraft hysteria and once declined the presidency of Harvard College.) Winslow next married Elizabeth Dixie Pemberton in 1722. A gold mourning ring commemorating her death, "16 Sep 1740 AE 71," probably made by Winslow, is owned by Yale University Art Gallery. Winslow's third wife, Susannah Furman Lyman (m. 1744), survived him to marry Nicholas Sever, a former Harvard tutor.

Winslow's early public service, between 1699 and 1715, ran the usual gamut. He was constable, fireward, tithing man, surveyor, overseer of the poor, and selectman. His military service included serving in the militia as captain, major, and, finally, as colonel of the Boston regiment with Jacob Wendell as lieutenant colonel and Samuel Sewall as major. He was also a member of the Artillery Company and served as its captain in 1714 and 1729. From 1728 to 1743, he served as sheriff of Suffolk County, Massachusetts, a post that Jonathan Belcher declared to be worth at least £600 to £700 a year. In 1740 he was given the unenviable task of impressing twenty seamen "not being inhabitants of this province, or belonging to any outward-bound fishing-vessel, or coaster" for the HMS *Astrea.* During the last ten years of his life, he was a judge of the Inferior Court of Common Pleas.

Winslow lived in a large house on King Street (purchased from the heirs of Gov. John Leverett) at what later became the corner of State and Congress streets. The inventory of his estate valued the mansion house at £666.13.4. He also owned a house in Middle Street valued at £200. His 222 ounces 5 pennyweight in wrought silver he directed to be sold to pay his debts and funeral expenses. In addition, he bequeathed to his surviving sons "as a token of remembrance" specific items of value: to Joshua "my silver hilt sword," to John "my clock," and to Isaac "my Watch." He also bequeathed to the grandson of his second wife, "two Belly Cups wrought" (no doubt what we today would call a cann). He further reserved from the plate to be sold a silver snuffer and stand and a spoon, all for the use of his wife. To the widows of his three deceased sons—Edward, Samuel, and William—he bequeathed £50 each. The total value of his estate, real and personal, was £1,083.18.5.

As a silversmith he is without peer. The wondrous chasing and brilliant design in the sugar boxes alone qualify him for a special place in the history of the craft. The three great communion dishes made for the Second Church of Boston display a grandeur that relies instead on pure form. Their imposing presence is hard to explain and cannot be captured in photographs. He was well patronized by the Hutchinson family, to which he was related through his mother. Through his three wives and his children he built an extended network of blood relatives and in-laws that served him well in his craft and his mercantile pursuits. Among them was the silversmith Samuel Vernon of Newport, Rhode Island, a second cousin.

Historians of American silver have theorized that Winslow served his apprenticeship under Jeremiah Dummer (1645–1718) because of similarities between some pieces made by each craftsman. Winslow's standing salt is much like Dummer's (both pieces in the Museum of Fine Arts, Boston); hence, it is said, we see the passing on of a tradition of craftsmanship and design. The trouble with this theory is that there are too many examples of nearly identical pieces made by different makers who had no such relationship with one another. The four flagons made for Boston's Brattle Street Church are, in the words of Kathryn C. Buhler, "as alike as if made by one man" but in fact were made by John Noyes, Nathaniel Morse, John Edwards, and Winslow. Perhaps Winslow did serve under Dummer, but until better evidence surfaces it remains an open question. Winslow's own apprentices included Moody Russell and Peter Oliver. A portrait of Winslow by John Smibert is owned by Yale University Art Gallery.

References: Buhler, *American Silver*, pp. 79–89. Buhler and Hood, *American Silver*, pp. 54–66. Helen Comstock, "Silver by Edward Winslow of Boston, 1669–1753," *Connoisseur* 33, no. 482 (December 1941): 205–9. Sewall, *Diary*, index. *DAB*, s.v. "Winslow, Edward"; "Winslow, Isaac." Ensko, *American Silversmiths III*, pp. 144, 175. Jones, *Old Silver*, pp. 9, 41, 65, 68, 97, 120, 225, 286, 405, 406, 483, 489, 491. Kane, *Dictionary*, s.v. "Winslow, Edward." John Marshall Phillips, "Edward Winslow, Goldsmith, Sheriff, and Colonel," *Bulletin of the Associates in Fine Arts at Yale University* 6, no. 3 (June 1935): 45, 46. Council proceedings, June 12, 1740, in *Proceedings of the Massachusetts Historical Society* 18 (1880–81): 370. Roberts, *Artillery Company*, 1:326–27. John H. Sheppard, "Genealogy of the Winslow Family," *NEH&GR* 17 (1863): 159–62. SCPR book 48, pp. 595–96; book 49, pp. 341–45. Edward Winslow to William Pepperrell, May 24, 1745, in "The Pepperrell Papers," in *Collections of the Massachusetts Historical Society*, 6th ser., 10 (1899): 216–17.

136
TANKARD, ca. 1703

H. 6¾" (17.2 cm), DIAM. base 5" (12.7 cm), W. 7³⁄₁₆" (18.3 cm)
23 oz. 11 dwt. 3 gr. (733.6 g)

Stamps: "EW" in roman letters, over a fleur-de-lis, all in a conforming shape resembling a shield, struck on body, left of handle, and on lid.

Engraved on body opposite handle: arms of the Chester family, griffin rampant in shield above ermine surmounted by helmet, crest, griffin rampant; mantling of bold scrolls.

Engraved on lid: "This/ Tankard/ with three large Flaggons where given/ to the Church in Charlestown/ by/ Richard Sprague, Esqʳ./ a liberal Benefactor to the Church & poor of/ said Town AD.1703. The Flaggons not being needed/ for Sacramental uses, were sold by Vote of the Church/ June 17.ᵗʰ 1800. & the property vested in a Town Note/ See Chh. Book. ᶠᵒˡⁱᵒ Nᵒ. 1. p. 58, & Chh. Book Nᵒ. 2.ᵗᵒ 4. p. 31" in script and roman letters.

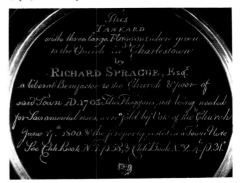

Engraved on base: "The gift of/ Capt. Richard Sprague/ to the Church of Charlstoune 1703" in script.

Description: raised body with straight sides; applied base molding rises from plain lower edge to a torus molding followed by a scotia molding with double-bead moldings above and below both; double-scored line encircles upper body below rim. Raised bottom with no centerpunch. Raised 2-step lid with centerpunches on both sides; crenate lip; 2 pairs of scored lines encircle lid at edge. Cast thumbpiece consists of a pair of dolphins flanking circular mask of man with drooping mustache; meander wire at base. Cast hinge with meander wire on each side. Raised-and-soldered hollow handle with tapered drop soldered to body below upper juncture of handle; cast cherub's head tailpiece; cast drop adjoining hinge; circular vent.

Spectrographic analysis:

	SILVER	COPPER	LEAD	GOLD
BODY	91.6	8.0	0.33	0.05
BOTTOM	92.7	6.7	0.41	0.12
LID	90.6	8.8	0.36	0.07
HANDLE	90.5	9.1	0.28	0.06
THUMBPIECE	92.8	6.5	0.29	0.11

History: Capt. Richard Sprague (ca. 1625–1703) was a sea captain and member of one of the founding families of Charlestown. Born in England, he was the son of Ralph Sprague (d. 1650) and the nephew of Richard Sprague (d. 1668). He commanded an armed vessel during the hostilities with the Dutch in 1674 and patroled Long Island Sound to protect Anglo-American shipping. When the Charlestown train band was split into 2 companies, he was chosen to command 1 of the companies. Sprague was prominent among those who opposed the repressive measures of Governor Andros following the revocation of the Massachusetts Bay Colony's charter in 1686. He was placed under house arrest, deprived of command of his militia company, and expelled from the House of Representatives. In 1689 simmering resentment broke into open rebellion. On April 18, 1689, Sprague led his militia company into Boston. Local government was saved, and Richard Sprague was a hero. Sprague's first wife was Eunice Chester, the daughter of Leonard and Mary Chester, which accounts for the Chester coat of arms on both tankards. The Spragues were not armigerous, but the Chesters were. Leonard Chester's tomb in Wethersfield, Conn., bears a crude armorial device and the inscription: "Here lyes the body of Leonard Chester Armiger late of the Town of Blaby and several other Lordships in Leistersheire deceased in Wethersfeild Anno Domini 1648 Etatis 39." In 1655 Mary Chester married Richard Russell of Charlestown, who died in 1676. This is the same Richard Russell who is memorialized in the 2 tankards made by Jeremiah Dummer for Charlestown Church (nos. 43, 44). When Mary died in 1688, she bequeathed £5 to her son-in-law Richard Sprague and "a silver plate with the Chester arms on it" to her servant John Coultman of Wethersfield.

Richard Sprague died October 7, 1703, at age 78. He had no children of his own, but in his will he provided for the children of his 2 brothers. A wealthy man for the time and place, he was a munificent benefactor. Of particular interest is his bequest to the Charlestown Church of £100 in money, "part thereof to be laid out and invested into four Sylver tankards for ye Sacramentall use and ye rest of s^d sum to be disposed of by ye Deacons of the s^d Church or their successours for ye best advantage of s^d Church." He bequeathed Harvard College £400, all in pieces of eight, £50 to the Reverend Simon Bradstreet, £20 to the Reverend Michael Wigglesworth, and £50 to the free school in Charlestown. The inventory of his estate included "money found in the house . . . £2243.12.0," 66 oz. of plate, and "two cocernuts tipt wt Silver."

William I. Budington indicates that in 1800 the "sacramental furniture" belonging to Charlestown Church consisted of 4 flagons, 14 tankards, 1 cup, 1 basin, and 1 spoon, all in silver; 8 pewter dishes; and 2 tablecloths. Three flagons, 7 tankards, and 4 pewter dishes, "not having been used for many years, were sold, and the proceeds loaned to the town of Charlestown, to be again invested in plate for the use of the communion table, at the pleasure of the church."

Provenance: In March 1926 the First Church of Charlestown, Mass., sold 14 pieces of communion plate to Alfred Stainforth of Winthrop, Mass., for $7,500. The lot included this and 1 other tankard by Winslow plus 2 tankards by Dummer (nos. 43, 44) and 2 by Josiah Austin (nos. 3, 4). H. F. du Pont purchased the 6 tankards from Israel Sack, April 1926.

Exhibitions: "American Church Silver," Museum of Fine Arts, Boston, 1911. "New England Meeting House and Church, 1630–1850," Currier Gallery of Art, Manchester, N.H., 1979.

Comments: See no. 137 for mate to this tankard.

References: American Church Silver, nos. 1013 or 1014. Peter Benes and Philip D. Zimmerman, *New England Meeting House and Church: 1650–1850* (Manchester, N.H., and Boston: Currier Gallery of Art and Boston University, 1979), no. 143. William I. Budington, *The History of the First Church of Charlestown* (Boston: By the author, 1845), pp. 192–93. Fales, *American Silver*, no. 35. Margery Somers Foster, *"Out of Smalle Beginnings . . .": An Economic History of Harvard College in the Puritan Period, 1636 to 1712* (Cambridge: Belknap Press, 1962), p. 61. Frothingham, *History of Charlestown*, esp. chap. 23. Jones, *Old Silver*, pp. 119–20, pl. 48. Roberts, *Artillery Company*, 1:267. Henry R. Stiles, *History of Ancient Wethersfield, Connecticut*, 2 vols. (New York: Grafton Press, 1904), 2:208–11. Robert Trent, "Silver Abstracts from Middlesex Probate," author's collection (a copy of this 1974 compilation was generously provided by Trent). Thomas B. Wyman, *Genealogies and Estates of Charlestown in the County of Middlesex and Commonwealth of Massachusetts, 1629–1818*, 2 vols. (Boston, 1879), 2:892.

59.3365 Gift of H. F. du Pont, 1965

137
TANKARD, ca. 1703

H. 6⅜" (16.8 cm), DIAM. base 5" (12.7 cm),
w. 7¼" (18.4 cm)
23 oz. 11 dwt. 22 gr. (733.9 g)

Stamps: "EW" in roman letters, over a fleur-de-lis, all in a conforming shape resembling a shield, struck on body, left of handle, and on lid.

Engraved on body opposite handle: arms of the Chester family, griffin rampant in shield above ermine surmounted by helmet, crest, griffin rampant; mantling of bold scrolls. *Engraved on base:* "The gift of/ Capᵗ. Richard Sprague/ to the Church of Charlstoune 1703" in script. *Scratched on lid:* "DL" in roman letters.

Description: raised body with straight sides; applied base molding rises from plain lower edge to torus molding followed by scotia molding with double-bead moldings above and below both; doubled-scored line encircles upper body below rim. Raised bottom with no centerpunch. Raised 2-step lid with centerpunches on both sides; crenate lip; 2 pairs of scored lines encircle lid at edge. Cast thumbpiece consists of a pair of dolphins flanking a circular mask of man with drooping mustache; meander wire at base. Cast hinge with meander wire on each side; arabic "6" struck into right side and underside of hinge. Raised-and-soldered hollow handle with tapered drop soldered to body below upper juncture of handle; cast cherub's head tailpiece; cast drop adjoining hinge; notched vent.

Spectrographic analysis:

	SILVER	COPPER	LEAD	GOLD
BODY	92.2	7.2	0.35	0.12
BOTTOM	93.8	5.7	0.35	0.08
LID	90.9	8.5	0.33	0.09
HANDLE	90.0	9.4	0.27	0.07
THUMBPIECE	93.5	5.9	0.21	0.12

History: Part of communion service owned by the First Church of Charlestown, Mass.; see no. 136.

Provenance: See no. 136.

Exhibitions: See no. 136.

Comments: See no. 136 for mate to this tankard.

References: See no. 136, but this tankard is not illustrated in Fales, *American Silver.*

59.3366 Gift of H. F. du Pont, 1965

ℰ 138
COMMUNION DISH, 1711

DIAM. 15 ⅛" (38.4 cm), H. 1 ¹³⁄₁₆" (4.6 cm)
42 oz. 10 dwt. 1 gr. (1322.0 g)

Stamps: "EW" in roman letters, over a fleur-de-lis, all in a conforming shape resembling a shield, struck on rim opposite engraved arms.

Engraved on rim opposite stamp: heraldic device consisting of a lion rampant in circular field with crosslets, all surrounded by foliate mantling (Hutchinson arms).

Engraved on underside: "The Gift of/ Edward Hutchinson/ To the Second Church in Boston. May 1711" in script.

Description: raised circular form, deeply dished in center, with broad rim; edge of rim folded; large centerpunch on inside, smaller one on bottom.

Spectrographic analysis:

	SILVER	COPPER	LEAD	GOLD
BOTTOM	92.5	7.0	0.33	0.03
INSIDE	94.8	4.7	0.35	0.04

History: Edward Hutchinson (1678–1752) was the son of Elisha Hutchinson and Lydia Foster and the half brother of Thomas Hutchinson, who presented an identical dish to Boston's Second Church (no. 139). Hutchinson was a successful merchant and an influential figure in the public life of Boston. He served in many public offices, including those of constable, selectman, justice of the peace, justice of the Court of Common Pleas, and judge of probate for Suffolk County. His name is associated with the development of public works such as markets, bridges, and fortifications. He was particularly interested in education, and in 1719 the town publicly thanked him and Thomas for donating "ye Writing Sch. House." For 30 years he was treasurer of Harvard College. In December 1721 Samuel Sewall, the diarist, objected to his appointment as treasurer on grounds of procedure rather than personal animosity. He was active in the militia, rising to the rank of lieutenant colonel, and he was a longtime member of the Artillery Company, as were so many of the Boston gentry. That he was personally acquainted with Edward Winslow is suggested by Sewall's comment in a letter to Wait Winthrop in 1711, wherein he notes the appointment of Captain Winslow as lieutenant and "Mr. Edward Hutchinson" as ensign. (Rank in the militia differed from rank in the Artillery Company.)

In 1706 Edward Hutchinson married Lydia Foster, the daughter of John Foster and Elizabeth Clarke (Freake) Foster, thus providing one more link between the 2 families. (Lydia's half sister Sarah had married Thomas Hutchinson in 1703.) What prompted the 2 brothers to present identical pieces of plate to the Second Church is unknown, but it could have been related to the death of their father-in-law, John Foster, in February 1711. Foster's third wife, Abigail, died only 3 weeks later. Her bequest of £20 to the Second Church was realized in a similar dish bearing the Foster arms. Also in 1711 the Second Church received by bequest from Elizabeth Wensley a large flagon made by Peter Oliver (no. 102). Wensley lived on property adjoining that of John Foster.

E. Alfred Jones reproduces a list of plate owned by the Second Church from a document dated March 2, 1729/30. The list includes 11 cups, 3 bowls, 12 tankards, 4 dishes, and 5 flagons. Jones observes that many pieces had disappeared by the time he conducted his survey.

Provenance: The Second Church in Boston sold the 2 dishes donated by Thomas and Edward Hutchinson, along with the flagon by Peter Oliver, to H. F. du Pont, 1966. The sale was attempted earlier but was blocked by a lawsuit on behalf of a disgruntled parishioner.

Exhibitions: "American Silver," Museum of Fine Arts, Boston, 1906. "American Church Silver," Museum of Fine Arts, Boston, 1911. "Masterpieces of American Silver," Virginia Museum of Fine Arts, Richmond, 1960.

Comments: See no. 139 for identical dish presented by Thomas Hutchinson. The Metropolitan Museum of Art owns a pair of cast candlesticks with the Hutchinson arms. The Museum of Fine Arts, Boston owns a mug that supposedly also belonged to him. Both pieces bear Winslow's stamp. Spink & Son, Ltd., of London, sold a nearly identical dish (15 ¼" diam.) made by Thomas Farren of London in 1717. (See Spink & Son, *Octagon* 23, no. 1 [March 1986]: 10.) Spink refers to the form as "a plain silver shallow bowl," but the pertinent early American documents call them dishes. As far as is known, the form was used exclusively for ecclesiastical purposes in colonial America, hence the term *communion dish*. The size of the dish reminds us that partakers of the Lord's Supper in Puritan Boston used real bread and not wafers.

References: American Silver, MFA, no. 327. *American Church Silver*, no. 1007 or 1008. John Booth, "Memoirs of a Magician's Ghost," *Linking Ring* (June 1974): 44–46, for an account of the litigation surrounding the sale. Buck, *Old Plate*, pp. 169–70. Sewall, *Diary*, p. 986. Jones, *Old Silver*, pp. 35–43, pl. xv. *Masterpieces of American Silver*, no. 140. Chandler Robbins, *History of the Second Church, or Old North, in Boston* (Boston, 1852), pp. 302–3. Roberts, *Artillery Company*, 1:341–42. "Samuel Sewall to Wait Winthrop," June 4, 1711, "The Winthrop Papers," in *Collections of the Massachusetts Historical Society*, 6th ser., no. 5 (1892): 230.

66.1053 Bequest of H. F. du Pont, 1969

139
COMMUNION DISH, 1711

DIAM. 15 ⅛" (38.4 cm), H. 2" (5.1 cm)
41 OZ. 14 dwt. (1297.0 g)

Stamps: "EW" in roman letters, over a fleur-de-lis, all in a conforming shape resembling a shield, struck on rim opposite engraved arms.

Engraved on rim opposite stamp: heraldic device consisting of a lion rampant in circular field with crosslets, all surrounded by foliate mantling (Hutchinson arms). *Engraved on underside:* "The Gift of/ Thomas Hutchinson/ To the Second Church in Boston May. 1711–" in script.

Description: raised circular form, deeply dished in center, with broad rim; edge of rim folded; large centerpunch on inside, smaller one on bottom.

Spectrographic analysis:

	SILVER	COPPER	LEAD	GOLD
BOTTOM	92.1	5.4	0.34	0.06
INSIDE	94.9	4.7	0.37	0.07

History: Thomas Hutchinson (1675–1739) was the son of Elisha Hutchinson and Hannah (Hawkins) Hutchinson and half brother of Edward Hutchinson, who presented an identical dish to the Second Church (no. 138). Thomas Hutchinson was a successful merchant and man of affairs. He was selectman, representative to the General Court, and for many years a member of the Provincial Council. In 1711 he offered to build a schoolhouse "at the North End of the town," but the project was not completed until 1719, at which time the town voted "The Thanks of this Town unto the doners of the Two North School Houses, viz. The Hon'ble Thomas Hutchinson Esqr for the Gramer Schoolhouse. And ye Sd Mr Thoms Hutchinson and also Edward Hutchinson Esqrs for ye Writing Sch. House." Like his half brother, Thomas was a member of the Artillery Company and the militia.

In 1703 Thomas Hutchinson married Sarah Foster, a daughter of John Foster by his first wife. Samuel Sewall noted the occasion in his diary in an entry dated December 23, 1703: "Dr. Mather marries Mr. Thomas Hutchinson and Mrs. Sarah Foster. A very great Wedding." Meanwhile, John and Abigail Foster were living in their elegant brick house on Garden Court Street that had been built a little over a decade earlier. Its symmetrical facade and 2½-story pilasters made it not only a very grand house but a highly innovative one for the time. In 1703 the Fosters settled the house on the young married couple, who did not move in until John and Abigail Foster's death in 1711. The first child born in the house was Thomas Hutchinson, Jr., who would become the ill-fated governor destined to spend his later years in exile. The mansion was nearly destroyed when it was sacked by a mob in 1765 during the Stamp Act crisis, and it was finally dismantled in 1833. Historian Abbott Lowell Cummings reproduces a woodcut of the house that appeared in *American Magazine* in 1836.

Thomas Hutchinson possessed a large quantity of wrought silver. He bequeathed to his wife Sarah "six hundred ounces of the Household Plate I am now Owner of, she to Chuse what pieces she pleases; the Remainder of my Plate I will to be divided into Seven Equal parts; my Son Thomas to have Two Seventh parts, my Son Foster one Seventh," with the remaining silver divided equally among his four married daughters. After various cash bequests to Boston clergymen and £20 to the master of the North Grammar School, he provided a generous bequest of £300 to Harvard College. The bulk of the estate was divided between sons Thomas and Foster, with the former receiving two-thirds and the latter one-third.

Provenance: See no. 138.

Exhibitions: "American Silver," Museum of Fine Arts, Boston, 1906. "American Church Silver," Museum of Fine Arts, Boston, 1911. "An Exhibition of American Silver and Art Treasures, English-Speaking Union," London, 1960.

Comments: See no. 138 for identical dish presented by Edward Hutchinson. The Metropolitan Museum of Art owns a coffeepot, also made by Winslow, with the Hutchinson arms. It is thought to have belonged to Thomas Hutchinson. For additional comments, see no. 138.

References: American Silver, MFA, probably no. 328. *American Church Silver*, no. 1007 or 1008. John Booth, "Memoirs of a Magician's Ghost," *Linking Ring* (June 1974): 44–46, for an account of the litigation surrounding the sale of silver by the Second Church. Buck, *Old Plate*, pp. 169–70. Abbott Lowell Cummings, "The Foster-Hutchinson House," *Old-Time New England* 54, no. 3 (January–March 1964): 59–76. Sewall, *Diary*, p. 493. Jones, *Old Silver*, pp. 35–43, pl. xv. Chandler Robbins, *History of the Second Church, or Old North, in Boston* (Boston, 1852), pp. 302–3. Roberts, *Artillery Company*, 1:304–5. *Sibley's Harvard Graduates*, s.v. "Hutchinson, Thomas."

66.1054 Bequest of H. F. du Pont, 1969

140
SUGAR BOX, 1702

L. 7 ⁷⁄₁₆" (18.9 cm), w. 6 ⅛" (15.6 cm), H. 5" (12.7 cm)
15 oz. 2 dwt. 20 gr. (471.0 g)

Stamps: "EW" in roman letters, over a fleur-de-lis, all in a conforming shape resembling a shield, struck twice on body on each side of hinge; similar but smaller version struck on rim of lid near hinge.

Engraved on underside of box: "O/ D•E/ Donum W:P 1702".

Description: oval box with hinged lid; stands on 4 cast feet. Sides richly adorned with chased and repoussé gadrooning broken by an acanthus leaf over each of the 4 feet and an oval boss featuring

a helmeted equestrian figure on each end; each foot consists of a double scroll and a double-cleft pad, suggesting an animal foot. The lid, also oval in plan, overhangs the rim of the box substantially and consists of stepped bands alternating between plain molded and highly articulated surfaces. The outermost band on the flange has a plain outside edge followed by a band of checkerboard punchwork; the next band is depressed below the plane of the flange and is untouched by chasing tools; this is followed by a vertical plain band forming the first step upward, which, in turn, is followed by a band of close-spaced gadrooning; midway up the lid is a broad area of plain step moldings; above this is a broad area of richly articulated acanthus leaves against a punchwork background; the upper central part of the lid, looking down, is framed by a bound wreath containing asymmetrical gadrooning

and punchwork with a cameo portrait of a helmeted figure on each side of the handle; the handle itself is cast in an arched, vinelike form with acanthus leaves sprouting from its upturned ends; 2 tendrils branch down to create a circular opening for lifting the lid; at the top of the arch is a small circular wreath. Attached to 1 side of the lid is a 5-segment hinge with a circular hasp for keeping the lid firmly closed; chased into the hasp is a landscape with an equestrian warrior brandishing a sword; a trifid tab extends from the lower edge of the hasp. The body and lid were raised; the handle, feet, and hinge were cast. It is the chasing and repoussé work, however, that make this piece truly monumental. Whether done by Winslow himself or by someone else, it represents a bravura performance seldom equaled in American silver.

Spectrographic analysis:

	SILVER	COPPER	LEAD	GOLD
SIDE	92.3	7.3	0.33	0.07
BOTTOM	92.1	7.3	0.36	0.11
LID	92.7	6.8	0.30	0.07
HANDLE	93.4	5.7	0.22	0.01
FOOT	91.6	7.7	0.30	0.01
HINGE	91.3	8.1	0.31	0.06

History: The inscription refers to Daniel and Elizabeth Oliver, who were given the box by William Partridge, probably on the occasion of the birth of their son Daniel, born June 13, 1702, who did not survive infancy. Daniel Oliver (1664–1732) was the son of Capt. Peter Oliver, Boston merchant, and Sarah Newdigate. In 1696 he married Elizabeth Belcher (1678–1735), daughter of Andrew Belcher, who was once described as "the most opulent merchant in the town of Boston." Elizabeth's brother Jonathan Belcher, who became governor of Massachusetts and later of New Jersey, married Mary Partridge, daughter of William Partridge, who served as lieutenant governor and acting governor of New Hampshire from 1697 to 1703. William Partridge was therefore Elizabeth (Belcher) Oliver's uncle-in-law. Given the Puritan habit of not distinguishing between blood relatives and those acquired by marriage, the relationship was more important than it might appear to today's readers.

Daniel Oliver was looked upon with awe by his contemporaries. Writing to his son and namesake, Jonathan Belcher said, "Your uncle Oliver was an uncommon instance of Christianity & exact piety." Much later John Langdon Sibley referred to him as "the ideal Puritan: a saint of unbounded charity." He was also a highly successful merchant as attested by Belcher's comment: "I knew him in very middling circumstances, but he died in opulency." Oliver was a selectman of Boston, overseer of the poor, justice of the peace, and a member of the governor's council. Both Daniel and Elizabeth were memorialized in sermons preached by the Reverend Thomas Prince and published in 1732 and 1735. Their portraits were painted twice by John Smibert, and all 4 portraits are still owned by descendants.

In his will, proved August 7, 1732, Oliver called for the income from his "Spinning House" to be used for "Learning the poor children of the Town of Boston to Read the Word of God and to write if need be." To his wife, Elizabeth, he bequeathed "my Brick Mansion House . . . also all my wrought Plate, Gold Rings, Linnen, Household Stuff and Provision in said House." He also specified that she "have her choice out of my Books for her own use." Elizabeth's will, proved June 3, 1735, bequeathed "for the use of the Communion Table of the Old South Church in Boston in which I have been an Unworthy Partaker my Silver Tankard Marked E:O." (The tankard is not recorded in E. Alfred Jones's enumeration of the silver in Old South.) The rest of her estate, "my wearing Apparell only Excepted," she divided between her sons Andrew and Peter.

Sons Andrew and Peter Oliver went on to preeminence as well. Andrew (1706–74) served the public cause faithfully, finally assuming the office of lieutenant governor under the ill-fated Thomas Hutchinson. Peter (1713–91) was a jurist who might have had a distinguished career had his conservative views not run counter to the prevailing mood. Although he became chief justice of Massachusetts in 1771, he was under constant attack for his Loyalist views. When British forces departed for Halifax in March 1776, he went with them. He proceeded to England, where he lived out his days in Birmingham. Before leaving Boston, Peter Oliver went to his elegant mansion in Middleboro, known as Oliver Hall, to retrieve a box of valuables. Among these valuables was, presumably, the sugar box that had been presented to his parents in 1702.

Provenance: William Partridge; Daniel and Elizabeth Oliver; Peter Oliver. The box was rediscovered in the 1930s in a Scottish church, where, according to Stephen G. C. Ensko, it had probably been deposited long ago for safekeeping. Ensko purchased it in 1937 and sold it to H. F. du Pont in 1951.

Comments: The sugar box is displayed at Winterthur in the Wentworth Room near an oval portrait of Chief Justice Peter Oliver. Painted by an unknown artist, ca. 1785, the portrait is reproduced in *Faces of a Family*, a catalogue of Oliver family portraits compiled by Andrew Oliver and published privately in 1960. It includes the Smibert portraits of Daniel and Elizabeth Oliver and a group portrait of sons Andrew, Peter, and Daniel (1704–27). (Note: This Daniel was the third child of Daniel and Elizabeth to bear the name; the other 2 died young.)

Edward Winslow made 4 of the 9 surviving American silver sugar boxes. (John Coney made 4, and Daniel Greenough made 1.) The small number of survivals suggests that the sugar box was a rare form, but from the number of times they are mentioned in inventories this was not the case. James Lloyd, a Boston merchant who died in 1693, owned 3. The form flourished during the late seventeenth and early eighteenth centuries, and then it ceased to be made at all. Presumably it lost its function when the price of sugar declined and sugar came into common use. Sugar was more conveniently served in a bowl and no longer required the security of a locked box. More importantly, perhaps, the rich symbolism associated with sugar boxes lost its meaning. Sugar was assumed to increase fertility, and, hence, sugar boxes were suitable gifts on the occasion of marriage or the birth of a child.

The amatory and marital associations surrounding this form are explored in detail by Edward J. Nygren in "Edward Winslow's Sugar Boxes: Colonial Echoes of Courtly Love." Nygren shows that the form derives from Italian *cassoni* of the sixteenth century, which were often decorated with paintings or carvings featuring battle scenes from epic poems and classical mythology.

He further demonstrates a relationship between the specific iconography of this Winslow sugar box and the art and literature of the seventeenth century. The equestrian warrior depicted on the hasp and on 3 bosses has usually been interpreted as Saint George slaying the dragon. Nygren dispels this idea by reproducing an illustration from John Ogilby's *Homer: His Iliads* (London, 1660) that bears a remarkable resemblance and could well be the source used by Winslow. Instead of a dragon, the figure on the ground is a wounded warrior. The

combination of martial and amatory allusions sounds awkward today but was common in such epic love poems as Torquarto Tasso's *Gerusalemme Liberta* and Edmund Spenser's *Faerie Queene*. Themes of courtly love and chivalry were embodied in such readily available books as Baldassare Castiglione's *Book of the Courtier* and Henry Peacham's *Complete Gentleman*.

The other 3 Winslow sugar boxes are owned by Yale University Art Gallery, Henry Ford Museum, and the Museum of Fine Arts, Boston. The Winterthur box most closely resembles the one at Yale, which descended in the Winslow family and was long thought to have been made by Edward Winslow for his family's use. Nygren disputes this contention on the grounds that its date of fabrication does not coincide with the dates of Winslow's 2 marriages and that in any case it would have been socially inappropriate for a man of his station to own such an elegant piece. He postulates that it was made for the Bouchers, who, owing to financial difficulties, sold the box back to Winslow at a later time. Sarah Middlecott married Louis Boucher in 1702, the year in which 3 of the 4 Winslow sugar boxes were made. Boucher, from one of Boston's Huguenot merchant families, went bankrupt in 1714. A portrait of Mrs. Boucher, painted by John Smibert in 1730, is owned by Winterthur (Edgar P. Richardson, *American Paintings and Related Pictures in the Henry Francis du Pont Winterthur Museum* [Charlottesville: University Press of Virginia, 1986], no. 15.)

Exhibitions: "New England Begins: The Seventeenth Century," Museum of Fine Arts, Boston, 1982.

References: Bernard Bailyn, *The Ordeal of Thomas Hutchinson* (Cambridge: Belknap Press of Harvard University Press, 1974). "The Belcher Papers," in *Collections of the Massachusetts Historical Society*, vol. 6 (1893), p. 167; vol. 7 (1894), p. 112. Kathryn C. Buhler, "The Nine Colonial Sugar Boxes," *Antiques* 85, no. 1 (January 1964): 88–91. *DAB*, s.v. "Oliver, Andrew" and "Oliver, Peter." Davidson, *Colonial Antiques*, p. 100. Fales, *American Silver*, no. 37. Fennimore, *Silver and Pewter*, no. 83. H. E. Keyes, "A New England Sugar Box of 1702," *Antiques* 32, no. 6 (December 1937): 309. Fairbanks and Trent, *New England Begins*, no. 467, where Daniel Oliver's wife is misidentified as Mary Belcher. Edward J. Nygren, "Edward Winslow's Sugar Boxes: Colonial Echoes of Courtly Love," *Yale University Art Gallery Bulletin* 33, no. 2 (Autumn 1971): 39–52. Andrew

Oliver, *Faces of a Family: An Illustrated Catalogue of Portraits and Silhouettes of Daniel Oliver, 1664–1732, and Elizabeth Belcher, His Wife, and Their Oliver Descendants and Their Wives Made Between 1727 and 1850* (Privately printed, 1960). John W. Raimo, *Biographical Dictionary of American Colonial and Revolutionary Governors, 1607–1789* (Westport, Conn.: Meckler Books, 1980). Helen Burr Smith, "New Light on a Silver Sugar Box," *Antiques* 49, no. 3 (March 1946): 178. Charles Messer Stow, "Edward Winslow Sugar Box Brought Back from England," *New York Sun*, September 18, 1937, p. 14. SCPR book 31, p. 56; book 32, pp. 52, 151. Thomas Prince, *The Faithful Servant: A Sermon . . . Occasion'd by the . . . Death of . . . Daniel Oliver* (Boston, 1732). Thomas Prince,

Precious in the Sight of the Lord: A Sermon upon the Death of Mrs. Elizabeth Oliver (Boston, 1735). Sewall, *Diary*, index, for numerous references to Daniel Oliver. *Sibley's Harvard Graduates*, 7:103–35, for Daniel Oliver, Jr.; 7:383–413, for Andrew Oliver; 8:737–63, for Peter Oliver. Thomas Weston, *History of the Town of Middleboro, Massachusetts* (Boston and New York: Houghton Mifflin Co., 1906), pp. 359–84, for a description of Oliver Hall. Thomas Weston, Jr., "Peter Oliver," *NEH&GR* 40, no. 3 (July 1886): 241–52; 40, no. 4 (October 1886): 349–59. W. H. Whitmore, "Notes on the Belcher Family," *NEH&GR* 27, no. 3 (July 1873): 239–45; W. H. Whitmore, "The Oliver Family," *NEH&GR* 19, no. 2 (April 1865): 100–106.

59.3363 Gift of H. F. du Pont, 1965

141
TANKARD, ca. 1730

H. 7 ⁷⁄₁₆" (18.9 cm), DIAM. base 4 ⅞" (12.4 cm),
w. 7 ⅛" (18.1 cm)
24 oz. 1 dwt. 22 gr. (749.4 g)

Stamps: "EW" in roman letters, over a fleur-
de-lis, all in a conforming shape resembling a
shield, struck on body near rim, left of handle.

Description: raised body with straight sides;
applied base molding consists of ogee topped
by 3 beads; fillet molding around body at ⅓
height; applied molding around rim. Raised
bottom with centerpunch outside. Raised
stepped-and-domed lid with no centerpunch;
cast finial. Cast double-spiral thumbpiece. Cast
5-segment hinge. Raised-and-soldered hollow
handle with cast drop on upper part of handle;
scroll on lower back; circular domed tailpiece;
circular vent.

Spectrographic analysis:

	SILVER	COPPER	LEAD	GOLD
BODY	90.1	8.6	0.57	0.25
BOTTOM	95.0	4.0	0.31	0.29
HANDLE	91.3	7.9	0.49	0.19

Comments: The Metropolitan Museum of Art
and Hood Museum at Dartmouth College own
tankards similar in almost all respects down to
and including base molding, low midband,
finial, thumbpiece, handle, and tailpiece. The
first of these is engraved with the Hutchinson
arms and crest.

77.226 Gift of Marshall P. Blankarn, 1977

142
COVER FOR PORRINGER, ca. 1720

DIAM. 5 ¾" (14.6 cm), H. ⅝" (1.6 cm)
3 oz. 1 dwt. 12 gr. (95.7 g)

Stamps: "EW" in roman letters, in 2 conjoined circles, struck once on upper side.

Engraved on upper side: "Winthrop Pyemont/ from his Aunt/ Augusta Clinton Winthrop" and "once belonging to the/ Johannets" in script.

Description: raised circular form; deeply dished with pronounced convex molding rising from narrow flat surface around edge; centerpunch on top.

Spectrographic analysis:

	SILVER	COPPER	LEAD	GOLD
INSIDE CENTER	93.0	6.3	0.36	0.14

History: The Pyemont/Winthrop inscription is modern (late nineteenth or early twentieth century), but the allegation of early ownership by the Johonnot family is likely. See *History* of accompanying porringer by Jonathan Reed, no. 108.

Provenance: See no. 108.

Comments: See no. 108.

References: See no. 108.

65.1370 Gift of H. F. du Pont, 1965

143
SERVING SPOON, ca. 1711

L. 14 ½" (36.8 cm)
7 oz. 16 dwt. 11 gr. (243.3 g)

Stamps: "EW" in roman letters, over a fleur-de-lis, all in a conforming shape resembling a shield, struck on back of handle near bowl.

Engraved on back of handle at widest part: "Francis Wardwell" in script. *Engraved below:* "8 oz."

Description: elongated deep oval bowl with rat-tail on back; long handle with spatulate upturned end; midrib on upper side.

Spectrographic analysis:

	SILVER	COPPER	LEAD	GOLD
BOWL BACK	92.0	7.6	0.31	0.11
HANDLE BACK	92.5	7.1	0.29	0.14

History: According to the history accompanying the spoon, the original owner was one Frances Cook who married Jonathan Wardwell on June 27, 1710. They had a son Francis, born October 12, 1711, and a daughter Frances, born January 20, 1713. Given the casual spelling of proper names at the time, Wardwell may be the Jonathan Wardell who advertised October 6, 1712, that he had "set up a Hackney Coach to accommodate all Persons on reasonable Terms." He could be found "at the sign of the Orange Tree in Hanover Street, Boston." Presumably this was his own establishment, for his name appears on a 1714 list of Boston tavern-keepers and innholders. Following his death in December 1721, his widow, Frances Wardell, was licensed as an innholder. In his diary Benjamin Lynde mentions dining at Wardell's on several occasions. One author notes that Wardwell and Wardell are used interchangeably in Boston records.

Provenance: Mrs. George F. Richardson, from whom it was purchased by Francis Hill Bigelow; Brooks Reed Gallery, Boston, sold to H. F. du Pont, April 1927.

References: Fales, *American Silver*, no. 95. *Diaries of Benjamin Lynde and Benjamin Lynde, Jr.* (Boston: Privately printed, 1880), p. 57. "Hackney Coach," *NEH&GR* 13, no. 2 (April 1859): 107. Jeremiah Colburn, "List of Innholders and Retailers of Spirits in Boston, 1714," *NEH&GR* 31, no. 1 (January 1877): 108. Chandler Robbins, *History of the Second Church, or Old North, in Boston* (Boston, 1852), p. 539.

59.3364 Gift of H. F. du Pont, 1965

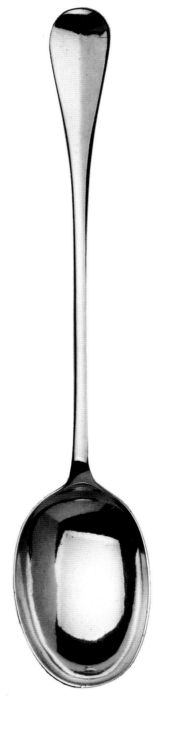

144
SPOON, ca. 1720

L. 7 15/16" (20.2 cm)
2 oz. 1 dwt. 4 gr. (64.0 g)

Stamps: "EW" in roman letters, over a fleur-de-lis, all in a conforming shape resembling a shield, struck once on back of handle.

Engraved on back of handle: "L*B" in shaded block letters.

Description: elongated oval bowl with plain swage-formed rattail on back; rounded upturned handle with midrib on front.

Spectrographic analysis:

	SILVER	COPPER	LEAD	GOLD
BOWL	92.4	7.3	0.24	0.10
HANDLE	92.8	6.9	0.24	0.08

Provenance: Mr. and Mrs. Stanley B. Ineson, New York City; Mr. and Mrs. Alfred E. Bissell, Wilmington, Del.

Comments: Made in 1 piece; clearly later in date than the 2 spoons in nos. 145, 146.

References: Belden, *Marks of American Silversmiths*, p. 451 a.

62.240.1550 Gift of Mr. and Mrs. Alfred E. Bissell, 1962–63

145
SPOON, ca. 1700

L. 7 11/16" (19.5 cm)
1 oz. 9 dwt. 12 gr. (45.9 g)

Stamps: "EW" in roman letters, over a fleur-de-lis, all in a conforming shape resembling a shield, struck once on back of handle.

Engraved on back of handle: "D/ T*S" in block roman letters.

Description: elongated oval bowl with swage-formed beaded rattail with converging ridges on back; trifid-end handle cut from sheet.

Spectrographic analysis:

	SILVER	COPPER	LEAD	GOLD
BOWL	95.2	4.2	0.41	0.09
HANDLE	95.2	4.2	0.40	0.09

Provenance: Mr. and Mrs. Stanley B. Ineson, New York City; Mr. and Mrs. Alfred E. Bissell, Wilmington, Del.

Comments: The maker's stamp is larger than usual; for this reason Belden called it "undoubtedly spurious." I disagree.

References: Belden, *Marks of American Silversmiths*, p. 452 c.

62.240.1551 Gift of Mr. and Mrs. Alfred E. Bissell, 1962–63

146
SPOON, ca. 1700

L. 7 5/16" (18.6 cm)
1 oz. 4 dwt. 12 gr. (38.1 g)

Stamps: "EW" in roman letters, over a fleur-de-lis, all in a conforming shape resembling a shield, struck once on back of handle.

Engraved on back of handle: "AB" in crude block roman letters.

Description: oval bowl with swage-formed decoration on back consisting of a ridged and beaded rattail flanked by foliation; trifid-end, slightly upturned handle cut from sheet and soldered to bowl.

Spectrographic analysis:

	SILVER	COPPER	LEAD	GOLD
BOWL	92.0	7.6	0.26	0.08
HANDLE	92.6	7.1	0.22	0.06

Provenance: Mr. and Mrs. Stanley B. Ineson, New York City; Mr. and Mrs. Alfred E. Bissell, Wilmington, Del.

References: Belden, *Marks of American Silversmiths*, p. 452 b.

62.240.1552 Gift of Mr. and Mrs. Alfred E. Bissell, 1962–63

❦ *New York*

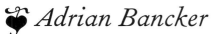# Adrian Bancker

1703–72
New York, New York

The son of Evert Bancker, mayor of Albany (1695–96, 1707–9), Adrian Bancker was apprenticed to Henricus Boelen, New York City, in 1718. He married Gertrude E. Van Taerling in New York in 1728 and became a freeman in 1731. In 1722 he witnessed the will of merchant Gerard Beekman, which suggests that Bancker was well connected. Active in local affairs, Bancker was elected collector for South Ward in 1733, 1735, and 1736. His advertisement in the *New York Journal*, October 23, 1766, placed his shop at Bridge Street, near the Exchange. He was memorialized in a 1769 inscription in the New York Dutch Church, where he had served as deacon. Bancker's set of three casters at the Museum of the City of New York is a rare survival, as is the pair of cast candlesticks once owned by Mr. and Mrs. Samuel Schwartz. Two bowls by Bancker, owned by the Metropolitan Museum of Art, are worthy of note: one was a gift to Christopher Bancker for services to the Roosevelt family; the other commemorates the fire of 1750 that destroyed the New Free School and the steeple of Trinity Church. E. Alfred Jones records a beaker for a church in Accord, New York, and a baptismal bowl for the New York Dutch Church.

References: Jones, *Old Silver*, pp. 1, 329. *NYHS Collections:* vol. 26 (1893) *Abstracts of Wills*, pp. 275–76. Von Khrum, *Silversmiths*, p. 9. James G. Wilson, *Memorial History of the City of New-York*, 4 vols. (New York: New-York History Co., 1892–93), 2:349.

147
PORRINGER, 1725–60

DIAM. bowl 5 ½" (14.0 cm), H. 2" (5.1 cm), w. 7⅝" (19.4 cm)
9 oz. 10 dwt. 21 gr. (296.8 g)

Stamps: "AB" in roman letters, in an oval, struck twice on underside of body.

Engraved on underside of body: "B/ TP" in shaded roman letters. *Scratched on underside of handle:* "AD 1708" in roman letters.

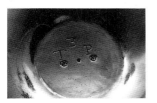

Description: raised circular bowl with bulging sides and a short, slightly angled rim; bottom domed in center; centerpunch on underside of body; cast handle pierced with 3 large voids and 1 small void at tip.

Spectrographic analysis:

	SILVER	COPPER	LEAD	GOLD
UNDERSIDE	89.4	9.7	0.24	0.16
HANDLE	92.4	7.1	0.16	0.08

Provenance: Charles K. Davis, Fairfield, Conn.

Exhibitions: "Masterpieces of American Silver," Virginia Museum of Fine Arts, Richmond, 1960.

Comments: Handle identical to one on Christopher Robert porringer, no. 247; both are slightly asymmetrical. See identical porringer by Bancker at Yale University Art Gallery. Engraved date added later.

References: Fales, *American Silver*, no. 54. Kauffman, *Colonial Silversmith*, p. 89. *Masterpieces of American Silver*, no. 152. *American Silver*, MFA, no. 633.

56.46.1 Gift of Charles K. Davis, 1956

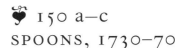

❦ 148
MILKPOT, 1750–70

H. 4 ⁵⁄₁₆" (11.0 cm), W. 4 ¹⁄₁₆" (10.3 cm)
4 oz. 9 dwt. 22 gr. (139.9 g)

Stamps: "AB" in roman letters, in an oval, struck once on underside of body. A second strike is illegible.

Engraved on side of body: "CNQ" in later script.

Description: raised pear-shape body with curvilinear flared rim and prominent curved pouring lip; centerpunch on underside. Cast C-curve handle with sprig and reverse C curves for upper and lower handle attachments; 3 legs cast as C scrolls with triple-pad feet and shell knees; circular vents under each shell.

Spectrographic analysis:

	SILVER	COPPER	LEAD	GOLD
BODY	87.5	11.5	0.20	0.19
HANDLE	93.1	6.2	0.11	0.21
FOOT	92.0	7.1	0.21	0.22

Provenance: H. F. du Pont.

References: Fales, *American Silver*, no. 23.

59.2307 Gift of H. F. du Pont, 1965

❦ 149 a, b
BUCKLES, ca. 1765

(a) L. 2 ⁹⁄₁₆" (6.5 cm), W. 1 ¹⁵⁄₁₆" (4.9 cm),
H. ¾" (1.9 cm)
1 oz. 5 dwt. 1 gr. (39.0 g)
(b) L. 2 ⁹⁄₁₆" (6.5 cm), W. 1 ¹⁵⁄₁₆" (4.9 cm),
H. ¾" (1.9 cm)
1 oz. 4 dwt. 10 gr. (38.0 g)

Stamps: "AB" in roman letters, in an oval, struck once on edge of each buckle near spring plunger. Incuse "88" struck on steel centerpiece.

Description: cast rectangular frame with rounded corners, convex front, concave back; obverse: beaded inner and outer borders flanking central braided border bound at corners and middle by double bands secured with pins through back; reverse: vertical steel plate in center with spring and catch for hinged frame with 2 hinged chapes, each with 2 tines. Pressure on spring plunger releases hinged frame.

Spectrographic analysis:

	SILVER	COPPER	GOLD	LEAD
(a)	97.9	1.1	0.96	0.04
(b)	96.6	1.9	1.41	0.04

Note: Traces of mercury were also found. The presence of mercury and a high gold content suggests that the buckles were gilded at some point.

Provenance: Ladd M. Levis, Boston.

77.169.1, .2 Gift of Ladd M. Levis, 1977

❦ 150 a–c
SPOONS, 1730–70

(a) L. 7 ⅞" (20.0 cm)
1 oz. 15 dwt. 1 gr. (54.4 g)
(b) L. 4 ⅛" (10.5 cm)
5 dwt. 6 gr. (8.2 g)
(c) L. 8" (20.3 cm)
1 oz. 17 dwt. 13 gr. (58.2 g)

Stamps: "AB" in roman letters, in an oval, struck twice on backs of handles (a) and (c), struck once on back of handle (b).

Engraved on back of handle: (a) "W / TC" in shaded roman letters; (b) "E•B" in roman letters; (c) "R / AM" in shaded roman letters.

Description: (a, c) oval bowl with swage-formed rattail and single drop; flat wavy-end upturned handle; (b) elongated oval bowl with swage-formed squared single drop; rounded upturned handle with midrib on front.

Spectrographic analysis: Silver content ranges from 90.0 to 91.7 percent.

Provenance: Mr. and Mrs. Stanley B. Ineson, New York City; Mr. and Mrs. Alfred E. Bissell, Wilmington, Del.

References: Belden, *Marks of American Silversmiths*, p. 47.

62.240.958, .27, .959 Gift of Mr. and Mrs. Alfred E. Bissell, 1962–63

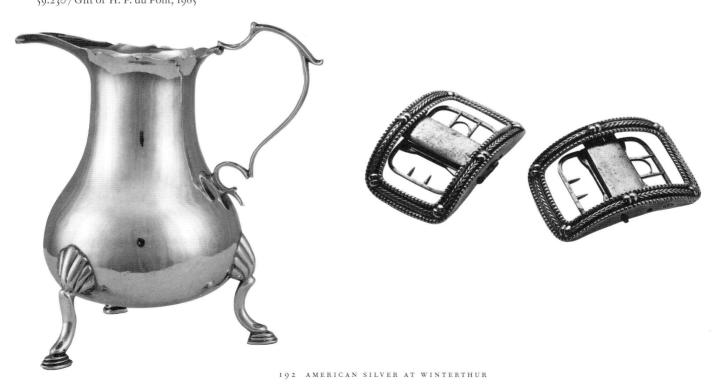

JB

Attributed to John Bedford
1757–1834
Fishkill, New York

Stephen Ensko claims that John Bedford
had a shop on Main Street, in Fishkill,
and that he advertised at that location in
1782. He is also listed in *New York State
Silversmiths* with a stamp very close to
that on the ring in the following entry.
No further information about him is
available. A John Barrett of New York
City has also been suggested as the
owner of this stamp. Barrett is listed
in *New York State Silversmiths* and in
volumes 3 and 4 of Ensko's *American
Silversmiths and Their Marks* but is not
mentioned in Paul von Khrum's *Silversmiths of New York City*. For this reason
I have discounted this theory. Although
a city craftsman seems more likely, the
scanty evidence points to John Bedford.
This is, however, a tentative attribution
pending the discovery of better data.

References: Ensko, *American Silversmiths IV*,
pp. 13, 278, for Barrett; pp. 17, 291, for John
Bedford. *New York State Silversmiths*, pp. 24,
28. Von Khrum, *Silversmiths*.

 151
GOLD RING, 1780–1820

DIAM. 13/16" (2.1 cm), W. 3/16" (0.5 cm)
1 dwt. 12 gr. (2.3 g)

Stamps: "JB" in script, in a rounded rectangle,
struck once inside ring.

Description: circular band, rounded on outside,
flat on inside.

Spectrographic analysis:

GOLD	SILVER	COPPER	
89.7	5.2	5.1	22 karat

Provenance: John D. Kernan, New Haven.

Comments: This is a form that changes little
over time and therefore does not provide stylistic clues to its date.

68.17 Museum purchase from John D. Kernan,
1968

Jurian Blanck, Jr.

1645–ca. 1699 or 1714
New York, New York

Jurian Blanck, Jr., is probably the son of Jeurisen (or Juriaen) Blanck, who, after learning his trade in Amsterdam, became the first documented silversmith to practice in New York City. The younger Blanck learned his trade from his father. Baptized in 1645, he was admitted to the Dutch Church in 1668. In 1672 he was appointed censor of weights and measures. He married Hester Vanderbeck in 1673 and became a freeman in 1695. For the years 1695 to 1699, his property in the West Ward was assessed at £40. In 1697 his wife was indicted for "Encouraging the servt of Mr. Clarke to steale mony & entertaining of negroes." In 1698 Blanck was named one of the executors of the estate of "Catharine Blank, widow of Jurian Blank"; she was either his mother or stepmother. She refers to him in the will as "my eldest son Jurian Blanck," and she bequeathed to him her Bible and one-seventh of her estate. He remains, however, a somewhat shadowy figure. His death date is claimed by some as 1699 and by others as 1714. From the latter year there is a will by a Jurian Blanck, yeomen, that was contested by the family on the grounds that the testator was non compos mentis.

There is a small but impressive body of silver associated with Jurian Blanck, Jr.; his work may be the earliest surviving New York silver. A few objects bearing the "IB" stamp over a quartrefoil seem likely to be his. This distinctive group includes a baptismal basin at the First Reformed Church of Tarrytown and a pair of casters and a tankard at the Museum of the City of New York. These pieces appear to date from the 1690s and perhaps somewhat earlier. Another group bears an "IB" stamp in a conforming surround, which some silver historians have associated the Boelens. Among this group is a funeral spoon at the Albany Institute supposedly made on the death of Kiliaen Van Rensselaer (1655–87). It has been attributed to Blanck, probably because of its date. Another example is a beaker at the First Reformed Church of Brooklyn (similar to no. 215, by the anonymous "HH") with an engraved donor's date of 1684.

References: Ensko, *American Silversmiths IV*, pp. 21, 278. *New York State Silversmiths*, p. 32. *NYHS Collections*: vol. 25 (1892) *Abstracts of Wills*, p. 296; vol. 35 (1902) *Abstracts of Unrecorded Wills*, p. 12; vol. 43 (1910) *New-York Tax Lists*, pp. 13, 48, 90, 127, 156, 186, 233, 291. *Minutes of the Common Council*, 1:31, 52, 61. Miller, *New York Silversmiths*, nos. 1–9.

152
TWO-HANDLED CUP AND COVER, ca. 1690

H. (with cover) 5 ½" (14.0 cm), H. (cover only) 1 ⁷⁄₁₆" (3.7 cm), W. 8 ⅞" (22.5 cm), DIAM. rim 5 ⅝" (14.3 cm)
23 oz. 20 dwt. (745.0 g)

Stamps: "IB" in roman letters, over 4 conjoined circles, all in a shield, struck once on upper body, left of handle, and once on upper surface of cover.

Engraved on side of body: armorial device consisting of a demi-lion rampant rising from a ducal coronet, the lion also wearing a coronet, all in a shield flanked by leafy scrolls. *Crest:* a closed helmet and leafy scrolls under ducal coronet with demi-lion rampant, also wearing a coronet. *Engraved on opposite side of body:* "C/ I∗E" in shaded script. *Engraved on underside:* "C/ I∗E" in shaded roman letters.

Description: raised circular form with slightly flared plain rim and straight sides that curve in to slightly rounded bottom; lower half of body decorated with continuous pattern of chased and repoussé acanthus leaves; centerpunch on underside. Seamed reeded base ring attached to foot flange; 2 cast C-curve handles; the upper portions are caryatids and have protruding scrolls, the lower portions end in double bud terminals. Raised circular cover, single stepped and slightly domed, with 3 cast scroll feet on top; cover decorated with elaborate chased and repoussé acanthus leaves with a large 6-petal rosette in center surrounded by stippling; bezel; no visible centerpunch.

Spectrographic analysis:

	SILVER	COPPER	LEAD	GOLD
BODY SIDE	91.7	7.5	0.34	0.12
BODY BOTTOM	94.3	5.2	0.28	0.11
LID	92.9	6.4	0.28	0.10
HANDLE	93.1	5.8	0.22	0.26
FOOT ON LID	92.2	7.2	0.23	0.12

History: The initials "C/ I∗E" refer to Jacobus and Eva (Philipse) Van Cortlandt, who were married in 1691. The coat of arms is that of the Philipse family. It is quite likely that the cup was commissioned by Frederick Philipse (1626–1702), Eva's father, who was arguably the wealthiest man in New York when he died. He owned Philipsburgh Manor, a portion of which survives today as a museum. In his will Philipse left "to my eldest daughter Eva, wife of Jacobus Van Cortlandt, all that house and ground with the appurtenances in ye city of New York where they at present live . . . And one quarter of all ships, plate goods, etc." Jacobus Van Cortlandt (1658–1739) was the youngest son of Oloff Stevenszen Van Cortlandt (1600–1684), founder of the family in America and a prominent merchant and colonial official. Jacobus was a merchant and landholder. He was appointed mayor of New York in 1710 and 1719. In this calling he followed in the steps of his older and more famous brother, Stephenus (1643–1700), who served as mayor in 1677, 1686, and 1687 and created Cortlandt Manor. Jacobus and Eva had 4 children: Frederick (who married the daughter of Augustus Jay), Margaret (who married Abraham De Peyster), Mary (who married Peter Jay), and Anna (who married John Chambers). Jacobus had extensive landholdings, both within the city and upriver, including a portion of Philipsburg Manor and a one-quarter share of 10,000 acres on Paltz River. Frederick, as the only male heir, received the bulk of the father's property, and it is likely that the cup passed through his line. Jacobus also bequeathed to Frederick "my boat 'Anna,' with the canoe, and all other tackling."

Provenance: Mrs. Arthur Iselin, New York City; Robert Ensko, Inc., New York City, sold to H. F. du Pont, 1947.

Exhibitions: "New York Silversmiths of the Seventeenth Century," Museum of the City of New York, 1962–63. Winter Antiques Show, New York City, January 1982.

Comments: An extraordinary tour de force in early American silver, this is 1 of 4 nearly identical cups that are peculiar to New York City. Two are by Gerrit Oncklebag (1 at Yale University Art Gallery, the other at Historic Deerfield). The fourth, by Cornelius Kierstede, is at the Art Institute of Chicago. All share the same form with acanthus leaf chasing around the lower body, cast caryatid handles, a heavily chased lid with a central rosette, and 3 cast scroll feet. Milo M. Naeve discusses them as a group in "Silver Syllabub Cups." He attributes

the design to a common English source of which there seems to be only 1 surviving example. The cup is now in the Kuntsindustrimuseum of Copenhagen; its stamps show that it was made in London, 1676–77, by an unknown silversmith with the initials "TK." The body and lid are nearly identical to the American examples, but the handles are C-curve scrolls. Louise Conway Belden claims that because of their covers, these cups were used for syllabub. A tankard at the Museum of the City of New York has the same stamp and the same engraved initials "C/ IE"; it is engraved with the Van Cortlandt coat of arms. There is also a tankard at Yale bearing the Philipse arms. Early records often use Cortlandt instead of Van Cortlandt.

References: Davidson, *Colonial Antiques*, p. 107. Fales, *American Silver*, no. 3. Fennimore, *Silver and Pewter*, no. 165. James G. Wilson, *Memorial History of the City of New-York*, 4 vols. (New York: New-York History Co., 1892–93), 2:144. Miller, *New York Silversmiths*, no. 5, pl. 7. Milo M. Naeve, "Dutch Colonists and English Style in New York City: Silver Syllabub Cups by Cornelius Kierstede, Gerrit Oncklebag, and Jurian Blanck, Jr.," *American Art Journal* 19 (1987): 40–53. *NYHS Collections*: vol. 27 (1894) *Abstracts of Wills*, pp. 307–10, for will of Jacobus Van Cortlandt, which notes a prenuptial agreement with Eva's father; vol. 25 (1892) *Abstracts of Wills*, pp. 369–73, for will of Frederick Philipse. For possible use of cup, see Louise Conway Belden, *The Festive Tradition: Table Decoration and Desserts in America, 1650–1900* (New York: W. W. Norton, 1983), p. 136, fig. 4:1.

59.2289 Gift of H. F. du Pont, 1965

Henricus Boelen

1697–1755
New York, New York

Henricus Boelen, son of silversmith Jacob Boelen, succeeded his father on the latter's death in 1729. In 1718 he married Janetje Waldron (1698–1776). Although he belonged to the Dutch Church for much of his life, Janetje and her family became intensely involved with the New York Moravian congregation, which Henricus finally joined in his later years.

There has been much confusion between Henricus Boelen and Hendrick Boelen (1661–91), and attempts to sort them out have proven inconclusive. Silver that was thought to be too early for Henricus was attributed to Hendrick but without much consistency. There seems to be no distinguishable difference between the stamps attributed to Henricus and those attributed to Hendrick. Therefore, I believe that there is only one *H.* Boelen responsible for this body of silver. Hendrick was identified in his will as a "smith," and Paul von Khrum has proven that he was a gunsmith rather than a silversmith. Moreover, there is evidence that New York silver in seventeenth-century styles continued to be made well into the eighteenth century. For example, in 1731 Henricus made two tall silver beakers for the Reforme Church in Bergen, New Jersey, to replace two pewter beakers of identical form.

Had their purchase not been documented, they too would have been given an earlier date. We think of drinking bowls, of the type in the following entries, as seventeenth-century objects and therefore have tended to date them earlier. Henricus's bowls are like those by his father, proving that the demand for them continued. As with certain other forms, like porringers, that change little over time, we must regard these small drinking bowls as having a wider date spread.

By establishing that the conjoined "HB" stamp in a crowned shield belongs to Henricus Boelen and not to Hendrick, we have enlarged the body of silver attributed to him and settled once and for all the long-standing debate. There is also a simpler form of the stamp using a conjoined "HB" in a rectangle. That this too is Henricus's stamp seems beyond doubt; both versions are found on a porringer with the owner's initials "TVBB." It is illustrated, along with both stamps, in Waddington's (Toronto) auction catalogue for a sale on June 12, 1984.

References: Howard S. Randolph and Mrs. Russell Hastings, "Jacob Boelen, Goldsmith, of New York and His Family Circle," *NYG&BR* 72, no. 4 (October 1941): 265–94. *NYHS Collections:* vol. 30 (1897) *Abstracts of Wills,* p. 76. Von Khrum, *Silversmiths,* p. 16. *Register of Members of the Moravian Church* (Bethlehem, Pa.: H. T. Clauder, 1873), pp. 140, 143. I am indebted to Deborah Dependahl Waters for calling to my attention the porringer with the 2 stamps.

153
DRINKING BOWL, ca. 1730

DIAM. 4 ½" (11.4 cm), H. (with handle) 2 1/16" (5.2 cm), w. 6 11/16" (17.0 cm)
3 oz. 5 dwt. 18 gr. (102.3 g)

Stamps: "HB" in conjoined roman letters, in a crowned shield, struck once in center of underside.

Engraved on underside: "IVB" in shaded roman letters. *Scratched on underside:* "GE[?]/ to/ AKE".

Description: raised circular shallow bowl with plain rim and flat bottom; centerpunch on underside; 2 twisted wire, C-scroll handles. Sides of body chased into 6 panels, each with a stylized leaf flanked by scrolls; tips of fronds and scrolls accented with punchwork.

Spectrographic analysis:

	SILVER	COPPER	LEAD	GOLD
UNDERSIDE	92.3	7.1	0.19	0.13
HANDLE	92.9	5.9	0.13	0.14

Provenance: F. & L. Schwartz, Philadelphia.

53.186 Museum purchase from F. & L. Schwartz, 1953

♥ 154

DRINKING BOWL,
ca. 1730

DIAM. 4 ¹¹⁄₁₆" (11.9 cm), H. (with handles) 2 ¹⁄₁₆"
(5.2 cm), W. 7 ¹⁄₁₆" (17.9 cm)
3 oz. 3 dwt. 13 gr. (98.8 g)

Stamps: "HB" in conjoined roman letters, in a
crowned shield, struck once in center of underside.

Engraved on underside: "AˣD" in shaded roman
letters.

Description: raised circular shallow bowl with
plain rim and flat bottom; centerpunch on
underside; 2 twisted wire, C-scroll handles.
Sides of body chased into 6 panels, each with
a stylized leaf flanked by scrolls; tips of fronds
and scrolls accented with punchwork.

Spectrographic analysis:

	SILVER	COPPER	GOLD	LEAD
UNDERSIDE	95.1	4.5	0.17	0.13
HANDLE	90.1	7.7	0.34	0.31

Provenance: Charles F. Montgomery, Wallingford, Conn., sold to Charles K. Davis, Fairfield,
Conn., 1941.

Comments: Similar to no. 153, but the handles
are made of heavier gauge wire.

References: Fales, *American Silver*, no. 40. Kauffman, *Colonial Silversmith*, p. 96.

56.46.4 Gift of Charles K. Davis, 1956

❦ 155
DRINKING BOWL, ca. 1730

DIAM. 4 ⅛" (10.5 cm), H. (with handles) 1 ¾"
(4.4 cm), W. 6 ⅜" (16.2 cm)
2 oz. 12 dwt. 12 gr. (81.6 g)

Stamps: "HB" in conjoined roman letters, in a
crowned shield, struck once in center of underside.

Scratched on underside: "C+R[?]" in roman
letters.

Description: raised circular shallow bowl with
plain rim and flat bottom with an applied band
around base; centerpunch on underside; 2 C-
curve flat-sided handles cut from sheet.

Spectrographic analysis:

	SILVER	COPPER	LEAD	GOLD
UNDERSIDE	94.4	4.9	0.21	0.13
BODY SIDE	88.6	10.2	0.35	0.22
HANDLE	93.6	5.8	0.10	0.09

Provenance: H. F. du Pont.

Comments: At first glance the bottom appears
to be a separate piece, but it is not. The applied
band was probably added later to reinforce the
bottom.

References: Fales, *American Silver*, no. 39.

59.2311 Gift of H. F. du Pont, 1965

❦ 156 a–c
SPOONS, ca. 1730

(a) L. 6 ¾" (17.2 cm)
1 oz. 14 dwt. 19 gr. (52.4 g)
(b) L. 7 ½" (19.1 cm)
1 oz. 9 dwt. 2 gr. (45.1 g)
(c) L. 7 ¾" (19.7 cm)
1 oz. 12 dwt. 9 gr. (50.3 g)

Stamps: "HB" in conjoined roman letters, in a
crowned shield, struck once on back of bowl
(a) and once on back of handles (b) and (c).

Engraved on back of bowl (a): "CR" in shaded
roman letters. *Engraved on back of handle:* (b)
"VH/ EA" in shaded roman letters; (c) "R∗F"
in shaded roman letters.

Description: (a) oval bowl with swage-formed
rattail on back; cast handle, triangular in section, with foliate decoration and stylized bud
at end; (b) elongated oval bowl with swage-
formed double rounded drop on back; rounded
upturned handle with midrib; (c) oval bowl
with swage-formed rattail with conforming
ridge and double rounded drop; upturned
wavy-end handle.

Spectrographic analysis: Silver content ranges
from 90.6 to 97.1 percent.

Provenance: Mr. and Mrs. Stanley B. Ineson,
New York City; Mr. and Mrs. Alfred E. Bissell,
Wilmington, Del.

Exhibitions: (a) Metropolitan Museum of Art,
New York City, 1939–42.

References: Belden, *Marks of American
Silversmiths*, p. 66.

62.240.971, .972, .1432 Gift of Mr. and Mrs.
Alfred E. Bissell, 1962–63

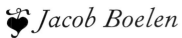
Jacob Boelen

ca. 1657–1729
New York, New York

Born in Amsterdam, young Jacob Boelen immigrated with his parents to New Amsterdam in 1659. Twenty years later he married Catherina Clock, and in 1698 he was admitted as a freeman of New York. Boelen was a member of the Dutch Church, where he was buried. His house and shop were on Broad Street, next to the home of Urseltje Schepmoes Van Dyck, whose son Peter became an important silversmith. In his will, dated July 31, 1725, and proved March 23, 1729/30, Boelen called himself a goldsmith. He was named executor or witness in numerous New York wills and was active in local affairs. He was repeatedly named alderman and assessor for the North Ward and served on numerous committees for public works, such as one to construct a new city hall in 1696. He was also a member of the Common Council.

Concern over the accuracy of weights and measures and the quality of gold and silver is expressed in a petition of 1695 affirming that such control was necessary and recommending the appointment of "Cornelius Vanderburgh & Jacob Boelen, Silver Smiths, as Persons of good Reputation and very fitt to be appointed . . . for the keeping of the Standard of Silver & Gold Weights and markeing all such as shall be used in this Citty & Province."

For the Ulster County town of Marbletown, Boelen made a silver seal, which is now at the Metropolitan Museum of Art, and in 1702 he was asked to make a gold box for Viscount Cornbury, the newly appointed governor. In 1733 the *New-York Gazette* carried a notice of silver stolen in Flatbush: "One Silver Tankard, a piece of Money in the Led of King Charles II, and the Led all engraved, a Coat of Arms, before (in it Man on a Waggon with two Horses) mark'd on the Handle, L P A. One Silver Tankard plain, with a Piece of Money in the Led, mark'd on the Handle A P or A L. One Cup with two twisted Ears chas'd with Skutchens, marked L P A. One Tumbler marked L P A. One Dutch Beker weighs about 28 Ounces, Engraved all around, marked L P A. All the above were made by Mr. Jacob Boele[n], Stamp'd IB."

References: DAB, s.v. "Boelen, Jacob." Gottesman, *Arts and Crafts, 1726–76*, p. 31. Howard S. Randolph and Mrs. Russell Hastings, "Jacob Boelen, Goldsmith, of New York and His Family Circle," *NYG&BR* 72, no. 4 (October 1941): 265–94. *NYHS Collections*: vol. 43 (1910); vol. 44 (1911) *New York Tax Lists*; vol. 18 (1885) *Burghers and Freemen*, for numerous references; vol. 35 (1902) *Abstracts of Unrecorded Wills*, pp. 153–54, for his will; see also vol. 25 (1892) and vol. 26 (1893) *Abstracts of Wills*, for references in other wills. *Minutes of the Common Council*, index. James G. Wilson, *Memorial History of the City of New-York*, 4 vols. (New York: New-York History Co., 1892–93), 1:510.

157
TANKARD, ca. 1710

H. 6 15/16" (17.6 cm), DIAM. base 5 7/16" (13.8 cm), w. 8 11/16" (22.1 cm)
30 oz. 8 dwt. 15 gr. (944.3 g)

Stamps: "ƗB" in roman letters, in a crowned shield, struck once on upper body, left of handle; once on underside of body; and once on top of lid.

Engraved on back of handle: "W / E∗E" in shaded roman letters. *Engraved on front of body opposite handle:* "W / EE" ("W" as a cypher, "EE" in shaded foliate script with a small floral device between the E's). *Scratched on top of lid and on front of body:* "PW" in roman letters. *Lightly engraved on top of lid:* 8-point star formed by interlocking triangles with cross-hatching inside, rudimentary florets between points, the whole enclosed in a plain circle and a wavy circle.

Description: raised body with straight tapering sides and flat bottom; 4-step molded applied rim; centerpunch on underside. Applied base molding consists of 4 concave sections divided by a band of wigglework; above a smaller concave molding is a band of cut-card work, each unit consisting of an anthemion with a ladder-like device in the center. Raised circular single-step lid with flat top crenellated at front; centerpunch on top; applied bezel. Cast cocoon thumbpiece. Cast 5-segment hinge between bands of wigglework. Raised-and-soldered hollow C-curve handle with cast lion couchant applied to upper back; above lion is an applied band of anthemia similar to cut-card work over base molding; lower end of handle forms a C curve in profile and terminates with a cast putto mask applied to a shield-shape plate; circular vent in center of engraved cross; larger circular upper vent.

Spectrographic analysis:

	SILVER	COPPER	LEAD	GOLD
BODY SIDE	92.2	7.3	0.16	0.12
UNDERSIDE	92.3	7.0	0.18	0.11
BASE MOLDING	93.0	6.5	0.17	0.14
LID	92.7	6.4	0.18	0.44
HANDLE	93.0	6.5	0.15	0.12

History: Owned by Evert and Engletie Wendell, who were married in 1710 and lived in Albany. See no. 265 by Jacob C. Ten Eyck for information on Evert and Engletie Wendell.

Provenance: Charles K. Davis, Fairfield, Conn.

Exhibitions: "Masterpieces of American Silver," Virginia Museum of Fine Arts, Richmond, 1960. "New York Silversmiths of the Seventeenth Century," Museum of the City of New York, 1962–63.

Comments: A similar tankard by Boelen, with a William III coin dated 1696 set into the lid, is owned by the Metropolitan Museum of Art.

References: Fales, *American Silver*, nos. 43, 45. Kauffman, *Colonial Silversmith*, p. 110. *Masterpieces of American Silver*, no. 158. Miller, *New York Silversmiths*, no. 18.

57.94 Gift of Charles K. Davis, 1957

❧ 158
CEREMONIAL SPOON, ca. 1700

L. 6 ½" (16.5 cm)
1 oz. 13 dwt. 17 gr. (52.4 g)

Stamps: "ƗB" in roman letters, in a crowned shield, struck once on back of bowl.

Engraved on back of bowl: "C/ Ɨ*L" in roman letters.

Description: broad oval bowl with a swage-formed rattail; cast handle, triangular in section, with foliate decoration and forward-bent stylized bud at end.

Spectrographic analysis:

	SILVER	COPPER	LEAD	GOLD
BOWL	89.7	9.0	0.24	0.12
HANDLE	92.5	6.6	0.24	0.17

Provenance: Charles F. Montgomery, Wallingford, Conn., sold to Charles K. Davis, Fairfield, Conn., 1945.

Exhibitions: "New York Silversmiths of the Seventeenth Century," Museum of the City of New York, 1962–63.

Comments: Similar to spoon no. 156 a, by Henricus Boelen, except that the Jacob Boelen spoon has more 3-dimensional decoration. Spoons of this type were often given as memorial presents at funerals.

References: Davidson, *Colonial Antiques*, p. 35. Fales, *American Silver*, no. 69. Fennimore, *Silver and Pewter*, no. 29. Miller, *New York Silversmiths*, no. 14.

56.46.2 Gift of Charles K. Davis, 1956

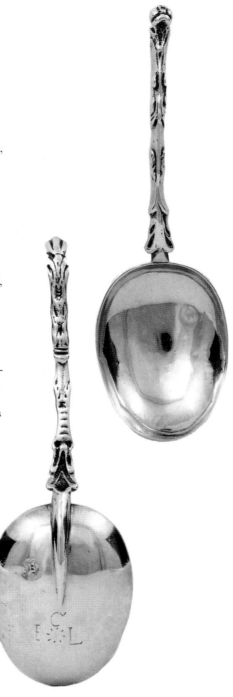

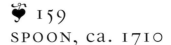

❧ 159
SPOON, ca. 1710

L. 7 ½" (19.1 cm)
1 oz. 12 dwt. 15 gr. (50.7 g)

Stamps: "ƗB" in roman letters, in a crowned shield, struck once on back of handle.

Engraved on back of handle: "L/ Ɨ*M" in roman letters. *Scratched on back of handle below engraved initials:* shaded roman "P".

Description: oval bowl with a swage-formed rattail, conforming ribs, and single rounded drop on back; straight wavy-end handle bent sharply upward at tip.

Spectrographic analysis:

	SILVER	COPPER	GOLD	LEAD
BOWL	92.5	7.4	0.10	0.08
HANDLE	92.3	7.5	0.18	0.00

Provenance: Mr. and Mrs. Stanley B. Ineson, New York City; Mr. and Mrs. Alfred E. Bissell, Wilmington, Del.

Comments: Same stamp as no. 158.

References: Belden, *Marks of American Silversmiths*, p. 66.

62.240.975 Gift of Mr. and Mrs. Alfred E. Bissell, 1962–63

 *Gerardus Boyce*

1795–1880

Boyce & Jones, w. late 1820s
New York, New York

Born in New York City, Gerardus Boyce is listed in directories at Grand near Crosby, 1820; 11 Leonard, 1821; Grand near Greene, 1822–23; 91 Grand near Greene, 1824; 110 Greene, 1825. He is also recorded at the last address from 1835 to 1857. During the late 1820s, he presumably was a partner in the firm of Boyce & Jones. He acquired an apprentice from the almshouse in 1844. He is recorded in the United States census of 1850 and in the 1855 New York state census.

In Boyce's long career he made many tea sets in the melon style and a number of pieces in rococo revival style. A five-piece service in the melon style is owned by the Manigault House in Charleston, South Carolina, and a three-piece tea service, owned in 1972 by dealers Arthur and Theresa Greenblatt, Amherst, New Hampshire, is decorated with chinoiserie designs. Boyce also made a traditional eighteenth-century–style cann (owned in 1972 by dealer Edwin Fitler, Ardmore, Pennsylvania) that was presented by William L. Van Zant to his son on his birthday in 1846. Yale University Art Gallery owns a boatswain's whistle made by Boyce. E. Alfred Jones records a beaker by Boyce that was the gift of Salmon Hubbell to the First Church of Bridgeport, Connecticut, in 1829. Although Boyce's silver is readily found, little is known about the man himself.

References: Buhler and Hood, *American Silver*, no. 775. Jones, *Old Silver*, p. 93. Arthur and Theresa Greenblatt advertisement, *Antiques* 110, no. 6 (December 1976): 1222. Von Khrum, *Silversmiths*, p. 18. I am indebted to Deborah Dependahl Waters for the census information.

 160
DISH CROSS, ca. 1835

H. 3" (7.6 cm), w. 12 ⅜" (31.4 cm)
15 oz. 8 dwt. 21 gr. (480.4 g)

Stamps: "G. BOYCE" in roman letters, in a rectangle, struck once on underside of spirit lamp.

Engraved on side of spirit lamp: "C.B." in shaded gothic letters.

Description: circular spirit lamp with 4 arms and supports for holding dishes. Lower body of lamp, from well to just above bulbous sides, raised; upper body of lamp seamed and inserted into lower body. Raised friction-fit circular lid with molded rim rises over interior well with a seamed conical wick holder and bezel. Upper body of lamp holds in place the 2 rings from which the 4 arms branch out, 2 from each ring. Cast arms, rectangular in section, soldered to center rings, both of which rotate freely; 6-point cast stars, held in place by rivets, serve as stops for leg sleeves; 4 cast 10-petal feet are attached to cast C scrolls that attach to sleeves. Cast 9-lobe shells, which serve as plate supports and which are plain on top, are attached to sleeves by cast scrolls. The sleeves slide freely on the arms to support different size plates.

Spectrographic analysis:

	SILVER	COPPER	LEAD	GOLD	ZINC
UNDERSIDE OF BURNER	85.9	13.4	0.27	0.11	0.02
FOOT	90.7	8.7	0.21	0.14	0.06

Provenance: Joseph B. Brenauer, New York City; Parke-Bernet sale of Brenauer's estate in 1946 to Mark Bortman; Jane Bortman Larus, Woburn, Mass.; William Core Duffy, New Haven.

Exhibitions: "Masterpieces of American Silver," Virginia Museum of Fine Arts, Richmond, 1960. Diplomatic Reception Rooms, Department of State, Washington, D.C., 1972–83.

Comments: Another dish cross by Boyce, with initials "ADP," was exhibited at the Museum of the City of New York, 1937–38, and was later acquired by the Metropolitan Museum of Art. The Winterthur dish cross is nearly identical to one made by Standish Barry that is in the Hammerslough collection at Wadsworth Atheneum. Boyce is the only American silversmith known to have made more than 1 dish cross.

References: Donald Fennimore, "Gerardus Boyce Dish Cross," *Silver* 18, no. 1 (January/February 1985): 16–17. Eleanor Gustafson, "Museum Accessions," *Antiques* 125, no. 1 (January 1984): 114. *Masterpieces of American Silver*, no. 159.

83.61 Museum purchase from William Core Duffy, 1983, with funds given by Mrs. Alfred E. Bissell in memory of her husband

🂱 161 a, b
SALTS, 1820–40

(a) H. 2 ⅛" (5.4 cm), w. 4 ¹³⁄₁₆" (12.2 cm)
3 oz. 19 dwt. 21 gr. (124.2 g)
(b) H. 2 ¹⁄₁₆" (5.2 cm), w. 4 ¾" (12.1 cm)
3 oz. 19 dwt. 15 gr. (123.9 g)

Stamps: "G. BOYCE" in roman letters, in a rectangle, struck once on underside of each body.

Engraved on side of each body: plain shield with 3 griffin heads on a field gules; crest consists of forearm on a heraldic band supporting a crown; motto: "VIRTUTIS GLORIA MERCES" in roman letters.

Description: raised oval body with slightly convex sides, flat bottom, and upward curving ends; applied gadrooned rim and foot. Handles on each end cast as acanthus leaves and scrolls. Centerpunch on underside of each body; gold wash inside each body.

Spectrographic analysis:

	SILVER	COPPER	LEAD	GOLD
BODY SIDE (a)	89.8	9.8	0.33	0.08
BODY SIDE (b)	89.2	10.4	0.26	0.06

Provenance: Marshall P. Blankarn, New York City.

Comments: Coat of arms is said to be that of the Robertsons. The motto translates, "Glory is the Recompense of Valor."

References: Hammerslough, *American Silver*, 2:28, for a similar set of 4 salts.

79.198.1, .2 Gift of Marshall P. Blankarn, 1979

🂱 162 a, b
SUGAR BOWL AND CREAMER, ca. 1834

(a) Sugar bowl and lid: H. 8 ¹³⁄₁₆" (22.4 cm), w. 9 ¹⁄₁₆" (23.0 cm)
Bowl: 18 oz. 19 dwt. 4 gr. (588.3 g)
Lid: 4 oz. 17 dwt. 18 gr. (151.7 g)
(b) Creamer: H. 7 ½" (19.1 cm), w. 7 ¾" (19.7 cm)
15 oz. 12 dwt. 23 gr. (485.6 g)

Stamps: (a) "NEW YORK" in roman letters, in a serrated rectangle; "N.Y" in roman letters, in a plain rectangle; also, a crude 4-point star containing 5 pellets and a rectangle containing 4 pellets, all struck on underside of body; (b) same stamps struck on underside of body, except city is given as "NEW YO[?]E" (illegible letter possibly "R").

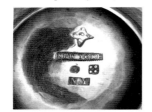

Engraved on sides of both bodies: "M•G•M" in large shaded gothic letters; "Made from ancient silver coin found by Mary E. Smith/ in a secret drawer of an old family desk at the/ Smith Homestead, Woodbury, Conn. in the year 1834" in script.

Description: raised circular lower bodies, wide at top, with nearly flat shoulders, tapering into small rounded bottom; centerpunch on underside of both bodies. Incurving necks. Raised, circular, stepped pedestals. Die-rolled decorative bands around rim, shoulders, top of pedestal, and footring consist of vertical spearlike leaves alternating with a single bud on a tall thick stalk, all on a ground with horizontal striations.

(a) Sugar bowl and lid: 2 vertically seamed, hollow, S-curve handles with 1 sprig; raised circular stepped-and-domed lid with large hollow bud finial; short bezel.

(b) Creamer: incurved neck flares toward rim and has broad extended pouring lip; single handle styled as on sugar bowl.

Spectrographic analysis:

	SILVER	COPPER	LEAD	GOLD
(a) Sugar bowl and lid				
BODY SIDE	81.6	18.2	0.22	0.04
FOOT	84.2	15.6	0.23	0.05
HANDLE 1	83.9	15.9	0.12	0.06
HANDLE 2	84.2	15.6	0.12	0.06
LID	84.3	15.6	0.06	0.06
(b) Creamer				
BODY SIDE	82.4	17.4	0.09	0.05
SPOUT	81.7	18.1	0.10	0.06
FOOT	84.3	15.6	0.10	0.07
HANDLE	84.0	15.9	0.11	0.05

History: Mary E. Smith was probably the same Mary E. Smith (b. July 2, 1820) who married John J. Monell. Her father was Nathaniel B. Smith (b. 1795), a lawyer, judge of probate, and representative to the General Assembly of Connecticut. His father was the distinguished jurist Nathaniel Smith (1762–1822). Both father and son read law with Tapping Reeve at Reeve's famous law school in Litchfield, Conn. Mary would have been 14 years old when she found the old coins (referred to in the engraving) in the Smith house. The initials "MGM," engraved later, no doubt refer to a member of the Monell family.

Provenance: Smith family of Woodbury, Conn.; Carl Kossack, North Haven, Conn.

Comments: Very well made and solid, the 2 pieces are handsome examples of late classical American silver. The attribution to Boyce is based on a bowl in a private collection bearing Boyce's stamp and the 4 pellets in a square. Silver content is unusually low but consistent.

References: William Cothren, *History of Ancient Woodbury, Connecticut* (1854; reprint, Baltimore: Genealogical Publishing Co., 1977), pp. 398–405, 677.

90.45.1, .2 Gift of Carl Kossack, 1990

❧ 163
BOWL, ca. 1835

H. 4 ¾" (12.1 cm), W. 7 ⅝" (19.4 cm)
14 oz. 16 dwt. 8 gr. (459.8 g)

Stamps: "G. BOYCE" and "N.YORK" in roman letters, each in a rectangle, struck once on underside of body.

Engraved on side of body: "Susan Chapman/ from her/ Mother" in script.

Description: raised circular body, incurved before curving sharply out to molded rim; sides formed into 8 panels so that rim is octagonal in plan; centerpunch on underside of body; 4 hollow cast scroll feet with water leaves. Body chased with crude C scrolls, acanthus leaves, and flowers, creating 2 reserves for engraving; 1 reserve is blank.

Spectrographic analysis:

	SILVER	COPPER	LEAD	GOLD
BODY SIDE	84.7	15.1	0.14	0.07
UNDERSIDE	84.8	15.0	0.14	0.07
FOOT 1	92.9	6.8	0.18	0.09
FOOT 2	92.9	6.9	0.13	0.06
FOOT 3	92.5	7.4	0.05	0.07
FOOT 4	92.7	7.2	0.05	0.09

Provenance: Carl Kossack, North Haven, Conn.

Comments: This is an early example of rococo revival with good form but rather crude chased decoration. Low silver content but very consistent.

90.46 Gift of Carl Kossack, 1990

❧ 164
LADLE, ca. 1830

L. 14 ⅜" (36.5 cm)
6 oz. 18 dwt. 7 gr. (214.6 g)

Stamps: "G. BOYCE" in roman letters, in a rectangle, accompanied by 3 additional stamps: a star in a circle, a male profile in a rounded rectangle, and an anchor in an oval. All stamps struck once on back of handle.

Engraved on front of handle: "JCM" in foliate script.

Description: oval bowl with swage-formed single rounded drop; downturned fiddle-shape handle with rounded shoulders at lower end and swage-formed basket of flowers on upper front.

Spectrographic analysis:

	SILVER	COPPER	LEAD	GOLD
BOWL	85.2	14.3	0.30	0.21
HANDLE	86.0	13.5	0.33	0.20

Provenance: Mr. and Mrs. Stanley B. Ineson, New York City; Mr. and Mrs. Alfred E. Bissell, Wilmington, Del.

References: Belden, *Marks of American Silversmiths*, p. 70.

62.240.1657 Gift of Mr. and Mrs. Alfred E. Bissell, 1965

Ephraim Brasher

1744–1810

Brasher & Alexander, w. 1800–1801
[Brasher & Riker], w. 1800–1801
New York, New York

Ephraim Brasher, the son of Ephraim and Catherina (Van Keuren) Brasher, was baptized in the New York Dutch Church in 1744. On November 10, 1766, he married Ann Gilbert (born Adriaantje), sister of silversmith William Gilbert. One child, also named Ephraim, is recorded from this marriage; the baptism was witnessed in 1777 by William Gilbert and Margaret Brasher. Following Ann's death in 1797, Brasher married Mary Austin. When he drew up his will in 1803, he bequeathed to his "beloved wife Mary" his entire estate, including his dwelling house on Cherry Street.

Like Gilbert, Brasher was a member of the Gold and Silversmiths Society in 1786. He appears in the directories at 1 Cherry Street, 1786; 77 Queen Street, 1787; 1 Cherry Street, 1789–90; 2 Cherry Street, 1791–93; 5 Cherry Street 1794–95; 350 Pearl Street, 1796; 5 Cherry Street, 1800–1802; 350 Pearl Street, 1803–7. In 1808–9 he was listed as excise officer at 350 Pearl Street. While at 1 Cherry Street he sold four silver skewers, two silver waiters, and a tea tray to George Washington, who lived only a few doors away on Cherry Street. (One of the waiters is owned by the Mount Vernon Ladies' Association.) Brasher's partnership with George Alexander, established in 1800, dissolved in early 1801.

Brasher is best known, perhaps, for his coins made for the State of New York, the so-called Brasher doubloon. He also countermarked foreign coins for fineness, of which a great many were in circulation at the time. In his domestic silver he worked in both the rococo and urn styles. His bellied coffee urn with three spigots and three C-and-S-scroll legs, owned by the Art Institute of Chicago, is a fine example of American rococo design. Amherst College owns a fish slice with an unusual pierced and bright-cut blade, and Yale University Art Gallery owns a large ladle with Onslow-pattern handle.

References: Stephen Decatur, "Ephraim Brasher, Silversmith, of New York," *American Collector* 7, no. 5 (June 1938): 8, 9, 17 (reprinted in Kurt M. Semon, ed., *A Treasury of Old Silver* [New York: Robert M. McBride, 1947], pp. 69–71). Walter H. Breen, "Brasher and Bailey: Pioneer New York Coiners, 1787–1792," in Harold Ingholt, ed., *Centennial Publication of the American Numismatic Society* (New York: By the society, 1958), pp. 137–45. James A. Rasmussen, "Gilbert Family of Albany and New York," *NYG&BR* 122, no. 3 (July 1991): 164–65. Von Khrum, *Silversmiths*, p. 19. I am indebted to Deborah Dependahl Waters for bringing the Gilbert genealogy to my attention.

165
SALVER, ca. 1780

DIAM. 7⅞" (20.0 cm), H. 1 1/16" (2.7 cm)
10 oz. 6 dwt. 19 gr. (320.9 g)

Stamps: "E•B" in roman letters, in a rectangle, struck 3 times on underside of body.

Scratched on underside of body: "oz 10   dwt 16 gr 12".

Description: flat circular body with elevated and shaped edge consisting of 6 wavy-edge bracket-like segments that form points where they meet. Cast ropelike border applied to upper edge of rim. Centerpunch on upper surface. 3 cast, equally spaced, short cabriole (or back-to-back C-scroll) legs with pad feet.

Spectrographic analysis:

	SILVER	COPPER	GOLD	LEAD
TOP	89.6	9.9	0.33	0.18
UNDERSIDE	88.7	10.3	0.37	0.26
FOOT	93.1	6.4	0.29	0.17

Provenance: Robert Ensko, Inc., New York City, sold to H. F. du Pont, 1930.

65.1384 Gift of H. F. du Pont, 1965

❧ 166 a–f
SPOONS, 1780–1810

(a) L. 8 ¹⁵⁄₁₆" (22.7 cm)
1 oz. 17 dwt. 13 gr. (58.3 g)
(b) L. 9" (22.9 cm)
6 dwt. 23 gr. (10.8 g)
(c) L. 5 ³⁄₁₆" (13.2 cm)
1 oz. 17 dwt. 3 gr. (57.7 g)
(d) L. 9 ⅛" (23.2 cm)
1 oz. 12 dwt. 20 gr. (51.0 g)
(e) L. 5 ¼" (13.3 cm)
8 dwt. 6 gr. (12.8 g)
(f) L. 7 ⁷⁄₁₆" (18.9 cm)
1 oz. 13 dwt. 13 gr. (52.1 g)

Stamps: (a) "E•BRASHER" in roman letters, in a rounded rectangle; "N•YORK" in roman letters, in a rectangle, each struck once on back of handle; (b) "BRASHER" in roman letters, in a rectangle, rounded on right end; "E•B" in roman letters, in an oval, both struck once on back of handle; (c) "E•B" in roman letters, in an oval, struck once on back of handle; (d–f) "EB" in roman letters, in a rectangle, struck twice on back of handles.

Engraved on front of handle: (a) "WMM" in script, in a bright-cut medallion with pendant drop; (b) "MIS" in foliate script, in a bright-cut medallion with pendant drop; (c) "M/ H•T" in crude roman letters. *Scratched on back of handle:* "1284H"; (d) "RMK" in foliate script, in a bright-cut medallion with pendant drop; (e) "S/ IA" in shaded roman letters, in a bright-cut medallion with pendant and bright-cut border; (f) "TAS" in foliate script, in a bright-cut medallion with foliate pendant drop.

Description: (a) pointed oval bowl with swage-formed pointed drop and rounded second drop; pointed downturned handle with midrib; (b) pointed oval bowl with swage-formed squared drop and faint rounded second drop; rounded downturned handle with midrib; (c) oval bowl with swage-formed pointed drop; rounded downturned handle; (d) elongated oval bowl with swage-formed pointed drop and faint rounded second drop; rounded downturned handle with midrib; (e) elongated oval bowl with swage-formed 9-lobe shell surmounted by a cross plus a rounded drop; pointed downturned handle with midrib; (f) deep oval bowl with swage-formed double rounded drop with straight incised line cut across drop; rounded downturned handle.

Spectrographic analysis: Silver content ranges from 89.9 to 92.3 percent.

Provenance: Mr. and Mrs. Stanley B. Ineson, New York City; Mr. and Mrs. Alfred E. Bissell, Wilmington, Del.

Exhibitions: (e) Metropolitan Museum of Art, New York City, 1935–61.

References: Belden, *Marks of American Silversmiths*, pp. 73, 74.

62.240.925, .924, .44, .967, .47, .968 Gift of Mr. and Mrs. Alfred E. Bissell, 1962–63

Charles Oliver Bruff

ca. 1735–1817
Elizabethtown, New Jersey,
w. prior to 1763
New York, New York, w. 1763–83
Shelburne, Nova Scotia, w. 1783–1817

Charles Oliver Bruff was one of many Maryland silversmiths with that surname. He was born in Talbot County, Maryland, the son of James Earl Bruff, who had interests in Elizabethtown, New Jersey, and apparently set up his son in business there about 1760. By January 1763 Bruff was working in New York City, where he advertised "at the sign of the teapot and tankard in Maiden-Lane." In the same year he married Mary Letellier, who may be related to silversmith John Letellier. During his twenty years in New York, Bruff's numerous newspaper advertisements stressed his capacity to provide fine quality jewelry; this, no doubt, is why by 1765 he listed himself as "at the Sign of the Teapot, Tankard, and Earring, the corner of King-street." Like silversmith Lewis Fueter, he catered to military clientele during the Revolution and offered "Small Swords Silver mounted, Cut-and-thrust and Cutteau De Chase, mounted with beautiful green Grips." Also, like Fueter, his Tory sympathies forced him to leave New York with the British in 1783. A person of means, he took with him a household consisting of seven family members and eight servants. In Shelburne he turned his hand to all kinds of smith's work, the proof of which is a wafer iron with his full name, now located in the Nova Scotia Museum in Halifax.

For someone so well documented, a small quantity of his silver survives. Major works include a covered sugar bowl (similar to the Myer Myers bowl, no. 231, at Winterthur) at the Museum of the City of New York and a silver shoe buckle owned by the American Pine Barrens Society.

References: "Collectors' Notes," *Antiques* 121, no. 2 (February 1982): 496–97. Gottesman, *Arts and Crafts, 1726–76*, pp. 32–36. Gottesman, *Arts and Crafts, 1777–99*, pp. 63–64. John E. Langdon, *American Silversmiths in British North America, 1776–1800* (Toronto: By the author, 1970), pp. 38–42. John E. Langdon, "New Light on Charles Oliver Bruff, Tory Silversmith," *Antiques* 93, no. 6 (June 1968): 768–69. Harry Peters and Donald MacKay, *Master Goldsmiths and Silversmiths of Nova Scotia* (Halifax: Antiquarian Club, 1948), pp. 117–21. Pleasants and Sill, *Maryland Silversmiths*, pp. 216–18. Von Khrum, *Silversmiths*, pp. 21–22. Williams, *Silversmiths of New Jersey*, pp. 48–49.

❧ 167
SCISSOR TONGS, ca. 1765

L. 5 1/16" (12.9 cm), 1 oz. 4 dwt. 23 gr. (38.8 g)

Stamps: "COB" in roman letters, in a conforming surround, struck once on each of 2 finger grips.

Engraved on circular hinge: "AT" in a cypher of foliate script; "JU" and "R" at the top of the "T" in smaller roman letters, all on azure ground.

Description: 2 cast arms joined off-center by a circular pivot hinge. Each arm consists of a shell tip on a plain shaft that is configured in C scrolls as it nears pivot hinge; circular sprigged finger grip is joined to pivot hinge by 2 C scrolls. Flat circular pivot hinge, with a pin in the center, is engraved on 1 side with an 8-petal flower.

Spectrographic analysis:

SILVER	COPPER	GOLD	LEAD
94.5	5.0	0.25	0.11

Provenance: Edward E. Minor; Mrs. Gregory S. Prince, Chevy Chase, Md., sold to H. F. du Pont, 1954.

Comments: Excellent example of rococo design applied to a small silver artifact.

References: Fales, *American Silver*, no. 87. Kauffman, *Colonial Silversmith*, p. 168. J. Hall Pleasants and Howard Sill, "Charles Oliver Bruff, Silversmith," *Antiques* 39, no. 6 (June 1941): 309–11, fig. 5.

54.7 Gift of H. F. du Pont, 1958

❧ 168
SPOON, ca. 1765

L. 5 1/16" (12.9 cm), 6 dwt. 5 gr. (9.7 g)

Stamps: "COB" in roman letters, in a conforming surround, struck once on back of handle.

Engraved on back of handle: "M/ ‡C" in crude shaded roman letters.

Description: elongated oval bowl with swage-formed double drop on back; rounded upturned handle with slight midrib.

Spectrographic analysis: Silver content is 89.0 percent.

Provenance: Mr. and Mrs. Stanley B. Ineson, New York City; Mr. and Mrs. Alfred E. Bissell, Wilmington, Del.

References: Belden, *Marks of American Silversmiths*, p. 82.

62.240.42 Gift of Mr. and Mrs. Alfred E. Bissell, 1962–63

❧ George Carleton

w. ca. 1820
New York, New York

Stephen Ensko, in *American Silversmiths and Their Marks III*, mentions George Carleton as working in New York City about 1810, while the Darling Foundation's *New York State Silversmiths* lists him as having worked in New York City circa 1820. Carleton's name was dropped, however, from the most recent edition of Ensko, possibly because Carleton does not appear in Paul von Khrum's listings drawn from New York City directories. Further research is required to document this maker—if indeed he is not a retailer. A salt spoon and a mustard ladle, both in private hands and both with the same stamp as the pitcher in the following entry, plus three teaspoons in the Kossack collection at Yale University Art Gallery, are Carleton's only known works. *New York State Silversmiths* also lists a partnership of Carleton & Kimball for 1810.

References: Ensko, *American Silversmiths III*, p. 35. Ensko, *American Silversmiths IV*. *New York State Silversmiths*, p. 47. Von Khrum, *Silversmiths*.

❧ 169
PITCHER, ca. 1810

H. 6 11/16" (17.0 cm), w. 7 3/4" (19.7 cm),
DIAM. base 4 1/16" (41.9 cm)
15 oz. 13 dwt. 12 gr. (487.6 g)

Stamps: "CARLETON" in roman letters, in a rectangle, struck once on underside of body; a 5-point star is struck on each side of the stamp.

Engraved on underside of body: "JA" (or "IA") in foliate script. *Engraved on side of body:* "W[?]" in foliate script (Fales, *American Silver*, lists "WC").

Description: circular seamed body in shape of Liverpool jug. Slightly concave in upper and lower body, bulbous in middle; applied molded rim; set-in, slightly domed bottom and molded base ring; inset V-shape spout with applied molded rim. Hollow C-curve handle, seamed vertically, with plain oval tailpiece; circular vent.

Spectrographic analysis:

	SILVER	COPPER	LEAD	GOLD
BODY SIDE	87.0	12.4	0.19	0.10
UNDERSIDE	92.2	7.3	0.12	0.14
SPOUT	86.8	12.6	0.20	0.06
HANDLE	87.8	11.7	0.17	0.09

Provenance: George Arons & Brothers, Ansonia, Conn.

Comments: This seamed vessel is nearly identical in appearance to a pitcher made by Paul Revere, Jr. (no. 112), which is raised.

References: Fales, *American Silver*, no. 123.

56.12 Museum purchase from George Arons & Brothers, 1956

 John Crawford

w. ca. 1815–45
New York, New York, w. 1815–37
Philadelphia, Pennsylvania, w. 1837–43
New York, New York, w. 1844–45

John Crawford appears in the New York City directories at 92 John Street, 1815; 406 Broadway, 1816–17; Bowery next to Vauxhall, 1818–25; 227 Grand Street, 1826–34; 99 Chrystie Street, 1835. He is thought to have worked in Philadelphia from 1837 to 1843 before returning to New York City. He seems to have preferred the lobate style, based on the small quantity of surviving silver. A four-piece lobate tea service by Crawford, with die-rolled decorative bands, is owned by the Art Institute of Chicago. A goblet with incurved neck and chased acanthus leaves on the lower bulbous body is owned by the Museum of the City of New York. Crawford also made a pair of beakers, engraved with the date 1826, for the Third Congregational Church in New Haven.

References: Jones, *Old Silver*, p. 308. Milo M. Naeve and Lynn Springer Roberts, *A Decade of Decorative Arts: The Antiquarian Society of the Art Institute of Chicago* (Chicago: Art Institute of Chicago, 1986), no. 64. Von Khrum, *Silversmiths*, p. 34.

♣ 170 a, b
SUGAR BOWL AND CREAMER, ca. 1830

(a) Sugar bowl and lid: H. 8 ⅞" (22.5 cm), w. 9 ¼" (23.5 cm)
16 oz. 17 dwt. 2 gr. (523.0 g) (lid: 130.8 g)
(b) Creamer: H. 7" (17.8 cm), w. 6 ¾" (17.1 cm)
10 oz. 18 dwt. 10 gr. (338.9 g)

Stamps: "J. CRAWFORD" in roman letters, in a rectangle, struck once on underside of each body.

Engraved on side of each body: "AEY" in foliate script.

Description: both pieces are oval in plan with 12 vertical lobes around lower bodies. Die-rolled decorative band of leaves, grapes, and blossoms, 11/16" wide, around upper bodies. Oval stepped bases with decorative bands around bottom and top; centerpunch on underside of both bodies.

(a) Sugar bowl and lid: raised stepped upper body between 2 decorative bands; 2 C-curve hollow handles, made in vertical halves, circular in section, swelling toward crimped centers; bulbous thumbpieces; single upper terminal, double lower handle terminals. Lid oval in plan, flat at edge, rises to high dome, elaborately chased with leaves and grapes; hollow finial cast in shape of a heaped basket of leaves and grapes. Die-rolled decorative band of leaves, grapes, and blossoms, ⅜" wide, around base and rim.

(b) Creamer: upper body seamed and incurved before flaring at rim, which is low on sides, higher at handle, and has extended wide rim for pouring lip. Applied ¼" die-rolled decorative band of meandering vine, grapes, leaves, and blossoms around rim and at top of base.

Spectrographic analysis:

	SILVER	COPPER	LEAD	GOLD
(a) Sugar bowl and lid				
BODY SIDE	85.8	13.5	0.27	0.05
LID	96.3	3.6	0.17	0.03
(b) Creamer				
BODY SIDE	87.0	12.3	0.26	0.08
LID	83.1	16.4	0.39	0.07

History: The initials "AEY" may refer to the Yates family; see no. 175.

Provenance: Helen De Lancey Watkins, Schenectady, N.Y.

Comments: Form and decoration nearly identical with hot water pot and teapot, no. 175, by Eoff & Shephard, which is also engraved with the initials "AEY."

68.133.1, .2 Museum purchase from estate of Helen De Lancey Watkins, 1968

Abraham Cuyler

1713–49
Albany, New York
Previously attributed to A. Carman,
unknown location in New York

An "AC" and an "IC" worked in the
Albany area in the early to middle years
of the eighteenth century. John D. Kernan, Jr., claims that both of these stamps
refer to Cuylers. He suggests that the
"IC" stamp belongs to Jacob Cuyler
and the "AC" stamp may belong to one
of two Abraham Cuylers: Abraham
(1663–1747), the father of Catherina
Cuyler, who married Jacob Ten Eyck;
or Abraham (1713–49), Catherina's
brother. Unfortunately, there is no
evidence to support the theory that
either Abraham Cuyler was a silversmith. Still, an Albany provenance for
the following objects seems likely; in
the absence of another identifiable "AC,"
the attribution to the younger Abraham
Cuyler seems plausible.

References: Rice, *Albany Silver*, p. 71. John D.
Kernan, Jr., "The Mystery of AC Silver," *An-
tiques* 71, no. 6 (June 1957): 554–55. John D. Ker-
nan, Jr., "More AC Silver," *Antiques* 75, no. 5
(May 1959): 463. John D. Kernan, Jr., "A New
Albany Smith and Further Light on AC and
IGL," *Antiques* 74, no. 2 (August 1958): 140–42.

171
SALT, ca. 1740

H. 1 ⅝" (4.1 cm), DIAM. rim 2 ⅝" (6.7 cm),
w. 2 ¹³⁄₁₆" (7.1 cm)
2 oz. 2 dwt. 7 gr. (65.8 g)

Stamps: "AC" in roman letters, in a rectangle,
struck once on underside of body.

Engraved on underside of body: "IG" in shaded
roman letters with a sprig between.

Description: raised circular body with bulbous
sides and an applied cast scalloped molding at
rim; double-scored line encircles body below
rim; centerpunch on underside; 3 cast cabriole
legs with triple pads at knees and feet.

Spectrographic analysis:

	SILVER	COPPER	GOLD	LEAD
BODY	93.3	6.6	0.14	0.03
FOOT	95.2	4.7	0.13	0.02

Provenance: Harry Arons, Ansonia, Conn.

Exhibitions: "Albany Silver," Albany Institute
of History and Art, 1964.

Comments: Several pieces survive that have
the "AC" stamp and are associated with the
Albany area. There is little question that this
salt relates to that group of artifacts. An identical salt with an Albany history is in a private
collection, and an identical salt in the Albany
Institute is stamped "IC". Kernan took issue
with the attribution to A. Carman and instead
ascribed the "AC" pieces to an Abraham Cuyler
of Albany. On stylistic grounds the salt is
attributed to Abraham Cuyler (1713–49). See
tankard by "AC" in Sotheby's, sale no. 5809
(January 27, 1989), lot 920.

References: Fales, *American Silver*, no. 104.,
where it is published as the work of A. Carman.
Kauffman, *Colonial Silversmith*, p. 159. See Kernan articles and Rice, *Albany Silver*, no. 50.

56.10.10 Museum purchase from Harry Arons,
1956

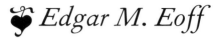

Edgar M. Eoff

1785–1858

Eoff & Phyfe, w. 1844–50
Eoff & Shephard, w. 1852–?
New York, New York

Edgar M. Eoff appears in New York City directories starting in 1844/45 at 5 Dey Street in partnership with William M. Phyfe. Eoff remained at this address through at least 1850, by which time he was listed alone. A small quantity of silver by Eoff & Phyfe survives. A bowl originally presented to Phineas Eldridge by the shipmasters of London, now at the Metropolitan Museum of Art, has the stamp of Baldwin & Company in addition to "E&P." Baldwin was the retailer. The Valentine Museum, Richmond, owns a goblet presented in 1847 to Col. C. Crozet by the students of Richmond Academy. In addition to the stamp "E&P," it has the retailer's stamp of Mitchell & Tyler.

By 1852/53 Eoff was at 83 Duane Street, where he is listed alone and as the partner of George L. Shephard. It is unclear how long the partnership lasted. Several of their tea services survive, most in the rococo revival style, including one at the Museum of the City of New York made for Mr. and Mrs. Amos Trowbridge, who were married in 1851. A heavily chased ewer in the rococo revival style is owned by the Museum of Fine Arts, Boston. Part of the inscription indicates that it was purchased at "the Great Metropolitan Fair" by John Quincy in 1864. Many of the Eoff & Shephard pieces also bear the stamp of "Ball, Black & Co.," and "Ball, Black & Tompkins," major silver retailers.

References: New York City directories. *New York State Silversmiths*, p. 71. Von Khrum, *Silversmiths*, which lists the partnership with Phyfe (but refers to Edward Eoff instead of Edgar) and does not list the partnership with Shephard. Jonathan Fairbanks, "A Decade of Collecting American Decorative Arts and Sculpture at the Museum of Fine Arts, Boston," *Antiques* 120, no. 3 (September 1981): 590–636, fig. 37, for ewer.

172
COFFEEPOT, 1844–48

H. 11 ⁵⁄₁₆" (28.7 cm), w. 9 ⅛" (23.2 cm)
28 oz. 11 dwt. 5 gr. (888.3 g)

Stamps: "E&P" in roman letters, in a rectangle, struck once on underside of body. *Retailer's stamp:* "BALL, TOMPKINS & BLACK" in roman letters, struck once on underside of body.

Engraved on side of body: "HHM" in foliate script.

Description: seamed pear-shape body with elongated neck and flared rim with applied molding; centerpunch on inset piece in bottom. Raised stepped-and-domed lid with plain rim (no overhang); bezel; cast urn-shape finial. Cast 5-segment hinge. Raised, circular, stepped foot with applied footring. S-curve seamed spout with 7 longitudinal panels merging to 4 at tip. High-loop, C-curve, hollow, seamed handle with 3 longitudinal panels on outside; 2 ivory insulators; 4 silver pins.

Spectrographic analysis:

	SILVER	COPPER	LEAD	GOLD
BODY	85.1	14.2	0.24	0.07
FOOT	88.8	10.2	0.38	0.06
SPOUT	89.2	10.1	0.27	0.07
LID	90.3	8.9	0.28	0.07

History: Initials "HHM" refer to Henrietta Hargraves Meigs, born September 25, 1845, in Macon, Ga.

Provenance: Mr. and Mrs. John J. Bradley, Wilmington, Del.

Comments: Interesting mix of traditional and later techniques of fabrication that tends to characterize silver of this period.

74.132 Gift of Mr. and Mrs. John J. Bradley, 1974

♣ 173
KNIFE, ca. 1844–48

L. 8 ¹⁄₁₆" (20.5 cm)
1 oz. 17 dwt. 23 gr. (58.9 g)

Stamps: "EOFF & PHYFE" in roman letters, in a rectangle, struck once on back of handle.

Engraved on side of handle: stag's head on a heraldic band.

Description: rectangular blade, wavy in outline, rounded at end. Seamed handle (pitch filled?) with chased and repoussé decoration consisting of 7-lobe shell surrounded by ribbon C scrolls at upper end; conforming double-thread border continues down handle to anthemion at lower end.

Spectrographic analysis: Silver content of handle is 91.0 percent.

Provenance: The Silver Shelf, Ardmore, Pa.

References: Belden, *Marks of American Silversmiths*, p. 158.

71.73 Museum purchase from the Silver Shelf, with funds from Mr. and Mrs. Alfred E. Bissell, 1971

♣ 174 a–e
TEA SERVICE, ca. 1855

(a) Urn: H. 15 ⅛" (38.5 cm), w. 10 ⅜" (26.4 cm)
60 oz. 12 dwt. 9 gr. (1881.0 g)
(b) Teapot: H. 9 ⅞" (25.1 cm), w. 9 ¹¹⁄₁₆" (24.6 cm)
29 oz. 6 dwt. 17 gr. (910.3 g)
(c) Sugar bowl and lid: H. 8 ¹³⁄₁₆" (22.4 cm), w. 7 ³⁄₁₆" (18.3 cm)
25 oz. 14 dwt. 3 gr. (797.7 g)
(d) Creamer: H. 8 ³⁄₁₆" (20.8 cm), w. 5 ⁹⁄₁₆" (14.1 cm)
16 oz. 2 dwt. 11 gr. (500.3 g)
(e) Waste bowl: H. 5 ⅛" (13.0 cm) w. 6 ⁷⁄₁₆" (16.4 cm)
18 oz. 15 dwt. 15 gr. (582.8 g)

Stamps: "E&S" in roman letters, in a rectangle, struck once on underside of each body. *Retailer's stamps:* "BALL. BLACK & CO." in roman letters, in an arched rectangular surround; "N.YORK" in roman letters, in a rectangle, both struck once on underside of each body. Incuse star struck under city name on (b); 1 incuse star on each side of city name on (d).

Description: circular wide-bellied forms with tall narrow necks and narrow bases (except the bowl, which is broad and flat bottomed). Cast applied rims, scalloped on outside, smooth on inside (except bowl); centerpunch on underside of each body, all pieces seamed except bowl, which is probably turned; 4 applied feet cast as vine loops with leaves and flowers. High-dome hinged lids divided on lower portions into lobes to match cast scalloped rims; asymmetrical finials cast in loop with a blossom above and leaves and flowers below. High-loop C-curve handles cast with woody texture, leaves, flowers, and vine loops. Extensive chased, repoussé, and engraved decoration covers bodies and lids with vines, leaves, flowers, and C-scroll cartouches; acanthus leaf borders on necks and lids done in punchwork. All lids have cast 3-segment hinges.

(a) Urn: double bellied with repoussé and punchwork acanthus leaves around lower body. Circular pedestal perforated with 8 holes for venting burner, spreads to lobed base with cast applied scalloped base ring. Base decorated with the same combination of chasing and punchwork leaves as lid; 2 high-loop C-curve handles. Cast spigot, standing straight out from lower body, is decorated with cast acanthus leaves; a cross in plan, the cylindrical arms (control for spigot) are attached to a bail handle cast as 2 S curves joined by a floral motif. Circular frame under base holds circular burner with removable lid and wick holder.

(b) Teapot: S-curve spout cast with woody texture, leaves, flowers, and vine loops; ivory insulators in handle; perforations in body at handle serve as strainer.

(c) Sugar bowl and lid: 2 handles.

(d) Creamer: short tubular spout cast in similar woody motifs.

(e) Waste bowl: flared and lobed upper body to match cast applied scalloped rim.

Spectrographic analysis:

	SILVER	COPPER	LEAD	GOLD
(a) Urn				
BODY	89.4	10.3	0.18	0.07
LID	91.3	8.5	0.11	0.06
FOOT	96.8	3.0	0.10	0.07
HANDLE	96.7	3.1	0.06	0.08
(b) Teapot				
BODY SIDE	88.0	11.8	0.21	0.05
LID	89.2	10.5	0.16	0.06
HANDLE	94.6	5.1	0.23	0.06
SPOUT	94.1	5.8	0.14	0.06
(c) Sugar bowl and lid				
BODY SIDE	92.4	7.5	0.11	0.08
LID	91.4	8.5	0.07	0.05
HANDLE	91.5	8.3	0.13	0.06
(d) Creamer				
BODY SIDE	85.0	14.9	0.14	0.03
LID	89.1	10.7	0.14	0.06
HANDLE	92.1	7.7	0.11	0.05
(e) Waste bowl				
BODY SIDE	90.1	9.7	0.15	0.07
FOOT	89.6	10.1	0.22	0.05

Provenance: James O'Hara Cazenove, Alexandria, Va.

Comments: Handsome full-blown rococo revival style.

72.306.1–.5 Bequest of James O'Hara Cazenove, 1972

❦ 175 a, b
TEA SERVICE, ca. 1855

(a) Hot water pot: H. 11 ¼" (28.6 cm), W. 11 ¾" (29.8 cm)
31 oz. 10 dwt. 7 gr. (977.9 g)
(b) Teapot: H. 10 ⅛" (25.7 cm), W. 12 ½" (31.8 cm)
34 oz. 9 dwt. 20 gr. (1070.3 g)

Stamps: "E&S" in roman letters, in a rectangle, struck once on underside of each body. *Retailer's stamps:* "BALL, BLACK & CO." in roman letters, in an arched rectangular surround; "N.YORK" in roman letters, in a rectangle, both struck once on underside of each body.

Engraved on side of each body: "AEY" in foliate script.

Description: both pieces are oval in plan with 11-lobe vertical sections around the lower body; raised upper body curved between die-rolled decorative bands; centerpunch on underside of each body. Oval lid, flat at edge, rises to high dome and is elaborately chased with leaves and grapes; hollow finial cast in shape of a heaped basket of leaves and grapes. Oval stepped base with applied decorative die-rolled bands around bottom and top. C-curve hollow handles made in 2 vertical halves; circular in section swelling toward crimped center; bulbous thumbpiece; single upper terminal and double lower terminals; 2 ivory insulators; 4 silver pins. S-curve spouts, made in vertical halves, banded in the middle and terminate in a beak. Die-rolled decorative band around bodies, ¹¹⁄₁₆" wide, consists of a meandering vine with leaves, grapes, and blossoms. Decorative bands with similar motifs around rims and bottoms, ⅜" wide, around top of base, ¼" wide. Hot water pot has large perforations in body for pouring. Teapot has small perforations in body to serve as strainer.

Spectrographic analysis:

	SILVER	COPPER	LEAD	GOLD
(a) Hot water pot				
BODY SIDE	82.1	17.7	0.19	0.07
LID	95.3	4.5	0.19	0.08
FOOT	96.1	3.6	0.28	0.06
HANDLE	84.3	15.4	0.20	0.07
(b) Teapot				
BODY SIDE	88.5	11.3	0.17	0.07
LID	95.9	3.9	0.15	0.10
FOOT	95.7	3.9	0.33	0.11
HANDLE	89.5	10.2	0.14	0.09

History: Initials may refer to the Yates family; see no. 170.

Provenance: Helen DeLancey Watkins, Schenectady, N.Y.

Comments: Decorative bands originally gilded.

68.132.1, .2 Museum purchase from estate of Helen DeLancey Watkins, 1968

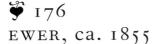 176
EWER, ca. 1855

H. 7⅜" (18.7 cm), W. 4⅜" (11.1 cm)
8 oz. 19 dwt. (277.7 g)

Stamps: "E•S" in roman letters, in a rectangle; "N.YORK" in roman letters, in a rectangle, both struck once on underside of body. *Retailer's stamps:* "B.B&Co." in roman letters, in a rectangle, struck once on underside of body. *Incuse stamps:* "42" and "95".

Engraved on side of body: "JSBT" in shaded script.

Description: circular bulbous main body with a plain molding and a beaded molding applied to upper edge; high concave neck with flared rim and extended pouring lip; plain molding on outside edge of rim. High, C-curve, vertically reeded handle with 2 acanthus leaves and 3 sprigs; cast in 2 vertical halves. Pedestal has a circular domed base with applied beading around top and base. Domed hinged lid of very thin metal with cast onion finial; 3-segment hinge. Repoussé decoration consists of long tapering trumpetlike flowers growing out of overlapping water leaves on lower half of body; water-leaf pattern is repeated around upper pedestal.

Spectrographic analysis:

	SILVER	COPPER	LEAD	GOLD
BODY SIDE	92.8	7.0	0.14	0.05
FOOT	95.8	4.1	0.09	0.06
HANDLE	95.5	4.3	0.12	0.05

Provenance: Marshall P. Blankarn, New York City.

78.151 Gift of Marshall P. Blankarn, 1978

Garret Eoff
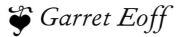

1779–1858

Eoff & Howell
Eoff & Connor
Eoff & Moore
New York, New York

The son of Garret and Sarah (Heyer) Eoff, the younger Garret Eoff served his apprenticeship with Abraham G. Forbes until 1798. He first appears in New York City directories in 1805–6 at 5 New Street; he is also listed for those years at 2 Wall Street with watchmaker Paul Howell. In 1834 he apparently took as partner one John Connor; they are both listed at 51 Morton Street. The following year his business associate was John C. Moore, a silversmith. Neither partnership lasted, and Eoff continued to be listed alone until at least 1846, when he would have been sixty-seven years old. He should not be confused with Edgar Eoff, who appears in the late 1840s and who formed a partnership with William Phyfe.

Garret Eoff made the communion silver for Trinity Church, New York City. The chalice, paten, flagon, and basin conform to traditional modes and look as if they had been made in the 1720s. His domestic silver made during the early decades of the nineteenth century is stylish, especially a teapot now in the Metropolitan Museum of Art. Its lobate body is supported by four curved legs resting on ball feet.

References: Ensko, *American Silversmiths III*, pp. 70, 267. Von Khrum, *Silversmiths*, pp. 44–45.

177 a–e
TEA SERVICE, ca. 1820

(a) Teapot: H. 10 ⁷⁄₁₆" (26.5 cm), w. 11 ³⁄₁₆" (28.4 cm)
30 oz. 13 dwt. 9 gr. (951.7 g)
(b) Tea caddy: H. 8 ¹⁵⁄₁₆" (22.7 cm), w. 6 ¹⁄₁₆" (15.4 cm)
18 oz. 19 dwt. 19 gr. (589.3 g)
(c) Sugar bowl and lid: H. 9 ¹⁄₁₆" (23.0 cm), w. 8 ⁵⁄₁₆" (21.1 cm)
15 oz. 14 dwt. 5 gr. (487.5 g) (cover: 203.5 g)
(d) Waste bowl: H. 5 ⁷⁄₁₆" (13.8 cm) w. 6 ¹³⁄₁₆" (17.3 cm)
16 oz. 19 dwt. 3 gr. (526.2 g)
(e) Creamer: H. 8" (20.3 cm), w. 6 ¹³⁄₁₆" (17.3 cm)
13 oz. 9 dwt. 13 gr. (418.2 g)

Stamps: "G.EOFF" in roman letters, in a rectangle, struck twice on underside of each body, except once on (d).

Engraved on side of each body: "ML" in foliate script.

Description: raised circular lower bodies, each with 12 vertical lobes and rounded bottoms; ¾" die-rolled decorative bands above; circular incurved pedestals and raised stepped feet; ½" die-rolled decorative bands around feet and lids consist of meandering vines with roselike blossoms, leaves, and buds on a stippled ground. The wider decorative bands are similar but more detailed and include thorns. Lids (where applicable) are flat with high-dome lobate centers with cast egg-shape finials partially enclosed by cast acanthus leaves.

(a) Teapot: raised convex upper body curves under circular rim; perforations in body at spout serve as strainer; centerpunch inside and out on lower body. Hinged lid has vent in center, a bezel, and a cast 5-segment hinge. S-curve spout, seamed off center, terminates in a beak. High-loop seamed hollow handle, rectangular in section, with a sprig, 2 wooden insulators, and 4 silver pins; lower portion of handle angles in before curving down to join body.

(b) Tea caddy: raised convex upper body curves under circular rim; centerpunch inside and out on lower body. Lid has a bezel, a cast 5-segment hinge, a catch released by push button, and no vent.

(c) Sugar bowl and lid: raised convex upper body curved under circular rim; centerpunch on inside and outside of lower body; 2 high-loop handles similar to those on (a) but without insulators. Friction-fit lid has a bezel but no vent outside (although there is a vent hole on the inside).

(d) Waste bowl: centerpunch on underside of body.

(e) Creamer: seamed incurved upper body, flared at rim; broad extended pouring lip, low on sides, higher at handle; centerpunch on underside of body. Applied ³⁄₁₆" die-rolled decorative band encircling rim has meandering vine-and-leaf pattern on a stippled ground.

Spectrographic analysis:

	SILVER	COPPER	LEAD	GOLD
(a) Teapot				
BODY SIDE	90.4	8.7	0.26	0.23
HANDLE	89.2	10.5	0.13	0.07
LID	91.6	8.0	0.15	0.11
BODY BAND	96.3	3.2	0.31	0.14
(b) Tea caddy				
BODY SIDE	90.0	9.4	0.30	0.11
LID	92.7	6.9	0.21	0.11
BODY BAND	95.8	3.9	0.15	0.11
(c) Sugar bowl and lid				
BODY SIDE	90.9	8.3	0.26	0.19
HANDLE	90.4	9.2	0.20	0.12
LID	91.8	7.6	0.22	0.15
BODY BAND	96.0	3.7	0.20	0.07
(d) Waste bowl				
BODY	86.9	12.2	0.28	0.17
BODY BAND	94.8	4.9	0.15	0.11
(e) Creamer				
BODY	89.6	9.8	0.26	0.12
HANDLE	91.5	8.0	0.16	0.15
BODY BAND	95.4	4.3	0.16	0.10

History: The initials "ML" refer to Mary (Riker) Leaycraft, who, in 1798, married Gamaliel Smith (1772–?), a New York merchant born in Suffield, Conn. Their daughter Eliza (1802–93) married Antoine Lentilhon (1796–1838). The service descended to the donor, who was a cousin of H. F. du Pont.

Provenance: Pauline Robinson, New York City.

References: Pauline Robinson, "New York One Hundred Years Ago" (typescript, Hagley Museum and Library, Wilmington, Del., 1923).

67.103.1–.5 Gift of Pauline Robinson, 1967

❦ 178 a, b
SERVING SPOON AND LADLE, ca. 1830

(a) Serving spoon: L. 12 ⅞" (32.7 cm)
5 oz. 11 dwt. 15 gr. (173.2 g)
(b) Ladle: L. 13 ¾" (34.9 cm)
8 oz. 9 dwt. 21 gr. (263.6 g)

Stamps: "G.EOFF" in roman letters, in a rectangle, struck once on the back of each handle, accompanied by 3 strikes: (1) a coarsely rendered head in profile in an oval; (2) a lion passant in a rectangle; and (3) a roman "S" in an oval.

Engraved on front of each handle: "AEL" in foliate script.

Description: pointed oval bowl on spoon; wide and deep oval bowl on ladle; swage-formed 14-lobe shell on back of each bowl; downturned fiddle-shape handles with shoulders and the following swage-formed design on the front of each: fiddle-shape cartouche with 9-lobe shell flanked by C scrolls on upper section; middle section flanked by stylized acanthus leaves; lower section has bold thread border that meets in lower center at 6-petal floret flanked by anthemia; plain backs.

Spectrographic analysis:

	SILVER	COPPER	LEAD	GOLD
(a) Spoon				
BOWL	86.7	12.8	0.35	0.10
HANDLE	88.3	11.0	0.38	0.14
(b) Ladle				
BOWL	85.4	14.0	0.46	0.12
HANDLE	87.5	11.8	0.43	0.12

History: The initials "AEL" refer to Antoine Lentilhon (1796–1838), who married Eliza Smith (1802–93) in 1824 in New York City. Lentilhon was a merchant from Lyons, Fr., and a business partner of Alphonse du Pasquier. The couple was married in Saint Peter's Roman Catholic Church in the morning, but in the evening the ceremony was performed again by the Smith family minister "who had done all the family christenings." In her old age Eliza was described as a "delightful raconteuse."

Provenance: Antoine and Eliza (Smith) Lentilhon, descending to Pauline Robinson, New York City.

Comments: The same initials appear on salt spoons no. 179 b, c.

References: Eugene Lentilhon, *The Lentilhons and Their Kinsmen of Forez, France, and the United States* (Paris, 1931). Pauline Robinson, "New York One Hundred Years Ago" (typescript, Hagley Museum and Library, Wilmington, Del., 1923).

67.209, .208 Gift of Pauline Robinson, 1967

179 a–c
FORK AND SPOONS,
ca. 1825

(a) Fork: L. 8 5/16" (21.1 cm)
3 oz. 6 dwt. 17 gr. (103.5 g)
(b) Salt spoon: L. 4 1/8" (10.5 cm)
10 dwt. 13 gr. (16.4 g)
(c) Salt spoon: L. 4 3/16" (10.6 cm)
10 dwt. 21 gr. (16.9 g)

Stamps: "G.EOFF" in roman letters, in a rectangle, struck once on back of each handle, accompanied by 3 strikes: (1) male head in profile in an oval; (2) lion passant in a rounded rectangle; and (3) roman "S" in an oval.

Engraved on front of fork: "MPL" in script.
Engraved on front of salt spoons: "AEL" in script.

Description: 4-tine fork with swage-formed 11-lobe shell on back. Gilded oval bowls on spoons; downturned fiddle-shape handles with the following swage-formed design on the front of each handle: fiddle-shape cartouche with 9-lobe shell flanked by C scrolls on upper section; middle section flanked by stylized acanthus leaves; lower section has bold thread border that meets in lower center at 6-petal floret flanked by anthemia; plain back.

Spectrographic analysis: Silver content ranges from 87.7 to 91.3 percent, with high mercury count on salt spoons because of gilding.

History: The salt spoons were owned by Antoine and Eliza (Smith) Lentilhon; see no. 178. The fork was owned by a member of the Lentilhon family.

Provenance: H. F. du Pont.

Comments: See no. 178.

70.1301.1, 70.1156.1, .2 Bequest of H. F. du Pont, 1969

180 a–c
SPOONS AND LADLE,
ca. 1825

(a) Spoon: L. 5 15/16" (15.1 cm)
13 dwt. 8 gr. (20.7 g)
(b) Mustard ladle: L. 4 7/8" (12.4 cm)
8 dwt. 15 gr. (13.4 g)
(c) Salt spoon: L. 3 13/16" (9.7 cm)
5 dwt. 22 gr. (9.2 g)

Stamps: "G.Eoff" in roman letters, in a conforming surround, struck once on the back of each handle; accompanied by 2 strikes: (1) spread-winged eagle in an oval; and (2) roman "C" in an oval.

Engraved on front of spoon: "HVV" in foliate script. *Engraved on front of salt spoon:* "MATB" in foliate script.

Description: (a) pointed oval bowl on spoon, with a swage-formed 12-lobe shell on back; downturned fiddle-shape handle with rounded shoulders and swage-formed 7-lobe shell, each lobe containing a stalk of wheat, center of shell has 3 stylized flowers; (b) plain circular bowl; downturned fiddle-shape handle with midrib and rounded shoulders; (c) plain oval bowl; downturned fiddle-shape handle with swage-formed 10-lobe shell.

Spectrographic analysis: Silver content ranges from 92.1 to 92.4 percent.

Provenance: Mr. and Mrs. Stanley B. Ineson, New York City; Mr. and Mrs. Alfred E. Bissell, Wilmington, Del.

Exhibitions: (c) Metropolitan Museum of Art, New York City, 1938–61.

References: Belden, *Marks of American Silversmiths*, p. 157.

62.240.229, .745, .750 Gift of Mr. and Mrs. Alfred E. Bissell, 1962–63

William Garret Forbes

1751–1840
New York, New York

There are a number of silversmiths by the name of Forbes, and silver historians have gone to some length to sort them out. William Garret Forbes, for example, was for some time mistakenly called William Graham Forbes. This dynasty of silversmiths began with the arrival of William Forbes from Scotland around 1712. His son Gilbert was the father of William Garret and Abraham Gerritse Forbes, both silversmiths. William married Catherine Van Gelder in 1771 and became a freeman in 1773. He was a member of the Gold and Silversmiths Society, headed by Myer Myers. New York City directories place him at 88 Broadway, 1786–93; 118 Broadway, 1794–95; 90 Broadway, 1796–1802; 99 Broadway, 1804; and 90 Broadway, 1805–9.

Forbes made quantities of silver in the new styles appearing around 1800, much of it very light in weight. It is doubtful that he continued as a working silversmith past 1810. His three silversmithing sons used the 90 Broadway address at various times before and after 1810: Colin Van Gelder Forbes (1776–1859); John Wolfe Forbes (1781–1864), whose work survives in quantity; and Garret Forbes (1785–1851). Colin's son William (b. 1799) also became a silversmith.

References: Rachel B. Crawford, "The Forbes Family of Silversmiths," *Antiques* 107, no. 4 (April 1975): 730–35. "Collectors' Notes," *Antiques* 103, no. 3 (March 1973): 561–62. Von Khrum, *Silversmiths*, pp. 48, 49.

♣ 181
TEA CADDY, ca. 1810

H. 5 ⅞" (14.9 cm), w. 6 ⅝" (16.8 cm), D. 4 ¹¹⁄₁₆" (11.9 cm), L. of key 1 ¹³⁄₁₆" (4.6 cm)
13 oz. 4 dwt. 23 gr. (412.1 g)

Stamps: "W. G. FORBES" in roman letters, in a rectangle, struck 3 times on underside of body.

Engraved on front of body: "CSH" in script, in a square frame with canted corners suspended from a swag of acorns and leaves; same frame and swag without initials on back of body. Engraved convex band circling upper body has acorns, leaves, and crossed ribbons against striated ground.

Description: seamed body rectangular in plan, convex sides, flat inset bottom, rolled rim. Lock attached to inside front by 3 rivets; keyhole between the 2 upper rivets. Raised 4-panel lid rises to flattened dome with cast urn finial; finial secured by a large rivet; applied wire bezel; 5-segment hinge connects lid to body on long side in back. Accompanied by silver key with elaborately pierced handle with central heart motif.

Spectrographic analysis:

	SILVER	COPPER	LEAD	GOLD
BODY SIDE	90.5	9.1	0.19	0.11
UNDERSIDE	94.5	5.3	0.14	0.08
LID	93.6	6.2	0.13	0.07
BAND	90.3	9.3	0.18	0.08
KEY	94.8	5.3	0.00	0.00

Provenance: Richard Gould Antiques, Santa Monica, Calif.

Comments: One of 3 known American locking tea caddies in silver. Analysis shows key to be a modern replacement.

References: Fennimore, *Silver and Pewter*, no. 89. Gregor Norman-Wilcox, "Some Unpublished American Silver," *Antiques* 31, no. 3 (March 1937): 126–28, fig. 13.

67.231 Museum purchase from Richard Gould Antiques, 1967

❦ 182
ETUI, ca. 1785

H. 4 ½" (11.4 cm), w. 2 ⅝" (6.7 cm), D. 1"
(2.5 cm)
5 oz. 15 dwt. 5 gr. (179.2 g)

Stamps: None. Attribution based on identical case, bearing Forbes's stamp, at Yale University Art Gallery, given by Elizabeth Delancey to Oliver Delancey, John Delancey's brother.

Engraved on front of body: "This/ MEMORI-AL/ was bequeathed/ by the best of/ MOTH-ERS/ to her Son/ John/ De Lancey." in roman letters. Inscription encircled by laurel branches crossed at the bottom and tied with a ribbon; overhead a crown with 5 points, each tipped with a star. *Engraved on back of body:* "Eliz[h]./ De Lancey/ ob[t], 23 Sept[r]/ 1784/ æt 64" in script, in a circle on a swag-draped urn. *Engraved on underside of body:* "When you Receive this Token,/ The Parent who gives it,/ Will be no Longer here on Earth./ Let us live so as to hope to meet/ in Heaven" in roman letters.

Description: tall rectangular body, tapered slightly from top to bottom, elongated oval in plan, with a high-dome hinged lid and flat bottom; body seamed. Lid attached to body at narrow end with a brass pin. Applied decorative bands around base, top, rim, and lower edge of lid have wheelwork guilloche, punched dots, and engraved *x*'s. Interior of body divided into 9 compartments by a wood matrix capped with a silver plate.

Five instruments remain: (1) steel scissors with oval silver grips; (2) silver, steel, and brass tweezers that look like dividers; (3) steel lancet blade, stamped "EVAN[?]" with a crown above, between tortoiseshell leaves; (4) steel corkscrew with eye and no handle; and (5) ivory memo leaves, joined at crest by a steel pin and cupro-silver washers, with pencil inscription: "John De Lancey/ N. Y." and "Miss A. A. Yates/ Schenectady/ N. Y."

Spectrographic analysis:

	SILVER	COPPER	LEAD	GOLD
BODY	88.6	10.0	0.55	0.20
LID	88.1	10.6	0.57	0.18
BASE BAND	87.7	10.7	0.58	0.21
BODY BAND	87.7	10.8	0.54	0.20
HANDLE	94.4	4.9	0.20	0.12

History: Elizabeth Colden (1720–84) married Peter De Lancey (1705–70) in January 1737/38. Her father was Cadwallader Colden (1688–1776), the Loyalist lieutenant governor of New York and amateur scientist and author. Peter was the son of Stephen De Lancey, founder of the De Lancey family in America. When Elizabeth drew up her will in 1782, she made the following bequest: "To my son Stephen, and each of my sons, John, James, Oliver and Warren, a silver pocket case of instruments to be made in the neatest manner, value 6 guineas, with the following engraving on them: 'When you receive this token, the parent who gives it will be no longer here on Earth. Let us live so as to hope to meet in heaven.'"

John De Lancey (1741–1820) succeeded his father in the New York Assembly, representing Westchester County from 1768 to 1775 and from 1793 to 1795. During the Revolution he served as high sheriff and captain of the 17th Dragoons, a Loyalist unit.

At least 3 of the 5 etuis survive. Oliver's is in the Garvan collection at Yale University Art Gallery, and James's was in Nova Scotia in a private collection as of 1931. Although all the De Lanceys inclined toward Loyalist views, James led a troop of horsemen known as the "Cowboys," who terrorized the supporters of the American cause in Westchester County from 1777 until 1781. James Fenimore Cooper based his novel *The Spy* on this partisan warfare. As a result of this disruptive activity, De Lancey was forced to leave New York in 1782. Like many other Loyalists, he went to Nova Scotia, where he settled on a farm in Annapolis.

Provenance: John De Lancey, New York City; descended to Helen De Lancey Watkins, Schenectady, N.Y.

References: Buhler and Hood, *American Silver*, no. 703. *DAB*, s.v. "Colden, Cadwallader," "De Lancey, James." Fennimore, *Silver and Pewter*, no. 202. D. A. Story, *The De Lanceys: A Romance of a Great Family* (London: Thos. Nelson and Sons, 1931), pp. 50–51.

68.136 Museum purchase from the estate of Helen De Lancey Watkins, 1968

❦ 183
SUGAR BOWL AND LID, ca. 1800

H. (with lid) 10 ¼" (26.0 cm), DIAM. rim 4 ¼" (10.8 cm), L. (one side of square base) 3 ³⁄₁₆" (8.1 cm)
11 oz. 18 dwt. 13 gr. (371.0 g)

Stamps: "W G Forbes" in script, in a conforming surround, struck once on side of base.

Engraved on side of body: "PML" in foliate script.

Description: raised circular urn-shape body mounted on a pedestal, flaring to a circular plinth that, in turn, becomes a square base. Beading around rim, top of pedestal, and plinth. Raised circular lid, flat at edge, curves up to narrow neck that flares to knop and domed top with cast urn finial. Beading around knop and finial. Bezel.

Spectrographic analysis:

	SILVER	COPPER	LEAD	GOLD
BODY SIDE	90.7	8.8	0.19	0.11
LID	94.6	4.3	0.51	0.18
FOOT	90.4	8.4	0.25	0.27

Provenance: Marshall P. Blankarn, New York City.

77.76 Gift of Marshall P. Blankarn, 1977

❧ 184
SUGAR BOWL AND LID, ca. 1810

H. (with lid) 6 11/16" (17.0 cm), w. 6 11/16"
(17.0 cm)
13 oz. 7 dwt. 7 gr. (415.7 g)

Stamps: "W.G Forbes" in slanted roman letters
and script, in a rectangle, struck once on underside of body.

Engraved on side of body: "HAR" in foliate
script, within a shield with a border of darts;
shield suspended from bowknot and flanked
by crossed leafy branches. *Engraved on opposite
side:* same shield without initials.

Description: seamed body, oval in plan, convex
sides, die-rolled decorative band inset between
main body and concave upper body with plain
rim reinforced by an applied strip inside. Applied oval base ring. Each handle a cast scroll
with a pendant hinged ring. Raised lid, oval
in plan, flat at rim, rising in center to applied
domed platform surmounted by a cast urn
finial. Bright-cut dart and wheel-turned border
on flat of lid. Bezel.

Spectrographic analysis:

	SILVER	COPPER	LEAD	GOLD
BODY SIDE	90.4	8.7	0.47	0.19
BASE	94.6	4.6	0.41	0.19
LID	91.1	8.1	0.45	0.18

Provenance: Marshall P. Blankarn, New York
City.

Comments: See no. 185 with same engraved
initials.

77.224 Gift of Marshall P. Blankarn, 1977

❧ 185
CREAMER, ca. 1810

H. 5 3/16" (13.2 cm), w. 4 11/16" (11.9 cm)
4 oz. 13 dwt. 12 gr. (145.4 g)

Stamps: "W G Forbes" (possibly a period after
"W") in slanted roman letters, in a rectangle,
struck once on underside.

Engraved on side of body: "HAR" in foliate
script, with same engraved shield as no. 184;
bright-cut border on upper body.

Description: seamed body, oval in plan, convex
sides, die-rolled decorative band inset between
main body and upper body, which rises to a
plain rim with extended pouring lip; flat bottom. Applied oval base ring. High-loop strap
handle, partially reeded on outside, tapers at
lower end.

Spectrographic analysis:

	SILVER	COPPER	LEAD	GOLD
BODY SIDE	91.3	8.2	0.23	0.10
BOTTOM	96.9	2.4	0.15	0.14
HANDLE	90.4	3.9	0.42	0.14

Provenance: Marshall P. Blankarn, New York
City.

Comments: Underside appears to be a separate
piece. Poorly made. See no. 184 with same
engraved initials.

77.75 Gift of Marshall P. Blankarn, 1977

❦ 186
CREAMER, ca. 1810

H. 4 13/16" (12.2 cm), w. 6 3/4" (17.1 cm)
6 oz. 10 dwt. 18 gr. (203.3 g)

Stamps: "W.G.FORBES" in roman letters, in a rectangle, struck once on underside.

Engraved on side of body: "[?]G" in script.
Engraved on underside of body: "AD" in shaded roman letters.

Description: seamed body, oval in plan, with 3 horizontal ridges on upper body curved to conform to profile of rim; concave neck with gently flared rim rising to point at handle and extended pouring lip in front; applied plain molding on outside of rim. Oval reeded base is integral with body except for underside, which is a separate piece. Curved strap handle, reeded on outside, is angular in upper section.

Spectrographic analysis:

	SILVER	COPPER	LEAD	GOLD
BODY SIDE	90.0	9.2	0.28	0.10
BASE	95.4	4.0	0.21	0.14
HANDLE	90.4	8.6	0.35	0.14

Provenance: Marshall P. Blankarn, New York City.

Comments: Poor design and execution. Hammer marks inside body.

77.74 Gift of Marshall P. Blankarn, 1977

❦ 187
LADLE, ca. 1800

L. 14 9/16" (37.0 cm)
6 oz. 14 dwt. 1 gr. (208.0 g)

Stamps: "W G Forbes" in italics, in a rectangle; an eagle's head, in an oval; a sheaf of wheat, in a rectangle, all struck once on back of handle.

Engraved on front of handle: "RIG" in foliate script.

Description: oval bowl with swage-formed rounded drop on back; pointed downturned handle with short midrib.

Spectrographic analysis:

SILVER	COPPER	LEAD	GOLD
93.2	6.5	0.19	0.12

Provenance: Mr. and Mrs. Stanley B. Ineson, New York City; Mr. and Mrs. Alfred E. Bissell, Wilmington, Del.

Comments: Device stamps, like the eagle and the sheaf of wheat, have traditionally been called pseudohallmarks. Christine Wallace Laidlaw's study of Teunis D. DuBois has shown that these stamps can sometimes indicate a maker other than the one whose name stamp appears on the object.

References: Belden, *Marks of American Silversmiths*, p. 173 c or d. See also Christine Wallace Laidlaw, "Silver by the Dozen: The Wholesale Business of Teunis D. DuBois," *Winterthur Portfolio* 23, no. 1 (Spring 1988): 25–50.

62.240.1614 Gift of Mr. and Mrs. Alfred E. Bissell, 1965

❦ 188
SPOON, ca. 1785

L. 5 ¼" (13.3 cm), 7 dwt. 22 gr. (12.3 g)

Stamps: "W•F" in roman letters, in a rectangle, struck once on back of handle.

Engraved on front of handle: "CK" in foliate script, in a bright-cut medallion with pendant drop.

Description: elongated oval bowl with swage-formed rounded drop; pointed downturned handle.

Spectrographic analysis: Silver content is 89.5 percent.

Provenance: The Silver Shelf, Ardmore, Pa.

References: Belden, *Marks of American Silversmiths*, p. 173 a.

73.190 Museum purchase from the Silver Shelf, 1973, with funds from the Ineson-Bissell Fund

❦ 189 a, b
SPOONS, ca. 1790

(a) L. 8 ⁵⁄₁₆" (21.1 cm), 1 oz. 14 dwt. 14 gr. (53.7 g)
(b) L. 5 ⁷⁄₁₆" (13.8 cm), 9 dwt. 1 gr. (14.0 g)

Stamps: "W•FORBES" in roman letters, in a rectangle, struck once on back of each handle.

Engraved on front of handle: (a) "B/ GS" in crude roman letters, in crude bright-cut medallion with pendant drop and featheredge border; (b) "IH" in foliate script, in a bright-cut medallion with pendant drop and featheredge border.

Description: oval bowls with swage-formed rounded drops on back; rounded downturned handles with faint midribs.

Spectrographic analysis: Silver content ranges from 88.1 to 90.8 percent.

Provenance: Mr. and Mrs. Stanley B. Ineson, New York City; Mr. and Mrs. Alfred E. Bissell, Wilmington, Del.

References: Belden, *Marks of American Silversmiths*, p. 173 b.

62.240.1114, .253 Gift of Mr. and Mrs. Alfred E. Bissell, 1962–63

❦ 190 a–e
SPOONS, ca. 1790

(a) L. 5 ¾" (14.6 cm), 8 dwt. 16 gr. (13.5 g)
(b) L. 5 ⁹⁄₁₆" (14.1 cm), 6 dwt. 13 gr. (10.2 g)
(c) L. 5 ⁵⁄₁₆" (13.5 cm), 6 dwt. 10 gr. (10.0 g)
(d) L. 8 ¾" (22.2 cm), 1 oz. 11 dwt. 10 gr. (48.8 g)
(e) L. 9 ¹⁄₁₆" (23.0 cm), 1 oz. 16 dwt. 14 gr. (56.8 g)

Stamps: "W.G.Forbes." in italics, in a rectangle, struck once on back of each handle; (c–e) accompanied by an eagle's head in an oval and a sheaf of wheat in a rectangle.

Engraved on front of handle: (a) "DB" in foliate script; (b) "MI" in foliate script, in a bright-cut medallion with pendant drop; (c) "RM" in shaded roman letters, in a bright-cut medallion with pendant drop; (d) "ICM" in shaded roman letters, in a bright-cut medallion with a pendant drop; and (e) "IAS" in foliate script.

Description: (a–c, e) pointed oval bowl with swage-formed pointed drop; (d) elongated oval bowl with swage-formed drop; (a, b) downturned coffin-end handle; (c–e) pointed downturned handle with short midrib.

Spectrographic analysis: Silver content ranges from 89.1 to 91.3 percent.

Provenance: Mr. and Mrs. Stanley B. Ineson, New York City; Mr. and Mrs. Alfred E. Bissell, Wilmington, Del.

Exhibitions: (a) "Silver by New York Makers," Museum of the City of New York, 1937–38.

Comments: See *Comments* no. 187.

References: Belden, *Marks of American Silversmiths*, p. 173 c. Miller, *Silver by New York Makers*, no. 107 a only.

62.240.239, .252, .251, .1112, .1113 Gift of Mr. and Mrs. Alfred E. Bissell, 1962–63

❦ 191 a–c
SPOONS, ca. 1800

(a) L. 5 ½" (14.0 cm), 9 dwt. 20 gr. (15.3 g)
(b) L. 5 ¼" (13.3 cm), 7 dwt. 14 gr. (11.8 g)
(c) L. 8 ¹⁵⁄₁₆" (22.7 cm), 1 oz. 17 dwt. 9 gr. (58.0 g)

Stamps: "W G Forbes" in script, in a conforming surround, struck once on back of each handle; accompanying (c): "N•YORK" in roman letters, in a rectangle with serrated edge.

Engraved on front of handle: (a) "IHMB" in shaded roman letters, in a bright-cut medallion with pendant; (b) "AM" in foliate script, in a bright-cut medallion with pendant drop; (c) "HVW" in foliate script, in a bright-cut medallion with pendant.

Description: oval bowls with single drops on back; (a) and (c) have rounded downturned handles with midrib; (b) has pointed downturned handle.

Spectrographic analysis: Silver content ranges from 90.4 to 92.1 percent.

Provenance: (a, b) Mr. and Mrs. Stanley B. Ineson, New York City; Mr. and Mrs. Alfred E. Bissell, Wilmington, Del.; (c) Philip Curtis, Newark, N.J.

References: Belden, *Marks of American Silversmiths*, p. 173 e.

(a, b) 62.240.249, .250 Gift of Mr. and Mrs. Alfred E. Bissell, 1962–63; (c) 77.186 Museum purchase from Philip Curtis, 1977

❦ 192 a–c
SPOONS, ca. 1800

(a) L. 9 ¹⁄₁₆" (23.0 cm), 1 oz. 18 dwt. 20 gr. (60.3 g)
(b) L. 9 ⁵⁄₁₆" (23.7 cm), 2 oz. 5 dwt. 21 gr. (71.2 g)
(c) L. 7 ⅛" (18.1 cm), 18 dwt. 8 gr. (28.5 g)

Stamps: "W.G.FORBES" in roman letters, in a conforming surround, struck once on back of each handle.

Engraved on front of handle: (a) "NAP" in crude shaded roman letters; (b) "CRM" in foliate script; (c) "EA" in foliate script.

Description: pointed oval bowls with a double drop on (a) and single drops on (b) and (c); downturned fiddle-shape handles on (a) and (b); coffin-end handle on (a); downturned coffin-end handle with midrib on (c).

Spectrographic analysis: Silver content ranges from 90.9 to 92.2 percent.

Provenance: Mr. and Mrs. Stanley B. Ineson, New York City; Mr. and Mrs. Alfred E. Bissell, Wilmington, Del.

References: Belden, *Marks of American Silversmiths*, p. 173 g.

62.240.1115, .1116, .1117 Gift of Mr. and Mrs. Alfred E. Bissell, 1962–63

❦ Daniel Christian Fueter

1720–85
New York, New York, w. 1754–65
Southbury, Connecticut, w. 1765–68
New York, New York, w. 1768–69

Daniel Christian Fueter was born in Bern, Switzerland, in 1720. The Fueter family had been in Bern at least since the sixteenth century and was well established in business and professions. Presumably apprenticed to a local silversmith, Fueter interrupted his career to join the military in 1740. In 1745 he married Caterina Elizabeth Meyer, and their first child, Ludwig Anton (known to us as Lewis), was born in 1746. Other children followed in 1747, 1748, and 1749. Daniel and other members of his family became involved in a conspiracy to overthrow the Bernese government. The plot was discovered and revenge exacted on the conspirators. To save his life, Fueter, along with his immediate family, left Bern and went into exile. By 1752 they were in London, where son Christian was born. Late in 1753 Daniel registered his stamp ("DCF" in roman letters, in an oval) with the Goldsmiths' Company. It was probably during his London sojourn that he joined the Moravian Church. In the spring of 1754, Daniel and his family sailed for New York aboard the Moravian ship *Irene*, which also carried several Moravian luminaries as well as painter J. Valentine Haidt.

By May 27, 1754, Fueter advertised in the *New-York Gazette* that he "makes all sorts of Gold and Silver work, after the newest and neatest Fashion; he also gilds Silver and Metal, and refines Gold and Silver after the best manner; and makes Essays on all sorts of Metal and Oar." Henceforth, until his departure for Europe fifteen years later, his movements are followed in the diaries of the New York Moravian congregation. As a result, no colonial craftsman's personal life is so well documented. The diaries provide little information about his professional life. He became a freeman in 1759.

In March 1763 Fueter advertised again in the *New-York Gazette*, this time to announce that he carried "a Beautiful Assortment of Jewellry, which for Elegance and Taste is greatly superior to any Thing hitherto brought to this Place . . . all extremely Cheap." The Moravian diaries chronicle but do not explain his move in December 1765 to Southbury, Connecticut. He remained there, or somewhere in Connecticut, for three years before returning to New York City. An advertisement in the January 1769 *New-York Gazette* announced the partnership of Daniel and his son Lewis as well as their return to the city. Later the same year (July 31), Daniel advertised the addition to his shop of one John Anthony Beau, a chaser from Geneva. John Kingston is Fueter's only known apprentice, other than his sons.

Daniel Fueter's American career ended suddenly with his family's departure for Europe on October 18, 1769. Only sons Lewis (Ludwig) and Daniel, Jr., remained. Apparently having patched things up with the authorities, Fueter eventually returned to Bern, where he lived out his days, dying December 31, 1785, at age sixty-five. Son Christian was educated as an artist and engraver; he studied under J. B. Greuze and J. M. Morikofer and was later appointed master of the mint in Bern.

Daniel Christian Fueter produced stylish, well-made silver. Although trained in Continental traditions, he adapted to Anglo-American tastes in all instances but one—candlesticks (no. 195), which are clearly based on Swiss prototypes. None of his English silver is known to have survived. A few pieces of silver made in Bern prior to his exile are known, among them two small covered bowls, a creamer, a sugar caster, and a soup ladle. Most bear the "DCF" stamp in an oval.

Outstanding examples of Fueter's work in other American collections include a magnificent bread basket at the Museum of Fine Arts, Boston; a large salver engraved with the Provost family coat of arms at the Metropolitan Museum of Art; a heavily chased gold whistle-coral-bells in the Garvan collection at Yale University Art Gallery; and an elegant rococo cruet stand engraved with the Van Voorhis crest at Historic Deerfield. He also cast medals in silver: the Montreal medal of 1761 and an Indian peace medal with the bust of George III in 1764.

References: Gottesman, *Arts and Crafts, 1726–76*, pp. 41–43. Arthur G. Grimwade, *London Goldsmiths, 1697–1837* (London: Faber and Faber, 1976), pp. 44, 516. "The Diary of the [Moravian] Congregation in New York," and related church documents, Moravian Archives, Bethlehem, Pa. Johan Rudolph Gruner, "Genealogia," 1752, manuscript genealogy of the Fueter family, Burgerbiliothek, Bern. Marie Roosen Runge, *Die Goldschmiede Der Stadt Bern* (Bern, 1951), p. 15. *NYHS Collections*: vol. 18 (1885) *Burghers and Freemen*, p. 194. Ulrich Thieme and Felix Becker, *Allgemeines Lexicon der Bildenden Künstler von der Antike bis zur Gegenwart*, 37 vols. (Leipzig: W. Engelmann, 1907–50), s.v. "Fueter, Christian." I am indebted to Martin Kiener of Kirchlindach, Switzerland, for bringing to my attention Swiss silver made by Fueter.

❦ 193
TEAPOT, 1754–69

H. 7 ¹¹⁄₁₆" (19.5 cm), w. 9 ¼" (23.5 cm)
23 oz. 9 dwt. 12 gr. (730.2 g)

Stamps: "DCF" in roman letters, in an oval;
"N:/ YORK" in slanted roman letters, in a
conforming surround. Both struck once on
underside of body.

*Engraved on underside of lower handle socket
terminal:* "AY" in crude stylized roman letters.

Engraved on side of body: "SBL" in foliate
script. *Scratched on underside of body:* "[1] 22 9".

Description: raised circular body with bulbous
lower half rising to a separately made, narrow,
concave neck with a slightly flared rim enclosed
in a 4-step molding; centerpunch on underside
of body. Perforations in body at spout serve as
strainer. Cast stepped footring. Cast S-curve
paneled spout terminates in a bird's head. Raised
circular high-dome stepped lid with vent; cast
pineapple-in-a-cup finial attached through top
of lid by a rivet; 8-point star escutcheon held in
place by finial; 5-segment cast hinge with brass
pin. C-curve hardwood handle has 1 scroll and
1 sprig; upper handle socket has thumbpiece;
lower socket includes a C-curve section terminating in a sprig and a scroll; both sockets cast
in vertical halves; both are secured to handle
by silver pins.

Spectrographic analysis:

	SILVER	COPPER	LEAD	GOLD
BODY	90.1	9.6	0.16	0.03
LID	90.1	9.6	0.13	0.08
SPOUT	95.1	4.5	0.12	0.22
FOOTRING	92.3	7.3	0.18	0.10
LOWER HANDLE				
SOCKET	96.4	3.3	0.12	0.22

History: History of ownership in the Lansing family of Albany. Probably originally owned by the Yates family and descended in the Lansing family. The engraved initials "AY" may refer to Abraham Yates, whose daughter Susannah married Abraham G. Lansing in 1779. The initials "SBL" may refer to their daughter Susan (or Sarah) B. Lansing.

Provenance: Robert Ensko, Inc., New York City, sold to H. F. du Pont, May 1940.

Exhibitions: "Tea: A Revolutionary Tradition," Fraunces Tavern Museum, New York City, 1980–81.

Comments: A similar teapot by Fueter, engraved with the name Teunis Tiebout, was in the Sotheby Parke-Bernet sale of November 19–22, 1980. Teapots of this form, commonly called Queen Anne, were made by several silversmiths, including Peter Van Dyck, Henricus Boelen, and Thauvet Besley of New York City and Jacob Jacobse Lansing of Albany. Some early attempts to create this form were not wholly successful, as the Boston-made example by John Allen of Boston (no. 2) proves. The Fueter example has superb balance and rhythm. The incurved neck serves as a perfect foil to the boldly projecting lower body. The teapot has all the solidity of a New York Chippendale armchair.

References: Fales, *American Silver*, no. 107. Kauffman, *Colonial Silversmith*, p. 125. Talcott, *Genealogical Notes*, pp. 124–25, 136.

59.2299 Gift of H. F. du Pont, 1965

❦ 194
CUP, 1754–55

H. 3 ³⁄₁₆" (8.1 cm), DIAM. rim 3 ⅛" (7.9 cm), DIAM. base 2" (5.1 cm)
2 oz. 13 dwt. 16 gr. (83.3 g)

Stamps: "DCF" in roman letters, in an oval; "N:/ YORK" in slanted roman letters, in a conforming surround. Both struck on underside of body.

Engraved around entire body: (1) head of beast with jaws agape, flame emerging from mouth, smoke from eyes and nostrils; amid flames: "Hell" in roman letters; (2) full-length male figure with hairy body, cloven feet, horns, and snakes for hair, a serpent entwined around his body; his left hand holds a flail with 3 snakes emerging from the end; the flail is directed toward the fires of hell; chain leads from this figure back through a gate of 2 fluted columns and an arch with a death's head and inscription: "DEATH" in roman letters; (3) the chain from the gate is attached to the nose of a standing male figure, wearing a miter and ecclesiastical garments, who carries a cross in his right hand and a rope in his left; (4) the rope runs from the mitered figure through a gallows to the neck of a standing male figure attired in tam-o'-shanter, plaid shawl, knee breeches, shoes, and a sword. All figures stand on rolling terrain.

Engraved around body below rim: 3 couplets in roman letters: (1) "I WISH THEY WERE ALL HANG'D IN A ROPE/ THE PRETENDER DEVIL AND THE POPE."; (2) "THREE MORTAL ENEMIES REMEMBER./ THE DEVIL POPE AND THE PRETENDER."; (3) "MOST WICKED DAMNABLE AND EVIL./ THE POPE PRETEND[E]R AND THE DEVIL." Each couplet is separated by vertical reeding.

Engraved on underside of body: "D/ IM" in shaded roman letters, with triangular dots. *Engraved around outside of lower body:* "This gift is to my Son Ro[?] Samuel by his father Saml. Samuel N. York 14 March/ 1778" in script. The son's first name appears to have been altered.

Description: raised circular body in shape of an inverted bell; molded rim; centerpunch on underside of body; cast circular stepped foot.

Spectrographic analysis:

	SILVER	COPPER	GOLD	LEAD
BODY	93.6	6.1	0.17	0.14
FOOT	95.8	4.0	0.11	0.10

History: No history of "D/ IM" in the Samuel family; a Levy Samuel, merchant, was admitted as a freeman in 1743, and in 1778 there was a business partnership of "Mssrs Samuel and Levy" at 856 Hanover Square.

Provenance: Sold in an estate sale at the auction house of William Morley, Philadelphia, to jeweler Harry Burke, Philadelphia; sold by Burke to Ginsburg & Levy, New York City; sold to Richard A. Loeb, New Brunswick, N.J.; reacquired by Ginsburg & Levy and sold to H. F. du Pont, December 1949.

Exhibitions: Winter Antiques Show, New York City, 1982. "Marks of Achievement: Four Centuries of American Presentation Silver," Museum of Fine Arts, Houston, 1987.

Comments: This form commonly occurs in French silver, where it is called a *gobelet*. It is intriguing that the Museum of the City of New York owns a similar cup with the same engraved imagery. That cup was made by Hugues Lossieux, St. Malo, Fr., 1707–8. It bears an engraved inscription on the underside reading "Ioseph Leddel sculpt. 1750." and what appears to be a conjoined "BL." The engraved scenes on both cups appear to be by the same hand. Joseph Leddel, Jr., pewterer and engraver, who probably engraved both cups, died May 10, 1754. Since Fueter arrived in New York on April 15, 1754, the Winterthur cup must have been made between these 2 dates. The French cup, dating much earlier but not engraved until 1750, must have been the source for both the form and imagery of the Winterthur cup.

Two other heavily engraved pieces of hollowware are signed by Joseph Leddel, and both are dated 1750. One, a tankard by William Vilant, owned by Historic Deerfield, bears scenes from Ovid and portrait heads of English nobility. The other, a cann by Bartholomew Le Roux II, from a Christie's sale, October 1990, has 6 engraved scenes from the Old Testament story of Joseph. It is assumed that both were engraved by Joseph Leddel, Jr., rather than by his father, who followed the same craft. The father's will was proved January 12, 1754, thus ruling Leddel, Sr., out as the engraver of the Fueter cup.

Pope's Day, or Guy Fawkes Day as it is known in England, was celebrated with gusto in British North America during the seventeenth and eighteenth centuries. Effigies of the pope and the devil were commonly carried in processions and usually burned. One account, written during the late 1760s, described a mob that "carried twenty Devils, Popes, & Pretenders thro the Streets" of Boston. The claim of the Catholic Stuarts to the English throne caused the pretender to be treated as an evil on a par with the pope and the devil. In 1750 and 1754, when both cups were engraved, no doubt the events of 1745 were fresh in the minds of Protestants throughout the Anglo-American world. Charles Edward Stuart ("Bonnie Prince Charlie") had led a Scottish army in an attempt to unseat George II. He was defeated at Culloden, but the threat remained in the minds of many Protestants, as did the hope among Jacobites that someday they might succeed.

This is the backdrop against which the highly charged message on the Fueter cup must be viewed. New York was strongly Protestant with its mix of French Huguenots, Dutch Calvinists, and various English Protestant denominations. There was no Catholic church in the city until after the Revolution. The complex devil-pope-pretender imagery surely had a print source, but it has yet to be discovered. There was a strong community of French Protestants in New York City, and 1 of its members must have brought over the older cup early in the eighteenth century.

References: Clayton, *Collector's Dictionary*, fig. 30. Davidson, *Colonial Antiques*, p. 253. Fales, *American Silver*, no. 101. Fennimore, *Silver and Pewter*, no. 171. Warren, Howe, and Brown, *Marks of Achievement*, p. 117. For references to Samuel, see *NYHS Collections*: vol. 18 (1885) *Burghers and Freemen*, p. 148; vol. 84 (1973) *Rivington's New York Newspaper: Excerpts from a Loyalist Press, 1773–1783*, p. 148. *Letters of a Loyalist Lady* (Cambridge: Harvard University Press, 1927), p. 8, for comment on Pope's Day in Boston. For Ledell, see Ledlie Irwin Laughlin, *Pewter in America*, 2 vols. (rev. ed., Barre, Mass.: Barre Publishers, 1969), 2:4.

56.521 Gift of H. F. du Pont, 1965

❦ 195 a, b
CANDLESTICKS,
ca. 1769

(a) H. 8 ⅜" (21.3 cm), DIAM. base 6 ¼" (16.0 cm)
14 oz. 2 dwt. 13 gr. (438.4 g)
(b) H. 8 ⅜" (21.3 cm), DIAM. base 6 ¼" (16.0 cm)
14 oz. 7 dwt. 23 gr. (446.8 g)

Stamps: "DCF" in roman letters, in an oval;
"N:/ YORK" in slanted roman letters, in a
conforming surround, struck once on socket
of each stick.

Engraved on upper portion of lower body: armorial device consisting of a boar's head; "SEC" in
script.

Description: lower body consists of a dished circular base, with cyma-curve molded rim, rising
in center to form a circular hollow tapering
shaft; remainder of stick constructed of built-
up sections connected by circular rivets; deep
cast socket with removable bobeche forms upper
body; central section has a knop in the middle
and applied gadrooning above and below.

Spectrographic analysis:

(a)	SILVER	COPPER	GOLD	LEAD
BASE	94.5	5.3	0.16	0.03
LOWER SHAFT	93.1	6.7	0.14	0.04
UPPER SHAFT	91.9	8.0	0.10	0.03
BOBECHE	92.5	7.3	0.13	0.05

(b)	SILVER	COPPER	GOLD	LEAD
BASE	94.2	5.7	0.13	0.03
LOWER SHAFT	94.4	5.5	0.13	0.05
UPPER SHAFT	90.7	9.1	0.20	0.05
BOBECHE	92.5	7.4	0.07	0.04

History: According to the last private owner,
the original owner of the candlesticks was
Samuel Campbell (1736–1813), a bookbinder
and bookseller from Edinburgh who moved to
New York City, where he carried on the same
trade. Campbell married Catherine Taylor.
Their son, Samuel Campbell, Jr. (1765–?), born
in Edinburgh, was a bookseller and papermak-
er. During the 1790s the firm of Campbell &
Smith made high-quality paper for banknotes.
Young Samuel married, first, Elizabeth Duyckinck and, later, Euphrenia Duyckinck. Catherine Campbell (1797–1881), a daughter from the
first marriage, married Marcus Wilbur in 1819;
their daughter Eliza married Benjamin Webster
in 1849; their son Albert married Mary Lawrence, and they became the parents of Aileen
(Webster) Payne.

Provenance: Samuel and Catherine (Taylor)
Campbell; Samuel and Elizabeth (Duyckinck)
Campbell; Catherine (Campbell) Wilbur; Eliza
(Wilbur) Webster; Albert and Mary (Lawrence)
Webster; Aileen (Webster) Payne; Sothebys,
New York City.

Comments: Unique in the American work of
Daniel Fueter and, indeed, unique in American
silver, the candlesticks are patterned on Swiss
models. (See, for example, candlesticks by
Philibert Pottin and Wilhelm Brenner of Lausanne in Marcel Grandjean et al., *L'Argenterie
du Vieux-Lausanne.*) Why this distinctly Swiss
form should appear in Fueter's New York
oeuvre remains a mystery. The crest is that of
Campbell. The initials "SEC" refer to Samuel
Campbell, Jr., and either Elizabeth or Euphrenia Duyckinck.

References: Sotheby's, "Americana" (January
24–27, 1990), lot 180. Marcel Grandjean et al.,
L'Argenterie du Vieux-Lausanne (Lausanne,
Switz.: Editions du Grand-Pont, Jean-Pierre
Laubscher, 1984), VL83A001 and VL83A020,
for similar candlesticks.

90.24 Museum purchase from Sotheby's, 1990

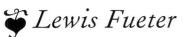

Lewis Fueter

1746–84
New York, New York

Lewis Fueter was born in Bern, Switzerland, where he was known as Ludwig Anton. The son of goldsmith Daniel Christian Fueter, he fled with his family when they were forced to leave Switzerland for political reasons. They went first to London and then to New York in 1754. During the family's three-year hiatus in Connecticut, Lewis completed his training under his father. Shortly after their return to the city, the *New-York Gazette* (January 1769) announced the partnership of Daniel and Lewis Fueter "in Dock-Street, next to Mr. G. Dykinck's." The partnership lasted only a few months, however, because Daniel and most of the family returned to Europe in autumn 1769, leaving only sons Lewis and Daniel, Jr. In May 1774 Lewis advertised that he had moved his shop "from the Coffee-House Bridge to the house in Queen-street, lately occupied by Mr. Judah, Silver Smith, and opposite Robert G. Livingston, Esq." He became a freeman in 1775.

Lewis might well be styled the Tory silversmith for the many commissions he received from, or for, British officers. One such work was the great salver, now at the New-York Historical Society, that was presented to Capt. Thomas Sowers by Governor Tryon and the General Assembly. During the war most of Fueter's commissions were for military accoutrements such as camp cups and at least one cross-belt plate (the latter being the only known American example, now in a private collection). Fueter paid for this patronage the hard way. In August 1776 it was noted: "The Persecution of the Loyalists continues unremitted: Donald M'Lean, Theophilus Hardenbrook, Young Fueter the Silversmith, and Rem Rappalye have been cruelly rode on Rails, a Practice most painful, dangerous, and till now peculiar to the *humane* Republicans of New-England."

When the British evacuated New York in 1783, Fueter went with them to Halifax. Shortly thereafter he went to Jamaica, where he drowned in 1784. Although the number of possessions at the time of his death was small, he was hardly destitute. He owned a gold watch, a silver-hilted sword, 130 ounces of silver, and "Sundry Silversmiths Tools much damaged with Saltwater." A severe hurricane hit Jamaica early in August 1784. The damage was extensive with twenty-three ships sunk and twenty more driven ashore. It is probable that the storm was the cause of Fueter's death. Fueter also made domestic silver, as the thirty-nine spoons and two ladles in the following entries attest. In addition to the usual canns, sugar bowls, and the like, he created an elegant set of silver mounts for a pair of mahogany knife cases made for the Stuyvesant family that include escutcheons, bail handles, and ball-and-claw feet. (The cases are at the Metropolitan Museum of Art.)

References: Gottesman, *Arts and Crafts, 1726–76*, p. 44. Gottesman, *Arts and Crafts, 1777–99*, pp. 66–67. Thomas Jones, *History of New York during the Revolutionary War*, 2 vols. (New York: New-York Historical Society, 1879), 1:596–97. *NYHS Collections*: vol. 18 (1885) *Burghers and Freemen*, p. 238. Carl Brun, *Schweizerisches Künstler-Lexicon*, 4 vols. (Frauenfeld, Switz., 1905–17), s.v. "Fueter, Ludwig"; see also references for Daniel C. Fueter. I am extremely grateful to Robert B. Barker, who provided me with a copy of the inventory of Fueter's estate from the Jamaica Archives (Probate Inventories, vol. 68, pp. 7, 7a, 8).

196 a, b
LADLES, ca. 1775

(a) L. 14⅝" (37.2 cm)
6 oz. 14 dwt. 9 gr. (209.0 g)
(b) L. 8¹/₁₆" (20.5 cm)
2 oz. 1 gr. (62.3 g)

Stamps: (a) "LFueter" in script, in a conforming surround, struck twice on back of handle; (b) "L Fueter" in roman letters, in a conforming surround, struck once on back of handle.

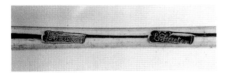

Engraved on front of handle: (a) "TAB" in foliate script; (b) armorial device consisting of a crescent moon with a face on a heraldic band (Deutch family crest).

Description: circular deep bowls, swage-formed drops on back; long handles curve back to downturned ends; midrib on back; (a) has double rounded drop with incised curved line across lower drop; (b) has a single drop with a curved incised line.

Spectrographic analysis:

	SILVER	COPPER	LEAD	GOLD
(a)				
BOWL	91.0	8.2	0.48	0.18
HANDLE	92.1	7.2	0.40	0.17
(b)				
BOWL	87.3	12.0	0.21	0.17
HANDLE	89.2	10.1	0.19	0.19

Provenance: Robert Ensko, Inc., New York City, sold 1 of the ladles to H. F. du Pont, May 1935.

References: Fales, *American Silver*, no. 96.

59.2309, 59.2310 Gift of H. F. du Pont, 1965

❦ 197 a–t
SPOONS, ca. 1775

(a–f) L. 8 9/16"–8 11/16" (21.8–22.1 cm)
1 oz. 19 dwt.–2 oz. 1 dwt. (60.4–62.6 g)
(g–r) L. 6 11/16"–6 3/4" (17.0–17.2 cm)
18 dwt. 15 gr.–1 oz. 19 gr. (28.9–32.3 g)
(s, t) L. 11 11/16"–11 3/4" (29.7–29.9 cm)
3 oz. 10 dwt. 1 gr.–3 oz. 10 dwt. 17 gr.
(108.7–109.7 g)

Stamps: "L FUETER" in roman letters, in a conforming surround, struck once on back of each handle.

Engraved on front of each handle: armorial device consisting of a crescent moon with a face on a heraldic band (Deutch family crest).

Description: oval bowls with swage-formed double drops; rounded downturned handles with midrib.

Spectrographic analysis: Silver content ranges from 86.5 to 92.4 percent, but most spoons are in the range of 87.0 to 89.0 percent.

Provenance: Robert Ensko, Inc., New York City, sold to H. F. du Pont, January 1935.

Comments: See nos. 198, 199 for total of 37 spoons with Deutch crest.

References: (g–r) Fales, *American Silver*, no. 77.

61.635.2, .4–.7, .9; 61.637.1–.12; 61.636.1, .2 Gift of H. F. du Pont, 1965

❦ 198 a–j
SPOONS, ca. 1775

(a–f) L. 8 9/16"–8 11/16" (21.8–22.1 cm)
2 oz. 16 dwt.–2 oz. 17 dwt. 5 gr. (86.9–88.8 g)
(g–j) L. 8 15/16"–9" (22.7–22.9 cm)
2 oz. 17 dwt.–2 oz. 17 dwt. 14 gr.
(88.5–89.4 g)

Stamps: "LFueter" in script, in a conforming surround, struck once on back of each handle.

Engraved on front of handles: (a–f) armorial device consisting of a crescent moon with a face on a heraldic band (Deutch family crest).

Description: oval bowl with swage-formed double drop on (a–f); oval bowl with swage-formed single drop on (g–j); rounded downturned handle with midrib.

Spectrographic analysis: Silver content ranges from 86.9 to 90.0 percent.

Provenance: (a–h) Robert Ensko, Inc., New York City, sold to H. F. du Pont, January 1935; (i, j) Mr. and Mrs. Stanley B. Ineson, New York City; Mr. and Mrs. Alfred E. Bissell, Wilmington, Del.; (g, h) Frederick T. Widmer, New York City, sold to H. F. du Pont, July 1936.

References: (i or j) Belden, *Marks of American Silversmiths*, p. 179.

Comments: See nos. 197, 199 for total of 37 spoons with Deutch crest.

(a–h) 61.635.1, .3, .8, .10–.12; 61.633.1, .2 Gift of H. F. du Pont, 1965; (i, j) 62.240.1120.1, .2 Gift of Mr. and Mrs. Alfred E. Bissell, 1962–63

❦ 199 a–k
SPOONS, ca. 1775

L. 5 1/16"–5 3/16" (12.9–13.2 cm)
8 dwt. 1 gr.–9 dwt. 17 gr. (12.5–15.1 g)

Stamps: "LF" in script, in a rectangle, struck once on back of each handle.

Engraved on front of each handle: armorial device consisting of a crescent moon with a face on a heraldic band (Deutch family crest).

Description: oval bowl with swage-formed double drop; rounded downturned handle with midrib.

Spectrographic analysis: Silver content ranges from 86.8 to 92.8 percent, but most are in the range of 89.0 to 91.0 percent.

Provenance: Robert Ensko, Inc., New York City, sold to H. F. du Pont, January 1935.

Comments: See nos. 197, 198 for total of 37 spoons with Deutch crest.

(a–f) 61.634.1–.6; (g–k) 61.936.1–.5 Gift of H. F. du Pont, 1965

William Gale

1799–1867

Gale, Wood & Hughes, w. 1833–45
Gale & Hayden, w. 1846–50
New York, New York

William Gale started his business in 1821. In 1833 he formed a partnership with his two former apprentices, Jacob Wood and Jasper Hughes, under the firm name of Gale, Wood & Hughes. The partnership lasted until 1845 when Wood and Hughes formed their own firm. Gale then formed a partnership with Nathaniel Hayden that lasted until 1850. They were located at 116 Fulton Street. Numerous examples of their silver bear the stamps of others, presumably retailers. Perhaps their best-known work is the large and elaborate presentation urn now owned by the Tennessee Botanical Garden and Fine Arts Center, Nashville. Weighing 307 ounces, it was presented to Henry Clay, "the Gallant Champion of the Whig Cause by the Whig Ladies of Tennessee." It also bears the stamp of Gowdey & Peabody of Nashville.

    The career of William Gale, Jr., overlaps with that of his father, under whom he probably served his apprenticeship. His advertisement in an 1857 city directory suggests continuity: "Established 1821. Wm. Gale Jr. (Late Wm. Gale & Son) Silversmith. 572 & 574 Broadway, Metropolitan Hotel. Manufactory at 447 Broome St." The Broome Street address was given in the 1858–59 and 1859–60 directories for William Gale, Sr.

References: New York City directories. David Bigelow, *History of Prominent Mercantile and Manufacturing Firms in the United States*, vol. 6 (Boston: D. Bigelow, 1857), p. 141. Von Khrum, *Silversmiths*, p. 52. Diana Cramer, "Wood and Hughes," *Silver* (November/December 1989): 28–32. Warren, Howe, and Brown, *Marks of Achievement*, no. 139, for Clay urn.

200
EWER, 1849

H. 12 ½" (31.8 cm), w. 7 ¹⁵⁄₁₆" (20.2 cm)
20 oz. 11 dwt. 12 gr. (639.9 g)

Stamps: "G&H" in roman letters, in a rectangle; "G/ &/ H" in roman letters, in a vertical oval with a pendant diamond containing "1849" (1 number in each corner), the last 2 stamps linked by a circle, all struck once on underside of body.

Engraved on body under pouring lip: "NYSAS/ Awarded to/ H. T. E. Foster, Lakeland/ 1st Premium on Farms/ January/ 1849" in script.

Description: urn-shape lower body seamed at handle; high concave neck with flared irregular rim and broad pouring lip; cast C scrolls, S scrolls, and fleurs-de-lis applied to outer surface of rim. Hollow cast C-curve handle with small back-to-back C scrolls forming the lower handle attachment, the whole handle partly covered by acanthus leaves. Raised circular trumpet-shape pedestal with applied bands of die-rolled decorative bands in acanthus leaf pattern at top and around base. Extensive repoussé work on 3 sides of body: inscription framed in a cartouche of C scrolls with a bouquet of flowers at bottom and a cluster of agricultural trophies at the top (sheaf of wheat, acanthus leaf, rake, sickle, and more leaves); left of inscription is a small masonry house with 2 windows and 1 door, all against a mountainous background, fenced yard in foreground, overarching tree at right; right of inscription is a small masonry house with 3 windows and 1 door plus a framed outbuilding, all set in a rocky landscape with small trees plus overarching tree on left; 4 equidistant bouquets of flowers around base.

Spectrographic analysis:

	SILVER	COPPER	LEAD	GOLD
BODY	94.6	5.3	0.18	0.00
HANDLE	93.0	6.6	0.33	0.02
BASE	96.2	3.5	0.20	0.07

History: Presented to Herman Ten Eyck Foster by the New York State Agricultural Society in 1849. This ewer was won at a fair held September 5–7, 1848. The New York State Agricultural Society was founded in 1832 and reorganized in 1841. Foster is H. F. du Pont's maternal grandfather.

Provenance: Herman Ten Eyck Foster; Mary Pauline Foster du Pont, Henry Algernon du Pont, Winterthur, Del.; H. F. du Pont.

References: Fales, *American Silver*, no. 127. Donald L. Fennimore, "Gale and Hayden Ewer," *Silver* 18, no. 2 (March/April 1985): 12–14. Fennimore, *Silver and Pewter*, no. 126.

Comments: Extensive hammerwork inside body in spite of seaming. Small circular portion of lower body let in. An elegant piece. The Museum of the City of New York owns a presentation pitcher made by the firm dated July 19, 1845. The Carnegie Museum of Art in Pittsburgh owns an elaborate rococo revival pitcher made by Gale & Hayden in 1849 and presented to Charles Avery, a Pittsburgh merchant.

61.964 Gift of H. F. du Pont, 1965

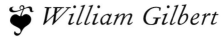

William Gilbert

1746–1832

William W. Gilbert & Son, w. 1791–95
New York, New York

William (Willem) Gilbert, son of William and Aeltie (Verdon) Gilbert, was baptized in 1746 in the Dutch Church. He married Catherina Cosine in 1767. (His sister Ann [Adriaantje] married silversmith Ephraim Brasher.) In 1802 Gilbert married Betsy Hawley (d. 1844). He fathered nineteen children by his two wives: eleven baptized at the New York Dutch Church (1768–90), four at Red Hook (1777–82), and two at Greenwich (1807–13). In his will, made in 1832, he referred to himself as "Gentleman." He was wealthy enough to leave $5,000 each to many of his children. Betsy received all the household goods, except for a desk given to son Garrit, plus one-third of the rents and profits from real estate.

In 1770 Gilbert's shop on Broadway was broken into and robbed of "near two Hundred Pounds in Plate" (*New York Gazette or Weekly Post-Boy*, August 27, 1770). He acquired a large parcel of land on Greenwich Lane. During the British occupation of New York, he left the city and served in the same regiment of New York militia as his brother-in-law Ephraim Brasher. When George Washington visited New York in December 1784, the Common Council presented him with a gold box symbolizing the freedom of the city. Made by Gilbert, for £45.16.0, it appears in Washington's inventory, but its whereabouts today are unknown. (Other gold freedom boxes were authorized at the same time for presentation to George Clinton, John Jay, Marquis de Lafayette, and Baron von Steuben. Silversmith Samuel Johnson is known to have made two and, perhaps,

all four of these boxes. The Jay box remained in private hands until sold at auction by Sotheby's in 1991. The Steuben box is at Yale University Art Gallery.)

For several years Gilbert was alderman of the West Ward. It was in this capacity that he was asked by the council to oversee the making of the gold freedom boxes. He also served in the State Assembly, 1789–93 and 1803–8. He held other civic offices, including the post of treasurer of the Saint Tammany Society, otherwise known as the American Museum, organized by John Pintard. He was also a member of the Gold and Silversmiths Society. A pastel portrait of Gilbert by James Sharples is owned by the Museum of the City of New York.

Directories list Gilbert at Broadway, 1786; 71 Broadway, 1787–89; 24 and 26 Dey Street, 1794–95; Greenwich, 1796–1818. For 1791–95 the firm is listed as William W. Gilbert & Son, Merchants.

Much of Gilbert's surviving work is in the early neoclassical style that had become so pervasive by the 1780s and 1790s, but some pieces in the rococo mode also survive. The Museum of the City of New York owns a cann and a salver that belonged to Nicholas Bayard (1736–98). A circular covered sugar bowl and creamer, in a private collection as of 1960, are heavily chased in the rococo manner.

References: Stephen Decatur, "William Gilbert, Silversmith of New York," in Kurt M. Semon, ed., *A Treasury of Old Silver* (New York: Robert M. McBride, 1947), pp. 61–63. Kathryn C. Buhler, *Mount Vernon Silver* (Mount Vernon, Va.: Mount Vernon Ladies' Association, 1957), p. 74. *Minutes of the Common Council. NYHS Collections*: vol. 18 (1885) *Burghers and Freemen*, pp. 251–52, 271–72. Miller, *Silver by New York Makers*, p. 41, for portrait. James A. Rasmussen, "Gilbert Family of Albany and New York," *NYG&BR* 122 (July 1991): 164–66. Von Khrum, *Silversmiths*, p. 55.

201
BOWL, ca. 1780

H. 3 1/16" (7.8 cm), DIAM. rim 5 5/16" (15.1 cm)
8 oz. 3 dwt. 19 gr. (254.7 g)

Stamps: "W.Gilbert" in script, in a rectangle; "Nev•York" in roman letters, in a rectangle. Both struck twice on underside of body.

Engraved on underside of footring: "EC" in shaded roman letters. *Engraved on side of body:* "Elizabeth Codwise./ —and—/ Major Ezra Starr./ Married, April 24, 1781." in script (probably added in the nineteenth century). *Scratched on underside of body:* "86".

Description: raised circular body with angled sides, flared rim, and rounded bottom; rim cut in pattern of back-to-back cyma curves; inside of rim engraved in pattern of leafy branches; centerpunch on underside; cast circular stepped footring.

Spectrographic analysis:

	SILVER	COPPER	LEAD	GOLD
BODY	87.0	12.1	0.32	0.26
FOOT	93.1	6.8	0.07	0.06

Provenance: Mary Lent Antiques, Wallington, N.Y.; sold through Louis G. Myers, New York City, to H. F. du Pont, 1930.

Comments: A similar bowl by Gilbert, complete with engraved floral border, is owned by the Museum of the City of New York. Another similar bowl, by Myer Myers, is owned by Yale University Art Gallery.

References: Fales, *American Silver*, no. 125. Fennimore, *Silver and Pewter*, no. 102.

61.933 Gift of H. F. du Pont, 1965

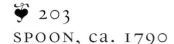 202
CREAMER, ca. 1780

H. 3 3/4" (9.5 cm), W. 4 3/16" (10.6 cm)
2 oz. 17 dwt. 20 gr. (89.9 g)

Stamps: "W.Gilbert" in script, in a rectangle, struck once on underside.

Engraved on side of body: "MET" in foliate script. *Engraved on other side of body:* "MET to ETC" in foliate script.

Description: raised pear-shape body with flared wavy-edge rim and extended pouring lip, centerpunch on underside; 3 cast cabriole legs with pad feet and pads at juncture with body; cast handle made in 3 C scrolls with a sprig.

Spectrographic analysis:

	SILVER	COPPER	GOLD	LEAD
BODY	92.1	6.8	0.59	0.19
HANDLE	93.0	6.5	0.27	0.15
FOOT	95.5	4.1	0.17	0.16

Provenance: Mary Lent, Wallington, N.Y., sold through Louis G. Myers, New York City, to H. F. du Pont, 1930.

57.1369 Gift of H. F. du Pont, 1965

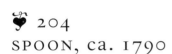 203
SPOON, ca. 1790

L. 7 1/2" (19.1 cm)
1 oz. 13 gr. (31.9 g)

Stamps: "Gilbert" in script, in a rectangle, struck once on back of handle.

Engraved on front of handle: "AED" in foliate script, in a bright-cut medallion with floral pendant drop; feather-cut and zig-zag border length of handle.

Description: oval bowl with swage-formed pointed drop and rounded second drop; pointed downturned handle with midrib.

Spectrographic analysis: Silver content is 89.7 percent.

Provenance: Mr. and Mrs. Stanley B. Ineson, New York City; Mr. and Mrs. Alfred E. Bissell, Wilmington, Del.

References: Belden, *Marks of American Silversmiths*, p. 192.

62.240.1155 Gift of Mr. and Mrs. Alfred E. Bissell, 1962–63

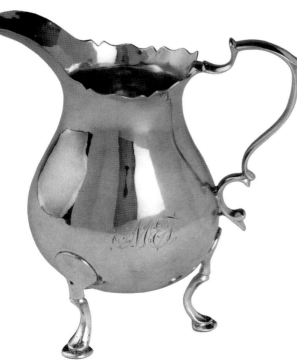

204
SPOON, ca. 1790

L. 3 7/8" (9.8 cm)
3 dwt. 21 gr. (6.1 g)

Stamps: "WG" in conjoined script, in a rectangle, struck once on back of handle.

Engraved on front of handle: "TC" in foliate script, in a bright-cut medallion with pendant drop.

Description: pointed oval bowl with swage-formed 9-lobe scallop shell on back; pointed downturned handle.

Spectrographic analysis: Silver content is 90.7 percent.

Provenance: Mr. and Mrs. Stanley B. Ineson, New York City; Mr. and Mrs. Alfred E. Bissell, Wilmington, Del.

References: Belden, *Marks of American Silversmiths*, p. 192.

62.240.766 Gift of Mr. and Mrs. Alfred E. Bissell, 1962–63

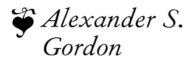

Alexander S. Gordon

d. 1803
New York, New York, w. ca. 1795–1803

Gordon advertised in the *American Citizen and General Advertiser*, April 21 and September 18, 1801: "In William street near the Post Office." He sold a silver polish of his own formula, complete with printed instructions, that "is wholesome to the Silver." He distinguished his polishing powder from "a mercurial preparation made and hawked in this city . . . which gives an instant gloss but which almost as instantaneously disappears; and, by the known corrosive property of the oxyd of that metal, the plate will eventually be destroyed." Sold for 50¢ a box, he offered a money-back guarantee if the purchaser was not satisfied. The inventory of his estate, dated November 9, 1803, included *The Goldsmiths Repository*, silversmith's tools, a pair of gold scales and weights, and a variety of wrought silver. The most valuable of his furnishings was "1 Billiard table and apparatus," valued at $125. Apparently Gordon was a Mason, for his inventory contained "2 Masonic medals, a mason's apron, &c."

The Essex Institute in Salem owns a silver tea service by Gordon, in the fluted style, that was made for James and Sally Dunlap, who were married in 1793. Sleepy Hollow Restorations owns a three-piece tea service, made in the late neoclassical style, for Catherine Clinton Taylor, who married Pierre Van Cortlandt in 1801.

References: "Inventory of the Effects of Alexander S. Gordon Deceased," March 9, 1804, Stanley B. Ineson Papers, Downs collection, Winterthur. Gottesman, *Arts and Crafts, 1800–1804*, pp. 97–98. Von Khrum, *Silversmiths*, p. 56.

205
GOBLET, ca. 1800

H. 6 ^{11}/₁₆" (17.0 cm), DIAM. rim 3 ⅞" (9.8 cm), DIAM. base 3 ⅛" (7.9 cm)
7 oz. 6 dwt. 12 gr. (227.3 g)

Stamps: "GORDON" in roman letters, in a serrated rectangle, struck once on underside of base.

Engraved on side of body: "F" in foliate script. *Scratched on underside of base:* "bny" twice in script.

Description: raised circular urn-shape body with plain rim; no centerpunch visible; 2-part stem flares to raised circular base with applied seamed footring encircled by 2 double-scored lines; upper part of stem seamed; 3 moldings in center of stem. Gilded interior.

Spectrographic analysis:

	SILVER	COPPER	LEAD	GOLD
BODY SIDE	93.1	6.2	0.46	0.29
FOOT	93.4	5.9	0.48	0.23

Provenance: Marshall P. Blankarn, New York City.

Comments: It is hard to tell how the body was formed. Although there are hammer marks inside, they cease two-thirds of the way down, and the lower body has turning marks.

76.277 Gift of Marshall P. Blankarn, 1976

206 a, b
SPOONS, ca. 1800

(a) L. 5 ⅜" (13.7 cm)
6 dwt. 12 gr. (10.1 g)
(b) L. 6" (15.2 cm)
9 dwt. 17 gr. (15.1 g)

Stamps: "Gordon" in script, in a rectangle, struck once on back of each handle.

Engraved on front of handle: (a) "MW"; (b) "THL". Both in foliate script.

Description: pointed oval bowls with swage-formed single rounded drops; downturned fiddle-shape handles with midribs on back.

Spectrographic analysis: Silver content ranges from 88.3 to 89.2 percent.

Provenance: (a) Mr. and Mrs. Stanley B. Ineson, New York City; Mr. and Mrs. Alfred E. Bissell, Wilmington, Del.; (b) Parke-Bernet Galleries, New York City.

62.240.288 Gift of Mr. and Mrs. Alfred E. Bissell, 1962–63; 72.53 Museum purchase from Parke-Bernet Galleries, 1972

Thomas Hammersly

1727–81
New York, New York

What we know of Thomas Hammersly is limited to a few newspaper advertisements, even fewer documentary references, and the silver that has survived. In August 1756 he advertised that "a negro fellow named Duke . . . [who] can work at the goldsmith's business" had run away. He offered 20s. if the workman was apprehended in the city, 40s. plus expenses if apprehended elsewhere. In 1757 he noted that he had moved his shop from "near the Change in Dock Street" to "Hanover-Square, next door to Mr. John Waters, Merchant." In 1766 Hammersly offered for rent "two commodious rooms." He married Sarah Colgan, the niece of Fleming Colgan, mariner, whose nephew Thomas Colgan became Hammersly's apprentice.

Hammersly's silver survives in quantity and is remarkable for a wide variety of forms. In addition to the usual tankards, teapots, and salvers, he made a mustard pot, a jigger cup, an apple corer, a strawberry dish, a bottle ticket, and what must be the earliest American syphon. E. Alfred Jones recorded a dish or communion plate at Grace Church, Jamaica, Long Island.

References: Gottesman, *Arts and Crafts, 1726–76,* p. 48. Jones, *Old Silver,* p. 231. *NYHS Collections:* vol. 31 (1898) *Abstracts of Wills,* p. 380. Von Khrum, *Silversmiths,* p. 62.

207
TEAPOT, ca. 1760

H. 6 3/16" (15.7 cm), W. 9 1/2" (24.1 cm)
19 oz. 15 gr. (590.6 g)

Stamps: "TH" in roman letters, in a rectangle, struck 3 times on underside of body.

Scratched on underside of body: "S∗E" in crude roman letters; "19 12 1/2".

Description: raised circular double-bellied body; centerpunch on underside. Cast circular stepped foot. Cast S-curve spout with 5 gadrooned panels; 2 C scrolls next to body. Cast circular domed lid with vent, flush mounted with a 5-segment hinge; finial cast in form of an artichoke and attached through lid with solder; 2 cast handle sockets, the upper with an acanthus leaf on top and scrolls on the side; 2 silver pins attach C-curve hardwood handle with 1 sprig.

Spectrographic analysis:

	SILVER	COPPER	LEAD	GOLD
BODY SIDE	91.4	8.5	0.18	0.16
LID	95.0	4.8	0.11	0.13
SPOUT	93.6	6.1	0.08	0.26

Provenance: Mr. and Mrs. Edward L. Cussler, Cavendish, Vt.

Comments: Similar to teapot by Samuel Edwards of Boston (no. 57).

75.88 Gift of Mr. and Mrs. Edward L. Cussler, 1975

208
SPOON, ca. 1760

L. 7 15/16" (20.2 cm), 2 oz. 12 gr. (63.0 g)

Stamps: "T•H" in roman letters, in a rectangle, struck twice on back of handle.

Engraved on back of handle: "I/ NM" in crude shaded roman letters.

Description: oval bowl with swage-formed double drop on back; upturned rounded handle with midrib.

Spectrographic analysis: Silver content is 91.1 percent.

Provenance: Mr. and Mrs. Stanley B. Ineson, New York City; Mr. and Mrs. Alfred E. Bissell, Wilmington, Del.

Exhibitions: "Silver by New York Makers, Late Seventeenth Century to 1900," Museum of the City of New York, 1937–38.

References: Belden, *Marks of American Silversmiths,* p. 212. Miller, *Silver by New York Makers,* no. 146.

62.240.1170 Gift of Mr. and Mrs. Alfred E. Bissell, 1962–63

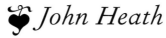 *John Heath*

w. 1760s
New York, New York

Information on John Heath is sparse. We do know that in 1760 he married Elizabeth Pell, in 1761 he became a freeman, and in 1763 he advertised in the *New York Mercury*, where he refers to himself as a "goldsmith, in Wall-street." In designating Heath as executor of his estate in 1762, Samuel Broadhurst called him "my friend and brother." A small but important body of his work survives, among which is a bowl at Yale University Art Gallery engraved with the Van Cortlandt coat of arms and crest and accompanied by an undated bill:

> *Pere Van Cortlandt*
> *to John Heath*
> To a Boole wt 29 oz 15 pwt
> Silver at 9/ 4 pr oz   13-17-8
> To Making the Boole at 3/ 6 pr oz   5-4-1
> To Engraving A Cot Armes & a Crist   1-0-0

Heath also made a double-bellied teapot similar to a Winterthur piece by Hammersly (no. 207). It was advertised in *Antiques* (December 1956) by Ginsburg & Levy. Heath made two outstanding examples of open work: a pair of salts with ball-and-claw feet in the Hammerslough collection at Wadsworth Atheneum and a mustard pot at Historic Deerfield.

References: Buhler and Hood, *American Silver,* no. 724. Flynt and Fales, *Heritage Foundation,* fig. 85. Hammerslough, *American Silver,* 1:49. *NYHS Collections:* vol. 18 (1885) *Burghers and Freemen,* p. 198; vol. 30 (1897) *Abstracts of Wills,* p. 145. Von Khrum, *Silversmiths,* p. 64. Ginsburg and Levy advertisement, *Antiques* 70, no. 6 (December 1956): 515.

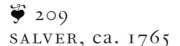 209

SALVER, ca. 1765

DIAM. 15 3/16" (38.6 cm), H. 1 5/8" (4.1 cm)
45 oz. 11 dwt. 4 gr. (1417.0 g)

Stamps: "J•HEATH" in roman letters, in a rounded rectangle, struck once on underside of body.

Engraved on upper side: heraldic device consisting of a falcon (facing right) on a falconer's hand (pointing left) on a vert ground, in an asymmetrical cartouche of 4 C scrolls flanked by stylized shells, flowers, and leaves. *Crest:* closed knight's helmet surmounted by a falcon. *Engraved on underside:* "oz/ 46"; *inscribed on underside, off-center near edge:* a circle about 5" in diameter.

Description: flat circular tray with elevated and shaped rim of 8 wavy-edge bracketlike segments that form points where they meet; inside border has gadrooning and chased scrolls and 5-petal flowers; cast ropelike border applied to outer edge of rim; 4 cast ball-and-claw feet on short cabriole legs.

Spectrographic analysis:

	SILVER	COPPER	GOLD	LEAD
UNDERSIDE	90.2	8.7	0.29	0.25
FOOT	91.2	7.9	0.23	0.21

History: Coat of arms is that used by the Schuyler family of New York City.

Provenance: Mrs. William Anderson, Pittsburgh, to Robert Ensko, Inc., New York City; sold to H. F. du Pont, February 1932.

Exhibitions: "American Rococo, 1750–1775: Elegance in Ornament," Metropolitan Museum of Art, New York City, and Los Angeles County Museum of Art, 1992. "Silver by New York Makers," Museum of the City of New York, 1937–38. On loan to Museum of the City of New York at the time of its sale to H. F. du Pont.

Comments: A similar salver, by William Grigg of New York City and Albany, bears the coat of arms of the Clarkson family and is owned by the Art Institute of Chicago. Closely related to both is a salver with the Philipse crest owned by Sleepy Hollow Restorations and made by Richard Rugg, London, 1763–64.

References: Fales, *American Silver,* nos. 46, 120. Fales, *Early American Silver,* fig. 120. Fennimore, *Silver and Pewter,* no. 4. Morrison H. Heckscher and Leslie Green Bowman, *American Rococo, 1750–1775: Elegance in Ornament* (New York: Metropolitan Museum of Art, 1992), no. 73. Hood, *American Silver,* fig. 135. Miller, *Silver by New York Makers,* no. 154. Quimby, "Silver," p. 76. Joseph T. Butler, *Sleepy Hollow Restorations: A Cross Section of the Collections* (Tarrytown, N.Y.: Sleepy Hollow Restorations, 1983), no. 209, for Rugg tray. Milo M. Naeve and Lynn Springer Roberts, *A Decade of Decorative Arts: The Antiquarian Society of the Art Institute of Chicago* (Chicago: By the institute, 1986), no. 194, for Grigg tray.

59.2301 Gift of H. F. du Pont, 1965

❧ 210
SPOON, ca. 1765

L. 8 ¼" (21.0 cm)
1 oz. 15 dwt. 5 gr. (54.7 g)

Stamps: "J•HEATH" in roman letters, in a rounded rectangle, struck once on back of handle.

Description: oval bowl with swage-formed single drop on back; rounded downturned handle with midrib on back.

Spectrographic analysis: Silver content is 88.1 percent.

Provenance: Mr. and Mrs. Stanley B. Ineson, New York City; Mr. and Mrs. Alfred E. Bissell, Wilmington, Del.

References: Belden, *Marks of American Silversmiths*, p. 221.

62.240.1190 Gift of Mr. and Mrs. Alfred E. Bissell, 1962–63

❧ 211 a, b
SPOONS, ca. 1765

(a) L. 4 ¾" (12.1 cm)
6 dwt. 4 gr. (9.6 g)
(b) L. 4 ³⁄₁₆" (10.6 cm)
4 dwt. 9 gr. (6.8 g)

Stamps: "J•H" in roman letters, in a rounded rectangle, struck once on back of each handle.

Engraved on back of handle: (a) "M•P" in crude shaded roman letters; (b) "EW" in shaded roman letters.

Description: (a) oval bowl with swage-formed single rounded drop; rounded upturned handle with short midrib on front; (b) oval bowl with swage-formed 7-lobe shell and single rounded drop; rounded straight handle with midrib on front.

Spectrographic analysis: Silver content ranges from 89.5 to 91.3 percent.

Provenance: Mr. and Mrs. Stanley B. Ineson, New York City; Mr. and Mrs. Alfred E. Bissell, Wilmington, Del.

References: Belden, *Marks of American Silversmiths*, p. 221.

62.240.308, .309 Gift of Mr. and Mrs. Alfred E. Bissell, 1962–63

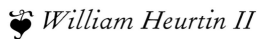# William Heurtin II

1703–65
New York, New York, w. ca. 1728–?
Newark, New Jersey, w. ?–1765

William Heurtin's father was Capt. William Heurtin, of New York City, who died in 1718. Young William married Susannah Kocherthal in 1728. They had two sons, William and Joshua, both of whom became silversmiths. (To distinguish the three generations, it is convenient to designate them by numerical suffixes.) William II was admitted a freeman of New York City in 1731. His shop was on the south side of John Street. The date of his removal to Newark has yet to be determined. Little of his silver survives. His son William III advertised in 1766 as a partner in the firm of Hurtin & Burgi, silversmiths and clockmakers, in Bound Brook, New Jersey, but by 1776 he too was back at the John Street address in New York City. It may not be possible to distinguish between the work of William II and William III.

References: J. Stewart Johnson, "Silver in Newark," *The Museum* [Newark, N.J.], n.s., 18, nos. 3, 4 (Summer/Fall 1966): 24. Von Khrum, *Silversmiths,* p. 66. Williams, *Silversmiths of New Jersey,* pp. 98–99.

212
CASTER, ca. 1750

H. 3 ½" (8.9 cm), w. 3 ³⁄₁₆" (8.1 cm)
3 oz. 3 dwt. 4 gr. (98.2 g)

Stamps: "WH" in roman letters, in an oval, struck once on underside of body.

Engraved on underside of body: "O / IH" in shaded roman letters.

Description: seamed cylindrical body with large flared base molding formed by raising; applied cast fillet ¼" below rim serves as lid stop; flat circular set-in bottom with centerpunch. S-curve plain cast handle. Circular domed friction-fit lid pierced with 5 rows of drilled holes; applied molded bezel; cast onion dome finial.

Spectrographic analysis:

	SILVER	COPPER	LEAD	GOLD
BODY SIDE	89.5	10.1	0.25	0.04
UNDERSIDE	94.4	5.1	0.17	0.12
LID	90.3	9.2	0.27	0.06
HANDLE	88.9	10.6	0.27	0.07

History: Tradition of ownership in the Ogden family.

Provenance: Mr. and Mrs. N. McLean Seabrease, Germantown, Pa., sold through Robert Ensko, Inc., New York City, to H. F. du Pont, 1929.

Comments: Most cylindrical casters and pepper boxes have let-in bottoms.

References: Fales, *American Silver,* no. 22.

59.2300 Gift of H. F. du Pont, 1965

❧ *William B. Heyer*

1776–1828
New York, New York

William B. Heyer appears as a silver-smith in New York City directories at 47 Warren Street, 1813–16; 202 Church Street, 1820; Broadway near Art Street, 1821; and Tammany Hall, 1822. Earlier he had been in partnership with Jesse Gale, but the ties were dissolved in 1808. Heyer & Gale made a jug for the Collegiate Church of New York. Heyer made two plates and two cups for the First Congregational Church of Providence, Rhode Island. On some of his tea services he used a distinctive die-rolled decorative band impressed with a continuous pictorial narrative that includes houses and human figures in a landscape. This band is on a sugar and creamer at the New-York Historical Society and on a tea service at Yale University Art Gallery. Heyer also made an unusual porringer, now in a private collection, that features an applied anthemion border on the rim and an odd square-shape handle with a heart-shape void in the center. A Heyer tea service at the Metropolitan Museum of Art also bears "H&N," the stamp of Hyde & Nevins, a prominent retailer and jeweler. Heyer used both name and initial stamps.

References: Jones, *Old Silver*, p. 388. Buhler and Hood, *American Silver*, no. 751. Von Khrum, *Silversmiths*, p. 66.

❧ 213 a–d
TEA SERVICE, ca. 1820

(a) Hot water pot: H. 11 ½" (29.2 cm), W. 12 ¼" (31.1 cm)
40 oz. 15 dwt. 8 gr. (1268.0 g)
(b) Teapot: H. 10 1/16" (25.6 cm), W. 11 5/16" (28.7 cm)
34 oz. 10 dwt. 1 gr. (1073.2 g)
(c) Sugar bowl and lid: H. 9 1/16" (23.0 cm), W. 8" (20.3 cm)
24 oz. 6 dwt. 3 gr. (756.0 g)
(d) Creamer: H. 6 1/8" (15.6 cm), W. 6" (15.2 cm)
12 oz. 19 dwt. 12 gr. (403.5 g)

Stamps: "W.B.HEYER" in roman letters, in an uneven rectangle, struck once on underside of body of each piece; "H&N" in roman letters, in a rectangle, struck once on underside of each piece.

Engraved on side of body: (a) "To Mary Hosack/ Given by Friend/ E Gracie" in script. *Engraved on opposite side of body:* "MH[?]".

Description: all pieces have squat bodies, rectangular in plan, with rounded corners, with plain bulbous lower bodies connected to upper bodies by a die-rolled decorative band; both sections raised. Circular flaring pedestals on rounded rectangular stepped bases. Die-rolled bands around foot and upper bodies, ½" wide, in pattern of opposed acanthus leaves and fleurs-de-lis on a stippled ground; band around rims in pattern of anthemia on stippled ground, ¼" wide except 3/16" on creamer. All lids have high flattened domes topped with heavily cast acanthus leaves and cast eagle finials; lids flush mounted with 5-segment hinges.

(a) Hot water pot and teapot: S-curve spouts with lower portion seamed, upper portion cast in design of acanthus leaves, feathers, and a duck's head. C-curve handles with central portion circular in section and seamed; upper portion cast with thumbpiece in overall pattern of acanthus leaves; lower portion cast in acanthus leaf pattern and terminating in an acorn drop; 2 ivory insulators and 4 silver pins. Rounded rectangular lids curve down before rising to dome. Centerpunch on underside of each body.

(c) Sugar bowl and lid: 2 hollow C-curve handles, seamed vertically, with acanthus leaves on lower half of handles and upper tips, which are not attached to body. Centerpunch on underside of body.

(d) Creamer: Upper body seamed and boldly incurved before flaring widely at rim; low on sides, higher at handle, extended in front for pouring lip; centerpunch on underside of body; single handle as on sugar bowl.

Spectrographic analysis:

	SILVER	COPPER	LEAD	GOLD
(a) Hot water pot				
BODY	90.0	9.6	0.29	0.05
HANDLE	91.1	8.5	0.25	0.02
SPOUT	90.5	9.1	0.23	0.02
LID	91.2	8.5	0.23	0.04
BODY BAND	93.0	6.7	0.21	0.07
(b) Teapot				
BODY	92.1	7.5	0.16	0.09
HANDLE	91.0	8.4	0.18	0.12
SPOUT	93.3	6.2	0.17	0.13
LID	91.1	8.4	0.20	0.14
BODY BAND	93.0	5.1	0.97	0.11

	SILVER	COPPER	LEAD	GOLD
(c) Sugar bowl and lid				
BODY	90.7	8.9	0.22	0.09
HANDLE	92.5	7.0	0.22	0.09
LID	93.2	6.4	0.22	0.11
BODY BAND	92.5	6.7	0.16	0.10
(d) Creamer				
BODY	91.6	7.8	0.30	0.08
HANDLE	94.5	5.0	0.17	0.10
BODY BAND	92.7	6.5	0.32	0.08

History: Mary Eddy Hosack (d. 1824) was the adopted daughter of Caspar Wistar and second wife of Dr. David Hosack (1769–1835), the eminent physician, botanist, teacher, and author. They were married in 1797 and had 9 children, 1 of whom was Alexander Eddy Hosack, an eminent surgeon. The senior Hosack created a botanical garden at his summer home in Hyde Park, N.Y. He was a founder of the New-York Historical Society and its president from 1820 to 1828. His portrait by Thomas Sully is at Winterthur.

Provenance: Gracie and Hosack families of New York City; Robert Carlen, art dealer, Philadelphia.

References: DAB, s.v. "Hosack, David."

66.71.1–.4 Museum purchase from Robert Carlen, 1966

❦ 214
STRAINER, ca. 1820

DIAM. bowl 3 1/16" (7.8 cm), w. 8 5/8" (21.9 cm), H. (with handles) 1 1/8" (2.9 cm)
1 oz. 10 dwt. 9 gr. (47.2 g)

Stamps: "W.B.HEYER" in roman letters, in a rectangle, struck once on underside of each handle.

Description: shallow circular raised bowl with applied molded rim and a secondary molding below. Body pierced with drilled holes in pattern of a 6-point star with a swirl in the center with double rows of holes arced from star points; 2 cast handles with wavy sides tapering to narrow rounded ends; teardrop void at end of each handle; handle attached to body at 3

points with voids between; outside attachments formed into scrolls; each handle drilled with holes in pattern of a conjoined "ID" (or "DI").

Spectrographic analysis:

	SILVER	COPPER	LEAD	GOLD
BODY	84.3	15.3	0.34	0.01
HANDLE	91.7	7.9	0.24	0.10

Provenance: Robert Ensko, Inc., New York City, sold to H. F. du Pont, March 1930.

Comments: Stylistically the strainer harks back to the eighteenth century.

57.829 Gift of H. F. du Pont, 1965

HH

Unidentified maker
New York, New York, or Hudson Valley

There are three versions of the "HH" stamp. Henry Hurst (1665–1717), the Swedish immigrant silversmith in Boston, used two separate *H*'s in an oval, and so he is an unlikely candidate as the author of the beaker described in the following entry. A conjoined "HH" stamp is found on only two pieces: a tumbler at Yale University Art Gallery engraved with the Van Schaick coat of arms and the beaker in no. 215. The style of the engraving on the tumbler indicates that it was made around 1700. The "HH" stamp on the tumbler is similar in character but not identical to that on the beaker. A search of both American and Dutch records has failed to reveal the identity of HH.

References: Rice, *Albany Silver*, p. 2. Buhler, *American Silver*, pp. 76–78. Buhler and Hood, *American Silver*, no. 992.

215
BEAKER, ca. 1690

H. 8" (20.3 cm), DIAM. rim 5 ⁵⁄₁₆" (13.5 cm), DIAM. base 3 ³⁄₁₆" (8.1 cm)
16 oz. 5 dwt. 6 gr. (505.8 g)

Stamps: "HH" in conjoined roman letters, in a square, struck twice on underside of body.

Engraved on outside of body: band of vines, leaves, and blossoms broken by 3 equidistant winged cherub heads below rim between border of double-incised lines. Beneath each cherub's head is an oval medallion portrait flanked by caryatidlike figures whose lower bodies terminate in C scrolls; pendant cluster of fruit hangs from each pair of C scrolls. Each of the 3 medallions contains a standing female figure displaying different attributes: (1) holds a bird in her right hand; (2) holds a child in her arms while another child stands next to her; and (3) holds a cross in her right hand. Between the medallions and suspended from the border below rim are pendant clusters of fruit and ribbons. Below each of these, near the base, is a bird, each one different: (1) is perched on a branch and eating from its tip; (2) is perched on a branch and reaching for a flying insect; and (3) is perched on a branch and looking back.

Engraved on underside of body: "I∗L" in shaded roman letters; "Jan: Lansÿn" in script.

Description: tall circular raised body, lower portion cylindrical, upper portion gently flared; plain rim; flat bottom; centerpunch on underside. Beneath reeded base molding is a bold molding that serves as a footring.

Spectrographic analysis:

	SILVER	COPPER	LEAD	GOLD
BODY SIDE	89.5	9.7	0.24	0.07
UNDERSIDE	91.8	7.6	0.22	0.02

History: Owned by Jan Lansing of Albany, who, according to Norman Rice, bequeathed the beaker to his daughter Engletie. She married Evert Wendell (1681–1750), a lawyer and com-

missioner of Indian Affairs from 1724 to 1734. The beaker descended through the Wendell family. (For other silver owned by them, see no. 265.) A Jan Lansing appears in Albany records for the 1670s and 1680s. He may have been a shopkeeper or merchant, for among the debts left by Nicholas van Renselaer when he died in 1678 was 13:12 florins "To Jan Lansingh for bread and candles." He was one of the burghers who consented February 17, 1680/81, to call a new minister and who later contributed to his support. Court records for 1689/90 reveal a Jan Lansingh charged (with 7 others) with having planted "a scandalous withered tree equipped with a straw wreath, from which hung a dried bladder with beans to which dried beaver testicles were attached" in front of the commissary's house but intended to embarrass one Gabriel Thomson, bridegroom. The offending object was referred to as a Maypole, and the court declared that such mischief should not be tolerated. As one of the lesser offenders, Lansingh paid a fine of 25 gilders and was warned not to do it again. Whether this is the Jan Lansing who owned the beaker, or his son, cannot be determined.

Provenance: Philip W. Birdseye, Utica, N.Y.

Comments: With images based on engravings in Dutch emblem books, this handsome beaker is 1 of a number of similar examples made in both Holland and the New York–New Jersey area. The tall beaker was used in the Dutch Reformed Church for serving communion wine. The 3 medallion portraits are allegorical representations of Faith, Hope, and Charity. The First Church of Albany owns 2 beakers with similar engraved decoration. One was made in Holland in 1660; the second, made to match the first, was created in New York City by Ahasuerus Hendricks in 1678. The tall beaker is 1 of the oldest silver forms, having been widely used in the ancient world.

References: Rice, *Albany Silver*, fig. 137, for beaker with similar engraving. *Minutes of the Court of Albany, Rensselaerwyck, and Schenectady*, 3 vols. (Albany: University of the State of New York, 1928), 2:288–90; 3:52, 73, 372. See also Edna Donnell, "A Seventeenth-Century New York Silver Beaker with Decoration from a Dutch Pattern Book," *Bulletin of the Metropolitan Museum of Art* 33, no. 2 (February 1938): 47–50.

58.95.1 Museum purchase from Philip W. Birdseye, 1958, with funds donated by H. F. du Pont

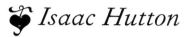

Isaac Hutton

1766–1855
Albany, New York, w. 1790–1817

Isaac Hutton was baptized in the New York Dutch Church, and we know little else about his early years. He was possibly the grandson of silversmith John Hutton. Isaac's parents were George and Anna Maria (Viele) Hutton of New York City. He first appears in Albany in 1790, keeping a jewelry store. His brother George was his business partner for many years. He took Gosen Van Schaick as an apprentice in 1792. Isaac is identified as the engraver of four copperplates in *A New History of the Grecian States* and "The Plan of the City of Albany," both published in 1794. In 1797 Hutton advertised for "Three silversmiths who may have constant employment in a very convenient shop and receive prompt pay" at 32 Market Street. Hutton was deeply involved with many local organizations, including the Albany Waterworks and the Society for the Promotion of Useful Arts, the latter being the predecessor of the Albany Institute of History and Art. He went bankrupt in 1817, probably marking the end of his silvermithing business.

Isaac Hutton was one of those entrepreneurs who started out making silver but who quickly became a merchandiser of all sorts of goods. One of his suppliers was Abraham Dubois of Philadelphia, who, in 1804, wrote to George Hutton, giving him prices on trumpets, clarinets, and "hautboys" (oboes). A large quantity of Hutton's silver survives, but much of it was probably made under his direction rather than by him personally. He was commissioned to design plate for use as prizes. A teapot by Hutton, now in the Metropolitan Museum of Art, was awarded by the Society for the Promotion of Useful Arts in 1813 to Nicholas Smith of Saratoga County for "the Second best Specimen of Woolen Cloth." Hutton also made a pair of communion dishes that Philip S. Van Rensselaer, mayor of Albany, presented to Saint Peter's Church in 1799. Although he made a wide variety of forms, Hutton is probably best known for his beakers and neoclassical hollowware. Of twenty-one pieces with the cypher of Elizabeth Van Rensselaer in the Glen-Sanders collection, Colonial Williamburg, nineteen were made by Hutton. He made, chased, and gilded a gold watch case in 1812 for Garret Van Schaick, cashier of Merchant's National Bank, Albany.

References: John Davis Hatch, "Isaac Hutton, Silversmith: Citizen of Albany," *Antiques* 47, no. 1 (January 1945): 32–35. Jones, *Old Silver*, p. 3. Rice, *Albany Silver*, pp. 37–46, 73, 74. Invoice to Van Schaick, 68x89, Downs collection, Winterthur Library. Abraham Dubois Letterbook, 1803–16, Hagley Museum and Library, Wilmington, Del.

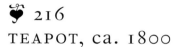

216
TEAPOT, ca. 1800

H. 6 ½" (16.5 cm), w. 11 ⅞" (30.2 cm)
17 oz. 8 dwt. 14 gr. (542.1 g)

Stamps: "HUTTON" in roman letters, in a rectangle, struck twice on underside of body; 2 unidentified stamps (possibly eagles) on body near handle.

Engraved on side of body (left of spout): "AMLG" in foliate script, in a shield suspended from a bowknot, crossed leafy branches below, dart motif swags above and on sides. *Engraved on opposite side:* plain shield containing a swastikalike device under a crescent and knight's helmet. Bright-cut dart and rollerwork border around upper and lower body and on rim of lid.

Description: fluted oval in plan, seamed vertically at handle end, flat bottom, incurved plain raised shoulders; no centerpunch. Raised flush-mounted oval lid, domed in center, with cast urn finial attached through lid by screw and nut; 3-segment hinge with pin penetrating sides. Straight tapered spout, oval in section, mounted at rakish angle, seamed on upper side; 2 seamed handle sockets, plain except for rollerwork next to handle. C-curve hardwood handle with sprig and scroll; 2 silver pins.

Spectrographic analysis:

	SILVER	COPPER	LEAD	GOLD
BODY SIDE	89.0	10.4	0.25	0.11
UNDERSIDE	96.1	3.4	0.25	0.13
LID	93.4	6.2	0.15	0.07
SPOUT	88.6	11.0	0.20	0.10

Provenance: Charles K. Davis, Fairfield, Conn.

Comments: An extraordinarily successful version of the neoclassical teapot form.

References: Rice, *Albany Silver*, fig. 67, for similar teapot by Hutton.

67.1444 Bequest of H. F. du Pont, 1969

❧ 217 a–d
TEA SERVICE, ca. 1815

(a) Teapot: H. 8" (20.3 cm), w. 12 ⅞" (32.7 cm) 25 oz. 12 dwt. 4 gr. (794.6 g)
(b) Creamer: H. 5 ⅞" (14.9 cm), w. 6 ⅝" (16.8 cm)
9 oz. 18 dwt. 7 gr. (307.7 g)
(c) Sugar bowl and lid: H. 7 ½" (19.1 cm), w. 9 ³⁄₁₆" (23.3 cm)
20 oz. 16 dwt. 7 gr. (645.9 g)
(d) Waste bowl: H. 4 ⅞" (12.4 cm), w. 6 ½" (16.5 cm)
13 oz. 16 dwt. 2 gr. (428.4 g)

Stamps: "HUTTON" in roman letters, in a rectangle, struck once on underside of each body, accompanied by stamps of an eagle, in an oval, struck twice on (a) and (c), 4 times on (b) and (d).

Engraved on panel on each body: "HCC" in foliate script. *Scratched on underside of body:* (c) "367"; (d) "357".

Description: raised bulbous lower bodies, oval in plan, no centerpunches. Upper bodies consist of plain, flat, horizontal panels angled to form an elongated octagon in plan; incurved necks. Bodies mounted on stepped pedestals, rectangular in plan with rounded corners and 4 ball feet.

(a) Teapot: plain partial lid with rectangular dome and oval cast finial; flush-mounted 3-segment hinge; circular vent. S-curve seamed spout cut away on upper front. Sharply angled hardwood handle with sprig attached to plain silver sockets with 2 silver pins.

(b) Creamer: neck curves up and out in front to form wide pouring lip; neck rises in back to meet reeded, sharply angled strap handle; rolled rim.

(c) Sugar bowl and lid: lid similar to teapot but friction fit and no vent; 2 reeded strap handles, both sharply angled.

(d) Waste bowl: circular lower body with centerpunch on underside; applied reeded rim above flat panels; raised, circular, stepped pedestal on reeded footring with 4 ball feet.

Spectrographic analysis:

	SILVER	COPPER	GOLD	LEAD
(a) Teapot				
UPPER BODY	91.8	7.9	0.24	0.05
LOWER BODY	91.4	8.4	0.19	0.05
UNDERSIDE	96.3	3.4	0.25	0.06
FOOT	91.0	8.7	0.23	0.06
SPOUT	95.6	4.1	0.28	0.04
LID	91.2	8.5	0.23	0.05

	SILVER	COPPER	GOLD	LEAD
(b) Creamer				
UPPER BODY	94.1	5.7	0.21	0.03
LOWER BODY	90.9	9.1	0.04	0.02
UNDERSIDE	95.1	4.7	0.18	0.05
FOOT	87.9	11.9	0.19	0.05
HANDLE	92.6	7.3	0.10	0.04
(c) Sugar bowl and lid				
UPPER BODY	94.2	5.6	0.14	0.04
LOWER BODY	92.0	7.7	0.19	0.04
UNDERSIDE	95.4	4.3	0.20	0.02
FOOT	92.1	7.7	0.14	0.03
HANDLE	94.3	5.4	0.18	0.05
LID	92.1	7.8	0.05	0.04
(d) Waste bowl				
BODY SIDE	91.3	8.6	0.11	0.01
UNDERSIDE	92.8	7.1	0.13	0.03
RIM	91.3	8.6	0.15	0.03
FOOT	93.1	6.7	0.17	0.03

Provenance: Carl Kossack, North Haven, Conn.

Comments: Hutton made teapots and related vessels in many variations of the oblong style.

90.42.1–4 Gift of Carl Kossack, 1990

❦ 218

BEAKER, ca. 1805

H. 3 ½" (8.9 cm), DIAM. rim 3 ¼" (8.3 cm)
3 oz. 17 dwt. 19 gr. (120.7 g)

Stamps: "HUTTON" in roman letters, in a rectangle, struck once on underside, accompanied by an eagle, in an oval, struck twice.

Engraved on side: armorial device consisting of a shield with 2 gates above a horizontal band and 1 below; *crest:* sheaf of wheat on a heraldic band; *motto on ribbon below:* "NE PARCAS/ NEC/ SPERNAS" in roman letters.

Description: raised circular vessel with gently bulging sides, incurved neck, flared plain rim, and slightly domed bottom; centerpunch on underside.

Spectrographic analysis:

	SILVER	COPPER	LEAD	GOLD
BODY SIDE	91.9	7.9	0.12	0.09
UNDERSIDE	95.5	4.3	0.11	0.10

History: Coat of arms, crest, and motto of the Yates family of Albany.

Provenance: John E. Langdon, Toronto.

Comments: Motto translates as "Neither Despair nor Hope." Henry Dawkins, Philadelphia engraver, did a bookplate for Peter Yates using this coat of arms.

References: James H. Halpin, Bronxville, N.Y., to John Langdon, April 28, 1975, Registration Division, Winterthur, for information on the armorial. Bolton, *Bolton's American Armory,* p. 186.

76.295 Gift of John E. Langdon, 1976

❦ 219

BEAKER, ca. 1805

H. 3 ¹³⁄₁₆" (9.7 cm), DIAM. rim 3 ⅜" (8.6 cm)
4 oz. 14 dwt. 10 gr. (146.5 g)

Stamps: "HUTTON" in roman letters, in a rectangle, struck once on underside, accompanied by an eagle, in an oval, struck once.

Engraved on side of body: "AMC" in script.

Description: seamed circular vessel with gently bulging sides, incurved neck, flared rim with applied molding, and flat inset bottom; no centerpunch.

Spectrographic analysis:

	SILVER	COPPER	LEAD	GOLD
BODY SIDE	89.6	10.0	0.24	0.11

Provenance: Marshall P. Blankarn, New York City.

References: Fennimore, *Silver and Pewter,* no. 170.

78.150 Gift of Marshall P. Blankarn, 1978

❦ 220 a–o

SPOONS, ca. 1800

(a–h, n) L. 5 ³⁄₁₆"–5 ⅝" (13.2–14.3 cm)
5 dwt. 2 gr.–9 dwt. 14 gr. (9.2–14.9 g)
(i–m, o) L. 8 ¾"–9 ³⁄₁₆" (22.2–23.3 cm)
1 oz. 12 dwt. 14 gr.–2 oz. 1 dwt. 19 gr. (50.6–64.9 g)

Stamps: "HUTTON" in roman letters, in a rectangle, struck once on back of each handle; "ALBANY" in roman letters, in a rectangle, struck once on back of handle (o).

Engraved on front of handle: (a, b) "IE" in foliate script, in a bright-cut medallion with diagonal feather-cut down the handle; (c) "LB" in foliate script; (d) "CE" in crude shaded roman letters, in a bright-cut medallion with pendant drop; (e) "NRVS" in foliate script, in a bright-cut medallion with pendant drop; (f) "SWB" in foliate script, in a bright-cut medallion with pendant drop and featheredge border down the handle; (g) "MS" in crude shaded roman letters, in a bright-cut medallion with pendant drop; (h) "NRVS" in foliate script, in a bright-cut medallion with pendant drop; (i) and (j) "MMT" in foliate script, in a bright-cut medallion with floral pendant drop; (k) "A/ I.F" in shaded roman letters, in a bright-cut medallion with pendant drop; (l) "M/ SG" in crude shaded roman letters; (m) "RH" in shaded roman letters, in a bright-cut medallion with pendant drop; (n) "HMTE" in foliate script, in a bright-cut medallion with pendant drop; (o) "FG" in foliate script, in a bright-cut medallion.

Description: oval bowls on all except (a), (b), and (n), which have pointed oval bowls; incised drops on bowls (a–d), (i), (k), and (n); swage-formed drops on (e), (f), (h), (j), (m), and (o); combination of incised and swage-formed drops on (g) and (l). Downturned pointed handles on (a), (b), (d), (f), (m), and (o); coffin-end handles on (c) and (l); rounded downturned handles on (e), (g–k), and (n).

Spectrographic analysis: Silver content ranges from 86.5 to 92.0 percent.

History: (n) Initials probably refer to Hermanus Ten Eyck, H. F. du Pont's great-grandfather on his mother's side.

Provenance: (n) Probably owned in the Ten Eyck family and inherited by H. F. du Pont. All others, Mr. and Mrs. Stanley B. Ineson, New York City; Mr. and Mrs. Alfred E. Bissell, Wilmington, Del.

References: Belden, *Marks of American Silversmiths,* pp. 243–44.

(a, c–m, o) 62.240.754, .348–.352, .681, .1207.1, .2, .1208–.1210, .1212 Gift of Mr. and Mrs. Alfred E. Bissell, 1962–63; (b) 68.28 Gift of Mr. and Mrs. Alfred E. Bissell, 1968; (n) 70.1265.1 Bequest of H. F. du Pont, 1969

Cornelius Kierstede

1674/75–1757
New York, New York, w. 1696–1704,
1706–22
Albany, New York, w. 1704–6
New Haven, Connecticut,
w. ca. 1724–ca. 1754
Bergen, New Jersey

Cornelius Kierstede, son of Dr. Hans Kierstede, "chyurgeon," and Jannetje Lockermans Kierstede, was baptized January 5, 1675; it is uncertain whether he was born late in 1674 or early in 1675. He is recorded as a freeman in both 1698 and 1702. (His father, grandfather, and brother were all named Hans Kierstede and were all surgeons. His brother Hans, who married Diana Van Schaick, was related by marriage to silversmith Gerrit Onklebag, to whom he bequeathed all but 5s. of his estate.) Cornelius married Sara Ellsworth in 1703; she was probably his second wife. In spite of his stays elsewhere, he is primarily known as a New York City silversmith whose work ranks with the best. Kierstede made a two-handled covered cup, owned by the Art Institute of Chicago, that is very similar to one by Jurian Blanck, Jr. (no. 152). He also made the magnificent columnar candlesticks, snuffer, and stand now in the Metropolitan Museum of Art. Created for the Schuyler family of Albany, the set is decorated with chinoiserie engraving, which is exceedingly rare in American silver. Notable commissions in Connecticut included a paneled bowl presented by the Yale College Class of 1746 to tutor Thomas Darling and communion silver for the church in Milford and two churches in New Haven. Exactly when he went to New Haven is unclear. By 1721 he was involved in a copper mining enterprise there along with James and Peter Ferris. By 1724 he may have been living there, although local records still referred to him as a goldsmith from New York. He spent his final days in Bergen, New Jersey.

References: New Haven Town Records, Ancient Town Records Series, vol. 3 (New Haven: New Haven Colony Historical Society, 1962), p. 466. Howard S. F. Randolph, "The Kierstede Family," NYG&BR 65, no. 3 (July 1934): 224–33. Gerald W. R. Ward, "The Dutch and the English Traditions in American Silver: Cornelius Kierstede," in Francis J. Puig and Michael Conforti, The American Craftsman and the European Tradition, 1620–1820 (Minneapolis: Minneapolis Institute of Arts, 1989), pp. 136–42.

221
TANKARD, ca. 1720

H. 7⅜" (18.7 cm), DIAM. base 5⅝" (14.3 cm),
w. 8¹¹⁄₁₆" (22.1 cm)
34 oz. 2 dwt. 9 gr. (1061.2 g)

Stamps: "CK" in roman letters, in a rectangle, struck once on upper body on each side of handle and once on top of lid.

Engraved on front of body opposite handle: armorial device consisting of lozenge shape divided vertically in center; on the left, a cross with a lozenge in each quarter on a gules ground; on the right, 3 roses with 9 teardrops scattered throughout; lozenge flanked by 2 large curling palmlike leaves with stems tied by a bowknot; a floral wreath, or chaplet, above.

Engraved on back of handle: "S/ R✳I [or R✳J]" (a shaded roman S) in script.

Engraved on top of lid: "RIS" (in a cypher) in a circular border of leaf forms.

Engraved on underside of body: "35=oünse A [?]" in script.

Description: raised circular body with straight tapering sides and flat bottom; 2-step molded rim with wigglework; centerpunch on underside. Applied base molding, flared at bottom, consists of broad concave molding with 2 narrow channels below and 2 above; band of wigglework under 2 more narrow channels; moldings above: a band of cut-card work, each unit consisting of an engraved leaf. Raised circular single-step lid with flat top, crenellated front and rear; centerpunch on top; bezel. Cast ram's horn thumbpiece. Cast 5-segment hinge between bands of wigglework. Raised-and-soldered hollow C-curve handle with cast lion couchant applied to upper handle back; above lion is a leaf form similar to cut-card border but larger; lower end of handle forms a C curve in profile and terminates with a cast putto mask applied to a shield-shape plate; teardrop-shape lower vent and circular upper vent.

Spectrographic analysis:

	SILVER	COPPER	LEAD	GOLD
BODY SIDE	90.3	8.8	0.29	0.19
UNDERSIDE	92.9	6.3	0.25	0.16
BASE MOLDING	90.5	8.5	0.32	0.27
LID	90.2	8.9	0.36	0.15
HANDLE	91.6	7.4	0.40	0.13

History: The coat of arms is taken from John Guillim's *Display of Heraldry*, where it is identified as belonging to "Jane Still, Baroness, Dowager Pile." Attempts to link the tankard with the Sill family of Connecticut have failed to produce any credible evidence, although a Connecticut provenance is likely. The initials "S/ RI" and accompanying cypher remain unidentified.

Provenance: Rockwell Gardner, Stamford, Conn., sold to Charles K. Davis, Fairfield, Conn., May 1951.

Exhibitions: "Silver by Early Connecticut Makers," Wadsworth Atheneum, Hartford, Conn., 1954. "American Silver and Art Treasures," Christie's, London, for the English-Speaking Union, 1960. "New York Silversmiths of the Seventeenth Century," Museum of the City of New York, 1962–63. "Georgian Canada: Conflict and Culture, 1745–1820," Royal Ontario Museum, Toronto, 1984.

Comments: This is the most elegant New York tankard at Winterthur. The cypher probably derives from Joseph Sympson, *Book of Cyphers* (London, 1726). The palmlike leaves tied in a bowknot and the chaplet above are similar in character to those on a caudle cup made by Gerrit Oncklebag (Christie's sale [January 23, 1988], lot 95). Instead of the usual cocoon thumbpiece found on New York tankards, Kierstede used the ram's horn thumbpiece that is associated with New England tankards.

References: American Silver and Art Treasures (London: Christie's for the English-Speaking Union, 1960), p. 97. Davidson, *Colonial Antiques*, p. 105. Fales, *American Silver*, no. 38. Fennimore, "Cornelius Kierstede Tankard," *Silver* 16, no. 3 (May/June 1983): 30–32. Fennimore, *Silver and Pewter*, no. 161. Miller, *New York Silversmiths*, no. 34. Donald Blake Webster, *Georgian Canada: Conflict and Culture, 1745–1820* (Toronto: Royal Ontario Museum, 1984), no. 60.

56.84 Gift of Charles K. Davis, 1956

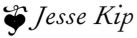

Jesse Kip

1660–1722
New York, New York

Baptized in the Dutch Church in New York City in 1660, Jesse Kip was the fourth son of Jacob Hendrickzen Kip and Maria de la Montagne. Jacob was secretary of the province and served on the council. Jesse married Maria Stevens (or Stevenson) in 1695. He was assessor for the North Ward in 1697, when silversmith Jacob Boelen served as alderman and Ahasureus Hendricks as collector. In 1698 Kip served as collector along with silversmith Gerrit Oncklebag. An indenture of 1696 refers to Kip as a merchant, but a land deed of 1704, discovered by John Marshall Phillips, identifies him as a goldsmith. Between 1709 and 1712, he moved from the city to Newtown, Queens County, Long Island, where he took over the fulling mill that had been owned by his brother Jacobus. His will was proved April 30, 1722.

Only about a dozen pieces of silver by Kip are known. He made two large drinking bowls with caryatid handles, one now in the Henry Ford Museum, Dearborn, Michigan, and one in the Metropolitan Museum of Art. He made a so-called birthday spoon, now at the New-York Historical Society, that was given to Cornelia Duyckinck in 1686 according to the inscription. Three tankards, three sucket forks, a mote spoon, a porringer, a saucepan lid, and, possibly, a teapot round out his surviving work.

References: John Marshall Phillips, "Identifying the Mysterious IK," *Antiques* 44, no. 1 (July 1943): 19–21. Frederic E. Kip, *History of the Kip Family in America* (Boston: Hudson Printing, 1928), pp. 385–86.

222

SUCKET FORK, ca. 1700

L. 5 7⁄16" (13.8 cm)
9 dwt. 7 gr. (14.5 g)

Stamps: "IK" in roman letters, in a rectangle, struck once on back of handle.

Engraved on back of spoon: "VR/ SE" ("VR" conjoined) in script.

Description: combination form with spoon at one end and fork at other end, joined by a straight shaft, rectangular in cross section. Elongated oval bowl with ridged rattail; 3-tine fork. Front: engraved vine and floral pattern on handle; crosshatched lamb's tongue and irregular figure with rays on fork end. Back: engraved vine and floral pattern on handle; featheredge engraving around rattail.

Spectrographic analysis:

	SILVER	COPPER	LEAD	GOLD
SPOON BOWL	88.5	10.4	0.41	0.13
FORK	89.7	9.2	0.41	0.11

History: Initials may refer to Stephen (1707–47) and Elizabeth (Grosbeck) (1710–56) Van Rensselaer, who were married in 1729. Stephen succeeded his brother Jeremiah as lord of the manor of Rensselaerwyck in 1745. Probable line of descent is through their son Stephen (1742–69), who married Catherine Livingston (1745–1810), and their son Gen. Stephen Van Rensselaer (1764–1839).

Provenance: Philip H. Hammerslough, West Hartford, Conn.

Exhibitions: "New York Silversmiths of the Seventeenth Century," Museum of the City of New York, 1962–63. "Remembrance of Patria: Dutch Arts and Culture in Colonial America, 1609–1776," Albany Institute of History and Art, 1986. "The Taste of Power: The Rise of Genteel Dining and Entertaining in Early Washington," The Octagon, Washington, D.C., 1990.

Comments: This is 1 of 3 sucket forks known to have been made by Kip. The other 2, 1 in the Garvan collection at Yale University Art Gallery and 1 at the Museum of the City of New York, are engraved "Maria Van Renslaer," possibly for Maria Van Cortlandt (b. 1680), who married Kiliaen Van Rensselaer (1663–1719) in 1701. Suckets were preserved fruit (plums, grapes, lemons, etc.). Some were wet and served in a syrup, hence the value of both spoon and fork. Gervase Markham, in *The*

English Housewife (1615), advised: "Your preserved fruites shall be disht up first, your Pastes next, your wet suckets after them, then your dried Suckets."

References: George Barton Cutten, "Sucket Forks," *Antiques* 57, no. 6 (June 1950): 440, 441, for general background on the form. *Oxford English Dictionary*, s.v. "sucket." Fennimore, *Silver and Pewter*, no. 34. Hammerslough, *American Silver*, 3:66. Miller, *New York Silversmiths*, no. 47. Blackburn and Piwonka, *Remembrance of Patria*, no. 308. *The Taste of Power: The Rise of Genteel Dining and Entertaining in Early Washington* (Washington, D.C.: The Octagon, 1990), no. 86. Kiliaen Van Rensselaer, *The Van Rensselaer Manor* (Baltimore: Privately printed, 1917).

63.52 Museum purchase from Philip H. Hammerslough, 1963

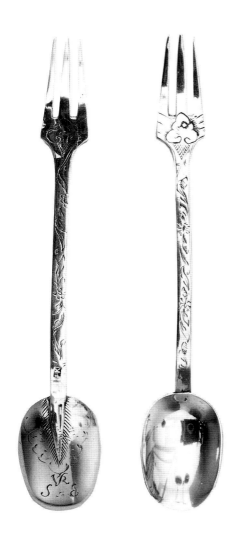

❦ 223
LID, 1685–1710

DIAM. 4 15/16" (12.5 cm), H. 1 11/16" (4.3 cm)
3 oz. 16 dwt. 6 gr. (118.6 g)

Stamps: "IK" in roman letters, in a rectangle, struck once on upper surface next to finial.

Engraved on underside of flange: "P / IC" in roman letters.

Description: raised circular 2-step lid, flat in center with plain flange and applied bezel; centerpunch inside; cast capstan-and-reel finial.

Spectrographic analysis:

SILVER	COPPER	LEAD	GOLD
89.9	9.5	0.32	0.11

History: Said by donor to have been made for John and Catherine Pintard, of New York City, whose initials are engraved on the lid and on the accompanying saucepan by Gerrit Oncklebag (no. 236). Both pieces descended to their son Lewis Pintard.

Provenance: John and Catherine Pintard; Lewis Pintard; Charles Albert Stevens; Mrs. Robert L. Stevens (1947); Mary Stevens Baird, New York City, and Bernardsville, N.J.

Exhibitions: "From Lenape Territory to Royal Province: New Jersey, 1600–1750," New Jersey State Museum, Trenton, 1971. According to the donor both the saucepan and lid were exhibited at Colonial Williamsburg, Fogg Art Museum, Metropolitan Museum of Art, and the New Jersey Historical Society.

References: From Lenape Territory, no. 203. "Some Rarities in American Silver and Gold," *Antiques* 51, no. 1 (January 1947): 48–50. Carolyn Scoon, "Cornelia Duyckinck's Birthday Spoon Inscribed and Dated: August 25, 1686," *New-York Historical Society Quarterly Bulletin* 34, no. 4 (October 1950): 315–17.

76.21b Gift of Mary Stevens Baird, 1976

Bartholomew Le Roux I

ca. 1662–1713
New York, New York

Bartholomew Le Roux I was born in Holland, probably in the early 1660s, and moved with his family to London about 1685. Since he went to New York shortly thereafter, it appears that he was trained in Holland rather than England. In New York he was admitted as a freeman in 1687. In 1688 Le Roux married Geertruyd Van Rollegom, whose sister married Tobias Stoughtenberg, Sr., father of the silversmith of the same name. The couple lived in the West Ward, where Bartholomew is listed as assessor, assistant, and collector from 1699 to 1711. He was designated in 1702 as one of "four or six Able Citizens to be the watch and Bellmen of this City." Le Roux witnessed the wills of several prominent New Yorkers. His sons John and Charles became silversmiths, as did his grandson Bartholomew (who is generally referred to as Bartholomew Le Roux II to distinguish him from his grandfather). Peter Van Dyck served his apprenticeship with Le Roux and married Le Roux's daughter Rachel.

Le Roux's most impressive accomplishment in silver is the large two-handled cup owned by the Minneapolis Institute of Arts and engraved with the coat of arms of the Marquess of Winchester. Its sides and lid are heavily chased in leaf patterns resembling those on the Jurian Blanck covered cup, no. 152. Four sucket forks by Le Roux are at Historic Deerfield, and a large bowl and elaborate caster are at Yale University Art Gallery.

References: Buhler and Hood, *American Silver*, nos. 564, 565. Flynt and Fales, *Heritage Foundation*, fig. 53. *Minutes of the Common Council.* Francis J. Puig et al., *English and American Silver in the Collection of the Minneapolis Institute of Arts* (Minneapolis: By the institute, 1989), no. 180. Von Khrum, *Silversmiths*, p. 79.

224
STRAINER, ca. 1730

DIAM. bowl 3 ⅞" (9.8 cm), w. 4 ⅜" (11.1 cm), H. 1 ¹¹⁄₁₆" (4.3 cm)
2 oz. 9 dwt. 15 gr. (77.2 g)

Stamps: "BLR" ("LR" conjoined) in roman letters, in an oval, struck once on inner arm of clip.

Engraved on shield (outer arm of clip): armorial device consisting of demi-lion rampant holding a staff with a coronet and pennant, all on a heraldic band.

Description: raised circular shallow bowl with applied molded rim; bottom of bowl pierced with 81 crosslets arranged in a square bordered by a single row of drilled holes; sides of bowl pierced at 4 compass points with symmetrical pattern of French curves, with drilled holes in center, alternating with stylized fleurs-de-lis with central drilled hole. Bar clip attached to side by C-curve upper section; outer arm in form of a shield.

Spectrographic analysis:

	SILVER	COPPER	GOLD	LEAD
BOWL SIDE	89.1	9.8	0.50	0.30
HANDLE	90.9	8.1	0.51	0.24

History: Tradition of ownership in the Bayard family of New York, according to donor. Crest identified in *Fairbairn's Crests* as belonging to the Nicholson family.

Provenance: Mary Stevens Baird, New York City and Bernardsville, N.J., whose great-grandmother was a Bayard. Owned in 1947 by Mrs. Robert L. Stevens.

Exhibitions: "From Lenape Territory to Royal Province: New Jersey 1600–1750," New Jersey State Museum, Trenton, 1971. According to donor, it was also exhibited at Colonial Williamsburg, Fogg Art Museum, Metropolitan Museum of Art, and the New Jersey Historical Society.

References: "Some Rarities in American Silver and Gold," *Antiques* 51, no. 1 (January 1947): 48–50. *From Lenape Territory*, no. 135. James Fairbairn, *Fairbairn's Crests of the Families of Great Britain and Ireland*, rev. Laurence Butters, ed. Joseph MacLaren (Edinburgh and London, 1860): 1:353, 2: pl. 81.

76.221 Gift of Mary Stevens Baird, 1976

❦ *Bartholomew Le Roux II*

1717–63
New York, New York

The son of Charles Le Roux and Catharina (or Magdalena?) Beekman, Bartholomew Le Roux was baptized in the New York Dutch Church, October 30, 1717. Charles Le Roux (1689–1745) had an illustrious career as a New York goldsmith, engraver, and die sinker. He made freedom boxes for the city of New York to give as presentation pieces. His son is referred to as Bartholomew Le Roux II to distinguish him from his grandfather, goldsmith Bartholomew Le Roux I, for whom he was named. Bartholomew II was admitted as a freeman in 1739.

Le Roux lacks the high visibility of his father and grandfather in New York City records, but he is recorded as colonel commandant of the Second Battalion of militia in 1759 and muster master for Dutchess County in 1760. Two pairs of silver candlesticks of his make were reported stolen in 1757 from "the House of Mr. Jacob Franks." Le Roux made the usual variety of mid eighteenth-century forms. A cann surfaced at Christie's in 1990 that is heavily engraved with panels of biblical scenes and winged heads and is signed "Ioseph Leddel fculp/ 1750." The Detroit Institute of Arts owns a set of three casters, and the New-York Historical Society has a pair of canns.

References: NYHS Collections: vol. 18 (1885) *Burghers and Freemen*, p. 139; vol. 24 (1891) *New York Muster Rolls*, pp. 259, 521; vol. 30 (1897) *Abstracts of Wills*, p. 223. Christie's (October 19, 1990), lot 100. Gottesman, *Arts and Crafts, 1726–76*, p. 51. Von Khrum, *Silversmiths*, p. 79.

❦ 225
TWO-HANDLED CUP AND LID, ca. 1745

H. (with lid) 13 ½" (34.3 cm), w. 11 ⅝" (29.5 cm), DIAM. rim 6 ¹¹⁄₁₆" (17.0 cm), H. lid 5 ⅝" (14.3 cm), DIAM. lid 7 ³⁄₁₆" (18.3 cm)
81 oz. 6 dwt. 5 gr. (2529.0 g)

Stamps: "BLR" ("LR" conjoined) in roman letters, in an oval, struck twice on underside of body. Part of another strike (with same "R") adjoins the 2 stamps.

Description: raised circular vase form with nearly straight sides and rounded bottom; slightly angled applied molded rim; applied molded midband; centerpunch on underside. Short incurved pedestal on cast stepped foot; 2 hollow cast double–C-curve handles; acanthus leaf, sprig, and scroll on upper handle; double scrolls and sprig on lower handle; seamed vertically. Raised circular stepped-and-domed lid with hollow cast finial (with stepped base, pedestal, bell, and knop); bezel applied to seamed flange; centerpunch inside.

Spectrographic analysis:

	SILVER	COPPER	LEAD	GOLD
BODY	91.8	7.8	0.23	0.17
HANDLE	93.1	6.4	0.26	0.23
LID	91.2	8.5	0.23	0.10
FINIAL	90.6	8.9	0.30	0.22

History: The first owner was probably Gulian Verplanck (1698–1751), who married Mary Crommelin (b. 1712), the daughter of an Amsterdam merchant. Gulian and Mary Verplanck lived in his house on Wall Street in New York City. They also owned a gambrel-roof house in Fishkill, N.Y., called Mount Gulian where, in 1783, the Society of the Cincinnati was formed. Mount Gulian burned in 1931. Gulian Verplanck was a merchant, active in trade with the West Indies and Holland, and a member of the New York Assembly. He bequeathed to his wife Mary all the "household furniture, jewels, plate, etc. and four Negro slaves together with an annuity of £200 and the use of the rents and profits of my house in Wall street wherein I now live . . . until my son [Samuel] shall attain the age of twenty-three." Samuel inherited the bequest and went on to become a wealthy importer and banker. The cup descended in Samuel's line.

Provenance: Gulian Verplanck and Mary Crommelin; their son Samuel Verplanck; eventually to Elizabeth Knevels, who sold it in 1941 to Gebelein Silversmiths, Boston; sold to H. F. du Pont, November 1966.

Comments: The heaviest piece of silver in the Winterthur collection and certainly one of noble design, the cup has posed some questions but nothing to seriously question its validity as a fine example of early American silver. The absence of an armorial device or inscription seems strange for a form that is usually a presentation piece, but the Art Institute of Chicago owns a similar cup by Myer Myers, also with no engraving. The highly buffed surface and the hint of other stamps have raised suspicions. Yet, the alloy is absolutely correct for American silver of the period, and there is no reason to doubt the maker's stamp. It also has a history of ownership in a distinguished American family.

References: Louise C. Belden, "The Verplanck Cup," *Antiques* 92, no. 6 (December 1967): 840–42. William Edward Verplanck, *The History of Abraham Isaacse Verplanck and His Male Descendants in America* (Fishkill Landing, N.Y.: J. W. Spaight, 1892).

66.127 Bequest of H. F. du Pont, 1969

Frederick Marquand

1799–1882
New York, New York, w. ca. 1820
Savannah, Georgia, w. 1820–26
New York, New York, w. 1826–39

Frederick Marquand's father, Isaac, had extensive business interests in New York and Savannah, and Frederick's early years were spent in Georgia. He learned silversmithing in his father's firms, probably in both cities. In 1820 he returned to Savannah, where he became the partner of Josiah Penfield, his cousin. He remained there until 1826, when he moved back to New York City and established himself at 166 Broadway under his own name, according to George Barton Cutten. Paul von Khrum found him in New York City directories at 166 Broadway, 1824–32, and at 181 Broadway, 1833–39, both times listed as a jeweler. A billhead of 1824 specifies "F. Marquand, successor to E. Barton & Co." as "Manufacturer of Jewelry, Silver Plate, Spoons, &&." (Erastus Barton & Co. is listed at 155 Broadway, 1814–17, 1819, and at 166 Broadway, 1820–23.) For a brief period around 1832, the firm was, first, Marquand & Brother and shortly thereafter Marquand & Brothers (Frederick, Isaac, and Henry), but by 1833 it was Marquand &

Company. The last change reflected the addition of William Black and Henry Ball, former apprentices, to the firm. Frederick and Henry Marquand withdrew in 1839 to pursue lucrative careers in real estate and banking. With the addition of yet another partner, the company became Ball, Tompkins & Black, billing itself as successor to Marquand & Company.

Frederick Marquand was a trained silversmith, but one suspects that he spent little time at the bench. Following in his father's footsteps, he had an entrepreneurial spirit that sought to maximize profits no matter where they lay. As a result, his mercantile pursuits made him a rich man. One of his many benefactions was Marquand Chapel at Yale University, given in memory of his wife. Yale owns a portrait bust of Marquand by Edward Sheffield Bartholomew, signed and dated 1856.

References: George Barton Cutten, *The Silversmiths of Georgia, Together with Watchmakers and Jewelers, 1733 to 1850* (Savannah, Ga.: Pigeonhole Press, 1958), pp. 85–90. Katharine Gross Farnham and Vallie Huger Efird, "Early Silversmiths and the Silver Trade in Georgia," *Antiques* 99, no. 3 (March 1971): 380–85. Invoice dated 1824, 76x453, Downs collection, Winterthur Library. *New York State Silversmiths*, pp. 122–23. Von Khrum, *Silversmiths*, p. 86. *Yale University Portrait Index, 1701–1951* (New Haven: Yale University Press, 1951), p. 74.

226 WINE SYPHON, ca. 1830

L. 22 ³⁄₁₆" (56.4 cm), w. 6" (15.2 cm)
13 oz. 3 dwt. 19 gr. (410.3 g)

Stamps: "F.M." in roman letters, in a rectangle, struck once on thumbscrew of cock.

Description: inverted U-shape tube with cylindrical pump attached to 1 side; sides of *U* formed by tubing; top of *U* formed by octagonal tubing joined on each end by double-reel castings. Lower end of shorter tube perforated with 8 holes on sides and capped on end; lower end of longer tube has cylindrical cock and scalloped thumbscrew. Pump attached to longer tube by a plate at upper end, abutting tube at lower end; small tube connects lower end of pump with main tube just above cock; pump plunger consists of a solid silver rod, lower end with leather (or cork) seal between 2 discs; upper end of plunger threaded and screwed into ivory ball-and-reel finial.

Spectrographic analysis:

	SILVER	COPPER	LEAD	GOLD
PUMP	89.3	9.8	0.42	0.20
LONG TUBE	91.7	7.6	0.31	0.13
SHORT TUBE	91.5	7.9	0.38	0.12
THUMBSCREW	92.6	6.7	0.37	0.15

Provenance: Robert Ensko, Inc., New York City, sold to H. F. du Pont, August 1941.

Comments: A nearly identical wine syphon by Marquand was advertised by Hinda Kohn in *Antiques* 125, no. 1 (January 1984): 173.

References: Fales, *American Silver*, no. 132. Fennimore, *Silver and Pewter*, no. 46. Kurt M. Semon, "Small but Useful American Silver," in Kurt M. Semon, ed., *A Treasury of Old Silver* (New York: Robert M. McBride, 1947), pp. 76–78.

61.651 Gift of H. F. du Pont, 1965

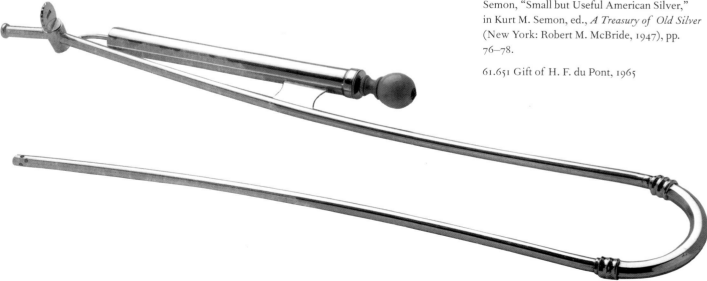

❦ 227
GOLD MEDAL, 1832–33

H. 6 5/16" (16.8 cm), W. 4 11/16" (11.9 cm), D. 7/16" (1.1 cm)
7 oz. 6 dwt. (226.6 g)

Stamps: None; Marquand & Brothers is the documented maker. See *History.*

Engraved on applied oval panels on front of medal: bust portraits of George Washington and Marquis de Lafayette. *Engraved shield quartered (clockwise from lower left):* (1) coat of arms of the city of New York consisting of windmill blades, 2 barrels, and 2 beavers; (2) variant of United States flag consisting of stars and stripes; (3) arms of the state of New York consisting of sun rising over mountains with water in foreground; and (4) "NYSA" (sideways) in script, on a field of gules, in the center a smaller shield sable with initials "NG" in script.

Engraved on C scroll, bottom front: "PRO•PAT-RIA•ET•GLORIA•" in roman letters. *Engraved on partial globe near top:* lines of latitude and longitude and squiggles suggesting continents plus inscription "N/ AMERICA" on left and "FRANCE" on right, both in roman letters. *Engraved on back of medal:* "THE/ National Guard/ 27th New York State Artillery,/ TO/ La Fayette,/ Centennial Anniversary/ of the Birth Day of/ Washington/ New York/ 22d February/ 1832" in script, gothic, and roman letters.

Description: cartouche-shape main body formed by 4 C scrolls for the upper half and 1 large C scroll for the bottom half. Flanking bust portraits are pairs of flags with spear points that extend beyond the edge of the medal; above flags on left are 2 spears and a pistol; above flags on right are 2 swords and an unidentified implement. The portraits are encircled by a wreath of stylized leaves and acorns on the left and a laurel on the right. Scallop shell at upper center with dependent fasces; stylized shell and leaves

at bottom. The main body of the medal is surmounted by a partial globe supporting a free-standing spread-winged eagle. Applied to plain back surface are 2 circular eyes that hold loops for attaching a ribbon for wearing. Accompanied by original red leather case with blue velvet and white satin interior shaped to accept medal. Hinged case has 3 closure hooks. Case stamped with diamond-in-oval at points. Front of body cast as 1 piece and chased. Portrait busts are applied. Back is a separate piece of plain gold sheet cut to fit the front. Interior is hollow.

Spectrographic analysis:

	GOLD	SILVER	COPPER
OBVERSE	71.3	16.7	12.0
REVERSE	81.6	10.6	7.8

History: The centennial of George Washington's birth was celebrated with parades, pageants, speeches, and commemorative artifacts. Lafayette, the memory of whose triumphal visit to America in 1824 was still fresh, was closely linked with Washington. During the festivities, officers of the 27th Regiment of New York State Artillery decided to present Lafayette "on the succeeding anniversary of American Independence" with a medal "embellished with appropriate devices and inscriptions." The medal was designed by a T. Brown, probably Thomas Brown, a stone seal engraver of New York City, and executed by Marquand & Brothers. It is said to be made of gold from the mines of North Carolina. The medal was committed to James Fenimore Cooper, American consul in Lyons, for presentation to Lafayette. Cooper did not receive it in time to present it on July 4, 1833, as the donors had planned. It was finally delivered to him in October, and on November 21, he made the presentation to the general in Paris in the presence of various diplomats and officers.

There was a precedent for such a medal. During Lafayette's 1824 American tour, he was presented with a similar gold medal, although it emphasized commerce rather than martial themes, "on behalf of the Young Men of Baltimore." It was made by Charles Pryce, a goldsmith in the employ of Samuel Kirk, and engraved by John Sands. It is now in the Maryland Historical Society, Baltimore. "Pro Patria et Gloria" is the motto of the 27th Regiment.

Provenance: Marquis de Lafayette; Christie's, New York City, October 1978.

Exhibitions: "Lafayette: Hero of Two Worlds," Queens Museum, New York City, 1989. Winter Antiques Show, New York City, January 1982.

References: Emmons Clark, *History of the Seventh Regiment of New York, 1806–1889* (New York: Seventh Regiment, 1890). Donald L. Fennimore, "A Solid Gold Testimonial: An American Medal for Lafayette," *Antiques* 117, no. 2 (February 1980): 426–30. See also "Collectors' Notes," *Antiques* 118, no. 1 (July 1980): 149. *Lafayette, Hero of Two Worlds: The Art and Pageantry of His Farewell Tour of America, 1824–1825* (Flushing, N.Y.: Queens Museum, 1989), fig. 77. *The New-York Mirror*, April 27, 1833, p. 1, for story of and engraved view of medal. For the Baltimore Lafayette medal, see Dorothy Welker, "The Lafayette Medal," *Journal of Early Southern Decorative Arts* 2, no. 1 (May 1976): 27–37; Goldsborough, *Silver in Maryland*, no. 227.

78.113 Museum purchase at auction through Christie's, 1978

❧ 228 a–e
SPOONS, ca. 1830

(a–c) L. 7 ⅛" (18.2 cm)
1 oz. 3 dwt. 17 gr.–1 oz. 4 dwt. 14 gr. (36.9–38.3 g)
(d) L. 7" (17.8 cm)
1 oz. 7 dwt. 23 gr. (43.0 g)
(e) L. 6 ³⁄₁₆" (15.7 cm)
10 dwt. 22 gr. (17.0 g)

Stamps: (a–d) "F.M." in roman letters, in a rectangle; accompanying each maker's stamp: (1) bust profile of male figure, in a horizontal oval; (2) lion passant, in a rectangle with canted corners; and (3) a roman "G" in a circle; (e) "F Marquand" in script, in a conforming surround. All stamps struck once on back of each handle.

Engraved on front of handle: (a–c) "A" in a foliate script; (d) "JEN" in script; (e) "MS" in foliate script.

Description: (a–d) pointed oval bowls with swage-formed 10-lobe shell on back, downturned fiddle-shape handle with swage-formed kings pattern on front with shell, acanthus leaf, and double anthemion; (e) pointed oval bowl with swage-formed pointed drop on back; downturned fiddle-shape handle with coffin end and engraved with dotted border and bright-cut pendant drop.

Spectrographic analysis: Silver content ranges from 88.8 to 92.7 percent.

History: (d) Initials "JEN" may refer to John Nicoll, father of Caroline Nicoll Lamar, great-grandmother of the donor.

References: Belden, *Marks of American Silversmiths*, p. 287 a, b.

Provenance: (a–c) Robert Ensko, Inc., New York City, sold to H. F. du Pont, June 1936; (d) Mr. and Mrs. William Anderson Henry, Wilmington, Del.; (e) Mr. and Mrs. Stanley B. Ineson, New York City; Mr. and Mrs. Alfred E. Bissell, Wilmington, Del.

(a–c) 61.632.1–.3 Gift of H. F. du Pont, 1965; (d) 73.318 Gift of Mr. and Mrs. William Anderson Henry, 1973; (e) 62.240.416 Gift of Mr. and Mrs. Alfred E. Bissell, 1962–63

❧ 229
FORK, ca. 1835

L. 8 ⅛" (20.6 cm)
3 oz. 23 gr. (94.6 g)

Stamps: "F.M." in roman letters, in a rectangle, struck once on back of handle; accompanying each marker's stamp: (1) bust profile of a male figure in a rectangle; (2) lion passant in a rectangle; and (3) a roman "G" in a square.

Engraved on back of handle: "JSL" in foliate script and a 3-masted schooner under full sail, with flags raised and waves lapping at sides.

Description: 4 tines with swage-formed 12-lobe shell on back; upturned fiddle-shape handle with swage-formed kings pattern on front with shell, acanthus leaf, and double anthemion.

Spectrographic analysis: Silver content is 87.7 percent.

Provenance: Robert Ensko, Inc., New York City, sold to H. F. du Pont, July 1936, as part of a set of 12.

70.1309.2 Bequest of H. F. du Pont, 1969

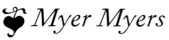

Myer Myers

1723–95
New York, New York, w. 1744–76

Halstead & Myers, w. 1763–64
Norwalk, Connecticut, w. 1776–80
Philadelphia, Pennsylvania,
w. 1780(?)–82
New York, New York, w. 1783–95

Myer Myers's parents were Solomon and Judith Myers, from Holland. Myer probably received his education at the school sponsored by Congregation Shearith Israel, where children of Jewish parents were taught Hebrew, Spanish, Dutch, and English. His brother Asher Myers became a brazier. Myers married Elkalah Cohen around 1762; they had five children. In 1767 he married Joyce Mears; they had eight children. Myers was listed as a freeman in 1746 and advertised in 1753, 1754, 1771, and 1773. He was an active member of Congregation Shearith Israel. A Freemason, he was appointed senior warden of King David Masonic Lodge in 1769. He was active in the Gold and Silversmiths Society and was elected chairman in 1786. He died at his house, 17 Pearl Street.

Myers had a long and productive career as a silversmith, and much of his work survives. He is noted for having made the Torah bells (rimonim) for what later became Touro Synagogue in Newport, Congregation Shearith Israel in New York, and Congegation Mikveh Israel in Philadelphia. He also made silver for Protestant churches, such as the First Presbyterian Church of New York City. Among his outstanding works are the following: four rococo cast candlesticks given to Catherine Livingston (two at Yale University Art Gallery; two at the Metropolitan Museum of Art); two superb cake baskets (one in a private collection and one at the Metropolitan Museum of Art); heavily chased sugar and creamer made to match a London coffeepot owned by the Brinckerhoff family (private collection); a rococo cruet stand, one of only three American stands (offered for sale by Bernard & S. Dean Levy in 1988); and the magnificent dish ring at Yale.

References: Rita Feigenbaum, "Craftsman of Many Styles," *American Art and Antiques* 2, no. 3 (May/June 1979): 58–59. Leo Hershkovitz, *Wills of Early New York Jews (1704–1799)* (New York: American Jewish Historical Society, 1967), pp. 67n, 71, 140–41, 147–48, 165n. Jones, *Old Silver*, pp. 320, 337. Jane Bortman Larus, *Myer Myers, Silversmith, 1723–1795* (Washington, D.C.: B'Nai B'rith, 1964). *Myer Myers: American Silversmith* (New York: Jewish Museum, 1965). Jeanette Rosenbaum, *Myer Myers, Goldsmith, 1723–1795* (Philadelphia: Jewish Publication Society of America, 1954). Alfred Werner, "Myer Myers: Silversmith of Distinction," *America Art and Antiques* 2, no. 3 (May/June 1979): 50–57.

230
COFFEEPOT, 1760–90

H. 13 1/16" (33.2 cm), w. 8 7/16" (21.4 cm)
32 oz. 4 dwt. 17 gr. (1002.6 g)

Stamps: "Myers" in script, in a conforming surround, struck once on underside of body.

Engraved inside footring: "M/ AM" (only upper portion of 2 lower letters included, perhaps because of a repair) in shaded roman letters.

Description: raised circular double-bellied body with incurving elongated neck rising to slightly flared rim with applied stepped molding. Raised circular foot with plain incurved pedestal and gadrooned outer edge; applied footring. Raised high-dome lid with cast gadrooned rim; double-scored lines encircle lid; hollow cast pineapple finial stands on circular plate set into top of lid; bezel. Cast 5-segment hinge. S-curve spout cast in 2 vertical sections: front and upper back with acanthus leaf pattern, lower front with shell pattern that extends back over body and around base of spout. S-curve hardwood handle with 1 scroll and 1 reverse curve; upper socket cast with dependent shell and drop; lower socket cast as a C curve with a scroll-and-sprig terminal.

Spectrographic analysis:

	SILVER	COPPER	LEAD	GOLD
BODY SIDE	88.4	10.9	0.41	0.18
FOOTRING	93.4	5.8	0.24	0.22
SPOUT	93.3	5.2	0.76	0.33
LID	92.1	7.3	0.51	0.07
LOWER HANDLE SOCKET	94.4	4.7	0.22	0.17

History: Initials "M/ AM" may refer to Alexander and Mary Mercer of Mercer County, N.J.

Provenance: Robert Ensko, Inc., New York City, sold to H. F. du Pont, September 1932.

Exhibitions: "Aspects of American Colonial Jewish Life," Fraunces Tavern Museum, New York City, 1979–80.

Comments: It is curious that the engraved inscription on the footring is cut off, but perhaps this happened when the foot was repaired. Jeanette Rosenbaum lists 7 coffeepots by Myers, of which this is 1. Although at first glance they appear to be very much alike, the coffeepots differ markedly in their details. Those at Historic Deerfield and at St. Louis Art Museum are identical to the Winterthur pot except for the bases.

References: Fales, *American Silver*, no. 112. Quimby, "Silver," p. 77. Jeanette Rosenbaum, *Myer Myers, Goldsmith, 1723–1795* (Philadelphia: Jewish Publication Society of America, 1954), p. 109.

59.2305 Gift of H. F. du Pont, 1965

♥ 231
SUGAR BOWL AND LID, ca. 1770

H. (with lid) 4 ³⁄₁₆" (10.6 cm), DIAM. 4 ½"
(11.4 cm)
9 oz. 5 dwt. 7 gr. (288.2 g)

Stamps: "Myers" in script, in a conforming
surround, struck once on underside of body
and once on top of lid. The stamp on the lid
is struck over another stamp, probably an earlier attempt to use the same stamp.

Engraved on underside of foot: "K/ WS" in
crude roman letters.

Description: raised circular double-bellied body
with straight vertical rim; centerpunch obscured
by maker's stamp; cast circular stepped foot.
Raised circular lid, stepped and domed, with
circular cast finial that serves as a foot when
the lid is inverted; rim of lid folded down to
fit over rim of bowl in a friction fit; no bezel.
When lid is removed from bowl and inverted,
it functions as a small serving dish.

Spectrographic analysis:

	SILVER	COPPER	LEAD	GOLD
BODY	91.4	8.2	0.27	0.14
LID	92.3	7.2	0.25	0.11

Provenance: Mr. and Mrs. N. McLean Seabrease,
Germantown, Pa.; sold through Robert Ensko,
Inc., New York City, to H. F. du Pont as part of
the Seabrease collection, August 1929.

Exhibitions: "The Jewish Community in Early
America, 1654–1830," DAR Museum, Washington, D.C., 1980–81.

Comments: At least 5 other bowls in this distinctive form are known to have been made by
Myers.

References: Fales, *American Silver*, no. 112.
Quimby, "Silver," p. 77. Jeanette Rosenbaum,
Myer Myers, Goldsmith, 1723–1795 (Philadel-
phia: Jewish Publication Society of America,
1954), p. 129. "The Jewish Community in Early
America, 1654–1830" (typescript, 1980, Daugh-
ters of the American Revolution, Washington,
D.C.), p. 15.

59.2306 Gift of H. F. du Pont, 1965

♥ 232
CREAMER, 1760–90

H. 4 ¹³⁄₁₆" (12.2 cm), W. 4 ¹³⁄₁₆" (12.2 cm)
5 oz. 23 gr. (157.0 g)

Stamps: "Myers" in script, in a conforming
surround, struck twice on underside of body.

Engraved on side of body: "EE" in shaded script.
Engraved on underside of foot: "T/ IS" in
roman letters.

Description: raised circular double-bellied body
with flared rim and extended pouring lip; applied
rope molding around outside of rim; remnant of
centerpunch on underside. Cast circular stepped
foot and incurved circular pedestal; rope molding applied around edge of foot. Cast S-curve
rococo handle with a series of C scrolls, twists,
and sprigs.

Spectrographic analysis:

	SILVER	COPPER	LEAD	GOLD
BODY	90.7	8.9	0.23	0.19
FOOT	94.0	4.5	0.33	0.25
HANDLE	94.3	4.1	0.27	0.28

Provenance: H. F. du Pont.

Exhibitions: "Masterpieces of American Silver," Virginia Museum of Fine Arts, Richmond, 1960. "The Age of Elegance: The Rococo and Its Effects," Baltimore Museum of Art, 1959. "Aspects of Colonial Jewish Life," Fraunces Tavern Museum, New York City, 1979–80.

Comments: One of 6 listed by Jeanette Rosenbaum, this is a superb example of American rococo silver.

References: The Age of Elegance: The Rococo and Its Effects (Baltimore: Baltimore Museum of Art, 1959), no. 442. Fales, *American Silver,* no. 112. Fennimore, *Silver and Pewter,* no. 122. *Masterpieces of American Silver,* no. 191. Quimby, "Silver," p. 77. Jeanette Rosenbaum, *Myer Myers, Goldsmith, 1723–1795* (Philadelphia: Jewish Publication Society of America, 1954), p. 111.

59.2304 Gift of H. F. du Pont, 1965

❦ 233 a, b
BEAKERS, 1760–90

(a) H. 4" (10.2 cm), DIAM. rim 3 3/16" (8.1 cm)
5 oz. 6 dwt. 11 gr. (165.2 g)
(b) H. 4" (10.2 cm), DIAM. rim 3 3/16" (8.1 cm)
5 oz. 9 dwt. 7 gr. (169.6 g)

Stamps: "Myers" in script, in a conforming surround, struck once on underside of each body.

Engraved on underside of each body: "M/ IR" in shaded roman letters. *Scratched on underside of (b):* "SM" in script.

Description: raised circular body with straight tapered sides and plain rim; double-scored lines encircle body just below rim; centerpunch on underside. Applied molded footring.

Spectrographic analysis:

	SILVER	COPPER	GOLD	LEAD
SIDE (a)	89.4	9.7	0.36	0.23
SIDE (b)	89.5	9.7	0.12	0.33

History: Initials "M/ IR" refer to Isaac Moses and his wife Reyna. Moses was a successful merchant who lived in New York and had a farm on the site of the future Pennsylvania Station. He provided financial support to the American cause during the Revolution. After the war Moses, Myers, and Hayman Levy were chosen to present a welcoming letter to Gov. George Clinton.

Provenance: Ginsburg & Levy, New York City, sold to H. F. du Pont, December 1949.

Exhibitions: "Myer Myers, Silversmith, 1723–1795," B'Nai B'rith, Washington, D.C., 1964.

Comments: These were part of a larger set, 1 of which is in the Bortman-Larus collection, Washington, D.C.

References: Fales, *American Silver,* no. 134. Kauffman, *Colonial Silversmith,* p. 80. Jeanette Rosenbaum, *Myer Myers, Goldsmith, 1723–1795* (Philadelphia: Jewish Publication Society of America, 1954), p. 101. Jane Bortman Larus, *Myer Myers, Silversmith, 1723–1795* (Washington, D.C.: B'Nai B'rith, 1964), p. 9.

61.957.1, .2 Gift of H. F. du Pont, 1965

❦ 234 a–d
SPOONS, 1760–90

(a) L. 8 5⁄16" (21.1 cm)
1 oz. 11 dwt. 21 gr. (49.5 g)
(b) L. 6 7⁄16" (16.4 cm)
1 oz. 5 dwt. 15 gr. (39.8 g)
(c) L. 7 11⁄16" (19.5 cm)
2 oz. 3 dwt. 1 gr. (66.8 g)
(d) L. 8 5⁄16" (21.1 cm)
1 oz. 13 dwt. 13 gr. (52.1 g)

Stamps: "Myers" in script, in a conforming surround, struck twice on back of handles (a), (c), and (d) and once on back of handle (b).

Engraved on front of handle: (a) "JB" in shaded roman letters connected by a bar with a circle in the center. *Engraved on back of handle:* (b) prancing horse on a heraldic band; (c) "NL/ S/ WA".

Description: oval bowls with swage-formed single rounded drop on back of (a), (b), and (d); single rounded drop and rattail on (c). Rounded downturned handle with midrib on (a); rounded upturned handle with midrib on (b) and (c); rounded upturned handle without midrib on (d). Spoon (d) is gilded and heavily chased with a vine-and-floral design in the bowl surrounded by an inner border of semicircular figures and an outer border of dots and darts; the handle has an oval sunburst near the tip, below which is a section of floral vine; the narrow part of the handle is incised in a diaper pattern; handle back is plain.

Spectrographic analysis: Silver content ranges from 87.5 to 92.4 percent.

Provenance: Mr. and Mrs. Stanley B. Ineson, New York City; Mr. and Mrs. Alfred E. Bissell, Wilmington, Del.

Exhibitions: (c) "Silver by New York Makers: Late Seventeenth Century to 1900," Museum of the City of New York, 1937–38.

Comments: (d) is an enigma, although it is clearly an authentic piece by Myers. Just when it was chased and gilded and for what purpose is open to question. The complexity of the decoration and the fact that no other example exists suggest that it may have been used for ceremonial purposes. The decoration was probably added in the mid to late nineteenth century. The chased floral decoration on the handle resembles the work of the shop of Samuel Kirk in Baltimore, but of course it could have been done in any number of shops by midcentury.

References: Belden, *Marks of American Silversmiths,* p. 311. (c) Miller, *Silver by New York Makers,* no. 213. Jeanette Rosenbaum, *Myer Myers, Goldsmith, 1723–1795* (Philadelphia: Jewish Publication Society of America, 1954), pp. 124 c, d, 125 b.

62.240. 1293, .1294, .1295, .1390 Gift of Mr. and Mrs. Alfred E. Bissell, 1962–63

234d

❦ 235
SPOON, 1760–90

L. 8 3⁄16" (20.8 cm)
2 oz. 10 dwt. 6 gr. (78.0 g)

Stamps: "MM" in conjoined roman letters, in a shield, struck twice on back of handle.

Engraved on back of handle: "R/ IC" in crude shaded roman letters, with a stylized palmette between.

Description: oval bowl with swage-formed double rounded drop and midrib on back; rounded upturned handle with midrib on front.

Spectrographic analysis: Silver content is 92.4 percent.

Provenance: Mr. and Mrs. Stanley B. Ineson, New York City; Mr. and Mrs. Alfred E. Bissell, Wilmington, Del.

References: Belden, *Marks of American Silversmiths,* p. 311.

62.240.1279 Gift of Mr. and Mrs. Alfred E. Bissell, 1962–63

❧ Gerrit Oncklebag

ca. 1670–1732
New York, New York, w. ca. 1690–1713
England, w. ca. 1713–32

Baptized in the New York Dutch Church, April 16, 1670, Gerrit Oncklebag was the son of Adam Onckelbagh and Neeltje Jans, who later married Ahasureus Hendricks, a silversmith and probably Oncklebag's master. Gerrit married Elizabeth Van Schaick in 1689 and was admitted as a freeman in 1698. Along with silversmith Jesse Kip he was named assessor for the North Ward in 1698. Hans Kierstede, surgeon and brother of goldsmith Cornelius Kierstede, named him executor and chief beneficiary in his will of March 31, 1712. (Hans was related by marriage to the Oncklebags.) Ocklebag's extensive activity in civic affairs ended abruptly in 1713, when he was declared "A Person of Evil fame and Reputation and hath been Convicted of Coyning the Current Money of this Province and since hath also been Convicted of Champerty," for which he was denied admission as an assistant from the North Ward. No doubt this is why he left for England, where he remained until his death.

Oncklebag's surviving silver is of the highest quality. Outstanding examples include two two-handled covered cups almost identical to the Jurian Blanck cup at Winterthur (no. 152); these are in the collections of Historic Deerfield and Yale University Art Gallery. In 1697 Oncklebag made a pair of tall beakers for the Dutch Church in Flatbush "to be used for the Lord's supper," for which he was paid 34 pieces of eight or 408 guilders; he was paid an additional 7.10 guilders "inasmuch as they were heavier than the pieces of eight" plus 94 guilders for making them.

References: NYHS Collections: vol. 35 (1901) *Unrecorded Wills*, p. 173; vol. 80 (1947) *Supreme Court Province of New York*, pp. 372–73. Jones, *Old Silver*, p. 181. Miller, *New York Silversmiths*, s.v. "Onckelbag." *Minutes of the Common Council*, 3:47. Milo M. Naeve, "Dutch Colonists and English Style in New York City: Silver Syllabub Cups by Cornelius Kierstede, Gerrit Oncklebag, and Jurian Blanck, Jr.," *American Art Journal* 19 (1987): 40–53. Von Khrum, *Silversmiths*, p. 97.

❧ 236
SAUCEPAN, ca. 1700

L. 10 3/16" (25.9 cm), H. 5 9/16" (14.1 cm), DIAM. bowl 4 3/4" (12.1 cm)
10 oz. 16 dwt. 22 gr. (337.3 g)

Stamps: "B/ G•O" in roman letters, in a trefoil surround with a straight bottom line, struck once on underside of body.

Engraved on underside of body: "P/ IC" in shaded roman letters, with a fleur-de-lis between the 2 lower letters. *Engraved on body below handle:* "LP/ 1733/ CAS" in shaded roman letters, with anthemionlike leaves following the "L" and "P" and between the letters "CAS." *Engraved on front of body:* heraldic shield with a band across the middle containing 3 roses, 2 stars above, and 1 star below on an azure ground; shield flanked by festoons of leaves. *Crest:* helmet flanked by leaves; banner above: "JE ESPERE" with 3 stars below; banner below: "FAIT BIEN CRAIN RIEN", all in roman letters.

Description: raised circular bowl with bulbous sides, rounded domed bottom, plain straight rim; centerpunch on underside. Seamed straight handle tapers to slightly larger diameter at tip; tip has a raised dome with a small cast finial; handle attached to body at angle with a curvilinear cut-card plate.

Spectrographic analysis:

	SILVER	COPPER	LEAD	GOLD
BODY SIDE	88.9	10.3	0.42	0.07
UNDERSIDE	91.7	7.2	0.24	0.08
HANDLE	90.0	9.3	0.39	0.08

History: Said by donor to have been made for John and Catherine Pintard of New York City, whose initials are engraved on the underside. John Pintard's father was Anthony Pintard, a Huguenot from La Rochelle, Fr., who settled in Shrewsbury, N.J., in the 1690s. John (d. 1753), a merchant, married Catherine Carré, daughter of Huguenot Louis Carré. Two of their children were John (1734–60) and Lewis (1732–1818) Pintard. John Pintard married Mary Cannon in 1757. Both parents died soon after the birth of their son John Pintard (1759–

1844), whereupon he was brought up by his uncle Lewis. Both Lewis and his nephew distinguished themselves in public service. It is this John Pintard whose memory is perpetuated because of his efforts to preserve and collect historical materials through the founding of the New-York Historical Society.

Two sets of engraved initials commemorate early members of the Pintard family: "P/ IC" (John and Catherine Pintard), "LP" (Lewis Pintard). The initials "CAS" refer to Charles Albert Stevens, uncle of the donor. The Pintard coat of arms was a later addition.

Provenance: John and Catherine Pintard; Lewis Pintard; John Pintard; Mrs. Robert L. Stevens; Charles Albert Stevens; Mary Stevens Baird, New York City and Bernardsville, N.J.

Exhibitions: "From Lenape Territory to Royal Province: New Jersey, 1600–1750," New Jersey State Museum, Trenton, 1971. According to donor, it was also exhibited at Colonial Williamsburg, Fogg Art Museum, Metropolitan Museum of Art, and the New Jersey Historical Society.

Comments: Accompanied by a lid made by Jesse Kip (no. 223) with initials "P/ IC" on flange.

References: Lockwood Barr, "Initials on Early American Silver," *Antiques* 51, no. 1 (January 1947): 45, 46. *Bolton's American Armory*, p. 132, for Pintard coat of arms. *DAB*, s.v. "Pintard, John" and "Pintard, Lewis." *From Lenape Territory*, no. 203. *NYHS Collections*: vol. 28 (1895) *Abstracts of Wills*, p. 441, for will of first John Pintard; vols. 70–73 (1940–41) *Letters from John Pintard to His Daughter*, 4 vols., 1:ix–xx, for biography and ancestry. "Some Rarities in American Silver and Gold," *Antiques* 51, no. 1 (January 1947): 48–50. Carolyn Scoon, "Cornelia Duyckinck's Birthday Spoon Inscribed and Dated August 25, 1686," *New-York Historical Society Quarterly Bulletin* 34, no. 4 (October 1950): 315–17, for mention of saucepan.

76.21a Gift of Mary Stevens Baird, 1976

✿ *Elias Pelletreau*

1726–1810
New York, New York, w. 1747–50
Southampton, Long Island, New York,
w. 1750–76
Simsbury, Connecticut, w. ca. 1776–80
Saybrook, Connecticut, w. 1780–82
Southampton, Long Island, New York,
w. 1782–1810

Elias Pelletreau was the son of Francis and Jane (Osborne) Pelletreau and a grandson of Elie Pelletreau, who came to America from France around 1700. Born in Southampton, Elias was sent to New York City in 1739 for a year of schooling with John Proctor. His indenture of apprenticeship to New York goldsmith Simeon Soumaine was signed in November 1741; it called for a term of seven years starting the following January. In 1748, the year he finished his apprenticeship, he married Sarah Gelston of Southampton, his stepsister. This may have prompted his return to Southampton late in 1750 but not before he became a freeman of New York City that same year. His shop in Southampton was attached to his house on Main Street and is preserved today; it may be visited during the summer months. Pelletreau left Southampton during the American Revolution to live temporarily in Connecticut. Various account books survive that reveal the nature of his business. In addition to silver, he sold buttons, buckles, and jewelry as well as carved whalebone. The surviving account books, which are incomplete, record the sale of fifty-seven tankards. He sold to customers over a wide area that included Long Island, Connecticut, New Jersey, and New York City and its hinterland. William Ustick, a hardware merchant in New York City and a relative by marriage, was especially helpful in selling his work. Pelletreau was active in the militia, even when he was

past the age when duty was expected, and was commonly called Captain Pelletreau. Sons John and Elias Pelletreau, Jr., also became silversmiths, as did grandson William Smith Pelletreau. Although Pelletreau remained active during the 1780s and, probably, the 1790s, his son John handled more and more of the business. John continued to use his father's stamp even after his father's death.

A large amount of Pelletreau's silver survives, including one of the few remaining large two-handled covered cups. This noble piece, engraved with the Van Cortlandt coat of arms, is on loan to the Museum of the City of New York. Pelletreau made numerous tankards, canns, porringers, and cups of various sorts, and he worked in the styles prevailing during the middle years of the eighteenth century. Pelletreau's life and work have been published extensively, as indicated below. His business is extraordinarily well documented. There are four account books: three in the East Hampton Free Library and a fourth account book plus other papers at the Long Island Historical Society.

References: Dean F. Failey, "Elias Pelletreau, Long Island Silversmith" (Master's thesis, University of Delaware, 1971). Dean F. Failey, *Long Island Is My Nation: The Decorative Arts and Craftsmen, 1640–1830* (Setauket, N.Y.: Society for the Preservation of Long Island Antiquities, 1976). *Elias Pelletreau: Long Island Silversmith* (New York: Brooklyn Museum, 1959). Benett W. Turpin, *Elias Pelletreau, 1726–1810: Goldsmith of Southampton, Long Island, New York* (Smithson, N.Y.: Exposition Press, 1984). Mabel C. Weaks, "Captain Elias Pelletreau, Long Island Silversmith," *Antiques* 19, nos. 5, 6 (May/June 1931), 5:365–68, 6:438–40.

✿ 237
TANKARD, 1760–90

H. 4⅝" (11.7 cm), DIAM. base 3 9⁄16" (9.0 cm),
w. 5⅛" (13.0 cm)
8 oz. 19 dwt. 23 gr. (279.9 g)

Stamps: "E•P" in roman letters, in a rectangle, struck once on underside of body in center.

Engraved on underside of body: "C/ W∗E" in shaded roman letters. *Lightly and crudely scratched on underside of body:* "63".

Description: raised circular body with straight tapering sides and nearly flat bottom; plain flared rim contiguous with body; centerpunch obscured by maker's stamp. Applied base molding consists of a wide convex molding with a 3-step molding above and flared molding below. Raised circular single-step lid with flat top; crenellated at front and decorated with traces of feathery engraving; centerpunch inside and outside; bezel. Cast thumbpiece, gently S curved in profile, with scroll motif across top edge. Cast 3-segment hinge with wavy drop. Raised-and-soldered C-curve hollow handle with plain back; lower end of handle forms a C curve in profile and terminates in a plain oval plate; circular lower vent; semicircular upper vent.

Spectrographic analysis:

	SILVER	COPPER	LEAD	GOLD
BODY	91.5	8.2	0.22	0.06
UNDERSIDE	95.5	4.2	0.20	0.05
HANDLE	90.7	8.9	0.33	0.09
LID	91.1	8.3	0.27	0.07

Provenance: Ginsburg & Levy, New York City, sold to H. F. du Pont, October 1930.

Exhibitions: "Elias Pelletreau: Long Island Silversmith," Brooklyn Museum, New York City, 1959.

Comments: Pint size rather than the usual quart size.

References: Elias Pelletreau: Long Island Silversmith (New York: Brooklyn Museum, 1959), no. 70. Kauffman, *Colonial Silversmith*, p. 111.

59.2514 Gift of H. F. du Pont, 1965

PORRINGER, 1760–80

DIAM. body 4 13/16" (12.2 cm), H. 2 1/4" (5.7 cm), w. 6 13/16" (17.3 cm)
6 oz. 17 dwt. 5 gr. (213.4 g)

Stamps: "EP" in roman letters, in a rectangle, struck twice on outside of rim flanking handle.

Engraved on front of handle: "P∗H" in shaded roman letters.

Description: raised circular bowl with bulbous sides and a short angled rim; bottom slightly domed in center; centerpunch inside and on underside; cast handle pierced with 3 large voids.

Spectrographic analysis:

	SILVER	COPPER	LEAD	GOLD
BODY	90.0	9.6	0.22	0.11
HANDLE	92.7	6.8	0.23	0.09

History: The initials "PH" may refer to Philip Howell of Southampton, who is recorded as a customer in the Pelletreau account books.

Provenance: Parke-Bernet Galleries, New York City, sold to H. F. du Pont, October 1964.

Exhibitions: Colonial Society of Southampton, N.Y., Pelletreau silver shop, summers of 1967 and 1968.

Comments: The body is higher in proportion to its diameter than most other porringers, but in an idiosyncratic way it is still a successful design.

References: Dean F. Failey, *Long Island Is My Nation: The Decorative Arts and Craftsmen, 1640–1830* (Setauket, N.Y.: Society for the Preservation of Long Island Antiquities, 1976), no. 244, for mate to this porringer with same initials.

66.114 Gift of H. F. du Pont, 1966

CANN, ca. 1780

H. 6 1/16" (15.4 cm), w. 6 1/4" (15.9 cm)
12 oz. 13 dwt. 23 gr. (394.9 g)

Stamps: "EP" in roman letters, in a rectangle, struck twice on upper body on each side of handle.

Engraved on body opposite handle: "EEC" in foliate script.

Description: raised circular form with bulbous lower body, incurving neck, flared rim with incised ring; centerpunch on underside of body. Cast circular stepped foot. Double–C-curve handle with scroll and acanthus leaf on upper end; scroll and pointed tailpiece on lower end; handle cast in 2 vertical sections; vents in both upper and lower sections; upper handle end attaches to body by a 3-step circular plate; lower handle end attaches to body by a plain circular plate.

Spectrographic analysis:

	SILVER	COPPER	LEAD	GOLD
BODY	92.1	7.6	0.20	0.10
FOOT	94.5	4.6	0.26	0.09
HANDLE	93.0	6.2	0.24	0.09

History: Tradition of ownership by the Reverend David S. Pierson of Long Island, N.Y., and New London, Conn. Descended in the family of M. H. Provost, Hamden, Conn.

Provenance: Parke-Bernet Galleries, New York City, sold to H. F. du Pont, October 1964.

Exhibitions: Colonial Society of Southampton, N.Y., Pelletreau silver shop, summers of 1967 and 1968.

Comments: A fine rococo handle distinguishes this otherwise plain form.

66.115 Gift of H. F. du Pont, 1966

❦ 240 a–f
SPOONS, 1750–76

L. 7⅞"–8" (20.0–20.3 cm)
1 oz. 12 dwt.–1 oz. 17 dwt. 20 gr. (51.0–58.8 g)

Stamps: "EP" in roman letters, in a rectangle, struck once on back of each handle.

Engraved on back of each handle: "B/ R∗P" in shaded roman letters.

Description: oval bowls with swage-formed double rounded drops with midrib between; rounded upturned handles with midrib.

Spectrographic analysis: Silver content ranges from 89.3 to 90.7 percent.

Provenance: Parke-Bernet Galleries, New York City, sold to H. F. du Pont, October 1964.

Exhibitions: Colonial Society of Southampton, N.Y., Pelletreau silver shop, summers of 1967 and 1968.

Comments: A clue to the engraved initials "B/ R∗P" may be found in the Pelletreau accounts, which record sales to "Richard Brown's wife" of Oyster Pond. I was unable to determine her given name.

66.116.1–.6 Gift of H. F. du Pont, 1966

❦ 241 a–g
SPOONS, 1750–76

(a, b) L. 4⁵⁄₁₆" (11.0 cm)
4 dwt. 20 gr. (7.6 g)
(c–g) L. 7⅝"–8" (14.4–20.3 cm)
1 oz. 8 dwt. 5 gr.–1 oz. 14 dwt. 14 gr.
(43.8–53.7 g)

Stamps: "EP" in roman letters, in a rectangle, struck once on back of each handle.

Engraved on back of handle: (a) "IM" in crude shaded roman letters; (b) "S+D" in crude roman letters; (d, e) "I∗B" in crude shaded roman letters; (f) "W/ C∗S" in crude roman letters; (g) "M/ S∗Z" in crude shaded roman letters. *Engraved on front of handle:* (c) "P. McDurmet" in script.

Description: oval bowls with swage-formed double rounded drops with midrib on (a, b, d–f); oval bowl with swage-formed single pointed drop on (c); oval bowl with swage-formed single rounded drop and rattail on (g); all handles rounded and upturned with midrib.

Spectrographic analysis: Silver content ranges from 89.9 to 92.1 percent.

Provenance: Mr. and Mrs. Stanley B. Ineson, New York City; Mr. and Mrs. Alfred E. Bissell, Wilmington, Del.

Exhibitions: (f) Metropolitan Museum of Art, New York City, 1935–61.

Comments: The initials "IB" may refer to John Butler of Oyster Bay, who is recorded as a customer in the Pelletreau accounts. P. McDurmet remains unidentified.

References: Belden, *Marks of American Silversmiths*, pp. 330–31.

62.240.453, .454, .1354, .1355, .1398, .1356, .1357
Gift of Mr. and Mrs. Alfred E. Bissell, 1962–63

Stephen Richard

New York, New York,
w. ca. 1802–ca. 1834

Stephen Richard is listed in directories at 160 Broadway, 1802–12; 12 Maiden Lane, 1813–15; 10 Maiden Lane, 1816; 153 Broadway, 1817–26; and 169 Broadway, 1828, usually as a jeweler and enameler. He advertised as jeweler, enameler, and hairworker in the *New-York Evening Post*, December 27, 1802. All of this does not suggest that he was a master silversmith, but the evidence from several surviving pieces of hollowware indicates otherwise. The cake basket that bears his engraved signature, along with the stamp of Hugh Wishart, was long thought to be a unique expression of an apprentice asserting his identity. With the appearance of at least three more pieces bearing Richard's engraved signature, it is time to recognize that we are dealing with quite a different situation and to give him the credit that is unquestionably his. In 1962 Ginsburg & Levy advertised an oval tray with the Wishart stamp and the Richard signature. An exhibition at Hirschl & Adler Galleries in New York City included a large neoclassical tea (or coffee) urn with no maker's stamp but with the following engraved inscription: "112 Oz./ S. Richard Fecit/ No 160 Broad Way New York Sterling Silver." Richard's shop was located at this address until 1812. The same exhibition included a presentation ewer and salver with no stamps but with the engraved inscription "S. Richard/ Maker/ New York" on the salver. Both pieces, which are of very high quality, are in private collections. Of the four known pieces bearing Richard's signature, two have Wishart's stamp. Rather than a relationship of master and apprentice, it appears that Wishart may have commissioned the two pieces for one of his customers. Not one to hide his light under a bushel, Richard boldly proclaimed his authorship.

Regrettably, little other work survives. A pair of pitchers presented by the firemen of New York City to their chief engineer, Jameson Cox, in 1829 is owned by the Museum of the City of New York. A pair of cake dishes (baskets?) was in the 1938 exhibition at the Museum of the City of New York, "Silver by New York Makers." A few examples of his flatware survive, some of it also bearing an "SW" stamp, which may refer to either Samuel or Stephen White.

References: Neo-Classicism in America: Inspiration and Innovation, 1810–1840 (New York: Hirschl & Adler Galleries, 1991), nos. 2, 18. Miller, *Silver by New York Makers*, no. 243. Von Khrum, *Silversmiths*, p. 107.

242
CAKE BASKET,
1793–1820

H. (with handle up) 10 15/16" (27.8 cm), H. (with handle down) 5" (12.7 cm), L. 18 7/16" (34.1 cm), W. 10 5/8" (27.0 cm)
38 oz. 8 dwt. 1 gr. (1194.5 g)

Stamps: "WISHART" in roman letters, in a rectangle, struck once on underside of body, once on upper surface of handle, and once on outside of base ring. For maker, see engraved inscription below.

Engraved on rim: "SSB"; *on opposite rim:* "HAACB". Both in foliate script.

Engraved on side of body: heraldic device consisting of a blasted oak tree with a medusa head shield hanging from a branch, all in a blank shield; crest: closed helmet surmounted by a spread-winged eagle and a medusa-head shield, the whole flanked by a mantle of leafy scrolls.

Engraved on underside of body: "S. Richard fecit" in italics.

Description: rectangular in plan with rounded corners, the raised body has a deep curved well and broad flat angled rim with applied reeded molding. Seamed pedestal, concave in section and conforming to shape of body, has an applied footring. Large bail handle hinged with silver pins on long sides of body; handle U shape in cross section in center, narrows to rectangular cross section toward hinges. No centerpunch.

Spectrographic analysis:

	SILVER	COPPER	LEAD	GOLD
BODY SIDE	90.3	8.7	0.38	0.24
UNDERSIDE	96.6	2.7	0.40	0.32
RIM	91.4	7.5	0.37	0.21
HANDLE	90.9	7.9	0.48	0.20
BASE RING	90.6	8.0	0.43	0.19

Provenance: Robert Ensko, Inc., New York City, sold to H. F. du Pont, December 1930.

References: Fales, *American Silver*, no. 141. Fennimore, *Silver and Pewter*, no. 105.

61.956 Gift of H. F. du Pont, 1965

❦ 243 a–c
FORK AND SPOONS, 1802–30

(a) Fork: L. 6 ¾" (16.4 cm)
1 oz. 14 dwt. 6 gr. (53.2 g)
(b) Salt spoon: L. 3 ¹³⁄₁₆" (9.7 cm)
4 dwt. 12 gr. (7.0 g)
(c) Spoon: L. 9 ⅛" (23.2 cm)
1 oz. 19 dwt. 4 gr. (60.8 g)

Stamps: "SRichard" in script, in a conforming surround, struck once on back of each handle. Gothic "P" struck once on back of handle (a). "S•W" in roman letters, in a rectangle, struck once on back of handles (b) and (c).

Engraved on back of handle: (a) "SW" in script. *Engraved on front of handle:* (c) "TM" in foliate script.

Description: (a) 4-tine fork with shoulders; upturned fiddle-shape handle with midrib on front; (b) wide oval bowl with no drop; rounded downturned handle with midrib on back; (c) oval bowl with swage-formed rounded drop; downturned fiddle-shape handle with midrib on back.

Spectrographic analysis: Silver content ranges from 88.3 to 92.0 percent.

Provenance: (a, b) Mr. and Mrs. Stanley B. Ineson, New York City; Mr. and Mrs. Alfred E. Bissell, Wilmington, Del.; (c) Gebelein Silversmiths, Boston.

References: Belden, *Marks of American Silversmiths*, p. 354.

(a) 62.240.514, (b) 62.240.815 Gift of Mr. and Mrs. Alfred E. Bissell, 1962–63; (c) 72.103 Museum purchase from Gebelein Silversmiths, 1972

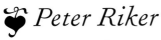

Peter Riker

w. ca. 1797–1817

Alexander & Riker, w. ca. 1797–1800
[Brasher & Riker], w. 1800–1801
Riker & Clapp (also Clapp & Riker),
w. 1802–8

Peter Riker is found in the directories at
378 Pearl Street, 1801–4/5; 65 Chatham
Street, 1808; 86 Chatham Street, 1809–11;
151 Cherry Street, 1812–14; 261 Water
Street, 1815–17; 123 Henry Street, 1818–
20; and 55 Hester Street, 1821. He was
associated with George Alexander from
1797 to 1800 at the Pearl Street address.
The firm was sometimes known as Alexander & Riker and at other times as Riker
& Alexander. The partnership was dissolved by mutual consent in March 1800.
Alexander then formed a partnership with
Ephraim Brasher that broke apart early
in 1801. Alexander died in April 1801.

Philip Clapp is found in the directo-
ries as a silversmith at 86 Chatham
Street, 1805/6–8; 65 Chatham Street,
1809–10; 44 Frankfort Street, 1811–16.
The firm of Clapp & Riker (also Riker
& Clapp) is found in the directories at 80
Cherry Street, 1802; 373 Pearl Street,
1803–5; and 86 Chatham Street, 1806–8.
A tea service by Riker & Clapp is illus-
trated in *New York State Silversmiths*.

References: Ensko, *American Silversmiths IV*,
p. 4. Gottesman, *Arts and Crafts, 1800–1804*,
p. 93. *New York State Silversmiths*, pp. 18, 19.
Von Khrum, *Silversmiths*, pp. 4, 28, 29, 108.

244
CREAMER, ca. 1797–99

H. 8 ¼" (21.0 cm), w. 5 ⅛" (12.9 cm)
8 oz. 6 dwt. 11 gr. (258.9 g)

Stamps: "A&R" in roman letters, in a rectangle,
struck once on side of base below spout. Intaglio stamp of spread-winged eagle on base next
to maker's stamp.

Engraved on body opposite handle: "AW" in
script, in a circular medallion with a leaflike
border of wheelwork and bright-cut engraving.

Description: raised helmet-shape body with high
pouring lip with ridge running down upper front
of body; low sides, back rising to point. Centerpunch inside and on underside of body. Applied
beaded band around outside of rim over band of
wheelwork. Body joined to base consisting of
trumpet-shape pedestal on square plinth; bead
moldings on upper and lower edges of pedestal.
High-loop strap handle tapers to point at bottom
and broadens to rounded shoulders and rectangle at upper join with body. Sides of square
plinth applied.

Spectrographic analysis:

	SILVER	COPPER	LEAD	GOLD
BODY SIDE	86.9	12.8	0.20	0.15
FOOT	91.7	8.0	0.22	0.10
HANDLE	91.4	8.1	0.25	0.15

Provenance: Marshall P. Blankarn, New York
City.

Comments: New York State Silversmiths gives
what appears to be the same stamp to both Alexander & Riker and Andras & Richards. Most
other reference works give the "A&R" stamp to
Alexander & Riker, a partnership documented
by newspaper advertisements. Furthermore, the
directories identify Alexander & Riker as silversmiths, whereas Andras alone, and when in partnership with Samuel Richard, is identified as a
jeweler. The stamp "A&RIKER" is on a privately owned spoon.

79.212 Gift of Marshall P. Blankarn, 1979

🌺 245
PIPE LIGHTER OR BRAZIER, 1800–1802

w. 8 ½" (21.6 cm), H. (incl. handle) 3 ³⁄₁₆"
(8.1 cm), DIAM. bowl (at rim) 4" (10.2 cm)
5 oz. 12 dwt. 8 gr. (174.7 g)

Stamps: "RIKER & CLAPP" in roman letters,
in a conforming surround, struck once on
underside.

Engraved on side of bowl opposite handle: heraldic device consisting of an embowed arm, the
hand clasping an arrow, above a heraldic band.

Description: raised circular hemispherical bowl
with applied reeded rim; bottom of bowl pierced
by circular void in center with circular voids
around it, these in turn are encircled by 8-point
elliptical voids. Centerpunch not visible because
of center void. Short cylindrical base with flat
bottom attached to underside of bowl; sides
pierced all around with triangular and circular
voids. No centerpunch. Seamed hollow tapered
cylindrical handle socket mounted to side of
body at upward angle; black balluster-turned
wooden handle secured to socket by 1 silver pin.

Spectrographic analysis:

	SILVER	COPPER	LEAD	GOLD
BODY SIDE	88.7	10.1	0.28	0.23
UNDERSIDE	94.0	4.9	0.17	0.43
BASE (UNDER HANDLE)	87.3	11.3	0.36	0.21
HANDLE	87.2	11.3	0.33	0.17

Provenance: Robert Ensko, Inc., New York City,
sold to H. F. du Pont, November 1934.

Comments: How this object works is not clear.
The pierced base is soldered to the body and,
hence, not removable.

References: Fales, *American Silver*, no. 136.

57.1268 Gift of H. F. du Pont, 1965

🌺 246 a, b
SPOONS, 1797–99

(a) Teaspoon: L. 5 ⁷⁄₁₆" (13.8 cm)
7 dwt. 8 gr. (11.4 g)
(b) Salt spoon: L. 4" (10.2 cm)
5 dwt. (7.8 g)

Stamps: "A & R" in roman letters, in a rectangle,
struck once on back of each handle. On (b) an
illegible adjoining stamp that may be the same
pseudohallmark as on the creamer (no. 244).

Engraved on front of handle: (a) bright-cut oval
with pendant outlined in wheelwork; (b) "SF"
(sideways) in script, in a bright-cut oval with a
bright-cut border the length of the handle, all
with an inner border of wheelwork.

Description: (a) pointed oval bowl with swage-
formed pointed oval drop; rounded downturned handle with midrib; (b) oval bowl with
swage-formed pointed drop; rounded downturned handle with midrib.

Spectrographic analysis: Silver content ranges
from 87.0 to 93.3 percent.

Provenance: Mr. and Mrs. Stanley B. Ineson,
New York City; Mr. and Mrs. Alfred E. Bissell,
Wilmington, Del.

62.240.528, .723 Gift of Mr. and Mrs. Alfred E.
Bissell, 1962–63

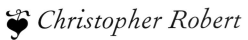

Christopher Robert

1708–93
New York, New York

Christopher Robert, son of Suzanne Nicholas du Cailleau and Daniel Robert from La Rochelle, France, was baptized in the French Church, New York City, on July 11, 1708. On May 8, 1723, he was apprenticed to John Hastier, "Sylversmyth," for a term of seven years. The indenture was witnessed by Elias Pelletreau, Sr. Under the terms of the indenture Robert was to receive a quarter of schooling every year and "Liberty to go sleep at his Mother's House Every Night." He became a freeman in 1731. His first wife, Elinor, died in 1743. Later that same year he married Mary Dyer. His son Daniel (1746–1804) went to Kings College (Columbia) and later to Edinburgh University. In his will, drawn up in September 1792, Robert called himself a merchant. He bequeathed his "three casters marked DRS, being old family plate," to his son Daniel. He instructed his executors to provide his wife Mary with "the use and income of all the residue of my estate during her life." After her death, however, "I give to my daughter, Mary Elizabeth, as much of my furniture as will furnish a drawing room and bedroom." The rest of the estate was to be divided equally between his children Daniel, Christopher, John, Mary Elizabeth, and Mary Rhinelander. Robert's silver is rare.

References: "The History of the Robert Family from Documents Collected by the Late Christopher Robert in 1859–60," manuscript, Huguenot Society of America, New York City. *NYHS Collections*: vol. 18 (1886) *Burghers and Freemen*, p. 117; vol. 39 (1906) *Abstracts of Wills*, p. 238; vol. 42 (1909) *Indentures of Apprentices*, pp. 178–79. Alfred V. Wittmeyer, ed., *Registers of the Births, Marriage, and Deaths of the Eglise Francoise á la Nouvelle York* (New York: Huguenot Society of America, 1886), p. 115; see also p. 100 for baptism of his brother Daniel, July 29, 1704. Von Khrum, *Silversmiths*, p. 109.

247
PORRINGER, ca. 1735

DIAM. bowl 5 ⁷⁄₁₆" (13.8 cm), w. 7 ½" (19.1 cm)
8 oz. 9 dwt. 16 gr. (263.2 g)

Stamps: "CR" in roman letters, in an oval, struck twice on underside of body.

Engraved on front of handle (facing out): "M∗W" in shaded roman letters.

Description: raised circular bowl with bulging sides and a short angled rim; bottom slightly domed in center; centerpunch on inside and underside; cast handle pierced with 3 large voids and 1 small void at tip.

Spectrographic analysis:

	SILVER	COPPER	LEAD	GOLD
BODY	87.0	12.6	0.25	0.15
HANDLE	92.4	7.2	0.24	0.18

History: Initials "M∗W" probably refer to Mary Whitwell, daughter of Oliver Whitwell, an ancestor of the donor. She married in 1768. Oliver Whitwell resided in both Newport, R.I., and New York City and is said to have fought in the Revolution.

Provenance: Whitwell family in New York City area; Mr. and Mrs. William Livingston Whitwell, Hollins College, Va.

Comments: The handle is identical to one on the Bancker porringer (no. 147). Both are slightly asymmetrical. It is also similar to the porringer by Elias Pelletreau in the Hogg collection at the Museum of Fine Arts, Houston.

References: David B. Warren, *Bayou Bend: American Furniture, Paintings, and Silver from the Bayou Bend Collection* (Houston: Museum of Fine Arts, 1975), no. 300, for similar piece.

76.80 Gift of Mr. and Mrs. William Livingston Whitwell, in memory of Mrs. Livingston Miller Whitwell, 1976

248 a, b
SPOONS, 1750–80

(a) L. 7 ⁹⁄₁₆" (19.2 cm), 1 oz. 17 dwt. 1 gr. (57.5 g)
(b) L. 8 ³⁄₁₆" (20.8 cm), 1 oz. 13 dwt. 17 gr. (52.3 g)

Stamps: "CR" in roman letters, in an oval, struck twice on back of handle (a); "CR" in roman letters, in a rectangle, struck twice on back of handle (b).

Engraved on back of handle: (a) "M/ WF" in shaded roman letters; (b) "T/ I∗P" in crude shaded roman letters.

Description: (a) oval bowl with swage-formed rounded drop and rattail; rounded upturned handle with midrib; (b) oval bowl with rounded drop and incised opposing arc at tip; rounded upturned handle with midrib.

Spectrographic analysis: Silver content ranges from 91.1 to 93.5 percent.

Provenance: Mr. and Mrs. Stanley B. Ineson, New York City; Mr. and Mrs. Alfred E. Bissell, Wilmington, Del.

62.240.1367, .1366 Gift of Mr. and Mrs. Alfred E. Bissell, 1962–63

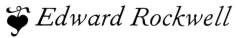

Edward Rockwell

w. 1803–14

Edward & Samuel Rockwell, w. 1815–47
New York, New York

Edward Rockwell is listed in the directories for 1803 through 1814. He advertised in 1807: "Jewellery and Silverware of his own manufacture at the shop at 4 Park Place." The partnership of Edward & Samuel Rockwell, the latter presumably Edward's brother, is listed from 1815 to 1847 at various locations. The Rockwell stamp is on a large tea urn, advertised by Robert Jackson and Ann Gilloly in 1983 and on a three-piece coffee set advertised by Blum's Antique Shop in 1951. An elaborate tureen bearing the Van Cortlandt arms is owned by the Museum of the City of New York. A heavily decorated standing cup in a private collection bears the Rockwell name stamp. It was presented to a Col. James A. Moore by the Second Company of Lafayette Guards, Second Regiment of New York Artillery, on November 10, 1828. It is not clear how to distinguish between the work of Edward and that of the partnership. In light of the tureen and cup, however, it appears that the single name stamp may apply to the partnership as well as to Edward Rockwell alone. Given the stylistic characteristics of known Rockwell silver, much of it was probably made in the 1820s and 1830s. There is also a Samuel D. Rockwell who appears in New York City directories from 1834 to 1850. A gold spoon with incuse stamp "S. D. ROCKWELL" is at Winterthur.

References: Ensko, *American Silversmiths IV*, p. 175. Blum's Antique Shop advertisement, *Antiques* 59, no. 5 (May 1951): 363. Robert Jackson and Ann Gilloly advertisement, *Antiques* 123, no. 4 (April 1983): 730. Von Khrum, *Silversmiths*, p. 110.

249
BEAKER, ca. 1820

H. 3" (7.6 cm), DIAM. rim 3 ⅛" (7.9 cm), DIAM. base 2 ⅜" (6.0 cm)
4 oz. 2 dwt. 16 gr. (128.6 g)

Stamps: "ROCKWELL" in roman letters, against a ground of diagonal striations, all in a rectangle, struck once on underside of body. Accompanied by an eagle in a circle and a roman "C" in a circle.

Engraved on side of body: "RT" in shaded script.

Description: raised cylindrical body with slight tapering toward bottom; plain flared rim; nearly flat bottom; applied footring of die-rolled decorative band with pattern of framed anthemia against a dotted ground.

Spectrographic analysis:

	SILVER	COPPER	LEAD	GOLD
BODY SIDE	91.8	7.8	0.26	0.16
BOTTOM	94.7	5.0	0.17	0.10

Provenance: Marshall P. Blankarn, New York City.

Comments: Device stamps, like the eagle and "C" here, may refer to another maker or retailer or they may have no meaning at all; see Christine Wallace Laidlaw, "Silver by the Dozen: The Wholesale Business of Teunis D. DuBois," *Winterthur Portfolio* 23, no. 1 (Spring 1988): 25–50.

79.203 Gift of Marshall P. Blankarn, 1979

❦ 250 a–c
SPOONS, ca. 1815

(a) L. 5 7⁄16" (13.8 cm)
7 dwt. 10 gr. (11.5 g)
(b) L. 6" (15.2 cm)
9 dwt. 16 gr. (15.0 g)
(c) L. 8 15⁄16" (22.7 cm)
1 oz. 11 dwt. (48.1 g)

Stamps: "ROCKWELL" in roman letters, in a serrated rectangle, struck once on back of each handle, plus sheaf of wheat in a rectangle on (a) and (b).

Engraved on front of each handle: (a) "WM" in foliate script; (b) "TEM" in foliate script, in a dotted border with a pendant; (c) empty shield-shape medallion with pendant drop.

Description: pointed oval bowls with swage-formed single drop on (a) and (c) and single incised drop on (b); rounded downturned fiddle-shape handle with midrib on (a); coffin-end downturned fiddle-shape handle on (b) and (c).

Spectrographic analysis: Silver content ranges from 85.4 to 91.0 percent.

Provenance: (a, b) Mr. and Mrs. Stanley B. Ineson, New York City; Mr. and Mrs. Alfred E. Bissell, Wilmington, Del.; (c) Avis and Rockwell Gardiner, Stamford, Conn.

Exhibitions: (b) "Silver by New York Makers," Museum of the City of New York, 1937–38.

References: Belden, *Marks of American Silversmiths*, p. 361. Miller, *Silver by New York Makers*, no. 249 b only.

(a, b) 62.240.575, .576 Gift of Mr. and Mrs. Alfred E. Bissell, 1962–63; (c) 65.39 Museum purchase from Avis and Rockwell Gardiner, 1965

❦ 251 a–c
SPOONS, ca. 1820

(a) L. 3 15⁄16" (10.0 cm)
5 dwt. 13 gr. (8.6 g)
(b) L. 3 15⁄16" (10.0 cm)
5 dwt. 9 gr. (8.3 g)
(c) L. 5 7⁄8" (14.9 cm)
9 dwt. 14 gr. (14.9 g)

Stamps: "Rockwell" in italics, in a rectangle, struck twice on back of handles (a) and (b), once on back of handle (c).

Engraved on front of handles: (a, b) "MC" in foliate script; (c) "SI" in script.

Description: (a, b) salt spoons with circular bowls and rounded downturned fiddle-shape handles with swage-formed 10-lobe shell on upper end of each; (c) oval bowl with swage-formed squared drop; rounded downturned fiddle-shape handle with midrib.

Spectrographic analysis: Silver content ranges from 88.5 to 91.9 percent.

Provenance: (a, b) Mr. and Mrs. Stanley B. Ineson, New York City; Mr. and Mrs. Alfred E. Bissell, Wilmington, Del.; (c) Julian B. Myers, New Milford, N.J.

References: Belden, *Marks of American Silversmiths*, p. 361; Belden attributes this stamp to S. D. Rockwell.

(a, b) 62.240.819.1, .2 Gift of Mr. and Mrs. Alfred E. Bissell, 1962–63; (c) 78.128 Gift of Julian B. Myers, 1978

Sayre & Richards

w. 1803–13

John Sayre
1771–1852
Thomas Richards
w. 1802–30
New York, New York

John Sayre was born in Southhampton, Long Island, the home of silversmith Elias Pelletreau and the Dominy dynasty of cabinetmakers. John's younger brother, Joel, also became a well-known New York silversmith. John first appears in New York City directories in 1796 at 437 Pearl Street. In November 1803, the first year of the partnership with Thomas Richards, the firm advertised "Watches, Plate and Jewellery, Sayre & Richards, No. 240 Pearl-street, corner of Burling slip, have for sale, wholesale and retail, a large assortment of English watches, direct from the manufactures; also Watch and clock Makers tools, watch and clock materials. . . . They manufacture silver tea setts of the newest and most approved patterns, and silver ware in general" (*Mercantile Advertiser* [New York City], November 23, 1803). After 1814 John worked in Cohoes, New York, and ended his years in Plainfield, New Jersey. One

of the partners was probably a clockmaker, although it is unclear which one. Little is known about Thomas Richards. He is identified in the directories as a watchmaker; yet, surviving bills from the 1820s show substantial sales of silver by him, including the following sale to "Captn Vanderbilt":

1 dozen Silver Tea Spoons	12"37
1 Gravy Spoon	3"50
Engraving Thistle on all	1"50

New York/ Oct. 8, 1824

Although a number of pieces by John Sayre survive, there are few from the partnership. The Newark Museum owns a bowl and a mug, and there are a few pieces of flatware in various collections. Many of the firm's pieces bear what appears to be a date stamp: a roman capital in a rectangular surround. This stamp could also represent the work of another silversmith; a lot of work was jobbed out at that time.

References: Ensko, *American Silversmiths IV*, pp. 172, 183, 323, 327. Gottesman, *Arts and Crafts, 1800–1804*, p. 99. Jones, *Old Silver*, p. 400. Von Khrum, *Silversmiths*, p. 115. 58x8.1–.12 and Ph 1154, Downs collection, Winterthur Library; see also Dominy Papers (59x9.153) for a watch paper for Sayre & Richards.

252
STAND FOR TEAPOT, 1802–13

L. 6 ½" (16.5 cm), W. 4 13/16" (12.2 cm), H. 1 ⅛" (2.9 cm)
4 oz. 10 dwt. 7 gr. (140.4 g)

Stamps: "S&R" in roman letters, in an oval, struck once on underside. Accompanied by a roman "G" in a square.

Scratched on underside: "oz 4 dwt 11".

Description: raised flat oval tray with convex rim divided into 4 segments; each segment consists of 3 creased and scalloped panels; center-punch obscured by maker's stamp; 4 broad flat ogee feet.

Spectrographic analysis:

	SILVER	COPPER	LEAD	GOLD
TOP	91.6	7.9	0.19	0.12
FOOT	93.9	4.9	0.37	0.13

Provenance: Robert Ensko, Inc., New York City, sold to H. F. du Pont, December 1931.

Comments: Trays of this type were used to support flat-bottom neoclassical teapots, thus protecting the surface of a tea table or sideboard.

61.1092 Gift of H. F. du Pont, 1965

❦ 253 a–e
SPOONS, 1802–13

(a) L. 6 ⅜" (16.9 cm)
14 dwt. 23 gr. (23.3 g)
(b) L. 6 ⅛" (15.6 cm)
9 dwt. 12 gr. (14.8 g)
(c) L. 9 ¹⁵⁄₁₆" (23.7 cm)
1 oz. 18 dwt. 3 gr. (59.2 g)
(d) L. 5 ¹¹⁄₁₆" (14.5 cm)
9 dwt. 7 gr. (14.5 g)
(e) L. 9 ½" (24.1 cm)
2 oz. 16 gr. (63.1 g)

Stamps: "S&R" in roman letters, in an oval, struck once on back of each handle. A roman "F" in a rectangle, struck on back of handle (c).

Engraved on front of handle: (a) "RES" in foliate script; (b) "AW" in foliate script, in a bright-cut medallion with rollerwork; (c) "SMC" in shaded roman letters, in a bright-cut medallion with rollerwork; (d) "PW" in script; (e) "JMB" in script.

Description: (a) pointed oval bowl with swage-formed rounded drop; rounded downturned handle with midrib; (b) pointed oval bowl with swage-formed pointed and rounded drops; rounded downturned handle; (c) oval bowl with swage-formed rounded double drop; coffin-end downturned handle; (d) pointed oval bowl with swage-formed pointed drop; coffin-end downturned handle; (e) pointed oval bowl with rounded drop; coffin-end downturned handle.

Spectrographic analysis: Silver content ranges from 85.9 to 93.4 percent.

Provenance: Mr. and Mrs. Stanley B. Ineson, New York City; Mr. and Mrs. Alfred E. Bissell, Wilmington, Del.

References: Belden, *Marks of American Silversmiths*, p. 374.

62.240.655, .657, .1429, .654, .1430 Gift of Mr. and Mrs. Alfred E. Bissell, 1962–63

❦ 254 a, b
SPOONS, 1802–13

(a) L. 5 ⁷⁄₁₆" (13.8 cm)
7 dwt. 8 gr. (11.4 g)
(b) L. 4 ¹⁄₁₆" (10.3 cm)
4 dwt. 7 gr. (6.7 g)

Stamps: "S&R" in roman letters, in a rectangle, struck once on back of each handle. A roman "F" in a rectangle, struck on handle (b).

Engraved on front of handle: (a) "ES"; (b) "K" in script. *Engraved on back of handle:* (a) "ELW" in script.

Description: oval bowl with swage-formed rounded drop on (a); wide oval bowl with swage-formed rounded drop on (b); coffin-end downturned handles on both.

Spectrographic analysis: Silver content ranges from 91.1 to 92.8 percent.

Provenance: Mr. and Mrs. Stanley B. Ineson, New York City; Mr. and Mrs. Alfred E. Bissell, Wilmington, Del.

References: Belden, *Marks of American Silversmiths*, p. 374 b.

62.240.656, .820 Gift of Mr. and Mrs. Alfred E. Bissell, 1962–63

AS

Albany, New York

Silver with an Albany provenance and stamped "AS" (with a V-shape crossbar on the "A") has puzzled silver historians for years. Norman S. Rice discovered a 1769 reference to Abraham Schuyler "of the City of Albany Silversmith." He thought that it might refer to Abraham Schuyler (1735–1812), the son of David and Maria (Hansen) Schuyler, who married Eva Beekman in 1763. Virtually nothing is known about him, and no other person of that name or initials appears in the Schuyler genealogies. The only piece of hollowware with the "AS" stamp is a tankard in the Albany Institute. It is similar to other New York tankards of the first half of the eighteenth century and is engraved "H V Driessen," probably for Hendrick Van Driessen, the first child baptized, in 1715, in the Dutch Church in Albany. The only other "AS" pieces known are two large spoons and a ladle. Although all three look to be too early for a silversmith who came of age in the 1750s, silver was often made in outdated styles, making style alone an unreliable indicator of age. Lacking further evidence, the attribution to Schuyler remains questionable. Therefore, the "AS" stamp, which was once attributed to Abraham Skinner of New York City, remains unidentified. As a footnote, the "A" in the "AS" stamp closely resembles the "A" in the seal of Albany (1686). Both have the V-shape crossbar.

References: Rice, *Albany Silver*, p. 6, figs. 59, 61. Ensko, *American Silversmiths IV*, pp. 184, 189, 239–40.

255

STUFFING SPOON, ca. 1755

L. 15 15⁄16" (40.5 cm)
7 oz. 1 dwt. 16 gr. (219.6 g)

Stamps: "AS" (with V-shape crossbar on the "A") in roman letters, in a rectangle, struck twice on back of handle.

Engraved on back of handle: "E/ I∗R∗B" in crude shaded roman letters. *Engraved at a later date on front of handle:* "John B. Sanders./ to/ Henry R. Sanders." in script.

Description: deep oval bowl with swage-formed rounded drop with an opposing arc; rounded upturned handle with midrib.

Spectrographic analysis:

	SILVER	COPPER	LEAD	GOLD
BOWL	85.7	14.1	0.12	0.10
HANDLE	88.7	11.1	0.15	0.13

History: Unknown, but original inscription may refer to the Elmendorf family, which was related to the Sanders family of upstate New York.

Provenance: Mr. and Mrs. Stanley B. Ineson, New York City; Mr. and Mrs. Alfred E. Bissell, Wilmington, Del.

References: Belden, *Marks of American Silversmiths*, p. 376 a, which accepts the attribution to Schuyler. Rice, *Albany Silver*, p. 36, for a similar spoon.

62.240.1663 Gift of Mr. and Mrs. Alfred E. Bissell, 1965

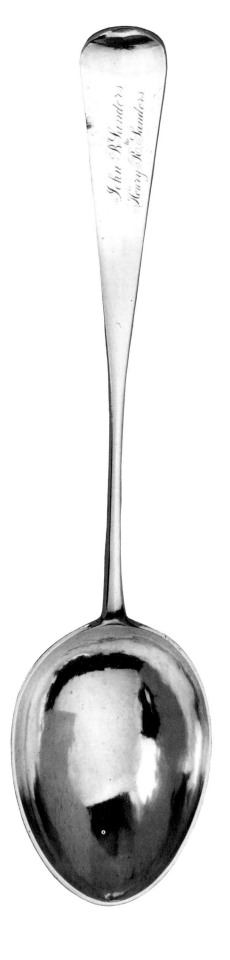

256

LADLE, ca. 1770

L. 14 ³⁄₁₆" (36.0 cm)
6 oz. 8 dwt. 20 gr. (199.7 g)

Stamps: "AS" (with V-shape crossbar on the "A") in roman letters, in a rectangle, struck once on back of handle.

Engraved at a later date on front of handle: "E Peebles" in script.

Description: shell-shape bowl with 18 lobes and a swage-formed rounded drop; rounded upturned handle with midrib.

Spectrographic analysis:

	SILVER	COPPER	LEAD	GOLD
BOWL	86.3	13.1	0.36	0.19
HANDLE	88.0	11.5	0.35	0.14

Provenance: Mr. and Mrs. Stanley B. Ineson, New York City; Mr. and Mrs. Alfred E. Bissell, Wilmington, Del.

Comments: An extraordinarily handsome ladle of majestic proportions.

References: Belden, *Marks of American Silversmiths*, p. 376.

62.240.1609 Gift of Mr. and Mrs. Alfred E. Bissell, 1965

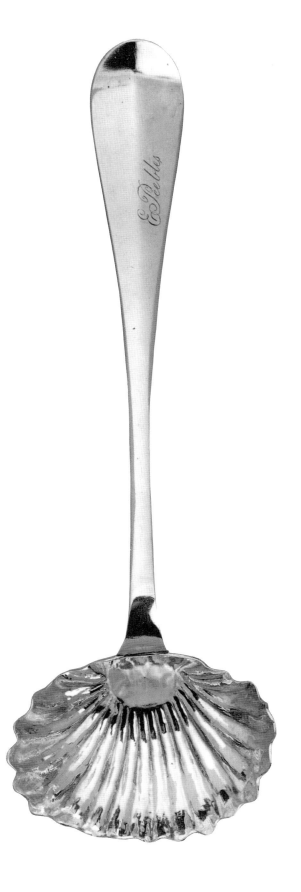

❧ *Simeon Soumaine*

ca. 1675–1750
New York, New York

Born in London to French parents, Simeon Soumaine is said to have arrived in New York City about 1690. His date of birth has been given as 1685, but this is unlikely in view of his admission as a freeman in New York City in January 1695/96. He was the master of William Anderson, Elias Boudinot, and Elias Pelletreau. A lottery was held at Perth Amboy, New Jersey, in 1727 for "£501 of Silver and Gold wrought by Simeon Soumaine of New-York, Gold-Smith, all of the newest Fashion." First prize was "an Eight square Tea-Pot, six Tea-spoons, Skimmer and Tongs, valued at £18 3s. 6d." The silver for the lottery was on display in Soumaine's shop, where it had been appraised by fellow silversmiths Peter Van Dyck and Charles Le Roux (*New-York Gazette*, April 3–10, 1727). Soumaine served as constable and assessor for Dock Ward and was on the vestry of Trinity Church. He witnessed numerous wills, and the names of the testators suggest that he moved freely among both the French and English communities.

Soumaine's surviving silver spans the fashions from the late seventeenth to the mid eighteenth centuries. His forms range from the typical massive New York tankard of 1690–1730 to the elegant tea caddies and octagonal tea-pots of the 1740s. He made communion silver for Saint Peter's Church in Perth Amboy, and Immanuel Church, New Castle, Delaware. A tankard owned by the Charleston Museum bears stamps of both Soumaine and Van Dyck. A tea caddy and a sugar box by Soumaine, both rectangular in plan with canted corners and both bearing the Bayard coat of arms, sold at auction in 1989.

References: Gottesman, *Arts and Crafts, 1726–76*, p. 61. Jones, *Old Silver*, pp. 175–76, 302, 363, 454. *NYHS Collections*: vol. 18 (1885) *Burghers and Freemen*, p. 449; vol. 26 (1893) *Abstracts of Wills*, p. 259; vol. 42 (1909) *Indentures of Apprentices*, pp. 124–25, 148; vols. 43, 44 (1910, 1911) *New York Tax Lists*. *Minutes of the Common Council*, 1:395. Christie's, "Americana Sale" (January 20, 1989), lots 300, 301.

❧ 257
TANKARD, ca. 1730

H. 6⅝" (16.8 cm), DIAM. base 5⅛" (13.0 cm),
w. 7⅞" (20.0 cm)
28 oz. 13 dwt. 17 gr. (892.2 g)

Stamps: "SS" in roman letters, in a rectangle, struck once on base of thumbpiece.

Engraved on front of body opposite handle: armorial device consisting of a shield divided vertically in the center; on the left: 2 greyhound heads above a chevron gules and 1 greyhound head below; on the right: 2 stars above a chevron argent, a horn below; shield enclosed in a frame of strapwork, scrolls, and acanthus leaves with a broken scroll pediment above with a lion rampant on a heraldic band between; area between shield and frame tinctured azure and has an irregular 4-sided reserve on each side.

Engraved on underside of body: "L/ WM" in shaded roman letters, "E.P.L.B." in foliate script; "From his/ Grandmother/ AB" in script.

Description: raised circular body with straight tapering sides and slightly concave bottom, plain flared rim contiguous with body; no centerpunch. Applied base molding consists of a wide ogee molding with a small 1-step molding below and a 2-step molding above. Raised circular single-step lid with flat top and crenellated front; centerpunch inside and outside; bezel. Cast cocoon thumbpiece. Cast 5-segment hinge. Raised-and-soldered hollow C-curve handle with beaded rattail on back; lower end of handle forms a C curve in profile and terminates without a tailpiece; lower vent conforms to center of cross; upper vent semicircular.

Spectrographic analysis:

	SILVER	COPPER	LEAD	GOLD
BODY SIDE	91.2	8.4	0.26	0.06
UNDERSIDE	91.6	8.1	0.26	0.08
LID	90.2	9.0	0.43	0.16
THUMBPIECE	92.8	6.2	0.36	0.27

History: Owned by the Ludlow and, later, Broome families, according to dealer. At the Metropolitan Museum of Art there is a tankard by Thomas Hammersly with the Broome coat of arms that is engraved with the initials "SPB." Charles Knowles Bolton's description of the coat of arms reflects that on the Hammersly

tankard. The coat of arms on the Soumaine tankard bears a superficial resemblance but differs in important details. Bolton's description of the Ludlow arms is closer if not the same: "Arg a chev sa bet 3 foxes' heads erased" with a rampant lion crest.

Provenance: Mr. and Mrs. N. McLean Seabrease, Germantown, Pa., through Robert Ensko, Inc., New York City, to H. F. du Pont, August 1929.

Comments: It is unusual to find the maker's stamp on a small appendage rather than on the body itself. This tankard is not alone among the works of Soumaine in this regard. A tankard at the Brooklyn Museum and one in a private collection are also stamped on the thumbpiece.

This tankard also closely resembles one owned by the Society for the Preservation of Long Island Antiquities. The thumbpiece also appears to be installed backwards, compared to other New York tankards, an irregularity that may have occurred during a repair. It seems that the upper part of the thumbpiece is separate from the lower part, where the stamp is located.

References: Bolton, *Bolton's American Armory*, pp. 23, 106. *Catalogue of Exhibition of Silver Used in New York, New Jersey, and the South* (New York: Metropolitan Museum of Art, 1911), no. 63.

63.524 Gift of H. F. du Pont, 1965

258
LADLE, ca. 1740

L. 14 ⅜" (36.5 cm)
3 oz. 15 dwt. 16 gr. (117.7 g) (includes wood handle)

Stamps: "SS" in roman letters, in a rectangle, struck once on underside of bowl.

Engraved on outside of bowl opposite handle: armorial device consisting of a shield divided vertically in center; on the left, a pile with 3 lozenges; on the right: a chevron in the center and a canton containing a saltire cross in the upper left corner.

Description: raised circular bowl with bulbous sides, rounded bottom, incurved neck, and flared molded rim; V-shape spout inset on 1 side. Tapering tubular handle socket with midrib attached to side of bowl at right angle to spout. Long turned hardwood handle with midband and bulbous upper end. Handle fixed in socket by 2 silver pins.

Spectrographic analysis:

	SILVER	COPPER	LEAD	GOLD
UNDERSIDE OF BOWL	93.6	5.8	0.36	0.18
SPOUT	93.7	5.4	0.28	0.20
SOCKET	95.5	3.6	0.34	0.16

Provenance: Avis and Rockwell Gardiner, Stamford, Conn.

Comments: The coat of arms is unidentified.

References: Kauffman, *Colonial Silversmith*, p. 157.

54.38 Museum purchase from Avis and Rockwell Gardiner, 1954

259
MARROW SCOOP, ca. 1740

L. 9" (22.9 cm)
1 oz. 5 dwt. 11 gr. (39.6 g)

Stamps: "SS" in roman letters, in a square, struck once on back.

Engraved on front of shaft: "K" in foliate script, over an armorial device consisting of a griffin's head on a heraldic band.

Description: 2 long grooved channels, one narrower than the other, connected by a half-round shaft.

Spectrographic analysis:

SILVER	COPPER	GOLD	LEAD
90.2	9.2	0.22	0.17

Provenance: Ginsburg & Levy, New York City, sold to H. F. du Pont, December 1949.

Comments: The stamp is not the same as that on the ladle or the tankard, but it is still believed to be Soumaine's. Silversmiths often had smaller versions of their stamps for use on small objects. Marrow scoops, or marrow spoons, were commonly used in the eighteenth century to dig the marrow out of bones. In England 1 scoop usually accompanied a set of 10 knives, and knife boxes often had 1 compartment reserved for the marrow scoop.

References: Fennimore, *Silver and Pewter*, no. 36. Clayton, *Collector's Dictionary*, s.v. "Marrow spoon."

58.2101 Gift of H. F. du Pont, 1965

Tobias Stoughtenburg

1700–1759
New York, New York

Baptized in the New York Dutch Church, December 22, 1700, Tobias was the son of Tobias Stoughtenburg, Sr., and Annetje (Van Rollegon) Stoughtenburg. His mother's sister Geertruyd married silversmith Bartholomew Le Roux I in 1688, who was possibly Tobias's master. Admitted as a freeman in 1731, Tobias married Maria Ten Broock in 1733. His advertisement in the *New-York Weekly Post Boy* (October 23, 1744) placed him "near the Spring Garden, New-York." It is often hard to distinguish between father and son in the records. Stoughtenburg left a small body of work of high quality. His engraved teapot in the Darling Foundation collection has a solid Dutch quality to it. It is one of two that are known to have survived (see Christie's sale [January 19, 1990], lot 223, for the other one). Two groups of silver that he made for New York families survive: a set of three tankards for the Marston family and a tankard, salt, beaker, caster, and two spoons for the Van Loon family.

References: Gottesman, *Arts and Crafts, 1726–76*, pp. 61–62. Miller, *Silver by New York Makers*, nos. 291–92. *Minutes of the Common Council. NYHS Collections*: vol. 18 (1885) *Burghers and Freemen*, p. 118. *New York State Silversmiths*, pp. 168, 172. Von Khrum, *Silversmiths*, pp. 124–25. Alice Winchester, "Some Heirloom Silver from an Old New York Family," *Antiques* 51, no. 6 (June 1947): 390–91.

260
STUFFING SPOON, ca. 1740

L. 14 %6" (37.0 cm)
7 oz. 9 gr. (217.8 g)

Stamps: "TSB" in roman letters, in an oval, struck twice on back of handle.

Engraved on back of handle: "M+M" in roman letters.

Description: large deep oval bowl with swage-formed double rounded drop on back; rounded upturned handle deeply creased on front for most of its length.

Spectrographic analysis:

	SILVER	COPPER	LEAD	GOLD
BOWL	93.7	6.1	0.13	0.10
HANDLE	90.8	9.0	0.17	0.08

Provenance: Mr. and Mrs. Stanley B. Ineson, New York City; Mr. and Mrs. Alfred E. Bissell, Wilmington, Del.

Exhibitions: Metropolitan Museum of Art, New York City, 1935–61.

References: Belden, *Marks of American Silversmiths*, p. 398. Buhler and Hood, *American Silver*, no. 602, for Soumaine spoon.

Comments: An uncommonly strong interpretation of a not uncommon form. A similar large spoon by Soumaine is owned by Yale University Art Gallery.

62.240.1666 Gift of Mr. and Mrs. Alfred E. Bissell, 1965

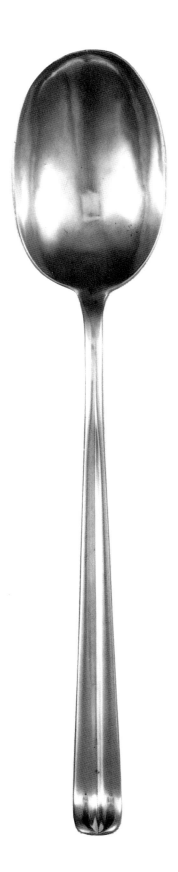

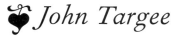

John Targee

w. 1797–ca. 1828

Peter Targee

w. 1808–14

John & Peter Targee, w. 1809–14
New York, New York

The Targee family came from Washington County, Rhode Island, and descended from seventeenth-century Huguenot émigrés from Port des Barques on the west coast of France. Beyond the family's origins, little is known about John Targee's life as a craftsman. It is uncertain whether Peter Targee was his brother or his son. Targee was somehow associated with silversmith John Vernon, who also used a similar pseudohallmark (a sailing ship). The association is confirmed by the fact that Targee's son was named John Vernon Targee. John is listed in New York City directories at 24 Gold Street, 1797–99, and at 192 Water Street, 1804–28, as a gold- and silversmith. From 1829 to 1839, his address is given as 27 Frankfort Street, without an occupation. Peter is listed at 71 and 96 John Street, 1808, and at 192 Water Street, 1809–14. The partnership was productive; more pieces survive from the partnership than by John Targee alone.

Although Targee remains a vague figure in the literature on silver, the following account, published in 1840 in a compilation of the richest citizens of New York City, suggests that he found a more profitable field of endeavor than that of silversmith:

John Targee—A young French adventurer, silversmith by trade, emigrated, some fifty years ago, to this country, and by good conduct and industry, and great shrewdness as a politician in the democratic ranks, to which he, as it turned out, wisely attached himself, rendered himself eminently conspicuous in that party, and for his untiring devotion to their interests, was richly rewarded with sundry profitable posts of honor. So distinguished had he become from the Jeffersonian triumph of 1800 upward, that Vice President Tompkins made him his confidential friend, and he was everywhere looked upon for a time as the most influential leader, if not chief of the party in this quarter of the state. Hence during the struggles to supplant Clinton, the poet Croaker wrote thus:

> *I'm sick of General Jackson's toast*
> *Canals are nought to me;*
> *Nor do I care who rules the roost,*
> *Clinton or Targee.*

According to the compiler of this account, Targee was said to be worth $150,000. Diarist Philip Hone mentions Targee as a leader of a celebration in honor of Van Buren's nomination for the presidency in 1840 and again as a pall-bearer for the funeral of William Henry Harrison in April 1841. John and Peter Targee made a tea set owned by the Museum of the City of New York; a beaker for the Irish Presbyterian Church in New York, given by Henry Rutgers; a snuffbox presented by the people of Kingston, New York, to Dewitt Clinton and now at the Metropolitan Museum of Art; and a gold sword and scabbard given by Governor Tompkins to Maj. Gen. Edmund Pendleton Gaines for the defense of Fort Erie in 1814 (present whereabouts unknown).

References: James Frances Dallett, "Corrected Attribution," in "Collectors' Notes," *Antiques* 89, no. 5 (May 1966): 734–35. Ensko, *American Silversmiths IV*, p. 201. Jones, *Old Silver*, p. 358. Von Khrum, *Silversmiths*, p. 126. *The Diary of Philip Hone, 1828–1851*, 2 vols. (New York: Dodd, Mead, 1889), 2:38, 75. *Wealth and Biography of the Wealthy Citizens of New York City* (New York: "Compiled with much care and published at the Sun Office," 1840), p. 28.

❦ 261 a, b
SUGAR BOWL AND CREAMER, ca. 1815

(a) Sugar bowl: H. (with lid) 8 ½" (21.6 cm), w. 9 ½" (24.1 cm)
26 oz. 20 gr. (808.1 g)
(b) Creamer: H. 6 ¼" (15.9 cm), w. 4 ¼" (10.8 cm)
13 oz. 17 dwt. 8 gr. (430.3 g)

Stamps: "I.T." in roman letters, in a rectangle, struck once on underside of each body; 2 illegible strikes in same location on each body.

Engraved on both sides of both bodies: "L" in foliate script.

Description: oval in plan with 12 vertical lobes around lower body; centerpunch on underside. Stepped base, rounded rectangle in plan, joined to body by circular pedestal. Both pieces have die-rolled decorative bands: all, except 1 around rim of sugar bowl, consist of repeat pattern of tall narrow panels set in round arches alternating with slender vertical darts. Bands are ⅜" around base, ⅝" around pedestal, and 9/16" around upper body.

(a) Sugar bowl and lid: sugar bowl has raised stepped upper body between 2 decorative bands; 2 double reversed C-scroll handles, made in vertical halves, rectangular in section, with thumbpiece at top and single plain terminals; vents in handles. Lid oval in plan with flat rim and single-step center; hollow cast finial in shape of a bouquet of flowers and leaves; vent into finial.

(b) Creamer: upper portion of body raised and incurved before flared rim; low sides, higher at handle, extended rim for wide pouring lip. Single handle same as on bowl. Applied decorative band, around outside of rim, 3/16" wide, consists of veined pointed leaves.

Spectrographic analysis:

	SILVER	COPPER	LEAD	GOLD
(a) Sugar bowl				
BODY SIDE	88.9	10.8	0.21	0.10
FOOT	93.7	5.4	0.44	0.31
HANDLE	87.4	11.6	0.26	0.09
(b) Creamer				
BODY SIDE	90.1	9.5	0.13	0.11
FOOT	94.8	4.5	0.17	0.29
HANDLE	90.3	9.3	0.10	0.05

Provenance: Marshall P. Blankarn, New York City.

78.143.1, .2 Gift of Marshall P. Blankarn, 1978

❦ 262 a–c
TEA SERVICE, 1809–14

(a) Teapot: H. 6 ¾" (17.2 cm), w. 11 ¼" (28.6 cm)
19 oz. 18 dwt. 1 gr. (617.6 g)
(b) Sugar bowl and lid: H. 4 ⅞" (12.4 cm),
w. 6 ⅛" (15.6 cm)
9 oz. 7 dwt. (290.2 g)
(c) Creamer: H. 6 ⅛" (12.5 cm), w. 7 ¹¹⁄₁₆"
(19.6 cm)
6 oz. 7 dwt. 20 gr. (198.4 g)

Stamps: "I&PT" in roman letters, in a rectangle, struck once on underside of each body. Accompanying each stamp are 2 illegible stamps.

Engraved on side of each body: "JS" in foliate script, in an oval enclosure of leaves formed by engraving and wheelwork.

Description: seamed bulbous lower bodies with flat bottoms; horizontal bulbous bands above; no centerpunches. Each piece mounted on 4 short, cast, animal paw feet. Oblong style.

(a) Teapot: upper body above plain horizontal band incurves to an oblong raised-and-domed partial lid, hinged on short side with a flush-mounted 5-segment hinge; oblong cast finial; circular vent. S-curve seamed spout cut away on upper front. Sharply angled hardwood handle attached to plain silver sockets. Body pierced at spout to form strainer.

(b) Sugar bowl: plain rolled rim. Lid similar to that on teapot except larger and without vent; 2 molded strap handles, both sharply angled.

(c) Creamer: neck rises and extends in front to form a narrow pouring lip; rises in back to meet sharply angled, molded strap handle; simple molded rim.

Spectrographic analysis:

	SILVER	COPPER	GOLD	LEAD
(a) Teapot				
UPPER BODY	93.7	6.2	0.12	0.03
LOWER BODY	92.9	7.0	0.11	0.04
BASE	93.6	6.2	0.15	0.04
LID	96.4	3.4	0.19	0.03
SPOUT	93.7	6.0	0.24	0.03
(b) Sugar bowl and lid				
UPPER BODY	92.0	7.9	0.02	0.03
RIM	92.3	7.6	0.02	0.03
BASE	93.9	5.9	0.18	0.04
HANDLE	93.8	6.0	0.17	0.03
LID	92.7	7.1	0.13	0.03
(c) Creamer				
BODY	93.3	6.4	0.32	0.05
UNDERSIDE	94.1	5.1	0.04	0.01
HANDLE	93.7	6.1	0.22	0.04

Provenance: Carl Kossack, North Haven, Conn.

References: Christie's (New York City) (January 23, 1982), lots 57, 58, for 2 3-piece tea services by Targee, 1 with similar bodies and animal-paw feet.

90.43.1–.3 Gift of Carl Kossack, 1990

❦ 263
SPOON, ca. 1810

L. 9 ¼" (23.5 cm)
2 oz. 4 dwt. 14 gr. (69.2 g)

Stamps: "I.T." in roman letters, in a rectangle, struck once on back of handle; accompanied by 2 strikes, 1 an illegible stamp (possibly a lion's head) in a shield, the other a roman "P" in a shield.

Engraved on front of handle: "CV" in foliate script.

Description: pointed oval bowl with swage-formed single-pointed drop; pointed down-turned handle with short midrib.

Spectrographic analysis: Silver content is 91.8 percent.

Provenance: Mr. and Mrs. Stanley B. Ineson, New York City; Mr. and Mrs. Alfred E. Bissell, Wilmington, Del.

References: Belden, *Marks of American Silversmiths,* p. 403.

62.240.1502 Gift of Mr. and Mrs. Alfred E. Bissell, 1962–63

Barent Ten Eyck

1714–95
Albany, New York

The fifth son of Koenraet Ten Eyck, one of the Albany area's first silversmiths, and Geertje Van Schaick, Barent could have learned his craft from his father or from his older brother, Jacob C. Ten Eyck. He married Elsie Gansevoort in 1752. He was heavily engaged in making silver for the Indian trade according to numerous references in the papers of Sir William Johnson. On August 16, 1756, for example, Johnson paid Ten Eyck £100 "for sundrys for Warriors." Apparently a well-made silver arm band could be bartered in the 1760s for three beaver pelts. A silver gorget by Ten Eyck with the royal coat of arms is in the Museum of the American Indian, New York City. He made a small quantity of domestic silver. Ten Eyck served in the militia before and during the Revolution. In 1795 he subscribed £40 toward the establishment of Union College in Schenectady.

References: Rice, *Albany Silver*, pp. 16, 68, 69. George Barton Cutten, "The Ten Eyck Silversmiths," *Antiques* 42, no. 6 (December 1942): 299–303. Henry Waterman George, "The Ten Eyck Family of New York," *NYG&BR* 63, nos. 2–4 (April, July, October, 1932): 269. Michael W. Hamilton, ed., *The Papers of Sir William Johnson*, 14 vols. (Albany: University of the State of New York, 1921–65), 2:589, 599, 637, 3:150, 4:298, 7:246, 453. Charlotte Wilcoxen, "Indian-Trade Silver of the New York Colonial Frontier," *Antiques* 116, no. 6 (December 1979): 1356–61, fig. 3.

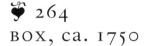 264
BOX, ca. 1750

L. 2 13/16" (7.1 cm), w. 2 ½" (6.4 cm), H. ½" (1.3 cm)
1 oz. 13 dwt. 3 gr. (51.4 g)

Stamps: "B•TE" ("TE" conjoined) in roman letters, in a rectangle, struck once inside bottom of body.

Engraved on underside of body: "I✶K" in shaded roman letters. *Engraved on lid:* preening bird with long neck and extended tail feathers standing on a hillock with flowers; conforming border in repeating pattern of geometric plant forms.

Description: heart-shape box with hinged lid; sides of body, formed from sheet silver, are attached to flat bottom with rolled edge; lid similarly made but sides molded; 3-segment hinge with brass pin soldered to body across lobes of heart.

Spectrographic analysis:

	SILVER	COPPER	LEAD	GOLD
BOTTOM	74.4	24.5	0.39	0.10
SIDE	83.9	15.3	0.29	0.11
LID	70.5	28.4	0.39	0.07

Provenance: H. F. du Pont.

Exhibitions: "Albany Silver" and "Remembrance of Patria: Dutch Arts and Culture in Colonial America, 1609–1776," Albany Institute of History and Art, 1964, 1986.

References: Rice, *Albany Silver*, fig. 3. Fales, *American Silver*, no. 18. Blackburn and Piwonka, *Remembrance of Patria*, no. 307.

Comments: Unusually low silver content.

52.291 Gift of H. F. du Pont, 1952

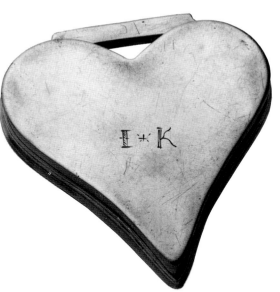

Jacob C. Ten Eyck

1705–93
Albany, New York

Jacob C. Ten Eyck was the son of silversmith Koenraet Ten Eyck of Albany. In 1719 he was apprenticed to Charles Le Roux of New York City for seven years. The text of his indenture is reproduced in Henry J. Kauffman, *The Colonial Silversmith: His Techniques and His Products*. Jacob returned to Albany and went into business with his father. Both were merchants as well as silversmiths; a surviving account book shows that they sold quantities of silver for the Indian trade. Forms mentioned include buckles, clasps, gorgets, crosses, arm bands, earrings, and buttons. Jacob also made extensive domestic silver, especially paneled bowls, salts, tankards, porringers, teapots, and canns. The Albany Institute owns a tankard stamped by Jacob Ten Eyck and Bartholomew Schaats. In 1736 Ten Eyck married Catharyna Cuyler (1709–90), daughter of Abraham and Catherine Cuyler. He served in a number of civic offices in Albany, including that of mayor and judge of the Court of Common Pleas. He was a member of the Albany Committee of Correspondence.

References: George Barton Cutten, "The Ten Eyck Silversmiths," *Antiques* 42, no. 6 (December 1942): 299–303. Henry Waterman George, "The Ten Eyck Family of New York," *NYG&BR* 63, nos. 2–4 (April, July, October, 1932): 164. Kauffman, *Colonial Silversmith*, p. 43. *NYHS Collections:* vol. 24 (1892) *Muster Rolls of the New York Provincial Troops*, p. 1; vol. 42 (1909) *Indentures of Apprentices*, p. 122; vols. 50 (1918) and 53 (1921) *Cadwalader Colden Papers*, pp. 155, 203. Cuyler Reynolds, *Albany Chronicles: A History of the City Arranged Chronologically* (Albany: J. B. Lyon, 1906), no. 22 (list of mayors), p. 383. Rice, *Albany Silver*, p. 68, figs. 5, 6, 13, 16.

265
BOWL, ca. 1735

H. (incl. handles) 4 13/16" (12.2 cm), DIAM. bowl 7 ½" (19.1 cm), W. 11 1/16" (28.1 cm)
18 OZ. 20 gr. (561.2 g)

Stamps: "[I]T[E]" in roman letters, in a circle, struck once on body above back center panel; "IT[E]" in roman letters, in a circle, struck once on body, above panel, left of center front. Stamps incomplete and partially illegible, but H. F. du Pont's records list "ITE" ("TE" conjoined).

Engraved on side of bowl under rim: "W / EE" (a sprig between the *E*'s) in script.

Description: circular raised bowl form with plain thickened rim; applied circular base with flat footring. Bottom of body chased with central star-pattern flower; sides of body decorated with 6 chased panels, each with a curvilinear border and each containing a different floral design; accents of heavy punchwork dots around lower body; 2 cast C-curve handles with caryatid figures, double C scrolls at bottom, scroll terminals at top, rows of large beads on sides. Center-punch obscured by chasing.

Spectrographic analysis:

	SILVER	COPPER	LEAD	GOLD
BODY SIDE	92.2	7.3	0.27	0.13
FOOTRING	93.8	5.3	0.21	0.11
HANDLE	90.0	8.7	0.90	0.11

History: Made for Evert and Engletie (Lansing) Wendell, who were married in 1710. Evert Wendell (1681–1750) lived and died in Albany. Wendell was a lawyer and commissioner of Indian Affairs from 1724 to 1734. His will, made in 1749, bequeathed his surveying instruments and law books to eldest son Johannes; extensive lands plus "pleasure sleigh and large Holland gun marked with his name on the lock" to son Abraham; and his dwelling house and lot in Albany's fourth ward to youngest son Philip. Wendell's account books, daybook, and ledger are in the New-York Historical Society. Engletie (1690–1769) was the daughter of Jan (Johannes) Lansing, the presumed owner of the tall beaker (no. 215) by the silversmith HH.

Provenance: According to Charles F. Montgomery, the bowl descended through Philip Wendell's line and remained in the Wendell family until sold.

Exhibitions: Winter Antiques Show, New York City, January 1982. "Albany Silver," Albany Institute of History and Art, 1964. Washington (D.C.) Antiques Show, 1986.

Comments: Similar bowls were made by Jesse Kip, Jacob Boelen, Bartholomew Le Roux I, Simeon Soumaine, Benjamin Wynkoop, and Cornelius Kierstede. Ten Eyck also made a bowl like this for Dirck and Margaret (Cuyler) Ten Broeck. Bowls of this type (*brandewijnskom*) were used in Friesland and Groningen, The Netherlands, for communal drinking on festive occasions. They were filled with brandy and raisins and passed around for each guest to serve himself with a silver spoon. For a tankard by Koenraet Ten Eyck, also made for Evert and Engletie Wendell, see Rice, *Albany Silver*, fig. 9. See no. 157 for a tankard made by Jacob Boelen for the same patron.

References: Rice, *Albany Silver*, fig. 11. *Antiques* 70, no. 5 (November 1956): frontispiece, p. 449. Clayton, *Collector's Dictionary*, pl. 5. Fales, *American Silver*, no. 42. Fennimore, *Silver and Pewter*, no. 95. Mrs. Emery Westervelt Dennis, "The Ten Eyck Bowl," *Bulletin of the Albany Institute of History and Art* 19, no. 5 (Fall 1967): 1–6, for essay on similar bowl. A. L. den Blaauwen, *Dutch Silver, 1580–1830* (Amsterdam: Rijksmuseum, 1979), no. 85, p. 370, for prototype *brandewijnskom*. John N. Pearce, "New York's Two-Handled Paneled Silver Bowls," *Antiques* 80, no. 4 (October 1961): 341–45. "Further Comments on the Lobate Bowl Form," *Antiques* 90, no. 4 (October 1966): 524–25. For portraits of both Wendells, see Blackburn and Piwonka, *Remembrance of Patria*, p. 244.

55.127 Gift of Charles K. Davis, 1955

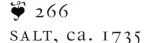

266
SALT, ca. 1735

H. 2 7/16" (6.2 cm), DIAM. base 3 ¾" (9.5 cm)
4 oz. 4 dwt. 7 gr. (131.1 g)

Stamps: "ITE" ("TE" conjoined) in roman letters, in an oval, struck once on upper surface in center.

Engraved on side of body: "TE/ H✲M" ("TE" conjoined) in shaded roman letters.

Description: raised circular form flared toward base, incurved toward top; shallow depression in top forms bowl with molded edge; bold gadrooned borders encircle upper and lower body; below upper gadrooning is a triple row of punchwork dots; above lower gadrooning is a decorative border of foliage, 4-petal florets, and punchwork dots. Bottom edge flattened to form footring; centerpunch on upper surface of bowl.

Spectrographic analysis:

SILVER	COPPER	LEAD	GOLD
90.4	8.9	0.36	0.12

History: Made for Hendrick Ten Eyck (1680–1772) and his wife Margarita (Bleeker) Ten Eyck (1680–1773), who were married in 1706. They were maternal ancestors of H. F. du Pont. Jacob Ten Eyck was Hendrick's cousin.

Provenance: Hendrick and Margarita (Bleeker) Ten Eyck; Jacob Henry (1708–76) and Anna (Wendell) Ten Eyck, married 1737; Harmanus (1750–1828) and Margaret (Bleeker) Ten Eyck, married 1776; Andrew (1772–1849) and Anna (Ten Eyck) Foster; Herman Ten Eyck (1822–69) and Mary Pauline (Lentilhon) Foster; Henry Algernon (1838–1926) and Mary Pauline (Foster) (1849–1902) du Pont, married 1874; H. F. (1880–1969) and Ruth (Wales) (1889–1967) du Pont, married 1916.

Exhibitions: "Albany Silver," Albany Institute of History and Art, 1964.

References: C. Louise Avery, *Early American Silver* (1930; reprint, New York: Russell and Russell, 1968), p. 344, fig. 60. Marshall Davidson, "A Colonial Silver Trencher Salt," *Bulletin, Metropolitan Museum of Art* 32 (July 1937): 186, 188, for a similar trencher salt by Ten Eyck. Pierre S. du Pont, *Genealogy of the du Pont Family, 1739–1942*, 3 vols. (Wilmington, Del.: By the author, 1943), 1: chart 86. Fales, *American Silver*, no. 105. Fennimore, *Silver and Pewter*, no. 57. Rice, *Albany Silver*, fig. 5. John Beverly Riggs, *A Guide to the Manuscripts in the Eleutherian Mills Historical Library* (Greenville, Del.: By the library, 1970), for genealogy.

59.2596 Gift of H. F. du Pont, 1965

❦ *William Thomson*

New York, New York, w. 1810–45

Little is known about William Thomson, although he worked for a long time and produced a good quantity of silver. He is listed in directories as a silversmith and a "manufacturing silversmith." He worked at 99 Broadway (1810–11), 399 Broadway (1812–14), 118 William Street (1815–20), 177 Broadway (1821–22), 129 William Street (1823–33, 1841–45). A privately owned mug, circa 1820, bears the stamp of Thomas Chester Coit of Natchez, Mississippi, in addition to Thomson's stamp. This reflects the practice common among major silversmiths of the day of making silver for resale elsewhere by another silversmith or jeweler. A tea service in the Hammerslough collection at Wadsworth Atheneum was commissioned by the vestry of Saint Michael's Church, Charleston, South Carolina, for presentation to the unknown "NMB." Thomson also made a pitcher that was presented to Capt. Samuel C. Reid for his spirited defense of the brig *General Armstrong* in the Azores

on September 26, 1814. The pitcher appeared in the 1937–38 exhibition "Silver by New York Makers" at the Museum of the City of New York. Thomson's holloware reflects the styles popular in the 1810s and 1820s with lobate bodies, die-rolled decorative bands, and fancy cast handles, feet, and finials. An elaborate pair of rococo candlesticks with an 1825 inscription is in the Metropolitan Museum of Art. Thomson also made the silver mounts for a covered coconut cup engraved with Masonic symbols in the Hammerslough collection. He is also credited with a silver medallion featuring the shield of Owen Glendower on one side and royal coat of arms on the other. It may have been used in one of the many secret societies of that time.

References: Graham Gallery advertisement, *Antiques* 108, no. 4 (October 1975): 673, for lobate-style neoclassial tea set. Jones, *Old Silver*, p. 462, for beaker made for First Church, Stonington, Conn. Hinda Kohn advertisement, *Antiques* 127, no. 4 (April 1985): 782, for silver medallion. "Masonic Mystery," *Antiques* 102, no. 6 (December 1972): 1077. Von Khrum, *Silversmiths*, p. 128.

❦ 267
BEAKER, 1833

H. 3 ⅜" (8.6 cm), DIAM. rim 3 3/16" (8.1 cm), DIAM. base 2 ⅝" (6.7 cm)
3 oz. 13 dwt. 6 gr. (113.9 g)

Stamps: "W.Thomson" in script, in a conforming surround; "NEW.YORK" in roman letters, in a rectangle; "1833" in a rectangle. All struck once on underside.

Engraved on side of body: armorial device consisting of a shield with a horizontal banner in center, a stringed horn above and 3 fleurs-de-lis below; *crest:* demi-lion rampant emerging from basket (or half globe); motto: "SUPERANDA FORTUNA FERENDO" in roman letters, around lower half of coat of arms.

Description: raised cylindrical body slightly tapered toward bottom; plain slightly flared rim; flat bottom; centerpunch on underside.

Spectrographic analysis:

	SILVER	COPPER	LEAD	GOLD
BODY SIDE	87.2	12.2	0.30	0.15
UNDERSIDE	88.2	11.2	0.25	0.15

Provenance: The Silver Shelf, Ardmore, Pa.

Comments: If "1833" refers to the year of manufacture, dates should logically appear on other Thomson pieces. One such instance is a ewer by Thomson advertised by Pillsbury, Michel & Associates with the statement "maker mark dated 1835." From this we presume that the year 1835 is struck into the body as 1833 is on the beaker. Another example is a coffeepot at the Yale University Art Gallery carrying Thomson's stamp and the strike "1831." Most of Thomson's silver does not carry these date stamps.

References: Pillsbury, Michel & Associates advertisement, *Antiques* 124, no. 3 (September 1983): 454, for ewer with 1835 stamp. Silver Shelf advertisement, *Antiques* 106, no. 6 (December 1972): 1092.

73.37 Museum purchase from the Silver Shelf, 1973

❧ 268
WASTE BOWL, ca. 1830

H. 5 7/16" (13.8 cm), DIAM. 6 ¾" (17.2 cm)
17 oz. 13 dwt. 14 gr. (548.7 g)

Stamps: "[W]Thomson" in script, in a conforming surround, struck once on underside of body.

Scratched twice on underside of pedestal: "18 6".

Description: raised circular bulbous lower body with 13 lobes; incurving neck and flared rim topped by die-rolled decorative band consisting of meandering vine with grapes and leaves; centerpunch on underside. Raised, circular, stepped pedestal with die-rolled decorative bands where pedestal meets body and around base; both bands consist of sheaves of wheat; the upper band 3/16" wide, the lower band 5/16" wide.

Spectrographic analysis:

	SILVER	COPPER	GOLD	LEAD
BODY SIDE (LOBE)	83.7	16.2	0.14	0.01
RIM BAND	95.0	4.9	0.10	0.04
BASE BAND	90.0	9.8	0.22	0.02
UNDERSIDE	95.4	4.5	0.17	0.01

Provenance: Carl Kossack, North Haven, Conn.

90.49 Gift of Carl Kossack, 1990

❧ 269
SUGAR TONGS, ca. 1825

L. 6 9/16" (16.7 cm)
2 oz. 1 dwt. 13 gr. (64.6 g)

Stamps: "W.Thomson" in script, in a conforming surround, struck once inside each arm.

Engraved on bow back: "M Mc" in foliate script.

Description: bow-type tongs; U-shape form with broad bow, fiddle-shape arms and shell grips; applied sheaf of wheat on outside of each arm.

Spectrographic analysis:

	SILVER	COPPER	LEAD	GOLD
BOW BACK	88.4	10.9	0.53	0.08
SHELL	87.4	11.9	0.42	0.11

Provenance: H. F. du Pont.

Comments: Same motif and inscription as no. 270.

57.1372 Gift of H. F. du Pont, 1965

❧ 270 a–c
SPOONS, ca. 1825

(a) L. 5 13/16" (14.8 cm)
11 dwt. 15 gr. (18.1 g)
(b) L. 5 13/16" (14.8 cm)
12 dwt. 12 gr. (19.4 g)
(c) L. 5 ⅞" (14.9 cm)
13 dwt. 3 gr. (20.4 g)

Stamps: "W.Thomson" in script, in a conforming surround, struck once on back of each handle.

Engraved on front of each handle: "M Mc" in foliate script.

Description: pointed oval bowl with swage-formed 12-lobe shell on back; rounded downturned fiddle-shape handle with swage-formed sheaf of wheat on upper end.

Spectrographic analysis: Silver content ranges from 84.9 to 86.9 percent.

Provenance: H. F. du Pont.

Comments: Same motif and inscription as no. 269.

57.1382–.1384 Gift of H. F. du Pont, 1965

❧ 271
SPOON, ca. 1825

L. 5 ¾" (14.6 cm)
11 dwt. 18 gr. (18.3 g)

Stamps: "Wm Thomson." in script, in a conforming surround, struck once on back of handle.

Engraved on front of handle: illegible script letters. *Engraved on back of handle:* "Hoxsey" in script.

Description: pointed oval bowl with swage-formed rounded drop; rounded downturned fiddle-shape handle with midrib.

Spectrographic analysis: Silver content is 87.7 percent.

Provenance: Mr. and Mrs. Stanley B. Ineson, New York City; Mr. and Mrs. Alfred E. Bissell, Wilmington, Del.

References: Belden, *Marks of American Silversmiths,* p. 408.

62.240.718 Gift of Mr. and Mrs. Alfred E. Bissell, 1962–63

Tiffany & Company

1851–
New York, New York

Charles Tiffany (1812–1902), along with partner John B. Young, opened a store at 259 Broadway in 1837. They sold stationery and fancy goods, which included a few small silver items like thimbles, card cases, and snuffboxes. In 1841 J. L. Ellis joined the firm, and it became Tiffany, Young & Ellis. By 1848 the firm ventured into jewelry, with substantial purchases made in Paris.

Shortly after the company moved to larger quarters at 271 Broadway in 1847, it began selling silver hollowwares. In 1848 the partners hired as their first designer Gustav Herter, who worked for the firm until 1851, when he left to become a cabinetmaker. Following Herter's departure, the firm contracted with John C. Moore, an established New York silversmith, to make silver exclusively for them. Later that same year, Moore turned his business over to his son Edward C. Moore (1827–91), a talented silversmith and designer. In the words of Charles and Mary Carpenter, the younger Moore was "the guiding genius of Tiffany's silverware business." Thus, for all practical, if not legal, purposes, 1851 may be considered the founding date of the company. In 1853 Charles Tiffany gained complete control of the company, which became known as Tiffany & Company. Later that year the firm moved again, this time to 550 Broadway, where it remained until 1870, before moving yet again to Union Square. The Tiffany factory, located on Prince Street, employed 500 workers during the 1870s and 1880s.

The period from the late 1860s to the late 1880s is regarded as the most creative for the company. There is no doubt that Edward C. Moore, who merged his own company with Tiffany and became general manager of the latter in 1868, was responsible for this flowering. He assembled a notable collection of oriental art, later bequeathed to the Metropolitan Museum of Art, that inspired many innovations in the design of Tiffany silver. The gothic "M" found on so much nineteenth-century Tiffany silver indicates that it was made under Moore's jurisdiction. He died in 1891.

As part of its search for quality, Tiffany & Company adopted the sterling standard in 1851. At that time much silver was stamped "Coin," "Coin Silver," "Dollar," or "STANDARD," all of which were well below the British sterling standard of 92.5 percent silver. Tiffany silver was stamped "ENGLISH STERLING" from 1854 until 1870, after which it was stamped "STERLING SILVER." In manufacturing, Tiffany combined modern techniques—die stamping, spinning, power tools, and the specialization of tasks—with hand work and strict quality control. Numbers stamped on the undersides of hollowware are pattern and order numbers and, sometimes, patent dates. Although these numbers can assist in dating, they are not consistently reliable indicators of dates of manufacture.

A vast amount of Tiffany silver survives, in both public and private collections. One excellent representative body of Tiffany silver is owned by the Musuem of the City of New York, and one of the more spectacular groupings is owed by the New York Yacht Club. Tiffany & Company made many important pieces of American presentation silver, including the monumental Bryant vase now at the Metropolitan Museum of Art. Curiously, it did not make flatware until 1869. The firm remains in existence and retains its archives, which are rich in drawings and other records.

Louis Comfort Tiffany (1848–1933), son of Charles, had little to do with designing Tiffany & Company products. As an artist and decorator he earned renown in his own right. His Tiffany Studios, not to be confused with Tiffany & Company, made about two dozen pieces of custom-designed silver, but the firm is better known for its work in glass and other metals.

References: Charles H. Carpenter, Jr., and Mary Grace Carpenter, *Tiffany Silver* (New York: Dodd, Mead, 1978). Carpenter, "Nineteenth-Century Silver in the New York Yacht Club," *Antiques* 112, no. 3 (September 1977): 496–505. Charles H. Carpenter, Jr., and Janet Zapata, *The Silver of Tiffany and Co., 1850–1987* (Boston: Museum of Fine Arts, 1987). John Howard Brown, ed., *The Cyclopedia of American Biographies*, 7 vols. (Boston, 1903), s.v. "Tiffany, Charles Louis."

☙ 272 a–h
BEVERAGE SERVICE, 1874

(a) Kettle on stand: H. 12 ½" (31.8 cm),
H. (stand only) 6 ¹⁵⁄₁₆" (17.6 cm), H. (kettle only)
9 ⅛" (23.2 cm), W. (kettle) 8 ⁷⁄₁₆" (21.4 cm)
Kettle: 29 oz. 2 dwt. 18 gr. (906.3 g)
Stand: 33 oz. 6 dwt. 20 gr. (1037.0 g)
(b) Teapot: H. 5 ³⁄₁₆" (13.2 cm), W. 9 ⁷⁄₁₆"
(24.0 cm)
22 oz. 13 dwt. 9 gr. (705.1 g)
(c) Coffeepot: H. 7 ⅜" (18.7 cm), W. 7 ¹⁄₁₆"
(17.9 cm)
17 oz. 8 dwt. 5 gr. (541.5 g)
(d) Hot milk pot: H. 8 ⁷⁄₁₆" (21.4 cm), W. 6 ⁹⁄₁₆"
(16.7 cm)
24 oz. 8 dwt. 17 gr. (760.0 g)
(e) Water pitcher: H. 8 ¹¹⁄₁₆" (22.1 cm), W. 7 ⅝"
(19.4 cm)
29 oz. 16 dwt. 8 gr. (927.4 g)
(f) Sugar bowl and lid: H. 4 ¹¹⁄₁₆" (12.0 cm),
W. 7 ⅛" (18.1 cm)
14 oz. 9 dwt. 22 gr. (451.0 g)
(g) Waste bowl: H. 3 ½" (8.9 cm), DIAM. 5 ½"
(14.0 cm)
11 oz. 19 dwt. 5 gr. (372.1 g)
(h) Creamer: H. 4 ⁵⁄₁₆" (11.0 cm), W. 5 ³⁄₁₆"
(13.2 cm)
9 oz. 7 dwt. 17 gr. (292.0 g)

Stamps: "TIFFANY & CO." and "UNION
SQUARE" in roman letters, each in an arched
rectangular surround; "QUALITY / 925•1000"
in roman letters, in a rectangle; an old English
"M" in an oval. All the foregoing struck once
on the underside of each piece. *Incuse stamps on
the underside:* (a) "1878" and "7203" (on both

kettle and stand); "STERLING" in incuse
roman letters, on underside of burner in stand;
(b) "1982" and "2722"; (c) "1984", "7203", and
"2 P'TS"; (d) "1982", "2722", and "3 P'TS";
(e) "1653" and "2852"; (f) "1982" and "3007";
(g) "1982" and "2772"; (h) "1982" and "3007".

Engraved on the side of all pieces in reserve panel:
"MPF" in foliate script. *Engraved on underside:*
(e) "1874". *Scratched on underside:* (c) "3317";
(e) "4/ 13/ 8"; (f) "160" and "10807"; (g)
"12/7"; (h) "160".

Description: all pieces have flattened hemispherical bodies made in halves and joined around
the middle with a die-rolled decorative band;
lower bodies are plain; upper bodies are flat
chased into 12 square panels with canted corners, each panel is filled with abstract curvilinear decoration. Die-rolled midbands consist
of beaded upper and lower borders, circular
medallions with abstract symmetrical designs
interspersed with 5-petal flowers and scrolls;
3 pieces (c–e) have tall cylindrical necks and
flared rims. Lids (where applicable) are circular, low domed, and flat chased in floral and
geometric pattern; cast lotus blossom finials;
4 of the 5 lids have 5-segment hinges.

(a) Kettle and stand: lid hinged on side. Large
3-part hollow bail handle with cast acanthus decoration, 2 ivory insulators, and 4 silver pins;
handle pivots on cast hinges attached to body
by cast anthemia. S-curve spout with abstract
anthemion on lower front; 2 pegs attached to
each side of body for mounting on stand. Body
domed in center bottom. Applied base ring.
Base of stand is square in plan with side panels
of applied die-rolled decorative bands; 4 cast
feet, each with a square pad, an anthemion at the
knee, and brackets. Cast kettle supports formed
as intertwining vines, acanthus leaves, and double anthemia, each with 2 C scrolls flanking a
central rectangular block with an egg-shape finial. Circular burner and reservoir in center of
base with removable circular cover with handle
and douter; perforated steel basket inside.

(b) Teapot: similar to kettle except for fixed C-
curve seamed handle with 2 ivory insulators
and 4 silver pins; no applied base ring.

(c) Coffeepot: high rise spout seamed in 3 sections with abstract athemion on lower front;
plain high-loop seamed handle with 2 ivory
insulators and 4 silver pins; plain neck; no
applied base ring.

(d) Hot milk pot: same handle and base as coffeepot; very short, cast, applied, V-shape spout
with scrolls, anthemia, bell flowers, and stippled
ground. Plain neck.

(e) Water pitcher: slightly domed base and applied footring. Lower part of neck decorated
with panels of flat-chased curvilinear designs.
Die-rolled decorative band inset in neck. Handle
as on coffeepot. Molded rim applied inside neck;
rim extended slightly to create pouring lip.

(f) Sugar bowl and lid: 2 solid cast rectangular handles, each with 2 arms curving outward into leaf forms at body; pendant leaf forms in center of each handle. Same base as coffeepot. Lid same as on teapot, except that it is not hinged.

(g) Waste bowl: body and base same as sugar bowl but with short concave neck and flared molded rim. It looks rather like a spittoon.

(h) Creamer: body and base similar to sugar bowl but small in scale and with short concave neck, flared irregular molded rim with a broad pouring lip; high-loop seamed handle.

Spectrographic analysis:

(a) Kettle

	SILVER	COPPER	LEAD	GOLD
UPPER BODY	92.1	7.6	0.06	0.01
LOWER BODY	91.7	7.8	0.12	0.02
INSET BAND	93.5	6.3	0.07	0.02
SPOUT	92.3	7.3	0.09	0.01
LID	92.5	7.1	0.12	0.00

(a) Stand

SUPPORT SIDE	92.6	6.9	0.11	0.01
SNUFFER LID	92.6	7.3	0.05	0.00

(b) Teapot

UPPER BODY	91.9	7.3	0.17	0.01
LOWERBODY	92.4	7.4	0.08	0.00
INSET BAND	94.0	5.1	0.11	0.00
SPOUT	93.5	5.9	0.52	0.02
LID	93.5	6.1	0.08	0.01

(c) Coffeepot

UPPER BODY	92.0	7.3	0.39	0.01
LOWER BODY	91.9	7.1	0.58	0.02
INSET BAND	93.8	5.1	0.79	0.04
SPOUT	92.6	6.6	0.57	0.03
LID	91.0	7.8	0.67	0.02

(d) Hot milk pot

UPPER BODY	92.8	6.2	0.51	0.02
LOWER BODY	91.6	7.2	0.59	0.03
INSET BAND	94.4	4.7	0.62	0.03
LID	92.3	6.8	0.66	0.03
HANDLE	92.0	7.1	0.60	0.04

(e) Water pitcher

UPPER BODY	92.6	6.5	0.50	0.02
LOWER BODY	91.6	7.3	0.61	0.03
INSET BAND	93.2	5.6	0.48	0.02
HANDLE	92.1	6.9	0.57	0.02
UNDERSIDE	93.9	5.2	0.42	0.04

(f) Sugar bowl and lid

UPPER BODY	92.1	7.1	0.21	0.00
LOWER BODY	92.2	7.3	0.10	0.01
INSET BAND	93.0	5.8	0.64	0.03
HANDLE	94.0	5.6	0.28	0.01
LID	92.7	7.0	0.10	0.01

	SILVER	COPPER	LEAD	GOLD

(g) Waste bowl

UPPER BODY	92.7	6.7	0.40	0.02
LOWER BODY	91.7	7.2	0.55	0.04
INSET BAND	93.1	6.0	0.63	0.03
UNDERSIDE	90.9	6.2	0.41	0.01

(h) Creamer

UPPER BODY	92.0	7.2	0.23	0.00
LOWER BODY	92.4	7.1	0.18	0.02
INSET BAND	93.8	6.0	0.09	0.00
UNDERSIDE	92.6	7.0	0.26	0.02

History: The initials "MPF" refer to Mary Pauline Foster (1849–1902), who married Henry Algernon du Pont (1838–1926) in 1874. They were the parents of H. F. du Pont.

Provenance: Mary Pauline (Foster) du Pont; Henry Algernon du Pont; H. F. du Pont.

Exhibitions: "Romanticism Reflected," Winterthur Museum student exhibition, 1972.

Comments: Made in the Islamic style as interpreted by Edward C. Moore, whose collection of oriental art had a profound influence on the designs of Tiffany silver.

References: Charles H. Carpenter, Jr., and Mary Grace Carpenter, *Tiffany Silver* (New York: Dodd, Mead, 1978), pp. 71, 72, fig. 69, but pattern and order numbers are incorrect; see p. 234ff for fabrication techniques for Tiffany hollowware; see fig. 29 for Islamic jug that may have served as the model for the tall-neck pieces in this service.

70.1039.1–.8 Bequest of H. F. du Pont, 1969

❦ 273 a, b
BUD VASES, ca. 1874

(a) H. 4 ⅞" (12.4 cm)
1 oz. 7 dwt. 15 gr. (42.9 g)
(b) H. 4 ¹⁵⁄₁₆" (12.5 cm)
1 oz. 8 dwt. 3 gr. (43.7 g)

Stamps: "TIFFANY & Co" in roman letters, in an arc over "3514" over "STERLING" in roman letters, all struck incuse, on 1 side of underside; roman "M" over "3507" over "UNION-SQUARE" in roman letters, all struck incuse on other side of underside.

Engraved on side of each body: "MPF" in foliate script. *Engraved around upper body:* a neogrec–inspired band of diamond panels, spikes, and anthemia.

Description: tall cylindrical seamed body mounted on spun circular trumpetlike pedestal; bulbous applied rim cut into a series of 8-point petals.

Spectrographic analysis:

	SILVER	COPPER	GOLD	LEAD
(a)	92.7	7.2	0.04	0.04
(b)	92.9	7.0	0.05	0.03

History: The initials "MPF" refer to Mary Pauline Foster (1849–1902), who married Henry Algernon du Pont (1838–1926) in 1874. They were the parents of H. F. du Pont.

Provenance: Mary Pauline (Foster) du Pont; Henry Algernon du Pont; H. F. du Pont.

References: Charles H. Carpenter, Jr., and Mary Grace Carpenter, *Tiffany Silver* (New York: Dodd, Mead, 1978), for background.

70.1124.1, .2 Bequest of H. F. du Pont, 1969

❦ 274 a–f
TEA AND COFFEE SERVICE, ca. 1861

(a) Kettle on stand: H. (with handle up) 15 ¹⁄₁₆" (38.3 cm), H. (stand only) 8 ³⁄₁₆" (20.8 cm), H. (kettle only with handle up) 10 ⁹⁄₁₆" (26.8 cm), w. (stand only) 8" (20.3 cm), w. (kettle only) 10 ¹¹⁄₁₆" (27.1 cm)
Kettle: 45 oz. 15 dwt. 21 gr. (1421.0 g)
Stand: 25 oz. 10 dwt. 12 gr. (792.1 g)
(b) Coffeepot: H. 11 ¹⁵⁄₁₆" (30.32 cm), w. 8 ¹³⁄₁₆" (22.4 cm)
35 oz. 6 dwt. (1095.4 g)
(c) Teapot: H. 10 ½" (26.7 cm), w. 9 ⅛" (23.2 cm)
31 oz. 10 dwt. 2 gr. (977.6 g)
(d) Creamer: H. 7 ⅝" (19.4 cm), w. 4 ¼" (10.8 cm)
12 oz. 2 gr. (372.5 g)
(e) Sugar bowl: H. 6 ⁹⁄₁₆" (16.7 cm), w. 7 ⅜" (18.7 cm)
19 oz. 15 dwt. 7 gr. (613.3 g)
(f) Waste bowl: H. 4 ⅞" (12.4 cm), DIAM. 5 ⁹⁄₁₆" (14.1 cm)
12 oz. (372.42 g)

Stamps: "TIFFANY & CO." and "550 BROADWAY" in roman letters, each in an arched rectangular surround; "ENGLISH STERLING/ 925•1000" in roman letters, in a conforming rectilinear surround with an old English *M*, in an oval on each side. All stamps struck on underside of all pieces except kettle stand and creamer. Incuse "524" on underside of all pieces except kettle stand and creamer. Incuse "6992" on coffeepot, teapot, and sugar bowl. Incuse "7596" on underside of kettle, on ring of kettle stand, and on underside of spirit lamp. Incuse "7754" inside base ring of sugar bowl.

Engraved on upper body of all pieces except the kettle stand: "MCW" (in a cypher) in shaded gothic letters. *Engraved inside base ring of all pieces except kettle and stand:* "From Samuel & Sophia Whitwell. June 12th 1861." in script. *Scratched on underside of spirit lamp:* "75372". *Scratched on underside of coffeepot, teapot, creamer, and sugar bowl:* "282" and "232" (latter crossed out). *Also scratched under body of creamer:* "18202". *Scratched on underside of waste bowl:* "282".

Description: all pieces have raised circular urn-shape lower bodies (except kettle) mounted on reel-like pedestals and circular domed bases; centerpunch on underside of each body. Upper bodies (except waste bowl and stand) consist of narrow cylindrical necks standing on gently sloping shoulders. Flared molded rims (except on creamer, stand, and waste bowl). High-dome hinged lids with cast finial of boy playing horn; 5-segment cast hinges. Seamed high-loop rectilinear handles, arched toward body at bottom (except on creamer), have cast female heads and beaded decoration on sides; upper ends attached to body by cast scrolls. Applied bands of Greek key and beading around base and upper edge of lower bodies. Chased decoration: 6 strapwork cartouches, each with an anthemion, on base against stippled ground; bold repoussé acanthus leaves on lower part of lower body; flat-chased swirled anthemia against stippled ground on upper part of lower bodies; alternating anthemia and bellflowers, connected by scrolls, against a stippled ground, on shoulders. Flat-chased alternating bellflowers and buds with stems forming intersecting circles (except on sugar bowl), all on a stippled ground. Lids divided into 6 panels with elongated anthemion in each.

(a) Kettle on stand: Lid hinged on side. Large fixed 3-part bail handle, seamed and hollow, reeded on upper surface; 2 ivory insulators and 4 silver pins; handle supports joined to handle by a reel with rosettes on each side; lower part of each support (where it attaches to body) consists of a cast acanthus leaf and scrolls. Seamed S-curve spout decorated with large repoussé anthemion on lower front and a small one on upper tip. Applied base ring with beading; 2 silver pegs attached to each side of body of kettle for mounting on stand. Circular stand has 3 cabriole legs and 2 support arms. Body ring has gently sloping shoulders with a chased border of darts and dots on a stippled ground; applied band of Greek key and beading. Small lamp support ring attached to inside of legs by scrolls. Seamed hollow cabriole legs with scrolled feet; repoussé acanthus leaves on knees flanked by volutes and scrolls. Seamed hollow support arms, rectangular in section, have an arched vertical void and a curved crest with ears; shell in center of crest flanked by foliage, a rosette on each ear, stippled ground; 2 small circular vents inside body ring where each support arm is attached. Circular lamp with bowl-shape body on a foot-ring; flat top with beaded edge, concave ring around circular opening in center; threaded opening receives circular cover with 2 cylindrical wick holders.

(b) Coffeepot: handle has 2 ivory insulators and 4 silver pins; spout as on kettle.

(c) Teapot: 2 ivory insulators on handle and 4 silver pins; spout as on kettle; body pierced in diamond pattern to serve as strainer.

(d) Creamer: cylindrical collar flares outward on back and sides, upward and out in front to form broad pouring lip; handle as on other pieces except portion below head continues straight.

(e) Sugar bowl: gilded interior; no lid.

(f) Waste bowl: gilded interior.

Spectrographic analysis:

(a) Tea kettle

	SILVER	COPPER	GOLD	LEAD
BODY	94.6	5.3	0.05	0.05
SPOUT	95.3	4.5	0.08	0.06
LID	95.9	4.0	0.09	0.04
HANDLE	93.7	6.2	0.13	0.15

(a) Stand

	SILVER	COPPER	GOLD	LEAD
FOOT	96.2	3.7	0.05	0.05
RING	95.3	4.6	0.04	0.05
ARM	96.2	3.8	0.03	0.02
BURNER	93.2	6.6	0.10	0.07

(b) Coffeepot

	SILVER	COPPER	GOLD	LEAD
BODY SIDE	94.2	5.7	0.07	0.04
FOOT	95.9	4.0	0.11	0.04
LID	96.0	4.0	0.04	0.03
HANDLE	94.3	5.6	0.05	0.04
SPOUT	95.1	4.7	0.10	0.05

(c) Teapot

	SILVER	COPPER	GOLD	LEAD
BODY SIDE	94.8	5.1	0.11	0.05
FOOT	95.6	4.3	0.07	0.04
LID	94.8	5.1	0.07	0.05
HANDLE	94.3	5.5	0.09	0.05
SPOUT	95.4	4.4	0.06	0.07

(d) Creamer

	SILVER	COPPER	GOLD	LEAD
BODY SIDE	93.7	6.1	0.12	0.04
FOOT	95.4	4.4	0.16	0.05
HANDLE	94.6	5.3	0.07	0.05

(e) Sugar bowl

	SILVER	COPPER	GOLD	LEAD
BODY SIDE	93.2	6.6	0.04	0.04
FOOT	96.0	3.8	0.09	0.05
HANDLE	94.9	5.0	0.10	0.05

(f) Waste bowl

	SILVER	COPPER	GOLD	LEAD
BODY SIDE	93.6	6.3	0.09	0.06
FOOT	95.3	4.5	0.12	0.05

History: The set was a gift from Samuel and Sophia Whitwell to "MCW," probably a Whitwell too. The set later belonged to the donor's godfather, Frederick S. Whitwell, who lived next door to Louise Crowninshield (H. F. du Pont's sister) in Boston and who was a frequent guest of Mr. and Mrs. H. F. du Pont.

Provenance: Samuel and Sophia Whitwell; MCW [Whitwell?]; Frederick S. Whitwell, Boston; Mr. and Mrs. T. Truxton Hare, Jr., Edgemont, Pa.

Comments: The set is made from high-quality heavy-gauge metal and exhibits fine craftsmanship. The sophisticated use of classical motifs shows the persistence of neoclassicism in American design.

References: Charles H. Carpenter, Jr., and Mary Grace Carpenter, *Tiffany Silver* (New York: Dodd, Mead, 1978), fig. 66.

83.178.1–.6 Gift of Mr. and Mrs. T. Truxton Hare, Jr., in memory of Mr. and Mrs. Frederick S. Whitwell, 1983

❦ William Van Buren

w. 1790s
New York, New York, w. ca. 1790, 1794–?
Newark, New Jersey, w. 1792–94

Little is known about William Van Buren, whose name is sometimes spelled Van Beuren. He appears in New York City directories for 1791–92, but he advertised in *Wood's Gazette* (Newark, New Jersey) October 25, 1792: "at the sign of the Gold Watch" where he "plates all kinds of Harness and Bridle Furniture." By 1794 he was back in New York City at 22 Maiden Lane. Few examples of his work survive.

References: Johnson, "Silver in Newark," p. 33. Williams, *Silversmiths of New Jersey*, pp. 102, 103. Von Khrum, *Silversmiths*, p. 130.

❦ 275
TEAPOT, ca. 1795

H. (with lid) 6 ¾" (17.1 cm), w. 12 ⅜" (31.4 cm) 22 oz. 16 dwt. 20 gr. (710.5 g)

Stamps: "W.V.B" in roman letters, in a cartouche, struck twice on underside of body.

Engraved on side of body: "TD" in foliate script, in a shield suspended from a bowknot and flanked by crossed leafy branches; engraved blossoms and dependant leaves also flank the shield. Bright-cut dart and rollerwork borders around lower and upper edges of body and on shoulders surrounding lid; rollerwork swags on outer edge of shoulders. *Scratched on underside:* "22 oz."

Description: seamed body, oval in plan, straight sides; concave shoulders; beading applied around base and upper edge; narrow applied base band. Flush-mounted, hinged, slightly domed lid with hollow urn finial cast in vertical halves. Straight tapered spout, oval in section, seamed on upper side; 2 seamed handle sockets with applied bead molding; 2 silver pins; C-curve hardwood handle with sprig.

Spectrographic analysis:

	SILVER	COPPER	GOLD	LEAD
BODY SIDE	89.2	10.5	0.21	0.15
UNDERSIDE	95.4	4.3	0.22	0.14
LID	90.2	9.6	0.21	0.09
SPOUT	89.5	10.2	0.21	0.16

Provenance: Marshall P. Blankarn, New York City.

Comments: See no. 276, which has the same engraved initials.

77.79 Gift of Marshall P. Blankarn, 1977

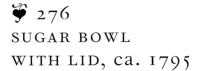

276

SUGAR BOWL
WITH LID, ca. 1795

H. 9 ⅞" (25.1 cm), DIAM. 4 ⁹⁄₁₆" (11.6 cm)
11 oz. 11 dwt. 4 gr. (358.7 g)

Stamps: "WVB" in roman letters, in a car-touche, struck once on side of square base.

Engraved on side of body: "TD" in foliate script, in a shield suspended from a bowknot and flanked by crossed leafy branches; engraved blossoms and dependant leaves flank the shield. Bright-cut dart and rollerwork border around upper edge of body.

Description: raised circular urn-shape body mounted on pedestal flared to circular plinth with beaded edge that, in turn, becomes a square base; entire pedestal and base appears to be fab-ricated from 1 piece of metal. Raised circular lid, flat at edge, curves up to tall narrow seamed neck that flares to a beaded molding and domed top; cast urn finial.

Spectrographic analysis:

	SILVER	COPPER	GOLD	LEAD
BODY SIDE	90.0	9.6	0.22	0.14
FOOT	90.4	9.2	0.22	0.24
LID	95.7	3.6	0.22	0.40

Provenance: Marshall P. Blankarn, New York City.

Comments: Similar to no. 275, which has same engraved initials.

80.182 Gift of Marshall P. Blankarn, 1981

❧ Jacobus Van der Spiegel

1668–1708
New York, New York

Unfortunately little is known about the brilliant craftsman Jacobus Van der Spiegel. He was admitted as a freeman in 1701/2, although he was certainly working in New York well before that date. In 1692 he married Anna Sanders in the Dutch Church in Albany, where his militia company had been sent in 1689 to defend against the French. He calls himself Johannes in his will, drawn November 29, 1708, in which he bequeathed 30s. to his eldest son Lawrence and the balance of his estate to his wife. Van der Spiegel made some of the most characteristic and spectacular silver of the period. A tankard owned by Yale University Art Gallery has the most lavishly engraved lid of any American tankard of the period. His standing salt (now in the Brooklyn Museum) is the only one made outside New England. The Metropolitan Museum of Art owns a baptismal basin, with a Dutch inscription, that was made in 1694 for the South Dutch Reformed Church. Van der Spiegel made communion silver for Saint Michael's Church, Trenton, New Jersey, and two outstanding salvers, now owned by Winterthur and the R. W. Norton Art Gallery in Shreveport, Louisiana. The Museum of the City of New York owns a tankard stamped by both Van der Spiegel and Jan Van Nieu Kirke.

References: Ensko, *American Silversmiths IV*, pp. 209, 288. Jones, *Old Silver*, p. 33. *NYHS Collections*: vol. 26 (1893) *Abstracts of Wills*, p. 165; vol. 18 (1885) *Burghers and Freemen*, p. 77. *Minutes of the Common Council*, 1:367, 381, 415; 2:60, 174, 177. Marvin D. Schwartz, "A Silver Salt by Jacobus Vander Spiegel," *Brooklyn Museum Annual* 6 (1964–65): 50–56.

❧ 277

TANKARD, ca. 1700

H. 6 15/16" (17.6 cm), DIAM. base 5 5/8" (14.3 cm), w. 8 1/8" (20.6 cm)
30 oz. 18 dwt. 15 gr. (962.1 g)

Stamps: "S/ IV" in roman letters, in a trefoil, struck once on underside of body and once on top of lid.

Engraved on front of body opposite handle: "H/ T*A" in shaded roman letters, enclosed by a single leafy branch forming a circle with the

ends crossed and 2 tassels below. *Scratched on lid side of hinge:* "AC[?]" in roman letters.

Description: raised body with straight tapering sides and slightly concave bottom; applied molded rim with large convex molding in center, small 2-step molding below and flared rim above; centerpunch on underside of body. Applied 6-step base molding below a band of cut-card work of which each unit consists of an anthemion with a ladderlike device in the center. Raised circular single-step lid with flat top

crenellated at front; bezel; centerpunch on top. Cast cocoon thumbpiece. Cast 5-segment hinge between bands of wigglework. Raised-and-soldered hollow C-curve handle with cut-card leaf form applied to upper back. Lower end of handle forms a C curve in profile and terminates with cast mask (male face with long hair) applied to an oval plate. Circular lower vent; 2 small circular upper vents.

Spectrographic analysis:

	SILVER	COPPER	LEAD	GOLD
BODY SIDE	92.5	6.8	0.32	0.09
UNDERSIDE	93.9	5.4	0.30	0.07
LID	91.3	8.1	0.29	0.13
BASE MOLDING	94.4	5.1	0.26	0.05
HANDLE	91.2	8.5	0.23	0.02

History: Isabelle Miller claims the initials "H/ T*A" refer to Thomas Havens (or Howell) and his wife Ananias, who were married in 1687.

Provenance: H. F. du Pont.

Exhibitions: "Silver by New York Makers," Museum of the City of New York, 1937–38.

References: Fales, *American Silver*, no. 31. Miller, *Silver by New York Makers*, p. 33, illus. no. 323. Marvin D. Schwartz, "A Silver Salt by Jacobus Vander Spiegel," *Brooklyn Museum Annual* 6 (1964–65): 52.

58.2103 Gift of H. F. du Pont, 1965

❧ 278
SALVER, ca. 1700

DIAM. 8 3/16" (20.8 cm), H. 2 7/8" (7.3 cm)
16 oz. 7 dwt. 3 gr. (508.8 g)

Stamps: "S/ I•V" in roman letters, in a trefoil, struck once on underside of foot.

Engraved on underside of body: "M+S" in roman letters. *Engraved on top of body:* "Myndert Schuyler/ b. 1672•d. 1755" in script.

Description: raised flat circular tray with boldly curved repoussé-gadrooned edge; centerpunch on upper and lower sides of tray; circular plain pedestal flares to repoussé-gadrooned base and flat footring.

Spectrographic analysis:

	SILVER	COPPER	LEAD	GOLD
TRAY TOP	93.3	6.4	0.26	0.11
FOOTRING	93.3	5.3	0.31	0.11

History: Myndert Schuyler (1672–1755), merchant, married Rachel Cuyler (d. 1747) in 1693. He was politically prominent in Albany, having served in the assembly in the periods 1702–10, 1713–15, 1724, and 1728–37; as alderman, 1718–19; as mayor, 1719–20 and 1723–25; and as commissioner of Indian Affairs, 1706–20 and 1728–46. He was a member of the Dutch Reformed Church, where he served as deacon.

Provenance: Robert Ensko, Inc., New York City, sold to H. F. du Pont, March 1947.

Exhibitions: "New York Silversmiths of the Seventeenth Century," Museum of the City of New York, 1962–63. "Albany Silver" and "Remembrance of Patria: Dutch Arts and Culture in Colonial America, 1609–1776," Albany Institute of History and Art, 1964, 1986.

Comments: The mate to this piece, now owned by the R. W. Norton Art Gallery, Shreveport, La., was made for Stephanus Van Cortlandt.

References: Cuyler Reynolds, *Albany Chronicles* (Albany: J. B. Lyon, 1906), no. 13, for Myndert Schuyler. Rice, *Albany Silver*, fig. 146. Davidson, *Colonial Antiques*, p. 106. Fales, *American Silver*, no. 7. Fennimore, *Silver and Pewter*, no. 11. Hood, *American Silver*, fig. 59. Miller, *New York Silversmiths*, no. 85. Blackburn and Piwonka, *Remembrance of Patria*, no. 320. Marvin D. Schwartz, "A Silver Salt by Jacobus Vander Spiegel," *Brooklyn Museum Annual* 6 (1964–65): 53.

59.2597 Gift of H. F. du Pont, 1965

❦ 279
DRINKING BOWL, ca. 1700

DIAM. bowl 4 ³⁄₁₆" (10.6 cm), H. (with handles)
2 ¹⁄₁₆" (5.2 cm), W. 6 ⁷⁄₁₆" (16.4 cm)
2 oz. 17 dwt. 15 gr. (89.7 g)

Stamps: "S/ [I]•V" in roman letters, in a trefoil,
struck once on underside of body. Lower left of
trefoil illegible.

Description: raised circular shallow bowl with
plain rim and flat bottom; centerpunch on
underside; 2 twisted-wire C-scroll handles.

Spectrographic analysis:

	SILVER	COPPER	LEAD	GOLD
BODY SIDE	91.7	7.6	0.38	0.15
UNDERSIDE	95.2	4.2	0.30	0.14

Provenance: Robert Ensko, Inc., New York City,
sold to H. F. du Pont, May 1941.

Exhibitions: "New York Silversmiths of the
Seventeenth Century," Museum of the City of
New York, 1962–63.

References: Fales, *American Silver*, no. 41. Miller,
New York Silversmiths, no. 80.

58.2102 Gift of H. F. du Pont, 1965

❦ 280
SPOON, ca. 1700

L. 7 ¾" (19.7 cm)
1 oz. 10 dwt. 5 gr. (46.9 g)

Stamps: "S/ I•V" in roman letters, in a trefoil,
struck once on back of handle.

Engraved on back of handle: "H/ W*L" in
shaded roman letters.

Description: oval bowl with swage-formed single rounded drop and reeded rattail on back;
upturned handle with wavy end.

Spectrographic analysis: Silver content is 90.8
percent.

Provenance: Mr. and Mrs. Stanley B. Ineson,
New York City; Mr. and Mrs. Alfred E. Bissell,
Wilmington, Del.

References: Belden, *Marks of American
Silversmiths*, p. 417.

62.240.1541 Gift of Mr. and Mrs. Alfred E.
Bissell, 1962–63

Peter Van Dyck

1684–1750
New York, New York

Baptized in New York on August 17, 1684, Peter Van Dyck was the son of Dirck Franszen Van Dyk (d. 1691) and Urseltje Shepmoes. Raised next door to silversmith Jacob Boelen, he was apprenticed to Bartholomew Le Roux I in 1700. In 1711 Van Dyck married Le Roux's daughter Rachel. Her brother was noted silversmith Charles Le Roux. Following Rachel's death, Van Dyck married heiress Cornelia Van Varick of Flatbush in 1715. Son Richard Van Dyck became a prominent goldsmith and engraver. Son Rudolphus, a merchant, helped to establish the Moravian Church in New York. Van Dyck was a prolific silversmith who made a wide variety of forms. In addition to the usual tankards, porringers, teapots, and spoons, he made a unique egg-shape mustard pot, which is at Yale University Art Gallery, and gold frames for miniature portraits. His three teapots at Yale show the progressive development of the so-called Queen Anne–style pot, culminating in a great octagonal example that is unique in American silver. A tankard in the Charleston Museum bears the stamps of both Van Dyck and Simeon Soumaine (*Antiques* [July 1978], p. 72).

References: Buhler and Hood, *American Silver*, nos. 587–98. *Catalogue of Exhibition of Silver Used in New York, New Jersey, and the South* (New York: Metropolitan Museum of Art, 1911), pp. 58–60. Mrs. Russell Hastings, "Peter Van Dyck of New York, Goldsmith, 1684–1750," *Antiques* 31, no. 5 (May 1937): 236–39; no. 6 (June 1937): 302–5.

281
CASTER, 1729–50

H. 3 ¼" (8.3 cm), w. 2 ⅚" (7.5 cm)
3 oz. 20 gr. (94.6 g)

Stamps: "PVD" ("VD" conjoined) in roman letters, in a rounded rectangle, struck once on body, left of handle.

Engraved on side of body opposite handle: "B/ N∗E" in shaded roman letters.

Description: seamed body, octagonal in plan, with straight sides and flat set-in bottom; no centerpunch. Stepped applied base molding; simple molding applied to body ¼" below rim serves as stop for lid. S-curve strap handle. Octagonal domed friction-fit lid pierced with circular arrangement of curvilinear voids and drilled holes in floral motifs; simple applied molded band around sides.

Spectrographic analysis:

	SILVER	COPPER	LEAD	GOLD
BODY SIDE	91.0	7.8	0.57	0.20
UNDERSIDE	93.3	5.3	0.56	0.24
LID	91.8	8.1	0.02	0.00
HANDLE	91.2	7.8	0.50	0.18

Note absence of gold and hardly any lead in lid.

History: The initials "B/ N∗E" refer to Nicholas and Elizabeth (Rynders) Bayard, who owned a large quantity of silver that was distributed after their deaths to their 6 grown children. Several lists were drawn up for "the allotment of the plate," which not only named the pieces but provided inscriptions, owners' initials, and sometimes makers' initials. Lots were drawn by the heirs, and the silver was then divided accordingly among Nicholas Bayard, Jr., his brother Stephen, and their sisters Judith (married to Jeremiah Van Rennselaer), Hester (married to John Van Cortlandt), Elizabeth, and Ann. Nicholas Bayard, Jr., got the caster. Other pieces in the Bayard collection by Peter Van Dyck included a small salver, 2 large tankards, and a teapot. There were also pieces by Richard Van Dyck, Cornelius Vanderburch, and others.

The documents covering the "allotment of the plate," now in the Nicholas Bayard Papers at Rutgers University, document one of the great collections of silver in colonial America. I am indebted to Nancy Goyne Evans for bringing them to my attention.

Provenance: Nicholas and Elizabeth Bayard; Nicholas Bayard, Jr. (1736–1813); Robert Ensko, Inc., New York City, sold to H. F. du Pont, September 1930.

Exhibitions: "Masterpieces of American Silver," Virginia Museum of Fine Arts, Richmond, 1960. "Remembrance of Patria: Dutch Arts and Culture in Colonial America, 1609–1776," Albany Institute of History and Art, 1986.

Comments: The caster is listed in the 1750 inventory of the Bayard silver with a somewhat heavier weight. This was puzzling until analysis revealed that the lid is a modern replacement. Presumably the original lid had a small finial, which would have accounted for the additional weight.

References: Fales, *American Silver*, no. 103. Blackburn and Piwonka, *Remembrance of Patria*, no. 305. *Masterpieces of American Silver*, no. 225. Nicholas Bayard Papers, Rutgers University Library, Camden, N.J.

58.2104 Gift of H. F. du Pont, 1965

🜍 282 a, b
SPOONS, ca. 1730

(a) L. 7 ¾" (19.7 cm)
1 oz. 11 dwt. (48.1 g)
(b) L. 8 3/16" (20.8 cm)
1 oz. 17 dwt. 23 gr. (58.9 g)

Stamps: "PVD" ("VD" conjoined) in roman letters, in a rectangle, struck twice on the back of each handle.

Engraved on back of handle: (a) "RM" in crude shaded roman letters; (b) "H/ H∗H" in shaded roman letters.

Description: oval bowl with swage-formed double rounded drop on back; rounded upturned handle with midrib on front.

Spectrographic analysis: Silver content ranges from 88.5 to 92.4 percent.

Provenance: Mr. and Mrs. Stanley B. Ineson, New York City; Mr. and Mrs. Alfred E. Bissell, Wilmington, Del.

References: Belden, *Marks of American Silversmiths*, p. 418.

62.240.1531, .1533 Gift of Mr. and Mrs. Alfred E. Bissell, 1962–63

🜍 283
SPOON, ca. 1710

L. 7 ⅝" (19.4 cm)
1 oz. 9 dwt. 21 gr. (46.4 g)

Stamps: "V/ P•D" in roman letters, in a trefoil, struck twice on back of handle.

Engraved on back of handle: "T/ I∗S" in shaded roman letters.

Description: oval bowl with swage-formed rounded drop and reeded rattail on back; rounded slightly upturned handle.

Spectrographic analysis: Silver content is 87.7 percent.

Provenance: Mr. and Mrs. Stanley B. Ineson, New York City; Mr. and Mrs. Alfred E. Bissell, Wilmington, Del.

References: Belden, *Marks of American Silversmiths*, p. 418.

62.240.1534 Gift of Mr. and Mrs. Alfred E. Bissell, 1962–63

🜍 284
SPOON, ca. 1710

L. 7 15/16" (20.0 cm)
1 oz. 17 dwt. 7 gr. (57.9 g)

Stamps: "P•V•D" ("VD" conjoined at top) in roman letters, in an oval, struck twice on back of handle.

Engraved on back of handle: "AC" in script.

Description: oval bowl with swage-formed rounded drop and rattail on back; rounded upturned handle with midrib on front.

Spectrographic analysis: Silver content is 88.7 percent.

Provenance: Mr. and Mrs. Stanley B. Ineson, New York City; Mr. and Mrs. Alfred E. Bissell, Wilmington, Del.

References: Belden, *Marks of American Silversmiths*, p. 418.

62.240.1535 Gift of Mr. and Mrs. Alfred E. Bissell, 1962–63

🜍 285 a, b
SPOONS, ca. 1730

(a) L. 8 ⅛" (20.6 cm)
1 oz. 17 dwt. 17 gr. (58.5 g)
(b) L. 7 15/16" (20.2 cm)
1 oz. 17 dwt. 15 gr. (58.4 g)

Stamps: "P•VD" ("VD" conjoined at top) in roman letters, in a rounded rectangle, struck twice on back of each handle.

Engraved on back of each handle: "C/ IM/ DC" in roman letters.

Description: deep oval bowl with swage-formed rounded double drop; rounded upturned handle with midrib.

Spectrographic analysis: Silver content ranges from 91.3 to 92.5 percent.

Provenance: Mr. and Mrs. Stanley B. Ineson, New York City; Mr. and Mrs. Alfred E. Bissell, Wilmington, Del.

References: Belden, *Marks of American Silversmiths*, p. 418.

62.240.1041, .1536 Gift of Mr. and Mrs. Alfred E. Bissell, 1962–63

Daniel Van Voorhis

1751–1824
New York, New York, w. ca. 1772–75
Philadelphia, Pennsylvania, w. 1775–82
Princeton, New Jersey, w. 1782–84
New York, New York, w. 1784–87
Bennington County, Vermont,
w. 1787–88
New York, New York, w. 1788–1803

Van Voorhis, Bayley & Coley,
w. 1784–85
Van Voorhis, Bayley, Coley & Cox,
w. 1785
Van Voorhis & Coley, w. 1786–87
Van Voorhis & Schanck, w. 1791–93
Van Voorhis & Son, w. 1797–1805

In spite of his peripatetic record, Daniel Van Voorhis is considered to be primarily a New York silversmith. He was born in Oyster Bay, probably apprenticed to a New York silversmith, and was living in the city in 1775 at the time of his marriage to Catharine Richards. Later that year he moved to Philadelphia. Almost immediately, and for the next several years, his name begins to appear in the accounts of Thomas Shields, who advanced him cash and paid him for making silver objects. Van Voorhis first appears publicly as a silversmith in his own right in 1780. Late in 1782 his move to Princeton coincided with the temporary relocation of Congress from Philadelphia to that city. In May 1784 he stopped briefly at New Brunswick before moving on to New York City. Once back in New York he formed a series of partnerships that make his career as a silversmith a complicated one. On December 18, 1784, the firm of Van Voorhis, Bayley & Coley announced itself as "Real Manufacturers in Gold, Silver, Jewellery, &c. at No. 27 Hanover-Square" and claimed "the Goods they manufacture will be sold on much lower Terms than those imported, and will be found equal in point of Workmanship." The firm was augmented in 1785 by the addition of a man named Cox. Both Simeon Bayley and Cox dropped out, but Van Voorhis and William Coley continued until at least 1787. They joined with the Rupert Mint in Vermont, making copper coins in 1787–88, another short-lived venture. Garret Schanck became Van Voorhis's business partner in 1791–92. By 1797 the firm was Daniel Van Voorhis & Son. With Van Voorhis's appointment as weigh master of New York City in 1803, the silver business became a sideline carried on with the help of his partner and stepson Daniel Richards Van Voorhis. The latter's death in 1805 probably ended the elder Van Voorhis's career as a silversmith; he died in Brooklyn in 1824.

Van Voorhis's work is mainly early neoclassical, with hollowware that is urn-shape or oval in plan and engraved with shields and swags. A substantial number of pieces survive and can be found in various public collections. A flat-top tankard made for Robert Lenox of New York is at the New-York Historical Society. It is surely one of the last examples of the form made in America.

References: Gottesman, *Arts and Crafts, 1777–99*, pp. 74–77. Rita S. Gottesman, "New Delvings in Old Fields: The Partnerships of Van Voorhis," *Antiques* 39, no. 6 (June 1941): 314–15. Jones, *Old Silver*, pp. 152, 337, 460, 509. John Marshall Phillips, Barbara N. Parker, and Kathryn C. Buhler, *The Waldron Phoenix Belknap, Jr., Collection of Portraits and Silver* (Cambridge: Harvard University Press, 1955), pp. 94–95. Prime cards, Winterthur. Von Khrum, *Silversmiths*, p. 132. Williams, *Silversmiths of New Jersey*, pp. 117–22. Waters, "Precious Metals Trades," pp. 73–74.

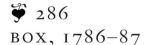

286
BOX, 1786–87

DIAM. 3 ³⁄₁₆" (8.1 cm), H. 1 ³⁄₁₆" (3.0 cm)
3 oz. 11 dwt. 8 gr. (110.7 g)

Stamps: "V&C" in roman letters, in a rectangle, struck once on underside of body.

Scratched on underside of body: "P7161".
Scratched on inside bottom of body: "18 1179".

Description: circular seamed body with flat bottom and straight sides; raised circular friction-fit lid fits over body; top of lid chased in pattern of 5 concentric circles.

Spectrographic analysis:

	SILVER	COPPER	GOLD	LEAD
BODY	92.9	6.7	0.22	0.15
LID	93.7	6.0	0.09	0.14

Provenance: Marshall P. Blankarn, New York City.

Comments: The "V&C" stamp was used during Van Voorhis's brief partnership with William Coley.

78.149 Gift of Marshall P. Blankarn, 1978

287
SKEWER, 1780–1805

L. 7 ¹¹⁄₁₆" (19.6 cm)
1 oz. 5 dwt. 11 gr. (39.6 g)

Stamps: "D.V.V." in roman letters, in a rectangle, struck once on shaft near loop. Adjoining stamp of a spread-winged eagle with a superimposed shield, all in a diamond-shape surround.

Description: thick flat body tapers from circular pierced handle to sharp point.

Spectrographic analysis:

SILVER	COPPER	LEAD	GOLD
87.0	12.0	0.39	0.17

Provenance: Sara H. Andrews, Ashaway, R.I.

Comments: Stephen Ensko attributed this combination of stamps to Van Voorhis's Philadelphia period, but there seems to be no corroborating evidence. Furthermore, the silversmith used the same set of stamps on a beaker, dated 1794, made for St. John's Church, Stamford, Conn.

References: Ensko, *American Silversmiths III*, p. 170.

61.68 Museum purchase from Sara H. Andrews, 1961

❦ 288
GOLD SPOON, 1785–1805

L. 4 ¹³⁄₁₆" (12.2 cm), 11 dwt. 17 gr. (18.2 g)

Stamps: "DVV" in roman letters, in a rectangle, struck once on back of handle.

Description: plain oval bowl; pointed down-turned handle.

Spectrographic analysis:

GOLD	SILVER	COPPER	
80.0	11.5	8.5	19 karat

Provenance: Mr. and Mrs. Donald Nalebuff, New York City.

Exhibitions: "American Gold, 1700–1860," Yale University Art Gallery, 1963.

Comments: The mate to this spoon remains in a private collection. The stamp seen here is not used on any of Van Voorhis's other work. The spoon is unusual for not having a drop or any other decorative element. The only other gold spoon at Winterthur is by S. D. Rockwell, New York City.

References: Bohan, *American Gold*, no. 29.

59.92 Gift of Mr. and Mrs. Donald Nalebuff, 1959

❦ 289 a–c
SPOONS, 1780–1805

(a) Spoon: L. 5 ³⁄₁₆" (13.2 cm), 7 dwt. 8 gr. (11.4 g)
(b) Salt spoon: L. 3 ¾" (9.5 cm), 4 dwt. 4 gr. (6.5 g)
(c) Salt spoon: L. 3 ¾" (9.5 cm), 4 dwt. 7 gr. (6.7 g)

Stamps: "D.V.V." in roman letters, in a rectangle, struck once on back of each handle. Adjoining stamp of a spread-winged eagle with a superimposed shield, in a diamond surround.

Engraved on front of handle: (a) "EO" in foliate script, in a bright-cut medallion with a pendant; (b, c) "RMV" (sideways) in script, in a bright-cut medallion with pendant.

Description: (a) oval bowl with swage-formed rounded drop; rounded downturned handle; (b, c) plain circular bowls; pointed downturned handles.

Spectrographic analysis: Silver content ranges from 90.9 to 92.5 percent.

Provenance: Mr. and Mrs. Stanley B. Ineson, New York City; Mr. and Mrs. Alfred E. Bissell, Wilmington, Del.

Exhibitions: (b) or (c) Metropolitan Museum of Art, New York City, 1938–61.

Comments: Traces of gilt on (b) and (c).

References: Belden, *Marks of American Silversmiths*, p. 419 c.

(a) 62.240.582, (b, c) 62.240.856.1, .2 Gift of Mr. and Mrs. Alfred E. Bissell, 1962–63

❦ 290 a, b
SPOONS, 1780–1805

(a) L. 8 ¹³⁄₁₆" (22.4 cm), 1 oz. 13 dwt. 17 gr. (52.4 g)
(b) L. 5 ½" (14.0 cm), 7 dwt. 18 gr. (12.0 g)

Stamps: "D.V" in roman letters, in a rectangle, struck once on back of each handle.

Engraved on front of spoon: (a) "WDL" in foliate script; (b) "L/ HA" in shaded roman letters.

Description: (a) oval bowl with swage-formed rounded drop with incised arc; (b) oval bowl with swage-formed rounded drop and, on back of bowl, standing bird with branch in its mouth. Rounded downturned handle with midrib on both.

Spectrographic analysis: Silver content ranges from 89.1 to 89.8 percent.

Provenance: (a) Mr. and Mrs. Stanley B. Ineson, New York City; Mr. and Mrs. Alfred E. Bissell, Wilmington, Del.; (b) Constance A. Jones, Philadelphia.

Comments: The "DV" stamp appears on numerous pieces with New York associations, especially the tankard at the New-York Historical Society made for Robert Lenox. It appears on other pieces in conjunction with the spread-winged eagle in a diamond. The latter stamp appears on the skewer having the "D.V.V." stamp.

References: Belden, *Marks of American Silversmiths*, attributes this stamp to David Vinton of Providence, but the weight of evidence favors Van Voorhis.

(a) 62.240.1521 Gift of Mr. and Mrs. Alfred E. Bissell, 1962–63; (b) 89.13.83 Bequest from Constance A. Jones, 1989

❦ 291 a–c
SPOONS, 1780–1805

(a) L. 5 ½" (14.0 cm), 8 dwt. 11 gr. (13.1 g)
(b) L. 7 ¼" (18.4 cm), 17 dwt. (26.4 g)
(c) L. 8 ¹⁵⁄₁₆" (22.7 cm), 1 oz. 18 dwt. 4 gr. (59.3 g)

Stamps: "D.V.VOORHIS" in roman letters, in a rectangle, struck once on back of each handle. On (b) and (c) the stamp is accompanied by a spread-winged eagle in a diamond surround.

Engraved on front of handles: (a, c) "JS" in script; (b) "ILT/ 1796./ 1870." in foliate script.

Description: pointed oval bowl with swage-formed double drop; pointed downturned handle with midrib on (a) and (c); (b) oval bowl with swage-formed rounded drop; pointed downturned handle with slight midrib.

Spectrographic analysis: Silver content ranges from 88.2 to 90.6 percent.

Provenance: Mr. and Mrs. Stanley B. Ineson, New York City; Mr. and Mrs. Alfred E. Bissell, Wilmington, Del.

References: Belden, *Marks of American Silversmiths*, pp. 418, 419 a, b.

62.240.587, .1431, .1540 Gift of Mr. and Mrs. Alfred E. Bissell, 1962–63

John Vernon

New York, New York, w. 1786–1817

Little is known about John Vernon, although a fair amount of his work survives. Directories place him at 41 Water Street in 1786 with Thomas Underhill in what was apparently a short-lived partnership. He remained at that address, although alone, through 1793. He was at 156 Water Street in 1794 and 93 John Street in 1795. Apparently he remained at the John Street address until 1803, when a fire devastated the neighborhood and "John Vernon & Co." suffered damage. From 1815 to 1817, he was in Gold Street. Vernon may have been John Targee's master, for Targee named his son John Vernon Targee. Vernon made several neoclassical tea services and a variety of other forms. He used poorly struck device stamps, usually incorporating an eagle's head, a date letter of sorts, and sometimes a sheaf of wheat.

References: Gottesman, *Arts and Crafts, 1800– 1804*, p. 100. Von Khrum, *Silversmiths*, p. 133.

292
STAND FOR TEAPOT, ca. 1800

L. 5 13/16" (14.8 cm), w. 4 11/16" (11.9 cm), H. 1 1/4" (3.2 cm)
4 oz. 13 dwt. 9 gr. (145.3 g)

Stamps: "I•V" in roman letters, in a rounded rectangle with a wavy top, struck once on underside of body. Accompanied by 2 strikes, 1 of which appears to be a roman "P"; the other is illegible.

Engraved on upper surface: "HT" in foliate script, in a circular medallion of rollerwork, the whole enclosed by a wreath of leaves against a striated ground.

Description: raised flat oval tray with a stepped concave rim with applied reeded molding; wheelwork borders on lower edge of step; centerpunch on underside; 4 short legs cast in curves with scroll feet.

Spectrographic analysis:

	SILVER	COPPER	LEAD	GOLD
BODY TOP	90.0	9.5	0.22	0.17
BODY BOTTOM	94.2	5.2	0.23	0.23
FOOT	91.9	6.8	0.41	0.33

Provenance: Robert Ensko, Inc., New York City, sold to H. F. du Pont, September 1935.

Comments: Tray made as a stand for an oval neoclassical teapot. See also no. 252.

References: Fales, *American Silver*, no. 137. Fennimore, *Silver and Pewter*, no. 6.

61.1091 Gift of H. F. du Pont, 1965

293
PORRINGER, ca. 1800

DIAM. bowl 5" (14.0 cm), H. 2 1/8" (5.4 cm), w. 8" (20.3 cm)
9 oz. 6 dwt. 17 gr. (306.0 g)

Stamps: "I•V" in roman letters, in a rectangle, struck once on underside of body and underside of handle; 2 illegible strikes on underside of body and underside of handle.

Engraved on front of handle: "AH/ to/ SPB" in shaded roman letters. *Engraved on body opposite handle:* "Anna Sophia Pope/ from her Grandmother/ Susanna P. Barstow/ 1848" in script.

Description: raised circular bowl with bulging sides and angled rim; bottom very slightly domed overall; centerpunch on underside; cast handle pierced in keyhole pattern with 11 voids.

Spectrographic analysis:

	SILVER	COPPER	LEAD	GOLD
BODY SIDE	90.6	9.1	0.20	0.13
HANDLE	94.2	5.7	0.08	0.10

Provenance: Susanna P. Barstow; Anna Sophia Pope; Robert Ensko, Inc., New York City, sold to H. F. du Pont, December 1930.

Comments: Two stamp-size areas on underside look as if they have been filled with solder.

References: Fales, *American Silver*, no. 124.

61.614 Gift of H. F. du Pont, 1965

❦ 294
CREAMER, ca. 1800

H. 6 15/16" (17.6 cm), w. 5 5/16" (13.5 cm)
6 oz. 9 dwt. 19 gr. (201.4 g)

Stamps: "I•V" in roman letters, in a rounded rectangle, struck once on side of foot; 2 illegible strikes in shields in same location.

Engraved on front of body below spout: "JL" in foliate script, in a shield suspended from a bow-knot and surrounded by a floral wreath with bright-cut swags on each side.

Description: raised helmet-shape body with high pouring lip, low sides, back rising to a point at handle; no centerpunch. Applied band of beading around rim. Body joined to base consisting of trumpet-shape pedestal on a square plinth; sides of plinth applied. High-loop strap handle tapers to point at bottom and broadens to angular shoulders near upper join with body.

Spectrographic analysis:

	SILVER	COPPER	LEAD	GOLD
BODY	91.4	8.2	0.23	0.17
HANDLE	91.2	8.6	0.19	0.11
FOOT	93.2	6.5	0.14	0.18

Provenance: Marshall P. Blankarn, New York City.

80.179 Gift of Marshall P. Blankarn, 1981

❦ 295
BEAKER, ca. 1800

H. 4 1/8" (10.5 cm), DIAM. rim 3 3/8" (8.6 cm)
7 oz. 16 dwt. 18 gr. (243.8 g)

Stamps: "I•V" in roman letters, against a stippled ground, in an oval with a wavy top, struck once on underside. Also on underside: roman "P" in a shield and an illegible figure on a shield, each struck once.

Scratched on underside: "G194 85".

Description: raised cylindrical body with slightly flared rim and flat bottom; centerpunch on underside; applied reeded base band.

Spectrographic analysis:

	SILVER	COPPER	LEAD	GOLD
BODY SIDE	89.1	9.9	0.52	0.23
BASE BAND	91.8	7.4	0.32	0.18

Provenance: H. F. du Pont.

61.971 Gift of H. F. du Pont, 1965

❦ 296
STRAINER, ca. 1800

DIAM. bowl 4 ½" (11.4 cm), H. (with handle)
1 ¹⁵⁄₁₆" (4.9 cm), W. 7 ⅛" (18.1 cm)
4 oz. 6 dwt. 13 gr. (134.3 g)

Stamps: "I•V" in roman letters, in a rounded
rectangle with wavy top, struck once on underside of handle. Accompanied by 2 strikes, one
probably a roman "P", the other illegible.

Engraved on underside of body: "AP" in foliate
script.

Description: shallow circular raised bowl with
slightly bulging sides and an angled rim with
applied reeded molding; no centerpunch visible.
Bottom of body pierced with drilled holes in
pattern of 7 concentric circles around a central
hole. Cast strapwork handle with 2 large shieldlike voids; handle angles up from body.

Spectrographic analysis:

	SILVER	COPPER	LEAD	GOLD
BOWL	93.9	5.8	0.15	0.13

Provenance: Marshall P. Blankarn, New York
City.

80.180 Gift of Marshall P. Blankarn, 1981

❦ 297
SUGAR TONGS, ca. 1800

L. 6 ⅜" (16.2 cm)
1 oz. 9 dwt. 15 gr. (46.0 g)

Stamps: "I•V" in roman letters, in a shield,
struck once on interior of arm. Accompanied
by 2 strikes, one a roman "P," the other an
eagle's head, both in shields.

Engraved on bow back: "HL" (or "THCL") in
foliate script.

Description: bow-type tongs; U-shape form with
straight tapering arms and plain oval bowl grips.

Spectrographic analysis:

SILVER	COPPER	GOLD	LEAD
89.0	10.8	0.21	0.04

Provenance: Mr. and Mrs. Stanley B. Ineson,
New York City; Mr. and Mrs. Alfred E. Bissell,
Wilmington, Del.

Comments: See tongs, no. 400 e (John Lynch),
which have the same monogram. Nearly identical tongs are in the Clearwater collection at the
Metropolitan Museum of Art.

References: Belden, *Marks of American
Silversmiths*, p. 421.

62.240.1632 Gift of Mr. and Mrs. Alfred E.
Bissell, 1965

❦ 298 a–d
SPOONS, ca. 1800

(a) L. 5 ¹¹⁄₁₆" (14.5 cm)
11 dwt. 19 gr. (18.4 g)
(b) L. 8 ⅝" (21.9 cm)
1 oz. 16 dwt. 20 gr. (57.2 g)
(c) L. 8 ⅞" (22.5 cm)
1 oz. 19 dwt. 5 gr. (60.9 g)
(d) L. 5 ¹⁵⁄₁₆" (15.1 cm)
10 dwt. 18 gr. (16.7 g)

Stamps: "I•V" in roman letters, struck once
on back of handle (a–c). Accompanied by 2
strikes, one a roman "P", the other an eagle's
head, both in shields. "IV" in roman letters,
in an oval, struck once on back of handle (d).
Accompanied by sheaf of wheat, in a rectangle,
struck twice.

Engraved on front of handle: (a) "HCT" in foliate script, in a bright-cut medallion with pendant; (b) "MH" in shaded roman letters, with
featheredge border; (c) "IHS" in foliate script;
(d) "CC" in foliate script.

Description: elongated oval bowls with swage-
formed single rounded drop on (a) and (c); oval
bowl with swage-formed double rounded drop
on (b); pointed oval bowl with swage-formed
single pointed drop on (d); rounded downturned handle with short midrib on (a) and (b);
pointed downturned handle with short midrib
on (c) and (d).

Spectrographic analysis: Silver content ranges
from 89.9 to 92.5 percent.

Provenance: Mr. and Mrs. Stanley B. Ineson,
New York City; Mr. and Mrs. Alfred E. Bissell,
Wilmington, Del.

Exhibitions: (c) Metropolitan Museum of Art,
New York City, 1935–61.

References: See Christine Wallace Laidlaw,
"Silver by the Dozen: The Wholesale Business
of Teunis D. DuBois," *Winterthur Portfolio* 23,
no. 1 (Spring 1988): 25–50, for argument attributing "IV"-stamped silver with sheaf of wheat
to DuBois.

62.240.584, .1537, .1538, .583 Gift of Mr. and
Mrs. Alfred E. Bissell, 1962–63

Hugh Wishart

New York, New York, w. ca. 1793–1824

Hugh Wishart is listed in directories at the following locations: 98 Market Street, 1794; 62 Wall Street, 1795; Cliff Street near Perry Street, 1796; 319 Pearl Street, 1797–98; 112 Broadway, 1799; 66 William Street, 1800–1802; 135 Broadway, 1803; 31 Liberty Street, 1804–7; 66 Maiden Lane, 1808–11; 31 Liberty Street, 1812–15; 29 Liberty Street, 1816–20; 63 Ann Street, 1821; Allen Street near Broome Street, 1822; 36 Spring Street, 1824. Although we know little about his life, a large body of his work survives. A fine neoclassical urn-shape soup tureen is owned by the Campbell Museum, Camden, New Jersey. A set of three tureens (unique in American silver), each engraved with the Lenox crest, is owned by the New-York Historical Society. The Museum of the City of New York owns a coffeepot inset with stamped panels that was made for Gen. Pierre Van Cortlandt (1762–1848). In the accompanying bill of sale, dated August 3, 1809, Wishart charged $51.12 ½, which included making and engraving.

In 1812 he made a pair of elegant cake baskets that are engraved "PCVC" for Pierre and Catherine Van Cortlandt and are now owned by the Museum of the City of New York.

Wishart's relationship with the younger silversmith Stephen Richard has been the subject of speculation. A cake basket at Winterthur with Wishart's stamp and Richard's engraved signature (no. 242) led previous authors to assume that Richard must have signed the piece when he was Wishart's apprentice. The appearance of three other pieces with Richard's signature, only one of them with Wishart's stamp and all of them important commissions, suggests that Richard made these pieces after he was well established.

References: Kathryn C. Buhler, "Silver Tureens in the Campbell Museum Collection," *Antiques* 97, no. 6 (June 1970): 904–9, fig. 15. Von Khrum, *Silversmiths*, p. 141.

299
CAKE BASKET, 1793–1810

H. (handle up) 10 ¾" (27.3 cm), H. (handle down) 4 ⅜" (11.1 cm), L. 13 ¾" (48.7 cm), W. 10 %6" (26.8 cm)
31 oz. 19 dwt. 2 gr. (991.6 g)

Stamps: "WISHART" in roman letters, in a rectangle, struck once on underside of body.

Engraved inside bottom of body: "GMW" in foliate script.

Description: oval in plan, the raised body has a deep curved well rising to a 2-step angled rim; the first step pierced in lattice pattern all around; the second step decorated in a repeating pattern of engraved and wheelwork flowers and leaves. Applied reed molding at rim. Seamed pedestal, concave in section and conforming to shape of body, has closely spaced pierced reeding; plain applied footring. Large bail handle hinged with silver pins on long sides of body; handle U shape in cross section in center, narrows and flattens toward hinges. Centerpunch inside body.

Spectrographic analysis:

	SILVER	COPPER	LEAD	GOLD
BODY SIDE	90.7	8.9	0.23	0.15
FOOTRING	95.2	4.5	0.17	0.07

History: According to the donor the cake basket was purchased from the Nicholas-Treadwell family of Shelton, Conn., a family that originally came from New York about 1800 and intermarried with the Warner family.

Provenance: Nicholas-Treadwell family, Shelton, Conn.; purchased in 1947 by members of donor's family; last private owner: Mr. and Mrs. Harold A. Mitchell, Old Saybrook, Conn.

86.133 Gift of Mr. and Mrs. Harold A. Mitchell, 1986

300
TEAPOT, 1793–1810

H. 7 15/16" (20.2 cm), w. 13 5/16" (33.8 cm)
19 oz. 2 dwt. 17 gr. (593.8 g)

Stamps: "WISHART" in roman letters, in a rectangle, struck once on underside.

Engraved on both sides of body: "BFG" in foliate script, with dart-motif swags below. *Scratched on underside:* "149" and "42122".

Description: oval in plan with straight plain sides seamed at handle end, flat bottom; concave shoulders (raised); applied bands around lower body (4 reeds) and upper body (3 reeds). Flush-mounted oval lid (raised), domed in center with urn finial cast in 2 vertical sections; 3-segment hinge. Straight tapered spout, oval in section, seamed on upper side; 2 seamed handle sockets with 3 reeds near handle. C-curve hardwood handle with sprig.

Spectrographic analysis:

	SILVER	COPPER	LEAD	GOLD
BODY SIDE	90.4	9.1	0.15	0.13
UNDERSIDE	96.3	3.5	0.09	0.09
SPOUT	91.9	7.9	0.10	0.08

Provenance: Marshall P. Blankarn, New York City.

79.192 Gift of Marshall P. Blankarn, 1979

301 a–f
FORKS, ca. 1810

L. 6 5/8"–6 11/16" (16.8–16.9 cm)
18 dwt. 2 gr.–19 dwt. 23 gr. (28.1–31.0 g)

Stamps: "H.WISHART" in roman letters, in a rectangle, struck once on back of each handle.

Engraved on front of each handle: "JMC" in foliate script, beneath heraldic device consisting of a 3-part leaf over a curved heraldic band.

Description: 3 tapered tines; rounded downturned fiddle-shape handle with slight midrib on back; no shoulders.

Spectrographic analysis: Silver content ranges from 88.0 to 90.2 percent.

Provenance: Mr. and Mrs. Stanley B. Ineson, New York City; Mr. and Mrs. Alfred E. Bissell, Wilmington, Del.

Comments: A seventh fork was returned to the donor. No doubt the set was larger, perhaps a dozen.

References: Belden, *Marks of American Silversmiths*, p. 453. Louise Conway Belden, *The Festive Tradition: Table Decoration and Desserts in America, 1650–1900* (New York: W. W. Norton, 1983), fig. 3:19, which refers to them as dessert forks. Fennimore, *Silver and Pewter*, no. 25.

62.240.517.1–.6 Gift of Mr. and Mrs. Alfred E. Bissell, 1962–63

❦ 302
SUGAR TONGS, ca. 1810

L. 8 1/16" (20.5 cm)
2 oz. 12 dwt. 23 gr. (82.2 g)

Stamps: "H.WISHART" in roman letters, in a rectangle, struck once inside each arm.

Engraved on bow back: "W" in foliate script.

Description: bow-type tongs; U-shape form with broad bow, fiddle-shape arms, and coffered rect-angular grips.

Spectrographic analysis:

SILVER	COPPER	GOLD	LEAD
91.3	8.4	0.16	0.09

Provenance: Mr. and Mrs. Stanley B. Ineson, New York City; Mr. and Mrs. Alfred E. Bissell, Wilmington, Del.

References: Belden, *Marks of American Silversmiths*, p. 453.

62.240.1619 Gift of Mr. and Mrs. Alfred E. Bissell, 1962–63

❦ 303 a–c
SPOONS, 1793–1815

(a) L. 5 7/16" (13.8 cm)
8 dwt. 3 gr. (12.6 g)
(b) L. 5 7/16" (13.8 cm)
7 dwt. 10 gr. (11.6 g)
(c) L. 8 13/16" (22.4 cm)
1 oz. 17 dwt. 11 gr. (58.1 g)

Stamps: "WISHART" in roman letters, in a rectangle, struck once on back of each handle.

Engraved on front of each handle: (a) "IS" in shaded roman letters; (b) "EC" (sideways) in foliate script, in a bright-cut medallion with pendant; (c) "JC" in foliate script.

Description: (a) pointed oval bowl with swage-formed double rounded drop on back; pointed downturned handle with short midrib; (b) pointed oval bowl with swage-formed single pointed drop on back; rounded downturned handle; (c) pointed oval bowl with swage-formed double rounded drop on back; pointed downturned handle with short midrib.

Spectrographic analysis: Silver content ranges from 90.0 to 92.7 percent.

Provenance: Mr. and Mrs. Stanley B. Ineson, New York City; Mr. and Mrs. Alfred E. Bissell, Wilmington, Del.

References: Belden, *Marks of American Silversmiths*, p. 452.

62.240.638, .639, .1594 Gift of Mr. and Mrs. Alfred E. Bissell, 1962–63

❦ 304 a, b
SALT SPOONS, 1793–1815

(a) L. 4" (10.2 cm)
6 dwt. 8 gr. (9.8 g)
(b) L. 4" (10.2 cm)
5 dwt. 18 gr. (9.0 g)

Stamps: "WISHART" in roman letters, in a rectangle, struck once on back of each handle.

Engraved on front of each handle: "S" in foliate script.

Description: broad oval bowl; rounded down-turned handle.

Spectrographic analysis: Silver content ranges from 90.2 to 90.4 percent.

Provenance: Mr. and Mrs. Stanley B. Ineson, New York City; Mr. and Mrs. Alfred E. Bissell, Wilmington, Del.

Exhibitions: (a) or (b) Metropolitan Museum of Art, New York City, 1938–61.

References: Belden, *Marks of American Silversmiths*, p. 452.

62.240.838.1, .2 Gift of Mr. and Mrs. Alfred E. Bissell, 1962–63

🍂 *Benjamin Wynkoop*

1675–1728
New York, New York

Benjamin Wynkoop married Femmetje Van de Heus in 1697 and became a freeman the following year. In 1728 Femmetje received a legacy from Marten Clock, who had married her sister. The will refers to her as "the wife of Benjamin Wynkoop, of New York, Goldsmith." Clock's sister married goldsmith Jacob Boelen. Wynkoop's son Cornelius (1701–40) succeeded his father, and son Benjamin, Jr. (1705–66) later worked as a silversmith in Fairfield, Connecticut, and married silversmith Jacobus Van der Spiegel's daughter. Benjamin was collector and assessor for the city's South Ward from 1703 to 1722. In the contested 1701 election for alderman, Wynkoop voted for fellow goldsmith Nicholas Roosevelt over Brandt Schuyler. Wynkoop made a paneled bowl very similar to the one by Jacob C. Ten Eyck (no. 265) and an elaborately engraved tankard with the Wynkoop coat of arms. He also made a beaker with the engraved date of 1711 for the First Reformed Church of Kingston, New York, that is now in the Metropolitan Museum of Art.

References: Ensko, *American Silversmiths IV*, pp. 230, 247, 341. Jones, *Old Silver*, p. 235. *Minutes of the Common Council*. Miller, *New York Silversmiths*, no. 102, for tankard with Wynkoop arms. Miller, *Silver by New York Makers*, p. 38. *NYHS Collections*: vol. 18 (1885) *Burghers and Freemen*, p. 63; vol. 26 (1893) *Abstracts of Wills*, pp. 86–87. *New York State Silversmiths*, p. 194. John N. Pearce, "New York's Two-Handled Paneled Silver Bowls," *Antiques* 80, no. 4 (October 1961): 341–45, fig. 1.

🍂 305
CUP, 1700–1728

H. 3" (7.6 cm), w. 4 1/16" (10.3 cm)
5 oz. 10 dwt. 19 gr. (172.3 g)

Stamps: "W∗K / •B•" in roman letters, in a heart, struck once on upper body, left of handle, and once on underside of body.

Engraved on handle: "RV / NH" ("RV" conjoined) in shaded roman letters.

Engraved on underside of body: "R" in a shaded roman letter. *Engraved on body opposite handle:* armorial device consisting of a tree in a meadow with 2 grazing horses against an azure ground; all in a shield with a banner below with motto "FORTI NONDEFICIT TALLUM" in sans serif letters; above: a closed helmet over a leafy wreath that hangs down both sides of shield; crest: a tree on a heraldic band.

Description: raised cylindrical body with straight tapering sides, slightly flared rim, and slightly concave bottom; centerpunch on underside. Broad 4-step molding around base; 3-element molding around rim. S-curve handle, flat on outside, curved on inside, plain triangular tailpiece.

Spectrographic analysis:

	SILVER	COPPER	LEAD	GOLD
BODY SIDE	94.0	5.7	0.21	0.02
UNDERSIDE	92.8	6.8	0.27	0.04
HANDLE	93.6	5.9	0.42	0.06

History: Initials "RV/ NH" are similar to those on a large paneled bowl by Wynkoop that was made for Nicholas and Hilletje Roosevelt, ca. 1707.

Provenance: Harrington family, Wilmington, Del.

Comments: See Wynkoop tankard with engraved initials "R/ NH" owned by Roosevelt Hospital and on loan to the Museum of the City of New York.

References: Louise Bartlett, "American Silver," *Bulletin, St. Louis Museum of Art* 17, no. 1 (Winter 1984): 6, for a similar mug.

73.236 Gift of Willis F. Harrington, George S. Harrington, and Charles J. Harrington, 1973

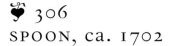 306
SPOON, ca. 1702

L. 8 ¹⁄₁₆" (20.5 cm)
1 oz. 10 dwt. 19 gr. (47.8 g)

Stamps: "WK/ B" in roman letters, in a heart, struck once on back of handle.

Engraved on back of handle: "S/ I∗E/ 1702/ ∗" in crude shaded roman letters.

Description: elongated oval bowl with swage-formed rounded drop and reeded rattail on back; wavy-end, slightly upturned handle.

Spectrographic analysis: Silver content is 94.9 percent.

Provenance: Mr. and Mrs. Stanley B. Ineson, New York City; Mr. and Mrs. Alfred E. Bissell, Wilmington, Del.

References: Belden, *Marks of American Silversmiths,* p. 457.

62.240.1558 Gift of Mr. and Mrs. Alfred E. Bissell, 1962–63

 307
SPOON, 1700–1728

L. 8" (20.3 cm)
1 oz. 7 dwt. 12 gr. (42.7 g)

Stamps: "W+K/ B" in roman letters, in heart with a double border, struck once on back of handle.

Engraved on back of handle: "E•D•W" in shaded roman letters.

Description: oval bowl with swage-formed rounded drop and reeded rattail flanked by foliation; wavy-end, slightly upturned handle.

Spectrographic analysis: Silver content is 90.9 percent.

Provenance: Mr. and Mrs. Stanley B. Ineson, New York City; Mr. and Mrs. Alfred E. Bissell, Wilmington, Del.

References: Belden, *Marks of American Silversmiths,* p. 457.

62.240.1557 Gift of Mr. and Mrs. Alfred E. Bissell, 1962–63

Pennsylvania and the South

Henry Andrews

Philadelphia, Pennsylvania, w. ca. 1795
Boston, Massachusetts, w. ca. 1830

Philadelphia directories indicate that Henry Andrews worked at 65 South Second Street during 1795 and 1796. The evidence for Stephen Ensko's claim that he worked in Boston is unclear. In addition to the beaker listed here, his documented work is limited to a gold picture frame in the Hammerslough collection at Wadsworth Atheneum and a gold mourning brooch at the Henry Ford Museum. Virtually nothing else is known about this artisan.

References: Brix, *Philadelphia Silversmiths*, p. 2. Ensko, *American Silversmiths IV*, pp. 6, 271. Belden, *Marks of American Silversmiths*, p. 32.

308
BEAKER, ca. 1795

H. 3 ½" (8.9 cm), DIAM. rim 3" (7.6 cm)
4 oz. 3 dwt. 3 gr. (129.0 g)

Stamps: "HA" in roman letters, in a rectangle, struck 4 times on underside of body.

Engraved on side of body: "ALB" in shaded foliate script.

Description: raised cylindrical body with slightly bowed tapering sides and flat bottom; center-punch on underside. Double molding around upper body; single molding around base is an extension of the seamed footring.

Spectrographic analysis:

	SILVER	COPPER	LEAD	GOLD
BODY SIDE	94.0	5.4	0.20	0.12
FOOTRING	93.8	5.3	0.19	0.14

Provenance: H. F. du Pont.

61.960 Gift of H. F. du Pont, 1965

309 a, b
SPOONS, ca. 1795

(a) L. 5 ¾" (14.6 cm)
9 dwt. 4 gr. (14.2 g)
(b) L. 5 %₁₆" (14.1 cm)
6 dwt. 19 gr. (10.5 g)

Stamps: "HA" in roman letters, in a rectangle, struck once on back of each handle.

Engraved on front of handle: (a) "EJ" ["EI"] in foliate script, in a bright-cut medallion with pendant; (b) "LC" in crude shaded roman letters.

Description: (a) pointed oval bowl with swage-formed single drop and bird with leafy sprig in beak, on branch; pointed downturned handle with midrib; (b) pointed oval bowl with swage-formed rounded drop; pointed downturned handle without midrib.

Spectrographic analysis: Silver content ranges from 88.2 to 92.4 percent.

Provenance: Mr. and Mrs. Stanley B. Ineson, New York City; Mr. and Mrs. Alfred E. Bissell, Wilmington, Del.

References: Belden, *Marks of American Silversmiths*, p. 32.

62.240.7, .8 Gift of Mr. and Mrs. Alfred E. Bissell, 1962–63

Joseph Anthony, Jr.

1762–1814
Philadelphia, Pennsylvania

Joseph Anthony's parents were Joseph and Elizabeth Anthony of a prosperous mercantile family from Newport, Rhode Island, who moved to Philadelphia in 1782. Presumably young Joseph had completed his apprenticeship in Newport and moved with them, for in 1783 he placed the first of many advertisements in Philadelphia newspapers. The notice (*Pennsylvania Packet*, October 4, 1783) mentions many different silver forms and numerous pieces of jewelry in addition to such nonsilver wares as buttons in various materials, memorandum books, shaving cases, corkscrews, fruit and pen knives, and other items. A japanned wooden jewel casket with gilt decoration, with Anthony's label inside, is owned by Independence National Historical Park. Notwithstanding his nonsilver merchandise, Anthony was a prolific silversmith. At the 1956 exhibition of Philadelphia silver at the Philadelphia Museum of Art (PMA), he was represented by eighteen pieces, which by no means exhausts his surviving silver. He made a tall double-bellied coffeepot for George Washington, now at Mount Vernon, and a hooped tankard commissioned by the Penns for presentation to Charles Jarvis, "for services rendered," in 1788 (now at PMA).

Joseph Anthony, Sr., ran his mercantile business in Philadelphia during the 1780s and is often confused with his son. In 1785 the younger Joseph married Henrietta Hillegas, daughter of Michael Hillegas, first treasurer of the United States.

Their three-story house on High (Market) Street, between Third and Fourth, had an elaborate showroom on the first floor and a workshop with forge on the third. In his final years Anthony was in partnership with sons Michael and Thomas. Portraits of Anthony and his wife, by Gilbert Stuart, are at the Metropolitan Museum of Art. A portrait miniature of Joseph by Benjamin Trott is at Yale University Art Gallery. One of his trade cards is reproduced here.

References: Philadelphia: Three Centuries, pp. 150–52, 177. *Philadelphia Silver*, nos. 2–18. Alfred Coxe Prime, comp., *The Arts and Crafts in Philadelphia, Maryland, and South Carolina, 1721–1785: Gleanings from Newspapers* (Topsfield, Mass.: Walpole Society, 1929), pp. 42–43. Alfred Coxe Prime, comp., *The Arts and Crafts in Philadelphia, Maryland, and South Carolina, 1786–1800: Gleanings from Newspapers* (Topsfield, Mass.: Walpole Society, 1932), pp. 85–87. Waters, "Philadelphia's Precious Metals Trades," pp. 20–21, 114. Prime cards, Winterthur. Joseph Anthony bills to Anthony Wayne, 1792, 64x80.1–.2, Downs collection, Winterthur. *Yale University Portrait Index*, p. 5.

310

COFFEEPOT, ca. 1790

H. 12⅝" (32.1 cm), w. 10⅛" (25.7 cm)
42 oz. 13 dwt. 8 gr. (1324.0 g)

Stamps: "JA" in script, on a stippled ground, all in a rectangle, struck 3 times on underside of body.

Engraved on side of body: "MM" in shaded foliate script. *Scratched on underside of body:* "44" and, more recently, "43319"; the last number is difficult to read because it is painted over by an accession number.

Description: raised circular double-bellied body with incurving elongated neck rising to a flared, heavily molded, applied rim; centerpunch on underside of body. Raised circular foot with plain incurved pedestal and gadrooned middle; cast stepped footring. Raised circular high-dome lid with applied cast gadrooned flange; elaborate hollow-cast finial of bunched acanthus leaves; vents outside and underneath. Lid attached to upper handle socket by a 5-segment cast hinge. S-curve spout cast in 2 vertical sections; molded acanthus leaf on upper back, shell pattern on lower front and around base of spout on body. S-curve hardwood handle with sprig. Cast upper handle socket has dependent shell and drop; C-curve lower socket with scroll and sprig attached to body by an oval plate.

Spectrographic analysis:

	SILVER	COPPER	GOLD	LEAD
BODY SIDE	90.0	9.8	0.11	0.10
LID	91.7	8.0	0.10	0.16
SPOUT	92.8	6.9	0.17	0.21

Provenance: Marshall P. Blankarn, New York City.

Exhibitions: "Philadelphia Silver," Philadelphia Museum of Art, 1956.

References: Philadelphia Silver, no. 7. Fennimore, *Silver and Pewter*, no. 134.

Comments: Handsome form. Unusual base: cast stepped foot attached just below gadrooning. See no. 312 b, which has the same engraved initials.

76.276 Gift of Marshall P. Blankarn, 1976

❦ 311
CREAMER, ca. 1785

H. 6 ⁷⁄₁₆" (16.4 cm), w. 5 ⁷⁄₁₆" (13.8 cm)
6 oz. 7 dwt. (197.1 g)

Stamps: "I•A" ("IA" conjoined at bottom) in roman letters, struck once on underside of body.

Engraved on body under pouring lip: "SMN" in foliate script.

Description: raised circular double-bellied body with narrow rounded bottom; high incurving neck flares to rim, extended in front for wide pouring lip; centerpunch on underside of body. Body mounted on a raised, circular, stepped pedestal with molded footring. Cast S-curve handle with C-scroll sections at top and bottom, 1 sprig, and leaf-pattern engraving.

Spectrographic analysis:

	SILVER	COPPER	GOLD	LEAD
BODY SIDE	89.2	10.6	0.16	0.05
FOOT	91.3	8.5	0.14	0.07
HANDLE	91.0	8.7	0.16	0.07

Provenance: Freeman's, Philadelphia, 1938; May and Howard Joynt, Alexandria, Va.; Christie's, New York City, 1990.

Comments: The creamer is part of a set that includes a teapot and sugar bowl made by Joseph and Nathaniel Richardson; see no. 459 a, b. Note the simplicity of fabrication using traditional techniques to achieve a handsome vessel.

References: Christie's (New York City), Joynt sale (January 19–20, 1990), lot 254.

90.2.3 Museum purchase from Christie's, 1990

❦ 312 a, b
SPOONS, ca. 1790

(a) L. 8 ¹⁵⁄₁₆" (22.7 cm)
1 oz. 15 dwt. 1 gr. (54.4 g)
(b) L. 8 ¾" (22.2 cm)
1 oz. 14 dwt. 8 gr. (53.3 g)

Stamps: "J Anthony" in script, in a conforming surround, struck once on back of each handle.

Engraved on front of handle: (a) "GRB" (crosswise) in script; (b) "MM" in foliate script, in a bright-cut medallion with floral pendant.

Description: oval bowl with swage-formed rounded drop; rounded downturned handle with midrib.

Spectrographic analysis: Silver content ranges from 90.3 to 90.5 percent.

History: Unknown, but (b) has same initials as no. 310.

Provenance: Mr. and Mrs. Stanley B. Ineson, New York City; Mr. and Mrs. Alfred E. Bissell, Wilmington, Del.

References: Belden, *Marks of American Silversmiths,* p. 33.

62.240.885, .886 Gift of Mr. and Mrs. Alfred E. Bissell, 1962–63

❦ 313
SPOON, ca. 1805

L. 9 ⅜" (23.8 cm)
1 oz. 11 dwt. 20 gr. (49.4 g)

Stamps: "JA" in script, in a rectangle, struck once on back of handle.

Engraved on front of handle: "NB" in foliate script.

Description: pointed oval bowl with incised pointed drop; coffin-end downturned handle.

Spectrographic analysis: Silver content is 88.7 percent.

Provenance: Mr. and Mrs. Stanley B. Ineson, New York City; Mrs. and Mrs. Alfred E. Bissell, Wilmington, Del.

References: Belden, *Marks of American Silversmiths,* p. 33.

62.240.872 Gift of Mr. and Mrs. Alfred E. Bissell, 1962–63

William Ball

1763–1815

Ball & Johnson, w. ?–1790
Baltimore, Maryland

Born in England and probably trained in Philadelphia, William Ball was long thought to be the son of the Philadelphia silversmith of the same name. Recent scholarship denies any relationship between the two. Ball was in Baltimore by 1790, when a notice appeared in the newspaper announcing dissolution of his partnership with Israel Johnson. By 1793 he was at "the Sign of the Golden Urn" on Market (later Baltimore) Street. He was among those silversmiths who, in 1814, signed a petition for the appointment of Thomas Warner as assay officer. He was active until his death on June 2, 1815. A great deal of his work survives, most of it in the neoclassical urn style. Notable examples include an oval tray, 32 ¾ inches long, engraved with the Ridgely arms.

References: Goldsborough, *Silver in Maryland*, pp. 72–77. Pleasants and Sill, *Maryland Silversmiths*, pp. 89–92. Prime cards, Winterthur.

314
VINAIGRETTE, ca. 1800

L. 1 ⁵⁄₁₆" (3.3 cm), w. ¹⁵⁄₁₆" (2.4 cm), H. ½" (1.3 cm)
1 oz. 17 dwt. 10 gr. (58.1 g)

Stamps: "W•Ball" in roman letters, in a conforming surround, struck once inside on bottom of body.

Engraved on lid: "F. St." in script, in an oval. *Scratched inside lid and body:* "IIIIV". *Scratched on underside of grill:* "VIIII". *Stamped on top edge of grill:* illegible arabic numbers.

Description: rectangular box with rounded corners and hinged lid. Exterior decorated with rollerwork pattern of wavy lines overall. Interior contains rectangular frame for grill, lower on right side to permit grill to slide over. Rectangular sliding grill is pierced and engraved in floral pattern with rollerwork border. Interior gilded. Applied lip on front of body; 5-segment hinge.

Spectrographic analysis:

	SILVER	COPPER	LEAD	GOLD
BODY	78.6	20.7	0.17	0.04
LID	76.8	22.4	0.19	0.03

Provenance: Philadelphia Antique Shop.

References: Fennimore, *Silver and Pewter*, no. 207. Eileen Ellenbogen, "Vinaigrettes," *Antiques* 83, no. 2 (February 1963): 214–17, for a discussion of this form.

Comments: Very low silver content. American vinaigrettes are rare.

66.8 Museum purchase from Philadelphia Antique Shop, 1966

315
SPOON, ca. 1800

L. 9 ¹¹⁄₁₆" (24.6 cm)
1 oz. 17 dwt. 15 gr. (58.4 g)

Stamps: "W•Ball" in roman letters, in a conforming surround, struck once on back of handle.

Engraved on front of handle: "AEH" in foliate script.

Description: oval bowl with swage-formed rounded drop; pointed downturned handle with midrib.

Spectrographic analysis: Silver content is 88.6 percent.

Provenance: Mr. and Mrs. Stanley B. Ineson, New York City; Mr. and Mrs. Alfred E. Bissell, Wilmington, Del.

62.240.902 Gift of Mr. and Mrs. Alfred E. Bissell, 1962–63

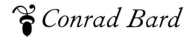

Conrad Bard

ca. 1800–1854

Bard & Hoffman, w. ca. 1837
Bard & Lamont, w. 1841–45
Conrad Bard & Son, w. 1849–ca. 1859
Philadelphia, Pennsylvania

Possibly trained under Thomas Fletcher, Conrad Bard first appears in the Philadelphia directories at 80 Locust Street in 1825. By 1837 he and Frederick Hoffman operated a watch, clock, and jewelry shop at 297 Arch Street. By 1841 Bard was in business with Robert Lamont at 205 Mulberry (later Arch) Street, a partnership that lasted four years. When Conrad's son, E. Milford Bard, joined the firm in 1849, it became Conrad Bard & Son, which it remained until about 1859. Although some surviving pieces are stamped "BARD & LAMONT" and some "C. BARD & SON," most are stamped "C. BARD 205 ARCH ST." A trade card for Conrad Bard & Son, circa 1855, shows a five-story building at 116 Arch Street, with a showroom on the first floor and the silver manufactory on the upper floors. The firm sold a full range of hollowwares (everything from communion sets to soup tureens) and flatware (butter knives to oyster ladles) in addition to Sheffield and Birmingham plated wares and watches from London, Liverpool, and Geneva. One of the British commissioners visiting the New York Industrial Exhibition of 1853 observed that the firm of Conrad Bard & Son not only manufactured

gold and silver plate, but a considerable trade is carried on by them in the manufacture of spoons and forks. For this purpose

they use a machine invented and manufactured upon their own premises, by which the production of these articles is much facilitated. Two circular dies or rollers are sunk with forms of the article to be rolled out. These are usually spoons of two sizes, a fork, and the side of a knife-handle. As the intaglio of one die is accurately adjusted to, and agrees with that of the other, one forming the obverse and the other the reverse of the pattern. . . . The rollers are about 5 inches in diameter, and are of course manufactured of the best steel and case hardened. . . . It is an ingenious and useful invention as applied to light articles in silver, taking up a small amount of space in a workshop and doing a much larger amount of work than a stamp press.

Bard evidently had a lifelong association with Fletcher; a silver-headed walking stick in a private collection is inscribed: "Presented/ to/ Thomas Fletcher/ by/ Conrad Bard,/ 1853." A silver teapot by C. Bard & Son was presented to Neal Dow (mayor of Portland, Maine, and a noted temperance leader), who, in 1851, achieved his long-sought goal of banning liquor sales statewide.

References: David A. Hanks, "Recent Acquisitions of American Silver," *Bulletin, Detroit Institute of Arts* 55, no. 2 (1977): 112–14, figs. 5 a, b, for a ewer and salver by Bard & Lamont dated 1841. Samuel Pennington, "A Mail/ Phone Auction," *Maine Antique Digest*, April 1987, p. 32-C. "Mr. George Wallis's Special Report," in *Report of the British Commissioners to the New York Industrial Exhibition of 1853* (London, 1854), pp. 52–53. Waters, "Philadelphia's Precious Metals Trades," pp. 171–73. Trade card, 74x144, Downs collection, Winterthur.

316 a, b
BEAKERS, 1845–49

H. 3 9/16" (9.0 cm), DIAM. rim 3 5/16" (8.4 cm)
(a) 5 oz. 7 dwt. 5 gr. (166.5 g)
(b) 5 oz. 5 dwt. 19 gr. (164.0 g)

Stamps: "C. BARD 205 ARCH ST." in roman letters, in a rectangle, struck once on underside of each body.

Engraved on side of body: (a) "J.F.W." in sans serif roman letters.

Description: seamed octagonal body with straight tapering sides rising to a circular molded rim; centerpunch on underside; conforming molded footring.

Spectrographic analysis:

	SILVER	COPPER	LEAD	GOLD
BODY SIDE (a)	89.0	10.8	0.10	0.06
BODY SIDE (b)	88.9	11.0	0.09	0.05

History: Donor said beakers were part of a set of at least 8 plus a water pitcher. Tradition of ownership by Caleb Jones (d. 1883), who in 1826 moved from Kentucky to Cooper County, Mo. Jones was a banker, farmer, and stockman in Arrow Rock, Mo., one of the eastern terminals of the Santa Fe Trail, and had close ties with Philadelphia wholesalers. "JFW" remains unknown.

Provenance: Charles van Ravenswaay, Wilmington, Del.

Comments: In 1843 silversmith John McMullin bequeathed to his heirs 5 inscribed silver tumblers. They were made by Bard & Lamont at a cost of $45.55.

References: Waters, "Philadelphia's Precious Metals Trades," p. 172, for reference to McMullin bequest.

69.208.1, .2 Gift of Charles van Ravenswaay, 1969

317
SPOON, 1845–49

L. 6" (15.2 cm)
13 dwt. 12 gr. (21.0 g)

Stamps: "C. BARD 205 ARCH [ST.]" in incuse roman letters, struck once on back of handle.

Engraved on front of handle: "WMAR" in foliate script.

Description: pointed oval bowl with swage-formed rounded drop; rounded upturned fiddle-shape handle with short midrib.

Spectrographic analysis: Silver content is 87.9 percent.

Provenance: Willowdale Antiques, Kennett Square, Pa.

References: Belden, *Marks of American Silversmiths*, p. 48.

70.261 Museum purchase from Willowdale Antiques, 1970

318
SPOON, 1841–45

L. 9 ¼" (23.5 cm)
1 oz. 16 dwt. 9 gr. (56.5 g)

Stamps: "BARD & LAMONT" in roman letters, in a rectangle, struck once on back of handle.

Engraved on front of handle: "IAT" in foliate script.

Description: pointed oval bowl with swage-formed rounded drop; rounded downturned fiddle-shape handle with midrib.

Spectrographic analysis: Silver content is 88.6 percent.

Provenance: The Silver Shelf, Ardmore, Pa.

References: Belden, *Marks of American Silversmiths*, p. 48.

73.185 Museum purchase from the Silver Shelf, 1973

John Bayly

Philadelphia, Pennsylvania, w. ca. 1750–90

John Bayly was the son of cordwainer John Bayly of Philadelphia. The name of his master remains unknown. In 1750 he married Jane Watkins in Christ Church, Philadelphia. They had a son named John who also became a silversmith and who worked in Philadelphia and New Castle County, Delaware. (The son's work has often been confused with that of his father.) Bayly advertised extensively in the Philadelphia newspapers from 1757 to 1783. In all that time he was at only three locations: "At the sign of the Tea-pot, at the lower end of Front-street, near the Draw-bridge"; at the corner of Front and Chestnut streets; and in Fetter Lane. He was a member of the Library Company of Philadelphia and the Fishing Company of Fort Saint Davids. His petition to the court of quarter sessions (1773) to operate a public house in Yellow Springs, Chester County, was signed by, among others, silversmiths Joseph Richardson, Jr., and Philip Syng. A miniature portrait of Bayly by David Boudon is at Yale University Art Gallery. Unlike many portraits of the period, which tended to gentrify the subject, Bayly is shown wearing his hair in the traditional craftsman's pigtail. A large quantity of his work survives. I am indebted to Barbara Soltis for sharing information from her forthcoming book on John Bayly. She corrects a number of statements published previously.

References: Hindes, "Delaware Silversmiths," who confuses father and son. *Philadelphia Silver*, nos. 31–37. Prime cards, Winterthur. Nancy Richards, "'A Most Perfect Resemblance at Moderate Prices': The Miniatures of David Boudon," in Ian M. G. Quimby, ed., *Winterthur Portfolio 9* (Charlottesville: University Press of Virginia for the Henry Francis du Pont Winterthur Museum, 1974), pp. 77–101, fig. 9. *Yale University Portrait Index*, p. 9.

319
TANKARD, ca. 1765

H. 7⁵⁄₁₆" (18.6 cm), DIAM. base 5⁷⁄₁₆" (18.8 cm), w. 7⁷⁄₁₆" (18.9 cm)
31 oz. 14 dwt. 9 gr. (986.5 g)

Stamps: "IB" in roman letters, in an oval, struck once on upper body, left of handle; "I•BAYLY" in roman letters, in a rectangle, struck once on underside of body.

Engraved on back of handle: "D/ I∗E" in roman letters. *Engraved on underside of body:* "oz 32 - 11 Pwt".

Description: raised body with straight tapering sides and slightly concave bottom; 2-step, applied, molded, flared rim with double-scored lines below; centerpunch on underside of body. Applied seamed base molding, flared at bottom, consists of concave-over-convex moldings divided by 3 sets of double-scored lines. Raised circular stepped-and-domed lid with 2 sets of double-scored lines encircling edge and overlap; applied crenate lip; bezel; centerpunch on top of lid. Cast ram's horn thumbpiece attached to 5-segment hinge with pendant drop. Raised-

and-soldered hollow S-curve handle terminating in a flat shield-shape tailpiece; circular vent with 4 notches on lower end; circular vent under upper handle attachment.

Spectrographic analysis:

	SILVER	COPPER	LEAD	GOLD
BODY SIDE	92.3	7.5	0.11	0.05
UNDERSIDE	91.8	8.0	0.10	0.07
LID	90.4	9.4	0.12	0.05
HANDLE	92.7	7.2	0.08	0.06

History: The tankard, along with a cann (no. 320), was made for Isaac (d. 1790) and Elizabeth (d. 1792) Dushane of Red Lion Hundred, Del. The silver was deeded to the Presbyterian Church near Saint Georges, Del., in 1790, for the communion table.

Provenance: Isaac and Elizabeth Dushane, Red Lion Hundred, Del.; Presbyterian Church of Saint Georges, Del.

Comments: Descriptions and weights of the tankard and cann are given in the deed of gift from Elizabeth Dushane to the church, and the maker is mentioned by name. Both the documentation and the presence on the tankard of both the name stamp and the "IB" stamp prove conclusively that the "IB" stamp is Bayly's. This stamp had heretofore been credited by some to Jacob Boelen, Jr., of New York City. Barbara Soltis was instrumental in finding this well-documented silver.

References: Donald L. Fennimore, "A John Bayly Tankard and Cann," *Silver* 19, no. 3 (May/June 1986): 18–19.

85.3 Gift of Saint Georges Presbyterian Church, 1985

🍶320
CANN, ca. 1765

H. 4 13/16" (12.2 cm), w. 5 ½" (14.0 cm)
12 oz. 8 dwt. 13 gr. (386.6 g)

Stamps: "IB" in roman letters, in an oval, struck twice on upper body, left of handle.

Engraved on back of handle: "D/ I∗E" in shaded roman letters. *Engraved on underside of body:* "oz 12 = dwt 14".

Description: raised circular form with bulbous lower body, incurving neck, flared rim with double-molded edge and double-incised line below; centerpunch on underside of body; seamed, circular, stepped footring. Double–C-scroll handle with sprig on upper portion, scroll and sprig at lower end, single drop with vent at upper handle attachment; handle cast in 2 vertical sections.

Spectrographic analysis:

	SILVER	COPPER	LEAD	GOLD
BODY SIDE	91.2	8.5	0.19	0.13
FOOT	97.1	2.8	0.09	0.05
HANDLE	92.7	6.9	0.30	0.13

For *History, Provenance, Exhibitions, Comments,* and *References,* see no. 319.

85.4 Gift of Saint Georges Presbyterian Church, 1985

321
TANKARD, ca. 1765

H. 7 1/16" (17.9 cm), DIAM. base 5 ½" (14.0 cm),
w. 7 ½" (19.1 cm)
30 oz. 18 dwt. 20 gr. (962.4 g)

Stamps: "I•B" in roman letters, in an oval,
struck once on upper body, left of handle.

Engraved on body opposite handle: "To/ Dr.
William Rumsey/ in/ grateful memory/ of/
kindness, skill and devoted service./ April 22.
1846". *Scratched on underside of body:* "1760"
(twice); "18=15=7" (twice); "31 02"; and
"31 [?]".

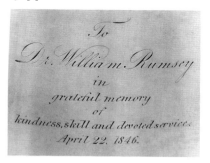

Description: raised circular body with straight
tapering sides and slightly concave bottom; 2-
step, applied, molded, flared rim; centerpunch
on underside of body. Applied seamed base
molding, flared at bottom, consists of concave-
over-convex moldings. Raised circular stepped-
and-domed lid with 2 sets of scored lines on top
edge; single-scored line on overlap; applied
crenelated lip; bezel; centerpunch on top. Cast
ram's horn thumbpiece attached to 5-segment
hinge with pendant drop. Raised-and-soldered
hollow S-curve handle terminating in a flat
shield-shape tailpiece; circular vent with 2
notches.

Spectrographic analysis:

	SILVER	COPPER	LEAD	GOLD
BODY SIDE	93.5	6.1	0.14	0.02
LID	93.1	6.6	0.13	0.04
HANDLE	93.1	6.6	0.12	0.06
BASE MOLDING	92.3	7.5	0.12	0.03

History: William Rumsey (1789–1871) was born
at the Rounds, a house on Sassafras Neck, Md.
He was the son of John Rumsey, who moved to
Wilmington, Del., in 1807. Rumsey graduated
from Yale in 1812 and attended medical school
at the University of Pennsylvania. By 1817 he
was practicing medicine in Philadelphia and
lived at 225 Coates St. He married his cousin
Anna Rumsey Dunlap. The donor is a great-

niece of Rumsey. In 1845 a colleague described
him as "a physician in full practice, [who] married a Miss Reeves [possibly an error]—related
to the late Dr. Physick—a good whig." No
doubt the tankard was presented to Rumsey
by a grateful patient.

Provenance: Dr. William Rumsey, Philadelphia;
descended to his great-niece Gertrude Brinckle,
Wilmington, Del.

Exhibitions: "Philadelphia Silver," Philadelphia
Museum of Art, 1956. On long-term loan to the
Historical Society of Delaware, Wilmington,
1940s to 1966.

References: Philadelphia Silver, no. 36. *Wealth
and Biography of the Wealthy Citizens of Philadelphia* (Philadelphia: G. B. Zieber, 1845), p. 7.

66.72 Gift of Gertrude Brinckle, 1966

Asa Blanchard

Lexington, Kentucky, w. 1808–38

Although Asa Blanchard is the best known and perhaps the most prolific of Kentucky silversmiths, his early life remains unknown. He was in Lexington by 1808, when he took William Grant and Andrew Anderson as apprentices. From 1809 until his death in 1838, his shop was on the corner of Mill and Short streets. In his will he bequeathed to his wife Hester, "two pair of Gold Spectacles and my sopha"; "unto my two apprentices Eli C. Garner and George Easley all of my tools to be equally divided." He made a pair of candlesticks for Isaac Shelby, Kentucky's first governor; they are now owned by the J. B. Speed Museum, Louisville, Kentucky. He made numerous beakers of the type often called, mistakenly, julep cups, but he also made pitchers, ewers, bowls, tea services, flatware, clock parts, and communion cups for the Presbyterian Church of Frankfort. In 1930 the Wilderness Trail Antique Shops, Frankfort, Kentucky, offered H. F. du Pont a pitcher and six beakers made by Blanchard, but he declined to purchase them. A portrait of Blanchard by Matthew Harris Jouett was in a private collection as of 1980.

References: Boultinghouse, *Silversmiths of Kentucky*, pp. 69–74. Margaret M. Bridwell, "Asa Blanchard, Early Kentucky Silversmith," *Antiques* 37, no. 3 (March 1940): 135–36. Margaret M. Bridwell, "Kentucky Silver," *Antiques* 52, no. 5 (November 1957): 364–66, for a receipted bill by Blanchard. William Barrow Floyd, "Kentucky Coin-Silver Pitchers," *Antiques* 105, no. 3 (March 1974): 576–80, figs. 1, 2. Henry H. Harned, "Ante-bellum Kentucky Silver," *Antiques* 105, no. 4 (April 1974): 818–24, figs. 2–6, for silver; fig. 7, for portrait. Jones, *Old Silver*, p. 182. *Silver in Kentucky Life*, pp. 14–15, 58.

322
BEAKER, ca. 1825

H. 3⅛" (7.9 cm), DIAM. rim 3 1/16" (7.8 cm)
5 oz. 4 dwt. 17 gr. (162.5 g)

Stamps: "A BLAN[CHARD]" in roman letters, in a rectangle, struck once on underside.

Engraved on side of body: "C" in foliate script.

Description: seamed barrel-shape body with flat bottom; centerpunch on underside; single applied molding at base and rim; 2 bands of 5 closely spaced scored lines encircle body.

Spectrographic analysis:

	SILVER	COPPER	LEAD	GOLD
BODY SIDE	89.6	10.2	0.17	0.09
UNDERSIDE	90.3	9.4	0.19	0.14

Provenance: Marshall P. Blankarn, New York City.

78.138 Gift of Marshall P. Blankarn, 1978

323 a, b
SPOONS, ca. 1825

(a) L. 7 3/16" (18.3 cm)
1 oz. 15 gr. (32.0 g)
(b) L. 7 5/16" (18.6 cm)
1 oz. 1 dwt. 1 gr. (32.7 g)

Stamps: "A•BLANCHARD" in roman letters, in a rectangle, struck once on back of each handle.

Description: (a) pointed oval bowl with no drop; rounded downturned fiddle-shape handle; (b) pointed oval bowl with swage-formed rounded drop; downturned coffin-end handle.

Spectrographic analysis: Silver content ranges from 89.9 to 92.4 percent.

Provenance: (a) Charles van Ravenswaay, Wilmington, Del.; (b) Mr. and Mrs. Stanley B. Ineson, New York City; Mr. and Mrs. Alfred E. Bissell, Wilmington, Del.

References: Belden, *Marks of American Silversmiths*, p. 64.

(a) 67.121 Gift of Charles van Ravenswaay, 1967; (b) 62.240.920 Gift of Mr. and Mrs. Alfred E. Bissell, 1962–63

🐝 Daniel Carrell

w. ca. 1782–98
Philadelphia, Pennsylvania,
w. ca. 1782–85
Charleston, South Carolina,
w. ca. 1785–96
Philadelphia, Pennsylvania,
w. ca. 1796–98

Daniel Carrell first appears in 1782 as a subscriber for new pews and a gallery at Saint Mary's Church, Philadelphia. Throughout his apparently brief tenure in Philadelphia, he advertised with his brother John, who, it may be inferred from the advertisements, was a clockmaker. In December 1784 they were located on Market Street "two doors above the Coffee House." By May 1785 they had moved to Front Street "to the house formerly occupied by Mr. Philip Syng, where they carry on the clock and watch makers, goldsmith and jewellers business." Their last advertisement in Philadelphia was in August 1785. From January 6, 1790, to August 8, 1796, Daniel Carrell advertised in Charleston, South Carolina, newspapers on his own. One of his first offerings to Charlestonians was "Philadelphia made Whips . . . of whale-bone and cat-gut, strongly mounted with silver." In 1791 he advertised "silver spoons of all kinds finished equal in every respect and sold cheaper than those imported . . . [and] Indian work made very cheap by the quantity." In 1794 he refers to his "manufactory and store, at the Sign of the Coffee Pot." He was an importer and retailer as well as a manufacturing silversmith. Little of his work survives.

References: Burton, *South Carolina Silversmiths,* pp. 34–35. Prime cards, Winterthur.

🐝 324 a, b
SNUFFERS AND TRAY, ca. 1790

(a) Snuffers: L. 6 ⅜" (16.2 cm), w. 2 ⅝" (6.7 cm), H. 1 %6" (4.0 cm)
3 oz. 13 dwt. 7 gr. (114.0 g)
(b) Tray: L. 8 ¹⁵⁄₁₆" (22.7 cm), w. 2 ½" (6.4 cm), H. 1" (2.5 cm)
7 oz. 16 dwt. 19 gr. (243.8 g)

Stamps: "CARREL" in roman letters, in a rectangle, struck once on blade of snuffers pan, struck twice on underside of tray.

Engraved on oval plate atop snuffers pan and in center of tray: "DH" in foliate script.

Description: (a) snuffers are a cast scissor form having a rectangular pan with canted corners on 1 arm and a conforming blade on the other; spear-point terminal on 1 arm; circular pivot; oval grips joined to arms by crescents and C scrolls; arms and handles cast; all on 3 cast ball feet; (b) elongated octagonal tray with outward-flaring sides higher at small ends; applied reeded molding on inside edge; flat bottom; heavy-gauge metal; no centerpunches.

Spectrographic analysis:

	SILVER	COPPER	LEAD	GOLD
SNUFFER HANDLE	93.0	6.1	0.24	0.21
SNUFFER BOX	89.0	9.9	0.40	0.23
UNDERSIDE OF TRAY	91.4	7.4	0.31	0.33

History: Possibly owned by the Hart family.

Provenance: Mr. and Mrs. N. McLean Seabrease, Germantown, Pa.; Robert Ensko, Inc., New York City, sold to H. F. du Pont, August 1929.

Comments: It is difficult to ascertain whether the tray was raised or seamed.

References: Fales, *American Silver,* no. 135. Fennimore, *Silver and Pewter,* no. 229.

59.3360 Gift of H. F. du Pont, 1965

Chaudron & Rasch

Philadelphia, Pennsylvania, w. 1809–12

Simon Chaudron
1758–1846
Philadelphia, Pennsylvania, w. 1795–1819
Demopolis, Alabama, w. 1819–25
Mobile, Alabama, w. 1825–46

Anthony Rasch
ca. 1778–ca. 1859
Philadelphia, Pennsylvania, w. 1804–20
New Orleans, Lousiana, w. 1820–ca. 1859

Chaudron & Bilon
Philadelphia, Pennsylvania,
w. 1795–ca. 1797

Jean Simon Chaudron was born in France, studied watchmaking in Switzerland, and in 1784 went to Saint-Domingue (Haiti). There he married Jeanne Geneviève Mélanie Stollenwerck, by whom he had thirteen children. After visiting Philadelphia in 1790 and 1793, he moved there in late 1793, most likely to escape the effects of the slave rebellion then occurring in Saint-Domingue. In Philadelphia he appears to have been primarily a jeweler, watchmaker, and importer of French silver, at least in his first phase. In 1795 he formed a partnership with Charles Fredric Bilon, another French silversmith and watchmaker; their shop was located at 12 South Third Street. Around 1797 Bilon moved to St. Louis, and Chaudron continued alone for some years. It is unclear when he began manufacturing silver. Surely he was doing so when, if not before, he took Anthony Rasch as an indentured servant, probably around 1797.

Born in Bavaria and trained as a silversmith in Germany, Rasch arrived in Philadelphia in 1804. In March 1809 Chaudron and Rasch announced their partnership. Their work carried the distinctive stamps "Chaudron's & Rasch" and "Ster[ling] Ameri[can] Man[ufacture]." The partnership was dissolved in August 1812, and the men went their separate ways.

Chaudron is listed in the 1818 Philadelphia directory as editor of *L'Abeille Americaine*. That he also remained active in silver production is indicated by an 1817 document in which Chaudron certified, along with silversmith William Seal and Christian Wiltberger, for the benefit of Baltimore authorities, that "there is no assay law in this City [Philadelphia], that our Word & stamp are sufficient to all our Customers with regard to the quality of the Silver manufactured by us; that we never manufacture any Silver of a lower quality than Spanish Dollars." Sometime between 1817 and 1819, Chaudron moved to Demopolis, Alabama, which had been established for Bonapartist refugees. He moved to Mobile in 1825. The National Portrait Gallery owns a portrait of Chaudron engraved by Saint-Mémin. The latter is known to have sold his prints at Chaudron's Philadelphia shop around 1801.

Anthony Rasch defined his business as a silver-plate manufactory in bills of 1814 and later. George Willig, Jr., became his partner briefly in 1818–19. By early 1820 he had moved to New Orleans, where he operated a shop at 75 Chartres Street until his death in 1859.

Together and separately Chaudron and Rasch made important American silver in late neoclassical styles that often reflected the latest French fashion. One example of their joint efforts is a double-spouted punch pot owned by the Metropolitan Museum of Art. Another is the extraordinary ewer by Chaudron, showing the influence of major French silversmith Jean-Baptiste Claude Odiot, which was advertised in *Antiques* in 1986. A tea caddy by Rasch, owned by the St. Louis Museum of Art, combines severity of form with cast classical decoration of a high order.

References: Louisa Bartlett, "American Silver," *Bulletin of the St. Louis Museum of Art* 17, no. 1 (Winter 1984): 32–33, for tea caddy by Rasch. James R. Cormany, "Jean Simon Chaudron, Silversmith, Poet, and American Pioneer," *Silver* 25, no. 4 (July/August 1992): 8–11. Goldsborough, *Eighteenth- and Nineteenth-Century Maryland Silver*, p. 18, for certification by Chaudron, Seal, and Wiltberger. Hilda Kohn advertisement, *Antiques* 129, no. 1 (January 1986): 124, for ewer by Chaudron. *Philadelphia: Three Centuries*, pp. 213–14, 226–27. Prime cards, Winterthur. Rasch's bills to Mr. Ashurst, September 17, December 17, 1814, 68x28.2, 65x28, Downs collection, Winterthur.

🌶 325 a–e
COFFEE AND TEA SERVICE, 1809–12

(a) Coffeepot: H. 13" (33.0 cm), W. 12⅝" (32.1 cm)

49 oz. 6 dwt. 10 gr. (1534.0 g)

(b) Teapot: H. 9⅞" (25.1 cm), W. 11" (27.9 cm)

34 oz. 5 dwt. 10 gr. (1066.0 g)

(c) Sugar urn with lid: H. 10⅝" (27.0 cm), W. 6³⁄₁₆" (15.7 cm)

32 oz. 5 dwt. (1003.1 g)

(d) Creamer: H. 7⅛" (18.1 cm), W. 5⁹⁄₁₆" (14.1 cm)

12 oz. 15 dwt. 4 gr. (396.8 g)

(e) Waste bowl: H. 6¼" (15.9 cm), W. 7⁵⁄₁₆" (18.6 cm)

18 oz. 19 dwt. 11 gr. (590.1 g)

Stamps: "CHAUDRON'S & RASCH" in roman letters, in a banner, struck once on underside of base on (a), (c), and (d); struck twice on underside of base on (b) and (e). "STER• AMERI•MAN•" in roman letters, in a banner, struck twice on underside of base of (a) and (d); struck once on underside of base on (b), (c), and (e).

Engraved on side of each body: a crescent moon (open end up) over a curved heraldic band; banner beneath with motto: "LUX VENIT AB ALTO" in roman letters. (Note: Engraving is to right of spout; hence it is visible to a left-handed pourer.) *Scratched on underside of each base:* "2242".

Description: raised circular bulbous bodies with upper concave section attached to a die-rolled decorative band in a guilloche pattern with 8-point stars inside loops and leaves above and below the intersections, all on a striated ground; all pieces except (c) have centerpunches on undersides of bodies. All bodies except (c) stand on trumpet-shape pedestals that are integral with tripartite bases; in plan, bases resemble a triangle with its points squared off and sides incurved; a die-rolled band with a small leaf pattern is applied to the skirt of the base; 3 hollow ball feet, each with a circular vent, support each base.

(a) Coffeepot: incurved neck decorated with repoussé pattern of leaves and grapes arranged in swags; die-rolled decorative band around rim has heart-shape leaf-and-dot pattern. Heart-shape opening in body at spout. Raised circular partial lid with flattened dome in center encircled by applied gadrooned molding; cast pomegranate finial; 5-segment flush-mounted hinge; short bezel. S-curve angular spout with cast dog's head at pouring end. Hardwood handle rises to 2 right angles before curving in toward body, where it meets a curved lower section; carved acanthus leaf and sprig on upper part of handle. Sockets shaped on outside as acanthus leaves and scrolls; 2 silver pins.

(b) Teapot: identical to (a) except smaller in scale, handle is C curved with 2 sprigs, upper socket is mounted at an angle, and body is pierced behind spout to serve as a strainer.

(c) Sugar urn and lid: raised hemispherical body with die-rolled guilloche band serving as rim; circular repoussé pattern of lotus leaves centered on underside of body with a cast pine-applelike drop over location of centerpunch. Body mounted on 3 long slender incurving legs with a cast goat's head at the top of each leg and a cloven hoof at the bottom. Cast figure of a seated dog mounted on circular plinth in center of base. Raised circular loose-fitting lid with short bezel is similar to lids on (a) and (b), except flattened dome is encircled by a pierced gallery with a band above in the Greek key pattern.

(d) Creamer: incurving neck flares at rim, rises to point at handle, and spreads to a wide pouring lip in front; die-rolled band in pattern of heart-shape leaves and dots applied to rim. S-curve hollow handle assumes bizarre animal head at spout; curved extension connects to upper body.

(e) Waste bowl: similar to (a) and (b) except guilloche band serves as rim, and 2 cast ram's head handles are mounted on outside of rim.

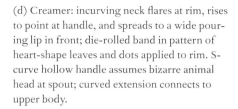

Spectrographic analysis:

	SILVER	COPPER	LEAD	GOLD
(a) Coffeepot				
BODY SIDE	93.6	5.3	0.18	0.10
INSET BAND	95.4	3.3	0.95	0.17
SPOUT	93.4	5.7	0.45	0.12
FOOT	94.9	4.5	0.19	0.10
(b) Teapot				
BODY SIDE	94.2	5.3	0.18	0.10
INSET BAND	95.4	3.3	0.95	0.17
SPOUT	93.4	5.7	0.45	0.12
FOOT	95.0	4.5	0.19	0.10
(c) Sugar urn				
BODY SIDE	94.4	5.0	0.24	0.10
INSET BAND	94.1	5.3	0.38	0.10
SPOUT	93.7	5.6	0.34	0.13
FOOT	93.1	6.0	0.39	0.11
(d) Creamer				
BODY SIDE	91.5	7.8	0.52	0.10
INSET BAND	94.1	4.8	0.76	0.18
FOOT	92.1	7.0	0.26	0.14
(e) Waste bowl				
BODY SIDE	93.9	5.4	0.48	0.12
INSET BAND	94.1	5.2	0.44	0.12
RAM'S HEAD	94.1	5.3	0.22	0.10
FOOT	92.1	7.1	0.51	0.11

History: The service was probably made for (or given to) Alexander James Dallas (1759–1817), not George Mifflin Dallas as held by family tradition. (George would have been only 20 years old in 1812, the last year of the Chaudron & Rasch partnership.) Born in Jamaica and educated in England and Scotland, Alexander came to Philadelphia in 1783 and was admitted to the Pennsylvania bar in 1786. In 1791 Governor

Mifflin appointed him secretary of the Commonwealth of Pennsylvania, the first of many appointed offices. From 1801 to 1814, he was U.S. district attorney for the Eastern District of Pennsylvania. In 1814 he succeeded Albert Gallatin as secretary of the treasury. He was influential in reestablishing national credit following the War of 1812 and in establishing the Second Bank of the United States. His son George Mifflin Dallas (1792–1864), who inherited the service, also had a distinguished career in public life. In 1813 he became secretary to Gallatin and was deeply involved in the peace negotiations of the War of 1812. He served as mayor of Philadelphia, district attorney, attorney general of Pennsylvania, minister to Russia, vice president under James Polk, and minister to Great Britain during the negotiations over British rights in Central America. The service descended in the Dallas and Wilkins families.

Provenance: Alexander James Dallas, Philadelphia; George Mifflin Dallas, Philadelphia; Matilda (Dallas) Wilkins; Henrietta Constanza Wilkins; Maria Saunders Wilkins; Maria Wilkins Smith (1884–1963); Mr. and Mrs. Henry Pleasants III, London.

Exhibitions: "In Praise of America: 1650–1825," National Gallery of Art, Washington, D.C., 1980.

Comments: The crest belongs to the Dallas family. The motto translates "Light cometh from on high." The use of the sterling stamp is unusual; it only became commonplace late in the nineteenth century. This service was in the vanguard of American neoclassicism at the time it was made. The sugar urn in particular, with its tripod legs and cloven feet, suggests the revival of antique forms based on archaeological discoveries. Note the possessive form of Chaudron used in the stamp. It suggests proprietorship while according recognition to Rasch, who was probably the working silversmith who made the service.

References: DAB, s.v. "Dallas, Alexander James" and "Dallas, George Mifflin." Wendy A. Cooper, *In Praise of America: American Decorative Arts, 1650–1830* (New York: Alfred A. Knopf, 1980), no. 300. Fennimore, "Chaudron's and Rasch Tea and Coffee Set," *Silver* 17, no. 3 (May–October 1984): 20–22. Fennimore, *Silver and Pewter*, no. 138, for description; no. 139, for illustration.

75.80.1–.5 Gift of Mr. and Mrs. Henry Pleasants III in memory of Maria Wilkins Smith, 1975

⚱ 326 a, b
CANDLESTICKS, 1809–12

(a) H. 11 15/16" (30.3 cm), DIAM. base 5 11/16" (14.5 cm)
21 oz. 10 dwt. 2 gr. (667.3 g)
(b) H. 12 1/16" (30.6 cm), DIAM. base 5 11/16" (14.5 cm)
22 oz. 12 dwt. 23 gr. (702.8 g)

Stamps: "CHAUDRON'S & RASC[H]" in roman letters, in a banner, struck once on side of each base; "STER•AMERI•MAN•" in roman letters, in a banner, struck once on opposite side of each base from name stamp.

Engraved on upper surface of each base: "UPL" in script. *Scratched under cast feet of shaft:* (a) "VII". *Scratched into upper part of base:* (a) "VII" (lower portion missing). *Scratched under cast feet of shaft:* (b) "IIII". *Scratched into upper part of base:* (b) what appears to be an incomplete "V".

Description: cast circular base with borders of beading, anthemia, and chevrons; shallow depression with pedestal rising in center to a circular platform with rolled gadrooned edge and a threaded socket to receive shaft. Tapered hexagonal shaft stands on 3 cast animal feet (4 toes each) with threaded shaft projecting below; upper shaft joined to a seamed drum-shape section with a border of anthemia between beaded borders. Shaft connected to socket by a pedestal. Cast cylindrical socket with 3 bold anthemia alternating with stemmed blossoms on outside, all on stippled ground; reeded molded rim. Removable bobeche with gadrooned edge.

Spectrographic analysis:

	SILVER	COPPER	LEAD	GOLD
(a)				
BASE	92.2	6.5	0.37	0.12
SHAFT	93.0	5.5	0.88	0.12
SOCKET	93.4	5.4	0.61	0.12
BOBECHE	88.2	9.0	0.02	1.4*
(b)				
BASE	92.2	6.5	0.49	0.11
SHAFT	93.0	5.5	0.44	0.14
SOCKET	93.4	5.4	0.49	0.11
BOBECHE	88.2	9.0	0.00	1.6*

*Probably gilded at one point.

History: Research by Berry Tracy, former curator of the American Wing, Metropolitan Museum of Art, suggests that the candlesticks were owned by naval officer Uriah Phillips Levy (d. 1862), who purchased Monticello in 1836.

Provenance: R. T. Trump & Co., Flourtown, Pa.

Exhibitions: "Nineteenth-Century America," Metropolitan Museum of Art, New York City, 1970.

Comments: Original bobeches were lost while candlesticks were on loan to the Metropolitan Museum of Art. Replacements were made by Harvey Stern & Co., Philadelphia, based on a similar pair of candlesticks sold by R. T. Trump & Co. to Richard P. Mellon. Roman numerals suggest the candlesticks were part of a set of at least 8.

References: Fennimore, *Silver and Pewter*, no. 183. *Nineteenth-Century America: Furniture and Other Decorative Arts* (New York: Metropolitan Museum of Art, 1970), no. 36. Merrill D. Peterson, ed., *Visitors to Monticello* (Charlottesville: University Press of Virginia, 1989), introd., for Levy family's ownership of Monticello.

74.3.1, .2 Museum purchase from R. T. Trump & Co., 1973

🌱 327
LADLE, 1809–12

L. 14 15/16" (37.9 cm)
11 oz. 7 dwt. 4 gr. (352.5 g)

Stamps: "CHAUDRON'S & RASCH" in roman letters, in a banner, struck once on back of handle; "STER•AMERI•MAN•" in roman letters, in a banner, struck once on back of handle.

Engraved on front of handle: "TP" in foliate script.

Description: raised deep oval bowl, mounted sideways, with broad pouring lips on either side; centerpunch on underside. Applied border of stylized leaves at rim; band of repoussé leaves, fruit, and clusters of grapes encircles midsection; 4 panels of repoussé acanthus leaves around lower body. Rounded downturned long handle with midrib is twisted into a spiral in lower section; handle forks near bowl and is attached by 2 cast clusters of grape leaves and a lap joint secured by 2 silver rivets.

Spectrographic analysis:

	SILVER	COPPER	LEAD	GOLD
HANDLE	92.3	7.5	0.19	0.11
BOWL	94.0	5.7	0.15	0.12

Provenance: Frank S. Schwartz & Son, Philadelphia.

Comments: Ladles are usually plain; the elaborate repoussé decoration on this one is rare. Method of attaching handle to bowl is also unusual.

References: Fennimore, *Silver and Pewter*, no. 17.

73.1 Museum purchase from Frank S. Schwartz & Son, with funds provided by George S. Kaufman, 1973

328 a–f
SALTS, 1795–1809, 1812–19

(a) H. 2 ¼" (5.7 cm), w. 4 ⅛" (10.5 cm)
2 oz. 8 dwt. 6 gr. (74.9 g)
(b) H. 2 ¼" (5.7 cm), w. 4 ¼" (10.8 cm)
2 oz. 10 dwt. 11 gr. (78.3 g)
(c) H. 2 ⅜" (6.0 cm), w. 4 ¼" (10.8 cm)
2 oz. 12 dwt. 18 gr. (81.9 g)
(d) H. 2 ¼" (5.7 cm), w. 4 1/16" (10.3 cm)
2 oz. 7 dwt. 19 gr. (74.2 g)
(e) H. 2 5/16" (5.9 cm), w. 4 3/16" (10.6 cm)
2 oz. 8 dwt. 22 gr. (75.9 g)
(f) H. 2 ¼" (5.7 cm), w. 4 ⅛" (10.5 cm)
2 oz. 12 dwt. 21 gr. (82.1 g)

Stamps: "CHAUDRON" in roman letters, on a stippled ground, all in a banner, struck once on underside of each pedestal.

Engraved on side of body: (a, b) a shaded gothic "B"; (c–f) "JBP" in shaded gothic letters.

Description: raised urn-shape body, oval in plan, with concave neck and flared rim with applied reeded molding inside; no centerpunch. Plain raised pedestal, oval in plan, with thick applied footring. Interior gilded.

Spectrographic analysis:

	SILVER	COPPER	LEAD	GOLD
(a)				
BODY OUTSIDE	90.3	9.0	0.21	0.14
BODY INSIDE	66.8	4.4	0.17	22.0
PEDESTAL	90.1	8.9	0.29	0.21

	SILVER	COPPER	LEAD	GOLD
(b)				
BODY OUTSIDE	91.1	8.2	0.21	0.12
BODY INSIDE	68.1	3.9	0.18	21.9
PEDESTAL	90.3	8.6	0.24	0.24
(c)				
BODY OUTSIDE	90.5	9.2	0.24	0.09
BODY INSIDE	77.8	4.2	0.23	12.9
PEDESTAL	89.9	9.2	0.40	0.18
(d)				
BODY OUTSIDE	91.9	7.7	0.24	0.13
BODY INSIDE	53.7	3.4	0.25	35.0
PEDESTAL	90.5	8.8	0.37	0.22
(e)				
BODY OUTSIDE	90.4	9.1	0.27	0.11
BODY INSIDE	68.9	4.7	0.23	20.1
PEDESTAL	89.9	9.3	0.45	0.16
(f)				
BODY OUTSIDE	90.7	9.0	0.25	0.14
BODY INSIDE	68.2	4.5	0.26	20.9
PEDESTAL	90.0	9.3	0.39	0.17

Provenance: (a, b) Philip H. Hammerslough, West Hartford, Conn.; (c–f) H. F. du Pont.

Comments: Although made for different customers, these salts were obviously made in quantity to the same specifications.

References: (a, b) Hammerslough, *American Silver*, 1:48.

(a, b) 63.7.1, .2 Museum purchase from Philip H. Hammerslough, 1963; (c–f) 70.1191.1–.4 Bequest of H. F. du Pont, 1969

329
SPOON, 1809–11

L. 8 13/16" (22.4 cm)
1 oz. 10 dwt. 4 gr. (46.8 g)

Stamps: "CHAUDRON'S & RASCH" in roman letters, in a banner, struck once on back of handle; "STER•AMERI•MAN•" in roman letters, in a banner, struck once on back of handle.

Engraved on front of handle crosswise: "RSL" in foliate script.

Description: pointed oval bowl with swage-formed pointed drop; rounded downturned handle with midrib.

Spectrographic analysis: Silver content is 87.3 percent.

Provenance: Mr. and Mrs. Stanley B. Ineson, New York City; Mr. and Mrs. Alfred E. Bissell, Wilmington, Del.

References: Belden, *Marks of American Silversmiths*, p. 105.

62.240.1013 Gift of Mr. and Mrs. Alfred E. Bissell, 1962–63

Samuel Coleman

1761–1842
Trenton, New Jersey

Born in Orange County, New York, Samuel Coleman and his brother Nathaniel both became silversmiths. Nathaniel, who worked in Burlington, New Jersey, is the better known of the two, and his work survives in greater quantity than Samuel's. Samuel placed an advertisement in *The New Jersey and Pennsylvania Almanac for the Year 1806*:

> SILVER WARE.
> SAMUEL COLEMAN,
> Gold & Silver-Smith
> TRENTON
>
> *Takes this method to inform the Public in general, that he continues the SILVER-SMITH'S BUSI-NESS in Warren-Street, Trenton, nearly opposite the STORE of Abraham Hunt, where he keeps for sale, and manufactures agreeably to orders, a variety of*
>
> Gold & Silver Work.

A creamer and sugar bowl by Samuel Coleman was advertised by Gebelein Silversmiths in 1958, and a chatelaine is in the Hammerslough collection, Wadsworth Atheneum. Otherwise, little of his silver survives.

References: Williams, *Silversmiths of New Jersey*, pp. 128–29. Gebelein Silversmiths advertisement, *Antiques* 74, no. 1 (July 1958): 11. Hammerslough, *American Silver*, 3:156.

330
SALVER, ca. 1800

L. 16 ¼" (41.3 cm), W. 12 ¹³⁄₁₆" (32.5 cm), H. 1 ¹¹⁄₁₆" (4.3 cm)
33 oz. 12 dwt. 1 gr. (1042.7 g)

Stamps: "S•C" in roman letters, in a rectangle, struck once on underside of body.

Engraved on upper surface: "I[?]TCR" in foliate script, in a vertical pointed oval flanked by floral and leaf motifs, all set within a horizontal wheel-work oval. *Scratched on underside:* "E8962".

Description: flat oval tray; no centerpunch; raised edge with applied reeded border; 4 short cast legs with acanthus leaves on outside; scroll feet.

Spectrographic analysis:

	SILVER	COPPER	LEAD	GOLD
UPPERSIDE	90.5	9.1	0.22	0.16
UNDERSIDE	94.7	4.9	0.22	0.12

Provenance: Marshall P. Blankarn, New York City.

References: Fennimore, *Silver and Pewter*, no. 5.

76.279 Gift of Marshall P. Blankarn, 1976

331 a, b
SPOONS, ca. 1800

(a) L. 5 ⅞" (14.9 cm)
8 dwt. 21 gr. (13.8 g)
(b) 9 ½" (24.1 cm)
1 oz. 15 dwt. 3 gr. (54.5 g)

Stamps: "S. COLEMAN" in roman letters, in a rectangle, struck once on back of each handle.

Engraved on front of handle: (a) "MH" in foliate script; (b) "LB" in foliate script.

Description: oval bowl with swage-formed rounded drop; downturned fiddle-shape handle with squared end on (a); rounded downturned handle on (b).

Spectrographic analysis: Silver content ranges from 89.5 to 90.7 percent.

Provenance: (a) The Collector, Centreville, Del.; (b) Mr. and Mrs. Stanley B. Ineson, New York City; Mr. and Mrs. Alfred E. Bissell, Wilmington, Del.

References: Belden, *Marks of American Silversmiths*, p. 118.

(a) 71.53 Museum purchase from the Collector, 1971; (b) 62.240.1029 Gift of Mr. and Mrs. Alfred E. Bissell, 1962–63

John Curry

w. 1820s–1830s

Curry & Preston, w. ?–1834
Philadelphia, Pennsylvania

On August 2, 1834, John Curry advertised in *Poulson's American Daily Advertiser* a "Silver Plate, Spoon & Fork Manufactory" at 76 Chestnut Street, stating that he was of the late firm of Curry & Preston. Both Curry and William Preston had been trained as silversmiths. They boasted that in their manufactory they employed "none but first rate workmen." They had a retail store at 103 Chestnut Street. Following dissolution of the partnership Curry continued to produce high-quality silver in Philadelphia. A typical transaction between silversmith and customer is seen in the following bill by Curry & Preston to a Mr. Ashurst:

Philad Sept 13th 1827

To 1 D⁊ Silver Shell & Threded forkes			.39	11
To 2 D⁊ Teas	D	25	2	
To 1 D⁊ Table Forkes	Do	.39	10	
To 1 D⁊ Desert Forkes	Do	24	18	
To 1 Fish Nife		6	10	chasing 1.25
Silver at—185 Cts per oⁿ	135	11	250.76 ½	
			$252.01 ½	

Contra By Silver forkes & Spoons	41	17	12	
By 6 Tumblers	41	8		
By 1 Fish Knife	3	1		
Old Silver at				
116 Cts per oⁿ	86	6	12	- $100 13 -
Balance due C & Preston			$151. 88 ½	
Receivd Payment		Curry & Preston		

Note the second part of the bill, where credit is given for the customer's "old" silver. Although there is an extra charge for chasing, fabrication costs are lumped together with the cost of the metal, unlike most eighteenth-century bills.

References: Waters, "Philadelphia's Precious Metals Trades," pp. 170–71. Curry & Preston bill, 75x171, Downs collection, Winterthur.

332
GOBLET, ca. 1830

H. 10 1/16" (25.6 cm), DIAM. rim 5 7/16" (13.8 cm)
26 oz. 18 dwt. 12 gr. (835.5 g)

Stamps: "J.CURRY•" and "PHILA." in roman letters, both in serrated rectangles, struck once on underside of body. Deep punchmark on either side of maker's name.

Description: raised, circular, bulbous lower body; cylindrical upper body flares sharply to rim; centerpunch on underside. Stepped-and-domed circular base with pedestal and knop. Lower body has continuous chased vine-leaf floral pattern on a stippled ground. Applied trophy of musical instruments, grapes, and leaves on upper body side. Bands of die-rolled decoration (grapes and leaves) around rim, at juncture of upper and lower bodies, at juncture of pedestal and body, and around outer edge of base. Footring is a die-rolled decorative band with shell and seaweed motif. Beading around knop and foot of pedestal.

Spectrographic analysis:

	SILVER	COPPER	LEAD	GOLD
PEDESTAL BASE	90.0	9.9	0.09	0.09
LOWER BODY	90.1	9.8	0.09	0.08
UPPER BODY	90.0	9.8	0.11	0.08

Provenance: Jonathan Trace, Putnam Valley, N.Y.

Comments: A successful form with superb chased decoration. Somewhat top-heavy. The grape-vine border appears on other Philadelphia silver of this period.

88.7 Museum purchase from Jonathan Trace, 1988

333
SPOON, ca. 1830

L. 5 7/8" (14.9 cm)
12 dwt. 10 gr. (19.3 g)

Stamps: "J. CURRY" in roman letters, in a rectangle, struck once on back of handle. Accompanied by a spread-winged eagle in an oval.

Engraved on front of handle: "MG" in foliate script.

Description: pointed oval bowl with swage-formed rounded drop; rounded downturned fiddle-shape handle.

Spectrographic analysis: Silver content is 93.2 percent.

Provenance: William J. Buckminster, Owls Head, Maine.

References: Belden, *Marks of American Silversmiths*, p. 126.

71.49 Museum purchase from William J. Buckminster, 1971

John David

1736–98
Philadelphia, Pennsylvania,
w. ca. 1755–93

John David's father, Peter David (1707–55), was the son of French Huguenot parents. Peter was apprenticed to New York silversmith Peter Quintard. Peter David moved to Philadelphia prior to John's birth in 1736. John probably learned his trade from his father and by 1755 was identified as a silversmith. He had a long career and advertised numerous times in Philadelphia newspapers. His October 7, 1772, advertisement in the *Pennsylvania Gazette* is illustrated with a coffeepot bearing a cypher. He advertised a spoon, thought to be stolen, that had "a dragon's head in a ducal coronet engraved on the handle" (*Pennsylvania Packet*, February 8, 1773). In 1787, late in his career, he received four major commissions from silversmiths Joseph and Nathaniel Richardson. We do not know what he made, but the last commission alone amounted to £77.10.7. John's son, his namesake and also a silversmith, took over the business in 1794. John, Jr., later went into business with Daniel Dupuy, to whom he was related through his father. Quantities of silver made by John David, Sr., survive. He made several of the tall double-bellied coffeepots that were so fashionable in the last third of the eighteenth century, including one now in the John Dickinson Mansion near Dover, Delaware. He also made the communion service for Saint Peter's Church in Lewes, Delaware. His Delaware connections included son-in-law Thomas Latimer of Newport, whom he named as one of the executors in his will made in Newport in 1793. His estate, proved in 1798, was sparse in terms of movable goods, but it did include houses on Pine and Front streets, Philadelphia, and an aggregate figure of £703.6.9 for stock on hand in the shop.

References: Fales, *Joseph Richardson and Family*, p. 303. *Philadelphia: Three Centuries*, pp. 44, 45, for information on Peter David. Kenneth Scott, "Advertising Woodcuts in Colonial Newspapers," *Antiques* 67, no. 2 (February 1955): 153, for illustrated advertisement from *Pennsylvania Gazette*, March 28, 1765. Prime cards, Winterthur. Student paper and copy of will provided by Aline Zeno.

334
CRUET STAND, ca. 1770

H. 10 %6" (26.8 cm), w. 9 ¹⁵/₁₆" (25.2 cm)
26 oz. 12 dwt. 12 gr. (828.1 g)

Stamps: "I•DAVID" in roman letters, in a rectangle, struck twice on underside of body.

Engraved on cartouche: "CR" (as a cypher) in foliate script.

Description: flat cinquefoil-shape platform reinforced underneath by 5 applied flat circular rings; no centerpunch. Central shaft, screwed through center of platform, shaped in ascending order: (1) a baluster with spiral grooves

alternating between plain and worked bands; (2) a plain baluster; (3) a plain shaft with rings at bottom, middle, and top; and (4) a cast bail-like fixed handle formed by 2 S curves with sprigs, leaves, and scrolls and joined at the top by an asymmetrical cast shell; 4 short legs cast as back-to-back C scrolls with acanthus scrolls at top and flat shell-shape feet; 5 large and 2 small cast gadrooned rings, supported by the 4 legs, are attached to one another and arranged in a circle around central shaft. A cast cartouche, attached to one ring and platform, consists of 2 C scrolls with shell edges.

Spectrographic analysis:

	SILVER	COPPER	LEAD	GOLD
PLATFORM	96.5	3.3	0.15	0.10
CARTOUCHE	91.1	8.2	0.36	0.16
RING	95.0	4.8	0.18	0.09
HANDLE	96.4	3.4	0.08	0.15
FOOT	93.5	6.1	0.17	0.16

History: Said by dealer to have belonged to the Ringgold family of New Jersey.

Provenance: Charles F. Montgomery, Wallingford, Conn., sold to H. F. du Pont, September 1948.

Exhibitions: "Philadelphia Silver," Philadelphia Museum of Art, 1956. "In the Style of the Signers: The Decorative Arts of Philadelphia," DAR Museum, Washington, D.C., 1987.

Comments: Includes bottles with London-made silver caps. An extraordinary example of American rococo silver. A nearly identical cruet stand, made by Myer Myers, was owned in 1988 by New York City antiques dealer Bernard & S. Dean Levy.

References: Fales, *American Silver*, no. 99. Fales, *Early American Silver*, fig. 24. Fales, *Joseph Richardson and Family*, p. 303. *Philadelphia Silver*, no. 47. Bernard & S. Dean Levy, catalogue 6 (January 1988), p. 109.

59.3362 Gift of H. F. du Pont, 1965

335 a, b
SAUCEBOATS, ca. 1770

(a) H. 4 ⅝" (11.7 cm), w. 7 ⅛" (18.1 cm) 10 oz. 5 dwt. 1 gr. (318.9 g)
(b) H. 4 ¹³⁄₁₆" (12.2 cm), w. 6 ¹⁵⁄₁₆" (17.6 cm) 9 oz. 10 dwt. 8 gr. (296.0 g)

Stamps: "I DAVID" in roman letters, in a rectangle with rounded corners, struck once on underside of each body.

Engraved off-center on side of each body: "TSC" in intertwined shaded foliate script.

Description: raised body, oval in plan, with bulbous sides, cyma-curve flaring rim, and a wide pouring lip; 3 equidistant punches, 1 in center, on underside of body. Double–C-curve handle, cast and seamed vertically, with acanthus leaf and scroll on free-standing upper end, sprig and scroll on lower end; 3 cast legs attached to body by shells; each curved leg terminates in a scroll on a flattened shell foot; shell feet pinned to legs.

Spectrographic analysis:

(a)	SILVER	COPPER	LEAD	GOLD
BODY SIDE	87.3	12.1	0.17	0.20
HANDLE	87.1	11.5	0.23	0.17
FOOT	94.5	5.4	0.12	0.11
(b)				
BODY SIDE	84.4	14.8	0.26	0.28
HANDLE	92.6	6.8	0.27	0.19
FOOT	95.1	4.6	0.16	0.15

History: Said to have been made for Thomas and Sarah Cooch of Cooch's Bridge near Newark, Del.

Provenance: Carl M. Williams, Philadelphia, sold to H. F. du Pont, November 1950.

Exhibitions: "Masterpieces of American Silver," Virginia Museum of Fine Arts, Richmond, 1960. "In the Style of the Signers: The Decorative Arts of Philadelphia," DAR Museum, Washington, D.C., 1987.

Comments: Fine examples of American sauceboats and a restrained version of the rococo style.

References: Fales, *American Silver*, no. 100. *Masterpieces of American Silver*, no. 237. Fennimore, *Silver and Pewter*, no. 118.

59.3351, .3352 Gift of H. F. du Pont, 1965

❦ 336
TANKARD, ca. 1765

H. 7⅛" (18.1 cm), w. 7⅝" (19.3 cm)
33 oz. 16 dwt. 12 gr. (1049.6 g)

Stamps: "DAVID" in roman letters, in a rectangle, struck 3 times on underside of body.

Engraved on front of body: "DEJ" in intertwined foliate script, in a rococo cartouche of C scrolls flanked by leafy flowering branches.

Engraved on underside of body: "1761 Charles G. Ridgely - 1785 Nicholas Ridgely - 1830 Anne Ridgely du Pont - 1898 Amelia Elizabeth du Pont./ 1924 Anne du Pont Peyton" in script; "BERNARD PEYTON - DEC. 18, 1975" in roman letters; armorial device consisting of a chevron with 3 stars in a strapwork shield; a blank banner below; crest of antlered animal head over a heraldic band. *Scratched on underside of body:* "3213"; "13".

Description: raised body with slightly bowed tapering sides and slightly concave bottom; 2-step applied molded rim with double fillet below; 2 centerpunches on underside of body. Applied seamed 2-step base molding consists, in descending order, of ogee and convex moldings separated by a fillet with a plain flat band at bottom. Circular stepped flat-topped lid with bracket-shape crenate lip; bezel; no centerpunch. Cast scroll thumbpiece attached to 5-segment hinge with a pendant drop.

Raised-and-soldered hollow S-curve handle terminating in a flat shield-shape tailpiece; notched vent on lower end.

Spectrographic analysis:

	SILVER	COPPER	GOLD	LEAD
BODY SIDE	90.6	9.1	0.16	0.15
UNDERSIDE	93.0	6.7	0.16	0.12
HANDLE	90.4	9.3	0.15	0.22
LID	92.8	7.0	0.05	0.07

Note low gold and lead content in lid.

History: Tradition of ownership in the Ridgley family as indicated by engraved inscriptions, donor's information, and Ridgely arms and crest.

Provenance: Ridgely, du Pont, and Peyton families to Bernard Peyton, to Mrs. Bernard Peyton, Princeton.

Comments: The oldest inscription, "DEJ," does not square with history as indicated in later inscriptions. The inscription for Bernard Peyton was requested by his wife, the donor, and was accomplished by Winterthur using a Philadelphia engraver named Mr. Gasparro. The coat of arms and crest are those used by Nicholas G. Ridgely of Baltimore.

References: Bolton, *American Armory*, p. 139, for Ridgley arms.

80.108 Gift of Mrs. Bernard Peyton, 1980

337
TEAPOT, ca. 1785

H. 10 ½" (26.7 cm), w. 10 ⅛" (25.7 cm)
23 oz. 1 dwt. 19 gr. (718.0 g)

Stamps: "I DAVID" in roman letters, in a rectangle, struck twice on underside of pedestal.

Engraved on one side of body: "AWC" in shaded foliate script. *Engraved on other side of body:* "JET" (intertwined) in crosshatched foliate script, in a bright-cut and wheelwork circle with flanking crossed branches, bowknots above and below.

Description: raised circular urn-shape lower body joined to short incurved neck by an applied beaded band; neck flares toward rim, which has an applied beaded band and a pierced gallery; centerpunch on underside of body. Trumpet-shape stepped pedestal with beading at top and at step; outer edge of pedestal encircled by fine gadrooning over an incised line on an applied footring. S-curve seamed spout with vertical rows of beading above and below. Raised, circular, trumpet-shape friction-fit lid with short bezel; rises to a beaded-and-domed knop surmounted by a cast pineapple finial with leaves

above and below; finial secured through top of lid by a silver bolt; vent. C-curve hardwood handle with a sprig; cylindrical sockets with beaded rims; silver pins.

Spectrographic analysis:

	SILVER	COPPER	LEAD	GOLD
BODY SIDE	89.5	10.1	0.21	0.11
FOOT	96.3	3.3	0.20	0.11
SPOUT	93.9	5.7	0.24	0.13
LID	90.1	9.5	0.34	0.10

Provenance: Marshall P. Blankarn, New York City.

Comments: Lid appears to have been formed by spinning process. It is uncertain whether these late pieces were made by John, Sr., or John, Jr. See no. 338, which has lid formed in the same way and the same owner's initials.

78.136 Gift of Marshall P. Blankarn, 1978

338
SUGAR URN WITH LID, ca. 1785

H. (with lid) 9 ⁹⁄₁₆" (24.3 cm), H. (without lid) 6 ⅛" (15.6 cm), DIAM. 4 ⅝" (11.7 cm)
13 oz. 5 dwt. 2 gr. (412.3 g)

Stamps: "JD" in roman letters, in an oval, struck 4 times on underside of pedestal.

Engraved on one side of body: "AWC" in foliate script. *Engraved on other side of body:* "JET" in intertwined shaded script, in a bright-cut and wheelwork circle with flanking crossed branches with a bowknot above.

Description: raised circular urn-shape body with applied beaded band and gallery at rim; centerpunch on underside. Trumpet-shape stepped

pedestal with a circular foot; beading around upper part and at step, rope molding on outer edge over scored line encircling footring. Circular trumpet-shape friction-fit lid, beaded step inside flange, rises to a beaded knop surmounted by a cast pineapple with leaves above and below; finial secured through top of lid by a silver bolt; no bezel.

Spectrographic analysis:

	SILVER	COPPER	LEAD	GOLD
BODY SIDE	91.6	7.7	0.31	0.12
FOOT	95.9	3.6	0.31	0.12
LID	92.6	6.6	0.38	0.14

Provenance: Marshall P. Blankarn, New York City.

Comments: Lid appears to have been formed by spinning process. It is uncertain whether these late pieces were made by John, Sr., or John, Jr. See no. 337, which has lid formed in the same way and the same owners' initials.

77.223 Gift of Marshall P. Blankarn, 1977

339
SKEWER, 1780–93

L. 11 ⅜" (28.9 cm), 3 oz. 8 dwt. 2 gr. (105.9 g)

Stamps: "I[or J] D" in roman letters, in an oval, struck once near ring.

Engraved near ring on side opposite stamp: armorial device consisting of a wyvern's head, facing left, on a heraldic band; motto above: "NON DE GENER" in roman letters, in an arc.

Description: elongated, triangular, flat pointed blade with a flat ring attached to broad end; ring decorated on both sides with bright-cut engraving.

Spectrographic analysis:

SILVER	COPPER	LEAD	GOLD
92.3	6.9	0.54	0.17

Provenance: Robert Ensko, Inc., New York City, sold to H. F. du Pont, December 1934.

Comments: Bright-cut decoration suggests a later date than the ca. 1760 date given by Martha Gandy Fales. Crest probably added at a later date.

References: Fales, *American Silver*, no. 94.

57.1269 Gift of H. F. du Pont, 1965

340
SPOON, 1780–93

L. 8 ⅞" (22.5 cm), 1 oz. 18 dwt. 16 gr. (60.0 g)

Stamps: "I•DAVID" ("VID" conjoined) in roman letters, in a rounded rectangle, struck once on back of handle.

Engraved on front of handle: "IAC" in foliate script.

Description: elongated oval bowl with swage-formed rounded drop and symmetrical foliate cartouche; rounded downturned handle with midrib.

Spectrographic analysis: Silver content is 89.7 percent.

Provenance: Mr. and Mrs. Stanley B. Ineson, New York City; Mr. and Mrs. Alfred E. Bissell, Wilmington, Del.

Exhibitions: Metropolitan Museum of Art, New York City, 1935–61.

62.240.1052 Gift of Mr. and Mrs. Alfred E. Bissell, 1962–63

James Duffel

1761–1835
Alexandria, Virginia, w. ca. 1781–90
Georgetown, South Carolina,
w. ca. 1790–1800
New York, New York, w. 1801–2
Fredericksburg, Virginia,
w. 1802–ca. 1810
Lynchburg, Virginia, w. ca. 1810–35

James Duffel came from Bucks County, Pennsylvania. During the American Revolution he enlisted at Alexandria, Virginia, and may, therefore, have served his apprenticeship in that city. In 1790 he appears in Georgetown, South Carolina, as a silversmith who could make "Any article of Gold or Silver . . . at short notice." The Georgetown area was a center for rice growing; presumably Duffel expected to capitalize on the wealth this represented. He was disappointed, however, and in 1799 announced his intention to leave. He asked people to settle their debts and, in the manner of the times, offered to take rice as payment. In 1801 he was in New York, at 349 Pearl Street, but in 1802 moved to Fredericksburg, Virginia, where his brother Edward was a merchant. When Edward moved to Lynchburg, James followed him, probably in 1810, when he bought a lot there. He quickly involved himself in local affairs, serving as a member of the city council in 1814 and a director of the Exchange Bank of Virginia. Numerous examples of his silver are found in the Lynchburg area, where he remained until his death in 1835.

References: Burton, *South Carolina Silversmiths*, pp. 235–36. George Barton Cutten, *The Silversmiths of Virginia, Together with Watchmakers and Jewelers from 1694 to 1850* (Richmond: Dietz Press, 1952), pp. 62–64. Von Khrum, *Silversmiths*, p. 42.

341
TEAPOT, ca. 1800

H. 12 ½" (31.8 cm), w. 9 ⁹⁄₁₆" (24.3 cm)
34 oz. 15 dwt. 6 gr. (1078.7 g)

Stamps: "I•DUFFEL" in roman letters, in a rectangle, struck twice on underside of body.

Engraved on side of body: "IW" (or "JW") in shaded foliate script. *Scratched on underside of base:* "27102".

Description: raised circular double-bellied body with incurving elongated neck rising to a slightly flared rim, which has a step molding applied on top; body pierced at spout to serve as a strainer; centerpunch on underside. Raised circular 1-piece foot with plain incurved pedestal and stepped outer edge. Raised circular high-dome lid with plain flange, bezel, and cast urn finial; vent in dome. Lid attached by a plain 3-segment hinge to upper handle socket. S-curve spout cast in 2 vertical sections; 3 rudimentary sprigs on spout, acanthus leaf on top, plain circular section with drop around base of spout on body. C-curve hardwood handle with sprig. Cast upper socket has dependant drop; C-curve lower socket has scroll and sprig attached to body by circular layers.

Spectrographic analysis:

	SILVER	COPPER	GOLD	LEAD
BODY SIDE	92.7	7.1	0.15	0.11
FOOT	93.6	6.2	0.11	0.11
SPOUT	95.6	4.1	0.14	0.14
LID	92.2	7.5	0.13	0.10

Provenance: H. F. du Pont.

Comments: Unusual foot for this form: raised in 1 piece and very plain. Pieces of this shape are usually coffeepots, but the strainer identifies it as a teapot. Given the maker's peregrinations, it is hard to say where this piece was made. Georgetown, S.C., or Fredericksburg, Va., are the most likely candidates.

70.1048 Bequest of H. F. du Pont, 1969

John B. Dumoutet

1761–1813
Philadelphia, Pennsylvania, w. 1793–97
Trenton, New Jersey, w. 1797
Philadelphia, Pennsylvania, w. 1797–1813
Charleston, South Carolina, w. 1802–13

Jean-Baptiste Dumoutet was one of a number of French silversmiths who found their way to the United States directly or indirectly via Saint-Domingue (Haiti). He first appeared in Philadelphia in 1793, worked briefly in Trenton during the yellow fever epidemic of 1797, and opened a shop in Charleston, South Carolina, in 1802. It is believed that the Charleston venture was a branch store rather than his primary base of operations. In 1799 Dumoutet called himself "Goldsmith and Jeweller," but later advertisements speak of his "Hair-work and Jewellery Manufactory" at 55 South Second Street, Philadelphia. In 1800 he offered "one thousand ounces of sterling silver Indian ornaments." In 1807 he opened a military store, next to his jewelry store, to sell gold braid, swords, and related goods. In 1810 he added a tortoiseshell comb manufactory. By 1811, however, his declining health prompted him to sell off some of these enterprises. Following his death in 1813, his widow Jane carried on the jewelry stores in both Philadelphia and Charleston until 1823.

The New York Public Library owns a Dumoutet trade card, drawn and engraved by James Akin, printed on silk, featuring a portrait of George Washington between two allegorical figures. A small amount of Dumoutet silver survives, mostly flatware and a few tea services. One important tea service, owned by Gebelein Silversmiths in 1978, has both his name stamp and "ID" stamp on the same pieces. A seven-piece beverage service, privately owned as of 1975, consists of both seamed and raised pieces. It was made for Samuel Sitgreaves (1764–1827), congressman from Pennsylvania and a diplomat under Washington and John Adams.

References: Burton, *South Carolina Silversmiths*, pp. 49–50. Maureen O'Brien Cole, "James Akin, Engraver and Social Critic" (Master's thesis, University of Delaware, 1967), pp. 254–55, for silk trade card. Waters, "Philadelphia's Precious Metals Trades," pp. 94, 133, 143. Williams, *Silversmiths of New Jersey*, pp. 129–30.

342
FOOTED BEAKER, ca. 1800

H. 3 ⅝" (9.2 cm), DIAM. 3 ¹⁄₁₆" (7.8 cm)
4 oz. 9 dwt. 21 gr. (139.8 g)

Stamps: "DUMOUTET" in roman letters, in a banner, struck once on underside.

Description: raised circular body broadening upward to convex shoulders, incurving neck, flared rim with applied double-reed band on outside; flat bottom with centerpunch on underside.

Spectrographic analysis:

	SILVER	COPPER	LEAD	GOLD
BODY SIDE	88.9	10.8	0.13	0.09
UNDERSIDE	96.2	3.7	0.11	0.00

Provenance: Robert Ensko, Inc., New York City, sold to H. F. du Pont, January 1934.

References: Fales, *American Silver*, no. 129.

61.1093 Gift of H. F. du Pont, 1965

343
SPOON, ca. 1800

L. 5 ¹⁵⁄₁₆" (15.1 cm)
9 dwt. 20 gr. (15.3 g)

Stamps: "DUMOUTET" in roman letters, in a banner, struck once on back of handle.

Engraved on front of handle: "LCS" in foliate script.

Description: pointed oval bowl with swage-formed rounded drop; pointed downturned handle.

Spectrographic analysis: Silver content is 90.8 percent.

Provenance: Mr. and Mrs. Stanley B. Ineson, New York City; Mr. and Mrs. Alfred E. Bissell, Wilmington, Del.

References: Belden, *Marks of American Silversmiths*, p. 145.

62.240.240 Gift of Mr. and Mrs. Alfred E. Bissell, 1962–63

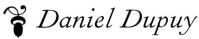

Daniel Dupuy

1719–1807
Philadelphia, Pennsylvania

Dr. John Dupuy, a Huguenot, was the founder of the Dupuy family in America. Having come from France by way of England and Jamaica, he arrived in New York sometime before 1709. Daniel Dupuy, the fourth child of John and Anne (Chardavoine) Dupuy, was born in New York City in 1719. His sister Jeanne married silversmith Peter David, father of John David, and it is believed that Daniel learned the craft from his brother-in-law, probably after Peter moved to Philadelphia in the 1730s. Daniel's son John (1747–1838) was probably a watch- and clockmaker, but Daniel, Jr. (1753–1826) was a silversmith. The careers of father and son overlap, and it is often difficult to separate their work. The several "Dupuy" and "DD" stamps are hard to assign with certainty. Newspaper notices after the Revolution generally specify Daniel Dupuy, Jr. Notices before and during the Revolution are considered to be the father's. They were working together in 1772 when father and son jointly took Joseph Evans as an apprentice. It is unclear when Daniel, Sr., gave up his business, but it has to be assumed that he made some silver in the neoclassical style—as did his son.

References: Charles Meredith Dupuy, *A Genealogical History of the Dupuy Family* (Philadelphia: Privately printed, 1910), pp. 26–32. *Philadelphia: Three Centuries,* pp. 161–62. Waters, "Philadelphia's Precious Metals Trades," pp. 13–15. Prime cards, Winterthur.

344
GOLD CLASP, ca. 1760

L. 1" (2.5 cm), w. (with tongue) ⅞" (2.2 cm), H. ³⁄₁₆" (0.5 cm)
15 dwt. 1 gr. (24.5 g)

Stamps: "DD" in roman letters, in a rectangle, struck once on backplate.

Engraved on frontplate: basket of flowers with a border of foliate scrolls. *Engraved on backplate:* "M•D" (originally "AB") in roman letters.

Description: clasp consists of slightly convex frontplate joined by sidewall to conforming backplate to create a hollow interior to receive tongue on right side. Backplate extends on left side into 3 eyelets reinforced with applied rings. Rectangular friction-fit tongue with 3 eyelets as above.

Spectrographic analysis:

GOLD	SILVER	COPPER
81.2	11.6	7.2

Provenance: Frank S. Schwarz, Philadelphia Antique Shop.

Exhibitions: "American Gold, 1700–1860," Yale University Art Gallery, New Haven, 1963.

Comments: Attached to a coral bracelet that is not original to it. Accompanied by a matching coral necklace without a clasp. Similar gold clasps by Dupuy are in the Hammerslough collection, Wadsworth Atheneum, and at the Philadelphia Museum of Art.

References: Bohan, *American Gold,* no. 54.

62.85.1 Museum purchase from Frank S. Schwarz, 1962

345 a–c
SPOONS, ca. 1770

(a) L. 4 ¾" (12.1 cm)
4 dwt. 22 gr. (7.7 g)
(b) L. 4 ⁷⁄₁₆" (11.3 cm)
5 dwt. 12 gr. (8.6 g)
(c) L. 4 ½" (11.4 cm)
4 dwt. 15 gr. (7.2 g)

Stamps: "DD" in roman letters, in an oval, struck twice on back of each handle. Incuse star between the 2 stamps on (b).

Engraved on back of handle: (a) "EC" in crude roman letters; (b) "ML" in crude shaded roman letters; (c) "SM" in crude shaded roman letters.

Description: oval bowl with swage-formed rounded drop outlined by ridges; (a) and (c) have shells on bowl back; rounded upturned handle with midrib.

Spectrographic analysis: Silver content ranges from 82.5 to 89.8 percent.

Provenance: Mr. and Mrs. Stanley B. Ineson, New York City; Mr. and Mrs. Alfred E. Bissell, Wilmington, Del.

Comments: There are a number of Dupuy spoons at Winterthur, but these are the only ones that seem likely to have been made by Daniel Dupuy, Sr.

References: Belden, *Marks of American Silversmiths,* pp. 146–47.

62.240.137, .138, .179 Gift of Mr. and Mrs. Alfred E. Bissell, 1962–63

William Faris

1728–1804
Annapolis, Maryland

London-born William Faris was in Annapolis by 1757, when he advertised in the newspaper as a "Watchmaker from Philadelphia." By late 1760 he had added both a clockmaker and a silversmith to his shop. Perhaps the latter did not work out, for in 1763 he noted that he had "procured from Philadelphia a very complete silversmith who has served a regular apprenticeship in that Business." In 1778 he offered for sale "a likely young negro fellow, by trade a Silversmith, Jeweller and Lapidary; there is very few if any better workman in America." The question is, did Faris become a silversmith himself, or did he rely entirely on hired craftsmen? That he oversaw the work and may have designed it is suggested by the survival in his papers of shop drawings (now in the Maryland Historical Society) for nineteen different silver forms. Among the forms represented are a cann, double-bellied coffeepot, teapot, tea kettle, bulbous tankard and cann, sugar bowl, sauceboat, caster, strainer, skewer, creamer, and soup ladle plus a teapot and stand in the neoclassical style. Three of his four sons trained with him: William, Charles, and Hyram. Saint John Faris, the fourth son, became a mariner. Faris's life is extraordinarily well documented, with the survival of some of his account books and a diary covering the last twelve years of his life. It is unfortunate that relatively few pieces of silver from his shop survive.

References: Lockwood Barr, "William Faris, 1728–1804," *Maryland Historical Magazine* 36, no. 4 (December 1941): 420–39. Lockwood Barr, "Family of William Faris (1728–1804), The Annapolis Silversmith," *Maryland Historical Magazine* 37, no. 4 (December 1942): 423–32. "Extracts from the Diary of William Faris of Annapolis, Maryland," *Maryland Historical Magazine* 28, no. 3 (September 1933): 197–244. Pleasants and Sill, *Maryland Silversmiths*, pp. 257–71, pls. 48–63.

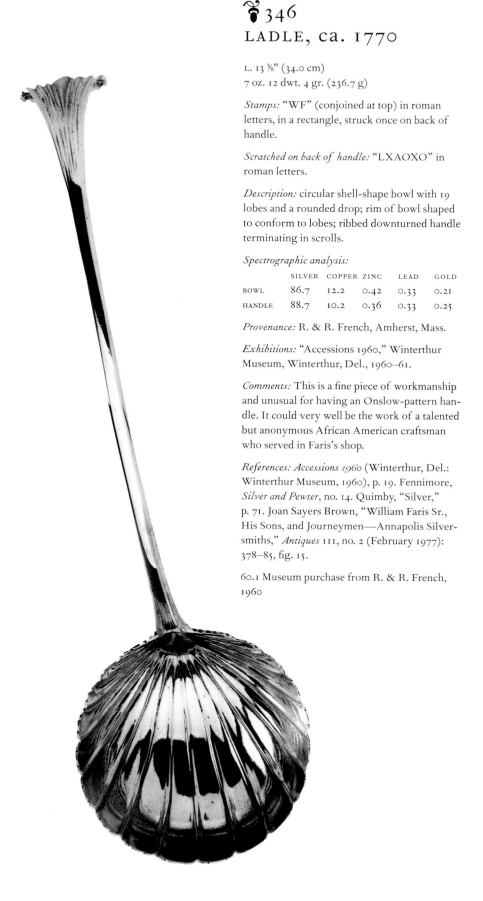

346
LADLE, ca. 1770

L. 13 ⅜" (34.0 cm)
7 oz. 12 dwt. 4 gr. (236.7 g)

Stamps: "WF" (conjoined at top) in roman letters, in a rectangle, struck once on back of handle.

Scratched on back of handle: "LXAOXO" in roman letters.

Description: circular shell-shape bowl with 19 lobes and a rounded drop; rim of bowl shaped to conform to lobes; ribbed downturned handle terminating in scrolls.

Spectrographic analysis:

	SILVER	COPPER	ZINC	LEAD	GOLD
BOWL	86.7	12.2	0.42	0.33	0.21
HANDLE	88.7	10.2	0.36	0.33	0.25

Provenance: R. & R. French, Amherst, Mass.

Exhibitions: "Accessions 1960," Winterthur Museum, Winterthur, Del., 1960–61.

Comments: This is a fine piece of workmanship and unusual for having an Onslow-pattern handle. It could very well be the work of a talented but anonymous African American craftsman who served in Faris's shop.

References: Accessions 1960 (Winterthur, Del.: Winterthur Museum, 1960), p. 19. Fennimore, *Silver and Pewter*, no. 14. Quimby, "Silver," p. 71. Joan Sayers Brown, "William Faris Sr., His Sons, and Journeymen—Annapolis Silversmiths," *Antiques* 111, no. 2 (February 1977): 378–85, fig. 15.

60.1 Museum purchase from R. & R. French, 1960

Fletcher & Gardiner

Boston, Massachusetts, w. 1808–11
Philadelphia, Pennsylvania, w. 1811–27

Thomas Fletcher (1787–1866) and
Sidney Gardiner (1785–1827) announced
their partnership in Boston during November 1808. In addition to a rich assortment of jewelry and imported fused
plate, they stressed silver of their own
manufacture: "Of the manufacturing
branch, they can speak with the fullest
confidence, as the whole attention of
one of the partners will be devoted to
this part of the business." That partner
would have been Gardiner, who had
been trained as a silversmith. Fletcher,
on the other hand, was trained as a
shopkeeper but also had a keen sense
of design. Although their business
prospered, in 1811 they moved to
Philadelphia, where they anticipated
even greater success. They were not

disappointed. With substantial capital,
aggressive marketing, and inspired purchases of foreign goods, they brought
a new entrepreneurial spirit to the business. Although new in town, they received the commission for making the
urn presented by the people of Philadelphia to Isaac Hull, captain of the United
States frigate *Constitution*, which had
defeated the *Guerriere*. The partners did
not fail to capitalize on the opportunity
to make an eye-catching showpiece that
would set the standard for presentation
silver for years to come. The Hull urn
is a full-blown expression of the empire style borrowed from France but
interpreted in an American idiom. An
engraved version of this design was used
on the company trade card. Many commissions for presentation silver followed,
one of the more important being a pair
of large urns presented by New York
merchants to De Witt Clinton in 1825.
The urns were modeled on the celebrated Warwick vase found in 1770 near
Hadrian's villa at Tivoli. (One urn is
at the Metropolitan Museum of Art;
the other is in a private collection.) As
spectacular as it was, the presentation
silver failed to earn the income derived
from the sale of domestic wares.

In 1815 Fletcher went to England to
see the full range of goods available, to
improve and augment business contacts,
and to increase his technical knowledge.
One result of this trip was the firm's
expanded list of imported goods that
included cutlery, brass, iron, lighting
fixtures, glass, and ceramics. By 1816 the
firm's annual sales were $102,000. Over
the next five to seven years a depressed
economy greatly reduced this income.
In 1825 Fletcher traveled to France and
England, returning with "a large assortment of Italian marble, alabaster and gilt
mantle time pieces" and French porcelain
in gold and salmon color made to order.
Meanwhile, in 1823, the partners had
begun to explore the potential market
in Mexico for both their domestic and
imported goods. This time Gardiner,

who had previously managed silver production in Philadelphia, was the emis-
sary. He was successful in opening new
markets, but on his second trip, in 1827,
he died. An auction was held in 1828 to
settle Gardiner's estate. Directories continued to list the firm as Fletcher &
Gardiner until 1836. Fletcher's nephew,
Calvin Bennett, became his partner from
1837 to 1839. Business was not good,
however, and in 1842 much of the firm's
inventory was sold at auction to satisfy
creditors. This event effectively ended
the professional life of what had been
America's premier manufacturer and
importer of silver and fused plate. A
later trade card, featuring the urn presented to Capt. Isaac Hull but with only
Fletcher's name, is owned by Winterthur. The Historical Society of Pennsylvania owns *The Gold and Silver Artificers
of Phila. in Civic Procession, 22d Feby
1832*, a lithograph showing the Fletcher
& Gardiner shop in the background.

References: Donald L. Fennimore, "Thomas
Fletcher and Sidney Gardiner: The Stylistic
Development of Their Domestic Silver,"
Antiques 102, no. 4 (October 1972): 642–49.
Donald L. Fennimore, "Elegant Patterns of
Uncommon Good Taste: Domestic Silver by
Thomas Fletcher and Sidney Gardiner" (Mas-
ter's thesis, University of Delaware, 1971).
Warren, Howe, and Brown, *Marks of Achieve-
ment*, pp. 90–91, for Clinton vases. Waters,
"Philadelphia's Precious Metals Trades," pp.
78–94. Elizabeth Ingerman Wood, "Thomas
Fletcher: A Philadelphia Entrepreneur of Pre-
sentation Silver," in Milo M. Naeve, ed., *Win-
terthur Portfolio 3* (Winterthur, Del.: Henry
Francis du Pont Winterthur Museum, 1967),
pp. 136–71. See also Berry B. Tracy, "Late Classical Styles in American Silver, 1810–1830,"
Antiques 86, no. 6 (December 1964): 702–6.

❦ 347
EWER, 1811–27

H. 15 ¾" (40.0 cm), w. 10 ⁵⁄₁₆" (26.2 cm)
76 oz. 7 dwt. 20 gr. (2376.0 g)

Stamps: "FLETCHER & GARDINER." and "PHILAD^A" in roman letters, both in rectangles, struck once on underside of square base in opposite corners.

Description: raised circular body with convex sides and rounded bottom; incurved neck rises and flares to broad pouring lip in front and cast dog's head terminal in back; continuous repoussé pattern of water leaves around lower body; a chased and repoussé band of meandering vine with flowers and leaves around shoulders; a die-rolled band of 8-point flowers is applied to the outside of the rim; centerpunch on underside of body. Raised double-dome partial lid; front edge, cut in alternating cyma curves, is short of covering entire pouring lip; rear edge attached to fixed portion of lid by a flush-mounted 5-segment hinge; repoussé waterleaf pattern in center of dome under cast dolphin finial; partial bezel. Trumpet-shape pedestal with applied band of dimpled pear-shape forms on upper edge of pedestal; lower edge worked in repoussé pattern of stylized acanthus leaves. Pedestal mounted on a square base that has sides decorated with rectangular repoussé panels, each with a central flower flanked by vines and leaves; 4 cast animal paw feet (5 toes each) support base at each corner. C-curve hollow handle, reeded in the middle, has scaled snakelike upper and lower sections: in upper section, snake's body curls around dog's head and drops down side of vessel to form upper handle attachment; in lower section, snake's tail coils into a circle before lying against body to form lower handle attachment.

Spectrographic analysis:

	SILVER	COPPER	LEAD	GOLD
BODY	92.2	7.6	0.13	0.04
BASE	95.9	3.9	0.11	0.09
HANDLE	95.7	4.3	0.06	0.06
LID	95.1	4.9	0.07	0.05
FOOT	96.5	3.9	0.00	0.06

History: Tradition of ownership in the Elkins family of Philadelphia.

Provenance: R. T. Trump & Co., Philadelphia.

Comments: An elegant design based on French prototypes. See, for example, Solange Brault and Yves Bottineau, *L'Orfevrerie Francaise du XVIIIe Siecle* (Paris: Presses Universitaires de France, 1959), pl. 24, for a 1784 *aiguiere et basin* by Robert-Joseph Auguste, Paris (Musée des

Arts Decoratifs), for overall shape, lid, and water leaves around lower body. On the Fletcher & Gardiner piece, note decorative bands that look die rolled but are hand worked. The same base with animal-paw feet was used on other major presentation pieces, such as the DeWitt Clinton urn, and on Fletcher's trade card. A tour de force of workmanship and design.

References: Donald L. Fennimore, "Thomas Fletcher and Sidney Gardiner: The Stylistic Development of Their Domestic Silver," *Antiques* 102, no. 4 (October 1972): fig. 3.

69.16 Museum purchase from R. T. Trump & Co., 1969

❦ 348
BOX, 1811–27

DIAM. 3 7/16" (8.7 cm), H. 5/8" (1.6 cm)
2 oz. 10 dwt. 8 gr. (78.3 g)

Stamps: "FLETCHER & GARDINER." in a circular surround with "PHILA" in center, in a rectangle; all in roman letters, stamped once on underside of body.

Engraved on top of lid: armorial device consisting of a lion rampant on gules in a cartouche of C curves with an inner border of or; flanked by crossed leafy branches; *crest:* a closed helmet flanked by leafy foliage; above, a pelican feeding its young in a nest, over a heraldic band.

Description: circular box with flat bottom; centerpunch inside body. Body side, formed from seamed sheet, flares toward bottom and has an applied fillet to stop lid. Low-dome (nearly flat) friction-fit lid, made like body, has a rolled edge.

Spectrographic analysis:

	SILVER	COPPER	LEAD	GOLD
BODY	92.2	7.5	0.23	0.13
LID	89.9	9.6	0.32	0.15

History: The arms and crest belong to the Lloyd family. The box is said by the donor to have been owned originally by James Lloyd (1769–1831) of Boston, a descendant of James Lloyd (d. 1693) founder of the Lloyd family in America. (See no. 50 for a ring made for his funeral by Jeremiah Dummer.) The younger James graduated from Harvard in 1787, was a merchant's clerk, and served in numerous political offices from state representative to U.S. senator from Massachusetts. He entertained Lafayette at his house on Somerset St. in 1825. He married Hannah Breck of Philadelphia and, after 1826, lived in that city.

Provenance: James Lloyd (1769–1831); descended in Lloyd family to Mrs. George L. Batchelder, Beverly, Mass.

Comments: Both the form and the engraving look back to the eighteenth century, but the box probably dates from the 1820s, probably after Lloyd moved to Philadelphia. The box was given to Winterthur with a collection of gold funeral rings that commemorated members of the Lloyd, Borland, Cutt, Comrin, and Foster families.

References: Fennimore, *Silver and Pewter*, no. 196. *Cyclopedia of American Biography*, 5:99.

72.75 Gift of Mrs. George L. Batchelder, 1972

❦ 349
SPOON, 1811–27

L. 5 15/16" (15.1 cm), 10 dwt. 22 gr. (17.0 g)

Stamps: "F&G" in roman letters, in a rectangle, struck once on back of handle. Accompanied by a spread-winged eagle in a rectangle with rounded corners.

Description: oval bowl with swage-formed rounded drop; rounded downturned fiddle-shape handle with swage-formed sheaf of wheat on end.

Spectrographic analysis: Silver content is 89.9 percent.

Provenance: The Silver Shelf, Ardmore, Pa.

Comments: Inscription removed.

References: Belden, *Marks of American Silversmiths*, p. 170.

74.99 Museum purchase from the Silver Shelf, 1974

❦ 350
SPOON, 1811–27

L. 6 1/8" (15.6 cm), 12 dwt. 17 gr. (19.8 g)

Stamps: "F.& G." in roman letters, in a rectangle, struck once on back of handle.

Engraved on front of handle: "B" in foliate script.

Description: pointed oval bowl with swage-formed rectangular drop with canted corners; downturned coffin-end fiddle-shape handle.

Spectrographic analysis: Silver content is 88.2 percent.

Provenance: Mr. and Mrs. Stanley B. Ineson, New York City; Mr. and Mrs. Alfred E. Bissell, Wilmington, Del.

References: Belden, *Marks of American Silversmiths*, p. 170.

62.240.219 Gift of Mr. and Mrs. Alfred E. Bissell, 1962–63

❦ 351 a, b
FORKS, 1827–42

(a) L. 6 15/16" (17.6 cm), 2 oz. 4 dwt. 5 gr. (68.6 g)
(b) L. 6 7/8" (17.5 cm), 1 oz. 19 dwt. 23 gr. (62.0 g)

Stamps: "T. FLETCHER" in roman letters, in a rectangle, struck once on back of handle.

Engraved on front of each handle: a demi-lion on a heraldic band.

Description: 4 tines with swage-formed 12-lobe shell on back; upturned wavy-end handle with double-thread border; 12-lobe shell with ribbon scrolls and acanthus leaf, and floral pattern.

Spectrographic analysis: Silver content ranges from 89.5 to 90.1 percent.

Provenance: Robert Ensko, Inc., New York City, sold to H. F. du Pont, June 1935.

Comments: Part of a set of 12 when purchased by H. F. du Pont.

References: Belden, *Marks of American Silversmiths*, p. 169.

(a) 65.3066, (b) 70.1323.1 Bequest of H. F. du Pont, 1969

Moritz Fürst

ca. 1782–after 1841
Philadelphia, Pennsylvania,
w. 1808–late 1820s
New York, New York, w. 1830s

Born in Czechoslovakia (then part of Hungary) and trained as a die sinker in Vienna, Moritz Fürst came to America in 1808 at the encouragement of Thomas Appleton, the American consul at Livorno. Fürst believed that he would become the official engraver and die sinker at the United States Mint in Philadelphia. Apparently the post had recently been given to John Reich, and Fürst was left to gather commissions as an independent die sinker. During the War of 1812, he was commissioned by both the United States government and the state of Pennsylvania to make dies for medals honoring the heroes of that war—among them the medal for Lt. Stephen Cassin described in the following entry. Eleven medals were for army officers, and twelve were for naval officers. All were struck in gold, but additional medals were struck in silver and copper. Later he made other medals, including Indian peace medals for presidents James Madison, Martin Van Buren, and John Quincy Adams; medals honoring distinguished Americans such as De Witt Clinton, Benjamin Rush, Alexander Hamilton, and Dr. David Hosack; and a medal celebrating the coronation of Queen Victoria. Fürst moved to New York City, probably during the late 1820s or early 1830s, before returning to Europe about 1840. Occasionally he employed his talents on more mundane work, such as cutting die rolls used for making the applied decorative bands on silver hollowware. Bands impressed with his name have been found on pieces by Collin Forbes, J. W. Forbes, and John or Allen Armstrong. A tea set by Hugh Wishart has stamped neoclassical panels for which Fürst made the dies. Winterthur owns a pitcher, lacking a maker's stamp, that has decorative bands that are impressed with Fürst's stamp.

References: Georgia S. Chamberlain, *American Medals and Medalists* (Annandale, Va.: Turnpike Press, 1963), pp. 26–47. William Dunlap, *History of the Rise and Progress of the Arts of Design in the United States*, 3 vols. (Boston: C. E. Goodspeed, 1918), 2:374–75. Leonard Forrer, *Biographical Dictionary of Medallists*, 8 vols. (London: Spink and Son, 1904), s.v. "Fürst, Moritz." Groce and Wallace, *Dictionary of Artists in America*, pp. 246–47. For stamped panels on Wishart tea set, see Sotheby's sale (October 9, 1985), lot 56.

352
GOLD MEDAL, ca. 1818

DIAM. 2 ½" (6.5 cm)
7 oz. 8 dwt. 8 gr. (230.7 g)

Stamps: "FURST. F." in roman letters, under bust portrait on obverse and under scene on reverse.

Description: circular flat form with raised rim and design in relief. Obverse: bust portrait, in profile, of man (facing right) in naval officer's uniform; inscription in roman letters, in relief around inside of rim: "STEP. CASSIN TICONDEROGA PRAEFECT. QUAE REGIO IN TERRIS NOS./ NON PLENA LAB." Reverse: at least 7 sailing ships and numerous galleys engaged in battle; burning town in background; clouds overhead; inscription in roman letters around inside of rim: "UNO LATERE PERCUSSO. ALTERUM/ IMPAVIDE VERTIT. [periods in form of stars]; inscription under scene: "INTER CLASS. AMERI./ ET BRIT. DIE XI SEPT./ MDCCCXIIII".

Spectrographic analysis:

GOLD	SILVER	
98.8	1.2	24 karat

History: Stephen Cassin (1783–1857) was a native of Philadelphia who entered the navy in 1800 as a midshipman. By 1804 he was master of the schooner *Nautilus*. Following service in the Tripolitan War and a reduction in naval forces, he found employment on various merchant ships. He was recalled during the War of 1812 but did not see action until 1814. In that year, with British military forces threatening invasion via the traditional route of Lake Champlain and the Hudson River, both sides built naval squadrons for use on the lake. Cassin was assigned to serve under Capt. Thomas Macdonough, commander of the American squadron. Cassin was given command of the *Ticonderoga*, one of Macdonough's 4 larger ships. The American ships were positioned off Plattsburg, N.Y., where American army units tried to block the British land advance. British naval forces moved in on the Americans, and a vicious battle ensued. All 4 of the larger British ships were disabled and surrendered. Only their galleys escaped. The British were so disheartened by this defeat that they gave up their invasion and withdrew their forces to Canada. It was a major—if not wholly expected—strategic victory for the United States.

Cassin was singled out for praise for his cool and effective leadership. In his *History of the Navy of the United States*, James Fenimore Cooper referred to the *Ticonderoga*'s "spirited commander" who "walked the taffrail . . . amidst showers of cannister and grape, directing discharges of bags of musket balls and other light missiles that had the effect of keeping the British effectually at bay."

Congress authorized a series of medals for military and naval officers who served in this and other actions during the war. Gold medals went to the commanders of the 3 surviving American ships: Macdonough, Cassin, and Robert Henley. Other commissioned officers received silver medals. Getting the medals made proved difficult. John Reich, at the U.S. Mint, was the logical choice to make the dies, but his work on Indian medals and on special medals for Isaac Hull and Stephen Decatur dragged on for several years after the war. Finally, in 1817, Fürst was engaged to help the project along. All but 1 of the dies was finished by October 1819, and most of the medals were struck by 1819.

Provenance: Sold at Parke-Bernet Galleries, New York City, 1960; David Stockwell, Wilmington, Del., 1963; Robert Carlen, Philadelphia, 1964.

Comments: Latin inscription on obverse: "Stephen Cassin, Commander of the Ticonderoga; what region on earth is not full of our works" (adapted from Virgil's *Aeneid)*. Latin inscription on reverse: "Beaten on one side, he fearlessly turns the other; between the American and British fleets September 11, 1814". The die sinker's byline on both sides: "Furst F[ecit]". In addition to the gold medals, 50 Macdonough medals were struck in silver and 100 in copper; Cassin's medal was struck only in gold. Winterthur also owns a copper version of the medal made to honor James Lawrence, captain of the *Hornet*, for his successful action against the *Peacock* in 1813; the die for this medal was also cut by Fürst.

References: Georgia S. Chamberlain, *American Medals and Medalists* (Annandale, Va.: Turnpike Press, 1963), p. 41, no. 10. R. W. Julian, *Medals of the United States Mint, 1792–1892* (El Cajon, Calif.: Token and Medal Society, 1977), pp. 147–48, 156. J. F. Loubatt, *The Medallic History of the United States of America, 1776–1876*, 2 vols. (New York: By the author, 1878), pp. 195–96, pl. 37. Edgar P. Richardson, "The Cassin Medal," in Richard K. Doud, ed., *Winterthur Portfolio 4* (Charlottesville: University Press of Virginia for the Henry Francis du Pont Winterthur Museum, 1968), pp. 75–82. Parke-Bernet Galleries, sale no. 1966 (April 9, 1960), lot 112. David Stockwell advertisement, *Antiques* 83, no. 1 (January 1963): 42.

64.145 Museum purchase from Robert Carlen, 1964

353
MEDAL, ca. 1839

DIAM. 2" (5.1 cm)
1 oz. 15 dwt. 4 gr. (54.6 g)

Stamps: "FURST.F:" in roman letters, on obverse in exergue.

Engraved on reverse: "Awarded to/ J. Hague./ for an Improvement in/ Ever Pointed Pencils/ Sep 1839" in script and italics.

Description: circular flat form with raised rim and design in relief. Obverse: left, a domed classical temple on a mountain top, at its foot 4 figures engaged in arts and crafts; sunburst in center; right, a seated female figure placing a crown of laurel (or bay) on head of standing child reading a book; overhead, horizontal angel blowing trumpet; inscription inside rim at top in relief: "MECHANICS INSTITUTE"; in exergue: "NEW-YORK/ FURST.F:". Reverse: inside rim, a wreath border consisting of an oak leaf branch on the left and an unidentified branch with long thin leaves on the right; stems tied with a bowknot; inscription inside rim at top in relief: "KNOWLEDGE IS POWER"; engraved inscription in center.

Spectrographic analysis:

SILVER	COPPER	GOLD	LEAD
96.9	2.9	0.10	0.12

History: The Mechanics Institute of the City of New York was founded in 1831 for the instruction of craftsmen. It had a library of roughly 1,200 volumes, including a 23-volume set of books on Egypt as well as newspapers, scientific journals, and literary magazines. In 1837 the institute was located in the basement of City Hall. Like similar societies elsewhere, it encouraged innovation in product development by holding an annual exhibition and by presenting awards. Silversmith John Hague, who began to manufacture pencil cases in 1835, was recognized by the society for his work.

Provenance: Frank S. Schwarz & Son, Philadelphia.

References: Frank S. Schwarz & Son advertisement, *Antiques* 102, no. 6 (December 1972): 950. Fennimore, *Silver and Pewter*, no. 213. Not listed in Georgia S. Chamberlain, *American Medals and Medalists* (Annandale, Va.: Turnpike Press, 1963), or J. F. Loubatt, *The Medallic History of the United States of America, 1776–1876*, 2 vols. (New York: By the author, 1878). *New-York as It Is in 1837* (New York: J. Disturnell, 1837), pp. 110–11, for the Mechanics Institute.

73.36 Museum purchase from Frank S. Schwarz & Son, 1973

🏵️354
MEDAL, ca. 1829

DIAM. 2" (5.1 cm)
1 oz. 14 dwt. 1 gr. (52.9 g)

Stamps: "FUR." in roman letters, on obverse under bust portrait.

Description: circular flat form with raised rim and design in relief. Obverse: bust portrait in profile of man (facing right) in civilian clothes; inscription inside rim: "ANDREW JACKSON PRESIDENT OF THE UNITED STATES A. D. 1829" in roman letters. Reverse: 2 clasped hands, military coat cuff with 3 buttons and braid on left hand, bare wrist on right hand; above, crossed tomahawk and pipe; inscription inside rim and in center: "PEACE/ AND/ FRIENDSHIP" in roman letters.

Spectrographic analysis:

	SILVER	LEAD	GOLD
OBVERSE	99.8	0.06	0.02
REVERSE	99.9	0.05	0.02

History: This is 1 of many presidential medals made for presentation to the Indians by the U.S. government. The actual history of this medal is unknown.

Provenance: Charlotte and Edgar Sittig, Shawnee-on-Delaware, Pa., sold to H. F. du Pont, March 1952.

Comments: The medal was also made in the 3" (7.6 cm) size. The hole and ring confirm that it was intended to be worn suspended from the neck. Fürst used an abbreviated version of his name on this medal.

References: Georgia S. Chamberlain, *American Medals and Medalists* (Annandale, Va.: Turnpike Press, 1963), p. 45, no. 4 c. J. F. Loubatt, *The Medallic History of the United States of America, 1776–1876*, 2 vols. (New York: By the author, 1878), p. 271, pl. 55, shows a larger version of medal.

52.34 Gift of H. F. du Pont, 1952

🏵️355
MEDAL, ca. 1837

DIAM. 2" (5.1 cm), W. 2 ½" (6.4 cm)
2 oz. 3 dwt. 8 gr. (67.3 g)

Stamps: "FURST" in roman letters, in exergue on obverse.

Engraved on reverse: "Awarded to/ Miss Martha Marvin/ for fine Specimens of Cacoons./ Reeled & Sewing Silk: 1837." in script.

Description: circular flat form with raised rim and design in relief. Small sphere soldered to upper edge has circular loop handle. Obverse: seated female figure (facing left), in classical dress, holding a laurel wreath in hand of outstretched right arm; left arm and hand hold a staff topped by a Phrygian cap; in front, a sailing ship, spinning wheel, sheaf of wheat, shuttle, and spool; behind her, a shield, eagle, caduceus, and cornucopia; inscription above figure (inside rim): "AMERICAN INSTITUTE" in roman letters, followed by a floret; in exergue: "NEW-YORK/ FURST" in roman letters. Reverse: inside rim, a wreath border consisting of an oak leaf branch on the left and an unidentified branch with long thin leaves on the right; stems tied in a bowknot; engraved inscription in center.

Spectrographic analysis:

	SILVER	COPPER	GOLD	LEAD
OBVERSE	98.1	1.7	0.19	0.02
REVERSE	98.3	1.5	0.22	0.01

History: The American Institute was created in 1828 in New York City to encourage and promote domestic industry "in agriculture, manufactures, and the arts; and any improvements made therein, by bestowing rewards and other benefits on those who shall make any such improvements or excell in any of the said branches." The institute's first fair of products and improvements was held in 1828; the last was in 1897. Medals of gold, silver, and bronze were awarded.

Provenance: Elwood Glass, Cleveland Heights, Ohio.

References: Andrew Harkness, "The American Institute—Catalyst for American Greatness," *TAMS Journal* 29, no. 4 (August 1989): 123–35.

91.31 Gift of Mr. and Mrs. Elwood Glass, Jr., 1991

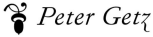

Peter Getz

1764–1809
Lancaster, Pennsylvania

Peter Getz, the son of John and Anna
Maria (Hammacher) Getz, was a jack of
many trades, mostly self-taught. The first
reference to him as a silversmith is in 1785,
but a newspaper notice of 1790 suggests
that he had only recently taken up the
trade on his own. He billed himself as a
goldsmith and jeweler and sold the usual
assortment of luxury items. He was also
an engraver and die sinker. In the latter
capacity he sought the directorship of
the United States Mint, but David Rittenhouse was appointed instead. He did
make the dies for a copper penny with
the profile of Washington. In 1796 he announced that he would make and repair
fire engines and, indeed, did make one of
his own design. On his death he was laud-
ed for having made significant improvements to the printing press by replacing
the large screw with rollers. Rittenhouse
referred to him as "a self-taught mechanic
of singular ingenuity." Several pieces of
Getz hollowware made for Aaron Levy
of Aaronsburg, Pennsylvania, are known
as well as a few other pieces.

References: Vivian S. Gerstell, *Silversmiths of
Lancaster, Pennsylvania, 1730–1850* (Lancaster,
Pa.: Lancaster County Historical Society, 1972),
pp. 22–37. Henry J. Kauffman, "Peter Getz of
Lancaster," *Antiques* 58, no. 2 (August 1950):
112–13.

356
BUTTON, 1790–1809

DIAM. 1" (2.5 cm)
2 dwt. 11 gr. (3.8 g)

Stamps: "P•G" in roman letters, in a rectangle,
struck once on back.

Engraved on front: "TD" (intertwined) in foliate
script.

Description: circular flat body with cast shank
applied to back.

Spectrographic analysis:

SILVER	COPPER	LEAD	GOLD
80.3	19.2	0.20	0.09

Provenance: Philip H. Hammerslough, West
Hartford, Conn.

Exhibitions: Hammerslough collection,
Wadsworth Atheneum, Boston.

Comments: Hammerslough owned 4 waistcoat
buttons and 1 sleeve button. It is the latter that
came to Winterthur. All have the same initials.

References: Fennimore, *Silver and Pewter*, no.
214. Hammerslough, *American Silver*, 2:92.

60.352 Museum trade with Philip H. Hammerslough, 1960

357
SPOON, 1790–1809

L. 7 3/16" (18.3 cm)
1 oz. 1 dwt. 4 gr. (32.9 g)

Stamps: "P•G" in roman letters, in a rectangle,
struck twice on back of handle.

Engraved on front of handle: "JMH" in foliate
script.

Description: oval bowl with swage-formed
rounded drop and an urn with a flame finial;
downturned rounded handle with midrib.

Spectrographic analysis: Silver content is 87.8
percent.

Provenance: Mr. and Mrs. Stanley B. Ineson,
New York City; Mr. and Mrs. Alfred E. Bissell,
Wilmington, Del.

Comments: Unusual decoration on bowl back.

References: Belden, *Marks of American
Silversmiths*, p. 189.

62.240.1128 Gift of Mr. and Mrs. Alfred E.
Bissell, 1962–63

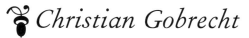

Christian Gobrecht

1785–1844
Philadelphia, Pennsylvania

Christian Gobrecht was born in Hanover, Pennsylvania, the son of John Christopher Gobrecht, a German clergyman who came to America in 1753. Young Gobrecht served his apprenticeship with a clockmaker in Manheim, Pennsylvania, and then moved to Baltimore. By 1811 he was in Philadelphia. Apparently he made ornamental work for clocks, such as engraved faces, which may have led him to specialize in engraving and, eventually, die sinking, in which he was largely self-taught. By 1816 he was employed by the engraving firm of Murray, Draper, Fairman & Company. Gobrecht is responsible for portrait prints of such notables as Alexander I of Russia, Benjamin Franklin, Abraham Rees, David Rittenhouse, Benjamin Rush, and George Washington. Seals, calico printer's rolls, typefounder's punches, and medals suggest the range of work that engaged this craftsman. He created medals for the Franklin Institute, the Massachusetts Charitable Mechanics Association, the New England Society for the Promotion of Manufactures, and the Carroll family of Maryland. In 1832 he applied to President Monroe for the position of engraver and die sinker at the United States Mint. Two years later he was appointed assistant engraver there, and in 1840 he became head of the engraving department. He retained that title until his death in 1844.

References: Charles Gobrecht Darrach, "Christian Gobrecht, Artist and Inventor," *PMHB* 30, no. 3 (July 1906): 355–58. Groce and Wallace, *Dictionary of Artists in America*, p. 263. Henry Simpson, *The Lives of Eminent Philadelphians Now Deceased* (Philadelphia: William Brotherhead, 1859), pp. 418–21.

358
MEDAL, ca. 1828

DIAM. 2" (5.1 cm)
1 oz. 11 dwt. 18 gr. (49.3 g)

Stamps: "GOBRECHT." in roman letters, on obverse under shoulder of portrait.

Description: circular flat form with raised rim and design in relief. Obverse: bust portrait in profile of man (facing left) with braided hair, wearing a fur-trimmed jacket; inscription around inside of rim: "TO CHARLES CARROLL OF CAR-ROLLTON". Reverse: circular wreath with pen and scroll at bottom; inscription inside wreath: "THE/ SURVIVING SIGNER/ OF THE/ DECLARATION OF/ INDEPEN-DENCE/ AFTER THE 50TH/ ANNIVER-SARY"; inscription between wreath and rim: "UPON ENTERING HIS 90TH YEAR/ SEP. XX MDCCCXXVI".

Spectrographic analysis:

SILVER	LEAD	COPPER
99.9	0.04	0.01

History: Charles Carroll of Carrollton (1737–1832) was the last surviving signer of the Declaration of Independence, following the deaths on July 4, 1826, of John Adams and Thomas Jefferson. As a Roman Catholic, Carroll had been barred from holding office in the colony of Maryland despite his extraordinary education. He accepted this limitation and planned to be a gentleman farmer on his 10,000-acre estate in Frederick County, called Carrollton Manor, but he was drawn into the debates preceding the Revolution and became a strong and effective advocate for independence. Eventually becoming U.S. Senator from Maryland, he had a distinguished career and was widely venerated. He called himself Charles Carroll of Carrollton to avoid being confused with relatives of the same name.

To honor Carroll's eighty-ninth birthday, September 19, 1826, his family commissioned Gobrecht to make this medal. It was not completed for at least 2 more years. Carroll saw a model of the medal in June 1828, and in August his grandson informed him that the dies were finally completed: "He [Gobrecht] wants money, but I think myself that it will be better not to pay him until the medals are received, as it may relax his energies. His part of the work is done, but I should like him to superintend the striking of the medals, which is done at the mint." Gold medals were struck for 4 close family members; 13 silver medals were struck for other family members. As of 1975, the original dies were still owned by the family.

Provenance: Lady Wigram, U.K.; Sotheby's, London.

Comments: The signature should read "GO-BRECHT. F. 1826" according to the catalogue cited above. The total absence of gold suggests a later electroplating.

References: Charles Carroll of Carrollton (Baltimore: Baltimore Museum of Art, 1975), pp. 156–57, which illustrates the dies and a gold version of the medal. *DAB*, s.v. "Carroll, Charles."

67.94 Museum purchase from Sotheby's, 1967

🜨 359
MEDAL, 1825–44

DIAM. 2" (5.1 cm)
1 oz. 19 dwt. 5 gr. (60.1 g)

Stamps: "GOBRECHT F." in roman letters,
under lower edge of bust portrait on obverse;
roman "G." on reverse below bowknot.

Engraved on reverse: "To/ Wm. F. Forepaugh/
Philadᵃ., Pᵃ/ For the Finishing of/ Bag Hides./
1844." in script and italics.

Description: circular flat form with raised rim
and design in relief. Obverse: bust portrait in
profile of man with long hair (facing left) who
is obviously Benjamin Franklin; inscription
around inside of rim: "FRANKLIN INSTI-
TUTE OF THE STATE OF PENNSYLVA-
NIA./ 1824". Reverse: inside rim, a wreath
border consisting of an oak leaf branch on the
right and a palm branch on the left; stems tied
with a bowknot; inscription inside rim:
"REWARD OF SKILL AND INGENUITY".

Spectrographic analysis:

SILVER	COPPER	GOLD	LEAD
99.7	0.19	0.08	0.03

History: In 1824 the Franklin Institute initiated
a series of exhibitions of domestic manufactures intended to stimulate technological development, particularly in Pennsylvania but also
in the United States generally. Starting in 1825,
medals in gold, silver, and bronze were awarded to individuals for innovative solutions to
technical problems or improved products. The
exhibitions were industrial fairs that became
popular with the public. The second fair, held in
1825, drew between 15,000 and 20,000 people.
Forepaugh was a currier in Philadelphia who
also received a medal in 1851 for his improvements in "shoe skirting and butts for belts."

Provenance: Garrison Kingsley, Wilmington,
Del.

Comments: The artist John Neagle wrote to
Gobrecht concerning the portrait of Franklin
on this medal: "I am delighted with it, and as a
specimen of art, am proud to acknowledge it
from the hands of a friend. I had an opportunity of giving it a severe test by comparing it in
one hand, with the same head by the celebrated
Dupre in the other, and it gives me great pleasure to say that, in my opinion, it surpasses the
other very far in merit. Yours has more of the
genuine character of our great philosopher
and statesman."

References: Bruce Sinclair, *Philadelphia's Philosopher Mechanics: A History of the Franklin
Institute, 1824–1865* (Baltimore: Johns Hopkins
University Press, 1974), chap. 4. Henry Simpson, *The Lives of Eminent Philadelphians Now
Deceased* (Philadelphia: William Brotherhead,
1859), pp. 419–20, for Neagle quotation.

84.27 Museum purchase from Garrison
Kingsley, 1984

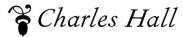

Charles Hall

1742–83
Lancaster, Pennsylvania

Charles Hall probably learned his trade from his brother, silversmith David Hall, who had a shop in Philadelphia on South Second Street at Hall's Alley. The alley was named for their father, Richard Hall, Jr. By 1763 Charles was in Lancaster, where he remained until he died as the result of a fall. In 1767 he married Maria Salome, daughter of Abraham LeRoy, a Swiss watchmaker. Few examples of his work survive, but among those that do are two high-style coffeepots; one superbly chased pot is in the Henry Ford Museum. A documented pair of his buckles is owned by the Rock Ford Foundation in Lancaster.

References: Vivian S. Gerstell, *Silversmiths of Lancaster, Pennsylvania, 1730–1850* (Lancaster, Pa.: Lancaster County Historical Society, 1972), pp. 37–44; see pp. 124–27, for facsimile of his inventory.

360
CANN, 1763–83

H. 4⅝" (11.7 cm), w. 4⅞" (12.4 cm)
8 oz. 10 dwt. 15 gr. (265.4 g)

Stamps: "CH" in roman letters, in a rectangle, struck twice on underside of body.

Engraved on body opposite handle: "TAR" in foliate script.

Description: raised circular form with bulbous lower body, incurving neck, flared rim with single-molded edge with single-incised line below. Centerpunch on underside of body. Cast, circular, stepped foot. Double–C-scroll handle with acanthus leaf and sprig on upper end, scroll and sprig on lower end; lower and upper handle ends attach to body by oval plates; vent in underside of upper handle, which is cast in 2 vertical sections. Pint size.

Spectrographic analysis:

	SILVER	COPPER	LEAD	GOLD
BODY SIDE	86.3	13.4	0.18	0.13
HANDLE	91.0	8.5	0.19	0.15
UNDERSIDE	92.7	7.0	0.13	0.12

Provenance: Probably Francis D. Brinton, West Chester, Pa., sold to H. F. du Pont, March 1930.

Exhibitions: "The Folk Arts and Crafts of the Susquehanna and Chenango River Valleys," Roberson Center for the Arts and Sciences, Binghamton, N.Y., 1978.

References: Fales, *American Silver*, no. 29.

65.1379 Gift of H. F. du Pont, 1965

312
SPOON, 1763–83

L. 4 11/16" (11.9 cm)
7 dwt. 2 gr. (11.0 g)

Stamps: "CH" in roman letters, in a rectangle, struck twice on back of handle.

Engraved on back of handle: "M+H" in shaded roman letters.

Description: oval bowl with swage-formed rounded drop and a 9-lobe shell; rounded downturned handle with midrib.

Spectrographic analysis: Silver content is 88.6 percent.

Provenance: Mr. and Mrs. Stanley B. Ineson, New York City; Mr. and Mrs. Alfred E. Bissell, Wilmington, Del.

References: Belden, *Marks of American Silversmiths*, p. 207.

62.240.300 Gift of Mr. and Mrs. Alfred E. Bissell, 1962–63

David Hall

ca. 1735–77
Philadelphia, Pennsylvania,
w. ca. 1759–77
Burlington, New Jersey, w. 1777–78

David Hall's shop was on South Second Street, between High (Market) and Chestnut streets, on the corner of Hall's Alley, which had been named for his father, Richard Hall, Jr. In 1766 he advertised himself as a "Goldsmith" who also sold chinaware and "drilled, clasped and wooden handles neatly affixed to china tea pots." His younger brother Charles probably learned the silversmithing trade from him prior to moving to Lancaster in 1763. David Hall moved to Burlington, New Jersey, in 1777, during the British occupation of Philadelphia. He died the following year, probably still in Burlington. His widow Hannah returned to Philadelphia, where William Ball, silversmith, and John Wood, clockmaker, served as bondsmen when letters of administration were granted by the court. A small quantity of Hall's silver survives, including a dish cross in a private collection, one of the few colonial examples of that form. He should not be confused with David Hall (1767–1814), son of his brother Charles Hall of Lancaster, who was also a silversmith.

References: Philadelphia: Three Centuries, pp. 122–23. Williams, *Silversmiths of New Jersey,* pp. 31–32.

362
CASTER, 1760–78

H. 5 5⁄16" (13.5 cm), DIAM. 2 ⅛" (5.4 cm)
4 oz. 1 dwt. 22 gr. (127.1 g)

Stamps: "D•HALL" in roman letters, in a rectangle, struck once on underside of body.

Engraved on side of upper body: "MA" in foliate script.

Description: raised bowl-shape lower body joined by midband to upper body, incurving to cylindrical neck; applied molded rim; centerpunch on underside of lower body. Cast, circular, stepped foot. Seamed high-dome friction-fit lid with flange and cast "spinning top" finial; sides divided into 6 diagonal panels with incised diaper pattern and drilled with 18 holes per panel.

Spectrographic analysis:

	SILVER	COPPER	GOLD	LEAD
BODY SIDE	90.7	8.9	0.22	0.19
LID	94.8	4.9	0.18	0.13

Provenance: Marshall P. Blankarn, New York City.

79.201 Gift of Marshall P. Blankarn, 1979

363
STUFFING SPOON, 1760–78

L. 15 ¹⁵⁄₁₆" (40.5 cm)
6 oz. 5 dwt. 5 gr. (194.3 g)

Stamps: "D Hall" in roman letters, in a rectangle, struck twice on back of handle.

Engraved on back of handle: "L*W" in shaded roman letters.

Description: deep oval bowl with swage-formed rounded drop; rounded upturned handle with midrib.

Spectrographic analysis: Silver content is 89.4 percent.

Provenance: Mr. and Mrs. Stanley B. Ineson, New York City; Mr. and Mrs. Alfred E. Bissell, Wilmington, Del.

References: Belden, *Marks of American Silversmiths,* p. 207.

62.240.1664 Gift of Mr. and Mrs. Alfred E. Bissell, 1962–63

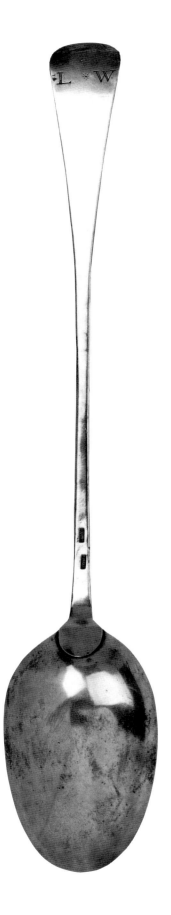

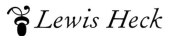

Lewis Heck

1755–1817
Lancaster, Pennsylvania

Lewis, or Ludwig, Heck first appears in Lancaster tax records in 1778 and as head of a household in 1779. He and his wife, Elizabeth, had seven children, the first in 1781. He was town clerk in 1781 and 1782 and secretary of the vestry of Trinity Lutheran Church in 1794. In 1802 his house and shop were located "next door to the northwest corner of the Statehouse Square." Little of his silver survives. A neoclassical creamer in a private collection has both his name stamp and his initial stamp.

References: Vivian S. Gerstell, *Silversmiths of Lancaster, Pennsylvania, 1730–1850* (Lancaster, Pa.: Lancaster County Historical Society, 1972), pp. 75–77; see pp. 129–30, for a facsimile of his inventory.

364
BUTTON, 1790–1817

DIAM. 15/16" (2.4 cm)
2 dwt. 2 gr. (3.3 g)

Stamps: "LH" in roman letters, in a rectangle, struck once on back.

Engraved on front: "TG" in foliate script, with a single-line border.

Description: circular, slightly domed body with a cast shank applied to back.

Spectrographic analysis:

ANTIMONY	SILVER	COPPER	LEAD	GOLD
61.4	32.1	6.2	0.11	0.06

Provenance: Edgar H. Sittig, Shawnee-on-Delaware, Pa.

Comments: Note the unusual composition of metal. Antimony was used as an additive in making pewter and Britannia ware. Winterthur purchased 2 identical buttons and traded 1 to Philip Hammerslough for no. 356.

References: Fennimore, *Silver and Pewter*, no. 214. Hammerslough, *American Silver*, 3:142, for illustration of one of the pair.

60.333.1 Museum purchase from Edgar H. Sittig, 1960

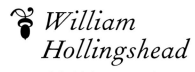

William Hollingshead

Philadelphia, Pennsylvania,
w. ca. 1757–85

Nothing is known about the early years of William Hollingshead. He first appears in 1762 when he offered "to be lett, A Plantation" in Kensington, Pennsylvania; prospects were to inquire of "William Hollingshead, Goldsmith, at the corner of Arch and Second streets." In 1774, still at the same address, he offered for sale on behalf of Thomas Jackson, potter, "A good assortment of Black Lead Crucibles." He was also at this address in the city directory for 1785. Hollingshead produced a significant number of pieces of high-quality silver hollowware in both the rococo and neoclassical styles. A drum-shape teapot and double-bellied sugar bowl and creamer were made in the early 1780s for the same family. Now owned by the Philadelphia Museum of Art, the set well illustrates the overlapping of styles that occurred at this time. Hollingshead's stamp, a distinctive "WH" in script, in a conforming surround, is quite unlike the half dozen or so other "WH" stamps. It does, however, bear a startling resemblance to the stamp of William Homer, who worked in Dublin from 1754 to 1773.

References: Douglas Bennett, *Collecting Irish Silver* (London: Souvenir Press, 1984), p. 179, for "WH" stamp. Prime cards, Winterthur. "Some Rarities in American Silver and Gold," *Antiques* 51, no. 1 (January 1947): 48, for illus. of 3-piece service.

🐝 365
SALVER, 1780–85

DIAM. 6 ⅞" (17.5 cm), H. 1 ¼" (3.2 cm)
9 oz. 8 dwt. 10 gr. (293.0 g)

Stamps: "WH" in script, in a conforming surround, struck once on underside.

Engraved on upper surface: "SIP" in foliate script.

Description: flat circular tray with raised-and-shaped edge consisting of 6 brackets with applied cast gadrooned border; chasing on underside repeats points and brackets on upper side; no centerpunch (but it could be covered by stamp); 3 short cabriole legs in the form of back-to-back C scrolls; triple-pad feet.

Spectrographic analysis:

	SILVER	COPPER	LEAD	GOLD
TOP	90.0	9.5	0.27	0.10
CAST BORDER	91.1	8.1	0.22	0.13
FOOT	92.5	6.7	0.19	0.18

History: Tradition of ownership in the Potts family of Philadelphia.

Provenance: Mr. and Mrs. N. McLean Seabrease, Germantown, Pa.; Robert Ensko, Inc., New York City, sold to H. F. du Pont, August 1929.

References: Philadelphia Silver, 1682–1800, nos. 145, 146, for 2 similar salvers by Hollingshead.

61.598 Gift of H. F. du Pont, 1965

🐝 366 a–d
SPOONS, 1760–85

(a) L. 5 ⁷⁄₁₆" (13.8 cm)
9 dwt. 18 gr. (15.2 g)
(b) L. 7" (17.8 cm)
1 oz. 1 dwt. 11 gr. (33.3 g)
(c) L. 6 ⅜" (16.2 cm)
1 oz. 1 dwt. 4 gr. (32.9 g)
(d) L. 8 ³⁄₁₆" (20.8 cm)
1 oz. 19 dwt. 16 gr.
(61.6 g)

Stamps: "WH" in script, in a conforming surround, struck twice on back of each handle.

Engraved on front of handle: (a) "MD"; (b) "SH"; (c) "WHB". All in foliate script. *Engraved on back of handle:* (d) "P/ PM" in shaded roman letters.

Description: elongated oval bowls with swage-formed rounded drop; rounded downturned handle with midrib on (a–c); rounded upturned handle with midrib on (d).

Spectrographic analysis: Silver content ranges from 89.8 to 94.9 percent.

Provenance: Mr. and Mrs. Stanley B. Ineson, New York City; Mr. and Mrs. Alfred E. Bissell, Wilmington, Del.

Comments: (d) is clearly earlier than the other 3 spoons, which have neoclassical engraving.

References: Belden, *Marks of American Silversmiths*, p. 230.

62.240.321, .1177, .1176, .1178 Gift of Mr. and Mrs. Alfred E. Bissell, 1962–63

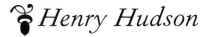

Henry Hudson

ca. 1818–88

Hudson & Dolfinger
Louisville, Kentucky, w. ca. 1855–88

Henry Hudson was a silversmith and jeweler who also manufactured silver for the wholesale market. He first appears as a jeweler in 1841 but by 1844 is listed as a silversmith. In the Census of Manufactures for 1850, Hudson was a gold- and silversmith who had six men and one woman working in his shop. Each year the shop used 5 pounds of gold, 650 pounds of silver, and 500 bushels of charcoal. By 1855 Hudson had formed a partnership with Jacob Dolfinger. Hudson & Dolfinger made pitchers, beakers, and flatware, a number of which are known today. The partnership was dissolved by 1888. Although he continued to be identified with the jewelry business until at least 1877, Hudson is no longer listed as a silversmith after 1860.

References: Boultinghouse, *Silversmiths of Kentucky,* pp. 159–60. Henry H. Harned, "Ante-bellum Kentucky Silver," *Antiques* 105, no. 4 (April 1974): 818–24, figs. 8, 15. William Barrow Floyd, "Kentucky Coin-Silver Pitchers," *Antiques* 105, no. 3 (March 1974): 576–80, fig. 10. *Silver in Kentucky Life,* pp. 35, 59.

367
BEAKER, ca. 1850

H. 3 ⅞" (9.8 cm), DIAM. rim 3 ⅜" (8.6 cm)
5 oz. 5 dwt. 7 gr. (163.4 g)

Stamps: "H. HUDSON/ LOUISVILLE" in incuse roman letters, struck once on underside.

Description: seamed cylindrical body with straight tapering sides, flat bottom set in; no centerpunch. Molded rim with sawtooth lower edge; molded footring with fine dentil upper edge.

Spectrographic analysis:

	SILVER	COPPER	LEAD	GOLD
BODY SIDE	86.4	13.3	0.18	0.07
UNDERSIDE	89.8	10.0	0.15	0.07

Provenance: H. F. du Pont.

70.1087 Bequest of H. F. du Pont, 1969

368 a, b
SPOONS, ca. 1850

(a) L. 8 ⁹⁄₁₆" (21.7 cm)
1 oz. 7 dwt. 12 gr. (42.7 g)
(b) L. 5 ¹³⁄₁₆" (14.8 cm)
1 oz. 7 dwt. 12 gr. (42.7 g)

Stamps: "H. HUDSON/ LOUISVILLE" in incuse roman letters, struck once on underside of (a); "LOUISVILLE" only on (b).

Description: elliptical bowl, plain on back; upturned rounded-end fiddle-shape handle and midrib.

Spectrographic analysis: Silver content ranges from 86.1 to 88.0 percent.

Provenance: Mrs. Endsley P. Fairman, Wilmington, Del.

References: Belden, *Marks of American Silversmiths,* p. 239.

70.184, .185 Museum purchase from Mrs. Endsley P. Fairman, 1970

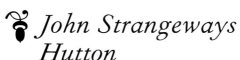

John Strangeways Hutton

1684–1792
Philadelphia, Pennsylvania

John Strangeways Hutton was remarkable for his longevity and, for the time, for having had two careers. He was born and raised in New York and apprenticed to a sea captain to become a mariner. He pursued a maritime career for several years. Somewhere along the line he learned the silversmith's trade and in 1720 was admitted a freeman of New York City as a goldsmith. In 1735, at age fifty-one, he went to work for Quaker goldsmith Joseph Richardson in Philadelphia. Richardson's records show payments to Hutton in the 1740s for making tumblers, sugar dishes, teapots, coffeepots, milk pots, salts, canns, and porringers. By the late 1740s—he was well over sixty—he went into semiretirement. This did not prevent him from continuing to make silver occasionally, and he is reputed to have made a silver tumbler at age ninety-four. By his first wife, Catherine Cheeseman of New York, he had eight children. At age fifty-one, following her death, he married Ann Vanlear (who was nineteen) and had seventeen more children. By the time Charles Willson Peale painted Hutton's portrait, he was a beloved and venerated figure in Philadelphia. His effigy joined those of Benjamin Franklin, Alexander Hamilton, and John Hancock at the New York Wax Work in 1793. Little of his silver survives.

References: Fales, *Joseph Richardson and Family*, pp. 62–63, 285–86. *NYHS Collections*: vol. 18 (1885) *Burghers and Freemen*, p. 100. John Fanning Watson, *Annals of Philadelphia and Pennsylvania in the Olden Time*, 3 vols., rev. Willis P. Hazard (Philadelphia: Leary, Stuart, 1927), 1:327–28.

369
SALVER, ca. 1750

DIAM. 5 13/16" (14.8 cm), H. 1 1/4" (3.2 cm)
8 oz. 6 dwt. 23 gr. (259.1 g)

Stamps: "I•H" in roman letters, in an oval, struck twice on underside of body.

Engraved on underside of body: "R/ IS" in shaded roman letters. *Scratched on underside of body:* "oz 61 10 g 18".

Description: flat circular tray with cast applied shaped edge consisting of 6 rudimentary bracketlike segments alternating with rectangular segments, each separated by shallow C-scroll indentations; centerpunch on underside; 3 short cast cabriole legs with triple-pad knees and triple-pad pointed feet.

Spectrographic analysis:

	SILVER	COPPER	LEAD	GOLD
UPPER SURFACE	93.2	5.9	0.45	0.30
RIM	95.2	4.6	0.14	0.11
FOOT	86.1	13.1	0.27	0.09

History: Inscription refers to Joseph and Sarah Richardson. Joseph was the son of John and Ann Richardson, who lived in New Castle County, Del., and was a contemporary of Joseph Richardson, Sr., the goldsmith.

Provenance: Joseph and Sarah Richardson; Sally Richardson, who married Nicholas Waln; Arthur M. Mason, Wilmington, Del., sold to H. F. du Pont, February 1932.

Comments: Similar to salvers made by Joseph Richardson, Sr. The discrepancy between the scratch weight and the current weight suggests that the feet were added later.

References: Fales, *American Silver*, no. 109. Fales, *Joseph Richardson and Family*, p. 63.

59.2909 Gift of H. F. du Pont, 1965

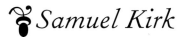

Samuel Kirk

1793–1872

Kirk & Smith, w. 1815–20
Samuel Kirk & Son, w. 1846–61, 1868–96
Samuel Kirk & Sons, w. 1861–68
Samuel Kirk & Son Co., w. 1896–1924
Samuel Kirk & Son, Inc., w. 1924–79
Kirk-Stieff, Inc., 1979–
Baltimore, Maryland

Samuel Kirk, a native of Doylestown, Pennsylvania, served his apprenticeship under Philadelphia silversmith James Howell, successor to Joseph Richardson, Jr. Kirk went to Baltimore in 1815 and entered into a partnership with John Smith until 1820. Kirk came to dominate the silver trade in Baltimore. By 1828 he made 93 percent of all the silver submitted to the Baltimore assay office. Although Kirk is best known for producing silver in the repoussé style, in fact he worked in traditional eighteenth-century styles: neoclassical, empire, and countless revival styles. An entrepreneur who became phenomenally successful, he brought his son into the business in 1846 to establish the firm Samuel Kirk & Son. In 1861, when two more sons joined, the firm became Samuel Kirk & Sons. The firm has become the longest-lived silver manufacturing enterprise in the United States, continuing today as Kirk-Stieff.

References: Louise Durbin, "Samuel Kirk, Nineteenth-Century Silversmith," *Antiques* 94, no. 6 (December 1968): 868–73. Goldsborough, *Eighteenth- and Nineteenth-Century Maryland Silver*, pp. 135–69. Goldsborough, *Silver in Maryland*, pp. 135–62. Patrick M. Duggan, "Marks on Baltimore Silver, 1814–1860: An Exploration," in Goldsborough, *Silver in Maryland*, pp. 26–37. Pleasants and Sill, *Maryland Silversmiths*, pp. 145–49.

370 a–f

COFFEE AND TEA SERVICE, 1828

(a) Coffeepot: H. 15" (38.1 cm), w. 10 ⅛" (25.7 cm)
57 oz. 11 dwt. 3 gr. (1786.0 g)
(b) Teapot: H. 12 ⅛" (30.8 cm), w. 9 ⅞" (25.1 cm)
38 oz. 12 dwt. 5 gr. (1198.1 g)
(c) Teapot: H. 11 ⅝" (29.5 cm), w. 9 ¹⁵⁄₁₆" (25.2 cm)
36 oz. 17 dwt. 19 gr. (1144.7 g)
(d) Sugar bowl with lid: H. 10" (25.4 cm), w. 7 ⁹⁄₁₆" (19.2 cm)
29 oz. 16 dwt. 17 gr. (925.8 g)
(e) Creamer: H. 8 ⅝" (21.9 cm), w. 6 ¾" (17.2 cm)
18 oz. 1 dwt. 6 gr. (560.5 g)
(f) Waste bowl: H. 3 ¹⁵⁄₁₆" (10.0 cm), DIAM. 7 ³⁄₁₆" (18.3 cm)
17 oz. 1 dwt. 20 gr. (530.4 g)

Stamps: "SAM͟L KIRK" in roman letters, in a rectangle, struck once on underside of body (a) and (f) and on outside of footring on (b), (d), and (e). "SK" in roman letters, in a rectangle; "11.OZ" in arabic numbers and roman letters, in a rectangle, struck once on underside of body (a) and (f), rim of (c), and on footring of (b), (d), and (e). Heraldic stamp consisting of a quartered oval with a star in the upper-right and lower-left quadrants and azure in the upper-left and lower-right quadrants, all in an oval, struck once on footring of (a), (b), and (d) and on underside of body (f). An incuse "F" struck once on footring of (a), (b), and (d) and on underside of body (f).

Engraved on side of each body: "M" in foliate script. Earlier engraving was removed in the twentieth century and replaced by the "M."

Description: all pieces except (f) have urn-shape main bodies. All pieces except (e) and (f) have incurved upper bodies. All pieces except (f) have trumpet-shape pedestals, sharp knops, and reeded footrings. All lidded pieces have circular domed lids with cast floral finials. All pieces have detailed repoussé work overall with flower-and-leaf patterns on pedestals, necks, and lids. Repoussé patterns on bodies feature people and structures in landscapes, but patterns differ from piece to piece. All bodies, lids, and pedestals are raised, and all bodies have centerpunches on their undersides.

All the repoussé decoration includes many trees of different types. All lids have finials attached through top by silver nuts and bolts. All lids have partial bezels except (d), which has no bezel.

(a) Coffeepot: elaborate seamed vertical spout terminating in a duck's head with an open bill for pouring; acanthus leaf on front; high-relief mask flanked by C scrolls and rocaille work below flowers and leaves. Handle rises vertically from shoulder to 2 right angles before curving gently toward lower body; flowers, leaves, and acanthus on sides; each end connected to sockets by 2 silver pins; ivory insulators; upper socket cast as a cowled female herm; lower socket cast as high-relief acanthus leaves. Repoussé design on body: side with handle to right, 2 arched bridges in a landscape of palm and other exotic trees with a male Asian figure carrying a spear and standing on the lower bridge; side with handle to left, a gabled frame house with an ell; in the front yard, a man carrying a scythe, a woman carrying a water bucket on her head, a dog, 2 overturned tubs, and a 4-wheel wagon; on left, a pup-tent–like structure under a tree dripping Spanish moss. Lid has 5-segment hinge within perimeter.

(b) Teapot: spout similar to (a) but without mask and rocaille work; perforations in body behind spout serve as strainer. Handle identical to (a) but smaller. Circular hinged lid as on (a). Repoussé design on body: side with handle to right, chinoiserie scene with standing male figure carrying a spear; woman with parasol behind wall; small pavilion on left; side with handle to left, a gabled frame house with an outbuilding and a pale fence; in foreground, a man carrying a pick over his shoulder, a dog, and a 2-wheeled cart; a brick monument on the left. Circular hinged lid as on (a).

(c) Teapot: spout similar to (b); perforations in body behind spout serve as a strainer. Handle identical to (b) but smaller. Repoussé design on body: side with handle to right, a turbaned male

figure carrying a spear leans on a wall; a hatted male figure also carrying a spear stands on a bridge; on left, a classical masonry niche holds a vase of flowers; side with handle to left, a thatched gabled frame house with leaded windows and an ell; in front yard, a dog, an overturned tub, and a man carrying a scythe; on left, a tentlike structure. Circular hinged lid as on (a).

(d) Sugar bowl with lid: rim is fitted with an applied crenelated rim with rectangular panels containing a diaper pattern; 2 handles, each rises straight up from body to 2 right angles, lower ends curve gently to meet body; floral decoration on sides. Repoussé design on body: side with engraved "M," 3 vaguely oriental structures, an arched bridge, and a baluster wall; male figure in foreground leans on what appears to be a hoe; a watering can nearby; other side, a circular building, vaguely oriental in character, and a classical building with columns and porch; in landscape, a woman with a basket, a dog, and a swan. Loose fitting lid.

(e) Creamer: incurving neck flares at rim and rises to a broad pouring lip in front and a peak in back; applied or folded rim. Handle similar to (d). Repoussé design on body: right of engraved "M," 2 men in a boat fishing, a gabled frame house in the background, a masonry house on the right; left of engraved "M," 2 vaguely Asian figures in landscape apparently gathering plant materials; small frame house with curved roof and pale fence in background; on the left an eagle stands on a C scroll.

(f) Waste bowl: circular bowl form has applied crenelated rim with dotted panels; short incurved pedestal with reeded footring. Repoussé design on body (clockwise from right of engraved "M"): a castlelike structure; flowers, leaves, and C scrolls; a vaguely oriental structure with a central tower and 2 wings, fenced yard in back; more flowers, leaves, and C scrolls; a blank reserve; a 2-story frame house with a smoking chimney; more flowers, leaves, and C scrolls; a 2-story frame house with wings on either side.

Spectrographic analysis:

	SILVER	COPPER	LEAD	GOLD
(a) Coffeepot				
BODY SIDE	93.4	6.4	0.13	0.10
FOOT	93.3	6.5	0.14	0.08
SPOUT	95.3	4.5	0.09	0.04
LID	95.7	4.0	0.16	0.09

	SILVER	COPPER	LEAD	GOLD
(b) Teapot				
BODY SIDE	92.4	7.3	0.31	0.05
FOOT	92.6	7.1	0.25	0.08
SPOUT	92.9	6.8	0.24	0.06
LID	92.8	6.8	0.29	0.08
(c) Teapot				
BODY SIDE	93.7	6.1	0.12	0.08
FOOT	93.5	6.3	0.10	0.10
SPOUT	93.2	6.5	0.12	0.13
LID	93.3	6.5	0.14	0.09
(d) Sugar bowl				
BODY SIDE	94.2	5.6	0.11	0.09
FOOT	93.3	6.5	0.16	0.11
HANDLE	97.2	2.7	0.08	0.08
LID	93.2	6.6	0.17	0.08
(e) Creamer				
BODY SIDE	93.0	6.9	0.10	0.05
FOOT	92.9	6.9	0.22	0.05
HANDLE	93.2	6.6	0.21	0.04
(f) Waste bowl				
BODY SIDE	93.4	6.3	0.18	0.06
FOOT	94.3	5.4	0.23	0.08

Provenance: Purchased from a Virginia family by Thomas Legget Moore, Richmond, ca. 1925, through jeweler Sol Scheer; Dr. and Mrs. W. Tyler Haynes, Richmond.

Exhibitions: (e) "Technological Innovation and the Decorative Arts," Hagley Museum, Wilmington, Del., 1973.

Comments: Probably one of the earliest services made by Samuel Kirk, it is a tour de force of traditional techniques. The pictorial repoussée work is a varied and compelling mix of chinoiserie and vernacular scenes. Although at first glance busy, these designs resolve into separate pleasing images. They have a dreamlike quality that is thoroughly charming. Note the graduated sizes—even between the 2 teapots. The heraldic stamp is the small oval version of the coat of arms of Maryland; it was used to represent the Baltimore assay office starting about 1824. The incuse "F" is the so-called dominical letter based on the old practice of designating the year by the dominical letter of the first Sunday after New Year's Day. Unlike the British system of letter dating, this one is much more complicated and, in fact, was used inconsistently. J. Hall Pleasants calculated that "F" referred to the year 1828, but recent research has cast doubt on this interpretation. The "11:OZ" stamp refers to the purity of the alloy, in this case 11 parts silver to 1 part copper, or 91.7 percent pure. This is close to the sterling standard of 92.5 percent, and spectrographic analysis proves that it is actually slightly above the sterling standard. Major collections of Kirk silver are held by the Peale Museum, Baltimore; the Maryland Historical Society; the Baltimore Museum of Art; and the Kirk-Stieff Company.

References: (e) *Technological Innovation and the Decorative Arts* (Wilmington, Del.: Eleutherian Mills–Hagley Foundation, 1973), no. 11.

72.297.1–.6 Gift of Dr. and Mrs. W. Tyler Haynes, 1972

371
BEAKER, ca. 1840

H. 3 ⅜" (8.6 cm), DIAM. rim 3" (7.6 cm)
3 oz. 19 dwt. 1 gr. (123.0 g)

Stamps: "SAML KIRK" in large roman letters, in a rectangle, struck once on underside. Accompanied by "10.15" in a serrated rectangle.

Engraved on side: "C. Carroll" in script.

Description: seamed cylindrical body with straight tapering sides, bottom set in; no centerpunch; double-molded rim; step-molded footring.

Spectrographic analysis:

	SILVER	COPPER	LEAD	GOLD
BODY SIDE	90.0	9.5	0.23	0.09
UNDERSIDE	92.9	6.6	0.26	0.09

History: In Samuel Kirk's daybook at the Maryland Historical Society, an entry for August 29, 1840, reads: "Mr. Carroll called; took his tumbler & paid 10$." Both present and earlier owners had hoped the beaker was owned by Charles Carroll of Carrollton (CCC) (1737–1832), the last surviving signer of the Declaration of Independence, but it is unlikely, especially in light of its probable purchase in 1840. Moreover, the first owner could not have been Carroll's son, Charles Carroll of Homewood (CCH), because he died before his father, in 1825. A more likely prospect is Charles Carroll of Doughoregan (CCD) (1801–62), grandson of CCC and son of CCH; he was known as "the Colonel." Doughoregan Manor was an estate of 13,500 acres in Howard County, Md. It was so much beloved by CCC that he requested burial there.

Provenance: The Wilderness Trail Antique Shops, Frankfort, Ky., sold to H. F. du Pont, November 1930.

Comments: The stamp "10.15" refers to the purity of silver based on 10 oz. 15 dwt. of silver to 1 oz. 5 dwt. of alloy, resulting in silver that is 89.6 percent pure. This is basically the standard for coin silver. I am indebted to Scott Erbes for bringing to my attention the reference to Kirk's daybook.

References: Fales, *American Silver*, no. 130, where it is erroneously referred to as one of a pair. *"Anywhere so Long as There Be Freedom": Charles Carroll of Carrollton, His Family and His Maryland* (Baltimore: Baltimore Museum of Art, 1975), pp. 254–55, for portrait of CCD. Kauffman, *Colonial Silversmith*, p. 81.

61. 961 Gift of H. F. du Pont, 1965

372
SPOON, 1824

L. 8 ¹³⁄₁₆" (22.4 cm)
3 oz. 3 gr. (93.3 g)

Stamps: "S. Kirk" in script, in a rounded rectangle, struck once on back of handle. Accompanied by the coat of arms of Maryland, in a quartered shield, in a rectangle with canted corners, and a roman "C" in a rectangle.

Engraved on back of handle: a spread-winged eagle perched on a stump atop a heraldic band.

Description: pointed oval bowl with swage-formed rounded drop; upturned wavy-end handle with double-thread border on lower end, 10-lobe shell with ribbon border at upper end, acanthus leaf and back-to-back anthemia in center.

Provenance: William J. Flather, Washington, D.C.

Comments: Dating based on Duggan.

References: Patrick M. Duggan, "Marks on Baltimore Silver, 1814–1860: An Exploration," in Goldsborough, *Silver in Maryland*, pp. 26–37.

84.59 Gift of William J. Flather, 1984

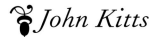

John Kitts

ca. 1805–63

Scott & Kitts, w. 1843–44
Smith & Kitts, w. 1844–45
Kitts & Stoy, w. 1851–52
Kitts & Werne, w. 1859–63
Louisville, Kentucky

John Kitts worked for John Lemon as a watchmaker from 1836 to 1841. He had various short-lived partnerships over the years, the most enduring one with Joseph Werne, Jr. Kitts made numerous pitchers, almost all with a bulbous lower body, a tall incurving neck, a C-curve handle, and mounted on a pedestal. Many came with beakers of the type shown in the following entry. In 1857 the Kentucky Agricultural Society paid "Jno. Kitts &n Co." $3,407.31 for silver. Immediately following in the same document is a list suggesting the silver forms purchased for the agricultural fairs:

There was after the State Fair at Henderson in October last the following amount to silverplate remaining, to wit:

1 silver pitcher cost	*$25*	*$25.00*
3 silver pitchers cost	*$20*	*60.00*
26 silver tumblers cost	*$10*	*260.00*
12 silver tumblers cost	*$5*	*60.00*
		$405.00

References: Boultinghouse, *Silversmiths of Kentucky*, pp. 179–80. William Barrow Floyd, "Kentucky Coin-Silver Pitchers," *Antiques* 105, no. 3 (March 1974): 576–80. Henry H. Harned, "Ante-bellum Kentucky Silver," *Antiques* 105, no. 4 (April 1974): 818–24. *Silver in Kentucky Life*, pp. 37, 59.

373
BEAKER, 1841–59

H. 3 13/16" (9.7 cm), DIAM. rim 3 ¼" (8.3 cm)
4 oz. 15 dwt. 23 gr. (148.9 g)

Stamps: "J. KITTS" in roman letters, struck incuse on underside.

Description: seamed cylindrical body with straight tapering sides; bottom set in; center-punch on underside; molded rim and footring, both with beading.

Spectrographic analysis:

	SILVER	COPPER	LEAD	GOLD
BODY SIDE	87.6	12.1	0.19	0.12
UNDERSIDE	90.8	9.0	0.10	0.10

Provenance: H. F. du Pont.

Comments: In the twentieth century the form has often been referred to as a julep cup, which is a misnomer, but in the nineteenth century it was known as a tumbler. Since the same form was called a beaker in the eighteenth century, that term has been used throughout this catalogue.

70.1150 Bequest of H. F. du Pont, 1969

William Kneass

1780–1840

Kneass & Delleker, w. 1817
Kneass, Young & Co., w. 1818–20
Philadelphia, Pennsylvania

Born in Lancaster, Pennsylvania, William Kneass learned engraving in Philadelphia, where he was working by 1804 as an engraver in line, stipple, and aquatint. He was also a die sinker. Kneass's business partner in 1817 was George Delleker, and the firm was known as Kneass & Delleker. From 1818 to 1820, his partner was James H. Young, and the firm was listed as Kneass, Young & Company. From 1824 until his death he was employed by the United States Mint in Philadelphia as both an engraver and die sinker. He succeeded Robert Scott in that position.

References: Groce and Wallace, *Dictionary of Artists in America*, pp. 173, 373, 710. David McNeely Stauffer, *American Engravers upon Copper and Steel*, 2 vols. (New York: Grolier Club, 1907), 1:153–54, for biographical information; 2:274–78, for prints. Fielding, *American Engravers*, pp. 168–72, for more prints.

374
MEDAL, ca. 1833

DIAM. 1 ¼" (3.2 cm)
9 dwt. 3 gr. (14.2 g)

Stamps: None. Attributed to William Kneass; see *History*.

Description: flat circular form with raised rim and design in relief. Obverse: bust portrait of man with long hair (facing left); inscription around inside of rim: "CHARLES WILLSON PEALE FOUNDER 1784". Reverse: circular wreath with ends tied in a bowknot; inscription inside rim: "PHILADELPHIA MUSEUM INCORPORATED 1821" with 2 florets between upper and lower parts of inscription.

Spectrographic analysis:

SILVER	COPPER	GOLD	LEAD
97.6	2.2	0.09	0.07

History: The medal refers to the museum in Philadelphia founded by Charles Willson Peale in 1784. Although often referred to as Peale's Museum, Peale preferred the name Philadelphia Museum. According to Charles Coleman Sellers, the trustees of the museum appointed a committee in 1829 to discuss a medal with Adam Eckfeldt, chief coiner at the U.S. Mint. Nothing appears in their minutes until 1833, when they authorized a gold medal. It must have pleased them for they subsequently authorized silver medals for Samuel Moore, director of the mint; Kneass, engraver; and Eckfeldt. Each trustee also received a silver medal. Other versions were struck in copper and copper gilt. While the copper versions have the phrase "ADMIT THE BEARER," that space was left blank on the gold and silver medals in order to accommodate the engraved names of the recipients.

Provenance: Mrs. J. Carson, Philadelphia.

References: Charles Coleman Sellers to E. P. Richardson, June 20, 1964, Winterthur object file. Charles Coleman Sellers, *Mr. Peale's Museum* (New York: W. W. Norton, 1980). R. W. Julian, *Medals of the United States Mint, 1792–1892* (El Cajon, Calif.: Token and Medal Society, 1977), p. 369, where it is attributed to Christian Gobrecht.

57.92.1 Museum purchase from Mrs. J. Carson, 1957

❦ *Peter L. Krider*

1821–95

Krider & Co., w. 1851–59
Krider & Biddle, w. 1859–ca. 1870
Philadelphia, Pennsylvania

Peter L. Krider began his apprenticeship with John Curry, circa 1835, and finished it under Robert and William Wilson. He remained with the Wilsons as a journeyman for approximately fifteen months. About 1842 he moved to Boston, where he worked for Obadiah Rich. He returned to Philadelphia about 1846 and served briefly as the Wilsons' foreman. The firm of Krider & Co. first appears in Philadelphia directories in 1851 at 51 Dock Street, which is also given as the home of Peter L. Krider. For the next four years, the firm is listed at 1 South Sixth Street. From 1859 to about 1870, John W. Biddle was his partner. During most of this time the firm was known as Krider & Biddle. In 1865 Krider is listed at Eighth and Jayne streets. The business was sold to August Weber around 1888.

Numerous examples of Krider's work survive. He seems to have specialized in beakers (tumblers). Many of them were shipped to retailers in other parts of the country, especially the South. One of Krider's good customers was John B. Akin of Danville, Kentucky, a jeweler who consistently had his own name stamped on Krider's beakers. Krider also made hollowware for such prominent Philadelphia retailers as Bailey & Company and J. E. Caldwell as well as the Baltimore firm of Canfield Brothers. The Krider firm made several important presentation pieces, including a pitcher given to Frederick Watts in 1867 by the farmers of Cumberland County, Pennsylvania (now at the Cumberland County Historical Society), and an elaborate repoussé fireman's trumpet dated 1852 (now at the Historical Society of Pennsylvania). A heavily chased tureen, reminiscent of the work of Samuel Kirk & Son of Baltimore, was published by Frank L. Schwarz.

References: Boultinghouse, *Silversmiths of Kentucky*, pp. 29, 30, for Akin. Diana Cramer, "Peter L. Krider, The Marks," *Silver* 21, no. 1 (January/February 1988): 31–33. *McElroy's Philadelphia City Directory for 1865. In Celebration of Fifty Years* (Philadelphia: Frank S. Schwarz & Son, 1980), no. 31.

❦ 375 a–f
BEAKERS, ca. 1860

(a) H. 3 9/16" (9.0 cm), DIAM. rim 3 1/4" (8.3 cm)
5 oz. 4 dwt. 20 gr. (163.0 g)
(b) H. 3 9/16" (9.0 cm), DIAM. rim 3 3/8" (8.6 cm)
5 oz. 4 dwt. 7 gr. (162.2 g)
(c) H. 3 9/16" (9.0 cm), DIAM. rim 3 5/16" (8.4 cm)
5 oz. 4 dwt. 16 gr. (162.8 g)
(d) H. 3 9/16" (9.0 cm), DIAM. rim 3 5/16" (8.4 cm)
5 oz. 7 dwt. 2 gr. (166.6 g)
(e) H. 3 11/16" (9.4 cm), DIAM. rim 3 1/4" (8.3 cm)
5 oz. 4 dwt. (161.9 g)
(f) H. 4" (10.2 cm), DIAM. rim 3 3/8" (8.6 cm)
5 oz. 2 dwt. 20 gr. (159.9 g)

Stamps: "∗P.L.K.∗" in roman letters, struck once on underside of each body. Accompanied by "STANDARD" and retailer's stamp "JOHN B. AKIN/ DANVILLE/ KY.". All in roman letters. All stamps incuse.

Description: cylindrical body with straight tapering sides and flat bottom; turn lines indicate that it was formed on a lathe by spinning; the chuck mark is visible. Molded rim and flared footring.

Spectrographic analysis:

	SILVER	COPPER	LEAD	GOLD
BODY SIDE (a)	90.3	9.1	0.20	0.11
BODY SIDE (b)	89.4	10.1	0.19	0.12
BODY SIDE (c)	90.8	8.8	0.21	0.06
BODY SIDE (d)	90.1	9.3	0.23	0.11
BODY SIDE (e)	89.0	10.4	0.26	0.06
BODY SIDE (f)	89.5	9.9	0.25	0.05

Provenance: H. F. du Pont.

Comments: Small beakers of this type were widely owned as personal items. Sets were often accompanied by large silver water pitchers, like the one owned by the J. B. Speed Museum in Louisville, Ky., which was made as a premium for the Kentucky State Agricultural Fair in 1859. Beakers too were commonly given as prizes at agricultural fairs and were sometimes referred to as calf tumblers, horse cups, or cattle cups. The term *julep cup* is a misnomer applied in the early twentieth century.

References: Fennimore, *Silver and Pewter*, no. 172. Letitia Hart Alexander, "The Myth of the Julep Cup," *Antiques* 8, no. 6 (December 1925): 364–65. Lockwood Barr, "Kentucky Silver and Its Makers," *Antiques* 48, no. 1 (July 1945): 25–27.

(a–d) 61.958.1–.4, (e, f) 61.1074, .1090 Gift of H. F. du Pont, 1965

376
BEAKER, ca. 1860

H. 3 ⅜" (9.2 cm), DIAM. rim 3 ⅜" (8.6 cm)
5 oz. 2 dwt. 11 gr. (159.0 g)

Stamps: "P. L. KRIDER/ STANDARD/ PHILADA" in roman letters, struck on underside of body. Accompanied by retailer's stamp: "JOHN B. AKIN/ DANVILLE/ KY." in roman letters. All stamps incuse.

Description: cylindrical body with straight tapering sides and flat bottom; turn lines indicate that it was formed on a lathe by spinning, but it also has a centerpunch on underside. Molded rim and molded footring integral with body.

Spectrographic analysis:

	SILVER	COPPER	LEAD	GOLD
BODY SIDE	90.9	8.9	0.12	0.06

Provenance: H. F. du Pont.

Comments: See no. 375.

References: See no. 375.

70.1088 Bequest of H. F. du Pont, 1969

John Letelier, Sr.

ca. 1750–?

John Letelier, Jr.

Philadelphia, Pennsylvania,
w. ca. 1770–93
Wilmington, Delaware, w. 1793–94
Chester County, Pennsylvania,
w. 1795–98
Wilmington, Delaware, w. 1799–1800
Washington, D.C., w. ca. 1802

John Letelier, Sr., appears in a Philadelphia advertisement in the January 29, 1770, issue of *Pennsylvania Chronicle* as "Goldsmith and Jeweller" on Second Street between Market and Chestnut streets, "next door to Captain Rankin's." In 1777, located on Market Street "nearly opposite the London Coffee-house," he advertised for a runaway "Negro wench named Nell," and in 1780 he offered watch crystals, main springs, and 35,000 shingles. The foregoing references undoubtedly refer to the father, as probably does an advertisement in the December 21, 1793, issue of *Delaware Gazette* for a John Letelier working in Wilmington on Market Street, "opposite Captain O'Flin's." He is said to have moved back to Philadelphia for a brief sojourn before turning up in Chester County, Pennsylvania, along with his son, from about 1795 to 1798. A John Leteleer, "farmer and silversmith," is listed on the Chester County tax lists, in West Marlboro township, in 1796. He owned 100 acres with an old log-and-stone house, an old log barn, and a shop. A freeman of the same name, also identified as a silversmith, lived at the same site. Both are listed again in 1798. They purportedly returned to Wilmington, but thereafter the record is ambiguous. A John la Teller, said to have been Wilmington's first dentist, was located in 1800 at what appears to be the same Market Street address. This business too was

moved to Philadelphia by the autumn of 1804. Abraham Dubois, Philadelphia merchant and silversmith, wrote to John Letelier twice in 1804 asking for payment for a turning lathe. In the letter of January 10, sent to Wilmington, Dubois suggested that the debt could be settled if Letelier made two creampots for him. "Let them be of the Urn kind[,] a large size with strong handles not to weigh above 5 oz to 5 oz 10 dwts." When this letter failed to elicit payment, or any other response, Dubois wrote him again in April. This letter was addressed to Washington City, where, Dubois learned, Letelier had moved. We do not know whether the debt was collected. A substantial quantity of silver bearing the Letelier name or initials survives. Most of it is in the Philadelphia neoclassical style and appears to have been made in the 1780s or 1790s. Sorting the silver by type of stamp, in order to distinguish between the work of the father and the son, has proven fruitless. No birth or death dates have been discovered for either Letelier.

References: Deborah Dependahl Waters, *Delaware Collections in the Museum of the Historical Society of Delaware* (Wilmington: Historical Society of Delaware, 1984), p. 75. Harrington, *Silversmiths of Delaware*, pp. 53–54. Hindes, "Delaware Silversmiths," pp. 275–76. Prime cards, Winterthur. Abraham Dubois letterbook, 1803–16, Hagley Museum and Library, Wilmington, Del.

377
CREAMER, ca. 1790

H. 6⁹⁄₁₆" (16.7 cm), w. 4⅝" (11.7 cm)
7 oz. 2 dwt. 12 gr. (221.1 g)

Stamps: "I•LT" in roman letters, in a rectangle, struck once on side of plinth.

Engraved on front of body below pouring lip: "ERT" in shaded foliate script.

Description: raised urn-shape lower body, high concave neck with flared rim and broad pouring lip; centerpunch inside body. Body joined to trumpet-shape pedestal mounted on a square plinth; sides of plinth applied. Applied beading around rim, top of lower body, and top of pedestal; integral beading around bottom of pedestal. High-loop handle cast as back-to-back C scrolls with a sprig and applied beading on upper top.

Spectrographic analysis:

	SILVER	COPPER	GOLD	LEAD
BODY SIDE	93.7	6.1	0.13	0.11
FOOT	94.6	5.2	0.11	0.10
HANDLE	96.3	3.6	0.07	0.10

Provenance: Mr. and Mrs. Harold J. Wilson, Oxford, Pa.; J. William and Jonathan Inslee, Downingtown, Pa.

83.86 Museum purchase in memory of Sally Moore from J. William and Jonathan Inslee, 1983

378
FLINT BOX, ca. 1780

L. 1 %16" (4.0 cm), w. 1 ³⁄₁₆" (3.0 cm), H. ⁵⁄₁₆"
(0.8 cm)
10 dwt. 14 gr. (16.5 g)

Stamps: "I•LT" in roman letters, in a rectangle,
struck twice on underside of lid.

Description: rectangular box with hinged flat
lid; sides formed from sheet silver, soldered to
a flat bottom; lid similarly made; 5-segment
hinge. Rectangular steel striker attached by 2
silver plates and 2 silver pins to side of box
below hinge; gilded interior; rollerwork decoration on top of lid and on underside of body.

Spectrographic analysis:

	SILVER	COPPER	LEAD	GOLD
UNDERSIDE	80.5	18.3	0.24	0.18
LID	80.1	18.2	0.22	0.15

Provenance: Joe Kindig, Jr., York, Pa., sold to
H. F. du Pont, August 1943.

Comments: Note the low silver content that is
often found in small wares such as this.

69.966 Bequest of H. F. du Pont, 1969

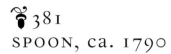

🜲 379
BOX, ca. 1780

L. 3 ¼" (8.3 cm), w. 2 ³⁄₁₆" (5.6 cm), H. ¹³⁄₁₆"
(2.1 cm)
1 oz. 19 dwt. 19 gr. (61.8 g)

Stamps: "I•LT" in roman letters, in a rectangle,
struck twice on underside of body.

Description: oval box with hinged lid; seamed
body has slightly bowed sides with sawtooth
engraved borders top and bottom; flat bottom
soldered to sides; no centerpunch. Slightly
domed lid with integral 5-segment hinge and
a silver pin; reinforcing band around underside with crenate-shape closing device; applied crescent over closing device.

Spectrographic analysis:

	SILVER	COPPER	LEAD	GOLD
LID	92.8	7.1	0.12	0.02
UNDERSIDE	92.4	7.4	0.12	0.04

Provenance: Mr. and Mrs. Stanley B. Ineson,
New York City; Mr. and Mrs. Alfred E. Bissell,
Wilmington, Del.

62.240.1712 Gift of Mr. and Mrs. Alfred E.
Bissell, 1965

🜲 380
SPOON, ca. 1780

L. 8 ⅜" (21.3 cm)
1 oz. 15 dwt. 14 gr. (55.2 g)

Stamps: "I•LT" in roman letters, in a rectangle,
struck twice on back of handle.

Engraved on back of handle: "S/ IA" in shaded
roman letters.

Description: elongated oval bowl with swage-
formed rounded drop and a bird perched on a
branch, holding a smaller branch in its beak;
rounded upturned handle with midrib.

Spectrographic analysis: Silver content is 89.5
percent.

Provenance: Mr. and Mrs. Stanley B. Ineson,
New York City; Mr. and Mrs. Alfred E. Bissell,
Wilmington, Del.

References: Belden, *Marks of American
Silversmiths*, p. 269.

62.240.1494 Gift of Mr. and Mrs. Alfred E.
Bissell, 1962–63

🜲 381
SPOON, ca. 1790

L. 9" (22.9 cm)
1 oz. 19 dwt. 5 gr. (60.8 g)

Stamps: "I. LE TELLIER" in roman letters, in a
conforming rectangle, struck once on back of
handle.

Engraved on front of handle: "SSH" in foliate
script.

Description: pointed oval bowl with swage-
formed pointed drop; downturned pointed
handle.

Spectrographic analysis: Silver content is 90.0
percent.

Provenance: Mr. and Mrs. Stanley B. Ineson,
New York City; Mr. and Mrs. Alfred E. Bissell,
Wilmington, Del.

Comments: Same stamp as on coffeepot and
teapot made for Thomas Kean (1747–1802)
and his wife, Mary, who lived in Wilmington,
Del. These pieces are now at the Historical
Society of Delaware, Wilmington.

References: Belden, *Marks of American
Silversmiths*, p. 269.

62.240.1253 Gift of Mr. and Mrs. Alfred E.
Bissell, 1962–63

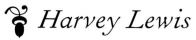

Harvey Lewis

ca. 1783–1835
w. ca. 1802–28

Lewis & Smith, w. 1805–ca. 1810
Philadelphia, Pennsylvania

The son of Curtis Lewis, a house carpenter, Harvey Lewis was probably apprenticed to Joseph Lownes. By 1802 he appeared in the tax records and by 1804 had taken his first apprentice, Henry Clark. The following year Lewis and Joseph Smith borrowed money from silversmith Joseph Richardson, Jr., to set up in business as partners. The partnership of Lewis & Smith lasted until about 1810. Thereafter Lewis was in business by himself. By March 1811 Lewis had built a new house, shop, and silversmith's wareroom on Second Street. He conducted his business there until 1818, when he removed to 143 Chestnut Street, the address shown in his pictorial advertisement in Joshua Shaw's *United States Directory* of 1822. In 1823 Lewis married Elizabeth Sellers, a cousin of Coleman Sellers, a longtime friend of Lewis. Sellers, married

to Charles Willson Peale's daughter Sophonisba, had named his third son Harvey Lewis Sellers (b. 1813). Starting about 1827, Lewis was plagued by illness, which continued until his death in 1835. He had, meanwhile, sold his business to Edward Lownes.

In 1822 Lewis was commissioned to make an elaborate vase for presentation to Frederick Graff, engineer of the Fairmount waterworks. Rich in iconography, if a bit awkward in design, the vase is now at the Historical Society of Pennsylvania. His best known work is the inkwell with supports of three winged sphinxes at Yale University Art Gallery. It is based on an ancient incense burner as interpreted by French goldsmiths of the Napoleonic era and English ceramic adaptations.

References: Philadelphia: Three Centuries, p. 267. Waters, "Philadelphia's Precious Metals Trades," pp. 46–48. Receipt for sale of flatware to Samuel Jarvis, 75x139, Downs collection, Winterthur.

382
CAKE BASKET, ca. 1820

L. 15 ¾" (40.0 cm), w. 10 ¹³⁄₁₆" (27.5 cm), H. 5 ¹³⁄₁₆" (14.8 cm)
51 oz. 1 dwt. 3 gr. (1588.0 g)

Stamps: "H. LEWIS" in roman letters, in a serrated rectangle, struck twice on underside of body.

Description: rectangular in plan with rounded corners, the raised body has a deep, curved well and broad flat angled rim; inner and outer edges of rim shaped to conform with applied

cast (or stamped and pitch-filled) gadrooned and floral borders; no centerpunch; 2 loop handles on short sides in form of double cornucopias with large floral motifs on either side and florets at corners. Raised concave pedestal on seamed base band; 4 feet cast in 2 parts as animal paws with flowers and leaves at knees.

Spectrographic analysis:

	SILVER	COPPER	LEAD	GOLD
BODY	94.2	5.2	0.16	0.15
BASE	93.8	5.6	0.28	0.14
HANDLE	95.5	4.2	0.18	0.08
FOOT	94.7	4.7	0.24	0.13

History: Tradition of ownership by the Wetherill family of Chalkley Hall, Frankford, Pa.

Provenance: Robert Carlen, Philadelphia.

Comments: A similar but larger basket with identical handles, also made by Lewis, was a bridal gift from Elizabeth Powell to her "great niece" Anne Francis. It was privately owned in 1976.

66.120 Museum purchase from Robert Carlen, 1966

383 a–e
SPOONS, ca. 1820

(a) L. 5 ⁹⁄₁₆" (14.1 cm), 7 dwt. 16 gr. (11.9 g)
(b) L. 5 ⁷⁄₁₆" (13.8 cm), 8 dwt. 7 gr. (12.9 g)
(c) L. 5 ½" (14.0 cm), 8 dwt. 9 gr. (13.0 g)
(d) L. 5 ½" (14.0 cm), 8 dwt. 13 gr. (13.3 g)
(e) L. 5 ½" (14.0 cm), 7 dwt. 12 gr. (11.6 g)

Stamps: "H. LEWIS" in roman letters, in a serrated rectangle, struck once on back of each handle.

Engraved on front of handle: "N" in foliate script.

Description: pointed oval bowl with swage-formed rounded drop; rounded downturned fiddle-shape handle with midrib.

Spectrographic analysis: Silver content ranges from 89.0 to 89.5 percent.

Provenance: Mrs. Duncan I. Selfridge, Wilmington, Del.

Comments: Of the 6 spoons given, 1 has since been deaccessioned.

69.200.1–.4, .6 Gift of Mrs. Duncan I. Selfridge, 1969

384
SPOON, ca. 1820

L. 7 ⁹⁄₁₆" (19.2 cm), 1 oz. 6 dwt. 23 gr. (41.9 g)

Stamp: "HARVEY.LEWIS" in roman letters, in a rectangle, struck once on back of handle.

Engraved on front of handle: "MC" in foliate script.

Description: pointed oval bowl with swage-formed rounded drop; downturned rounded fiddle-shape handle with midrib.

Spectrographic analysis: Silver content is 90.8 percent.

Provenance: Mr. and Mrs. Stanley B. Ineson, New York City; Mr. and Mrs. Alfred E. Bissell, Wilmington, Del.

References: Belden, *Marks of American Silversmiths*, p. 270.

62.240.1254 Gift of Mr. and Mrs. Alfred E. Bissell, 1962–63

385 a, b
SPOONS, 1805–10

(a) L. 9 ¹⁄₁₆" (23.0 cm), 1 oz. 17 dwt. 10 gr. (58.1 g)
(b) L. 8 ¹⁵⁄₁₆" (22.7 cm), 1 oz. 16 dwt. 23 gr. (57.4 g)

Stamps: "Lewis & Smith" in script, in a conforming surround, struck once on back of each handle. Accompanied by "WG" in roman letters, struck incuse.

Engraved on front of each handle: "MAC" in foliate script.

Description: elongated oval bowl with swage-formed rounded drop; rounded downturned handle.

Spectrographic analysis: Silver content ranges from 85.2 to 89.1 percent.

History: Engraved initials may refer to Mary Ann Corbit (1785–1828), niece of William Corbit, who married John Cowgill. The donor's wife, Susan Bowles Stickney, was a great-granddaughter of the Cowgills.

Provenance: P. W. Stickney, Evanston, Ill.

Exhibitions: On display at Corbit-Sharp House, Odessa, Del., for an unspecified period.

Comments: "WG" incuse stamp may possibly refer to John Ward Gethen, who usually used an "IWG" incuse stamp.

References: Belden, *Marks of American Silversmiths*, p. 189, for John Ward Gethen; p. 271, for Lewis.

67.280.1, .2 Gift of P. W. Stickney, 1967

Edward Lownes

1792–1834
Philadelphia, Pennsylvania

Edward Lownes, the son of Caleb Lownes, engraver and ironmonger, received his training in silversmithing from his uncle Joseph Lownes. By 1816 Edward had entered into partnership with Henry Irwin at 191 South Second Street. In 1817 Lownes was listed alone at 10 ½ South Third Street and in 1821 at 123 Chestnut Street. In 1824, along with Thomas Fletcher, Sidney Gardiner, and Harvey Lewis, he was one of the founding members of the Franklin Institute, which sponsored an annual exhibition of the "Products of National Industry" beginning that year. Lownes was one of the judges for the 1825 exhibition and an entrant himself in following years. Of the sixth exhibition, in 1830, the Committee on Premiums and Exhibitions noted: "We must not omit to mention the splendid display of silver plate from the workshops of Messrs. Thomas Fletcher, Edward Lownes, and R. and W. Wilson." Lownes worked in the currently fashionable styles, in particular the so-called round style, but he was also on the leading edge in producing examples of rococo revival silver. Two examples are the magnificent double-bellied, heavily chased coffeepot owned by Avis and Rockwell Gardner in 1972 and the Cadwalader tea kettle and stand described in the following entry.

References: Waters, "Philadelphia's Precious Metals Trades," pp. 45, 46, 48, 77, 78, 152, 164, 165.

386
KETTLE AND STAND, ca. 1830–34

H. (with handle up) 14 15/16" (37.9 cm), H. (with handle down) 12 13/16" (32.5 cm), w. 10 ½" (26.7 cm)
Kettle: 46 oz. 2 dwt. 2 gr. (1434.0 g)
Stand: 26 oz. 19 dwt. 9 gr. (838.8 g)

Stamps: "E•LOWNES" in roman letters, in a rectangle, struck twice on underside of kettle body. "E.LOWNES" in roman letters, in a rectangle, struck twice on underside of burner reservoir. Second set of stamps smaller than the first.

Engraved on side of body (with spout to right): an armorial device resembling a Maltese cross except that the lower arm is pointed instead of flared, tincture or, all over a curved heraldic band, which is over an assemblage of C scrolls, flowers, and leaves arranged asymmetrically in the rococo manner. *Engraved on side of body (with spout to left):* an asymmetrical blank cartouche of C scrolls, rocaille work, flowers, and leaves.

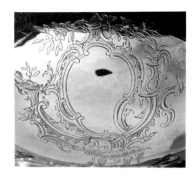

Description: raised circular form with bulbous upper body incurving down to smaller, nearly cylindrical lower body with a flat bottom; centerpunch on underside. Applied footring and applied overlapping ring to seat kettle in stand. Applied cast gadrooned molding forms rim and flange for seating lid. Circular raised domed lid, no bezel, has a bell-shape cast finial on a stepped base; lid attached on side with a flush-mounted 5-segment hinge. S-curve spout, cast in 2 vertical sections, has elaborate fluted base overlapping body with acanthus leaves and scrolls on its upper section. Elaborate hinged bail handle: hollow bow-shape grip with repoussé flowers and leaves on upper surface and flat chased leaves on underside; 2 vents on underside; handle legs are cast S curves with an acanthus leaf and beading on the outside, a spur inside, and scrolls at top and bottom that attach to cylindrical hinges with silver bolts; each hinge is attached to the body by a cast acanthus leaf.

The stand consists of a reeded circular ring that forms the seat for the kettle; below the ring is a skirt of cast gadrooned molding that is attached to a plain silver ring; attached to the outside of the plain ring are 3 equidistant sections of cast rococo openwork featuring C scrolls and leaves; between sections of the openwork ornament are the 3 legs, each cast in an S curve with scrolls, acanthus leaves, and sprigs and standing on a foot cast as an anthemion; upper end of each leg connected to body ring by a short C scroll; lower section of each leg connected to burner reservoir by strapwork with a scroll in the center. Burner in center was raised in 2 sections and has a band around the middle; lower body is double bellied; upper section is convex with a short cylindrical neck; single-scored line around outside of rim; circular burner cover made with a flange to sit on rim of reservoir; vertical cylindrical tube through center serves as wick holder.

Spectrographic analysis:

	SILVER	COPPER	LEAD	GOLD
BODY SIDE (KETTLE)	91.1	8.6	0.21	0.08
LID	94.1	5.6	0.17	0.10

	SILVER	COPPER	LEAD	GOLD
STAND HANDLE	93.6	6.0	0.20	0.09
RIM	95.2	4.0	0.35	0.13
LEG	94.2	4.8	0.33	0.13

History: Said by last private owner to have been made for Gen. Thomas (1779–1841) and Mary (Biddle) Cadwalader, who were married in 1804. Thomas was a Philadelphia lawyer who managed Penn family lands. He also served as lieutenant colonel of cavalry in the War of 1812 and later became major general of the Pennsylvania militia. The Cadwalader's son John (1805–79) became a renowned lawyer and jurist; their son George (1806–79) served as a general in the Mexican War and the Civil War.

Provenance: Thomas and Mary Cadwalader; descended to the estates of John Cadwalader Rowland and his sister Mrs. John L. Younger; their mother was the sister of John Cadwalader, Sr. Their heirs sold the kettle to Carl Williams, a Philadelphia dealer who, in turn, sold it to H. F. du Pont, May 1951.

Exhibitions: "Technological Innovation and the Decorative Arts," Hagley Museum, Wilmington, Del., 1973. "Tea: A Revolutionary Tradition," Fraunces Tavern Museum, New York City, 1980–81.

Comments: The arms are those of the Cadwalader family. The cast rococo decoration on the stand is very heavy and elaborate. Overall the kettle and stand partake strongly of the rococo style as it was practiced in the eighteenth century, with its careful modulation of plain and decorated surfaces. Rococo revival silver of the nineteenth century tends to underplay or ignore plain surfaces. The question of whether this piece represents survival or revival of the rococo style has often been raised. In my view it is clearly the former. Whatever its proper stylistic classification, it is a monumental piece of great beauty.

References: Fales, *American Silver*, no. 139. *DAB*, s.v. "Cadwalader, John." *The National Cyclopedia of American Biography*, 15 vols. (New York: J. T. White, 1893–1906), 12:269, for George Cadwalader and his father. Henry Simpson, *The Lives of Eminent Philadelphians Now Deceased* (Philadelphia: William Brotherhead, 1859), pp. 166–70, for Gen. Thomas Cadwalader. Sotheby Parke-Bernet, sale no. 3358 (April 28, 1972), lot 55, for a similar kettle and stand. *Technological Innovation and the Decorative Arts* (Wilmington, Del.: Eleutherian Mills–Hagley Foundation, 1973), no. 12.

51.50 Gift of H. F. du Pont, 1951

🥄 387
COVERED BOWL ON STAND, 1817–34

H. bowl 2 ⅜" (6.0 cm), DIAM. bowl 5 ¹³⁄₁₆" (14.6 cm), H. bowl (with lid) 3 ¹³⁄₁₆" (9.6 cm), DIAM. lid 5 ¹³⁄₁₆" (14.6 cm), H. stand 7 ¹⁄₁₆" (17.9 cm), DIAM. stand 6 ³⁄₁₆" (15.7 cm), H. stand (with covered bowl) 7 ⁹⁄₁₆" (19.2 cm), H. stand and covered bowl (handle up) 9 ³⁄₁₆" (23.3 cm) (all pieces) 16 oz. 7 dwt. 12 gr. (509.3 g)

Stamps: "E. LOWNES" in roman letters, in a rectangle, struck once on underside of bowl. Accompanied by incuse strike of fleur-de-lis with 3 stems below.

Scratched on underside of bowl and inside 1 leg of stand: "60806".

Description: raised circular bowl with flat bottom; lower body concave in profile; upper body straight in profile but tapering out toward rim; plain applied band inside rim; centerpunch on underside of body. Circular, friction-fit, slightly domed lid with a spherical finial; bezel; 3-legged stand consists of a circular frame with applied openwork and a large bail handle. Frame consists of 3 narrow circular bands to which all other parts are attached. Each leg is C curved in profile and convex in section; lower portion has applied stamped acanthus leaf and cloven hoof; upper portion consists of a stamped winged putto holding a bird in each hand, a floral swag and pointed shield below. Between each leg are 2 stamped decorative elements: upper one is a reclining female nude on a dolphin, the nude holding a paddle; lower one is a bearded male face on a stippled ground in a cartouche flanked by leaves with a shell and acanthus leaf below. Openwork handle is wide in the middle and tapers toward ends; contains 3 oval medallions, the center medallion chased with grapes and leaves, flanking ones chased with harps and masks; 2 silver pins connect shield-shape terminals to frame.

Spectrographic analysis:

	SILVER	COPPER	LEAD	GOLD
BOWL SIDE	93.5	6.2	0.18	0.13
BOWL SIDE	87.3	12.5	0.12	0.14
STAND HANDLE	77.6	22.1	0.22	0.06
STAND LEG	77.6	22.0	0.28	0.15
STAMPED FIGURE	76.6	23.2	0.17	0.05

Provenance: Michael Malley, East End Galleries, Pittsburgh.

Comments: Although the bowl was made by Lownes, the stand was probably imported from France. His inventory of 1834 includes "French stands," among other examples of imported French silver. These imports served as direct inspiration for silver made by Lownes and his contemporaries. The form is based on an ancient classical incense burner and is an example of archaeological classicism found in avant-garde American silver of the early nineteenth century. Note the low silver content of the stand as opposed to the bowl. The lid is extremely smooth and may have been formed by spinning, which raises the possibility that it may have been a later addition.

References: Fennimore, *Silver and Pewter*, no. 116. European Art and Antiques advertisement, *Antiques* 114, no. 6 (December 1978): 1245, for a tureen and stand by Martin Guillaume Biennais.

78.111 Museum purchase from Michael Malley, East End Galleries, 1978

☙ 388 a, b
SPOONS, 1817–34

(a) L. 6 ⅛" (15.6 cm)
14 dwt. 10 gr. (22.4 g)
(b) L. 8 ⅞" (22.5 cm)
1 oz. 18 dwt. 19 gr. (60.2 g)

Stamps: "E. LOWNES" in roman letters, in a serrated rectangle, struck once on back of each handle.

Engraved on front of handle: (a) "BRG" in foliate script; (b) "Corbit" in script.

Description: oval bowl with swage-formed rounded drops; rounded downturned fiddle-shape handle with midrib.

Spectrographic analysis: Silver content ranges from 87.1 to 87.3 percent.

History: (b) Probably owned by Corbit family of Odessa, Del.

Provenance: (a) Gebelein Silversmiths, Boston; (b) Mrs. Samuel F. Pryor III, Bedford Hills, N.Y.

References: Belden, *Marks of American Silversmiths*, p. 279.

(a) 70.308 Museum purchase from Gebelein Silversmiths, with funds from the Bissell Fund, 1970; (b) 86.6 Acquired in trade from Mrs. Samuel F. Pryor III, 1985

Joseph Lownes

1758–1820
Philadelphia, Pennsylvania

Born into a Quaker family, the son of John and Agnes Lownes, Joseph Lownes remained a practicing Quaker all his life. There is no record of his apprenticeship, but in all likelihood it was served with a Friend. In 1785 he married Esther Middleton of Crosswicks, New Jersey. In the same year he is listed in the first Philadelphia directory as a goldsmith on Front Street. By 1787 he had two apprentices, Samuel Williamson and Joseph Head, who was black. By this time Head had learned his craft well, for in the same year he showed a coffeepot of his own making to the Pennsylvania Abolition Society, which found him "a workman of distinguished abilities." During the last four years of Lownes's life, his son Josiah H. Lownes joined him as a business partner.

Lownes prospered from his shop work but even more so from his numerous investments in land and securities. He set the pattern for the entrepreneur silversmiths who followed. A large amount of his work survives, ranging in style from traditional rococo forms through the urn style and the many variants of the neoclassical style. One of his patrons was Elizabeth Willing Powell (1742–1830), widow of Samuel Powell. Another was Jacob Hiltzheimer, who recorded in his diary for March 29, 1794: "Before dinner took a walk down Third Street to South, then up Front Street and called on Lownes, the silversmith, and paid him for the six silver tankards which I had made for my children from the sale of my large ox." Looking back from 1860, Abraham Ritter recalled "Joseph Lowndes, though a prominent silversmith, was equally well known at No. 130 [Front St.], as an importer of China goods." Lownes's standing urn, now in the Hammerslough collection at Wadsworth Atheneum, was awarded to Capt. William Anderson by the Marine Insurance Office

of Philadelphia for staving off capture by a French privateer in 1799. Incorporated into the urn are features that we tend to think of as somewhat later, such as a cast lion mask and the cast eagle finial. Lownes's trade card is owned by the American Antiquarian Society.

References: Extracts from the Diary of Jacob Hiltzheimer of Philadelphia, 1765–1798 (Philadelphia: Press of Wm. F. Fell, 1893), p. 204. *Philadelphia: Three Centuries*, p. 187. Abraham Ritter, *Philadelphia and Her Merchants, as Constituted Fifty and Seventy Years Ago* (Philadelphia, 1860), p. 186. Waters, "Philadelphia's Precious Metals Trades," pp. 43, 46–48, 82, 119, 162–63, 170.

389
TANKARD, ca. 1800

H. 5 ⁵⁄₁₆" (13.5 cm), DIAM. base 3 ⁹⁄₁₆" (9.0 cm), W. 5 ¹¹⁄₁₆" (14.5 cm)
18 oz. 15 dwt. 9 gr. (583.8 g)

Stamps: "J•Lownes" in script, in a conforming surround, struck twice on underside of body.

Scratched on underside of base: "E 13086"; "61"; "D/ BC[?]".

Description: seamed cylindrical body with straight, slightly tapered sides and flat inset bottom; applied molded rim; wide bands of horizontal reeding around upper and lower body;

lower edge of body forms footring, centerpunch on underside. Flat lid, slightly domed in center; extended lip with V notch in front; 3 concentric scored lines circling dome; no centerpunch. Rectangular cast thumbpiece with incurving sides, wavy top, and 4 vertical voids; attached to 2 hinge arms pinned through handle and mounted flush with top of handle. Seamed hollow handle in back-to-back C scrolls. No vents.

Spectrographic analysis:

	SILVER	COPPER	LEAD	GOLD
BODY SIDE	93.1	6.8	0.13	0.05
UNDERSIDE	93.4	6.5	0.14	0.05
LID	92.6	7.2	0.15	0.06
HANDLE	93.1	6.7	0.10	0.02

Provenance: Robert Ensko, Inc., New York City, sold to H. F. du Pont prior to 1951.

Comments: This streamlined version of the tankard form was both new and old at the time of its fabrication. A flat-top tankard with straight tapering sides with 2 bands of scoring was made in London as early as 1626. A more cylindrical version came into vogue in the late eighteenth century, usually incorporating a pierced thumbpiece, and this was the final form assumed by the tankard before it disappeared altogether. Joseph Lownes made several like these, among which is the "hooped" tankard in the Green Tree collection at the Mutual Assurance Company that was presented to Capt. John C. Brevoor for recapturing his own ship after it had been taken by a French privateer in 1798.

References: Fales, *American Silver*, no. 119. Fennimore, *Silver and Pewter*, no. 158. Anthony N. B. Garvan and Carol A. Wojtowicz, *Catalogue of the Green Tree Collection* (Philadelphia: Mutual Assurance Company, 1977), pp. 94–95, for similar form by Lownes. *Octagon* 26, no. 2 (Autumn 1989): 46, for a Charles I example of the form.

61.615 Gift of H. F. du Pont, 1965

390
TEAPOT, ca. 1810

H. (with lid) 10 ⅞" (27.6 cm), w. 10 ¹¹⁄₁₆" (27.2 cm)
24 oz. 16 dwt. 6 gr. (771.7 g)

Stamps: "J Lownes" in script, in a conforming surround, struck 4 times on underside of foot, once in each corner.

Scratched on underside of foot: "4011"; "1111".

Description: raised urn-shape lower body, gadrooned all around on lower half, joined to stepped-and-incurved upper body by an applied molded band with beading; flared rim has beading on outside and an applied band on inside; body perforated at spout to serve as strainer; centerpunch on underside of body. Trumpet-shape pedestal mounted on a square foot; beading at top and bottom of pedestal. Raised, circular, trumpet-shape, friction-fit lid, stepped and incurved up to knop; cast urn-and-ball finial; beading around step, knop, and finial; bezel; no vent. Paneled S-curve spout with applied anthemion on upper end. C-curve hardwood handle with sprig; cylindrical sockets with beaded rims and silver pins.

Spectrographic analysis:

	SILVER	COPPER	LEAD	GOLD
BODY SIDE	90.1	9.7	0.14	0.08
FOOT	89.4	10.2	0.20	0.15
SPOUT	91.9	7.8	0.21	0.09
LID	89.3	10.4	0.15	0.09

Provenance: Marshall P. Blankarn, New York City.

78.137 Gift of Marshall P. Blankarn, 1978

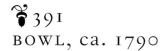

391
BOWL, ca. 1790

H. 5 ⁵⁄₁₆" (13.5 cm), DIAM. rim 6 ¼" (15.9 cm)
15 oz. 9 dwt. 18 gr. (481.7 g)

Stamps: "J Lownes" in script, in a conforming surround, struck twice on underside of foot.

Engraved on side of body: "JMC" in foliate script. Letters are formed by rollerwork and enhanced by engraving. *Scratched on underside of foot:* "oz 15 dwt 12".

Description: raised circular body with applied molded and beaded rim; centerpunch on underside of body. Body mounted on pedestal, flaring to a circular plinth that becomes a square foot; beading around top and bottom of pedestal.

Spectrographic analysis:

	SILVER	COPPER	GOLD	LEAD
BODY SIDE	91.7	8.0	0.19	0.15
FOOT	94.4	5.5	0.05	0.05

Provenance: Marshall P. Blankarn, New York City.

78.142 Gift of Marshall P. Blankarn, 1978

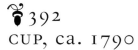

392
CUP, ca. 1790

H. 4" (10.2 cm)
6 oz. 3 dwt. 5 gr. (191.6 g)

Stamps: "J Lownes" in script, in a conforming surround, struck twice on underside of body.

Engraved on body opposite handle: "ML" in foliate script. *Engraved on underside of body:* "E•G/ to/ M•L" in shaded roman letters and script.

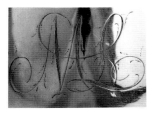

Description: raised circular bowl-like form with flat bottom, slightly domed in center; center-punch on underside. Applied beaded rim and footring. High C-curve strap handle with beaded edges flanking a groove; oval curved thumbpiece applied to top of handle.

Spectrographic analysis:

	SILVER	COPPER	LEAD	GOLD
BODY SIDE	91.7	8.0	0.16	0.13
UNDERSIDE	96.2	3.6	0.19	0.04
HANDLE	92.7	7.1	0.12	0.05

History: Initials "ML" refer to Mordecai Lewis (1748–99), a Philadelphia merchant who owned or managed 7 ships, most of which were engaged in the East India trade. At one point his firm included William Bingham. Lewis's counting house was at 112 S. Front St. (Lownes was at 130 S. Front St.). He married Hannah Saunders, daughter of merchant Joseph Saunders, in 1772, following a trip to Europe. Through his wife he was related to Thomas Morris and Samuel Coates, who served as executors of his estate. In his will, witnessed March 19, 1799, he bequeathed "to my beloved wife Hannah Lewis all and singular my household furniture, plate, wearing apparel, provisions, utensils, necessaries and conveniences." Lewis was a director of the Bank of North America, the Philadelphia Contributionship, the Library Company of Philadelphia, and Pennsylvania Hospital.

Provenance: Ronald Bourgeault Antiques, Hampton, N.H.

Comments: The cup appears to have been a small bowl to which a handle was added at a later date.

References: Henry Simpson, *The Lives of Eminent Philadelphians Now Deceased* (Philadelphia: William Brotherhead, 1859), pp. 652–55. Philadelphia wills, 1799, no. 127.

86.45 Museum purchase from Ronald Bourgeault Antiques, 1986

393 a–h
SPOONS, 1780–1820

(a) L. 9 ⅛" (23.2 cm), 1 oz. 18 dwt. (59.0 g)
(b) L. 9 ⅛" (23.2 cm), 1 oz. 15 dwt. 18 gr. (55.5 g)
(c) L. 9 ¼" (23.5 cm), 1 oz. 14 dwt. 23 gr. (54.3 g)
(d) L. 9 ½" (24.1 cm), 1 oz. 17 dwt. 7 gr. (57.9 g)
(e) L. 9 ¼" (23.5 cm), 1 oz. 14 dwt. 5 gr. (63.1 g)
(f) L. 8 ¹³⁄₁₆" (22.4 cm), 2 oz. 2 dwt. 22 gr.
(66.6 g)
(g) L. 8 ¹¹⁄₁₆" (22.1 cm), 1 oz. 17 dwt. (57.4 g)
(h) L. 2 ¹⁵⁄₁₆" (7.5 cm), 7 dwt. 4 gr. (11.1 g)

Stamps: "J Lownes" in script, in a conforming surround, struck once on back of each handle.

Engraved on front of handle: (a–e) "M" in foliate script; (g) "MM" in foliate script, in a bright-cut medallion with floral pendant drop and bright-cut border. No engraving on handles (f, h).

Description: (a–e) oval bowl with swage-formed rounded drop with molded double arch; rounded downturned handle with midrib; (f, g) oval bowl with swage-formed rounded drop; rounded downturned handle with midrib; (h) a caddy spoon with bowl in form of a 17-lobe scallop shell; flat shieldlike handle with beveled edges outlined in rollerwork.

Spectrographic analysis: Silver content ranges from 88.9 to 90.9 percent.

History: (a–e) Tradition of ownership by Robert Morris (1733–1806), the so-called financier of the Revolution.

Provenance: (a–e) Mrs. Duncan I. Selfridge, Wayne, Pa.; (f–h) Mr. and Mrs. Stanley B. Ineson, New York City; Mr. and Mrs. Alfred E. Bissell, Wilmington, Del.

Exhibitions: (h) Metropolitan Museum of Art, New York City, 1938–61.

References: Belden, *Marks of American Silversmiths*, p. 279. *DAB*, s.v. "Morris, Robert." (h) Fennimore, *Silver and Pewter*, no. 36.

(a–c) 69.12.1–.3 Gift of Mrs. Duncan I. Selfridge, 1969; (d, e) 62.80.1, .2 Gift of Mrs. Duncan I. Selfridge, 1962; (f–h) 62.240.1274, .1275, .818 Gift of Mr. and Mrs. Alfred E. Bissell, 1962–63

394 a–d
SPOONS AND TONGS, ca. 1790

(a) L. 5 ¾" (14.6 cm), 9 dwt. 18 gr. (15.2 g)
(b) L. 3 ⅝" (9.2 cm), 5 dwt. 19 gr. (9.0 g)
(c) L. 7" (17.8 cm), 1 oz. 10 dwt. 11 gr. (31.8 g)
(d) L. 6 ³⁄₁₆" (15.7 cm), 1 oz. 13 dwt. 23 gr.
(52.7 g)

Stamps: "J•Lownes" in script, in a conforming surround, struck on back of handles (a–c) and once inside each arm of (d).

Engraved on front of handle: (a) "IAR"; (b) "LC"; (c) "RSH". *Engraved on bow:* (d) "SR" in a bright-cut medallion with pendant drop and bright-cut border on each arm. All initials in foliate script.

Description: (a–c) oval bowl with swage-formed rounded drop; rounded downturned handle with midrib; (d) U-shape form with bow back, fiddle-shape arms, and oval spoon grips.

Spectrographic analysis: Silver content ranges from 90.0 to 91.6 percent.

Provenance: Mr. and Mrs. Stanley B. Ineson, New York City; Mr. and Mrs. Alfred E. Bissell, Wilmington, Del.

References: Belden, *Marks of American Silversmiths*, p. 279.

62.240.399, .799, .1273, .1655 Gift of Mr. and Mrs. Alfred E. Bissell, 1962–63

John Lynch

1761–1848
Baltimore, Maryland

Nothing is known of John Lynch's origins or training. On the basis of the harp stamp that sometimes accompanies his name stamp, it has been suggested that he came from Ireland. There was heavy Irish immigration into Maryland in the 1770s —in one two-week period in 1773 some 3,500 arrived in Baltimore—and Lynch might have been one of them. He first appears in the records as a silversmith in 1786, when he purchased a lot on Lexington Street near Howard Street. In 1796 he was on Boundary Street and in 1800 on Howard Street, but from 1801 on, he was located on Franklin Street. In 1804 he married Naomi Willey. He died in 1848 in his eighty-sixth year after having been a silversmith, jeweler, and clockmaker for at least sixty-two years. Most of Lynch's work was in the various neoclassical styles that we associate with the period 1785 to about 1830. In 1815 he joined nineteen other "manufacturers & Venders of Silver Ware in the City of Baltimore" to protest the Assay Act, not so much because they feared having their work subjected to scrutiny but because of the levy of 6¢ per ounce on all silver sold or manufactured in the city. Notwithstanding, in 1818 he had 495 ounces of silver assayed.

References: Goldsborough, *Eighteenth- and Nineteenth-Century Maryland Silver*, pp. 54–57. Goldsborough, *Silver in Maryland*, pp. 167–69. Pleasants and Sill, *Maryland Silversmiths*, pp. 158–60, pl. 34.

☙395 a, b
CANDLESTICKS, ca. 1800

(a) H. 9 ⅛" (23.2 cm)
14 oz. 3 dwt. 8 gr. (440.7 g)
(b) H. 9 ¹⁄₁₆" (23.0 cm)
12 oz. 19 dwt. 11 gr. (403.5 g)

Stamps: "I•L" in roman letters, in a rectangle, struck once on side of each base.

Description: square 1-piece cast base with ga-drooned edges; incurved up to reeded pedestal topped by a square plinth; 2-part cast shaft: lower end tapered toward base, looks like a banded bundle of reeds under a plain circular knop scribed with 3 pairs of lines; plain incurved neck of shaft supports reeded-and-banded socket with flared molded rim; inset with circular drip pan with a molded edge.

Spectrographic analysis:

	SILVER	COPPER	LEAD	GOLD
(a)				
BASE	84.2	14.8	0.30	0.15
SHAFT	91.3	7.8	0.32	0.17
(b)				
BASE	89.0	10.1	0.36	0.15
SHAFT	91.3	7.8	0.36	0.16

Provenance: David Stockwell, Philadelphia, sold to H. F. du Pont, December 1949.

Exhibitions: "Silver in Maryland," Maryland Historical Society, Baltimore, 1983–84.

References: Fales, *American Silver*, no. 116. Goldsborough, *Silver in Maryland*, no. 214.

Comments: Goldsborough notes that 2 more identical pairs are known, 1 possibly by Daniel You of Charleston, suggesting that the form was based on a popular British model.

59.676.1, .2 Bequest of H. F. du Pont, 1969

☙396 a, b
BEAKERS, 1790–1840

(a) H. 3 ⁹⁄₁₆" (9.0 cm), DIAM. rim 3 ³⁄₁₆" (8.1 cm)
3 oz. 10 dwt. 16 gr. (109.9 g)
(b) H. 3 ⁹⁄₁₆" (9.0 cm), DIAM. rim 3 ³⁄₁₆" (8.1 cm)
3 oz. 12 dwt. 1 gr. (112.1 g)

Stamps: "[I LY]NCH" on (a); "I LYN[CH]" on (b); both in roman letters, in a rectangle, struck once on underside of each base. Possibly a pellet after the "I."

Description: raised cylindrical body with slightly bowed tapering sides and flat bottom; center-punch on underside; small molded rim and footring.

Spectrographic analysis:

	SILVER	COPPER	LEAD	GOLD
(a)				
BODY SIDE	87.3	11.9	0.31	0.19
UNDERSIDE	92.2	7.3	0.26	0.16
(b)				
BODY SIDE	88.0	11.4	0.31	0.17
UNDERSIDE	93.1	6.4	0.26	0.20

Provenance: How of Edinburgh, Ltd., London; Eric-Douglas sale, Parke-Bernet Galleries, New York City, sold to H. F. du Pont, 1949.

Comments: Beakers are relatively timeless and, therefore, virtually impossible to date within the broad time span of Lynch's career.

References: Parke-Bernet Galleries, Eric-Douglas sale (December 2, 1949), lot 74.

61.959.1, .2 Gift of H. F. du Pont, 1965

❦ 397
SPOON, 1830–35

L. 8 15⁄16" (22.7 cm)
2 oz. 2 dwt. 19 gr. (66.4 g)

Stamps: "J•LYNCH" in roman letters, in a serrated rectangle, struck once on back of handle. Accompanied by stamps: "pillars of Hercules"; roman "D"; and a spread-winged eagle, all in squares with canted corners.

Description: pointed oval bowl with swage-formed rounded drop; rounded downturned handle with midrib.

Spectrographic analysis: Silver content is 91.3 percent.

Provenance: William J. Flather III, Washington, D.C.

Comments: The 3 smaller stamps were used by the Baltimore assay office from about 1830 to 1835. The "D" is thought to indicate that the silver was equal in fineness to Spanish dollars.

References: Patrick M. Duggan, "Marks on Baltimore Silver, 1814–1860: An Exploration," in Goldsborough, *Silver in Maryland*, pp. 26–37.

86.38 Gift of William J. Flather III, 1986

❦ 398
SPOON, ca. 1830

L. 8 ⅝" (21.9 cm)
2 oz. (62.2 g)

Stamps: "I LYNCH" in roman letters, in a rectangle, struck once on back of handle. Accompanied by an eagle's head in a rectangle.

Engraved on front of handle: "G" in foliate script.

Description: oval bowl with swage-formed rounded drop; downturned handle with midrib.

Spectrographic analysis: Silver content is 89.4 percent.

Provenance: William J. Flather III, Washington, D.C.

References: Duggan, "Marks on Baltimore Silver, 1814–1860: An Exploration," in Goldsborough, *Silver in Maryland*, pp. 26–37.

86.69 Gift of William J. Flather III, 1986

❦ 399
SPOON, ca. 1790–1840

L. 7 ⅛" (18.1 cm)
17 dwt. 9 gr. (27.0 g)

Stamps: "I•LYNCH" in roman letters, in a rectangle, struck once on back of handle.

Engraved on front of handle: "EAR" in foliate script.

Description: oval bowl with swage-formed rounded drop; rounded downturned handle.

Spectrographic analysis: Silver content is 92.5 percent.

Provenance: Margo Antiques, St. Louis.

69.22 Museum purchase, with funds from the Bissell Fund, from Margo Antiques, 1969

❦ 400 a–e
SPOONS AND TONGS, 1790–1840

(a) L. 5 ⅞" (14.9 cm)
8 dwt. 6 gr. (12.8 g)
(b) L. 5 ⅞" (14.9 cm)
8 dwt. 12 gr. (13.2 g)
(c) L. 5 ½" (14.0 cm)
8 dwt. 4 gr. (12.7 g)
(d) L. 3 13⁄16" (9.7 cm)
3 dwt. 20 gr. (6.0 g)
(e) L. 6 ⅞" (17.5 cm)
1 oz. 3 dwt. 15 gr. (36.7 g)

Stamps: "I•L" in roman letters, in a rectangle, struck once on back of handles (a–d) and once inside each arm of (e).

Engraved on front of handle: (a) "ETB" in foliate script, in a conforming bright-cut border with pendant drop; (b) "WRW" in foliate script, in a conforming bright-cut border with pendant drop; (c) "A•M•C" in shaded roman letters, in a conforming bright-cut border with a floral drop; (d) "SH" (sideways) in foliate script. *Engraved on bowback:* (e) "AT" in foliate script, in a bright-cut rectangular medallion with pendant drops on each side.

Description: (a, b) pointed oval bowl with swage-formed rounded drop; rounded downturned fiddle-shape handle with midrib; (c) pointed oval bowl with swage-formed pointed drop; downturned coffin-end handle; (d) wide oval bowl with drop; rounded downturned handle with midrib; (e) U-shape form with bow back, fiddle-shape arms, and wide oval spoon grips.

Spectrographic analysis: Silver content ranges from 86.2 to 91.6 percent.

Provenance: Mr. and Mrs. Stanley B. Ineson, New York City; Mr. and Mrs. Alfred E. Bissell, Wilmington, Del.

(a–d) 62.240.378–.380, .801 Gift of Mr. and Mrs. Alfred E. Bissell, 1962–63; (e) 62.240.1649 Gift of Mr. and Mrs. Alfred E. Bissell, 1965

Seraphim Masi

Washington, D.C., w. ca. 1822–52

Seraphim Masi advertised in the 1822 Washington directory as a "Watch Maker & Jeweller" who sold silver work, spectacles, and "a variety of other fancy goods." Most of what we know about him occurred during the 1820s. A chalice, paten, and baptismal bowl bearing the "S. MASI" stamp were presented to Christ Church in 1826. (They were still owned by the church in 1979.) In 1827 he had in his employ watchmaker Jacob Leonard. A spur with Masi's stamp, owned by Wilmer McLean (at whose house in Appomattox, Virginia, Lee surrendered to Grant) is now owned by Appomattox County Courthouse National Historical Park. More important for the following entries is that in 1825 Masi was paid $100 for a die of the great seal of the United States, and he is known to have made a number of skippets (boxes to hold wax seals) for the State Department. The last known commission was in 1852 for the skippet and rosewood box carried by Commodore Perry when he went to Japan. Masi is known to have placed his stamp on silver made by others. A coffeepot and teapot, now in the DAR Museum and probably made by Fletcher & Gardiner, bear the Baltimore pillars stamp, a Baltimore date letter, and Masi's stamp. Masi appears in the Washington directories for 1830 and 1843 on Pennsylvania Avenue. He placed display ads in the back of the directories for 1822 and 1830.

References: Joan Sayers Brown, "Skippets," *Antiques* 114, no. 1 (July 1978): 140–41. Edith Gaines, "Collectors' Notes," *Antiques* 103, no. 2 (February 1973): 365. Goldsborough, *Silver in Maryland,* p. 170. Debra A. Hashim, "American Silver at the DAR Museum," *Antiques* 117, no. 3 (March 1980): 634–41. Karen M. Jones, "Collectors' Notes," *Antiques* 112, no. 1 (July 1977): 84–85. *Washington City Directory* (William Duncan, 1822; S. A. Elliott, 1830; Anthony Reintzel, 1843).

401 a, b
SKIPPETS, ca. 1825–52

(a) DIAM. 5 1/16" (12.9 cm), H. 1 7/16" (3.7 cm)
Lid: 9 oz. 5 dwt. 7 gr. (287.5 g)
Box with cords: 14 oz. 10 dwt. 14 gr. (450.9 g)
(b) DIAM. 5 1/16" (12.9 cm), H. 1 3/8" (3.5 cm)
Lid: 8 oz. 9 dwt. 15 gr. (263.2 g)
Box: 10 oz. 1 dwt. 5 gr. (312.2 g)

Stamps: None. Attribution based on circumstantial evidence; see *Comments.*

Description: circular box with friction-fit lid. Body sides formed from 2 pieces of seamed sheet silver, the inside piece rising to form a bezel to receive lid; flat bottom consists of 2 pieces of sheet silver; applied molded base ring; no centerpunch on (a), centerpunch inside on (b). Lid sides formed from a single sheet of seamed silver with 2 small circular holes, 1 on either side, for seal cord; top consists of 2 pieces of sheet silver, the upper piece stamped with a relief image of the seal of the United States; applied molding joins top and sides. Cord attached through body; red wax seal removable on (a).

Spectrographic analysis:

	SILVER	COPPER	LEAD	GOLD
(a)				
LID	91.9	7.9	0.16	0.05
BODY	92.2	7.6	0.19	0.05
(b)				
LID	91.7	7.8	0.28	0.06
BODY	91.6	8.0	0.31	0.08

Provenance: (a) John Kenneth Danby, Wilmington, Del.; sold through Parke-Bernet sale of Danby estate, 1956; (b) probably sold by Robert Ensko, Inc., New York City, to H. F. du Pont, June 1935.

Exhibitions: (a) "A Celebration of Work: Craftsmen in the District of Columbia, 1790–1860," DAR Museum, Washington, D.C., 1991–92.

Comments: Commonly called seal boxes, the correct term for this form is *skippet.* They were intended to hold the wax seal attached by a cord to a treaty negotiated by the Department of State. While he was in Paris in 1783, John Adams was impressed by the British minister's commission: "very magnificent, the Great Seal in a Silver Box with the Kings Arms engraven on it, with two large gold Tassels &c. as usual." The first known American skippet was made for the Treaty of Ghent, which ended the War of 1812. It was made by Charles A. Burnet of

Georgetown, D.C., and is now in the Public Record Office, London. It was made to contain a 2 ½" seal. Several silversmiths including Masi are recorded as having made skippets. Although Burnet stamped his skippet, most have no makers' stamps. It is, therefore, impossible to attribute them with certainty. In Masi's favor, however, is the fact that, in 1825, he made a die that was 4 ¹¹/₁₆" in diameter for the Great Seal of the United States. Known as the "Old Treaty Seal," according to Joan Sayers Brown, it was used on all pendent seals until 1871. It was made to impress the wax, but its size suggests that it might also have been used to emboss the lids that would then have been finished by chasing. In 1871 Secretary of State Hamilton Fish decreed there would be no more metallic seal boxes. Because the form shows no discernible pattern of change over time, dating them remains difficult. The lids are interchangeable on these 2 skippets.

References: (a) Fales, *American Silver*, no. 128. Fennimore, *Silver and Pewter*, no. 198. Joan Sayers Brown, "Skippets," *Antiques* 114, no. 1 (July 1978): 140–41. Parke-Bernet Galleries, sale no. 1722, Danby estate sale (December 14, 1956), lot 285. Lyman C. Butterfield et al., eds., *Diary and Autobiography of John Adams*, 4 vols. (Cambridge: Belknap Press of Harvard University Press, 1961), 3:120.

(a) 56.98.1 Museum purchase from Parke-Bernet Galleries, 1956; (b) 57.1419 Gift of H. F. du Pont, 1965

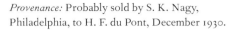

402
SKIPPET, ca. 1825–52

DIAM. 5 ⅛" (13.0 cm), H. 1 ½" (3.8 cm)
Lid: 9 oz. 11 dwt. 21 gr. (297.7 g)
Box: 11 oz. 15 dwt. 4 gr. (364.9 g)

Stamps: None. Attribution based on circumstantial evidence; see *Comments* in no. 401.

Scratched on underside of body and lid: what appears to be a roman "N" inside a parallelogram.

Description: circular box with friction-fit lid; body sides formed from 2 pieces of seamed sheet silver, the inside piece rising to form a bezel to receive lid; flat bottom consists of 2 pieces of sheet silver; fine gadrooned border inside applied molded base ring; centerpunch on underside. Lid sides formed from a single sheet of seamed silver with 2 small circular holes, 1 on either side, for seal cord; top consists of 2 pieces of sheet silver, the upper piece stamped and chased with the relief image of the seal of the United States; fine gadrooned border around top edge with an inner border of 24 equidistant stars in relief on a stippled ground; narrow inner border in rope motif; centerpunch inside.

Spectrographic analysis:

	SILVER	COPPER	GOLD	LEAD
LID TOP	99.1	0.75	0.31	0.06
LID INSIDE	89.6	9.4	0.24	0.59
BODY	85.9	12.9	0.18	0.68

Provenance: Probably sold by S. K. Nagy, Philadelphia, to H. F. du Pont, December 1930.

Comments: Although this skippet is similar to the 2 in no. 401, it is not identical. The lid is exceptionally heavy, and its irregularities suggest more hand chasing. Some people have attempted to date skippets using the hoary tradition of correlating the number of stars in the border with the number of states. Regrettably, this does not work; skippets with the same number of stars in their borders are documented for 1839 and 1851. An earlier skippet, used for pendant seals from 1782 until 1825, had a seal 2 ½" in diameter and also had the 24 stars. One of these, owned by the Library Company of Philadelphia, is attached to the Slave Trade Convention of 1824 with Great Britain. A larger box, for which Masi made the die in 1825 and which has no stars, was presumably used for an 1856 treaty with the Netherlands. Although this die was supposedly used until 1871, it was not used exclusively, as the boxes with stars from 1839 and 1851 demonstrate. There is, then, no way of dating these boxes more precisely than between 1825 and 1871. Portions of the lid are almost pure silver, which may suggest a later date or, possibly, electroplating.

References: Joan Sayers Brown, "Skippets," *Antiques* 114, no. 1 (July 1978): 140–41.

57.1420 Gift of H. F. du Pont, 1965

403
SPOON, ca. 1830

L. 8 ½" (21.6 cm), 1 oz. 13 dwt. 1 gr. (52.0 g)

Stamps: "S MASI" in roman letters, in a rectangle, struck once on back of handle.

Engraved on front of handle: "BMG" in foliate script.

Description: pointed oval bowl with swage-formed rounded drop; rounded downturned fiddle-shape handle with midrib.

Spectrographic analysis: Silver content is 89.0 percent.

Provenance: William J. Flather III, Washington, D.C.

Comments: A similar spoon in a private collection has the Masi stamp with a period after the "S."

85.25 Gift of William J. Flather III, 1985

Charles Maysenhoelder

Philadelphia, Pennsylvania, w. 1810–25

Charles Maysenhoelder appears in Philadelphia directories from 1810 to 1825, and in 1824 he was at 54 Chestnut Street. In 1991 the Philadelphia Museum of Art acquired an elaborate tea service with his stamp. This is the only known hollowware by this maker, aside from the box in the following entry.

References: Brix, *Philadelphia Silversmiths*, p. 70.

🐝 404
BOX, ca. 1815

L. 2 11/16" (6.9 cm), W. 1 9/16" (4.0 cm), H. 13/16" (2.1 cm)
1 oz. 15 dwt. 20 gr. (55.6 g)

Stamps: "C. MAYSENHOELDER" and "PHILADA." in roman letters, both in rectangles, struck once on underside of body; "STERLING" in sans serif letters, struck incuse on bezel.

Scratched inside body in corner: "4".

Description: rectangular box with hinged lid; seamed straight sides with bezel; flat bottom and lid; top and bottom plates overlap body. Lid decorated with anthemia at corners with wheelwork between at edge; 7-segment hinge with silver pin runs length of body. Interior and bezel gilded.

Spectrographic analysis:

	SILVER	COPPER	LEAD	GOLD
UNDERSIDE	87.6	12.2	0.13	0.12
LID	98.3	1.4	0.00	0.37

Provenance: H. F. du Pont.

Comments: Sterling stamp and high silver content of lid indicate that it was replaced at a much later date.

69.1473 Bequest of H. F. du Pont, 1969

🐝 405
SPECTACLES, ca. 1815

W. 4 ¾" (12.1 cm), Min. L. of temple 4 ½" (11.4 cm), Max. L. of temple 5 ⅞" (14.9 cm)
Weight not included because of lenses.

Stamps: "C. MAYSENHOELDER" and "PHILADA." in roman letters, both in rectangles, struck once on inside of right temple.

Description: oval frames connected by arched bridge; magnifying clear lenses; 2 large cast 3-segment hinges, middle section integral with temple; metal pin and screws either side; 2 2-piece temples connected by slide.

Spectrographic analysis:

	SILVER	COPPER	LEAD	GOLD
TEMPLE	93.2	6.6	0.17	0.07

Provenance: Forge Antiques, Downingtown, Pa.

References: Malcolm Watkins, "Antique Spectacles," *Antiques* 54, no. 6 (December 1948): 429–31. Jerome Redfearn, "American Silver and Gold Spectacles of the Nineteenth Century," pt. 1, *Silver* 18, no. 6 (November/December 1985): 8–12, for general background.

77.121 Museum purchase from Forge Antiques, 1977

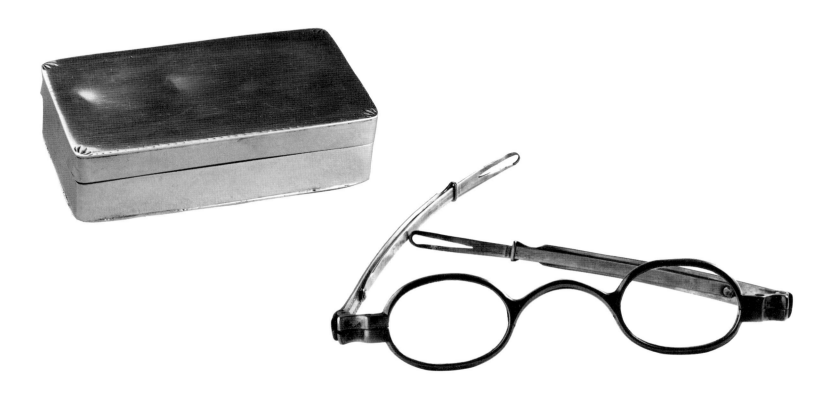

🐝 John McAllister

1753–1830

McAllister & Matthews, w. 1798–1811
John McAllister & Son, w. 1811–?
Philadelphia, Pennsylvania

John McAllister, born in Glasgow, came to New York in 1775 at age twenty-two. Ten years later he moved to Philadelphia, where he established a firm on Market Street, between Front and Second streets, for manufacturing canes and whips. That his business thrived is suggested by Daniel Carrell's advertisments, April 20, 1790, in the South Carolina *Charleston City Gazette and Advertiser*, which noted: "Just received, A number of M'Allester's Philadelphia Whips, Horseman's chair and switch kind, strongly mounted with silver." James Matthews of Baltimore was McAllister's partner from 1798 to 1811. Following Matthews's retirement, John McAllister, Jr., entered the firm, which became known as John McAllister & Son. Spectacles and other optics were a sideline introduced in 1799, but because of their profitability, they eventually became the main thrust of the business. The change is reflected in McAllister's trade card, which was altered not only

for a change of address but also to eliminate the image of whips and canes and add a pocket compass and spectacles. The firm remained in business under various McAllisters until 1941. John McAllister's portrait was painted by James Peale, and a circa 1843 photograph of the McAllister store on Chestnut Street appears in Robert Looney's *Old Philadelphia in Early Photographs.* A gossipy commentator of 1845 noted that the McAllisters were worth $50,000: "Made their money as opticians in part, and married the balance; good whigs and good citizens."

References: Trade card with notes by John McAllister, Jr., and 2 billheads, 75x318.2–.4, Downs collection, Winterthur. Robert F. Looney, *Old Philadelphia in Early Photographs, 1839–1914* (New York: Dover Publications, 1976), no. 116. "Memorial Notice of John McAllister, Jr.," *PMHB* 2 (1878): 91–95. Prime cards, Winterthur. C. G. Sloan & Co. advertisement, *Antiques* 94, no. 2 (August 1978): 182, for portrait of McAllister by James Peale. Henry Simpson, *The Lives of Eminent Philadelphians Now Deceased* (Philadelphia: William Brotherhead, 1859), pp. 731–33. Harold E. Gillingham, "Old Business Cards of Philadelphia," *PMHB* 53 (1929): 203–29, illus. p. 219. John Fanning Watson, *Annals of Philadelphia and Pennsylvania in the Olden Time*, 3 vols., rev. Willis P. Hazard (Philadelphia: Leary, Stuart, 1927), 3:454. *Wealth and Biography of the Wealthy Citizens of Philadelphia* (Philadelphia: G. B. Zieber, 1845), p. 16.

🐝 406 a–d
SPECTACLES, 1820–60

(a) w. 4⅜" (11.1 cm), Min. L. of temple 4¼" (10.8 cm)
(b) w. 4 9/16" (11.6 cm), Min. L. of temple 4 7/16" (11.3 cm)
(c) w. 4⅜" (11.1 cm), Min. L. of temple 4 5/16" (11.0 cm)
(d) w. 4⅜" (11.1 cm), Min. L. of temple 4" (10.2 cm)
Weights not included because of lenses.

Stamps: "McALLISTER" in roman letters, struck incuse on inside of right temple on all. "PHILAD." in roman letters, struck incuse inside left temple (a) and inside right temple (b); 8-point star inside left temple and "27" on outside right temple (b). Incuse sun inside left temple and "10" outside left temple (c). Incuse sun inside left temple and "36" outside right temple (d).

Engraved on outside of left temple: (b) "RD" in roman letters.

Description: oval frames connected by arched bridge on (a, b); rounded rectangular frames connected by arched bridge on (c); elongated octagonal frames connected by arched bridge on (d). All frames with magnifying clear lenses. All have cast 3-segment hinges with middle section integral with temples; metal pin and screw either side; 2-piece temples connected by slide; loop ends on (a–c); forked end on (d). (a) in a red paper and leather case with gilt inscription: "McALLISTER,/ MAKER,/ 48 Chestnut-st./ Philada."

406a

406c

406b

406d

Spectrographic analysis:

	SILVER	COPPER	ZINC	GOLD	LEAD
FRAME (a)	92.2	7.6	0.0	0.13	0.09
FRAME (b)	93.0	6.8	0.0	0.06	0.14
TEMPLE (c)	94.2	5.1	0.0	0.19	0.12
FRAME (d)	82.4	10.2	7.0	0.10	0.30

Provenance: (a, c, d) H. F. du Pont; (b) Richard H. and Virginia A. Wood, Baltimore.

Comments: McAllister made spectacles in "gold, silver, tortoise, plated or steel frames with concave or green glasses or pebbles."

(a) 57.1271 Gift of H. F. du Pont, 1965; (b) 61.75 Museum purchase from Richard H. and Virginia A. Wood, 1961; (c, d) 66.1473, 64.587 Bequest of H. F. du Pont, 1969

🦗 407 a, b
GOLD SPECTACLES, (a) ca. 1840, (b) ca. 1865

(a) w. 4 ¼" (10.8 cm), Min. L. of temple 4 ¼" (10.8 cm)
(b) w. 4 5⁄16" (11.0 cm), Min. L. of temple 4 ½" (11.4 cm)
Weights not included because of lenses.

Stamps: "McALLISTER" in roman letters, stamped incuse inside right temple; bar under "c" on (b). Partial anthemion and roman "B" incuse inside left temple (a). Crescent stamped inside left temple; "91" stamped outside right temple; "27" stamped outside left temple on (b).

Engraved inside left temple: (b) "Dr. Robert Burns." in script. *Scratched inside right temple:* (b) "23140".

Description: (a) rounded rectangular frames connected by an arched bridge; magnifying clear lenses. Cast 3-segment hinges with middle section integral with temples; gold pin and steel screw on either side; 2-piece temples with loop ends connected by slide; (b) elongated octagonal frames connected by arched bridge with scroll ends; magnifying clear lenses. Cast 3-segment hinges with middle section integral with temples; metal pin and screw on either side (not gold); 2-piece temples with loop ends connected by slide.

Spectrographic analysis:

	GOLD	SILVER	COPPER	KARAT
(a)				
FRAME	70.5	16.4	13.1	17
TEMPLE	71.4	16.3	12.3	17
(b)				
FRAME	41.8	28.4	29.9	10
TEMPLE	63.3	19.0	17.8	15

History: (a) Unknown; (b) a Robert Burns, M.D., on Frankford Ave., is listed in Philadelphia directories for 1865 and 1866. A search of earlier directories found no physician of this name. A display ad for "McAllister & Bros., Opticians, 728 Chestnut St." complete with linecut of spectacles appeared in the 1865 edition. In the 1866 edition, the name of the firm had changed to "W. Y. McAllister, Optician, 728 Chestnut Street."

Provenance: (a) H. F. du Pont; (b) Baldwin's Book Barn, West Chester, Pa., sold to H. F. du Pont, October 1951.

Comments: The spectacles illustrated in the 1865/66 McAllister ads are identical to (b), suggesting that the form changed little throughout the nineteenth century. This fact, when combined with the dates of the owner, show once again how difficult it can be to date objects that are unresponsive to fashion.

References: McElroy's Philadelphia City Directory for 1865, p. 114, supp. 30. *McElroy's Philadelphia City Directory for 1866,* p. 117, front supp. 14.

(a) 69.528 Bequest of H. F. du Pont, 1969; (b) 64.1203 Gift of H. F. du Pont, 1951

407b

407a

Thomas McConnell

1768–1825
Wilmington, Delaware, w. ca. 1790–1818
Richmond, Virginia, w. 1818–25

There were two silversmiths by the name of McConnell working in the Delaware Valley in the early years of the nineteenth century. Hugh McConnell appears in Philadelphia directories from 1811 to 1813, but little, if any, of his silver survives. Thomas McConnell of Wilmington is highly visible in the records, and he is most likely responsible for all the silver with the "M:Connell" or "McConnell" stamp. He advertised in 1806 that he had recently moved "to the house next door below the Town Hall, Market Street [Wilmington], where he sells all kinds of Gold and Silver Work, viz. Plate of the newest fashion, Table and Tea Spoons, Ladles, cream ladles, plain and shelled, etc. etc. He also makes and keeps constantly on hand a handsome assortment

of well finished jewelry." McConnell was active in civic affairs and the militia and was elected to the Wilmington Borough Council three times (1814, 1817, 1818). He is known to have sold the work of Ziba Ferris, another local goldsmith. In 1818 he moved to Richmond, where he spent the rest of his life. One argument in favor of McConnell silver being made by Thomas McConnell is that so many of the surviving pieces have Delaware histories. As many as twenty McConnell pieces are owned by the Historical Society of Delaware, whereas none are owned by the Historical Society of Pennsylvania or the Philadelphia Museum of Art.

References: Brix, *Philadelphia Silversmiths*, p. 66, for Hugh McConnell. Harrington, *Silversmiths of Delaware*, pp. 45–48, and Hindes, "Delaware Silversmiths," pp. 276–78, for Thomas McConnell.

408 a–d
COFFEE SERVICE, ca. 1806

(a) Coffeepot: H. 11 7/16" (29.1 cm), W. 13 5/8" (34.6 cm)
44 oz. 1 dwt. 17 gr. (1368.0 g)
(b) Sugar bowl: H. 7 11/16" (19.6 cm), W. 8 1/16" (20.5 cm)
14 oz. 19 dwt. 4 gr. (464.2 g)
(c) Creamer: H. 5 15/16" (15.1 cm), W. 5 13/16" (14.8 cm)
6 oz. 2 dwt. 11 gr. (190.0 g)
(d) Sugar tongs: L. 6 1/4" (99.2 cm)
1 oz. 15 dwt. 7 gr. (54.8 g)

Stamps: "M:CONNELL" (possibly a period under the "C") in roman letters, in a rectangle, struck once on footring on hollowware and once inside arm of sugar tongs.

Engraved on both sides of each body: "AJ" in foliate script. *Engraved inside pedestal:* (a) "AJ 1806 TO M.C.W. 1847 TO M.C.C. 1876" in a mix of script and small roman letters. *Engraved inside footring:* (c) "M.W.C. 1806–1847 to

M.C.W. 1876" in script; also on footring: "[?]ta" (the illegible portion having been deliberately covered with solder). *Engraved on outside:* (d) "MWC 1847 AJ 1806 MCC 1876" in script.

Description: raised oval urn-shape lower bodies divided into 6 vertical panels; bodies joined to raised oval flared-and-stepped pedestals on curvilinear applied footrings.

(a) Coffeepot: upper body, of a piece with lower body, is articulated by chasing into wide and narrow horizontal bands; uppermost portion has convex shoulders joined to main body; vertical rim with applied gadrooned band; centerpunch on underside of body. Raised oval hinged lid, flat at edge, domed in center with a cast urn finial; 4-segment hinge inset within circumference of lid. S-curve, vertically seamed spout with applied cast oval medallion at top. Curvilinear hardwood handle, upper portion rectangular in profile with carved acanthus leaf and sprig; lower portion has back-to-back C curve and S curve; seamed tubular sockets with silver pins.

(b) Sugar bowl: upper body, of a piece with lower body, articulated by chasing into a single plain horizontal band; vertical rim consists of an applied gadrooned band; centerpunch on underside of body; 2 strap handles reeded on outside down to applied sprigged medallion, tapers to point below; upper portion of handles square in profile. Raised oval lid, stepped and domed, with bezel and cast urn finial.

(c) Creamer: upper body, of a piece with lower body, is articulated by chasing into a plain horizontal band; high incurved neck flares at rim decorated with applied gadrooned band; deep extended pouring lip, low sides, back rises to meet handle; 2 off-center punches on underside of body. Strap handle has 2 pairs of double-incised lines on outside down to sprig; tapers to point below; upper portion angular in profile.

(d) Sugar tongs: U-shape form with bow back, tapered arms, and oval spoon grips; bright-cut borders.

Spectrographic analysis:

	SILVER	COPPER	LEAD	GOLD
(a) Coffeepot				
BODY SIDE	92.8	6.7	0.35	0.12
LID	94.0	5.6	0.23	0.13
SPOUT	92.5	7.1	0.26	0.12
FOOT	92.3	7.3	0.32	0.09
(b) Sugar bowl				
BODY SIDE	91.5	8.2	0.13	0.11
LID	92.9	6.9	0.06	0.20
HANDLE	91.6	8.1	0.16	0.14
FOOT	91.1	8.6	0.14	0.13
(c) Creamer				
BODY SIDE	89.3	10.4	0.20	0.11
HANDLE	90.3	9.4	0.17	0.10
FOOT	94.5	5.2	0.16	0.14
(d) Sugar tongs				
	92.2	7.4	0.23	0.17

History: "AJ" refers to Ann Jefferis, who married David Wilson, Jr., whose father built a brick house in Odessa, Del., that today is called the Wilson-Warner House. "M.C.W." refers to Mary Corbit Wilson, their daughter. "M.C.C." is Mary Clark Corbit, who married Edward Tatnall Warner.

Provenance: Descended in the Corbit, Wilson, and Warner families to Mrs. Earl R. Crowe, Wilmington, Del.

Exhibitions: Wilson-Warner House, Odessa, Del.

Comments: The handle of the creamer differs markedly from the handles on the sugar bowl and is probably a replacement. Note attempt to cover part of inscription inside footring of creamer. All maker's stamps on hollowware are on footring.

References: John A. H. Sweeney, *Grandeur on the Appoquinimink: The House of William Corbit at Odessa, Delaware* (Newark: University of Delaware Press, 1959), for information on Corbit and Wilson families.

72.108–.111 Gift of Mrs. Earle R. Crow, 1972

🥄 409 a, b
SPOONS, ca. 1800

(a) L. 6 15⁄16" (17.6 cm)
1 oz. 1 dwt. 3 gr. (33.1 g)
(b) L. 5 5⁄8" (14.3 cm)
9 dwt. 2 gr. (14.1 g)

Stamps: "MᶜCONNELL" in roman letters, in a rectangle, struck once on back of each handle.

Engraved on front of handle: (a) "MH" in script; (b) "HM" (as a cypher) in script.

Description: pointed oval bowl with swage-formed drop; rounded downturned handle.

Spectrographic analysis: Silver content ranges from 90.1 to 92.4 percent.

Provenance: (a) Mr. and Mrs. C. Laylor Burdick, Wilmington, Del.; (b) Mr. and Mrs. Stanley B. Ineson, New York City; Mr. and Mrs. Alfred E. Bissell, Wilmington, Del.

(a) 70.14 Gift of Mr. and Mrs. C. Laylor Burdick, 1970; (b) 62.240.207 Gift of Mr. and Mrs. Alfred E. Bissell, 1962–63

George W. McDannold

ca. 1801–after 1863
Mount Sterling, Montgomery County,
Kentucky, w. ca. 1826–?
Winchester, Kentucky, w. ?
Covington, Kentucky, w. ca. 1850–63

Born in Virginia, George W. McDannold
was a working silversmith when he appeared in a Montgomery County deed
book on March 16, 1829: "a house and lot
occupied by G. W. McDannold as a silversmith's shop" having been there since
1826. When he moved to Winchester and
how long he may have resided there has
yet to be determined. He appears next in
the census of 1850 in Covington, Kentucky, as a silversmith. Listed as part of
his household was a twenty-five-year-
old German-born silversmith and an
eighteen-year-old male, the elder probably a journeyman and the younger man
probably an apprentice. By 1859 he is listed in the *Kentucky State Gazetteer and
Business Directory* as a jeweler and watchmaker. McDannold sold his business in
1863 and became a railroad freight agent.
He made a wide variety of hollowware
and the inevitable beakers.

References: Boultinghouse, *Silversmiths of
Kentucky*, pp. 196–97, 304. *Silver in Kentucky
Life* (Lexington, Ky.: Transylvania University,
1980), pp. 40, 60.

410
BEAKER, 1850–63

H. 3 ⅜" (8.6 cm), DIAM. rim 3 ⅛" (7.9 cm)
4 oz. 5 dwt. 18 gr. (123.1 g)

Stamps: "McDANNOLD" in roman letters,
struck incuse on underside of body.

Description: seamed cylindrical body with
straight tapering sides, bottom let in; small centerpunch on underside. Rim and footring have
1 large and 2 small moldings.

Spectrographic analysis:

	SILVER	COPPER	LEAD	GOLD
BODY SIDE	87.1	12.7	0.18	0.09
UNDERSIDE	92.0	7.8	0.12	0.07

Provenance: H. F. du Pont.

References: Boultinghouse, *Silversmiths of Kentucky*, p. 196, for a discussion of stamps.

Comments: This is thought to be the last stamp
McDannold used.

70.1029 Bequest of H. F. du Pont, 1969

411
SPOON, 1830–50

L. 6 ¼" (15.9 cm)
12 dwt. 1 gr. (18.7 g)

Stamps: "G. W. McDANNOLD" in roman
letters, in a rectangle, struck once on back of
handle.

Description: pointed oval bowl with no drop;
rounded upturned fiddle-shape handle with
midrib.

Spectrographic analysis: Silver content is 91.9
percent.

Provenance: Gary E. Young, Lexington, Mo.

Comments: Probably the second stamp used
by McDannold, this one is thought to have been
in use from 1830 to 1850.

References: Boultinghouse, *Silversmiths of
Kentucky*, p. 196, for discussion of stamps.

76.115 Museum purchase from Gary E. Young,
1976

John McMullin

1765–1843

McMullin & Black, w. 1811–13
John & James McMullin, w. 1813–14
Philadelphia, Pennsylvania

John McMullin's origins remain obscure. He was probably one of a number of Scots or Scotch-Irish who came to the Delaware Valley in the postrevolutionary era. His presence is first recorded in the census of 1790, and he is listed in city directories from 1795 to 1841. In 1802 he was located next door to silversmith Samuel Williamson, whose address was 118 Front Street. McMullin's business flourished, and quantities of his silver survive. He was one of several American silversmiths who purchased silver from Thomas Bradbury & Son, Sheffield; transactions occurred between 1807 and 1811. He took as partners John Black, from 1811 to 1813, and James McMullin, from 1813 to 1814. As a devout

Presbyterian he was a member of the church on Spruce Street near Sixth. He also made communion silver for Philadelphia's First Presbyterian Church (Northern Liberties), the Third Presbyterian Church, the Central Presbyterian Church, and the Presbyterian church in New Castle, Delaware. These commissions ranged in date from 1810 to 1833. McMullin was active in benevolent and philanthropic enterprises as well. During the 1820s he served on a committee to raise funds to rebuild the Orphans' Asylum, was on the board of managers of the American Sunday School Union, and played a leadership role in the Pennsylvania Society for Promoting the Abolition of Slavery. McMullin worked initially in the urn style but moved quickly into the series of interpretations of classicism that followed. An urn-style creamer chased with the Great Seal of the United States is owned by the St. Louis Art Museum. His empire cruet stand with paw feet, owned by the Philadelphia Museum of Art, was selected for the Newark Museum's landmark exhibition "Classical America" in 1963. In 1994 Freeman Fine Arts, Philadelphia, offered for

sale a large tray presented in 1799 to Dr. Philip Syng Physick for his services during the yellow fever epidemic of 1798. The tray, accompanied by the receipt for its purchase, is engraved "John McMullin/ Fecit/ Philada. 1799." McMullin is listed in Philadelphia directories for 1833 and 1839 as a silversmith at 114 South Front Street. This is probably the same three-story house that he insured in 1810, in which the first-floor front room served as his shop.

References: Louisa Bartlett, "American Silver," *Bulletin of the St. Louis Art Museum* 27, no. 1 (Winter 1984): 28. *Classical America, 1815–1845* (Newark, N.J.: Newark Museum, 1963), no. 105. Loren Eitner, *Catalogue: The Mrs. John Emerson Marble Collection of Early American Silver* (Stanford, Calif.: Stanford University Museum, 1976), pp. 60–62. Freeman Fine Arts, Philadelphia, sale no. 641 (April 14–16, 1994). Jones, *Old Silver*, pp. 301, 370–73. Philadelphia directories for 1833 and 1839. Waters, "Philadelphia's Precious Metals Trades," pp. 115, 159–60.

412
BASKET, ca. 1820

L. 12 ⅝" (32.1 cm), w. 8 ⅜" (21.3 cm), h. 4" (10.2 cm)
22 oz. 8 dwt. 21 gr. (698.1 g)

Stamps: "I• M͡C M[ullin]" in italics, in a rectangle, struck once on underside of body. Stamp only partially legible.

Engraved on rim: "RTC" in foliate script.
Scratched on underside of body: "oz 22 13"; "11479".

Description: rectangular in plan with rounded corners, the raised body has a deep curved well and broad flat-angled rim; rim extends at each end to hollow cylindrical handles, each with a vent underneath; no centerpunch. Applied spray of 7 feathers over each handle end; applied gadrooned molding on edge of rim all around. Concave angular seamed pedestal with applied gadrooned footring.

Spectrographic analysis:

	SILVER	COPPER	LEAD	GOLD
BODY SIDE	94.7	5.0	0.22	0.13
HANDLE	92.4	7.1	0.20	0.07
FEATHERS	95.0	4.3	0.23	0.13
FOOTRING	93.3	6.3	0.23	0.10

Provenance: David Stockwell, Philadelphia, sold to H. F. du Pont, September 1949.

Exhibitions: "Masterpieces of American Silver," Virginia Museum of Fine Arts, Richmond, 1960.

Comments: The difference between the scratch weight and the actual weight is about 4 dwt., no doubt from polishing.

References: Fales, *American Silver*, no. 140. Kauffman, *Colonial Silversmith*, p. 138. *Masterpieces of American Silver*, no. 250. Hammerslough, *American Silver*, 1:127, for a wire basket by McMullin.

59.3350 Gift of H. F. du Pont, 1965

413
NURSING TUBE, ca. 1830

L. 7" (17.8 cm), w. 1 ⁹⁄₁₆" (4.0 cm)
16 dwt. 5 gr. (25.2 g)

Stamps: "[?]•McMULLIN" in roman letters, in a serrated rectangle, struck once on underside of convex disk. Accompanied by a spreadwinged eagle in a conforming surround and 2 incuse 6-point stars.

Description: cylindrical tube, seamed in 2 vertical sections, slip cut at lower end; 90 degree curve in upper end, which is fitted with a convex disk with rolled edge and a flattened nipple with a small hole. Drum-shape bottle cap centered on tube just below curve; a short secondary air tube extends below cap.

Spectrographic analysis:

	SILVER	COPPER	LEAD	GOLD
TUBE	95.8	4.1	0.11	0.06
NIPPLE	92.0	7.8	0.13	0.09

Provenance: Golden Eagle Shop, Wilmington, Del.

Comments: Made to fit over a bottle, this is a rare form in silver.

References: See Buhler, *American Silver*, no. 529, and Buhler and Hood, *American Silver*, no. 870, for similar nursing tubes by McMullin.

82.313 Museum purchase from the Golden Eagle Shop, 1982

414 a, b
SPOONS, 1800–1830

(a) L. 6 ⅜" (16.2 cm)
11 dwt. 17 gr. (18.2 g)
(b) L. 9 ⅝" (24.4 cm)
2 oz. 14 gr. (63.0 g)

Stamps: "I•M'MULLIN" in roman letters, in a serrated rectangle, struck once on back of each handle. Accompanied on (a) by 4 pellets in a diamond-shape surround.

Engraved on front of handle: (a) "ETR"; (b) "PAC". Both in foliate script.

Description: oval bowl with swage-formed rounded drop; rounded downturned fiddle-shape handle with midrib on (a); pointed downturned handle on (b).

Spectrographic analysis: Silver content ranges from 88.5 to 90.7 percent.

Provenance: Mr. and Mrs. Stanley B. Ineson, New York City; Mr. and Mrs. Alfred E. Bissell, Wilmington, Del.

References: Belden, *Marks of American Silversmiths*, p. 285.

62.240.436, .1314 Gift of Mrs. and Mrs. Alfred E. Bissell, 1962–63

James Musgrave

w. 1794–1813

Parry & Musgrave, w. 1794–95
Philadelphia, Pennsylvania

James Musgrave first appears in a December 1794 newspaper advertisement for the firm of Parry & Musgrave as "Goldsmiths and Jewellers, No. 42 South Second Street." By late 1795 the partnership was dissolved, and Rowland Parry moved to 36 Chestnut Street. Simultaneously, Musgrave announced that he was "at the old stand" and advertised for an apprentice. In November 1796 Musgrave offered "Plated Tea and Coffee Urns, Coffee Pots, Tea ditto, Castors from 5 to 8 bottles, Sugar and Cream Basons, Bottle Stands, Baskets, high Candlesticks, Brackets and Chamber ditto, Branches, Sconces, a variety of Silver and Plated Shoe Latchets, Spurs . . . [and] All kinds of work in the gold and silver line." Between 1798 and 1809, Musgrave's shop was at 44 South Second Street; from 1810 to 1813, he was at 74 Spruce Street. During this time he ceased to be a working goldsmith and spent the rest of his life in the brokerage business. Partly as a result of his short career as a silversmith, relatively little silver survives, most of it in the Philadelphia urn style and its derivatives. His coffee and tea service made for Irish-born John Barry, a naval hero of the Revolution, is in a private collection. It is in the urn style as modified by broad vertical flutes. A tall teapot in the same style, bearing the arms of the Roberdeau family, is owned by the Historical Society of Pennsylvania.

References: Philadelphia: Three Centuries, p. 171. Prime cards, Winterthur. Waters, "Philadelphia's Precious Metals Trades," pp. 34–35, 151.

415 a–c
TEA SERVICE, ca. 1810

(a) Teapot: H. 6 %₁₆" (16.7 cm), w. 10 ¹⁵⁄₁₆" (27.8 cm)
24 oz. 13 dwt. 1 gr. (766.8 g)
(b) Sugar urn with lid: H. 6 %₁₆" (16.7 cm), w. 5 ⅞" (14.9 cm)
15 oz. 2 dwt. 6 gr. (470.1 g)
(c) Waste bowl: H. 5 ³⁄₁₆" (13.2 cm), w. 6 ½" (16.5 cm)
13 oz. 7 dwt. 6 gr. (415.6 g)

Stamps: "Musgrave" in script, in a conforming surround, struck twice on underside of body (a) and once on underside base on (b) and (c).

Engraved on side of each body: "IRI" (or "JRJ") in shaded foliate script, in a cartouche of wheelwork and bright-cut engraving with small flanking branches and tripartite leaf above and below.

Description: all pieces have 4 equidistant plain vertical panels, each separated by 3 concave flutes. All pieces are decorated by a broad wheelwork and bright-cut band around the upper body. Panels are also articulated by wheelwork dots.

(a) Teapot: seamed body, oval in plan, with flat bottom and incurved neck; applied band inside rim provides flange for lid; body pierced at spout to serve as strainer; no centerpunch. Raised-and-domed partial lid, no bezel, cast floral finial secured through lid by a silver rivet; lid engraved around edge with flames on striations; 3-segment flush-mounted hinge, silver pin. S-curve seamed-and-paneled spout with hood over pouring end. C-curve and reverse C-curve hardwood handle with paneled tapered sockets with silver pins.

(b) Sugar urn: raised urn-shape body, oval in plan, with incurved neck and plain applied rim; centerpunch on underside. Lid similar to (a) except finial secured through lid by silver nut and bolt. Trumpet-shape pedestal with wheelwork and bright-cut border on lower edge, all on base with sides that repeat body panels.

(c) Waste bowl: raised circular hemispherical bowl, paneled like other bodies but with a plain applied conforming rim; centerpunch on underside. Pedestal and base as on (b) except it is circular in plan and has a worked band of beading outside engraved border.

Spectrographic analysis:

	SILVER	COPPER	LEAD	GOLD
(a) Teapot				
BODY SIDE	91.1	8.8	0.15	0.07
UNDERSIDE	94.7	4.8	0.24	0.10
SPOUT	94.3	5.4	0.14	0.08
LID	91.7	8.0	0.16	0.09
(b) Sugar urn				
BODY SIDE	88.5	10.9	0.23	0.09
FOOTRING	93.8	6.0	0.32	0.00
LID	88.5	10.4	0.30	0.12

	SILVER	COPPER	LEAD	GOLD
(c) Waste bowl				
BODY SIDE	83.8	15.2	0.32	0.08
FOOTRING	90.2	9.0	0.41	0.09
RIM	89.5	9.6	0.34	0.11

Provenance: A. J. Pennypacker, American Antique Shop, Pennsburg, Pa., sold to H. F. du Pont, February 1929.

Exhibitions: "Georgian Canada: Conflict and Culture, 1745–1820," Royal Ontario Museum, Toronto, 1984.

Comments: Set missing a creamer. Bill of sale to H. F. du Pont called for 4 pieces in set, but all other records show only these 3. Note mix of seamed and raised forms.

References: Fales, *American Silver*, no. 142. Donald Blake Webster, *Georgian Canada: Conflict and Culture, 1745–1820* (Toronto: Royal Ontario Museum, 1984), no. 140.

65.1381.1–.3 Gift of H. F. du Pont, 1965

416
SPOON, ca. 1800

L. 6" (15.2 cm)
10 dwt. 14 gr. (16.5 g)

Stamps: "Musgrave" in script, in a conforming surround, struck once on back of handle.

Engraved on front of handle: "ML" in foliate script.

Description: elliptical bowl with swage-formed rounded drop with incised line; pointed downturned handle.

Spectrographic analysis: Silver content is 90.3 percent.

Provenance: Mr. and Mrs. Stanley B. Ineson, New York City; Mr. and Mrs. Alfred E. Bissell, Wilmington, Del.

References: Belden, *Marks of American Silversmiths*, p. 310.

62.240.435 Gift of Mr. and Mrs. Alfred E. Bissell, 1962–63

417
SPOON, ca. 1794

L. 5" (12.7 cm)
5 dwt. 10 gr. (8.4 g)

Stamps: "P&M" in roman letters, in a rectangle, struck once on back of handle.

Engraved on front of handle: "A•R" in roman letters.

Description: oval bowl with swage-formed drop with pendant anthemion; rounded downturned handle with vestigial midrib.

Spectrographic analysis: Silver content is 88.7 percent.

Provenance: Mr. and Mrs. James H. Dawson, Wilmington, Del.

78.162 Gift of Mr. and Mrs. James H. Dawson, 1978

Johannes Nys

ca. 1671–1734
New York, New York, w. ca. 1692–98
Philadelphia, Pennsylvania,
w. ca. 1698–1723
Kent County, Delaware, w. 1723–34

Johannes Nys is one of the more difficult silversmiths to research because so many variants of his name appear in the record. *Denise*, *de Nyce*, and *Neuss* are only three of the fourteen known versions of the name given to this silversmith. In his own will the name appears as John Nis, but it is signed Johannes Nys. The signature, then, has become for most silver historians the justification for using Johannes Nys as the definitive spelling. Further compounding the problem is the presence of a John de Nys, joiner, in Philadelphia at about the same time. The facts as assembled by various authors seem to be these. Of French Huguenot ancestry, it is thought that the family arrived in New York during the 1660s. A Johannis Nys was baptized in the New York Dutch Church in 1671. Since so much of Nys's silver, especially his tankards, uses the forms and ornament found on early New York silver, it is assumed that he trained in New York City and that he worked there before moving to Philadelphia. While still in New York, he married Margrietie Keteltas in 1693 and appear in the tax records for 1695. He first appears in Philadelphia in a 1698 list of craftsmen that included silversmith Cesar Ghiselin, which means that he may have been the second silversmith to establish a business in that city.

Nys made silver for prominent Philadelphians such as William Penn, Isaac Norris, James Logan, Andrew Hamilton, and Anthony Morris. A handsome pair of braziers, made for Morris, is owned by the Philadelphia Museum of Art. Nys had many transactions with silversmith Francis Richardson, from whom he purchased supplies and wrought silver; in turn he made silver

porringers and spoons for Richardson. Martha Gandy Fales suggests that Richardson may have apprenticed with Nys. In 1723 Nys moved to Kent County, Delaware, where he remained until his death in 1734.

References: Fales, *Joseph Richardson and Family*, pp. 5, 8–9, 267, 269–70, 272. Harrington, *Silversmiths of Delaware*, pp. 5–8. Hindes, "Delaware Silversmiths," pp. 283–84. "Johannis Nys, Silversmith, ca. 1671–1734," brochure, Historical Society of Delaware, Wilmington, 1978. *Philadelphia: Three Centuries*, pp. 7–9. *Philadelphia Silver*, nos. 287–312. Samuel Woodhouse, "John De Nys, Philadelphia Silversmith," *Antiques* 21, no. 5 (May 1932): 117–18.

418
TANKARD, ca. 1720

H. 7 1/16" (17.9 cm), DIAM. base 5 7/16" (13.8 cm), w. 8 1/8" (20.6 cm)
30 oz. 15 dwt. 12 gr. (955.0 g)

Stamps: "I·N" in roman letters, in a heart, struck once on underside of body.

Engraved on body opposite handle: "MS" in foliate script. *Engraved on underside of body:* "on/ 33 = pe/ 3".

Description: raised body with straight tapering sides and slightly concave bottom; 2-step, applied, molded, flared rim; centerpunch on underside of body. Applied reeded base molding with cut-card border of inverted hearts above. Raised circular stepped-and-domed lid with rudimentary crenelated lip, small hole drilled through center; bezel. Cast cocoon thumbpiece. Cast 5-segment hinge between bands of wigglework; raised-and-soldered hollow S-curve handle terminates with a cast mask applied to a shield-shape plate pierced in 2 upper corners; notched vent.

Spectrographic analysis:

	SILVER	COPPER	LEAD	GOLD
BODY SIDE	88.0	11.6	0.39	0.09
UNDERSIDE	89.4	10.1	0.35	0.12
LID	88.8	10.8	0.35	0.06
HANDLE	87.3	12.2	0.39	0.14

History: Tradition of ownership in the Shippen family of Philadelphia. The tankard may have been owned by Jane Galloway (1745–1801), who married Joseph Shippen (1732–1810) in 1768. Since she was born in 1745, she would not have been the first owner. Given the style of the initials "MS," the tankard was either handed down or presented to a younger relative with those initials, probably about 1790. Joseph and Jane Shippen had 2 daughters, Mary (1773–1809) and Margaret (1782–76). The inscription could refer to either of them. Mary married Samuel Swift in 1793 and, as the eldest daughter, may have been given this heirloom at that time.

Provenance: Edwin S. Buckley, Lake Worth, Fla.

Comments: The use of cut-card work, cocoon thumbpiece, broad proportions, and powerful mask tailpiece show Nys working in his typical New York idiom. The lid, however, is more characteristic of Philadelphia silver, suggesting that it is either a replacement or that the tankard is a genuine hybrid. This is the only tankard by Nys without a flat lid.

References: Randolph Shipley Klein, *Portrait of an American Family: The Shippens of Pennsylvania across Five Generations* (Philadelphia: University of Pennsylvania Press, 1975), chart B-3.

79.219 Museum purchase from Edwin S. Buckley, 1979

🥄 419
PORRINGER, ca. 1700

DIAM. bowl 4 ½" (11.4 cm), w. 6 ⅝" (16.8 cm), H. 1 ¹¹⁄₁₆" (4.3 cm)
5 oz. 1 dwt. 9 gr. (157.7 g)

Stamps: "IN" in roman letters, with 4 pellets below (arranged 3 across and 1 above), all in an oval or shield, struck once in center of underside.

Engraved on front of handle: "M+S/ to E+D" in shaded roman letters and script. *Engraved on underside of body:* "aperil 28/th day = 17[?]" in script, third digit of year possibly 0 or 6.

Description: raised circular bowl with bulging sides and angled rim; bottom slightly domed in center; centerpunch obscured by stamp; cast handle pierced in geometric pattern with 7 closed and 4 open voids.

Spectrographic analysis:

	SILVER	COPPER	LEAD	GOLD
BODY SIDE	89.5	10.3	0.25	0.02
UNDERSIDE	93.8	5.7	0.26	0.07
HANDLE	92.4	6.9	0.35	0.13

History: According to information furnished by the dealer, the initials "M+S/ to E+D" refer to Mary Skyrin and Eliza Downing (1781–1882).

Provenance: Mary Skyrin; Eliza Downing, who married Robert V. Sharpless; their daughter Catherine, who married William Augustus White; their daughter Laura, who sold the porringer to Francis Brinton, who sold it to H. F. du Pont, 1930.

Exhibitions: "Masterpieces of American Silver," Virginia Museum of Fine Arts, Richmond, 1960. "Johannis Nys, Silversmith, ca. 1671–1734," Historical Society of Delaware, Wilmington, 1978.

Comments: It is unclear why the last 2 digits of the date were obliterated. The style of the engraving suggests a date around 1700.

References: Fales, *American Silver*, no. 53. "Johannis Nys, Silversmith, ca. 1671–1734," exhibition checklist, Historical Society of Delaware, Wilmington, 1978. *Masterpieces of American Silver*, no. 255.

59.2302 Gift of H. F. du Pont, 1965

🐝 420
PORRINGER, ca. 1710

DIAM. bowl 5 ½" (14.0 cm), w. 7 ⅞" (20.0 cm), H. 1 ¹⁵⁄₁₆" (4.9 cm)
8 oz. 14 dwt. 9 gr. (271.2 g)

Stamps: "⊥N" in roman letters, in a circular surround, struck once on underside of body. Overlaps centerpunch.

Engraved on front of handle facing in: "E∗G" in shaded roman letters.

Description: raised circular bowl with bulging sides and angled rim; bottom slightly domed in center; centerpunches inside and outside; cast handle pierced in geometric pattern with 16 voids.

Spectrographic analysis:

	SILVER	COPPER	GOLD	ZINC	LEAD
BOWL	88.5	10.8	0.18	0.05	0.01
HANDLE	75.7	22.9	0.09	0.32	0.06

History: According to Stephen Ensko the initials "E∗G" refer to Elizabeth "Griffitts," "who is recorded in Dr. Moon's book." The book in question is a genealogy of the Morris family, but it has a small section on the Griffits family. An Elizabeth Griffits was born in 1748(?) to Thomas Griffits, who had married the daughter of Isaac Norris in 1717. From Ireland by way of Jamaica, Thomas was in the lumber business, served as keeper of the Great Seal, and was elected mayor of Philadelphia on 4 occasions.

Provenance: Robert Ensko, Inc., New York City, sold to H. F. du Pont, September 1932.

Exhibitions: "Johannis Nys, Silversmith, ca. 1671–1734," Historical Society of Delaware, Wilmington, 1978.

Comments: More Nys porringers survive than all other forms together.

References: "Johannis Nys, Silversmith, ca. 1671–1734," exhibition checklist, Historical Society of Delaware, Wilmington, 1978. Robert C. Moon, *The Morris Family of Philadelphia*, 3 vols. (Philadelphia, 1898), p. 459; a 2-vol. supplement was published in 1908–9.

59.2303 Gift of H. F. du Pont, 1965

John Owen

1801–28
Philadelphia, Pennsylvania

Little is known about John Owen or his short-lived career. His advertisement in *Poulson's American Daily Advertiser* for May 3, 1820, featured illustrations of spectacles ("lenses to suit every sight"), a thimble, and a pile of fiddle-handled spoons. He also carried Sheffield plate wares and gold seals and watch keys. In September 1822 he filed for insolvency, owing to "the hardness of the times and having a Large Family to support." He managed to continue working as an independent silversmith until his death in 1828. His final location was on Callowhill Street near Second Street. His modest estate—$354.12 for everything including land and shop—included a rolling mill and a turning lathe, suggesting that he was adapting to the new technology.

References: Waters, "Philadelphia's Precious Metals Trades," pp. 103–4, 122.

421 a, b
CANDELABRA, ca. 1825

(a) H. 15 ⁷⁄₁₆" (39.2 cm), W. 17 ¹⁄₁₆" (43.3 cm), DIAM. base 5 ¹⁄₈" (13.0 cm)
With candles, wires, and wood reinforcing rods: 43 oz. 17 dwt. 17 gr. (1365.0 g)
(b) H. 16 ¼" (41.3 cm), W. 16 ¼" (41.3 cm), DIAM. base 5 ¹⁄₈" (13.0 cm)
With candles, wires, and wood reinforcing rods: 45 oz. 7 dwt. 23 gr. (1412.0 g)

Stamps: "J.OWEN" in roman letters, in a rectangle, struck once on outside of each footring.

Description: single candlestick with double-branch insert; raised, circular, stepped base with applied footring; chased acanthus leaf design on upper part of base. Columnar shaft with knop and reel at bottom and midband at center; upper end of shaft has chased acanthus leaf border. Double-walled seamed socket, fitted over top of shaft, has 2 rows of beading. Repeating diagonal-line border cut into socket midband, knop, pedestal, and footring; 2 tubular branches attached to central shaft with bobeche base. Seamed tubes spiral out from central shaft to plain double-walled cylindrical sockets and drip pans with acanthus leaf borders. Midway on each branch is a bud-shape sleeve, formed as an acanthus leaf, and at the end is a decorative cap. Both branch sockets have a bobeche. Central socket has a bell-shape lid with a bud finial cast as an acanthus leaf.

Spectrographic analysis:

	SILVER	COPPER	LEAD	GOLD
(a)				
LOWER SHAFT	92.8	6.7	0.28	0.18
FOOTRING	92.4	7.1	0.31	0.15
BRANCH	96.1	3.3	0.08	0.05
FINIAL	94.5	5.3	0.11	0.05
(b)				
LOWER SHAFT	93.4	5.9	0.28	0.17
FOOTRING	93.4	6.0	0.28	0.13
BRANCH	94.0	5.5	0.19	0.13
FINIAL	93.7	6.1	0.15	0.09

Provenance: H. F. du Pont.

Comments: Wood reinforcing rods in main shafts. Metal has a yellow cast.

References: Marshall B. Davidson, *The American Heritage History of Antiques: From the Revolution to the Civil War* (New York: American Heritage Publishing, 1968), p. 148. Fennimore, *Silver and Pewter*, no. 187.

61.952.1, .2 Bequest of H. F. du Pont, 1969

422
SUGAR TONGS, ca. 1825

L. 6 ¾" (17.1 cm), 2 oz. 7 dwt. 15 gr. (73.9 g)

Stamps: "I•OWEN" in roman letters, in a rectangle, struck once on each arm.

Engraved on bow back: "TEH" in shaded foliate script. *Engraved on each arm:* "SR" in foliate script, in a shield-shape reserve.

Description: U-shape form with bow back, flat tapered arms at right angles, and oval spoon grips; bright-cut borders with bellflower drops.

Spectrographic analysis: Silver content is 91.5 percent.

Provenance: Marshall P. Blankarn, New York City.

References: Fennimore, *Silver and Pewter*, no. 37.

79.213 Gift of Marshall P. Blankarn, 1979

423 a–g
SPOONS, ca. 1825

(a–f) average L. 5 ¼" (13.3 cm), 7 dwt. 7 gr. (11.3 g) average
(g) L. 9 ³⁄₁₆" (23.3 cm), 1 oz. 15 dwt. 2 gr. (54.5 g)

Stamps: "I•OWEN" in roman letters, in a rectangle, struck once on back of each handle.

Engraved on front of handle: (a–f) "DP" in foliate script; (g) "WDS" in foliate script.

Description: (a–f) pointed oval bowl with swage-formed rounded drop and, on back of bowl, a bird perched on leafy branch holding another branch in its beak; downturned fiddle-shape handle; (g) oval bowl with swage-formed rounded drop; pointed downturned handle.

Spectrographic analysis: Silver content ranges from 89.6 to 92.7 percent.

Provenance: (a–f) Francis D. Brinton sold to H. F. du Pont, March 1930; (g) Mr. and Mrs. Stanley B. Ineson, New York City; Mr. and Mrs. Alfred E. Bissell, Wilmington, Del.

Comments: The first 6 spoons are a set; all have bird-back bowls.

References: (g) Belden, *Marks of American Silversmiths*, p. 322.

(a–f) 56.582.1–.6 Gift of H. F. du Pont, 1965; (g) 62.240.135 Gift of Mr. and Mrs. Alfred E. Bissell, 1962–63

⚘ Henry J. Pepper

ca. 1789–1853
Wilmington, Delaware, w. ca. 1813–25
Philadelphia, Pennsylvania, w. 1825–49

Henry J. Pepper was born in Ireland and was, no doubt, the son of Henry Pepper, the Dublin-educated schoolmaster who taught languages in Wilmington during the 1790s. In 1797 Pepper, Sr., moved to Philadelphia, where he contracted yellow fever and died. His widow and children then returned to Wilmington. Henry J. Pepper surfaced as a silversmith in Wilmington with an advertisement in the *Delaware Statesman*, March 17, 1813. How and with whom he learned the craft is unknown. In 1817 he married Keziah Moore; later he married Sarah Bassett. In 1816 he added to his business "a large and general assortment of moroccos; Boot, Shoe, and Sole Leather from the manufactory of Messers A. Cardon & Co." An advertisement of 1824 illustrated spectacles with the caption: "See for Yourselves. Silver Spectacles, Silver Plate, Silver Spoons, and all kinds of Silver and Gold work are manufactured and kept constantly for sale." He became a friend and business associate of E. I. du Pont, the black powder manufacturer, for whom he made silver on numerous occasions. Hagley Museum owns six tiny teaspoons and tongs made by Pepper as an 1818 New Year's Day gift for Sophie du Pont from her sister Victorine, both daughters of E. I. du Pont. A Pepper tea service in the round style, purchased in 1972 for Eleutherian Mills, the family seat and now part of Hagley Museum, was stolen in 1981. Pepper's connection with the du Ponts was due in large part to his wife's position as nursemaid and seamstress for the du Pont children. In 1825 Pepper moved to Philadelphia, where he continued to practice his craft for another twenty-four years. In *Desilver's Philadelphia Directory and Stranger's Guide* (1833) he is located at 103 Chestnut Street, and his display advertisement features "Jewelry, Watches, Silverware, &c." In 1839 he is at 66 Chestnut Street. His death notice is in the *Public Ledger*, July 19, 1853.

References: Harrington, *Silversmiths of Delaware*, pp. 61–64. Hindes, *Delaware Silversmith*, pp. 286–87 plus plates. Ruthanna Hindes, "The Documentation of a Friendship: Pepper–du Pont," Delaware Antiques Show catalogue (December 2–4, 1971), pp. 79–85. *Life of Eleuthère Irénée du Pont from Contemporary Correspondence, 1819–1834*, trans. B. G. du Pont (Newark: University of Delaware Press, 1926), pp. 159–60, for letter from Pepper to E. I. du Pont, January 6, 1827. Elizabeth Montgomery, *Reminiscences of Wilmington* (Philadelphia: T. K. Collins, Jr., 1851), for discussions of the Pepper family. For further documentation, see John Beverly Riggs, *A Guide to the Manuscripts in the Eleutherian Mills Historical Library* (Greenville, Del.: By the library, 1970).

⚘ 424
SPECTACLES AND CASE, 1813–25

(a) Spectacles: w. 4 ½" (11.4 cm), L. of temple 4 ½" (11.4 cm)
Weight not included because of lenses.
(b) Case: L. 5 ⅛" (13.0 cm), w. 1 ⁵⁄₁₆" (3.3 cm), D. ¾" (1.9 cm)
2 oz. 10 dwt. 2 gr. (77.9 g)

Stamps: "HJP" in roman letters, in a rectangle, struck once on outside of left temple on (a).

Engraved on outside of right temple of (a), upside down, and on lid of (b): "Dr. Didier." in script.

Description: (a) oval frames connected by an arched bridge; magnifying clear lenses; cast 3-segment hinge with middle section integral with temple; metal pin and screw on either side; 2-piece temple connected by slide; circular hole at end; (b) flat elongated oval box with straight sides; one end of box hinged to serve as a lid; fabricated from sheet silver; 3-segment hinge; push-button spring-lock closure; rectangular exterior molding and bezel at rim.

Spectrographic analysis:

	SILVER	COPPER	LEAD	GOLD
(a) Spectacles				
LEFT TEMPLE	93.3	5.6	0.29	0.17
RIGHT TEMPLE	95.1	4.0	0.22	0.15
(b) Case				
BODY	91.5	8.3	0.22	0.14
LID	92.2	7.5	0.16	0.13

History: Owned by physician Pierre Didier (1741–1830), who came to the United States in 1794 from Saint-Domingue (Haiti) and who became a popular figure in Wilmington's French community. He had served with the French army and was wounded several times in

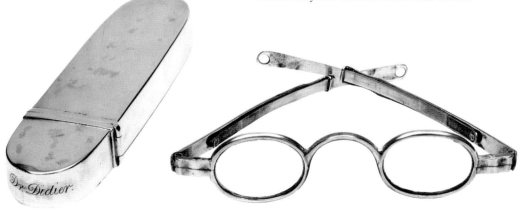

the Seven Years War. At an unspecified time he went to the Caribbean, where in 1774, after a 3-year apprenticeship, he was granted permission to practice medicine in Cap-François, Saint-Domingue. He also became involved in mercantile pursuits that began to bear fruit just as the revolution led by Toussaint L'Overture broke out. Like so many others, he came to North America, and he settled permanently in Wilmington, where he established a private medical practice. Didier befriended the du Pont family, especially E. I. du Pont, with whom he shared an interest in botany. To Madame du Pont he was known as "Papa Didier" and, when the doctor himself became ill, E. I. du Pont cared for him. Didier and du Pont made arrangements for caring for workers at the du Pont powder yards, unwittingly, perhaps, instituting what may be the earliest practice of industrial medicine in the United States. Didier was granted the exceptional privilege of burial in the du Pont family cemetery.

Provenance: H. F. du Pont.

References: Fales, *American Silver*, no. 131. Fennimore, *Silver and Pewter*, no. 200. Polly Jose Scafidi, "Doctor Pierre Didier and Early Industrial Medicine," *Delaware History* 15, no. 1 (April 1972): 41–54.

59.2698a, b Gift of H. F. du Pont, 1960

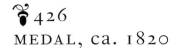

425
SPECTACLES, ca. 1813–25

w. 4 ¹¹⁄₁₆" (11.9 cm), Min. L. of temple 4 ¹¹⁄₁₆" (11.9 cm), Max. L. of temple 6 ¹¹⁄₁₆" (17.0 cm) 17 dwt. 23 gr. (28.0 g)

Stamps: "H.I. PEPPER" in roman letters, in a rectangle, struck once on right temple, upside down.

Engraved on right temple: "S" (or "L"); *on left temple:* "J" (or "I"); both in foliate script.

Description: oval frames connected by arched bridge; no lenses. Cast 3-segment hinge with middle section integral with temples; metal pin and screw on each side; 2-piece temple connected by slide; loop end.

Spectrographic analysis:

	SILVER	COPPER	LEAD	GOLD
LEFT TEMPLE	89.6	9.2	0.64	0.12
RIGHT TEMPLE	89.6	9.0	0.67	0.18

Provenance: Charlotte and Edgar Sittig, Shawnee-on-Delaware, Pa.

66.9 Museum purchase from Charlotte and Edgar Sittig, 1966

426
MEDAL, ca. 1820

DIAM. 1 ⁵⁄₁₆" (3.3 cm), W. (incl. loop) 1 ¹¹⁄₁₆" (4.3 cm)
4 dwt. 2 gr. (6.4 g)

Stamps: None. Attributed to Pepper on basis of other documentation; see *History.*

Engraved on both sides: "Good Behaviour" in script. Obverse has 6-point compass-formed star in a circle in the center with wheelwork guilloche border. Reverse has wheelwork circle in center and an engraved laurel leaf border.

Description: circular thin flat form with ring attached to edge; centerpunch on reverse.

Spectrographic analysis:

	SILVER	COPPER	LEAD	GOLD
OBVERSE	90.0	9.6	0.20	0.06
REVERSE	90.2	9.5	0.19	0.07

History: Note in nineteenth-century hand accompanying medal reads: "Silver Medal/ Sister Victorine had/ made (by Mr H Pepper)/ when she educated her/ younger sisters & brothers—to/ hang round the neck into/ the button hole of the best/ behaved of her[?] scholars/ Her pupils were/ Eleuthera DuPont/ Sophie M DuPont/ Henry DuPont/ Alexis I DuPont/ Mary Edith Simmens." All except the last were the children of E. I. du Pont. Victorine, the eldest daughter, married Ferdinand Bauduy in 1813 but was widowed the following year. She then devoted herself to caring for her siblings. Mary Edith Simmons was the daughter of a neighboring farmer and a ward of Jacques

Antoine Bidermann following her father's death. Bidermann married Evelina du Pont, Victorine's sister, who was close in age to Victorine. After her younger siblings grew up, Victorine turned her attention to the children of powder workers. She became one of the founders of the Brandywine Manufacturers Sunday School; the building survives and is open to the public at the Hagley Museum.

Provenance: Descended in du Pont family to H. F. du Pont.

Comments: Silver medals for good academic performance or behavior were awarded by private schools during the early nineteenth century. Victorine herself received a gold medal from Madame Rivardi's Seminary in Philadelphia in 1807 (see no. 465).

References: Betty-Bright Low and Jacqueline Hinsley, *Sophie du Pont, A Young Lady in America: Sketches, Diaries, and Letters, 1823–1833* (New York: Harry N. Abrams, 1987), for information on the du Pont daughters.

67.617 Bequest of H. F. du Pont, 1969

427
SPOON, ca. 1813–25

L. 12 ⅜" (31.4 cm)
4 oz. 12 dwt. 5 gr. (143.1 g)

Stamps: "HJP" in roman letters, in a rectangle, struck once on back of handle.

Engraved on front of handle: "EIDP" in foliate script.

Description: pointed oval bowl with swage-formed rounded drop; rounded downturned fiddle-shape handle with midrib.

Spectrographic analysis: Silver content is 90.4 percent.

History: Initials refer to E. I. du Pont, Wilmington, Del.

Provenance: Descended in du Pont family to H. F. du Pont.

Comments: Engraved initials identical to those on 428 a–f.

70.1253 Bequest of H. F. du Pont, 1969

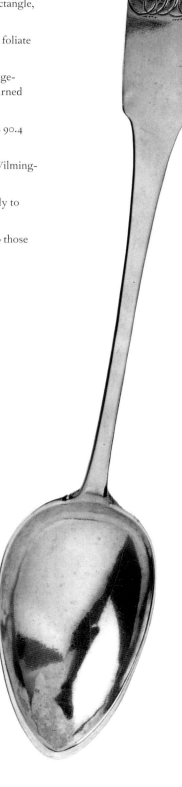

428 a–o
SPOONS, 1813–25

(a–k) average L. 5 ⅝" (14.3 cm)
(a) 9 dwt. 19 gr. (15.2 g)
(b) 10 dwt. 4 gr. (15.8 g)
(c, j, k) 9 dwt. 8 gr. (14.5 g)
(d) 6 dwt. 19 gr. (10.6 g)
(e) 9 dwt. 9 gr. (14.6 g)
(f) 10 dwt. 4 gr. (15.8 g)
(g) 9 dwt. 22 gr. (15.4 g)
(h) 9 dwt. (14.0 g)
(i) 9 dwt. 6 gr. (14.4 g)
(l–o) average L. 7 ½" (19.1 cm)
(l) 1 oz. 1 dwt. 18 gr. (33.8 g)
(m) 1 oz. 1 dwt. 9 gr. (33.2 g)
(n) 1 oz. 2 dwt. 4 gr. (34.4 g)
(o) 1 oz. 4 dwt. 8 gr. (37.8 g)

Stamps: "H•J•PEPPER" in roman letters, in a rectangle, struck once on back of each handle.

Engraved on front of handle: (a–f) "EIDP"; (g–k) "JP"; (l–o) "DAW/ 1806/ MWC/ 1847/ MCC/ 1876". All in foliate script.

Description: pointed oval bowl with rounded drop on (a–f), squared drop on (g–k), incised rectangular drop on (l–m); rounded down-turned fiddle-shape handles with midrib.

Spectrographic analysis: Silver content ranges from 89.7 to 91.3 percent.

History: (a–f) Initials refer to E. I. du Pont, Wilmington, Del.; see above; (g–k) possibly owned in the Pepper family; (l–o) "DAW" refers to David and Anne Wilson, Odessa, Del., who were married in 1806; "MWC" refers to their daughter Mary Wilson Corbit, who was married in 1847; "MCC" refers to Mary C. Corbit, daughter of Mary Wilson Corbit, who married E. Tatnall Warner in 1876. See no. 408 and next group of Pepper spoons, no. 429, for other Corbit family silver.

Provenance: (a–f) Descended in du Pont family to Mrs. Francis B. Crowninshield, Wilmington, Del. Louisa du Pont Crowninshield was H. F. du Pont's sister; (g–k) Dr. Margaret I. Handy, Chadds Ford, Pa.; (l–o) descended in Wilson, Corbit, and Tatnall families to Mrs. D. Meredith Reese, Wilmington, Del.

Exhibitions: (l–o) Wilson-Warner House, Odessa, Del.

Comments: Engraved initials on (a–f) identical to those on no. 427; 2 sets of the engraved initials on (l–o) are on no. 429 e–g and on no. 408.

References: John A. H. Sweeney, *Grandeur on the Appoquinimink: The House of William Corbit at Odessa, Delaware* (Newark: University of Delaware Press, 1959), for information on the Corbit and Wilson families.

(a–f) 57.7.1–.6 Gift of Mrs. Francis B. Crowninshield, 1957; (g–k) 61.427.1–.5 Gift of Dr. Margaret I. Handy, 1961; (l–o) 78.47.1–.4 Gift of Mrs. D. Meredith Reese, 1978

429 a–i
SPOONS, 1813–25

(a, b, d) average L. 8 ¹¹⁄₁₆" (22.1 cm)
(a) 1 oz. 13 dwt. 15 gr. (52.2 g)
(b) 1 oz. 13 dwt. 20 gr. (53.0 g)
(d) 1 oz. 13 dwt. 13 gr. (52.1 g)
(c) L. 8 ¹⁵⁄₁₆" (22.7 cm)
1 oz. 12 dwt. 19 gr. (50.9 g)
(e–g) average L. 9 ⅝" (24.4 cm)
(e) 2 oz. 4 dwt. 8 gr. (68.8 g)
(f) 2 oz. 5 dwt. 4 gr. (70.1 g)
(g) 2 oz. 4 dwt. 20 gr. (69.6 g)
(h) L. 9 ⅜" (23.8 cm)
2 oz. 1 dwt. 2 gr. (63.8 g)
(i) L. 4 ⁵⁄₁₆" (10.9 cm)
4 dwt. 22 gr. (7.6 g)

Stamps: "H. J. PEPPER" in roman letters, in a rectangle, struck once on back of each handle. On (i) only: "STANDARD" in roman letters, in a wavy banner.

Engraved on front of handle: (a–d) "SCC"; (e–g) "MCW/ 1847/ MCC/ 1876"; (h) "RM"; (i) "L". All in foliate script.

Description: (a–d) pointed oval bowl with swage-formed rounded drop; downturned fiddle-shape handle with swage-formed sheaf of wheat on front; (e–g) elongated pointed oval bowl with 2 incised lines simulating a drop; rounded downturned fiddle-shape handle; (h) oval bowl with incised squared drop; rounded downturned fiddle-shape handle; (i) salt spoon bowl formed as a 9-lobe shell; rounded downturned fiddle-shape handle.

Spectrographic analysis: Silver content ranges from 89.8 to 90.6 percent.

History: (a–d) "SCC" refers to Sarah Clarke Corbit (1810–71), daughter of Pennell and Mary (Clark) Corbit and granddaughter of William Corbit of Odessa, Del. She married Anthony Madison Higgins; (e–g) "MCW" refers to Mary Corbit Wilson of Odessa, Del., who married Daniel Corbit in 1847. "MCC" refers to Mary C. Corbit of Odessa, who married E. Tatnall Warner in 1876; (h) "RM" refers to Rachel Mendenhall, who married Thomas Garrett in 1830. Quaker-born Thomas Garrett (1789–1871) moved from Upper Darby, Pa., to Wilmington, Del., in the early 1820s. He was an avid abolitionist who helped more than 2,700 slaves to escape bondage. He was so revered by blacks that in 1870 he was hailed as "Our Moses."

Provenance: (a–d) Mrs. Samuel F. Pryor III, Bedford Hills, N.Y.; (e–g) descended in Wilson, Corbit, and Tatnall families to Mrs. D. Meredith Reese, Wilmington, Del.; (h) Mrs. Cazenove G. Lee, Washington, D.C.; (i) Mr. and Mrs. Stanley B. Ineson, New York City; Mr. and Mrs. Alfred E. Bissell, Wilmington, Del.

Exhibitions: (a–d) Corbit-Sharp House, Odessa, Del.; (e–g) Wilson-Warner House, Odessa, Del.

Comments: (e–g) See nos. 428 and 408 for silver with similar histories.

References: John A. H. Sweeney, *Grandeur on the Appoquinimink: The House of William Corbit at Odessa, Delaware* (Newark: University of Delaware Press, 1959), for history of Corbit and Wilson families. (h) *DAB*, s.v. "Garrett, Thomas." (i) Belden, *Marks of American Silversmiths*, p. 332.

(a–d) 86.5.1–.4 Museum trade with Mrs. Samuel F. Pryor III, 1985; (e–g) 78.46.1–.3 Gift of Mrs. D. Meredith Reese, 1978; (h) 70.96 Gift of Mrs. Cazenove G. Lee, 1970; (i) 62.240.789 Gift of Mr. and Mrs. Alfred E. Bissell, 1962–63

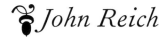
John Reich

1768–1833
Philadelphia, Pennsylvania

Born Johann Mathias Reich in Bavaria, John Reich was the son of Johann Christian Reich, an accomplished die sinker and medalist from whom he learned the craft and with whom he collaborated for many years. The younger Reich came to Philadelphia about 1800 at the urging of Henry Voight, chief coiner for the United States Mint. Voight lacked the technical skills, having been a watch- and clockmaker, to be a first-class die sinker, but he was a good administrator who recognized the need for a more talented hand. Thus Reich came to the mint, first "to make scales and other fine work" and later to become assistant engraver under Robert Patterson. His first major commission was the presidential Indian medals made during Thomas Jefferson's administration for the Lewis and Clark expedition. During the War of 1812, he cut the dies for the gold medals for Commodore Preble and Capt. Isaac Hull. He is also responsible for medals celebrating George Washington and Benjamin Franklin and for half-eagle and half-dollar coins. In 1811 Reich and Moritz Fürst exhibited medals at the first annual exhibition of the Society of Artists of the United States. Failing health and eyesight cut short his career, although he did not die until 1833. His work is highly regarded and is also rare.

References: Chamberlain, *American Medals and Medalists*, pp. 54–63. Groce and Wallace, *Dictionary of Artists in America*, p. 529.

430
MEDAL, 1807

DIAM. 1 ⁹⁄₁₆" (4.0 cm)
1 oz. 4 dwt. 5 gr. (37.6 g)

Stamps: Roman "R" on obverse, on subject's arm.

Description: circular flat form with raised rim and design in relief. Loop soldered into upper edge. Obverse: bust portrait in profile of man (facing right) in civilian clothes; inscription inside rim: "G. WASHINGTON PRES. UNIT. STA." in roman letters. Reverse: a pedestal with 1 side bearing the shield of the United States, draped over it a fringed cloth upon which are fasces and sword encircled by an olive wreath; inscription inside rim: "COMMISS. RESIGNED: PRESIDENCY RELINQ." in roman letters; in exergue: "1797".

Spectrographic analysis:

SILVER	COPPER	GOLD	LEAD
95.5	1.0	2.4	0.81

History: This is the fourth in a series of medals commissioned by Philadelphia merchant Joseph Sansom. It is a copy of a medal designed and executed by the English die sinker Thomas Halliday after a Stuart portrait of Washington. Since the medal was issued in multiples, the history of this particular one is unknown.

Provenance: H. F. du Pont.

Comments: The mint reproduced this medal in 1859 using new dies. In the reproduction, "Q" is above the base of the pedestal, and the sword points to the "C." In the original, the "Q" is close to the base of the pedestal, and the sword points between the "C" and "Y."

References: Chamberlain, *American Medals and Medalists*, pp. 58, 61. W. S. Baker, *Medallic Portraits of Washington* (Philadelphia: Robert M. Lindsey, 1885), no. 71.

67.616 Bequest of H. F. du Pont, 1969

Samuel Richards, Jr.

w. 1793–1818

Richards & Williamson, w. 1797–1800
Philadelphia, Pennsylvania

Nothing is known of Samuel Richards's background and training beyond the fact that he was a Quaker. From 1793 to 1818, advertisements place him at 136 South Front Street. The accounts of fellow Quaker goldsmith Joseph Richardson, Jr., show a number of transactions with Richards; in 1798 Richards purchased two teapots, a slop bowl, a sugar bowl, and a creamer from Richardson. In 1799 Richards's purchases of plate amounted to £99.18.2, which he paid in cash and goods (an iron plate stove and wharfage of 17,250 bricks). In 1797 Richards formed a partnership with Samuel Williamson that dissolved in 1800. In 1802 Richards took Thomas Whartenby as an apprentice for a term of six years, eleven months, and twenty-two days. A spoon in the William Penn Memorial Museum is stamped with both the "SR" and "S. RICHARDS" stamps, thus confirming the identity of the "SR" stamp. A number of other pieces from the partnership survive, including a large teapot in the urn style owned by the Baltimore Museum of Art. Examples of Richards's work include a cake basket at the Art Institute of Chicago and a six-piece beverage service in the round style, once owned by New York dealer Eric Shrubsole.

References: Fales, *Joseph Richardson and Family*, pp. 159, 305. *Philadelphia Silver*, nos. 318, 319. Waters, "Philadelphia's Precious Metals Trades," pp. 43–44, 133. *The Antiquarian Society: The First Hundred Years* (Chicago: Art Institute of Chicago, 1977), no. 206, for cake basket.

431
SUGAR BOWL, ca. 1800

H. (with lid) 7 1/16" (17.9 cm), H. (without lid) 5 1/16" (12.9 cm), W. 5 9/16" (14.1 cm)
14 oz. 14 dwt. 18 gr. (458.4 g)

Stamps: "S[.] RICHARDS" in roman letters, in a rectangle, struck once on underside of body.

Engraved on side of body: "MFG" in shaded foliate script.

Description: raised urn-shape body, oval in plan, with curved rim (concave in elevation); 2 bands around upper body formed by plain chasing; applied reeded band at rim; no centerpunch. Raised, oval, stepped foot rises to body; applied seamed footring. Raised oval friction-fit lid, curved to conform to body, is stepped and domed with a cast urn finial; bezel.

Spectrographic analysis:

	SILVER	COPPER	LEAD	GOLD
BODY SIDE	93.1	6.5	0.22	0.10
FOOTRING	93.5	6.0	0.26	0.14
LID	95.2	4.4	0.22	0.18

Provenance: Marshall P. Blankarn, New York City.

77.225 Gift of Marshall P. Blankarn, 1977

432
KNITTING NEEDLE CASE, ca. 1815

L. 9 ½" (24.1 cm), DIAM. ⁷⁄₁₆" (1.1 cm)
18 dwt. 5 gr. (28.3 g)

Stamps: "SR" in roman letters, in an oval, struck once on closed end of case.

Engraved on side of body: "Sarah Kaighn" (surname appears to have been altered from "Knight") in script.

Description: tubular body with ⅛"-wide slit along whole length; lower end terminates in fixed cylindrical seamed cap with a reel-like collar at juncture with body; upper end has removable cap matching fixed cap.

Spectrographic analysis:

	SILVER	COPPER	LEAD	GOLD
BODY	91.9	7.6	0.36	0.08
CAP	93.2	6.3	0.40	0.13

History: A Sarah Knight, Byberry Township, Pa., died in 1847. There is no inventory of her estate. A John Kaighn is listed in Philadelphia directories from 1785 to 1805.

Provenance: Philip H. Bradley Co., Downingtown, Pa.

Comments: A rare form in silver. Contains 6 steel knitting needles. Goldsmith Joseph Richardson sold 5 pairs of knitting sheaths in 1747 (Fales, *Joseph Richardson and Family*, p. 297).

77.204 Museum purchase from Philip H. Bradley, 1977

433 a, b
SPOONS, 1793–1818

(a) L. 6" (15.2 cm), 10 dwt. 19 gr. (16.8 g)
(b) L. 9 ¹¹⁄₁₆" (24.6 cm), 2 oz. 22 gr. (63.5 g)

Stamps: "S•RICHARDS" in roman letters, struck once on back of each handle.

Engraved on front of handle: (a) "RR"; (b) "JSL/ EFL/ EVS". All in foliate script.

Description: (a) pointed oval bowl with swage-formed rounded drop; rounded downturned fiddle-shape handle with midrib; (b) oval bowl with swage-formed pointed drop; rounded downturned handle.

Spectrographic analysis: Silver content ranges from 90.1 to 90.8 percent.

Provenance: (a) Gebelein Silversmiths, Boston; (b) Mr. and Mrs. Stanley B. Ineson, New York City; Mr. and Mrs. Alfred E. Bissell, Wilmington, Del.

Comments: This is the same stamp that is on the basket owned by the Art Institute of Chicago.

References: Belden, *Marks of American Silversmiths*, p. 354.

(a) 72.97 Museum purchase from Gebelein Silversmiths, 1972; (b) 62.240.1406 Gift of Mr. and Mrs. Alfred E. Bissell, 1962–63

434 a, b
SPOONS, 1793–1818

(a) L. 6" (15.2 cm), 12 dwt. 4 gr. (18.9 g)
(b) L. 9 ³⁄₁₆" (23.3 cm), 1 oz. 17 dwt. 9 gr. (58.0 g)

Stamps: "S. RICHARDS" in roman letters, in a rectangle, struck once on back of each handle. Accompanied by an 8-petal incuse floret on (a). Name stamps are not identical.

Engraved on front of handle: (a) "ACH"; (b) "SS". All in foliate script.

Description: (a) pointed oval bowl with swage-formed rounded drop; rounded downturned fiddle-shape handle with midrib; (b) oval bowl with swage-formed rounded drop; rounded downturned handle.

Spectrographic analysis: Silver content ranges from 90.2 to 92.5 percent.

Provenance: (a) The Silver Shelf, Ardmore, Pa.; (b) Mr. and Mrs. Stanley B. Ineson, New York City; Mr. and Mrs. Alfred E. Bissell, Wilmington, Del.

References: Belden, *Marks of American Silversmiths*, p. 355.

(a) 73.194 Museum purchase from the Silver Shelf, 1973; (b) 62.240.1408 Gift of Mr. and Mrs. Alfred E. Bissell, 1962–63

435 a, b
SPOONS, 1793–1818

(a) L. 9 ¼" (23.5 cm), 2 oz. 1 dwt. 21 gr. (65.0 g)
(b) L. 6 ¹⁄₁₆" (15.4 cm), 12 dwt. 1 gr. (18.7 g)

Stamps: "SR" in roman letters, in a rectangle, struck twice on back of handle (a). "S.R" in roman letters, in a rectangle, struck once on back of handle (b).

Engraved on front of handle: (a) "LS"; (b) "RRS". All in foliate script.

Description: (a) deep oval bowl with swage-formed squared drop and a spread-winged bird perched on a heraldic band; pointed downturned handle; (b) pointed oval bowl with swage-formed rounded drop; pointed downturned fiddle-shape handle with midrib.

Spectrographic analysis: Silver content ranges from 90.1 to 92.4 percent.

Provenance: (a) Mr. and Mrs. Stanley B. Ineson, New York City; Mr. and Mrs. Alfred E. Bissell, Wilmington, Del.; (b) Gebelein Silversmiths, Boston.

References: Belden, *Marks of American Silversmiths*, p. 355.

(a) 62.240.1424 Gift of Mr. and Mrs. Alfred E. Bissell, 1962–63; (b) 72.96 Museum purchase from Gebelein Silversmiths, 1972

Francis Richardson

1681–1729
Philadelphia, Pennsylvania

Born in New York City shortly after the arrival from England of his parents, Francis and Rebecca (Haward) Richardson, young Francis Richardson spent most of his childhood in the elegant Philadelphia house of his stepfather, Edward Shippen. (His father having died suddenly in 1688, Richardson's mother married Shippen the following year.) Although there is no record of his apprenticeship, there are various opinions. Martha Gandy Fales argues that he served it with Johannes Nys, whose name later appears in Richardson's records and whose stamp closely resembles Richardson's. Beatrice Garvan argues that the similarity of his stamp and his work to Newport and Boston work suggests training in one of those centers. Richardson did find it necessary to travel to Boston in 1703 to purchase the tools for his trade, although in 1701 he had made and sold a pair of shoe buckles to William Penn. In 1705 Richardson married Elizabeth Growden, and they lived in Letitia Court, off what is now Market Street. Following her death in 1714, he took two trips to London. Thereafter his mercantile practice became more important than silversmithing. In 1726 he married Letitia Swift and moved to Front Street. Richardson's silver is rare today. Of his children, Francis, Jr., the eldest, became a silversmith and a merchant, but it was his son Joseph who became one of the most important silversmiths of colonial America.

References: Fales, *Joseph Richardson and Family*, pp. 2–21. *Philadelphia: Three Centuries*, pp. 17–19. Richardson family papers, Downs collection, Winterthur.

436
CANN, ca. 1720

H. 5 11/16" (14.5 cm), w. 6 13/16" (17.3 cm)
17 oz. 12 dwt. 20 gr. (548.8 g)

Stamps: "FR" in roman letters, in a shield with a crown above, in its own conforming surround, struck once on back of handle.

Engraved on back of handle: "P∗S" in shaded roman letters. *Scratched on underside of body:* a roman "B".

Description: raised body with straight tapering sides, slightly flared rim, and concave bottom; single applied molding at rim; centerpunch on underside of body. Applied seamed 2-step base molding consists of a concave over a convex molding with a small fillet above and a plain straight base. Raised-and-soldered hollow S-curve handle terminating in a plain shield with ears (shield concave in profile); sprig formed by extra layer of silver on upper handle; circular vent inside lower end.

Spectrographic analysis:

	SILVER	COPPER	LEAD	GOLD
BODY SIDE	93.5	6.0	0.29	0.15
HANDLE	94.5	5.1	0.30	0.18
BASE MOLDING	91.5	7.8	0.29	0.13

History: According to family tradition, the initials "P∗S" refer to Phebe Sharpless (1701/2–72), who married Benjamin Hibberd (1707–85) of Chester County, Pa., in 1732. Hibberd's inventory included "a Silver kan & teaspoons." The cann descended in the Hibberd family.

Provenance: Josiah Hibberd, East Whitelands, Pa.; Willoughby Farr; Mr. and Mrs. N. McLean Seabrease, Germantown, Pa., through Robert Ensko, Inc., New York City, to H. F. du Pont, August 1929.

Comments: Fales argues convincingly that this "FR" stamp belongs to Francis Richardson rather than his son Frank (1706–82). The latter used "FR" in a rectangle. There is no record in the Richardson manuscripts at Winterthur of the sale of a cann to the Sharpless or Hibberd families, but of course it could have been purchased by someone else as a gift. The placement of the maker's stamp is unusual; it could hardly have been done after the handle was assembled.

References: Francis Richardson account book, Richardson family papers, Downs collection, Winterthur. Fales, *American Silver*, no. 44. Fales, *Joseph Richardson and Family*, fig. 6, pp. 13, 271. Fennimore, *Silver and Pewter*, no. 159. Kauffman, *Colonial Silversmith*, p. 106.

58.2382 Gift of H. F. du Pont, 1965

☙437
GOLD CLASP, ca. 1720

L. 1 1/16" (2.7 cm), w. 3/4" (1.9 cm), H. 1/4" (0.6 cm) 18 dwt. 1 gr. (28.0 g)

Stamps: "FR" in roman letters, in a heart, struck once on back.

Engraved on backplate: "SC" in crude roman letters. *Engraved on frontplate:* 6-petal flower with cross-hatching in center and pointed leaves between each petal; double-scored line border.

Description: clasp consists of a convex oval frontplate joined by sidewalls to a concave backplate to create a hollow interior to receive tongue on left side. Backplate extends on right to a tab pierced with 5 holes. Rectangular friction-fit tongue with tab as above.

Spectrographic analysis:

GOLD	SILVER	COPPER	
87.0	9.4	3.6	21 karat

Provenance: Arthur J. Sussell, Philadelphia; Parke-Bernet Galleries, New York City, October 1958.

Exhibitions: "American Jewelry," sponsored by the National Society of Colonial Dames at the Wilmington Fine Arts Center, Wilmington, Del., 1962. "American Gold," Yale University Art Gallery, New Haven, 1963.

Comments: The clasp is attached to 3 strands of coral beads that are not original to it. The same engraved floral design is found on a box with the same stamp now owned by the Philadelphia Museum of Art. The sale of 3 gold lockets is recorded in Francis Richardson, Sr.'s, account book. For the one sold May 20, 1720, he charged £1.0.8 for the gold and £1.8.8 for the making.

References: Bohan, *American Gold*, no. 48. Fales, *Joseph Richardson and Family*, fig. 11, pp. 13–14. Parke-Bernet Galleries, sale no. 1847, Arthur J. Sussell sale, pt. 1 (October 23–25, 1958), lot 440.

58.120.3 Museum purchase from Parke-Bernet Galleries, 1958

Joseph Richardson, Sr.

1711–84
Philadelphia, Pennsylvania

Son of Francis Richardson (1681–1729), who together with his sons and grandsons constituted a dynasty of silversmithing in Philadelphia, Joseph Richardson produced large quantities of silver for nearly half a century. His brother, Francis Richardson (known as Frank), began as a silversmith but quickly turned most of his attention to mercantile pursuits. It was Joseph who inherited his father's tools and who remained active with the hammer throughout his career—notwithstanding substantial imports of English silver. Joseph married Hannah Worril in 1741, but she died about five years later. In 1748 he married Mary Allen, who became the mother of Joseph, Jr., and Nathaniel, both of whom learned the craft from their father. In the 1730s John Hutton, at the rather advanced age of fifty-one, began working for Joseph, Sr., and continued to do so through the 1740s. In 1760 Joseph joined fellow silversmiths Daniel Dupuy, William Ball, John Leacock, Edmund Milne, and James Satterthwaite in a shipping venture to Guadaloupe. Joseph was active in the Society of Friends and a supporter of the Pennsylvania Hospital and other charities. Being a devout Quaker did not prevent him from making an elaborate teakettle-on-stand for the Plumstead family (now at Yale University Art Gallery), perhaps the most thoroughgoing example of eighteenth-century American rococo silver. In fairness, however, most of Richardson's work is restrained rather than flamboyant, often to the point of plainness. His life and work is covered in great detail in Martha Gandy Fales's book *Joseph Richardson and Family: Philadelphia Silversmiths*. She has arranged his various stamps in chronological order, which greatly aids in dating.

References: Fales, *Joseph Richardson and Family*. Martha Gandy Fales, "Some Forged Richardson Silver," *Antiques* 79, no. 5 (May 1961): 466–69. *Philadelphia Silver*, nos. 333–99. Richardson Family Papers, Downs collection, Winterthur. Joseph Richardson, account books for 1733–40, 1745–48, Historical Society of Pennsylvania, Philadelphia.

438
WHISTLE-CORAL-BELLS, ca. 1740

L. 5" (12.7 cm)
1 oz. 1 dwt. (48.2 g)

Stamps: "IR" in roman letters, in a rectangle, struck once on mouthpiece of whistle.

Description: body consists of 2 hollow cylinders joined by a baluster form. Octagonal baluster has bells dangling from shanks at each of 4 corners. Upper cylinder fitted with a whistle, shank, and ring; crudely incised lines divide cylinder into panels. Lower cylinder fitted with curvilinear shanks with dangling bells; pink coral extension fitted into scalloped lower end. Total of 8 bells.

Spectrographic analysis:

	SILVER	COPPER	LEAD	GOLD
MOUTHPIECE	92.4	5.9	1.1	0.12
BALUSTER	90.3	7.7	1.4	0.17
CYLINDER	94.0	5.0	0.30	0.11
CORAL SOCKET	95.5	3.2	0.12	0.06
BELL	94.6	5.0	0.27	0.09

Provenance: Joe Kindig, Jr., York, Pa.

Exhibitions: "Colonial Silversmiths, Masters and Apprentices," Museum of Fine Arts, Boston, 1956. "Philadelphia Silver, 1682–1800," Philadelphia Museum of Art, 1956. "Christmas Exhibition," Abby Aldrich Rockefeller Folk Art Center, Williamsburg, Va., 1958–59. "Children in America: A Study of Images and Attitudes," High Museum of Art, Atlanta, 1978–79.

Comments: Whistle-coral-bells are found in children's portraits from the sixteenth to the nineteenth centuries. Paul Van Somer's portrait of Elizabeth, daughter of James I, at Temple Newsam House, Leeds, Eng., and a pastel portrait of James Hopkinson by his father, Francis Hopkinson, the Signer, at the Maryland Historical Society, are 2 examples. Whistle-coral-bells are relatively fragile objects and usually show signs of repair. Smoothed coral apparently is pleasant for infants to suck on, while auditory pleasure was obtained from shaking the bells and blowing the whistle. In eighteenth-century America these objects were termed variously *coral and bells*, *socket and bells*, or *whistle and bells*. Logically, perhaps, they should be referred to as coral-whistle-and-bells.

References: Bernice Ball, "Whistles with Coral and Bells," *Antiques* 80, no. 6 (December 1961): 552–55, fig. 6. Buhler, *Masters and Apprentices*, no. 320. Fales, *American Silver*, no. 19. Fales, *Joseph Richardson and Family*, p. 135, fig. 119. Fennimore, *Silver and Pewter*, no. 219. Rosamond Olmsted Humm, *Children in America: A Study of Images and Attitudes* (Atlanta: High Museum of Art, 1978), p. 55. *Philadelphia Silver*, no. 363. See also Abby Hansen, "Coral in Children's Portraits: A Charm Against the Evil Eye," *Antiques* 120, no. 6 (December 1981): 1424–31.

56.560 Gift of H. F. du Pont, 1965

❦ 439
GOLD CLASP, ca. 1750

L. (with tongue) 1 ⅛" (2.9 cm), w. ¾" (1.9 cm), H. ¼" (0.6 cm)
3 dwt. 20 gr. (6.0 g)

Stamps: "IR" in roman letters, in a rectangle, struck once on backplate.

Engraved on backplate: "EC" in crude roman letters. *Engraved on frontplate:* basket of fruit atop 2 scrolls and flanked by larger leafy scrolls; border consists of alternating diagonal lines and dots within double-scored lines.

Description: clasp consists of a convex oval frontplate joined by sidewalls to a conforming backplate to create a hollow interior to receive tongue on right side. Backplate extends on left into 5 pierced lobes reinforced with applied rings. Rectangular friction-fit tongue with 5 lobes as above.

Spectrographic analysis:

GOLD	SILVER	COPPER	
85.7	8.6	3.9	21 karat

History: "EC" refers to Elizabeth Coultas, whose manuscript cookbook dated January 4, 1749/50, was also acquired by Winterthur at the same time. She is probably the wife of James Coultas, who was commissioned sheriff of Philadelphia on October 4, 1755, for a term of 3 years. The manuscript is boldly inscribed on the cover: "Elizabeth Coultas/ Her Receipt Book/ January ye 9th 1749/50." Its 24 leaves include recipes for cooking meatballs, "white Frigacy of Chickens," a rump of beef (stewed), pigeon pie, mushrooms, sauces for fish, venison, and woodcock, and many puddings. Pickling instructions are provided for walnuts, cucumbers, and nasturtium buds. There are several cures for scalds and burns and one for "a pain in the stomach and a heavy heart" that calls for a brew of rose water, sugar, and saffron.

Provenance: Arthur J. Sussell, Philadelphia; H. F. du Pont purchased from Parke-Bernet Galleries, New York City, January 23, 1959.

Exhibitions: "American Gold, 1700–1860," Yale University Art Gallery, New Haven, 1963.

References: Bohan, *American Gold*, no. 51. Peter J. Bohan, "Early American Gold," *Antiques* 88, no. 6 (December 1965): fig. 12. Parke-Bernet Galleries, sale no. 1872, Arthur J. Sussell sale, part 2 (January 22–24, 1959), lot 330 (illus.). Fales, *Joseph Richardson and Family*, p. 144, fig. 127. "Shop Talk," *Antiques* 54, no. 3 (September 1948): 152 (illus.), which mistakenly states that it is stamped "JR." John Thomas Scharf and Thompson Westcott, *History of Philadelphia, 1609–1884* (Philadelphia: L. H. Everts, 1884), 3:1737, for list of sheriffs of Philadelphia in colonial period. Manuscript cookbook, 60x25, Downs collection, Winterthur.

59.17.3 Museum purchase, with funds provided by H. F. du Pont, 1959

440
BOWL, ca. 1735–50

H. 2⅞" (7.3 cm), DIAM. rim 4⁹⁄₁₆" (11.6 cm)
5 oz. 1 dwt. (157.1 g)

Stamps: "IR" in roman letters, in a rectangle, struck twice on underside of body.

Engraved on side of body: "W / T•R" in shaded roman letters. *Scratched on underside of body:* "256".

Description: raised circular hemispherical body with slightly flaring sides and applied molded rim; centerpunch on underside; seamed molded footring.

Spectrographic analysis:

	SILVER	COPPER	LEAD	GOLD
BODY SIDE	92.2	7.1	0.46	0.10
FOOTRING	91.4	7.5	0.42	0.10

History: Tradition of ownership in the Wistar family. Research by Fales at the time of acquisition failed to turn up any Wistar with these initials. She did, however, find a reference in Joseph Richardson's accounts to the sale of a silver bowl to one Thomas Willard in 1738.

Provenance: Tiffany & Co., New York City.

Comments: Probably made for use as a waste bowl.

References: Fales, *Joseph Richardson and Family*, fig. 60.

58.56 Museum purchase from Tiffany & Co., 1958

❧ 441
PORRINGER,
ca. 1750–70

DIAM. bowl 5 $^{11}/_{16}$" (14.5 cm), H. 2" (5.1 cm),
W. 8 $^{1}/_{32}$" (20.4 cm)
7 oz. 9 dwt. 1 gr. (231.8 g)

Stamps: "IR" in roman letters, in a rectangle,
struck twice on underside of handle. Accompanied by 2 incuse acanthus-type curved leaves.

Engraved on front of handle (facing outward):
"S/ +H" in shaded roman letters. *Engraved on
side of body opposite handle:* "Joseph & Hannah.
Saunders. Married January 8th/ 1740–41./ A
Legacy from Hannah Paul to Saunders Lewis
1854." in script.

Description: raised circular bowl with bulging
sides and angled rim; bottom domed in center;
centerpunch outside and inside; cast handle
pierced in keyhole pattern with 9 voids.

Spectrographic analysis:

	SILVER	COPPER	GOLD	LEAD
BODY	94.0	5.3	0.56	0.21
HANDLE	94.6	5.1	0.05	0.20

History: The initials may refer to Hannah
Reeves (1717–88) and Joseph Saunders, whose
marriage was sanctioned by the Philadelphia
Monthly Meeting in 1740.

Provenance: Marshall P. Blankarn, New York
City.

References: Crane, *Diary of Elizabeth Drinker*,
p. 2208, for the Reeves-Saunders marriage.

79.209 Gift of Marshall P. Blankarn, 1979

❧ 442
MEDAL, 1757

DIAM. 1 ¾" (4.4 cm), H. ⅛" (0.3 cm)
4 dwt. 2 gr. (6.4 g)

Stamps: "WG" in roman letters, in a rectangle,
struck once on obverse in middle of date.
Struck by Richardson; see *History.*

Description: circular coin with hole in upper
edge; double-molded edge both sides. Obverse:
bust portrait of man (facing left) wearing
crown of laurel; relief inscription around edge:
"GEORGIUS•II•DEI•GRATIA•" in roman
letters. Reverse: seminude male figure seated
on ground (on left) facing male figure seated
on stool (on right) and wearing frock coat and
tricorn hat; both figures have upraised right
arms; tree on right; sun with rays at upper left;
relief inscription "J7[WG]7"; relief inscription around edge: "[LET US] LOOK TO
THE [MOST HIGH] WHO BLESSED OUR
FATHERS WITH [PEACE]" in roman letters.

Spectrographic analysis:

	SILVER	COPPER	GOLD	LEAD
OBVERSE	92.4	7.0	0.23	0.18
REVERSE	91.7	7.6	0.29	0.24

History: This medal was commissioned by the
Friendly Association for Regaining and Preserving Peace with the Indians by Pacific Measures, a largely Quaker organization formed in
Philadelphia in 1757; Richardson was a member.
The die was cut by Edward Duffield, clockmaker, at a cost of £15. In 1813 Joseph Richardson,
Jr., wrote to Thomas Wistar concerning the
medal: "The impressions which I now respectfully offer for thy acceptance are from dies that
have long been in the possession of my predecessor and myself; at the early time they were
engraved, coining presses were unknown in this
country, they were therefore cut on punches,
fixed in a socket, and struck with a sledge hammer. . . . I remember well the striking of the
Indian medal by my father, it was executed in
silver and presented to the Indians by the Society." It is recorded that the Friendly Association
paid Richardson £32.11.6 on July 14, 1757, and
£35.5.0 on October 26, 1757. In subsequent years
he made some 2,860 silver armbands, wristbands, hair plates, ear bobs, hair bobs, brooches,
crosses, gorgets, moons, and rings for presentation to Native Americans.

Provenance: H. F. du Pont.

Comments: The "WG" stamp may refer to William Ghiselin, grandson of Philadelphia's first silversmith, Caesar Ghiselin. William Ghiselin advertised in 1751 and 1752 and was an active Mason. It is unclear why his stamp should appear on the medal when its origins are so well documented. Silversmiths occasionally stamped a countermark on coins to verify their full value in an age when coins were often debased by clipping.

References: Fales, *Joseph Richardson and Family*, pp. 140–41, 297–98, fig. 124, for a better impression of the medal. Ensko, *American Silversmiths* IV, pp. 85, 339, for William Ghiselin.

67.615 Bequest of H. F. du Pont, 1969

443
SPOON, ca. 1730–50

L. 7 %6" (19.2 cm), 1 oz. 8 dwt. 23 gr. (45.0 g)

Stamps: "IR" in roman letters, in an oval, struck twice on back of handle.

Engraved on back of handle: "B/ GC" in shaded roman letters.

Description: elongated oval bowl with swage-formed rattail; rounded upturned handle with midrib.

Spectrographic analysis: Silver content is 91.1 percent.

Provenance: Mr. and Mrs. Stanley B. Ineson, New York City; Mr. and Mrs. Alfred E. Bissell, Wilmington, Del.

Comments: This is Richardson's earliest stamp.

References: Fales, *Joseph Richardson and Family*, p. 73. Belden, *Marks of American Silversmiths*, p. 356.

62.240.1378 Gift of Mr. and Mrs. Alfred E. Bissell, 1962–63

444 a–e
SPOONS, ca. 1750–80

(a) L. 7 ¹³⁄₁₆" (19.8 cm), 1 oz. 11 dwt. 23 gr. (49.6 g)
(b) L. 8 ⅛" (20.6 cm), 2 oz. 19 dwt. 15 gr. (92.6 g)
(c) L. 6 ¾" (17.1 cm), 1 oz. 1 dwt. 22 gr. (35.0 g)
(d) L. 4 ⅝" (11.7 cm), 5 dwt. 22 gr. (9.2 g)
(e) L. 4 ⅝" (11.7 cm), 6 dwt. 15 gr. (10.3 g)

Stamps: "IR" in roman letters, in a rectangle, struck twice on (b, d, e), 3 times on (a), and once on (c), all on back of handle.

Engraved on back of handle: (a) "R/ IM"; (b) "E/ IM"; (c) "MM"; (d) "MB"; (e) "HH", all in shaded roman letters.

Description: oval bowls; rounded drop with 14-lobe shell and arc on (a, c); double rounded drop on (b); rounded drop on (d); rounded drop with 9-lobe shell on (e); rounded upturned handles with midribs.

Spectrographic analysis: Silver content ranges from 88.0 to 92.6 percent.

Provenance: Mr. and Mrs. Stanley B. Ineson, New York City; Mr. and Mrs. Alfred E. Bissell, Wilmington, Del.

Comments: This is the most common version of Richardson's stamp; variations of it were used from about 1750 onward. This group of spoons bears early characteristics, such as engraved inscriptions in roman letters on the backs of upturned handles.

References: Belden, *Marks of American Silversmiths*, p. 357. Fales, *Joseph Richardson and Family*, p. 73.

62.240.1376, .1382, .1435, .549, .548 Gift of Mr. and Mrs. Alfred E. Bissell, 1962–63

445 a–e
SPOONS, ca. 1780

(a) L. 5 ½" (14.0 cm), 7 dwt. 7 gr. (11.4 g)
(b) L. 4 ¾" (12.1 cm), 6 dwt. (9.3 g)
(c) L. 8 ¼" (21.0 cm), 1 oz. 16 dwt. 6 gr. (56.3 g)
(d) L. 4 ¹⁵⁄₁₆" (12.5 cm), 5 dwt. 9 gr. (8.4 g)
(e) L. 4 ⅞" (12.4 cm), 5 dwt. 7 gr. (8.3 g)

Stamps: "IR" in roman letters, in a rectangle, struck once on back of handles (a, d, e) and twice on back of handles (b, c). Stamps on (d, e) have a notch in lower right side of surround.

Engraved on front of handle: (a) "RG" in script, in a wheelwork medallion with bright-cut pendant drop; (b) "SB" in crude shaded roman letters; (c) "ML" in shaded roman letters; (d, e) "B" in foliate script.

Description: (a) pointed oval bowl with swage-formed pointed drop; pointed downturned handle with midrib; (b) oval bowl with swage-formed rounded drop; rounded downturned handle with midrib; (c) elongated oval bowl with swage-formed rounded drop and 14-lobe shell and arc; rounded downturned handle with midrib; (d, e) oval bowl with no drop; rounded straight handles.

Spectrographic analysis: Silver content ranges from 88.5 to 95.6 percent.

Provenance: Mr. and Mrs. Stanley B. Ineson, New York City; Mr. and Mrs. Alfred E. Bissell, Wilmington, Del.

Comments: While the stamps are similar to those on the last group of spoons, these spoons all bear late characteristics, such as downturned handles with script initials on the front.

References: Belden, *Marks of American Silversmiths*, p. 357. Fales, *Joseph Richardson and Family*, p. 73.

62.240.543, .547, .1379, .540, .542 Gift of Mr. and Mrs. Alfred E. Bissell, 1962–63

❦ Joseph Richardson, Jr.

1752–1831
Philadelphia, Pennsylvania
See Joseph & Nathaniel Richardson,
w. 1777–90

Joseph Richardson, Jr., along with his brother Nathaniel, learned the craft of silversmithing from their father, Joseph Richardson, Sr., with whom they continued to work for several years beyond the normal term of service. In 1780 Joseph married Ruth Hoskins at the Friends Meeting in Burlington, New Jersey. It is unclear when the two brothers formed their partnership, perhaps around 1780, but it ended in 1790 when Nathaniel decided to become an ironmonger. Joseph continued in business by himself until at least 1801, making large quantities of silver, much of it contracted by the United States government for presentation to the Indians. In 1795 George Washington appointed him second assayer of the United States Mint, a position he held for more than thirty-five years. From about 1801 he devoted most of his time to the mint (although he continued to pursue other business ventures and, indeed, took an apprentice in 1801). Most of the silver made by him, therefore, dates between 1790 and 1801. In view of the large number of surviving pieces, he must have had a very active shop. In 1805 he moved to a new house on Market Street between Ninth and Tenth, then on the outskirts of town. His old house on Front Street was occupied by James Howell, a silversmith who did business for a time under the name of Richardson & Company. Howell may in fact have been making and marketing silver with Joseph Richardson's stamp. This possibility is suggested by the fact that Howell was in debt to Richardson and that his business operation carried the Richardson name. Joseph owned stock in the Schuylkill Navigation Company,

the City of Philadelphia, the Bank of Pennsylvania, the Bank of North America, and the Chesapeake and Delaware Canal Company. With Joseph's death in 1831, the Richardson dynasty of goldsmiths came to an end.

The urn style dominated his work, as it had during the partnership with Nathaniel, a quintessential example being the tea service in no. 446. But he continued making traditional objects, such as the gold clasp in no. 448, which looks similar to those made by his father and grandfather. He also sold imported silver

and fused plate, and, like most silversmiths, he made many repairs. Elizabeth Drinker noted in her diary for October 7, 1794: "A silver Coffee pot from J. Richardson's, cost 20 guineas, a present from H. D. to [J. C—ne]."

References: Fales, *Joseph Richardson and Family*, chaps. 6, 7. Joseph Richardson, Jr., letterbook, 53.165.209, and other Richardson family papers, Downs collection, Winterthur. See also Richardson family papers at Historical Society of Pennsylvania. Crane, *Diary of Elizabeth Drinker*, p. 602.

446 a–s
COFFEE AND TEA SERVICE, ca. 1795

(a) Coffeepot: H. 13 1/16" (33.2 cm), W. 12 7/8" (32.7 cm)

40 oz. 12 dwt. 3 gr. (1263.0 g)

(b) Teapot: H. 5 7/8" (14.9 cm), W. 11 5/8" (29.5 cm)

22 oz. 17 dwt. 1 gr. (710.8 g)

(c) Teapot: H. 5 3/8" (13.7 cm), W. 10 15/16" (27.8 cm)

20 oz. 7 dwt. 16 gr. (632.5 g)

(d) Sugar urn with lid: H. 10 1/2" (26.7 cm), W. 4 13/16" (12.2 cm)

16 oz. 13 dwt. 23 gr. (518.2 g)

(e) Creamer: H. 7" (17.8 cm), W. 5 3/16" (13.2 cm)

5 oz. 9 dwt. 8 gr. (170.0 g)

(f) Waste bowl: H. 5 3/4" (14.6 cm), DIAM. 6 1/2" (16.5 cm)

15 oz. 3 dwt. 9 gr. (471.8 g)

(g) Tongs: L. 6 1/4" (15.9 cm)

1 oz. 6 dwt. (40.4 g)

(h–s) Spoons: average L. 5 3/4" (13.6 cm)

1 oz. 3 dwt. (17.9 g) average

Stamps: "J•R" in roman letters, in a rectangle, struck 4 times on underside of bases (a, e, f); struck twice on underside of base (d); struck 4 times on underside of body (b); struck twice on underside of body (c); struck once inside bow of (g); struck twice on back of each handle (h–s).

Engraved on side of all hollowware, on outside of bow (g), and on front of all spoon handles: "AE" in shaded foliate script. On hollowware, initials are flanked by crossed leafy branches tied with a ribbon. On spoons they are enclosed in an oval bright-cut medallion. *Scratched on underside of pedestal:* (a) "oz 38"; *underside of body:* (b) "oz 24 dwts 17"; *underside of body:* (c) "oz 18 dwts 11"; *inside pedestal:* (d) "oz 17"; *inside pedestal:* (e) "[?]/ dwts 10"; *inside pedestal:* (f) "oz 15 dwts 8".

Description: all lidded pieces have pierced galleries and beading around rim; all other hollowware has applied bands of beading around rim, at top and bottom of pedestal, or around foot (b, c only). All lids loose fitting.

(a) Coffeepot: raised urn-shape body, oval in plan, with incurved neck and beading at shoulders; no centerpunch. Oval trumpet-shape pedestal on a rectangular base with plain applied sides. S-curve seamed spout with beading on upper and lower sides. C-curve hardwood handle with carved acanthus leaf and sprig on upper side; cylindrical upper socket, cone-shape lower socket, both with beading, 2 silver pins. Raised circular lid, oval in plan, short bezel, curves in and up to beaded knop; cast pineapple finial over 5 splayed leaves secured through lid by silver nut and bolt.

(b, c) Teapots: seamed body, oval in plan, with straight sides, flat top and bottom; body pierced at spout to serve as strainer; no centerpunch. Seamed, straight, tapering spout mounted at angle. Raised-and-domed lid, oval in plan, with short bezel and finial as on (a). C-curve handles as on (a); cylindrical sockets with beading; 2 silver pins per vessel.

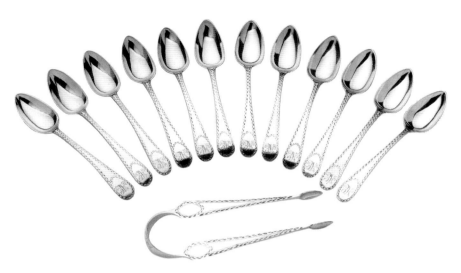

	SILVER	COPPER	GOLD	LEAD
(e) Creamer				
BODY SIDE	90.5	8.3	0.11	0.84
BASE	90.8	8.4	0.14	0.36
HANDLE	89.1	9.9	0.13	0.86
(f) Waste bowl				
BODY SIDE	89.3	9.9	0.04	0.17
BASE	90.6	8.3	0.07	0.28
(g) Tongs				
	90.5	8.5	0.11	0.51

(h–s) Spoons: Silver content ranges from 89.6 to 91.4 percent.

Provenance: H. F. du Pont.

Exhibitions: (c) "Decorative Arts of the Federal Period," Currier Gallery of Art, Manchester, N.H. (b or c) "Technological Innovation and the Decorative Arts," Hagley Museum and Library, Wilmington, Del., 1973.

Comments: This is the most complete service known to have been made by an American silversmith in the eighteenth century. It is the perfect expression of the Philadelphia urn style, with its pierced galleries, beaded borders,

(d) Sugar urn with lid: raised circular urn-shape body; centerpunch on underside of body. Circular trumpet-shape pedestal mounted on square base with plain applied sides. Raised circular lid similar to (a) except that it has a cast urn-shape finial.

(e) Creamer: raised helmet-shape body with high pouring lip, low sides, and a high back that rises to a point; no centerpunch. Pedestal and base as on (d). High-loop strap handle with a sprig tapers to point at bottom.

(f) Waste bowl: raised circular bowl form; centerpunch on underside. Pedestal and base as on (d).

(g) Tongs: U-shape form with bow back, flat tapered arms at right angles, and oval spoon grips; bright-cut borders with pointed oval medallions enhanced by wheelwork.

(h–s) Spoons: pointed oval bowl with swage-formed rounded drop; rounded downturned handle with midrib on back; bright-cut borders and oval medallion enhanced by wheelwork on front.

Spectrographic analysis:

	SILVER	COPPER	GOLD	LEAD
(a) Coffeepot				
BODY SIDE	89.5	9.5	0.20	0.23
SPOUT	92.4	7.2	0.19	0.15
HANDLE SOCKET	92.4	6.3	0.19	0.17
FINIAL	91.9	7.6	0.20	0.22
(b) Teapot				
BODY SIDE	91.0	7.6	0.70	0.16
SPOUT	90.8	7.6	0.65	0.21
BASE	93.6	5.0	0.72	0.26
LID	89.0	9.3	0.92	0.25

Note unusually high gold content.

	SILVER	COPPER	GOLD	LEAD
(c) Teapot				
BODY SIDE	95.3	4.4	0.19	0.17
SPOUT	90.2	9.5	0.17	0.17
BASE	95.3	4.3	0.17	0.17
LID	91.0	8.7	0.14	0.14
(d) Sugar urn				
BODY SIDE	88.7	10.7	0.20	0.37
GALLERY	84.0	15.7	0.11	0.23
BASE	88.9	10.6	0.20	0.32
LID	94.1	5.5	0.18	0.20

steepled lids, and circular pedestals on square bases. Both teapots have strainers (hence the names), but one was probably used as a hot water pot. Note that one is slightly smaller than the other.

References: Fales, *American Silver*, nos. 80, 81, 86, 118. Fales, *Joseph Richardson and Family*, fig. 166. Fales, *Early American Silver*, fig. 136. Donald L. Fennimore, "Joseph Richardson, Junior, Tea and Coffee Set," *Silver* 16, no. 6 (November/December 1983): 20–21. Fennimore, *Silver and Pewter*, no. 139, but illustrated under no. 138. Kauffman, *Colonial Silversmith*, p. 133. *Technological Innovation and the Decorative Arts* (Wilmington, Del.: Eleutherian Mills–Hagley Foundation, 1973), no. 10.

57.825, .823, .822, .827, .826, .824, .828, and .830.1–.12 Gift of H. F. du Pont, 1965

🍃 447 a–c
TEA SERVICE, ca. 1797

(a) Teapot: H. 9 %6" (24.3 cm), w. 10 ⅜" (26.4 cm)
26 oz. 2 dwt. 15 gr. (810.9 g)
(b) Sugar urn with lid: H. 8 ¹³⁄₁₆" (22.4 cm), DIAM. 4 ½" (11.4 cm)
15 oz. 5 dwt. 2 gr. (473.4 g)
(c) Creamer: H. 6 ⅞₆" (16.4 cm), w. 4 ¹¹⁄₁₆" (11.9 cm)
5 oz. 8 dwt. 8 gr. (168.1 g)

Stamps: "JR" in roman letters, in an irregular surround, struck 4 times on underside of base (1 in each corner) of (a, b). "JR" in roman letters, struck incuse twice on underside of base (in opposite corners) of (c).

Engraved on sides of (a, b) and on front of (c): "SM" in foliate script. *Engraved inside sidewall of all bases:* "Sarah Marshall, 1797" in slanted roman letters. *Scratched on underside of pedestal:* (a) "oz 24 dwt 19"; (b) "oz 15 dwt 7".

Description: raised circular urn-shape bodies joined to trumpet-shape pedestals on square applied foot; beading at top and bottom of pedestals. (a) Teapot: body joined to incurving

neck by an applied molded band with beading; concave molding applied to rim; body perforated at spout to serve as strainer; ringlike centerpunch on underside of body. Raised circular lid curves in and up to beaded-and-domed knop; acorn finial; vent; 3-segment hinge inset within circumference of lid. Plain S-curve seamed spout terminates in beak. C-curve hardwood handle with sprig; cylindrical sockets with beaded rims; silver pins.

(b) Sugar urn with lid: body has an applied molded band with beading at rim; ringlike centerpunch on underside of body. Friction-fit lid same as (a) but without vent and with a larger bezel.

(c) Creamer: raised circular helmet-shape body with high pouring lip, low sides, and high back rising to a point; applied band of beading around rim; centerpunch on underside of body. High-loop strap handle with sprig tapers to point at bottom.

Spectrographic analysis:

	SILVER	COPPER	LEAD	GOLD
(a) Teapot				
BODY SIDE	94.1	5.6	0.13	0.14
SPOUT	96.5	3.3	0.16	0.12
FOOT	96.4	3.4	0.14	0.13
FINIAL	96.5	3.3	0.08	0.07
(b) Sugar bowl				
BODY SIDE	95.6	4.2	0.13	0.11
FOOT	94.7	5.0	0.14	0.12
LID	95.9	3.9	0.16	0.07

	SILVER	COPPER	LEAD	GOLD
(c) Creamer				
BODY SIDE	93.4	6.4	0.13	0.11
FOOT	95.5	4.2	0.13	0.11
HANDLE	94.8	4.9	0.15	0.12

History: "SM" refers to Sarah Marshall Morris; see no. 457.

Provenance: Sarah and Thomas Morris; Mrs. Henry G. Morris; Mr. and Mrs. Anthony Saunders Morris, Bryn Mawr, Pa.

Exhibitions: Wilson-Warner House, Odessa, Del.

Comments: See waste bowl no. 488, by Thomas Whartenby, which is part of the set.

References: Louise C. Belden, "Sallie Morris' Silver," *Antiques* 100, no. 2 (August 1971): 214–16, fig. 2.

70.192.1–.3 Gift of Mr. and Mrs. Anthony Saunders Morris, 1970

448
GOLD CLASP, ca. 1790

L. (with tongue) 1" (2.5 cm), w. ½" (1.3 cm), H. ¼" (0.6 cm)
2 dwt. 1 gr. (3.2 g)

Stamps: "JR" in roman letters, in a rectangle, struck once on backplate.

Engraved on backplate: "DG/ to/ HGR" in roman letters and script. The first "G" is reworked from another initial, possibly "E."
Engraved on frontplate: bird perched on a leafy branch with head turned toward tail, a sprig in its beak; bright-cut featheredge border.

Description: clasp consists of a convex oval frontplate joined by sidewalls to a concave oval backplate to create a hollow interior to receive tongue on left side. Backplate extends on right to a tab pierced with 3 holes. Rectangular friction-fit tongue with tab, as above.

Spectrographic analysis:

GOLD	SILVER	COPPER	
85.3	8.2	6.4	20 karat

Provenance: Eugene J. Sussel, Philadelphia.

Exhibitions: "American Gold, 1700–1860," Yale University Art Gallery, New Haven, 1963.

Comments: Tabs are simpler in construction than those on no. 439 by Joseph Richardson, Sr. In the older one the piercing is reinforced by applied rings; in the later one it is not.

References: Bohan, *American Gold*, no. 58.

58.94 Museum purchase from Eugene S. Sussel, 1958

449
WRISTBAND, ca. 1795

DIAM. 2 13/16" (7.1 cm), H. 1 9/16" (4.0 cm)
1 oz. 5 dwt. 3 gr. (39.1 g)

Stamps: "JR" in roman letters, in a rectangle, struck once on inside of band.

Engraved on outside in center: spread-winged eagle with shield, cluster of arrows in left claw, olive branch in right claw, arc of 15 stars above (Great Seal of the United States).

Description: forged; circular open band pierced with a hole at each end; both outer edges reeded.

Spectrographic analysis:

SILVER	COPPER	LEAD	GOLD
93.7	5.3	0.45	0.17

Provenance: H. F. du Pont.

Exhibitions: "Decorative Arts of the Federal Period," Currier Gallery of Art, Manchester, N.H., 1979. "The American Eagle: Symbol and Spirit, 1782–1882," Katonah Gallery, Katonah, N.Y., 1988–89.

Comments: An entry in Joseph Richardson's accounts for October 29, 1796, is typical of the sales of silver to the U.S. government for presentation to the Indians:

To 30 pair Indian Arm bands weight 185 oz. 2 dwt.
To 60 pair ditto Wrist bands   98 oz. 3 dwt.
to 36 ditto Gorgets   59 oz. 15 dwt.
                               343 oz. 0 dwt.

@£0/12/6   £214/7/6

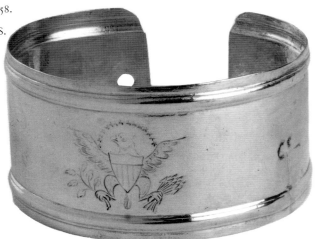

To 30 dozen Broaches	16 oz. 13 dwt. 12 gr.
@ £0/9/0	7/10/0
To making Ditto @ £0/7/6 per dozen	11/12/0
To 9 ½ dozen pair Ear bobs	5 oz. 19 dwt. 0 gr.
@ £0/9/0	2/13/6
To making ditto @ £0/36/0 per dozen pair	17/12/0
To Chasing 96 Eagles @ 0/2/0	9/12/0
To ditto 120 ditto @ 0/1/3	7/10/0
	£270/0/0

Winterthur owns a portrait by Saint-Mémin of an Osage warrior wearing a similar silver armband.

References: Fales, *American Silver*, no. 64. Fales, *Joseph Richardson and Family*, fig. 132, p. 307. John A. H. Sweeney, *The Treasure House of Early American Rooms* (New York: W. W. Norton, 1963), p. 85. See also Harold Gillingham, "Indian Trade Silver Ornaments Made by Joseph Richardson, Jr.," *PMHB* 67, no. 1 (January 1943): 83–91.

59.2308 Gift of H. F. du Pont, 1965

☙ 450
MEDAL, ca. 1789

H. (incl. loop) 5 ⅝" (14.3 cm), W. 4 ³⁄₁₆" (10.6 cm), D. ³⁄₁₆" (0.5 cm)
2 oz. 2 dwt. 9 gr. (65.9 g)

Stamps: None. Attributed to Richardson because he is known to have made and sold quantities of the "large" medals; see *Comments.*

Engraved on obverse: partially draped standing male figure wearing feather headdress, a tomahawk dropping from his right hand, a long-stemmed pipe in his left hand, which is extended toward a standing female figure; she wears a short-sleeve tunic, a long skirt, a short sword at her waist, and a plumed helmet with an emerging snake; a human face is on her left shoulder. On the ground to her left is a plow; below the 2 figures is a detached male head, lying on its side, with a spear below. Inscription: "G. WASHINGTON. PRESIDENT." in shaded roman letters, in an arc overhead; "1789" below. *Engraved on reverse:* Spread-winged eagle clasping an olive branch in his right claw and a bundle of arrows in his left claw; a shield with horizonal and vertical stripes superimposed on his body. Around the eagle's head are 13 stars partially encircled by cloudlike shapes emanating rays. Inscription: "THE UNITED, STATES OF AMERICA." in shaded roman letters.

Description: flat oval plate with a plain applied band as a rim; circular loop applied to uppermost portion.

Spectrographic analysis:

	SILVER	COPPER	GOLD	MERCURY	LEAD
OBVERSE	93.9	5.0	0.32	0.03	0.35
REVERSE	93.8	5.1	0.30	0.03	0.37
RIM	87.0	2.8	1.7	6.1	0.41
LOOP	85.1	4.3	0.40	2.3	6.1

Unusually high amounts of gold and mercury on the rim and loop reveal that they were once gilded.

Provenance: H. F. du Pont.

Exhibitions: Exhibition on federal New York, Fraunces Tavern Museum, New York City, 1986–87.

Comments: This was the first design for a presidential Indian medal. Indians allegedly objected to the allegorical female figure, which is why later versions show the figure of a man. Perhaps, also, Minerva, goddess of war, was an inappropriate symbol of the new nation. The symbolism on both sides of the medal is fairly clear, except for the detached head lying on the ground.

Although the medal has long been attributed to Joseph Richardson, Jr., that attribution is by no means a certainty. A 1793 "List of Silver Ware purchased by Tench Francis, agent, by direction of Alexander Hamilton Esqr Secretary of the Treasury and delivered for the Treaty with the Indians" includes: "18 large Medals Stamp'd JL" and "50 large Medals Stamp'd JR." "JR" is obviously Joseph Richardson; "JL" is, possibly, John Leacock of Philadelphia. Whether an unstamped medal is by yet a different silversmith is a moot point. The fact remains that Richardson was the most prolific supplier at that time.

An identical medal is owned by the American Numismatic Society, New York City.

References: Fales, *American Silver*, no. 61. Fales, *Joseph Richardson and Family*, fig. 134. Kauffman, *Colonial Silversmith*, p. 154. For similar medals, see Bauman L. Belden, *Indian Peace Medals Issued in the United States* (New York: American Numismatic Society, 1927), pl. 1, pp. 11–13; Francis Paul Prucha, *Indian Peace Medals in American History* (Madison: State Historical Society of Wisconsin, 1971), p. 75. John A. H. Sweeney, *The Treasure House of Early American Rooms* (New York: Viking, 1963), p. 85. "List of Silver," Timothy Pickering Papers, box 4, Essex Institute, Salem, Mass.; I am indebted to Nancy Goyne Evans for calling it to my attention.

61.1055 Gift of H. F. du Pont, 1965

451
BOX WITH SILVER FITTINGS, ca. 1794

L. 4 9/16" (11.6 cm), w. 2 5/8" (6.7 cm), H. 1 1/4" (3.2 cm)

Stamps: None. Attributed to Joseph Richardson, Jr., because of inscription; see *Provenance.*

Engraved on oval plaque on lid: "The Gift of Sarah Richardson/ WR/ 1794" in script and foliate script.

Description: oval leather box with straight sides and flat top and bottom; larger portion of lid is hinged flush to smaller, fixed lid. Oval silver medallion in center of lid has bright-cut and wheelwork border; silver trim on front edge of lid has bright-cut decoration.

Spectrographic analysis:

	SILVER	COPPER	LEAD	GOLD
MEDALLION	86.3	11.9	0.60	0.05
TRIM	99.0	0.51	0.02	0.02

Provenance: Acquired by Robert Carlen, a Philadelphia dealer, from a descendant of Joseph Richardson living in southern New Jersey.

Comments: Joseph Richardson, Jr., had a daughter named Sarah (1787–1855). Because its last private owner was a descendant of Joseph Richardson, Jr., the piece is assumed to be made by him for a member of his family. The possibility that it may have been imported should not be ruled out.

References: Fales, *Joseph Richardson and Family*, p. 2.

68.111 Museum purchase from Robert Carlen, 1968

452 a–f
SPOONS, ca. 1797

average L. 9" (22.9 cm)
2 oz. 2 dwt. (65.2 g) average

Stamps: "J•R" in roman letters, in irregular rectangles, struck once on back of each handle. Illegible additional stamp partially patched over on (e).

Engraved on front of each handle: "SM" in foliate script.

Description: elongated oval bowl with swage-formed rounded drop; rounded downturned handle with midrib.

Spectrographic analysis: Silver content ranges from 89.0 to 91.0 percent.

History: "SM" refers to Sarah Marshall Morris; see no. 457.

Provenance: Descended in Morris family to Anthony Saunders Morris, Bryn Mawr, Pa.

Exhibitions: Wilson-Warner House, Odessa, Del.

Comments: Part of set with spoons no. 453 and tea service no. 447.

References: Louise C. Belden, "Sallie Morris' Silver," *Antiques* 100, no. 2 (August 1971): 214–16.

70.193.1–.6 Gift of Mr. and Mrs. Anthony Saunders Morris, 1970

453 a–f
SPOONS, ca. 1797

L. 5 ¾" (14.6 cm) average
10 dwt. (16.9 g) average

Stamps: "JR" in roman letters, in a rectangle, struck twice on back of each handle.

Engraved on front of each handle: "SM" in foliate script.

Description: oval bowl with swage-formed rounded drop; rounded downturned handle with midrib.

Spectrographic analysis: Silver content ranges from 89.4 to 89.9 percent.

History: "SM" refers to Sarah Marshall Morris; see no. 457.

Provenance: Descended in Morris family to Anthony Saunders Morris, Bryn Mawr, Pa.

Exhibitions: Wilson-Warner House, Odessa, Del.

Comments: Part of a set with spoons no. 452 and tea service no. 447, all by Joseph Richardson, Jr.

References: Louise C. Belden, "Sallie Morris' Silver," *Antiques* 100, no. 2 (August 1971): 214–16.

70.194.1–.6 Gift of Mr. and Mrs. Anthony Saunders Morris, 1970

454 a–f
SPOONS AND LADLE, 1790–1801

(a) L. 9 ³⁄₁₆" (23.3 cm)
1 oz. 19 dwt. 16 gr. (61.6 g)
(b) L. 8 ⅞" (22.5 cm)
1 oz. 15 dwt. 16 gr. (55.4 g)
(c) L. 5 ⁷⁄₁₆" (13.8 cm)
10 dwt. 8 gr. (16.0 g)
(d) L. 5 ¼" (13.3 cm)
6 dwt. 15 gr. (10.3 g)
(e) L. 6 ¾" (17.1 cm)
15 dwt. 3 gr. (24.18 g)
(f) L. 6 ⅜" (16.2 cm)
1 oz. 3 dwt. 14 gr. (36.6 g)

Stamps: "J•R" in roman letters, in a rectangle, struck twice on back of all handles, except once on (d).

Engraved on front of handle: (a, c) "TRW" in foliate script; (b) "BAM" in foliate script, in a bright-cut medallion; (d) "MG" in foliate script; (e) "AC" in shaded roman letters; (f) "JSH" in foliate script, in a bright-cut medallion plus "T.H.E.M." in roman letters, below the medallion.

Description: (a–e) oval bowls with swage-formed rounded drops; rounded downturned handles with midribs; (f) shallow circular bowl with swage-formed rounded drop; rounded downturned handle with midrib.

Spectrographic analysis: Silver content ranges from 87.7 to 91.0 percent.

Provenance: (a–d, f) Mr. and Mrs. Stanley B. Ineson, New York City; Mr. and Mrs. Alfred E. Bissell, Wilmington, Del.; (e) H. F. du Pont.

References: Belden, *Marks of American Silversmiths*, p. 357.

(a–d, f) 62.240.1384, .1385, .551, .555, .1671 Gift of Mr. and Mrs. Alfred E. Bissell, 1962–63; (e) 65.3057 Bequest of H. F. du Pont, 1969

455 a–g
SPOONS, ca. 1790–1801

(a) L. 4 ⁷⁄₁₆" (11.3 cm)
6 dwt. 18 gr. (10.5 g)
(b) L. 5 ¼" (13.3 cm)
10 dwt. 13 gr. (16.4 g)
(c) L. 5 ⁹⁄₁₆" (14.1 cm)
11 dwt. (17.1 g)
(d) L. 5 ½" (14.0 cm)
10 dwt. 20 gr. (16.8 g)
(e) L. 6 ⅞" (17.5 cm)
18 dwt. 16 gr. (29.0 g)
(f) L. 8 ¹³⁄₁₆" (22.4 cm)
1 oz. 19 dwt. 1 gr. (60.6 g)
(g) L. 11 ⁹⁄₁₆" (29.4 cm)
4 oz. 3 dwt. 9 gr. (129.4 g)

Stamps: "JR" in roman letters, in a rectangle, struck once on back of handles (a, b, g), and twice on back of handles (c–f).

Engraved on back of handle: (a) "ED" in shaded roman letters; (g) "CHH" in foliate script. *Engraved on front of handle:* (b) demi-lion rampant on a heraldic band; (c) "BE" in shaded roman letters, in a bright-cut medallion; (d, f) "GMS" in foliate script; (e) blank bright-cut medallion; (g) pelican on a heraldic band.

Description: oval bowl and swage-formed rounded drop on (a, e–g); oval bowl with swage-formed rounded drop with incised line on (b–d); rounded upturned handle with midrib on (a); rounded downturned handle with midrib on (b–g).

Spectrographic analysis: Silver content ranges from 89.3 to 92.2 percent.

Provenance: Mr. and Mrs. Stanley B. Ineson, New York City; Mr. and Mrs. Alfred E. Bissell, Wilmington, Del.

References: Belden, *Marks of American Silversmiths*, p. 357.

(a–f) 62.240.559, .546, .553, .557, .1383, .1386 Gift of Mr. and Mrs. Alfred E. Bissell, 1962–63; (g) 62.240.1665 Gift of Mr. and Mrs. Alfred E. Bissell, 1965

456 a, b
SPOONS, 1790–1801

(a) L. 5 ⅝" (14.3 cm)
9 dwt. 16 gr. (15.0 g)
(b) L. 5 ⁹⁄₁₆" (14.1 cm)
9 dwt. 7 gr. (14.5 g)

Stamps: "JR" in roman letters, struck incuse on back of each handle.

Engraved on front of each handle: "M" in script.

Description: pointed oval bowl with swage-formed rounded drop; rounded downturned handle with midrib.

Spectrographic analysis: Silver content ranges from 89.8 to 90.6 percent.

Provenance: Mr. and Mrs. Stanley B. Ineson, New York City; Mr. and Mrs. Alfred E. Bissell, Wilmington, Del.

Comments: The incuse stamp is rare, but it is found on tea service no. 447.

References: Belden, *Marks of American Silversmiths*, p. 357.

62.240.550, .552 Gift of Mr. and Mrs. Alfred E. Bissell, 1962–63

Joseph & Nathaniel Richardson

w. 1777–90
Philadelphia, Pennsylvania
See individual biographies

The sons of Joseph Richardson, Sr., and grandsons of Francis Richardson, Joseph and Nathaniel came of age during the difficult years of the Revolution after having served a long apprenticeship with their father. Their business was hampered until 1783, when they began ordering goods from the silversmithing firm of John Masterman in London, with whom their father had also done business. With the death of Joseph, Sr., in 1784, Joseph, his small family (he had married in 1780), and Nathaniel moved into their father's house on Front Street. The business prospered, not only from silver they made for their customers but also from the sale of imported items and from investments in shipping. They purchased wrought silver for resale from other goldsmiths, such as John David, Abraham Carlisle, and Christian Wiltberger. By 1790 Nathaniel had given up silversmithing to become an ironmonger. The inventory of their shop, made when the partnership broke up, survives and is reprinted in Martha Gandy Fales's study *Joseph Richardson and Family: Philadelphia Silversmiths*.

Included were many spoons, sugar tongs, buckles (shoe, knee, and stock), pincushions, buttons, thimbles, gold lockets, lots of plated ware, and many scales and weights. Joseph continued in business until about 1801, as his duties at the United States Mint occupied more of his time. Nathaniel died in 1827 unmarried. With Joseph's death in 1831, the Richardson dynasty of goldsmiths came to an end.

The urn style predominates in the work of Joseph and Nathaniel Richardson, but the rococo style lingered, as in their tall double-bellied coffeepots (see no. 457) and a few other earlier forms.

References: Fales, *Joseph Richardson and Family*, chaps. 6, 7, apps. Richardson family papers, Downs collection, Winterthur, and Historical Society of Pennsylvania, Philadelphia.

457
COFFEEPOT, ca. 1790

H. 12 15/16" (32.9 cm), w. 9 ¾" (24.8 cm)
38 oz. 3 dwt. 10 gr. (1187.2 g)

Stamps: "I•NR" ("NR" conjoined) in roman letters, in a rectangle, struck twice on underside of body.

Engraved on side of body: "SM" in foliate script. *Engraved inside footring:* "Sarah Marshall 1797" in script. *Scratched on underside of body:* "oz 37 dwt 10".

Description: raised circular double-bellied body with incurving elongated neck rising to a flared molded rim; centerpunch on underside of body. Raised circular foot with plain incurved pedestal and gadrooned outer edge; applied footring. Raised circular high-dome lid with cast gadrooned finial; small vent in lid. Lid attached by a 5-segment cast hinge to upper handle socket. S-curve spout cast in 2 vertical sections; molded acanthus leaf on upper back; shell pattern on lower front and around base of spout on body. S-curve hardwood handle with sprig. Cast upper socket with dependent shell and drop; C-curve lower socket with double scrolls attached to body by curvilinear plate.

Spectrographic analysis:

	SILVER	COPPER	LEAD	GOLD
BODY SIDE	92.3	7.3	0.12	0.05
SPOUT	94.8	4.8	0.18	0.12
FOOT	93.8	5.8	0.15	0.08
LID	91.5	8.0	0.15	0.10

History: "SM" refers to Sarah Marshall Morris (d. 1824), daughter of Charles and Patience Marshall, Philadelphia Quakers. In 1797 Sarah married Thomas Morris (1774–1841). The couple lived in a mansion house at 86 N. Second St. in Philadelphia. Thomas served as prison inspector, member of the city council, treasurer of the Library Company of Philadelphia, and manager of the Pennsylvania Hospital. A sportsman, he was active in the State in Schuylkill Fishing Company and became governor in 1828. On his death in 1841, his inventory included several guns and 41 volumes of *Sporting Magazine*. The Morrises lived part of the year in a country retreat called Swarthmore on York Rd.

Provenance: Sarah and Thomas Morris; Anthony Morris (1803–93); his daughter Sallie M. Morris, who married H. Gurney Morris; their son Anthony Saunders Morris, Bryn Mawr, Pa.

Comments: A superb example of a late rococo form that remained popular even after neoclassical forms had become common. Although there is no reason to doubt that the coffeepot was made in the Richardsons' shop, it is interesting to note that in 1784 the Richardsons ordered from their London supplier "3 Silver Pollished 3 pint Coffee potts double bellied with cast spouts to weigh about 38 oz a piece." The description and weight perfectly fit this Morris piece. The discrepancy between the end of the brothers' partnership in 1790 and the engraved date of 1797 suggests that the pot was either left over from the days of the partnership or was purchased initially by someone else and later presented to Sally Morris. See nos. 447, 452, and 453 for other silver owned by Sarah Marshall Morris.

References: Louise C. Belden, "Sallie Morris' Silver," *Antiques* 100, no. 2 (August 1971): 214–16. Robert C. Moon, *The Morris Family of Philadelphia*, 3 vols. (Philadelphia, 1898), pp. 574–75. See also 2-vol. supplement issued in 1908–9 that reproduces silhouettes of the Morrises (pl. 153).

70.19 Gift of Mr. and Mrs. Anthony Saunders Morris, 1970

458
TANKARD, ca. 1787

H. 8 11/16" (22.1 cm), DIAM. base 4 5/8" (11.7 cm), w. 8" (20.3 cm)
30 oz. 3 dwt. (937.7 g)

Stamps: "I•NR" ("NR" conjoined) in roman letters, in a rectangle, struck twice on underside of body.

Engraved on back of handle: "M•Newbold" in shaded roman letters.

Description: raised circular form with bulbous lower body, incurving neck, flared rim with molded edge; 22 circular perforations in body at applied pouring spout; centerpunch on underside of body. Cast, circular, stepped foot; raised circular stepped-and-domed lid with double-scored lines on overlap; applied crenate lip; bezel; centerpunch inside and on top of lid. Cast openwork thumbpiece consisting of a pair of C scrolls surmounted by a shell; attached to a 5-segment hinge with a pendant drop. Raised-and-soldered hollow handle in back-to-back C scrolls terminating in a shield-shape tailpiece; lower handle end attached to body by oval plate; circular vent under lower handle.

Spectrographic analysis:

	SILVER	COPPER	LEAD	GOLD
BODY SIDE	93.1	6.2	0.41	0.12
LID	93.2	6.2	0.32	0.09
HANDLE	94.3	5.1	0.30	0.10
SPOUT	94.3	4.9	0.55	0.13

History: According to family tradition it was made for Martha Newbold (1761–91) at the time of her marriage to Josiah Reeve (1762–1840) in 1787. Descended in Reeve and Wistar families.

Provenance: Martha (Newbold) and Josiah Reeve; Martha Reeve (1791–1886), who married Clayton Webster Wistar (1793–1840); their son Josiah Wistar (1829–1915); his grandson Richard Wistar, Inverness, Calif.

Comments: Engraving, spout, and perforations added later. Many eighteenth-century tankards were converted in the nineteenth century to pitchers. As a tankard, it is similar in form to no. 473 by Philip Syng.

References: Fennimore, *Silver and Pewter*, no. 131. Eleanor Gustafson, "New Accessions," *Antiques* 112, no. 1 (July 1977): 58.

76.71 Gift of Richard Wistar, 1976

459 a, b
TEAPOT AND SUGAR BOWL, ca. 1785

(a) Teapot: H. 5 ⁷⁄₁₆" (13.8 cm), w. 9 ¾" (24.8 cm) 17 oz. 3 dwt. 22 gr. (533.6 g)
(b) Sugar bowl: H. 6 ¾" (17.2 cm), w. 4 ½" (11.4 cm)
10 oz. 5 dwt. 13 gr. (318.9 g)

Stamps: "I•NR" ("NR" conjoined) in roman letters, in a rectangle, struck twice on underside of each body.

Engraved on side of each body: "SMN" in foliate script.

Description: teapot has a raised cylindrical body with flat bottom and slightly domed top; center-punch on underside. C scrolls and leaves engraved on top of body surrounding lid. Slightly domed, loose-fitting, circular lid with cast pineapple finial and spreading leaves above and below. Beading around base, shoulders, and lid. Drawn-and-molded footring. Seamed straight tapering spout mounted at an angle. C-scroll hardwood handle with sprig mounted in circular sockets; 2 silver pins.

Sugar bowl has a raised circular double-bellied body with an overhanging molded rim; centerpunch on underside. Circular stepped pedestal on horizontal molded footring; raised circular friction-fit stepped-and-domed lid with cast finial as on teapot secured through lid by silver nut and bolt; broad flanges; bezel. Beading around edge of lid and footring.

Spectrographic analysis:

	SILVER	COPPER	GOLD	LEAD
(a) Teapot				
BODY SIDE	91.5	8.3	0.12	0.05
UNDERSIDE	96.4	3.5	0.11	0.04
SPOUT	92.0	7.8	0.15	0.07
LID	96.8	3.1	0.15	0.04
(b) Sugar bowl				
BODY SIDE	89.2	10.6	0.16	0.05
FOOT	91.3	8.5	0.14	0.07
HANDLE	91.0	8.7	0.16	0.07

Provenance: Freeman's, Philadelphia, ca. 1938; May and Howard Joynt, Alexandria, Va.; Christie's, New York City, 1990.

Comments: The 2 pieces are part of a set that also includes a creamer by Joseph Anthony (no. 311) with the same owner's initials. The neoclassical drum-shape teapot is accompanied by a sugar bowl and creamer with rococo bodies. The large beading applied to all 3 pieces suggests an attempt to unify them stylistically. This type of beading, called pearl work in the Richardson papers, required considerable labor.

Each bead was made individually with a punch, resulting in slightly varying distances between beads. The smaller and tighter beading found on so much Philadelphia neoclassical silver was stamped in strips that were then cut to fit and soldered in place. The combination of flat surfaces and surfaces curved in 1 dimension made it possible for the silversmith to take advantage of newly available sheet silver for making neoclassical forms. Yet this drum-shape teapot is raised in the traditional manner. The entire service is, therefore, on the cusp of both stylistic and technological change.

References: Christie's (New York City), Joynt sale (January 19–20, 1990), lot 254. Fales, *Joseph Richardson and Family*, fig. 136, for similar teapot and sugar bowl at the Philadelphia Museum of Art.

90.2.1, .2 Museum purchase from Christie's, 1990

🦢 460
TUMBLER, dated 1790

H. 2 ¾" (7.0 cm), DIAM. rim 3 ⅝" (9.2 cm)
5 oz. 15 dwt. 15 gr. (179.8 g)

Stamps: "I•NR" ("NR" conjoined) in roman letters, in a rectangle, struck twice on underside.

Engraved on side: grinning skull, wearing a laurel wreath, superimposed over crossed bones. Flanking skull and behind bones are 2 candlesticks, the left one with a short, recently extinguished candle that is still smoking, the right one with a lighted candle. *Engraved above skull and crossbones:* "Sic transit Gloria/ MUNDI" in script and shaded roman letters. *Engraved around rest of body:* "Magdalen Swift died 27th March 1790 = aged 67." in script.

Description: raised circular form with straight sides curving down to narrow flattened bottom; centerpunch on underside.

Spectrographic analysis:

	SILVER	COPPER	ZINC	LEAD	GOLD
BOTTOM	87.3	10.8	1.4	0.47	0.06

History: Magdalen Swift died at her husband's home, Croydon Lodge, in Bucks County, Pa. She was the daughter of Jacob Kollack (1693–?) of Lewes, Del., a prominent citizen of Sussex County when it was 1 of Pennsylvania's 3 lower counties. Born in 1724, Magdalen married Jasper McCall in 1745; he died 2 years later. In 1749 she married John Swift, collector of the Port of Philadelphia.

Provenance: Marshall P. Blankarn, New York City.

Comments: The motto, by Thomas à Kempis in his *Imitation of Christ* (ca. 1424), translates as "How swiftly passes the glory of this world." The skull and crossbones had long been symbols of death. The fact that the skull is crowned with laurel suggests death's victory over life. The 2 candles, 1 lighted, 1 recently snuffed, also refer to the brevity of life and the certainty of death. At first glance the engraving seems anachronistic and appears to be derived from sixteenth- and seventeenth-century emblem books. It is gruesome even for the iconography of death, which enjoyed a revival starting in the late eighteenth century. The iconography here partakes more of the seventeenth-century memento mori than of the early nineteenth-century's mourning art with willows and urns. Tumblers of this type were made during the late seventeenth and eighteenth centuries. One with London hallmarks for 1686–87 was in the exhibition "New England Begins" at the Museum of Fine Arts, Boston. They enjoyed a brief revival in late eighteenth-century America.

The engraving may be the work of James Smither, Jr., an engraver and seal cutter who in 1790 was located on Walnut Street near Front. He figures prominently in the Richardson account books. He engraved silver for the Richardsons and also purchased silver, including tumblers, that he presumably engraved and sold himself.

References: Fennimore, *Silver and Pewter*, no. 169. Gregory B. Keen, *Descendants of Jöran Kyn of New Sweden* (Philadelphia: Swedish Colonial Society, 1913), pp. 179–80. See Fairbanks and Trent, *New England Begins*, no. 227, and *Octagon* 11, no. 3 (Autumn 1974): 18, for similar forms with armorial engraving. I am indebted to Katie Davis for information on Magdalen Swift.

77.78 Gift of Marshall P. Blankarn, 1977

461 a, b
LADLES, 1777–90

(a) L. 15 ⅛" (38.4 cm)
6 oz. 7 dwt. 21 gr. (198.4 g)
(b) L. 14 ³⁄₁₆" (36.0 cm)
6 oz. 7 dwt. 20 gr. (200.1 g)

Stamps: "I•NR" ("NR" conjoined) in roman letters, in a rectangle, struck 3 times on back of each handle.

Engraved on front of handle: (a) "DB" in foliate script; (b) "MP" in elaborate foliate script, in a bright-cut medallion.

Description: (a) deep circular bowl with swage-formed double rounded drop; rounded down-turned handle with midrib; (b) circular shell-shape bowl with 19 lobes and a rounded drop; rounded downturned handle with featheredge border and midrib.

Spectrographic analysis: Silver content ranges from 91.6 to 92.1 percent.

Provenance: Mr. and Mrs. Stanley B. Ineson, New York City; Mr. and Mrs. Alfred E. Bissell, Wilmington, Del.

Comments: (b) is a ladle of exceptional beauty. Initials and style of engraving on (a) match those on no. 462 a.

References: Fales, *Joseph Richardson and Family*, fig. 162. Belden, *Marks of American Silversmiths*, p. 356.

62.240.1610, .1611 Gift of Mr. and Mrs. Alfred E. Bissell, 1965

462 a–e
SPOONS, 1777–90

(a) L. 8 ¾" (22.2 cm), 1 oz. 19 dwt. 5 gr. (60.9 g)
(b) L. 8 ³⁄₁₆" (20.8 cm), 1 oz. 17 dwt. 5 gr. (59.3 g)
(c) L. 8 ⅝" (21.9 cm), 1 oz. 19 dwt. 13 gr. (61.4 g)
(d) L. 8 ¹¹⁄₁₆" (22.1 cm), 1 oz. 16 dwt. 15 gr. (56.8 g)
(e) L. 8 ¾" (22.2 cm), 2 oz. 8 gr. (62.6 g)

Stamps: "I•NR" ("NR" conjoined) in roman letters, in a rectangle, struck twice on back of each handle.

Engraved on front of handle: (a) "DB" in foliate script; (c) "EA" in foliate script, in a bright-cut medallion; (e) "F/ WM" in shaded roman letters. *Engraved on back of handle:* (b) "AB/ AT" in shaded roman letters; (d) "TS/ ES" in crude shaded roman letters.

Description: (a, e) oval bowl with rounded drop and 11-lobe shell; rounded downturned handle with midrib; (b) oval bowl with rounded drop and setting sun with 14 rays; rounded upturned handle with midrib; (c) oval bowl with rounded drop; rounded downturned handle with midrib; (d) oval bowl with rounded drop and 11-lobe shell; rounded upturned handle with midrib.

Spectrographic analysis: Silver content ranges from 90.3 to 94.0 percent.

Provenance: Mr. and Mrs. Stanley B. Ineson, New York City; Mr. and Mrs. Alfred E. Bissell, Wilmington, Del.

Comments: Initials and style of engraving on (a) match those on no. 461 a.

62.240.1388, .1389, .1391, .1392, .1393 Gift of Mr. and Mrs. Alfred E. Bissell, 1962–63

463 a–c
SPOONS, 1777–90

(a) L. 5 ⁵⁄₁₆" (13.5 cm), 9 dwt. 23 gr. (15.5 g)
(b) L. 4 ⅞" (12.4 cm), 7 dwt. 12 gr. (11.7 g)
(c) L. 4 ¹³⁄₁₆" (12.2 cm), 7 dwt. (10.9 g)

Stamps: "I NR" ("NR" conjoined) in roman letters, in a rectangle, struck twice on back of each handle.

Engraved on front of handle: (a) "[?]T" in foliate script; (b, c) "MW" in shaded roman letters.

Description: (a) oval bowl with swage-formed rounded drop; rounded downturned handle with midrib; (b, c) oval bowl with swage-formed rounded drop, arc, and an 11-lobe shell; rounded downturned handle with midrib.

Spectrographic analysis: Silver content ranges from 91.1 to 94.8 percent.

Provenance: Mr. and Mrs. Stanley B. Ineson, New York City; Mr. and Mrs. Alfred E. Bissell, Wilmington, Del.

62.240.536, .537, .858 Gift of Mr. and Mrs. Alfred E. Bissell, 1962–63

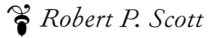

Robert P. Scott

1745–1823

Scott & Allardice, w. ca. 1793–97
Philadelphia, Pennsylvania

Robert P. Scott was born in Edinburgh and trained there as an engraver and watchmaker. By 1778 he was in Fredericksburg, Virginia, where he probably made plates for Virginia currency. In 1780 Jefferson, as governor of Virginia, commissioned him to cast and engrave an Indian medal. Jefferson was so impressed by the results that he proposed paying Scott £3,206.14. The governor commissioned at least six more pieces of silver for presentation to Native American officials who visited him at Monticello. Scott arrived in Philadelphia in 1781, where he practiced general engraving. His shop was initially at Front and Vine streets (1781–85), but in subsequent moves he was at Chestnut and Second streets (1785–87), 36 Chestnut Street (1787–92), 2 Carters Alley (1793), 4 Carters Alley (1795), 115 Walnut Street (1799–1807), 7 North Twelfth Street (1808), 13 North Twelfth Street (1809–11), 9 North Twelfth Street (1813–14), 11 North Twelfth Street (1816–17). The first product of his labors in Philadelphia was a map showing the disposition of forces at Yorktown. He also engraved a membership certificate for the Saint Andrews Society that is still in use today. In 1789 he took as an apprentice Samuel Allardice, who later became his partner. Scott & Allardice made numerous plates for Dobson's *Encyclopedia*. In 1793 Scott was appointed engraver to the United States Mint, where he made the dies for the copper cent issued that year. He remained at the mint until at least 1820.

References: Arner, *Dobson's Encyclopaedia*, pp. 116–29. Groce and Wallace, *Dictionary of Artists in America*, p. 566. David McNeely Stauffer, *American Engravers upon Copper and Steel*, 2 vols. (New York: Grolier Club, 1907), 1:242–43, for biography, pp. 471–74, for 16 of his prints. Fielding, *American Engravers*, pp. 238–40, for 16 more prints.

464
MEDAL, ca. 1801

DIAM. 2 ¼" (5.7 cm), w. (incl. loop) 2 ½" (6.4 cm)
1 oz. 3 dwt. 17 gr. (36.8 g)

Stamps: None. Attributed to Robert Scott; see *Comments*.

Description: circular form made of 2 die-stamped disks mounted back-to-back in a seamed raised rim; design in relief. Hole in upper body inside rim fitted with a silver loop for hanging medal; small hole drilled in edge of rim at loop. Obverse: half-length portrait of man (facing left) wearing his hair long and tied with a ribbon; inscription around inside of rim: "TH. JEFFERSON PRESIDENT OF THE U.S. A.D. 1801" in roman letters. Reverse: 2 clasped hands; the left wrist has a military coat cuff with 3 buttons and braid; the right wrist has a silver wristband chased with an eagle; above, crossed tomahawk and pipe; inscription inside rim and in center: "PEACE/ AND/ FRIENDSHIP" in roman letters.

Spectrographic analysis:

SILVER	LEAD
99.9	0.07

History: Following a policy begun in colonial times, presidents had medals struck for presentation to the Indians as tokens of amity. Jefferson's were the first such medals struck in this country. (As governor of Virginia, Jefferson had commissioned Scott to make cast medals.) The initial extensive distribution of the Jefferson medal was by Lewis and Clark on their expedition of 1804–6. Although dies were prepared for 2", 3", and 4" medals, the 3" and 4" medals were abandoned because of the difficulty in striking them. Even solid medals proved too time consuming. The solution was found in striking 2 thin disks, 1 for each side, and putting them together as a sandwich. Some are known to have had wooden cores. (This one is hollow.) The history of this medal is unknown.

Provenance: Charlotte and Edgar Sittig, Shawnee-on-Delaware, Pa., sold to H. F. du Pont, March 1952.

Comments: New dies for the reverse were cut in 1809. These have a hammerhead on the tomahawk, something lacking in the earlier version. Although some historians of American medallic art feel that John Reich made the dies, documentary evidence supports the attribution to Scott.

References: R. W. Julian, *Medals of the United States Mint, 1792–1892* (El Cajon, Calif.: Token and Medal Society, 1977), pp. 32–34, IP-4.

52.33 Gift of H. F. du Pont, 1952

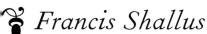

Francis Shallus

1773–1821
Philadelphia, Pennsylvania

Unlike many craftsmen practicing in Philadelphia, Francis Shallus was a native of the city. His father, Jacob, served in the Continental Army and later became assistant clerk to the Pennsylvania House of Representatives. In 1792 Francis was apprenticed to Robert Scott, engraver at the United States Mint in Philadelphia. In addition to his work at the mint, Scott did a lot of freelance work. He provided many of the plates for illustrations in Thomas Dobson's *Encyclopaedia*, many of which carry the initials of other workers along with Scott's name. Sixteen of these plates bear the initials "FS," and a few have "Shallus." Shallus appears on his own in the city directory for 1797. He is listed at various addresses over the next few years: 40 Vine Street, 63 Walnut Street, 104 Race Street, 30 Strawberry Street, 12 Prune Street, 83 and 89 South Front Street, 49 and 90 South Third Street, and 161 Chestnut Street. His principal work was book illustration, especially volumes of a scientific or technical nature. He was best known in his own time as the compiler of *The Chronological Tables for Every Day of the Year* (1811). He engraved a few trade cards but, unlike many engravers of the time, made few portrait prints. He is not a medalist, but he did engrave three medals: Madame Rivardi's award to Victorine du Pont, one masonic medal, and a plate or token for the Philadelphia Typographical Society. The last item is a medal only in the most marginal sense. Samuel Williamson's daybook, acquired by Winterthur, shows that Shallus bought blank medals from him and sometimes had Williamson gild them. Shallus then engraved and sold the medals himself.

Shallus also did the engraving on a race cup awarded by the Washington Jockey Club in 1805. It was made in, or for, Williamson's shop but sold through Burnet & Rigden of Georgetown, D.C. Shallus's wife operated a circulating library that, apparently, became the mainstay of the family as Francis's health declined.

References: Arner, *Dobson's Encyclopaedia*, pp. 129–30. Mary E. Holt, "A Checklist of the Work of Francis Shallus, Philadelphia Engraver," in Richard K. Doud, ed., *Winterthur Portfolio 4* (Charlottesville: University Press of Virginia for the Henry Francis du Pont Winterthur Museum, 1968), pp. 143–58. Rachel E. C. Layton, "Samuel Williamson's Presentation Silver: Important New Discoveries," *Silver* 25, no. 1 (January/February 1992): 8–13. Samuel Williamson daybook, Downs collection, Winterthur; see, for example, December 1804.

465
GOLD MEDAL, 1807

DIAM. 1 3/16" (3.0 cm)
5 dwt. 3 gr. (8.0 g)

Stamps: None. "F Shallus/ fecit" engraved on reverse under banner.

Engraved on obverse: a wreath consisting of 2 different flowering branches tied in a bowknot below; inscription in center: "Desert/ Rewarded" in script; inscription inside rim (above): "Mrs. Rivardi's Semy." in shaded roman letters; (below): "Philadelphia 1807." in slanted roman letters. Reverse: an arm extends from cloud to hold banner engraved: "Victorine/ Dupont/ de Nemours" in script; left hand extends from cloud to hold scales.

Description: circular flat form with raised applied rim milled inside on both sides; fixed circular loop integral to rim at top with loose ring attached.

Spectrographic analysis:

GOLD	COPPER	SILVER	
69.9	20.4	9.7	17 karat

History: Madame Rivardi's Seminary, as it was usually known, was founded in Philadelphia in 1802. A prestigious school for young women of affluent families, it was patterned after Madame Campan's pension in Paris, "the first secular school in France to provide women with a sound academic and moral education." Unlike at Mme Campan's, English was the first language of instruction, although French was taught as a foreign language and used extensively by immigrant students. Arithmetic, penmanship, English and French grammar, history, and geography alternated with dance instruction, needlework, drawing, and music. Above all, Mme Rivardi imparted social skills appropriate to wealthy young matrons. There was a talented faculty that included, for example, Denis Volozan, an artist of some repute who taught design skills. The school's trustees included Bishop William White, Benjamin Rush, Anthony Morris, and Peter Duponceau. In 1811 the school moved into Gothic Mansion, a new house at 12th and Chestnut streets owned by Godfrey Haga and designed by John Dorsey with help from Robert Mills. The house created a sensation with its pointed arches, recessed center, quatrefoil guilloches, and pinnacles. The school was, however, short-lived. In financial difficulty and never really comfortable in America, Mme Rivardi returned to Europe in 1815, as did many other transplanted French families, following the restoration of the Bourbons.

The recipient of this medal, Victorine du Pont (1792–1861), was the eldest daughter of Eleuthère Irénée du Pont (1771–1834), manufacturer of black powder on Brandywine Creek, just outside Wilmington, Del. The honorific "de Nemours" derived from her grandfather, Pierre Samuel du Pont de Nemours (1739–1817) and is perpetuated in the name of the giant chemical company that eventually grew out of the original enterprise: E. I. du Pont de Nemours & Co. Victorine attended Mme Rivardi's school from 1806 to 1808. Her father, in a letter to her grandfather, wrote in 1807: "Victorine wins everyone's affection; she is Madame Rivardy's best pupil; every month her name is at the head of her class in every subject . . . I have no doubt that next month I shall have the pleasure of telling you that she has earned the school's first prize."

In November 1813 Victorine married Ferdinand Bauduy, son of a business associate of her father's. Only 11 weeks later Bauduy was stricken with pneumonia and died. Victorine never remarried. She devoted the rest of her life to serving others—her sisters and brothers and the children of her father's employees through the Brandywine Manufacturers' Sunday School, which her father had proposed as a way for her to overcome her grief. She supervised her younger siblings and gradually supplanted her mother as mistress of Eleutherian Mills, the family seat. She and her sisters created a family journal called *Tancopanican Chronicle* that reported on the minutiae of daily life on the Brandywine. Her portrait, painted by Rembrandt Peale, is at Winterthur.

Provenance: Descended in the du Pont family to H. F. du Pont.

Exhibitions: "American Gold," Yale University Art Gallery, New Haven, 1963.

Comments: For a "Good Behavior" medal awarded by Victorine to 1 of her siblings, see no. 426.

References: Bohan, *American Gold*, no. 134. Fales, *American Silver*, no. 63. Mary Johnson, "Madame Rivardi's Seminary in Gothic Mansion," *PMHB* 104, no. 1 (January 1980): 1–38. Betty-Bright Low and Jacqueline Hinsley, *Sophie du Pont, A Young Lady in America: Sketches, Diaries, and Letters, 1823–1833* (New York: Harry N. Abrams, 1987), for information on life in the du Pont household. Mary Johnson, "Madame E. I. du Pont and Madame Victorine du Pont Bauduy, the First Mistresses of Eleutherian Mills: Models of Domesticity in the Brandywine Valley during the Antebellum Era," in "Industrious Women: Home and Work in the Nineteenth-Century Mid-Atlantic Region," Working papers from the Regional Economic History Research Center, vol. 5, nos. 2 / 3 (Wilmington, Del.: Eleutherian Mills-Hagley Foundation, 1982), pp. 13–38. Trade card for Mme Rivardi's school, 72x43, Downs collection, Winterthur.

59.625 Bequest of H. F. du Pont, 1969

George B. Sharp

Philadelphia, Pennsylvania, w. 1844–70

George B. Sharp appears in Philadelphia directories during the middle of the nineteenth century. In 1844 and 1847, he was at 19 North Rittenhouse Street. In 1865 his shop was at 819 Jayne Street, and his home was at 1634 Vine Street. Little of his silver is recorded, although more probably exists in private hands. A coffee urn on stand, owned privately, is in the neo-grec style and features a wonderful cast female head on each handle. Sharp also revived earlier styles rather successfully. In addition to the creamer in the following entry, there is a pair of salvers with gadrooned edges and hairy paw feet at the Historical Society of Pennsylvania. Sharp often used stamped pseudohallmarks along with his incuse name stamp.

References: Brix, *Philadelphia Silversmiths*, p. 92. Dorothy T. Rainwater, *American Silver Manufacturers* (Hanover, Pa.: Everybodys Press, 1966), p. 161. See Diana Cramer's series on Sharp in *Silver*: "Bailey and the Mysterious Philadelphia Marks," 21, no. 4 (July/August 1988): 12–15; "George Sharp," 22, no. 4 (July/August 1989): 36–37; "George Sharp and the Lion S Shield Mark," 22, no. 6 (November/December 1989): 26–27; "George Sharp: The Products," 24, no. 5 (September/October 1991): 24–30.

466
CREAMER, ca. 1850

H. 4" (10.2 cm), w. 3 ¼" (8.3 cm)
4 oz. 4 dwt. 19 gr. (131.6 g)

Stamps: "GEORGE SHARP" in roman letters, struck incuse on underside of body. Accompanied by "[S]TERLING" in roman letters, struck incuse; 3 stamps: 1 appears to be a lion passant; the other 2 are illegible. Remnants of stamped numbers also present: "37[?]7".

Description: raised pear-shape body with flaring rim and extended pouring lip, plain molded band around rim; centerpunch on underside of body; 3 legs, cast as C scrolls with shell feet, attached to stems of water leaves applied to body. Cast S-curve handle attached to body by reverse C curves; single sprig on upper handle and lower handle at tail.

Spectrographic analysis:

	SILVER	COPPER	LEAD	GOLD
BODY SIDE	92.5	7.2	0.31	0.02
HANDLE	93.2	6.5	0.34	0.02
FOOT	95.9	4.0	0.18	0.00

Note: Low gold content reflects better refining techniques practiced in the mid to late nineteenth century.

Provenance: Mrs. Duncan I. Selfridge, Wayne, Pa.

Comments: The neck is extremely narrow on this traditional eighteenth-century form, but it is similar to no. 148, made by Adrian Bancker a century earlier. It is a fine example of the revival of eighteenth-century forms.

69.13 Gift of Mrs. Duncan I. Selfridge, 1969

467
LADLE, 1850–70

L. 8 ¾" (22.2 cm)
2 oz. 1 dwt. 13 gr. (64.5 g)

Stamps: "GEORGE SHARP" in roman letters, struck incuse on back of handle. Accompanied by 3 stamps: in the center, a roman "S" in an oval; on either side, a lion passant in a rectangle, each facing the center.

Engraved on front of handle: "FTF" in gothic letters, with a bright-cut border.

Description: deep pointed oval bowl with flaring sides and 2 notches in edge near handle; rounded downturned handle with midrib.

Spectrographic analysis:

SILVER	COPPER	LEAD	GOLD
92.6	7.2	0.18	0.08

Provenance: Mrs. Endsley P. Fairman, Wilmington, Del.

Comments: The spoon partakes of the neogrec style while harking back to the neoclassical style.

78.6 Gift of Mrs. Endsley P. Fairman, 1978

Thomas Shields

1743–1819
Philadelphia, Pennsylvania

The son of James Shields of Newlin Township, Chester County, Pennsylvania, Thomas Shields, at age seventeen, was placed with John Bayly of Philadelphia to learn the "art and mystery" of silversmithing. Shields opened his own shop on Front Street, "the Third Door above the Drawbridge," in 1765. In 1771 he was "at the sign of the Golden Cup and Crown." In 1777 he signed the oath of allegiance (the original document survives in private hands). He is listed in Philadelphia directories from 1785 to 1791 at 126 South Front Street. He had extensive land interests in Wayne County, where he erected a house and grist and saw mills. He called his holdings Damascus, the manorial name given to the area by William Penn; locals called his complex Shields's Mills. He seems to have moved back and forth between Philadelphia and Wayne County.

Among the relatively small number of surviving pieces by Shields are a pair of canns made for the First Baptist Church of Philadelphia in 1794, an elegant repoussé salver once owned by collector Walter Jeffords, and a ladle for Thomas McKean, the Signer (of the Declaration of Independence). His account book for 1775–93 survives and shows him repairing silver, jewelry, and ceramics. He had customers in Delaware and Maryland as well as Philadelphia. Among his local clients were silversmiths Abraham Dubois, Daniel Van Voorhis, John Letelier, and John Carnan. During the war years he had a flourishing business in sword sales and repairs.

References: Thomas Shields daybook, 1775–91, Downs collection, Winterthur. *Philadelphia Silver*, nos. 456–69. Waters, "Philadelphia's Precious Metals Trades," pp. 71–73.

468
SUGAR BOWL, ca. 1785

H. (with lid) 8 ½" (21.6 cm), H. (without lid) 5 ⅝" (14.3 cm), DIAM. 5 ⅛" (13.0 cm)
15 oz. 10 dwt. 11 gr. (481.7 g)

Stamps: "TS" in roman letters, in a rectangle with rounded corners, struck twice on underside of body.

Engraved on side of body: "REH" in shaded foliate script, with swags below. *Scratched into underside of body:* "15 oz 10"; "£11 = [15]".

Description: raised circular double-bellied bowl with a flanged lip surmounted by beading and a gallery with arched voids; centerpunch on underside. Raised circular stepped foot with beading around edge rises to circular concave pedestal; 1 set of double-scored lines and 1 single-scored line encircle foot. Raised circular stepped-and-domed lid with cast pineapple finial supported in a star-shape cluster of leaves; 1 set double-scored lines and a single-scored line encircle lid; foldover rim becomes an angled bezel.

Spectrographic analysis:

	SILVER	COPPER	GOLD	LEAD
BODY SIDE	90.5	9.3	0.08	0.10
FOOT	94.6	5.1	0.17	0.15
LID BODY	89.6	10.0	0.22	0.22
FINIAL	92.9	7.0	0.05	0.05

Provenance: Mrs. N. McLean Seabrease, Germantown, Pa.; Robert Ensko, Inc., New York City, sold to H. F. du Pont, August 1929.

Comments: The elongation of the lower body and the height of the dome on the lid are unusual. The voids in the gallery are quite irregular, and the beading below the gallery is uneven, rising in some areas, dipping in others. The piece is a hybrid of rococo and neoclassical elements.

70.1082 Bequest of H. F. du Pont, 1969

469
LADLE, ca. 1785

L. 13 ¹¹⁄₁₆" (34.8 cm)
5 oz. 3 dwt. 4 gr. (160.1 g)

Stamps: "TS" in roman letters, in a rectangle, struck 3 times on back of handle.

Engraved on front of handle: "TJN" in foliate script.

Description: shallow circular bowl with swage-formed triple drop; rounded downturned handle with midrib.

Spectrographic analysis: Silver content is 90.9 percent.

Provenance: Mr. and Mrs. Stanley B. Ineson, New York City; Mr. and Mrs. Alfred E. Bissell, Wilmington, Del.

Comments: See no. 470 c for a spoon with the same owner's initials.

62.240.1658 Gift of Mr. and Mrs. Alfred E. Bissell, 1965

470 a–e
SPOONS, 1765–90

(a) L. 9" (22.9 cm), 1 oz. 19 dwt. 4 gr. (60.8 g)
(b) L. 9" (22.9 cm), 1 oz. 18 dwt. (59.0 g)
(c) L. 8 ¹³⁄₁₆" (22.4 cm), 1 oz. 17 dwt. 23 gr. (58.9 g)
(d) L. 3 ⅞" (9.8 cm), 4 dwt. 23 gr. (7.7 g)
(e) L. 5 ⁹⁄₁₆" (14.1 cm), 8 dwt. (12.5 g)

Stamps: "TS" in roman letters, in a rectangle, struck twice on back of each handle, except once on handle (e).

Engraved on back of handle: (a) upraised arm holding a laurel wreath, all on a heraldic band, motto in semicircular banner above: "NOBILI•ESTIRA•LEONIS" in roman letters; (d) "IR" in script. *Engraved on front of handle:* (b) "M∗K" in crude roman letters; (c) "TJN" in foliate script; (e) "RS" in foliate script, in a bright-cut medallion with pendant drop.

Description: (a) elongated oval bowl with swage-formed rounded drop with faint midrib; rounded upturned handle with midrib; (b) oval bowl with swage-formed rounded drop and 13-lobe shell; rounded downturned handle with midrib; (c) elongated oval bowl with swage-formed rounded drop with incised line; rounded downturned handle with midrib; (d) shovel-shape bowl; rounded upturned handle with midrib; (e) oval bowl with swage-formed rounded drop; rounded downturned handle.

Spectrographic analysis: Silver content ranges from 90.0 to 92.0 percent.

Provenance: Mr. and Mrs. Stanley B. Ineson, New York City; Mr. and Mrs. Alfred E. Bissell, Wilmington, Del.

Exhibitions: (a), (b), or (c) Metropolitan Museum of Art, New York City, 1935–61; (d) Metropolitan Museum of Art, 1938–61.

Comments: See no. 469 for same initials as on (c).

62.240.1452–.1454, .827.1, .663 Gift of Mr. and Mrs. Alfred E. Bissell, 1962–63

Robert Swan

Philadelphia, Pennsylvania, w. ca. 1799

Although nothing is recorded about Robert Swan's early life, we do know that he was working in Philadelphia on South Second Street in 1799. A small body of objects survives with his name stamp. Among them is a pair of goblets in a Delaware collection and a large coffeepot in the Philadelphia urn style in a California collection (as of 1954). A creamer, sugar bowl, and tongs in the urn style, made for Gen. John Kelso (1776–1819) of Erie County, Pennsylvania, went up for auction in 1969.

Sources have placed Swan in Worcester and Andover, Massachusetts, prior to Philadelphia. Recent research by Janine Skerry shows that there were two Robert Swans in Essex County, Massachusetts, but there is no evidence that either of them worked in precious metals. One was a bucklemaker who died in 1732 at age eighty-four. Whether the other Robert Swan sojourned in Philadelphia as a silversmith seems doubtful. All of Swan's surviving silver that shows regional characteristics speaks of Philadelphia rather than Massachusetts.

References: Brix, *Philadelphia Silversmiths,* p. 100. Flynt and Fales, *Heritage Foundation,* p. 334. Gregor Norman-Wilcox, "American Silver, 1690–1810, in California Collections," *Antiques* 65, no. 1 (January 1954): 48–51, fig. 12. *Philadelphia Silver,* nos. 486, 487. John A. H. Sweeney, "Silver from the Sewall C. Biggs Collection," *Antiques* 119, no. 4 (April 1981): 906–8, fig. 5. Janine Skerry's work was brought to my attention by Patricia E. Kane.

471
CREAMER, ca. 1815

H. 6 ³⁄₁₆" (15.7 cm), w. 5 ⁷⁄₁₆" (13.8 cm)
7 oz. 10 dwt. 20 gr. (234.6 g)

Stamps: "R•SWAN" in roman letters, in a rectangle, struck twice on underside of foot. Illegible stamp on outside of upper body.

Engraved on side of body: "TLC" in foliate script.

Description: raised urn-shape main body, oval in plan, joined to raised upper body, concave in profile; rim low on sides, high on handle side and at extended pouring lip; applied ropelike band around outside of rim and between upper and main bodies; no centerpunch. Oval stepped base with circular pedestal. High-loop C-curve handle with slight ridge on back.

Spectrographic analysis:

	SILVER	COPPER	LEAD	GOLD
BODY SIDE	91.9	7.8	0.14	0.15
FOOT	95.2	4.4	0.15	0.10
HANDLE	95.3	4.5	0.09	0.03

Provenance: Marshall P. Blankarn, New York City.

79.205 Gift of Marshall P. Blankarn, 1979

Philip Syng, Jr.

1703–89
Philadelphia, Pennsylvania, w. 1724–72

Philip Syng, Jr., was born in Cork, Ireland. He was the first son of Philip Syng, Sr. (1676–1739), a silversmith who brought his family to America in 1714. Philip and his brothers John and Daniel became silversmiths with all presumably having trained under their father. Philip, Sr., worked in Philadelphia, perhaps from late 1714 to the early 1720s. When young Philip reached his majority, his father re-married and moved to Cape May, New Jersey, later moving to Annapolis, where he was joined by son John. (John's son, also named Philip, became a brass founder.) The only documented work of Philip Syng, Sr., is the flagon he made for Christ Church, Philadelphia, in 1715. Philip, Jr., went on to a long career, and a good deal of his silver survives. The Syngs carried the characteristic Irish tankard form with them to Philadelphia. (See a tankard by Philip Tough, Dublin, 1708, advertised by Hobart House, Haddam, Connecticut, in the September 1990 issue of *Antiques*.) Syng added a professional engraver to his staff prior to advertising "Engraving on Gold, Silver, Copper or Pewter done by Laurence Herbert from London at Philip Syng's, Goldsmith, in Front Street" (*Pennsylvania Gazette*, May 19, 1748).

Philip Syng, Jr., personified the ideal of the philosopher mechanic. Fine craftsman, good citizen, supporter of intellectual and philanthropic enterprises, he was one of a small group that transformed Philadelphia into a cultural center by the eve of the Revolution. He was a member of Benjamin Franklin's junto, and the two became close personal friends. Syng was one of the original directors of the Library Company of Philadelphia, named in 1731, and one of the original trustees of the Public Academy of Philadelphia, later to become the University of Pennsylvania. Along with Franklin he was a founding member of the Union Fire Company and the Philadelphia Contributionship for the Insurance of Houses ("Hand-in-Hand"). He was a Mason, Saint John's Lodge of Philadelphia, rising to Grand Master in 1741 and Junior Grand Warden for Pennsylvania in 1749 while Franklin was Provincial Grand Master. He was on the vestry for Christ Church and the first treasurer of the American Philosophical Society.

Syng made the inkstand for the Provincial Assembly, perhaps the best known piece of American colonial silver, now in Independence Hall. He made the dies for the medal celebrating the capture of Kittanning in 1756 and seals for several customers. The administration of his estate shows £117.2.8 from silversmiths Joseph and Nathaniel Richardson "for Indian Plate sold them." He made numerous tankards, coffeepots, and salvers. Among his customers was Gen. John Cadwalader. He collaborated with Joseph Richardson, Sr., in the settlement of the estate of Philadelphia goldsmith Philip Hulbeart, transactions of which are preserved in the account book of Joseph Richardson, Sr., at Winterthur. The sale of Hulbeart's shop contents was announced in the *Pennsylvania Journal* for March 17, 1763. Among Syng's apprentices was Matthew Pratt, who went on to become a portrait painter. In 1772 Syng retired and moved to Upper Merion, Pennsylvania. His shop was taken over by Richard Humphreys, who received Syng's blessing in an advertisement in the *Pennsylvania Journal* for August 26, 1772. He died intestate, possessed of much property, including several houses in Philadelphia. The papers of administration are owned by Winterthur. Syng had eighteen children, all by his wife Elizabeth Warner, but only five, all daughters, survived to see their father's death. His eldest daughter Elizabeth married Edmund Physick, agent for the Penns and Receiver General and Keeper of the Great Seal of Pennsylvania.

References: Administration of estate of Philip Syng, 56x13.4, Downs collection, Winterthur. *DAB*, s.v. "Syng, Philip." Fales, *Joseph Richardson and Family*, app. B, for "Settlement of the Hulbeart Estate"; see index for other references. Wayne A. Huss, *The Master Builders: A History of the Grand Lodge of Free and Accepted Masons of Pennsylvania*, 3 vols. (Philadelphia: Grand Lodge F&AM of Philadelphia, 1986–89), 3:35–37. John W. Jordan, ed., *Colonial Families of Philadelphia*, 2 vols. (New York and Chicago: Lewis Publishing, 1911), 1:858–61. *Philadelphia Silver*, nos. 491–553. *Philadelphia: Three Centuries*, pp. 19–20, 30–31. Helen Burr Smith, "Philip Syng, Jr., Silversmith, Man of Divers Civic Interests," *New York Sun*, November 7, 1941. Nicholas Wainwright, *Colonial Grandeur in Philadelphia, The House and Furniture of General John Cadwalader* (Philadelphia: Historical Society of Pennsylvania, 1964). Note: Elizabeth S. Hamlin, "Philip Syng, Junior, Philadelphia Silversmith" (Master's thesis, University of Delaware, 1969), could not be located at either Winterthur or the University of Delaware.

🏺 472
TANKARD, 1741–47

H. 6⅞" (17.5 cm), w. 8¾" (22.2 cm),
DIAM. base 5⅝" (14.3 cm)
33 oz. 10 dwt. 6 gr. (1042.4 g)

Stamps: "PS" in roman letters, in a heart, struck
3 times on upper body, left of handle.

Engraved on back of handle: "EN" in shaded
roman letters.

Description: raised body with straight tapering
sides and flat bottom; flared molded rim with
single-scored line below; 2 centerpunches on
underside. Applied seamed 3-step base molding, flared at bottom, consists (in descending
order) of a convex molding, a fillet, a concave
molding, and a convex molding. Raised circular
stepped-and-domed lid with double-scored
and single-scored lines encircling edge; bezel;
no centerpunch. Cast scroll thumbpiece attached to 5-segment hinge with pendant drop.
Raised-and-soldered hollow S-curve handle
terminating in a flat shield-shape tailpiece that
conforms to cross section of upturned handle;
circular notched vent on lower end; circular
vent under upper handle attachment.

Spectrographic analysis:

	SILVER	COPPER	LEAD	GOLD
BODY SIDE	93.4	6.2	0.26	0.04
UNDERSIDE	94.1	5.8	0.18	0.05
LID	93.1	6.6	0.25	0.02
HANDLE	93.3	5.6	0.28	0.08
THUMBPIECE	93.3	6.0	0.31	0.14

History: According to the last private owner, the
initials on the tankard refer to Edith Newbold
(the daughter of Marmaduke Coate and Ann
Pole, who came to America early in the eighteenth century). In 1724 Edith married Thomas
Newbold.

Provenance: Edith and Thomas Newbold; their
daughter Mary, who married Anthony Sykes;
their son Thomas Sykes, who married Mary
Laurie; their daughter Edith, who married Earl
Gibbs; their son Thomas Gibbs, who married
Martha Eugle; their daughter Edith, who married Walter L. Reeder; the Reeders, of Colum-
bus, N.J., sold to H. F. du Pont, October 1930.

Comments: Long attributed to Philip Syng, Sr.,
this tankard is now given to Philip Syng, Jr.;
all evidence indicates that the heart stamp was
used by the son only. See especially the article
by Helen Burr Smith. Thomas Newbold died
in 1741, and Edith married Daniel Doughty in
1747. The tankard is thought to have been made
during the period of her widowhood.

References: Fales, *American Silver*, no. 25. Helen
Burr Smith, "Philip Syng Jr. Proved to Use
Disputed Heart-shaped Mark," *New York Sun*,
November 21, 1941, illus.

61.619 Gift of H. F. du Pont, 1965

🐚 473
TANKARD, 1750–72

H. 8" (20.3 cm), W. 7 3/16" (18.3 cm),
DIAM. base 5" (12.7 cm)
34 oz. 3 dwt. 21 gr. (1063.5 g)

Stamps: "PS" in roman letters, in a rounded rectangle, struck twice on underside of body. Accompanied by 2 incuse asymmetrical leaves.

Engraved on back of handle: "S/IR" in shaded roman letters. *Scratched on underside of body:* "oz 34 dwt 11".

Description: raised circular form with bulbous lower body, incurving neck, flared rim with molded edge with single-incised line below; centerpunch on underside of body. Cast, circular, stepped foot. Raised circular stepped-and-domed lid with double-scored lines encircling molded edge; centerpunch on top of lid, cast ram's horn thumbpiece attached to 5-segment hinge with pendant drop. Raised-and-soldered hollow handle in back-to-back C scrolls terminating in a shield-shape tailpiece; circular notched vent on lower end; circular vent under upper handle attachment.

Spectrographic analysis:

	SILVER	COPPER	LEAD	GOLD
BODY SIDE	92.5	7.3	0.22	0.04
UNDERSIDE	93.0	6.7	0.17	0.06
LID	93.3	6.5	0.14	0.05
HANDLE	90.8	8.9	0.19	0.04
THUMBPIECE	93.3	6.5	0.16	0.08

Provenance: H. F. du Pont.

Comments: The leaf stamps are frequently found on Syng's work. Their meaning, if any, is unclear.

References: Fales, *American Silver*, no. 97 (left). Kauffman, *Colonial Silversmith*, p. 111.

61.620 Gift of H. F. du Pont, 1965

⚜ 474
TANKARD, 1740–72

H. 7 ⅛" (18.1 cm), W. 7 ¾" (19.7 cm),
DIAM. base 5 ⁵⁄₁₆" (13.5 cm)
28 oz. 11 dwt. 1 gr. (888.1 g)

Stamps: "PS" in roman letters, in a shield,
struck 3 times on upper body (1 upside down)
perpendicular to handle.

Engraved on back of handle: "B/ I*S" in shaded
roman letters. *Engraved on front of body:* "JB"
in foliate script. *Engraved on underside of body:*
"oz 29 9". *Scratched twice on underside of body:*
"D7764".

Description: raised body with straight tapering
sides and slightly concave bottom; flared molded rim with single-scored line below; centerpunch on underside of body. Applied seamed
3-step base molding, flared at bottom, consists
(in descending order) of ogee, convex, and
ogee moldings, each separated by a fillet. Raised
circular stepped-and-domed lid; bezel; centerpunch inside and outside. Cast scroll thumbpiece attached to 5-segment hinge with a long
pendant drop. Raised-and-soldered hollow S-
curve handle terminating in a flat shield-shape
tailpiece; circular vent with notch on lower end.

Spectrographic analysis:

	SILVER	COPPER	LEAD	GOLD
BODY SIDE	90.8	8.1	0.26	0.07
UNDERSIDE	92.1	7.8	0.28	0.07
LID	94.3	5.5	0.08	0.03
HANDLE	87.3	11.2	0.34	0.14

Provenance: Marshall P. Blankarn, New York
City.

77.71 Gift of Marshall P. Blankarn, 1977

475
GOLD BUCKLE, ca. 1750

L. 1 9⁄16" (4.0 cm), W. 1 ¼" (3.2 cm),
D. 5⁄16" (0.8 cm)
11 dwt. 12 gr. (17.9 g̃)

Stamps: "PS" in roman letters, in a shield,
struck once on chape.

Engraved on back of frame: "SS" in roman
letters.

Description: cast open frame, rectangular in
plan with 2 rounded corners; gold pin across
center supports a 3-segment hinge: 2 segments
for chape with heart-shape void and 1 segment
for 2-tine prong. Obverse of frame elaborately
chased: scallop shells at 4 compass points, with
leafy scrolls between, and 2 masks, all in relief
on a stippled ground.

Spectrographic analysis:

GOLD	SILVER	COPPER	
85.9	9.8	4.2	21 karat

History: Family tradition holds that "SS" refers
to Sarah (Jervis) Sandwith (1708–56), who married William Sandwith (1700–1756) in 1731.
Sandwith was an Irish Quaker involved in shipping who came to Philadelphia shortly before
his marriage. Their daughter Elizabeth (1735–
1807), said to be the next owner of the buckle,
married Henry Drinker (1734–1809) in 1761.
Elizabeth (Sandwith) Drinker kept a diary for
almost her entire adult life, from 1758 to 1807.
On March 23, 1759, she recorded: "Called after
dinner at P. Syng's, bought a pair of Buckles."
The diary is a detailed and valuable account of
life in Philadelphia from the 1750s to the early
years of the nineteenth century. According to
family tradition the buckle was always worn by
the eldest daughter on her wedding day. It descended in the family to Mrs. Francis D. Brinton.

Provenance: Sarah (Jervis) and William Sand-
with; their daughter Elizabeth, who married
Henry Drinker in 1761; their daughter Sarah
("Sally") (1761–1807), who married Jacob
Downing (1756–1823) in 1787; their daughter
Elizabeth (1789–1882), who married Robert
Sharpless (d. 1822) in 1810; their daughter Cath-
erine, who married the Rev. William August
White in 1844; descended to Mrs. Francis D.
Brinton; David Stockwell sold to Lammot
du Pont Copeland, Mt. Cuba, Greenville, Del.

Exhibitions: "American Gold, 1700–1860," Yale
University Art Gallery, New Haven, 1963.

Comments: This is an extraordinary example of
craftsmanship on a small scale and, arguably, the
finest piece of colonial American gold. It is solid
gold except for the steel tines, which are plated
with gold (some delamination is visible). There
is, unfortunately, no mention of a gold buckle
in Elizabeth Drinker's diary. Given the size, elegance, and expense of this buckle, it was presumably worn at a woman's waist. Dating the buckle
is difficult. Syng could have made it for the marriage of Sarah and William Sandwith in 1731, although on stylistic grounds this seems unlikely.
Since the initials reflect her married name, the
buckle could have been given to Sarah Sandwith
anytime prior to her death in 1756.

References: Bohan, *American Gold*, no. 78, illus.
p. 19. Samuel W. Woodhouse, Jr., "American
Craftsmanship in Gold," *Antiques* 20, no. 1 (July
1931): 32–33, fig. 3. Crane, *Diary of Elizabeth
Drinker*, p. 15. The manuscript diaries are at
the Historical Society of Pennsylvania, Philadelphia.

68.304 Gift of Lammot du Pont Copeland, 1968

476
SALVER (OR PATEN), 1730–72

DIAM. 6" (15.2 cm), H. ¼" (0.6 cm)
5 oz. 13 dwt. 12 gr. (176.5 g)

Stamps: "PS" in roman letters, in a shield,
struck 3 times on upper surface.

Engraved on underside: "C/ I*E" in shaded
roman letters.

Description: circular flat tray with elevated,
probably applied, molded rim; centerpunch
on upper surface.

Spectrographic analysis:

	SILVER	COPPER	LEAD	GOLD
UPPER SURFACE	93.8	5.5	0.33	0.13
UNDERSIDE	96.5	3.0	0.25	0.11

Provenance: Baldwin's Book Barn, West
Chester, Pa.

Comments: If this piece had an ecclesiastical
provenance, it would be called a paten, the
small plate used in Anglican and Roman Catholic communion services to serve the wafers
and to cover the chalice. It is of appropriate
size. Furthermore, salvers without feet are rare.

References: Fales, *American Silver*, no. 108.

52.3 Museum purchase from Baldwin's Book
Barn, 1952

477
SPOON, ca. 1730

L. 8" (20.3 cm), 1 oz. 15 dwt. 10 gr. (55.0 g)

Stamps: "PS" in roman letters, in a heart, struck
twice on back of handle.

Engraved on back of handle: "W/ LP" in shaded
roman letters.

Description: elongated oval bowl with swage-
formed rattail; rounded upturned handle with
midrib.

Spectrographic analysis: Silver content is 89.0
percent.

Provenance: Mr. and Mrs. Stanley B. Ineson,
New York City; Mr. and Mrs. Alfred E. Bissell,
Wilmington, Del.

References: Belden, *Marks of American
Silversmiths*, p. 400.

62.140.1446 Gift of Mr. and Mrs. Alfred E.
Bissell, 1962–63

478 a–d
SPOONS, ca. 1750–72

(a) L. 8 3/16" (20.8 cm), 1 oz. 9 dwt. 13 gr. (45.9 g)
(b) L. 7 13/16" (19.8 cm), 1 oz. 12 dwt. 7 gr. (50.1 g)
(c) L. 8 1/8" (20.6 cm), 1 oz. 11 dwt. 6 gr. (48.5 g)
(d) L. 8" (20.3 cm), 1 oz. 18 dwt. 16 gr. (60.0 g)

Stamps: "PS" in roman letters, in a rectangle, struck once on back of handles (a–c) and twice on back of handle (d); accompanied on (d) by asymmetrical leaf struck incuse.

Engraved on front of handle: (a) "SH" in shaded roman letters; (b) "T/ NS" in shaded roman letters; (c) "JSJ" in foliate script. *Engraved on back of handle:* (d) "L/ IH" in shaded roman letters.

Description: (a–c) oval bowl with swage-formed rounded drop; rounded downturned handle with midrib; (d) elongated oval bowl with swage-formed rounded drop and an 11-lobe shell; rounded upturned handle with midrib.

Spectrographic analysis: Silver content ranges from 90.6 to 92.7 percent.

Provenance: (a, b, d) Mr. and Mrs. Stanley B. Ineson, New York City; Mr. and Mrs. Alfred E. Bissell, Wilmington, Del.; (c) H. F. du Pont.

References: Belden, *Marks of American Silversmiths*, p. 401.

(a, b, d) 62.240.1444, .1448, .1445 Gift of Mr. and Mrs. Alfred E. Bissell, 1962–63; (c) 65.3056 Bequest of H. F. du Pont, 1969

479 a, b
SPOONS, ca. 1750

(a) L. 4 7/16" (11.3 cm), 6 dwt. 9 gr. (9.9 g)
(b) L. 4 1/2" (11.4 cm), 6 dwt. 2 gr. (9.5 g)

Stamps: "PS" in roman letters, in a shield, struck once on back of handle (a), struck twice on back of handle (b).

Engraved on back of handle: (b) "ES" in crude roman letters.

Description: (a) elongated oval bowl with swage-formed rounded drop and shell; rounded up-turned handle with midrib; (b) elongated oval bowl with swage-formed rattail; rounded upturned handle with midrib.

Spectrographic analysis: Silver content ranges from 88.2 to 92.5 percent.

Provenance: (a) Mr. and Mrs. Stanley B. Ineson, New York City; Mr. and Mrs. Alfred E. Bissell, Wilmington, Del.; (b) Charlotte and Edgar Sittig, Shawnee-on-Delaware, Pa.

References: Belden, *Marks of American Silversmiths*, p. 401.

(a) 62.240.651 Gift of Mr. and Mrs. Alfred E. Bissell, 1962–63; (b) 64.114 Museum purchase from Charlotte and Edgar Sittig, 1964

480
SPOON, ca. 1770

L. 8 1/4" (21.0 cm), 1 oz. 19 dwt. 23 gr. (62.0 g)

Stamps: "PS" in script, in a conforming sur-round, struck once on back of handle. Accompanied by an asymmetrical leaf form struck incuse.

Engraved on back of handle: "W/ BS" in shaded roman letters.

Description: elongated oval bowl with swage-formed rounded drop and shell; rounded upturned handle with midrib.

Spectrographic analysis: Silver content is 93.0 percent.

Provenance: Mr. and Mrs. Stanley B. Ineson, New York City; Mr. and Mrs. Alfred E. Bissell, Wilmington, Del.

References: Belden, *Marks of American Silversmiths*, p. 401.

62.240.1447 Gift of Mr. and Mrs. Alfred E. Bissell, 1962–63

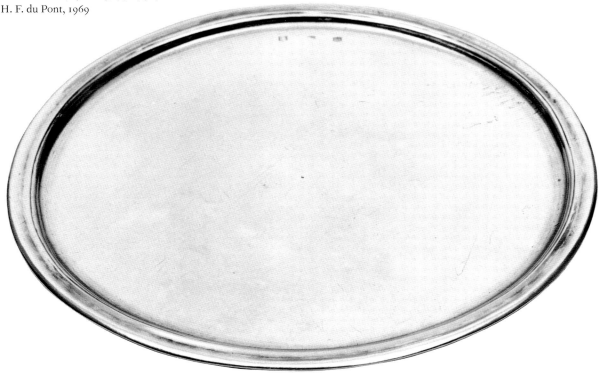

Taylor & Lawrie

w. 1837–?
Philadelphia, Pennsylvania

In 1857 Robert Taylor and Robert Dickson Lawrie issued a display advertisment featuring examples of their wares displayed in a rococo cartouche. Located at 114 Arch Street, above Fifth Street, they announced that "T. & L. having manufactured for the firm of Bailey and Kitchen 20 years, and owning all the Dies and Patents from which their work was made, are enabled to match all work finished by them during that time." The firm had, therefore, been in business at least since 1837. The advertisement suggests a recent break with Bailey & Kitchen, and indeed Taylor & Lawrie henceforth had close relationships with George Sharp and other Philadelphia silversmiths. Starting in 1858, the firm was located at 520 Arch Street. The 1857 ad noted, "All silver waranteed to which they affix their original . . . mark." Three stamps are reproduced in the ad: a spread-winged eagle in an octagon, a thistle in a rectangle, and a harp in a rectangle. This has proven to be an important clue to identifying their silver, which often carried the stamps of retailers, especially Bailey & Kitchen. Taylor and Lawrie imported large quantities of plated goods as well as manufacturing their own solid silver. In 1852 they received a patent on a flatware design.

Joseph T. Bailey and Andrew B. Kitchen were partners from 1832 to 1840 in a store on Chestnut Street, but the firm name persisted for six years after Kitchen's death in 1840. Although they offered for sale watches, jewelry, silver plate, plated wares, and fancy goods, they promoted themselves as manufacturers of fine quality silver. In 1847 Joseph Bailey founded Bailey & Co., a prestigious firm that had a lavish display of silver at the Crystal Palace exhibition in New York in 1853. One observer said of the firm on that occasion: "Their manufactory is one of the most extensive in the United States." Joseph died in 1854, but the firm was continued by his brothers. In 1878 it became Bailey, Banks & Biddle. Bailey & Kitchen clearly functioned as manufacturers as well as subcontractors in order to meet the needs of their customers for silver. With Taylor & Lawrie having taken over Bailey & Kitchen's dies and patents by 1857, the reorganized Bailey firm apparently became exclusively a retailer.

References: D. Albert Soeffing, "Taylor and Lawrie, Philadelphia Silversmiths," *Silver* 21, no. 5 (September/October 1988): 18, 19. *Gleason's Pictorial Drawing-Room Companion*, October 8, 1853, p. 232. *Philadelphia: Three Centuries*, p. 326. Waters, "Philadelphia's Precious Metals Trades," pp. 119, 169, 171, 174. Diana Cramer, "Bailey and the Mysterious Philadelphia Marks," *Silver* 21, no. 4 (July/August 1988): 12–15.

481
CHILD'S CUP, ca. 1840

H. 3 1/16" (7.8 cm), w. 3 9/16" (9.0 cm)
2 oz. 9 dwt. 15 gr. (77.0 g)

Stamps: 3 pseudohallmarks consisting of a spread-winged eagle in an octagon, a thistle in a rectangle, and a harp in a rectangle. All struck on underside of body. "BAILEY & KITCHEN" in roman letters, in a rectangle, struck once on underside of body.

Engraved on body opposite handle: "HAduP" in foliate script, in a wheelwork shield with a central acanthus leaf flanked by ferns above and a bowknot below. Pattern of branches with leaves and flowers extends from each side of shield around body almost to handle; pattern is formed by wheelwork highlighted by bright-cut engraving. *Scratched on underside of body:* "£E£/ — / $LHKO/ MKK".

Description: seamed cylindrical body with straight tapering sides and slightly concave bottom; centerpunch on underside. Applied molded rim; die-rolled base band with pattern of shells and leaves on a stippled ground. Cast S-curve handle with leaf and sprig on upper side and scroll at upper handle join.

Spectrographic analysis:

	SILVER	COPPER	LEAD	GOLD
BODY SIDE	91.4	8.2	0.19	0.04
UNDERSIDE	93.1	6.4	0.25	0.06
HANDLE	93.9	5.6	0.25	0.07

History: Purchased for Henry Algernon du Pont (1838–1926) when he was a child. He was raised at Eleutherian Mills, the family seat near Wilmington, Del., next to the family-owned gunpowder works. He went to West Point, served in the Civil War, and later became U.S. Senator from Delaware. He married Mary Pauline Foster; they became the parents of H. F. du Pont.

Provenance: Henry A. du Pont, Wilmington and Winterthur, Del.; H. F. du Pont.

Comments: The cup was previously attributed to Bailey & Kitchen. Small cups or mugs were modest forms of presentation silver that were usually given to infants and children.

References: Fennimore, *Silver and Pewter,* no. 154.

57.1370 Bequest of H. F. du Pont, 1969

482 a, b
MINIATURE SUGAR TONGS AND KNIFE, ca. 1840

(a) Tongs: L. 3 ¹⁄₁₆" (7.8 cm)
4 dwt. 16 gr. (7.3 g)
(b) Knife: L. 7 ⅝" (19.4 cm)
1 oz. 13 dwt. 10 gr. (51.9 g)

Stamps: 3 pseudohallmarks consisting of a spread-winged eagle in an octagon, a thistle in a rectangle, and a harp in a rectangle. Struck once inside arm of tongs and once on side of knife blade. "B & K" in roman letters, in a rectangle, struck once inside arm of tongs and once on side of knife blade.

Engraved on bowback of tongs: "EMH" in foliate script.

Description: bow-type tongs; U-shape form with wavy fiddle-shape arms and oval grips. Flat knife blade, rectangular in plan with rounded end; plain handle with double-thread border.

Spectrographic analysis: Silver content for both objects is 90.6 percent.

Provenance: (a) Edwin A. Fitler, Exton, Pa.; (b) The Silver Shelf, Ardmore, Pa.

(a) 80.51 Museum purchase from Edwin H. Fitler, 1980; (b) 71.72 Museum purchase from the Silver Shelf, 1971

483 a, b
SPOON AND FORK, ca. 1840

(a) Spoon: L. 6 ¹⁄₁₆" (15.4 cm)
11 dwt. 11 gr. (23.4 g)
(b) Fork: L. 7" (17.8 cm)
1 oz. 17 dwt. 22 gr. (58.9 g)

Stamps: 3 pseudohallmarks consisting of a spread-winged eagle in an octagon, a thistle in a rectangle, and a harp in a rectangle. Struck once on back of each handle. "BAILEY & KITCHEN" in roman letters, in a rectangle, struck once on back of each handle.

Engraved on front of handle: (a) "MAW" in foliate script; "AAM" in later script; (b) "MPB" in foliate script.

Description: (a) pointed oval bowl with swage-formed rounded drop; downturned fiddle-shape handle; (b) 4 tines; rounded upturned fiddle-shape handle with swage-formed 10-lobe shell on end and double-thread border.

Spectrographic analysis: Silver content ranges from 88.4 to 90.5 percent.

Provenance: (a) Margo Antiques, St. Louis; (b) Mr. and Mrs. Laylor Burdick, Wilmington, Del.

References: Belden, *Marks of American Silversmiths,* p. 42, for Bailey & Kitchen.

(a) 69.88 Museum purchase from Margo Antiques, 1969; (b) 70.18 Gift of Mr. and Mrs. Laylor Burdick, 1970

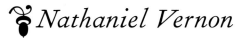

Nathaniel Vernon

1777–1843

Vernon & Company
Charleston, South Carolina

Nathaniel Vernon's origins are unknown, but Milby Burton speculates that he was related to John Vernon of New York City. When Nathaniel first appeared in Charleston, about 1802, he advertised under the name of Vernon & Company. Burton suggests that this may indicate that John Vernon was his backer and partner. Later, around 1808, he appears as simply Nathaniel Vernon. He imported large quantities of silver in addition to the work he made himself. At one point he proclaimed that he had employed "an Artist of the first rate ability" who could execute "any article in Gold and Silver . . . equal to that which is imported from Europe . . . particularly Large Plate, such as Waiters, Coffee Biggins, Tea-Pots, Sugar Dishes, Slop Bowles, Tanckards, &c. &c." In 1820 Vernon tried to sell his business. After a hiatus of seven years he appears again advertising imported goods, and as late as 1835, he was still referred to as a silversmith. Little of his silver is known outside the South. One of his most important commissions is the pair of covered urns made for the Independent Church of Charleston but now at Yale University Art Gallery.

References: Burton, *South Carolina Silversmiths*, pp. 187–89.

484
CUP, 1808–20

H. 3 ¼" (8.3 cm), w. 3 ⅞" (9.8 cm)
6 oz. 15 dwt. 23 gr. (211.0 g)

Stamps: "N. VERNON" in roman letters, in a serrated rectangle, struck once on underside.

Engraved on body: "Edward Phillips" in script.
Engraved on underside of body: "The gift of Mrs. Marion to her Son" in script. Scratched under the latter is a crescent moon; scratched above inscription is "6".

Description: seamed cylindrical body with straight, slightly tapering, sides and set-in slightly domed bottom; no centerpunch. Triple bands applied to outside of body at rim, midway, and around bottom. S-curve strap handle.

Spectrographic analysis:

	SILVER	COPPER	GOLD	LEAD
BODY SIDE	93.0	6.3	0.38	0.15
UNDERSIDE	94.1	5.1	0.41	0.16
HANDLE	89.9	9.7	0.12	0.31

Provenance: Mrs. J. Frederick M. Stewart, Upperville, Va., who found the mug in Savannah, Ga.

Comments: Very heavy for its size.

64.107 Gift of Mrs. J. Frederick M. Stewart, 1964

☙ 485
BOTTLE LABEL, 1802–8

W. 1⅝" (4.1 cm), H. ⅞" (2.2 cm) (not incl. chain)
3 dwt. 6 gr. (5.1 g)

Stamps: "N. VERNON & C?" in roman
letters, in a rectangle, struck once on reverse.

Engraved on obverse: "LEMON" in shaded
roman letters.

Description: curved oval plate with wavy wheelwork border; 2 drilled holes on upper edge, each
with a ring attached to secure ends of chain.

Spectrographic analysis:

SILVER	COPPER	LEAD	GOLD
91.3	7.6	0.52	0.21

Provenance: Margo Antiques, St. Louis.

References: Fennimore, *Silver and Pewter*, no.
44. See also Raphael A. Weed, "Silver Wine
Labels," *NYHSQB* 13, no. 1 (April 1929):
47–67, for information on the form.

68.273 Museum purchase, with funds from the
Bissell Fund, from Margo Antiques, 1968

☙ 486
SPOON, 1815–35

L. 8⅞" (22.5 cm)
1 oz. 17 dwt. 12 gr. (58.2 g)

Stamps: "N. VERNON" in roman letters, in
a serrated rectangle, struck once on back of
handle.

Engraved on front of handle: "JEB" in script.

Description: oval bowl with swage-formed
rounded drop; rounded downturned fiddle-
shape handle with midrib.

Spectrographic analysis: Silver content is 91.0
percent.

Provenance: The Silver Shelf, Ardmore, Pa.

71.66 Museum purchase, with funds from the
Bissell Fund, from the Silver Shelf, 1971

Thomas Whartenby

ca. 1788–ca. 1852

Whartenby & Bumm, w. 1816–18
Thomas Whartenby & Company,
w. 1847–52
Philadelphia, Pennsylvania

Thomas Whartenby's family lived in Duck Creek (Smyrna), Delaware. Upon the death of his father, Whartenby's mother consented to having Thomas and his three younger brothers placed under the guardianship of silversmith Samuel Richards, Jr., of Philadelphia. Thomas's apprenticeship with Richards began in March 1802 and ended in March 1809. By 1811 Whartenby had his own shop at 159 South Seventh Street. Silversmith Peter Bumm was in business with Whartenby from 1816 to 1818. Whartenby's extensive debts caused him to become insolvent in 1829. His creditors were, principally, jewelers Thibault & Brothers, Richards & Dubosq, Samuel Cameron, and the estate of Richard C. Woolworth. Whartenby managed, however, to continue his business until about 1852. From 1847 through 1852, the firm was known as Thomas Whartenby & Company. Perhaps his most important commission was a service, consisting of two wine coolers, two waiters, and twelve goblets, presented on behalf of the citizens of Philadelphia to Stephen Decatur in 1818. In 1968 Parke-Bernet Galleries offered a five-piece tea and coffee service by Whartenby. It featured round bodies, with die-rolled decorative bands, mounted on square, paw-footed plinths.

References: Brix, *Philadelphia Silversmiths*, p. 109. Waters, "Philadelphia's Precious Metals Trades," pp. 42, 133. Parke-Bernet Galleries, sale no. 2781, "Fine English and American Silver" (December 17, 1968), lot 28.

487
PAP BOAT, ca. 1815

L. 6 3/16" (15.7 cm), w. 3 1/16" (7.8 cm), H. 2 1/4" (5.7 cm)
2 oz. 17 dwt. 21 gr. (90.0 g)

Stamps: "T.W." in roman letters, in a rectangle, struck once on underside of body. Accompanied by a spread-winged eagle in a circle and, possibly, a crowned leopard's head in a conforming surround.

Description: generally circular, flat-bottomed, bowl-like body with an extended pouring lip opposite handle; applied molding on outer edge of rim all around except at end of pouring lip; no centerpunch. Cast S-curve handle, upper end terminates in a scroll, lower end terminates in a small shield; handle attached to body by sprig and lower curve of handle; a second sprig is on upper part of handle.

Spectrographic analysis:

	SILVER	COPPER	LEAD	GOLD
BODY	88.9	10.6	0.20	0.07
HANDLE	84.4	14.7	0.26	0.16

Provenance: R. T. Trump & Co., Philadelphia.

Comments: At the time it was acquired, there was some concern that the maker's stamp did not match the published "TW" stamp given to Whartenby. Further research shows that it matches the stamp on one of the goblets presented to Stephen Decatur (in the Amherst College collection), which lays to rest any doubt that the pap boat is by Whartenby. Pap boats were apparently used for feeding pap, a soft food, to infants and invalids. The form is rare in American silver.

69.9 Museum purchase from R. T. Trump & Co., 1969

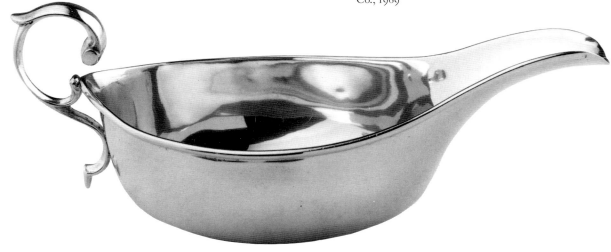

❦ 488
WASTE BOWL, ca. 1815

H. 5 %₆" (14.1 cm), w. 6 ¾" (17.1 cm)
18 oz. 16 gr. (559.6 g)

Stamps: "WHARTENBY" in roman letters, in a rectangle, struck twice on underside of body.

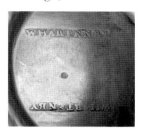

Engraved on side of body: "SM" in foliate script.

Description: raised hemispherical body with an applied molded band with beading at rim; centerpunch on underside of body. Trumpet-shape pedestal on a square applied foot; beading at top and bottom of pedestal.

Spectrographic analysis:

	SILVER	COPPER	LEAD	GOLD
BODY SIDE	92.5	7.1	0.28	0.11
FOOT	94.7	5.1	0.18	0.08

History: "SM" refers to Sarah Marshall Morris, who is discussed in no. 457.

Provenance: Sarah and Thomas Morris; Sarah Morris; Mr. and Mrs. Anthony Saunders Morris, Bryn Mawr, Pa.

Exhibitions: Wilson-Warner House, Odessa, Del.

Comments: Part of tea service, no. 447.

References: Louise C. Belden, "Sallie Morris' Silver," *Antiques* 100, no. 2 (August 1971): 214–16, fig. 2.

70.192.4 Gift of Mr. and Mrs. Anthony Saunders Morris, 1970

❦ 489
SPOON, ca. 1825

L. 8 ¾" (22.2 cm)
2 oz. 1 dwt. 23 gr. (65.1 g)

Stamps: "WHARTENBY" in roman letters, in a rectangle, struck once on back of handle.

Engraved on front of handle: "CM" in foliate script.

Description: pointed oval bowl with swage-formed rounded drop; rounded upturned fiddle-shape handle with midrib.

Spectrographic analysis: Silver content is 89.5 percent.

Provenance: Mr. and Mrs. Stanley B. Ineson, New York City; Mr. and Mrs. Alfred E. Bissell, Wilmington, Del.

References: Belden, *Marks of American Silversmiths*, p. 439.

62.240.1574 Gift of Mr. and Mrs. Alfred E. Bissell, 1962–63

William Whetcroft

ca. 1735–90
Annapolis, Maryland, w. 1766–67
Baltimore, Maryland, w. 1767–69
Annapolis, Maryland, w. 1769–76

Whetcroft & Higginson, w. 1774
Annapolis, Maryland

From Cork, Ireland, where he is recorded by Charles Jackson for 1759, William Whetcroft appears in Annapolis in March 1766 as goldsmith, jeweler, and lapidary in the house of William Knapp, watchmaker. In December 1767 he announced the opening of a shop in Baltimore while retaining the Annapolis shop. By 1769 he was back in Annapolis, having purchased Knapp's watchmaking equipment and having married Knapp's widow. Whetcroft's advertisement in the *Maryland Gazette* for May 13, 1773, is a lengthy recitation of silver, jewelry, and watch and clock repairing services. In 1774 he formed a partnership with Samuel Higginson, a coppersmith and silversmith. Shortly thereafter Whetcroft went into the ironmaking business with someone named M'Fadon. Apparently he left off being a silversmith by about 1776. By 1777 he was operating the Patapsco Slitting Mill and had acquired a foundry at Elk Ridge Landing. His prosperity is suggested by the portrait painted in 1791 by Charles Willson Peale (now at Yale University Art Gallery), which depicts him as a fashionable gentleman.

A small number of pieces by Whetcroft survive. An elegant pierced silver basket bearing his stamp is at Winterthur. The basket has traces of English hallmarks that he had apparently tried to obliterate. Enough remains, however, to determine that the basket was made by William Plummer of London about 1766. Although it was common for American silversmiths to import and sell English silver, this is a rare instance of passing off imported work as one's own. Whether unmarked imported plate was stamped by American craftsmen is another question.

References: Goldsborough, *Eighteenth- and Nineteenth-Century Maryland Silver*, p. 38. Goldsborough, *Silver in Maryland*, nos. 332–34. Charles James Jackson, *English Goldsmiths and Their Marks* (1921; reprint, New York: Dover Publications, 1964), p. 699. Pleasants and Sill, *Maryland Silversmiths*, pp. 74–77, pl. 8, for portrait.

490
SALVER, 1766–76

DIAM. 6 ⅛" (15.6 cm), H. 1 ¼" (3.2 cm)
8 oz. 11 dwt. 12 gr. (277.7 g)

Stamps: "W•W" (conjoined at top) in roman letters, in a rectangle, struck 4 times on underside of body.

Engraved on underside of body: "M/ B=A" in shaded roman letters. *Scratched on underside:* "10".

Description: flat circular tray with cast applied edge consisting of 6 bracketlike segments alternating with rectangular segments, each separated by deep semicircular indentations; no centerpunch; 3 short cast cabriole legs with paw feet and an animal mask on each knee.

Spectrographic analysis:

	SILVER	COPPER	GOLD	LEAD
UNDERSIDE OF BODY	88.3	10.9	0.24	0.24
FOOT	93.2	5.9	0.34	0.22

Provenance: Marian Coffin, Watch Hill, R.I., and New Haven, landscape architect to H. F. du Pont; H. F. du Pont.

Comments: The legs, with the very detailed grimacing face on the knees and the hairy paw feet, are unusual in American silver.

References: Fales, *American Silver*, nos. 48, 111.

57.42 Gift of H. F. du Pont, 1957

491
BOX, 1766–76

L. 3 3/16" (8.1 cm), w. 2 9/16" (6.5 cm), H. 13/16" (2.1 cm)
2 oz. 4 dwt. 2 gr. (68.4 g)

Stamps: "WW" (conjoined at top) in roman letters, in a rectangle, struck once inside bottom of body.

Description: oval box with flat bottom, molded sides, and hinged lid that consists of a molded frame inset with nacre (mother of pearl) carved as a scallop shell on its upper surface; crenate lip on lid; no centerpunch; 5-segment hinge with silver pin.

Spectrographic analysis:

SILVER	COPPER	LEAD	GOLD
87.7	11.1	0.48	0.25

Provenance: Charlotte and Edgar Sittig, Shawnee-on-Delaware, Pa.

Comments: On January 28, 1777, the printer of the *Maryland Journal and Baltimore Daily Advertiser* offered a $1 reward to whomever found and returned his "Silver Snuff Box with a Mother of Pearl Top."

References: Quimby, "Silver," p. 75.

66.289 Museum purchase from Charlotte and Edgar Sittig, 1966

492
SPOON, 1766–76

L. 4 3/4" (12.1 cm)
8 dwt. 9 gr. (13.0 g)

Stamps: "W•W" (conjoined at top) in roman letters, in a rectangle, struck once on back of handle.

Engraved on front of handle: "TC/ IM" in foliate script.

Description: oval bowl with swage-formed rounded drop and shell with ears; rounded downturned handle with midrib.

Spectrographic analysis: Silver content is 92.8 percent.

Provenance: Philip H. Hammerslough, Hartford, Conn.

57.89.3 Gift of Philip H. Hammerslough, 1957

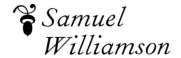 *Samuel Williamson*

1772–1843
w. 1794–1813

Williamson & Richards, w. 1797–1800
Philadelphia, Pennsylvania

Samuel Williamson completed his six-year apprenticeship with Joseph Lownes in 1793 and appears the next year in the city directory as a silversmith. His shops were at 70 South Front Street, 136 South Front Street, and 118 South Front Street. He was in partnership with Samuel Richards from 1797 to 1800. Williamson was one of the early entrepreneurs in the silversmithing trade, and he routinely employed the services of other silversmiths. In 1810 twelve different smiths worked for him at various times, and his shop is credited with producing 1,770 pieces of hollowware in that year alone. His business connections were extensive and included contacts in Boston, New York, Baltimore, Washington, London, and Sheffield. He had transactions with silversmiths John Dumoutet, John McMullin, Daniel Carrell, and Samuel Richards, not to mention extensive sales to Burnet & Rigden and later to Charles A. Burnet alone in Alexandria, Va., and Georgetown, D.C. He sent large quantities of silver to New Orleans on speculation (what he called an "adventure"); he agreed to split the proceeds with the ship's captain. Late in 1813, probably after having become well-to-do, he closed his business and moved to Uwchlan Township in Chester County, Pennsylvania, where he remained as a farmer for the rest of his life.

Williamson worked in the urn, lobate, and oblong styles. He also made at least two porringers with very light pierced handles. The Maryland Historical Society owns a six-piece beverage service in the lobate style that has a Maryland provenance. This is but one of numerous examples of Philadelphia silver finding a market in Maryland. Parts of a beverage service owned by the Smithsonian Institution were made by Williamson; the other parts were made by John McMullin, whose shop, in 1802, adjoined Williamson's on Front Street. Recent research by Rachel Layton established that Williamson made three racing cups and a punch urn for the Washington Jockey Club. The transaction was handled by Burnet & Rigden, who were previously credited with making them.

Williamson is a particularly well-documented maker because portions of his business records survive at both the Chester County Historical Society and Winterthur, which owns two ledgers (1800–1813) and a daybook (1803–11).

References: Ellen Beasley, "Samuel Williamson, Philadelphia Silversmith, 1794–1813" (Master's thesis, University of Delaware, 1964). *Philadelphia: Three Centuries*, pp. 167–68. Rachel E. C. Layton, "Samuel Williamson's Presentation Silver: Important New Discoveries," *Silver* 25, no. 1 (January/February 1992): 8–13. Waters, "Philadelphia's Precious Metals Trades," pp. 43–45. Williamson ledgers and daybook, Downs collection, Winterthur. Williamson collection, Chester County Historical Society, West Chester, Pa., microfilm in Downs collection, Winterthur.

🌱 493
BASKET, 1794–1813

L. 8 ¾" (22.3 cm), W. 5 ¹⁵⁄₁₆" (15.1 cm), H. 3 ⅜" (8.6 cm)
11 oz. 8 dwt. 2 gr. (353.9 g)

Stamps: "WILLIAMSON" in roman letters, in a rectangle, struck twice on underside. Accompanied by "PHIADDELPIILADE" in roman letters, in a circular band struck in center.

Scratched on underside: "oz 11   dw 8"; "7889".

Description: wire basket, rectangular in plan with rounded corners, with a solid base in the form of an oval tray with flaring sides, extended ends, and flat bottom; centerpunch on underside. Rectangular base band with an applied reeded footring. Sides of basket formed by 28 vertical wire loops (closed at top) bowed out and upward to a thin reeded rim.

Spectrographic analysis:

	SILVER	COPPER	LEAD	GOLD
LOWER BODY	96.8	2.8	0.31	0.12
RIM	95.0	4.7	0.14	0.24

Provenance: Marshall P. Blankarn, New York City.

Comments: This light and airy design is uncommon in American silver; the form is more often found in English silver. American baskets of this period are usually solid silver. It is unclear why Philadelphia is spelled so oddly.

References: Donald Fennimore, "Samuel Williamson Cake Basket," *Silver* 17, no. 2 (March/April 1984): 14–15.

78.141 Gift of Marshall P. Blankarn, 1978

🌱 494
BOWL, ca. 1810

H. 4 ⁵⁄₁₆" (11.0 cm), W. 6 ½" (16.5 cm)
14 oz. 22 gr. (435.9 g)

Stamps: "WILLIAMSON" in roman letters, in a rectangle, struck once on underside of body.

Engraved on side of body: "WAW" in foliate script.

Description: raised circular body with convex shoulders under an applied gadrooned rim; centerpunch on underside of body; raised stepped pedestal on a seamed footring.

Spectrographic analysis:

	SILVER	COPPER	LEAD	GOLD
BODY SIDE	89.1	10.5	0.26	0.08
FOOT	89.1	10.3	0.31	0.10

Provenance: Marshall P. Blankarn, New York City.

Comments: Probably a waste bowl and once part of a tea service.

78.158 Gift of Marshall P. Blankarn, 1978

🌱 495 a–c
SPOONS, 1794–1813

(a) L. 9 ⁷⁄₁₆" (24.0 cm), 1 oz. 17 dwt. 13 gr. (58.3 g)
(b) L. 9 ⅜" (23.8 cm), 2 oz. 2 gr. (62.2 g)
(c) L. 5 ⅝" (14.3 cm), 9 dwt. 15 gr. (15.0 g)

Stamps: "WILLIAMSON" in roman letters, in a rectangle, struck once on back of each handle; stamp on (c) is slightly smaller.

Engraved on front of handle: (a, b) "HS"; (c) "TAL", all in foliate script.

Description: pointed oval bowl with rounded drop; pointed downturned handle on (a, b); rounded downturned handle with midrib on (c).

Spectrographic analysis: Silver content ranges from 86.9 to 93.3 percent.

Provenance: Mr. and Mrs. Stanley B. Ineson, New York City; Mr. and Mrs. Alfred E. Bissell, Wilmington, Del.

Comments: (a) and (b) are a pair.

References: Belden, *Marks of American Silversmiths*, p. 447.

(a, b) 62.240.1580.1, .2; (c) 62.240.632 Gift of Mr. and Mrs. Alfred E. Bissell, 1962–63

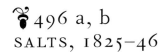

Robert Wilson
d. ca. 1846

William Wilson
d. after 1858

R. & W. Wilson, w. ca. 1825–46
William Wilson & Son, w. 1858–?
Philadelphia, Pennsylvania

R. & W. Wilson, as their firm was known, quickly became one of the most important manufacturers of fine silver in Philadelphia. The sons of silversmith Robert Wilson (1766–1824), Robert and William Wilson grew up in the business and, indeed, claimed to be the "only manufacturers in this city who have been brought up in this business exclusively." They clearly had the capital to invest in a modern facility that employed division of labor and power machinery. As they said, they had "facilities and conveniences not equalled in Philadelphia." Their Philadelphia Silver Spoon and Fork Manufactory at Fifth and Cherry streets produced large quantities of flatware and a substantial amount of hollowware. The firm also imported plated goods from the Sheffield firm of James Dixon & Son. Much of

their hollowware is in rococo- and neo-classical-revival styles dating from the 1840s and 1850s. The Smithsonian Institution owns a goblet presented to Franklin Peale in 1851 by the "Ladies of the U.S. Mint" that combines a Greek key border with rococo designs. Their presentation urn given to Robert Taylor Conrad in 1856, first mayor of Philadelphia following absorption of all communities in Philadelphia County, is a tour de force of midcentury design. Loosely based on the Warwick Vase, the footed urn is mounted on fasces and topped by the figure of Justice. Clearly this firm was a competitor of Bailey & Kitchen for top-of-the-line commissions. Robert Wilson is not listed in directories after 1846, and it is assumed that he died in that year. William Wilson continued to run the firm, which, when he brought in his son in 1858, became William Wilson & Son. In 1860 the firm employed forty-eight males and six females.

References: Philadelphia: Three Centuries, pp. 336–37, 355–56. Waters, "Philadelphia's Precious Metals Trades," pp. 170–71, 174.

496 a, b
SALTS, 1825–46

(a) H. 1 ¹³⁄₁₆" (4.6 cm), w. 3 ¹⁄₁₆" (7.8 cm)
2 oz. 1 dwt. 16 gr. (64.8 g)
(b) H. 1 ⅞" (4.8 cm), w. 3 ¹⁄₁₆" (7.8 cm)
2 oz. 1 dwt. 22 gr. (65.2 g)

Stamps: "R. & W. WILSON" in roman letters, struck incuse once on underside of each base. Accompanied by "PHILADA." in roman letters, struck incuse.

Engraved on outside of each body: "LMM" in foliate script.

Description: circular deep body in form of a scallop shell (raised or stamped); no centerpunch. Body supported by a cast leg, in form of an irregular S curve, with a stippled finish and a sprig. Leg stands on a base in the form of a hollow acanthus leaf heavily decorated with punchwork on a stippled ground. Thin flat baseplate with 2 circular vents conforms to shape of base.

Spectrographic analysis:

	SILVER	COPPER	LEAD	GOLD
(a)				
SHELL BODY	92.2	7.2	0.38	0.08
BASE	92.1	6.5	0.25	0.09
BASEPLATE	92.5	6.8	0.32	0.08
(b)				
SHELL BODY	91.7	7.8	0.29	0.09
BASE	95.0	3.7	0.21	0.15
BASEPLATE	93.9	5.8	0.32	0.08

Provenance: Robert Carlen, Philadelphia.

Comments: Purchased with salt spoons 497 a, b. These elegant salts were probably part of a larger set. Yale University Art Gallery owns an almost identical pair by the same makers, also purchased from a Philadelphia dealer.

67.133.1, .2 Museum purchase from Robert Carlen, 1967

❦ 497 a–d
SPOONS, 1825–46

(a) L. 3 ¹¹⁄₁₆" (9.4 cm)
5 dwt. 23 gr. (9.3 g)
(b) L. 3 ¹¹⁄₁₆" (9.4 cm)
5 dwt. 2 gr. (9.5 g)
(c) L. 6 ⅜" (16.2 cm)
16 dwt. 22 gr. (26.3 g)
(d) L. 7 ⅛" (18.1 cm)
19 dwt. 18 gr. (30.7 g)

Stamps: "R & W. WILSON" in roman letters, struck incuse on back of each handle.

Engraved on front of handles: (a, b) "LMM"; (c) "E I F"; (d) "HHM", all in foliate script.

Description: (a, b) salt spoon with shallow oval gilded bowl and a swage-formed acanthus leaf drop; pointed upturned handle with 10-lobe shell and double-thread and beaded border; (c) shell-shape bowl with 14 lobes; rounded up-turned fiddle-shape handle with swage-formed sheaf of wheat; (d) pointed oval bowl with swage-formed rounded drop; rounded up-turned fiddle-shape handle with swage-formed sheaf of wheat and sickle.

Spectrographic analysis: Silver content ranges from 91.7 to 93.4 percent.

Provenance: (a, b) Robert Carlen, Philadelphia; (c, d) Mr. and Mrs. Stanley B. Ineson, New York City; Mr. and Mrs. Alfred E. Bissell, Wilmington, Del.

Exhibitions: (c, d) Metropolitan Museum of Art, New York City, 1938–61.

Comments: (a, b) Salt spoons came with salts, no. 496 a, b.

References: Belden, *Marks of American Silversmiths*, p. 450 a.

(a, b) 67.134.1, .2 Museum purchase from Robert Carlen, 1967; (c, d) 62.240.733, .1560 Gift of Mr. and Mrs. Alfred E. Bissell, 1962–63

❦ 498 a–d
SPOONS AND KNIFE, 1825–46

(a) L. 7 ¹⁄₁₆" (17.9 cm)
1 oz. 8 dwt. 7 gr. (43.9 g)
(b) L. 6" (15.2 cm)
1 oz. 2 dwt. 8 gr. (34.7 g)
(c) L. 5 ¾" (14.6 cm)
10 dwt. 8 gr. (16.1 g)
(d) L. 7 ¼" (18.4 cm)
1 oz. 6 dwt. (40.4 g)

Stamps: "R & W. W." in roman letters, in a rectangle, struck once on back of each spoon handle and once on side of blade of (d). Accompanied on (a) by "5. FRANCS." in roman letters, in a rectangle.

Engraved on back of handle: (a) "IMF"; (b) "CF"; both in foliate script. *Engraved on front of handle:* (c) "AMP" in foliate script. *Engraved on side of handle:* (d) "Davis" in script.

Description: (a) pointed oval bowl with swage-formed rounded drop; rounded upturned fiddle-shape handle with 10-lobe shell; (b) pointed oval bowl with swage-formed 12-lobe shell; rounded upturned fiddle-shape handle with double-thread border, 11-lobe shell, and back-to-back anthemia; (c) pointed oval bowl with swage-formed rounded drop; rounded down-turned handle with swage-formed 10-lobe shell; (d) butter knife with flat curved blade, rounded on end; hollow rectangular handle with rounded end and double thread borders.

Spectrographic analysis: Silver content ranges from 89.4 to 92.2 percent.

Provenance: (a) Charlotte and Edgar Sittig, Shawnee-on-Delaware, Pa.; (b) H. F. du Pont; (c, d) Mr. and Mrs. Stanley B. Ineson, New York City; Mr. and Mrs. Alfred E. Bissell, Wilmington, Del.

Comments: The "5 FRANCS" stamp on (a) reflects one of the many attempts to create standards of metal quality during the first half of the nineteenth century. Robert and William Wilson manufactured their flatware to 4 standards, in descending order: crowns, 5 francs, Spanish dollars, and standard. The first 2 were French coins that, for a time, were legal tender in the United States. Spanish dollars, always available in great quantity, actually varied in

quality but were perceived as having a silver content of roughly 90.0 percent. Standard referred to the silver coinage of the United States that, prior to 1837, was 89.2 percent pure silver (afterward raised to 90.0 percent).

References: Belden, *Marks of American Silversmiths*, p. 450 b, c. (a) Deborah Dependahl Waters, "From Pure Coin: The Manufacture of American Silver Flatware, 1800–1860," in Ian M. G. Quimby, ed., *Winterthur Portfolio 12* (Charlottesville: University Press of Virginia for the Henry Francis du Pont Winterthur Museum, 1977), pp. 19–33, figs. 2, 3.

(a) 72.467 Museum purchase from Charlotte and Edgar Sittig, 1972; (b) 65.3054 Bequest of H. F. du Pont, 1969; (c, d) 62.240.606, .497 Gift of Mr. and Mrs. Alfred E. Bissell, 1962–63

499 a–k
SPOONS AND FORK, 1825–46

(a–e) L. 8 ½" (21.6 cm)
1 oz. 18 dwt. (59.0 g) average
(f) L. 6 3/16" (15.7 cm)
15 dwt. 1 gr. (23.4 g)
(g) L. 7 3/16" (18.3 cm)
2 oz. 6 gr. (62.5 g)
(h) L. 5 7/8" (14.9 cm)
1 oz. 5 dwt. 9 gr. (39.4 g)
(i) L. 7 3/16" (18.3 cm)
1 oz. 16 dwt. 10 gr. (56.6 g)
(j) L. 8 ¾" (22.2 cm)
1 oz. 9 dwt. 20 gr. (46.3 g)
(k) L. 7 11/16" (19.6 cm)
1 oz. 14 dwt. 10 gr. (55.1 g)

Stamps: "R & W. WILSON" in roman letters, in a rectangle, struck once on back of each handle.

Engraved on back of handle: (a–e) "EAR" in foliate script; (g, i) "Van Syckel" in script; (h) "Field" in script; (k) "ETR" in foliate script. *Engraved on front of handle:* (f) "T[? ?]R"; (j) "MEH". Both in foliate script.

Description: (a–e, g) pointed oval bowl with swage-formed 12-lobe shell; wavy upturned fiddle-shape handle with double-thread border, 11-lobe shell, and back-to-back anthemia; (f) pointed oval bowl with swage-formed rounded drop; rounded downturned fiddle-shape handle with midrib; (h, i) pointed oval bowl with swage-formed 12-lobe shell; rounded upturned fiddle-shape handle with double-thread border, 11-lobe shell, and back-to-back anthemia; (j) wide oval bowl with swage-formed rounded drop; rounded downturned fiddle-shape handle with midrib; (k) 4-tine fork with swage-formed 12-lobe shell; rounded upturned fiddle-shape handle with double-thread border, 11-lobe shell, and back-to-back anthemia.

Spectrographic analysis: Silver content ranges from 88.6 to 91.3 percent.

Provenance: (a–e, g–i) H. F. du Pont; (f) Mrs. Samuel F. Pryor III, Bedford Hills, N.Y.; (j, k) Mr. and Mrs. Stanley B. Ineson, New York City; Mr. and Mrs. Alfred E. Bissell, Wilmington, Del.

Comments: Spoons (a–e) are a set.

References: Belden, *Marks of American Silver-smiths*, p. 450 a.

(a–e) 61.628.1–.5 Gift of H. F. du Pont, 1965; (f) 86.9 Trade with Mrs. Samuel F. Pryor III, 1985; (g, h, i) 70.1318.2, 65.3051, .3059 Bequest of H. F. du Pont, 1969; (j, k) 62.240.1587, .479 Gift of Mr. and Mrs. Alfred E. Bissell, 1962–63

500
SPOON, 1825–46

L. 8 7/16" (21.4 cm)
2 oz. 14 dwt. 20 gr. (85.1 g)

Stamps: "R&WW" in roman letters, in a rectangle, struck once on back of handle. Accompanied by profile bust portrait (male), a roman "W", and a lion passant; all in rectangles with canted corners.

Engraved on back of handle: "W[?]S" in foliate script.

Description: pointed oval bowl with swage-formed rounded drop and shell; rounded upturned fiddle-shape handle with double-thread border and 2 shells on front; double-thread border with single shell on back.

Spectrographic analysis: Silver content is 91.7 percent.

Provenance: Mr. William Inslee, Downingtown, Pa.

80.53 Gift of Mr. William Inslee, 1980

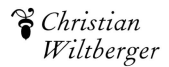

Christian Wiltberger

1766–1851

Wiltberger & Alexander, w. ?–1797
Philadelphia, Pennsylvania

Christian Wiltberger's father, Johan Peter Wiltberger (1731–77), was born at "Offenbach, in the Dominions of Prince Zary Bruken," of Castle Wildeburg in "Lower Austria." He came to Philadelphia, where he married Anne Caterina (last name unknown) in 1755. Their fifth child, John Christian, was born in 1766. By the time he appeared as a silversmith in Philadelphia newspapers in 1793, he had dropped his given name, completed an apprenticeship, and married Anne Warner. (Their fifth son, John Christian Wiltberger, Jr. (1798–1855), started his career as a silversmith, but at the age of twenty-one he was sent to Liberia with a group of African Americans by the Colonization Society. This led to his ordination as a minister, and in 1831 he became pastor of a Washington, D.C., church.)

Christian Wiltberger appeared in the press in 1797 when his partnership with Samuel Alexander was dissolved on less than friendly terms. Alexander felt compelled to state in his public notice that "as Mr. Wiltberger has authorized himself to settle the business without my knowledge, I therefore think it is my duty to inform my friends and the public that I am neither dead, insolvent, or run away, but that I have lately removed to the house formerly occupied by Mr. Wiltberger, in South Second Street, No. 33, where I mean to carry on the business" (*Federal Gazette*, June 5, 1797). Wiltberger, meanwhile, moved to 13 North Second Street, "nearly opposite Christ Church," advertising the usual selection of imported jewelry and plated wares plus "a considerable quantity of Silver Wares manufactured immediately under his own inspection" (*Federal Gazette*, June 7, 1797). Prior to the breakup, in May of the same year, the partners had referred to their "Manufactory and warehouse." All of this suggests a more entrepreneurial approach to the business and opens the question of the extent to which Wiltberger was a hands-on silversmith. He was one of three Philadelphia silversmiths (along with Simon Chaudron and William Seal) to sign an 1817 statement opposing the Baltimore assay law and certifying that "we never manufacture any Silver of a lower quality than Spanish Dollars." (The statement documents the interest of Philadelphia silversmiths in the Baltimore market.) Wiltberger's career as a silversmith ended relatively early; it is quite likely that he devoted his later years to mercantile activities. That he fared well financially is suggested by the fact that he was one of a handful of current or former silversmiths to be taxed by the state in 1832 for a "pleasure carriage." Wiltberger worked largely in the urn style but also made a number of more traditional forms. He made communion silver for Saint Paul's, Saint James's, and Saint John's churches in Philadelphia. The Saint John's service is now at Yale University Art Gallery. Stylistically speaking, his most advanced work is a large coffee urn with lion mask handles and ball feet now owned by the Virginia Historical Society.

References: Brix, *Philadelphia Silversmiths.* Belden, *Marks of American Silversmiths*, p. 451. "History of the Wiltberger Family," notes compiled by Ellen Sampson Magoun, 1936, Historical Society of Pennsylvania. *Philadelphia Silver*, nos. 576–94. Prime cards, Winterthur. Waters, "Philadelphia's Precious Metals Trades," pp. 115, 169.

501

SUGAR URN WITH LID, ca. 1800

H. (with lid) 10 ⁵⁄₁₆" (27.8 cm), H. (without lid) 6 ⁹⁄₁₆" (16.7 cm), DIAM. 4 ¾" (12.1 cm)
13 OZ. 16 dwt. 1 gr. (429.3 g)

Stamps: "C. Wiltberger" in roman letters, in a conforming surround, struck twice on footring.

Engraved on side of body: "MM" in foliate script. *Scratched on underside of pedestal:* "OZ 14 dwt 3".

Description: raised circular urn-shape body with concave panels (flutes) all around; narrow shoulders support a plain seamed rim; centerpunch on underside of body. Trumpet-shape pedestal mounted on scalloped-edge footring with concave panels all around. Raised circular lid, stepped inside flange, curves in and up to a large knop supporting a cast, paneled urn finial; bezel. Combination of wheelwork and bright-cut engraved decoration: band of paired circles with sunburst centers, each pair in a rectangle at the top of each body panel, tripartite dependent leaf on each panel; double row of wheelwork dots on each ridge between panels; lid and base of pedestal encircled by swags of wheelwork with single leaf motif.

Spectrographic analysis:

	SILVER	COPPER	LEAD	GOLD
BODY SIDE	95.0	3.5	0.27	0.15
FOOTRING	94.0	4.4	0.25	0.17
LID	94.5	4.0	0.28	0.16
FINIAL	93.3	4.9	0.33	0.19

Provenance: John Kenneth Danby, Wilmington, Del.; Parke-Bernet Galleries, New York City.

References: Fales, *American Silver*, no. 126. Parke-Bernet Galleries, sale no. 1722, Danby estate sale (December 13–15, 1956), lot 443.

56.98.2 Museum purchase from Parke-Bernet Galleries, 1956

502
SUGAR TONGS,
ca. 1800

L. 6 ½" (16.5 cm), 1 oz. 3 dwt. 20 gr. (37.0 g)

Stamps: "C. Wiltberger" in roman letters, in a conforming surround, struck once on inside of each arm.

Engraved on back of bow: "P" in foliate script, in an oval, with pendant drops and bright-cut borders on each arm; triple bellflower drop on each grip.

Description: U-shape form with bow back, straight tapered arms, and oval spoon grips.

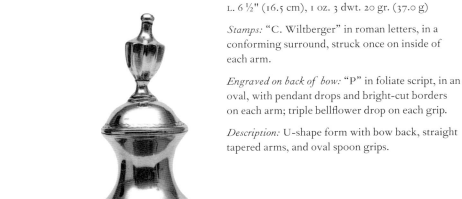

Spectrographic analysis:

SILVER	COPPER	LEAD	GOLD
91.7	7.9	0.24	0.14

Provenance: H. F. du Pont.

70.1052 Bequest of H. F. du Pont, 1969

503 a–j
SPOONS, 1793–1817

(a) L. 6 3/16" (15.7 cm), 10 dwt. 5 gr. (15.9 g)
(b) L. 5 ¾" (14.6 cm), 8 dwt. 1 gr. (12.5 g)
(c) L. 6" (15.2 cm), 9 dwt. 3 gr. (14.2 g)
(d) L. 7 ¼" (18.4 cm), 16 dwt. 9 gr. (25.4 g)
(e) L. 9 ⅛" (23.2 cm), 1 oz. 16 dwt. 14 gr. (56.8 g)
(f) L. 9 15/16" (23.7 cm), 1 oz. 17 dwt. 7 gr. (58.0 g)
(g) L. 6 15/16" (17.6 cm), 1 oz. 3 gr. (31.3 g)
(h) L. 5 ⅛" (13.0 cm), 5 dwt. 20 gr. (9.1 g)
(i) L. 5 ⅛" (13.0 cm), 5 dwt. 18 gr. (8.9 g)
(j) L. 5 3/16" (13.2 cm), 5 dwt. 11 gr. (8.5 g)

Stamps: "C. Wiltberger" in roman letters, in a conforming surround, struck once on back of each handle.

Engraved on front of handle: (a) "ME"; (b) "MW"; (c) "MR"; (d) "R"; (f) "CSR"; (g) "RW", all in foliate script; (e) a foliate script "B" over superimposed "FG" in gothic letters (added later). No engraving on (h–j).

Description: oval bowl with swage-formed rounded drop on all; (b, c) also have bird with branch in beak perched on a limb; (e) also has an urn; (h–j) also have an 11-lobe shell. Pointed downturned handles on (a–f); rounded downturned fiddle-shape handle on (g); rounded downturned handle on (h–j).

Spectrographic analysis: Silver content ranges from 89.2 to 91.6 percent.

History: (h–j) Descended to Bertina Atherton from a William McKenzie, ca. 1813.

Provenance: (a–g) Mr. and Mrs. Stanley B. Ineson, New York City; Mr. and Mrs. Alfred E. Bissell, Wilmington, Del.; (h–j) Bertina Atherton, Milford, Del.

Exhibitions: (c) Metropolitan Museum of Art, New York City, 1935–61.

Comments: (h–j) are a set.

References: Belden, *Marks of American Silversmiths*, p. 451.

(a–g) 62.240.633–.635, .1592, .1589, .1590, .1591 Gift of Mr. and Mrs. Alfred E. Bissell, 1962–63; (h–j) 71.138.1–.3 Gift of Bertina Atherton, 1971

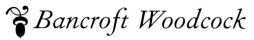

Bancroft Woodcock

1732–1817
w. 1754–94

Woodstock & Byrnes, w. 1790–ca. 1794
Wilmington, Delaware

Bancroft Woodcock's parents, Robert and Rachel (Bancroft) Woodcock, were Irish Quakers from County Wellford. They came to America in 1726, and at a later date moved to Wilmington, Delaware, where the births of their children are recorded in the records of the Wilmington Monthly Meeting. There is no record of Woodcock's apprenticeship. He appears on the scene as a silversmith in 1754 with a notice in the *Pennsylvania Gazette* that he has "set up his business in Wilmington, near the upper Market House, where all persons that please to favour him with their custom, may be supplied with all sorts of Gold and Silver work." As a practicing Quaker, he ran afoul of the law during the American Revolution when he refused to pay his muster fine, causing some contents of his shop to be seized. He also gained the attention of the local Quaker meeting when he accepted pay certificates in lieu of money from Continental soldiers. For this offense he was read out of meeting.

Richard Humphreys, later to become a noted Philadelphia silversmith, was one of his apprentices. It was not a happy relationship, for Humphreys was apparently given to strong drink and disorderly conduct. Another apprentice was Thomas Byrnes, Woodcock's nephew, who became his partner about 1790. It is quite likely that Woodcock trained his own son Isaac, who went on to become a silversmith. Elijah Wansey, described as a "mulatto apprentice lad," ran away from Woodcock's shop in 1790.

Woodcock left Wilmington in 1794 for Bedford County, Pennsylvania, where he had long owned land. Since his will was filed in Bedford County Court in 1817, he presumably spent the intervening years there. It is doubtful, as some sources have proposed, that he returned to Wilmington. Elizabeth Montgomery recalled that Bancroft was "a remarkably plain, stiff looking Friend, reminding one of bones and sinews, yet famous for his agility. In skating he excelled the youths of his day; no one could equal him. It was a novel sight to see such a person flourishing on the ice . . . performing feats to the amazement of beholders. . . . He was also famous for walking. . . . and more than once walked to Philadelphia. . . . Long before the Revolution he was a noted silversmith here. In 1774, he made plate for my mother; his workmanship was superior." Woodcock was a good friend of Henry and Elizabeth Drinker, Philadelphia Quakers, whose home he visited regularly. Elizabeth Drinker recorded his numerous visits in her diary.

For a silversmith who began his career in 1754, there is relatively little surviving work that appears to date earlier than the 1770s. Although he worked in the late rococo style before turning to neoclassical forms, his sugar bowls and coffeepots in the rococo style could just as well have been made in the 1780s. Two outstanding examples are a creamer and covered sugar bowl (now owned by the Art Institute of Chicago) that are both heavily chased with floral decoration. Another is a cruet stand (owned by the Delaware State Museum) that has an asymmetrical rocaille handle. His neoclassical silver follows the Philadelphia preference for the urn style with pierced galleries. Creamers and canns seem to have come from his shop in abundance. Several of his pieces are marked with scratch dates, all from the 1780s or early 1790s.

References: Harrington, *Silversmiths of Delaware*, pp. 9–13. Hindes, "Delaware Silversmiths," pp. 302–4 plus plates. *Bancroft Woodcock Silversmith* (Wilmington: Historical Society of Delaware, 1976), with essays by Roland Woodward ("Bancroft Woodcock Silver in the Collections of the Historical Society of Delaware") and David Warren ("Bancroft Woodcock: Silversmith, Friend, and Landholder"). Stuart L. Warter, "The Wandering Woodcocks of Pennsylvania: Bancroft, Isaac, and John," *Silver* 24, no. 5 (September/October 1991): 9–12. See also Elizabeth Montgomery, *Reminiscences of Wilmington* (Philadelphia: T. K. Collins, Jr., 1851), pp. 54–55; Crane, *Diary of Elizabeth Drinker*.

504 a, b
CANNS, ca. 1780

(a) H. 5 ¼" (13.3 cm), w. 5 ¼" (13.3 cm)
13 oz. 13 dwt. 18 gr. (425.7 g)
(b) H. 5 ³⁄₁₆" (13.2 cm), w. 5 ⁵⁄₁₆" (13.5 cm)
13 oz. 14 dwt. 16 gr. (427.2 g)

Stamps: "B•W" in roman letters, in a conforming surround, struck once on underside of body.

Engraved on side of body: armorial device consisting of a spread-winged bird with crest (not an eagle) standing on a snake whose upper body curves up so that it is looking at the bird. Snake's body rests on a heraldic band. *Engraved at a later date below:* "MꞱK" in shaded gothic letters.

Description: raised circular form with bulbous lower body, incurving neck, flared rim with single-molded edge with double-incised line below; centerpunch on underside of body. Cast, circular, stepped foot. Double–C-scroll handle with acanthus leaf and sprig on upper end, scroll and sprig on lower end, molded edges, lower and upper handle ends attach to body by built-up oval sections; vent in underside of upper handle, which is cast in 2 vertical sections.

Spectrographic analysis:

	SILVER	COPPER	LEAD	GOLD
(a)				
BODY SIDE	91.3	8.2	0.36	0.11
HANDLE	91.7	7.8	0.31	0.14
FOOT	93.2	5.2	0.54	0.35
(b)				
BODY SIDE	92.7	6.8	0.33	0.15
HANDLE	92.9	6.6	0.22	0.10
FOOT	93.5	5.0	0.58	0.27

History: The crest and initials are those of the McKean family of Delaware and Pennsylvania. The most famous member of the family, Thomas McKean (1734–1817), was a brilliant lawyer, politician, and jurist who spent the first half of his life in Delaware, where he would have had ample opportunity to patronize Bancroft Woodcock. He was in the first Delaware delegation to the Continental Congress, along with George Read and Caesar Rodney, and was a signer of the Declaration of Independence. Shortly thereafter he wrote the constitution for the state of Delaware. He went on to become chief justice for the state of Pennsylvania, serving in that capacity for 22 years, and represented Delaware in the congress. He served as governor of Pennsylvania for 9 years, from 1799 to 1808, following which he retired. His will refers to "my steel-seal ring with my coat of Arms cut thereon." Probably these are the arms that appear on an engraved portrait of him by David Edwin. The accompanying crest is described as "an eagle crested, with wings displayed, perched upon a snake, with head erected." This description fits the crest engraved on these 2 canns. Whether the canns were purchased directly by McKean or by another member of his family is uncertain. The family motto is "Mens sana in corpore sano" ("A healthy mind in a healthy body").

Provenance: Joe Kindig, Jr., York, Pa., sold to H. F. du Pont, October 1935.

References: DAB, s.v. "McKean, Thomas." Fales, *American Silver,* no. 113. Harrington, *Silversmiths of Delaware,* p. 12. Roberdeau Buchanan, *Genealogy of the McKean Family of Pennsylvania* (Lancaster, Pa., 1890), pp. 13–123, for biography; pp. 116–17, for discussion of the coat of arms. *Bolton's American Armory,* p. 112.

61.693.1, .2 Gift of H. F. du Pont, 1965

505
CANN, ca. 1780

H. 5 ³⁄₁₆" (13.2 cm), w. 5 ⁵⁄₁₆" (13.5 cm)
13 oz. 1 dwt. (405.0 g)

Stamps: "B•W" in roman letters, in a conforming surround, struck once on underside of body.

Engraved on underside of body: "S/ B✶S" in shaded roman letters.

Description: raised circular form with bulbous lower body, incurving neck, flared rim with single-molded edge with double-incised lines below; centerpunch amid a scratched circle on underside of body. Cast, circular, stepped foot.

Double–C-scroll handle with acanthus leaf and sprig on upper-end, scroll and sprig on lower end, molded edges, lower and upper handle ends attached to body by built-up oval sections; vent in underside of upper handle attachment; handle cast in 2 vertical sections.

Spectrographic analysis:

	SILVER	COPPER	LEAD	GOLD
BODY SIDE	90.9	8.8	0.18	0.08
HANDLE	90.5	8.9	0.28	0.15
FOOT	93.5	5.4	0.21	0.13

Provenance: H. F. du Pont.

References: Harrington, *Silversmiths of Delaware*, p. 12.

61.695 Gift of H. F. du Pont, 1965

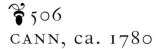

506
CANN, ca. 1780

H. 5 ⁵⁄₁₆" (13.5 cm), w. 5 ³⁄₈" (13.7 cm)
13 oz. 5 dwt. 19 gr. (413.4 g)

Stamps: "B•W" in roman letters, in a conforming surround, struck once on underside of body.

Engraved on underside of body: "IRD" in shaded roman letters with leaves between the letters.

Description: raised circular form with bulbous lower body, incurving neck, flared rim with convex molded edge and a single incised line below; centerpunch amid 2 scratched concentric circles on underside of body. Cast circular stepped foot. Double–C-scroll handle with acanthus leaf and sprig on upper end, scroll and sprig

on lower end, molded edges, lower and upper handle ends attached to body by built-up oval sections; 2 vents in underside of upper handle, which is cast in 2 vertical sections.

Spectrographic analysis:

	SILVER	COPPER	LEAD	GOLD
BODY SIDE	90.1	9.6	0.27	0.04
HANDLE	92.6	7.0	0.23	0.07
FOOT	94.6	3.9	0.24	0.09

Provenance: H. F. du Pont.

Comments: In 1930 Robert Ensko, Inc., New York City, removed the spout and some later initials from a cup, probably this one, for H. F. du Pont.

References: Harrington, *Silversmiths of Delaware*, p. 12.

61.694 Gift of H. F. du Pont, 1965

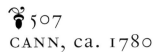

507
CANN, ca. 1780

H. 4 ⁷⁄₁₆" (11.3 cm), w. 4 ⅜" (11.1 cm)
9 oz. 17 dwt. 4 gr. (306.7 g)

Stamps: "B•W" in roman letters, in a conforming surround, struck once on underside of body.

Engraved on underside of body: "V / BR" ("V" has what may be a conjoined "L") in shaded roman letters. *Scratched on underside of footring:* "1 11 10".

Description: raised circular form with bulbous lower body, incurving neck, flared rim with single-molded edge and double-incised line below; 2 centerpunches on underside of body, 1 in a scratched circle. Cast, circular, stepped foot.

Double–C-scroll handle with scroll, acanthus leaf, and sprig on upper end, scroll and sprig on lower end, molded edges, lower and upper ends attached to body by built-up oval sections, vent in underside of upper handle, which is cast in 2 vertical sections.

Spectrographic analysis:

	SILVER	COPPER	LEAD	GOLD
BODY SIDE	90.1	9.3	0.31	0.13
HANDLE	90.6	8.7	0.45	0.19
FOOT	91.7	6.2	0.31	0.16

Provenance: H. F. du Pont.

References: Harrington, *Silversmiths of Delaware*, p. 12.

61.696 Gift of H. F. du Pont, 1965

508

SALVER, ca. 1770

DIAM. 9 ⅟₁₆" (23.0 cm), H. 1 ⁹⁄₁₆" (4.0 cm)
12 OZ. 18 dwt. 1 gr. (401.3 g)

Stamps: "B•W" in roman letters, in a conforming surround, struck once on underside of body.

Engraved on top of body: "CSM" (as a cypher) in foliate script. *Engraved on underside of body:* "M/ CS" in shaded roman letters. Accompanied by "13 = 12". *Scratched over "13": "oz"; scratched after "12": "12"; and scratched elsewhere on underside:* "oz/ 13–dwt/ 11".

Description: flat circular tray with raised-and-shaped edge consisting of cyma-recta and cyma-reversa curves; centerpunch partially covered by stamp. Applied cast border conforms to edge and has 6 equidistant shells; 3 short cast cabriole legs with acanthus leaves on the knees and ball-and-claw feet; the ball portion of each foot is stippled; 3 evenly spaced small circles on underside may be rivets added to secure applied molding to body.

Spectrographic analysis:

	SILVER	COPPER	LEAD	GOLD
UPPER SIDE	90.9	8.5	0.27	0.07
LEG	94.5	4.9	0.22	0.08

Provenance: James A. Lewis & Son, New York City, sold to H. F. du Pont, November 1951.

Comments: An excellent example of an American rococo salver with superbly detailed feet.

References: Fales, *American Silver*, no. 113. Donald L. Fennimore, "Bancroft Woodcock Salver," *Silver* 16, no. 5 (September/October 1983): 15–17.

51.63 Gift of H. F. du Pont, 1951

𝕭 509
CREAMER, ca. 1770

H. 4 ³⁄₁₆" (10.6 cm), w. 4 ⅜" (11.1 cm)
4 oz. 15 dwt. 21 gr. (149.1 g)

Stamps: "B•W" in roman letters, in a conforming surround, struck once on underside of body.

Engraved on front of body under pouring lip: "SMC" (in a cypher) in foliate script.

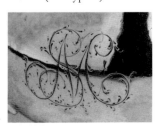

Description: raised circular double-bellied body with incurving neck, flaring wavy-edge rim, and extended pouring lip with crease in center; centerpunch obscured by maker's stamp; 3 legs, cast as C curves, have triangular triple-pad feet; legs attached to body by circular plates and stems. Cast S-curve handle attached to body by reverse C curves; 2 sprigs on upper handle, 1 on lower handle.

Spectrographic analysis:

	SILVER	COPPER	LEAD	GOLD
BODY SIDE	91.3	8.5	0.34	0.15
LEG	92.2	7.4	0.21	0.11
HANDLE	91.6	7.6	0.25	0.14

Provenance: S. J. Shrubsole, New York City, who found it in England and sold it to H. F. du Pont, March 1952.

References: Fales, *American Silver*, no. 113.

61.618 Gift of H. F. du Pont, 1965

𝕭 510
CREAMER, ca. 1785

H. 6 ¹³⁄₁₆" (17.3 cm), w. 5 ⅜" (13.6 cm)
6 oz. 15 dwt. 19 gr. (211.2 g)

Stamps: "B•WOODCOCK" in roman letters, in a rectangle, slightly scalloped inside, struck once on underside of base.

Scratched on underside of base: "1785/ ce/ Ge"; "1789".

Description: raised helmet-shape body with extended pouring lip; no centerpunch. Circular trumpet-shape pedestal mounted on square base with plain applied sides; high-loop C-curve handle attached to body at upper end by reverse C scroll; 1 sprig. Beading around rim, upper end of pedestal, circular base of pedestal, base, and on handle.

Spectrographic analysis:

	SILVER	COPPER	LEAD	GOLD
BODY SIDE	93.9	5.6	0.26	0.06
BASE	93.9	5.2	0.28	0.09
HANDLE	95.5	3.3	0.29	0.10

Provenance: Possibly the "Silver Pitcher (Bancroft Woodcock 1754)" sold by Arthur Sussel, Philadelphia, to H. F. du Pont, February 1930.

Comments: This is a very conservative version of a creamer in the urn style. It lacks the high-rising back and a higher pouring lip. It echoes rococo design in the reverse C curve in the handle. Compare with no. 511. The Art Institute of Chicago owns a similar creamer made for Myriah James of Wilmington, Del.

References: Harrington, *Silversmiths of Delaware*, p. 12.

61.650 Gift of H. F. du Pont, 1965

🌰511
CREAMER, ca. 1785

H. 6⅛" (15.6 cm), w. 4⅛" (10.5 cm)
6 oz. 5 dwt. 22 gr. (195.4 g)

Stamps: "B•WOODCOCK" in roman letters, in a rectangle, struck once on side of base.

Engraved on side of body: "JLT" in foliate script. *Engraved on side of base:* "1793"; last 2 numbers are larger and cruder than the first 2, and it appears that the "3" was originally a "6." *Scratched on underside of base:* "oz/ 6 [?]/ 8".

Description: raised helmet-shape body with high pouring lip, low sides, rises slightly at back; no centerpunch. Circular trumpet-shape pedestal mounted on a square base with plain applied sides; high-loop molded strap handle attached to body at upper end by reverse C scroll, tapers to point at bottom; sprig in middle. Beading around rim, upper end of pedestal, and around circular base of pedestal.

Spectrographic analysis:

	SILVER	COPPER	LEAD	GOLD
BODY SIDE	92.4	7.3	0.23	0.16
BASE	95.4	4.3	0.16	0.10
HANDLE	93.0	6.7	0.24	0.10

Provenance: Mrs. Leslie N. Gay; Dr. Leslie N. Gay, Baltimore.

Comments: Considered a better example of the form than no. 510.

77.168 Gift of Dr. Leslie N. Gay, 1977

512 a–j
FORKS, ca. 1780

L. 8 ¼" (21.0 cm)
2 oz. 2 dwt. (65.8 g) average

Stamps: "B•W" in roman letters, in a rectangle with incurving sides, struck twice on back of each handle.

Engraved on back of each handle: "W / I*M" in shaded roman letters.

Description: 4 tines with plain back; rounded upturned handle with pronounced midrib.

Spectrographic analysis: Silver content ranges from 93.0 to 93.4 percent.

Provenance: Edmund Bury, Philadelphia, sold to H. F. du Pont, May 1940.

Comments: Eighteenth-century forks are rare and sets even more so. The weight of these forks suggests that Woodcock may have followed a French model. The same initials are on spoon no. 513 b and on a porringer in the Delaware State Museum.

61.640.1–.10 Gift of H. F. du Pont, 1965

☙513 a–c
SPOONS, ca. 1770

(a) L. 8 3/16" (20.8 cm)
1 oz. 14 dwt. 8 gr. (53.3 g)
(b) L. 8" (20.3 cm)
1 oz. 17 dwt. 16 gr. (58.5 g)
(c) L. 8 5/16" (21.1 cm)
1 oz. 17 dwt. 23 gr. (58.9 g)

Stamps: "B•W" in roman letters, in a rectangle, struck once twice on back of handle (a), once on back of handles (b, c).

Engraved on back of handle: (a) "L/ A∗M"; (b) "W/ I∗M"; (c) "JL", all in shaded roman letters.

Description: elongated oval bowl with swage-formed rounded drop, arc, and shell on (a); double-rounded drop with midrib on (b); rounded drop, 2 crescents, and an 11-lobe shell on (c). Rounded upturned handle with midrib.

Spectrographic analysis: Silver content ranges from 87.3 to 92.6 percent.

History: (b) has the same initials as forks no. 512. Initials "JL" on (c) refer to John Lewden, an ancestor of Margaret Janvier Hort. The Lewdens lived in Christiana, Del., and were related to the Janviers and Corbetts of Odessa, Del.

Provenance: (a, b) Mr. and Mrs. Stanley B. Ineson, New York City; Mr. and Mrs. Alfred E. Bissell, Wilmington, Del.; (c) John Lewden, Margaret Janvier Hort, Bryn Mawr, Pa.

References: Belden, *Marks of American Silversmiths*, p. 454.

(a, b) 62.240.1544, .1545 Gift of Mr. and Mrs. Alfred E. Bissell, 1962–63; (c) 75.24 Gift of Margaret Janvier Hort, 1975

☙514 a, b
SPOONS, ca. 1780

(a) L. 8 1/8" (20.6 cm)
1 oz. 7 dwt. 4 gr. (42.2 g)
(b) L. 8 11/16" (22.1 cm)
2 oz. 17 gr. (63.2 g)

Stamps: "B•WOODCOCK" in roman letters, in a conforming surround, struck once on back of each handle.

Engraved on front of handle: (b) "AT" in foliate script.

Description: elongated oval bowl with swage-formed rounded drop, arc, and shell on (a); rounded drop and bird, with branch in beak, perched on limb on (b). Rounded upturned handle with midrib on (a); rounded down-turned handle with midrib on (b).

Spectrographic analysis: Silver content ranges from 90.0 to 90.2 percent.

Provenance: Mr. and Mrs. Stanley B. Ineson, New York City; Mr. and Mrs. Alfred E. Bissell, Wilmington, Del.

Exhibitions: (b) Metropolitan Museum of Art, New York City, 1935–61.

References: Belden, *Marks of American Silversmiths*, p. 454.

62.240.1595, .1596 Gift of Mr. and Mrs. Alfred E. Bissell, 1962–63

Freeman Woods

ca. 1766–1834
New York, New York, w. 1791–94
New Bern, North Carolina,
w. 1794–ca. 1827

Nothing is known of Freeman Woods's origins except, according to his death notice, that he was a native of New Jersey. He first appeared in New York City directories for 1791 to 1793 at 11 Smith Street and in 1794 at 19 William Street. By December 1794, he advertised in New Bern, North Carolina, as a goldsmith and silversmith from New York City whose offerings included waiters, tankards, teapots, sugar dishes, milk pots, tablespoons, teaspoons, and sugar tongs. In 1809 he promoted his silver spoons "of every description, he warrants lower than they can be bought anywhere to the northward—and of superior workmanship." Further advertisements in 1818, 1822, 1824, and 1826 show that he continued to practice his craft. He remained in New Bern for the rest of his days. A small amount of Woods's silver survives. An elegant sugar urn is owned by the Minneapolis Institute of Arts, and a pair of openwork salts is in the Hammerslough collection at Wadsworth Atheneum. Both are handsome expressions of the neoclassical style. There has been a tendency to attribute much of Woods's silver to his New York period, perhaps because of its sophistication. Given the fact that he worked in New York for fewer than four years but in New Bern for at least twenty-three years, there is a good chance that any silver with the Woods stamp was made in North Carolina.

References: George Barton Cutten, *Silversmiths of North Carolina, 1696–1850,* rev. Mary Reynolds Peacock (Raleigh: North Carolina Department of Cultural Resources, 1973), pp. 130–32. Von Khrum, *Silversmiths,* p. 142.

515
CREAMER, ca. 1800

H. 6⅜" (16.2 cm), w. 5⅛" (13.0 cm)
4 oz. 11 dwt. 22 gr. (143.0 g)

Stamps: "Wood[s]" in script, in a conforming surround, struck once on side of base.

Engraved on front of body below pouring lip: "DMT" in foliate script, in a bright-cut pointed oval with a bowknot above. *Scratched on underside of base:* "oz 4 wd 15"; "£4-3-6" (illegible marks above). *Scratched on underside of pedestal:* "C1351".

Description: raised helmet-shape body with high pouring lip and low sides, rising to a point in back at handle; no centerpunch. Applied band of beading around rim. Trumpet-shape pedestal with bands of beading around top and bottom; all on a square base. High-loop molded strap handle tapers to point at bottom.

Spectrographic analysis:

	SILVER	COPPER	LEAD	GOLD
BODY SIDE	85.9	13.9	0.14	0.12
FOOT	87.7	12.0	0.19	0.10
HANDLE	86.9	12.8	0.21	0.12

Provenance: Wunsch Americana Foundation, New York City.

Comments: Closely resembles Philadelphia creamers in the urn style.

75.96 Gift of Wunsch Americana Foundation, 1975

516
SPOON, ca. 1800

L. 5⅛" (13.0 cm)
7 dwt. 2 gr. (11.0 g)

Stamps: "Woods" in script, in a conforming surround, struck once on back of handle.

Engraved on front of handle: "BF" (crosswise) in foliate script, in a bright-cut medallion with pendant drop.

Description: oval bowl with swage-formed rounded drop; rounded downturned handle with midrib.

Spectrographic analysis: Silver content is 92.8 percent.

Provenance: George B. Cutten, Amherst, Mass., and Hamilton, N.Y.; Eric Shrubsole, Ltd., New York City.

References: Belden, *Marks of American Silversmiths,* p. 456.

71.88 Museum purchase from Eric Shrubsole, Ltd., 1971

Jesse Zane

ca. 1773–1852
Wilmington, Delaware, w. ca. 1794–1813

Jesse Zane's parents were Joel and Esther Zane, who probably moved to Wilmington in the 1770s. Joel was in the hardware business, which Jesse took over when he came of age. He had, meanwhile, learned the silversmith craft and combined the two occupations. *Delaware Gazette* for July 5, 1796, carried the following notice: "Just Received, and for sale by the subscriber, at his store, the corner of Third and Market-street (Opposite Patrick O'Flin's tavern) a neat and general assortment of Iron-mongery, Sadlery, Cutlery, Brass Ware, And Painters Colours, Jesse S. Zane. Who carries on the silversmith's Business in all its various branches, and gives The highest price for old silver."

In 1794 Zane married Susannah Hanson, the union having been sanctioned by the Society of Friends in the Wilmington Meeting. Following Quaker practice he absented himself from the Delaware militia in 1799 and was fined for doing so. In 1813 he moved to Philadelphia and apparently gave up the silversmith trade. A small quantity of his work survives.

References: Harrington, *Silversmiths of Delaware*, pp. 49–50. Hindes, "Delaware Silversmiths," pp. 305–6 plus plates.

517 a–d
TEA SERVICE, ca. 1800

(a) Teapot: H. 11⅛" (28.3 cm), w. 11⅞" (30.2 cm)
27 oz. 16 dwt. 13 gr. (865.5 g)
(b) Sugar urn with lid: H. 10⅛" (25.7 cm), w. 4 9/16" (11.6 cm)
15 oz. 9 dwt. 12 gr. (481.3 g)
(c) Creamer: H. 7⅝" (19.4 cm), w. 5 3/16" (13.2 cm)
5 oz. 16 dwt. 8 gr. (180.9 g)
(d) Waste bowl: H. 5 7/16" (13.8 cm), DIAM. 6 13/16" (17.3 cm)
13 oz. 17 dwt. 22 gr. (432.2 g)

Stamps: "ZANE" in roman letters, in a rectangle with rounded ends, struck once on side of each base.

Engraved on side of each body and on front of creamer: "ARG" in shaded foliate script.
Scratched on underside of base: (a) "9 86"; (b) "oz 16 dwt 5"; (c) illegible scratch weights.

Description: raised circular forms on trumpet-shape pedestals with beading around top and bottom, square base with plain sides.

(a) Teapot: urn-shape body with applied molded-and-beaded band at shoulders; a short stepped-and-incurved neck with an applied band of beading at rim; body pierced at spout to serve as strainer; centerpunch on underside of body. Raised circular friction-fit lid, stepped and incurved up to knop; both step and knop trimmed with beading; cast footed-urn finial secured through lid by a silver rivet. Seamed S-curve paneled spout. Elongated C-curve hardwood handle with carved acanthus leaf and 2 scrolls; 2 cylindrical sockets and 2 silver pins.

(b) Sugar urn with lid: raised urn-shape body with applied pierced gallery over a beaded border at rim; centerpunch on underside. Raised circular lid similar to (a) but not stepped.

(c) Creamer: raised helmet-shape body with high pouring lip, low sides, back rising slightly at handle; applied beaded molding at rim; no centerpunch. High-loop strap handle with a sprig and dual incised lines; tapers to point at bottom.

(d) Waste bowl: raised hemispherical body with applied beaded molding at rim; if centerpunch is there, it is obscured by an applied piece of scrap.

Spectrographic analysis:

	SILVER	COPPER	LEAD	GOLD
(a) Teapot				
BODY SIDE	91.6	7.0	0.18	0.13
BASE	91.8	6.7	0.21	0.13
NECK	94.5	4.0	0.18	0.14
SPOUT	91.7	6.9	0.18	0.11
LID	92.3	6.4	0.19	0.11
(b) Sugar urn with lid				
BODY SIDE	89.4	10.1	0.22	0.12
BASE	88.7	10.4	0.29	0.15
LID	88.7	10.3	0.25	0.08
FINIAL	88.6	8.7	0.20	0.06
(c) Creamer				
BODY SIDE	90.0	9.3	0.25	0.05
BASE	90.3	9.3	0.16	0.10
HANDLE	90.4	9.3	0.13	0.06
(d) Waste bowl				
BODY SIDE	89.5	10.1	0.22	0.07
BOTTOM	95.0	3.9	0.17	0.13
FOOTRING	88.9	10.3	0.25	0.10

Provenance: Parke-Bernet Galleries, New York City, through Robert Ensko, Inc., New York City, to H. F. du Pont.

Exhibitions: "Delaware Silver," Historical Society of Delaware, Wilmington, 1979; (a) "Selections from Winterthur Museum: Change and Choice in Early American Decorative Arts," IBM Gallery of Science and Art, New York City, 1989–90.

Comments: The set has the feeling of pieces assembled one at a time and not made en suite. Typical in form and decoration of the Philadelphia urn style.

References: Parke-Bernet Galleries, sale no. 848 (March 13–15, 1947), lot 87. Hindes, "Delaware Silversmiths," p. 305 and plate.

(a–d) 64.1151.1, .3, .2, .4 Gift of H. F. du Pont, 1965

Several years ago I asked George Reilly, head of the analytical lab at Winterthur, if he would measure the wall thickness of certain hollowwares in the hope of providing some reliable data on the consistency or variability of wall thicknesses in hand-raised silver. George responded with his usual enthusiasm and diligence.

The very nature of hand-made silver suggests that the wall thickness of an object should vary from one spot to another. How, then, would Reilly go about taking the measurements in such a way as to provide reliable and meaningful data? He created a diagram for each object that consisted of five concentric circles with the first, innermost, circle representing all points at one inch below the rim, the second circle representing two inches below the rim, and so forth. The concentric circles were divided into quadrants of 45 degrees, each separated by radii. Each radii was labeled: A, B, C, etc. The intersections between the radii and the concentric circles became the points at which wall thickness measurements were taken on all pieces. The average of the eight readings for each circle became the average wall thickness at that height on the vessel. Since taller vessels have more circles than shorter vessels, they show more readings. The results for selected hollowwares are displayed in tables 1 through 6. Body thicknesses for salvers, trays, and stands appear in table 7.

Measurements were taken using a Starett Universal Dial Indicator equipped with a special C-shape jig. Straight-sided hollowwares were the easiest to measure; bellied bodies sometimes posed problems, not to mention decorative surfaces that, falling in the wrong place, precluded a measurement.

Weights are provided to give a sense of scale. Here, as elsewhere in the catalogue, objects were weighed using a Mettler top-loading balance, Model P1200, which is capable of measurements to the nearest hundredth gram. (Weights were rounded off to the nearest tenth of a gram.)

Perhaps the most remarkable result of the study is the overall consistency of wall thickness maintained by silversmiths in the hand-raising process. The pair of Austin tankards (nos. 3, 4) shows a variance of only 0.004" in the walls of both pieces. The six Revere tankards have an internal consistency that is even more amazing:

No.	Range	Variance
111 a	0.012"–0.014"	0.002"
111 b	0.016"–0.018"	0.002"
111 c	0.015"–0.018"	0.003"
111 d	0.018"–0.019"	0.001"
111 e	0.014"–0.019"	0.005"
111 f	0.014"–0.016"	0.002"

Given this consistency, one might suspect the presence of sheet silver in the tankards, but the physical evidence points to hand raising. Looking at the much earlier work of Edward Winslow and New York silversmiths Cornelius Kierstede and Simeon Soumaine, we find a similar consistency:

No.	Silversmith	Range	Variance
136	Winslow	0.023"–0.025"	0.002"
137	Winslow	0.021"–0.025"	0.004"
221	Kierstede	0.020"–0.022"	0.002"
257	Soumaine	0.022"–0.025"	0.003"

The New York sample is small, however. Philadelphia tankards fail to show a similar consistency, although here again the sample is small compared with the number of tankards from Boston.

Looking at all tankards (tables 1–3), one quickly senses other patterns. Frequently, wall thicknesses decrease from top to bottom. Also, larger and heavier pieces have thicker walls than smaller and lighter pieces. See, for example, the difference between the half-size Elias Pelletreau tankard (table 2) and the oversize Benjamin Hiller tankard (table 1). See also the massive two-handled cup by Bartholemew Le Roux II with wall thicknesses ranging from 0.037" to 0.057" versus the small goblet or cup by Daniel Christian Fueter with a range from 0.014" to 0.018".

With the technological innovations of the nineteenth century, one might expect greater uniformity in the wall thicknesses of hollowwares. The Gordon goblet (table 5) has an average thickness of 0.019" at all levels, which strongly suggests sheet silver, although no seam is visible. On the other hand, the beakers by Peter L. Krider (table 6), almost surely formed by spinning on a lathe, show as much variation as those made by Myer Myers, which were formed by hand raising:

No.	Silversmith	Range	Variance
375 a	Krider	0.015"–0.016"	0.001"
375 b	Krider	0.014"–0.020"	0.006"
375 c	Krider	0.017"–0.019"	0.002"
375 d	Krider	0.017"–0.020"	0.003"
233 a	Myers	0.016"–0.019"	0.003"
233 b	Myers	0.017"–0.019"	0.002"

Across the board the wall thickness of tankards and other hollowware of similar size was in the range of 0.020"–0.025". Two one-hundredths of an inch seems fairly thin for a vessel designed to hold a quart of liquid, but thick rims and solid base moldings provided structural integrity. Even those tankards that have unusually thick metal one inch below the rim fall into the normal range in their lower measurements (Conyers and Dummer [no. 43], table 1). The anomaly is, of course, the six Revere tankards, which are unusually thin, with an average wall thickness of about 0.017".

Four of the five servers (table 7) show a heavier gauge metal, between 0.030" and 0.038" thickness. Since these flat bodies lack a reinforcing structure, the requisite rigidity could be obtained only by using a thicker metal. A worked or cast edge was of limited value.

The results of the wall thickness study suggest that silversmiths had considerable knowledge of the structural properties of silver and were ingenious in apportioning this precious metal according to the intended function of the form.

TABLE 1

Wall Thickness: New England Tankards
Average Thickness Below Rim in 1" Increments

No.	Silversmith	1 in.	2 in.	3 in.	4 in.	Wt.
3	Austin	0.022"	0.021"	0.020"	0.019"	789.6g
4	Austin	0.022"	0.023"	0.021"	0.020"	789.4g
37	Coney	0.028"	0.027"	0.020"	0.023"	968.6g
39	Conyers	0.046"	0.033"	0.026"	0.023"	1305.0g
43	Dummer	0.038"	0.022"	0.018"	0.019"	760.5g
44	Dummer	0.026"	0.017"	0.018"	0.019"	650.9g
45	Dummer	0.029"	0.023"	0.024"	0.016"	788.0g
74	Hiller	0.038"	0.035"	0.032"	0.032"	1842.0g
109	Revere, Sr.	0.024"	0.020"	0.017"	0.019"	894.7g
111 a	Revere, Jr.	0.013"	0.013"	0.012"	0.014"	745.6g
111 b	Revere, Jr.	0.018"	0.017"	0.017"	0.016"	776.5g
111 c	Revere, Jr.	0.015"	0.016"	0.018"	0.016"	771.8g
111 d	Revere, Jr.	0.019"	0.019"	0.019"	0.018	775.0g
111 e	Revere, Jr.	0.015"	0.019"	0.018"	0.014"	768.2g
111 f	Revere, Jr.	0.016"	0.016"	0.016"	0.014"	762.3g
118	Russell	0.026"	0.024"	0.019"	0.018"	931.9g
136	Winslow	0.024"	0.023"	0.023"	0.025"	733.6g
137	Winslow	0.025"	0.021"	0.023"	0.025"	733.9g
141	Winslow	0.016"	0.008"	0.005"	0.010"	749.4g

TABLE 2

Wall Thickness: New York Tankards
Average Thickness Below Rim in 1" Increments

No.	Silversmith	1 in.	2 in.	3 in.	4 in.	Wt.
157	Boelen	0.027"	0.026"	0.020"	0.018"	944.3g
221	Kierstede	0.022"	0.021"	0.021"	0.020"	1061.2g
237	Pelletreau	0.009"	0.009"	0.016"	—	279.9g
257	Soumaine	0.025"	0.022"	0.022"	0.023"	892.2g

TABLE 3

Wall Thickness: Philadelphia Tankards
Average Thickness Below Rim in 1" Increments

No.	Silversmith	1 in.	2 in.	3 in.	4 in.	Wt.
319	Bayly	0.025"	0.019"	0.022"	0.020"	986.5g
321	Bayly	0.031"	0.029"	0.021"	0.021"	962.4g
389	Lownes	—[1]	0.036"	0.034"	—[1]	583.8g
418	Nys	0.028"	0.037"	0.029"	0.022"	955.0g
458	Richardson, J. & N.	0.022"	0.025"	—[2]	—[2]	937.7g
472	Syng	0.032"	0.028"	0.024"	0.024"	1042.4g
473	Syng	0.040"	—[2]	—[2]	—[2]	1063.5g
474	Syng	0.025"	0.025"	0.021"	0.016"	888.1g

1 Unable to measure because of ribbed bands.
2 Unable to measure because of body shape.

TABLE 4

Wall Thickness: Other Hollowware

New England

Average Thickness Below Rim in 1" Increments

No.	Silversmith	Form	1 in.	2 in.	3 in.	4 in.	Wt.
35	Coburn	cann	0.019"	—	0.032"	—	403.5g
70	Greene	cann	0.022"	0.022"	0.020"	—	230.0g
79	Hurd, J.	coffeepot	0.016"	0.018"	0.020"	0.023"	923.9g
86	Hurd, J.	cann	0.021"	—	0.017"	—	354.8g
102	Oliver	flagon	0.038"	0.033"	0.029"	0.030"	1471.0g
117	Rouse	cup	0.020"	0.017"	—	—	156.1g

TABLE 5

Wall Thickness: Other Hollowware

New York

Average Thickness Below Rim in 1" Increments

No.	Silversmith	Form	1 in.	2 in.	3 in.	4 in.	Wt.
194	Fueter	cup	0.018"	0.014"	—	—	83.3g
205	Gordon	goblet	0.019"	0.019"	0.019"	—	227.3g
225	Le Roux II	cup	0.037"	0.039"	0.057"	0.037"	2529.0g
233 a	Myers	beaker	0.019"	0.016"	0.019"	—	165.2g
233 b	Myers	beaker	0.018"	0.017"	0.019"	—	169.6g
239	Pelletreau	cann	0.019"	0.023"	0.019"	—	394.9g

TABLE 6

Wall Thickness: Other Hollowware

Pennsylvania and the South

Average Thickness Below Rim in 1" Increments

No.	Silversmith	Form	1 in.	2 in.	3 in.	4 in.	Wt.
371	Kirk	beaker	0.017"	0.015"	0.014"	—	123.0g
375 a	Krider	beaker	0.016"	0.015"	0.016"	—	163.0g
375 b	Krider	beaker	0.020"	0.020"	0.014"	—	162.2g
375 c	Krider	beaker	0.019"	0.017"	0.017"	—	162.8g
375 d	Krider	beaker	0.019"	0.020"	0.017"	—	166.6g
396 a	Lynch	beaker	0.017"	0.015"	0.014"	—	109.9g
396 b	Lynch	beaker	0.017"	0.016"	0.014"	—	112.1g
436	Richardson	mug/cann	0.020"	0.019"	0.022"	0.016"	548.8g
505	Woodcock	cann	0.018"	0.018"	0.022"	—	405.0g
506	Woodcock	cann	0.016"	0.016"	0.024"	—	413.4g
507	Woodcock	cann	0.020"	0.018"	0.018"	—	306.7g

TABLE 7

Average Thickness of Salvers, Trays, Stands

No.	Silversmith	City	Thickness	Wt.
63	Edwards, T.	Boston	0.038"	792.4g
82	Hurd, J.	Boston	0.036"	275.0g
252	Sayre & Richards	New York	0.031"	140.4g
278	Van der Spiegel	New York	0.021"	508.8g
476	Syng	Philadelphia	0.034"	176.5g

Short-title Bibliography

Includes sources used more than three times in entries. Works cited in essays and works pertaining to only one silversmith or owner are not included here.

American Church Silver. Boston: Museum of Fine Arts, 1911.

American Silver and Art Treasures. London: Christie's for the English-Speaking Union, 1960.

American Silver: The Work of Seventeenth and Eighteenth Century Silversmiths. Boston: Museum of Fine Arts, 1906. Cited as *American Silver*, MFA.

Arner, Robert D. *Dobson's Encyclopaedia: The Publisher, Text, and Publication of America's First Britannica, 1789–1803*. Philadelphia: University of Pennsylvania Press, 1991.

Belden, Louise Conway. *Marks of American Silversmiths in the Ineson-Bissell Collection*. Charlottesville: University Press of Virginia for the Henry Francis du Pont Winterthur Museum, 1980.

Bigelow, Francis Hill. *Historic Silver of the Colonies and Its Makers*. 1917. Reprint. New York: Macmillan Co., 1941.

————. Scrapbook containing photographs and notes on silver sold to H. F. du Pont through Brooks Reed Gallery, Boston. Winterthur Library.

Blackburn, Roderick H., and Ruth Piwonka. *Remembrance of Patria: Dutch Arts and Culture in Colonial America, 1609–1776*. Albany: Albany Institute of History and Art, 1988.

Bohan, Peter J. *American Gold, 1700–1860*. New Haven: Yale University Art Gallery, 1963.

Bohan, Peter, and Philip Hammerslough. *Early Connecticut Silver, 1700–1840*. Middletown, Conn.: Wesleyan University Press, 1970.

Bolton, Charles Knowles. *Bolton's American Armory*. Boston: F. W. Faxon, 1927.

Boultinghouse, Marquis. *Silversmiths, Jewelers, Clock and Watch Makers of Kentucky, 1785–1900*. Lexington, Ky., 1980. Cited as Boultinghouse, *Silversmiths of Kentucky*.

Brix, Maurice. *List of Philadelphia Silversmiths and Allied Artificers from 1682 to 1850*. Philadelphia: Privately printed, 1920.

Buck, J. H. *Old Plate, Ecclesiastical, Decorative, and Domestic: Its Makers and Marks*. New York: Gorham Manufacturing Co., 1888.

Buhler, Kathryn C. *American Silver, 1655–1825, in the Museum of Fine Arts, Boston*. 2 vols. Boston, 1972.

————. "John Edwards, Goldsmith, and His Progeny." *Antiques* 59, no. 5 (April 1951): 288–92.

Buhler, Kathryn C., and Graham Hood. *American Silver: Garvan and Other Collections in the Yale University Art Gallery*. 2 vols. New Haven: Yale University Press for Yale University Art Gallery, 1970.

[Buhler, Kathryn C.]. *Colonial Silversmiths, Masters and Apprentices*. Boston: Museum of Fine Arts, 1956. Cited as Buhler, *Masters and Apprentices*.

Burton, E. Milby. *South Carolina Silversmiths, 1690–1860*. 1942. Reprint. Rutland, Vt.: Charles E. Tuttle, 1968.

Clarke, Hermann Frederick. *John Hull, A Builder of the Bay Colony*. Portland, Maine: Southworth-Anthoensen Press, 1940.

Clayton, Michael. *The Collector's Dictionary of Silver and Gold of Great Britain and North America*. New York and Cleveland: World Publishing Co., 1971.

Crane, Louise Forman, ed. *The Diary of Elizabeth Drinker*. 3 vols. Boston: Northeastern University Press, 1991.

Davidson, Marshall B., ed. *The American Heritage History of Colonial Antiques*. New York: American Heritage Publishing, 1967. Cited as Davidson, *Colonial Antiques*.

Dictionary of American Biography. 20 vols. New York: Charles Scribner's Sons, 1928–36. Cited as *DAB*.

Dow, George Francis. *The Arts and Crafts of New England, 1704–1775: Gleanings from Boston Newspapers*. Topsfield, Mass.: Wayside Press, 1927.

Ensko, Stephen G. C. *American Silversmiths and Their Marks III*. New York: Robert Ensko, 1948. Cited as Ensko, *American Silversmiths III*.

———. *American Silversmiths and Their Marks IV*. Boston: David R. Godine, 1989. Cited as Ensko, *American Silversmiths IV*.

Fairbanks, Jonathan L., and Robert F. Trent, eds. *New England Begins: The Seventeenth Century*. 3 vols. Boston: Museum of Fine Arts, 1982.

Fales, Martha Gandy. *American Silver in the Henry Francis du Pont Winterthur Museum*. Winterthur, Del.: By the museum, 1958.

———. *Early American Silver*. New York: E. P. Dutton, 1973. A revised and enlarged edition of *Early American Silver for the Cautious Collector* (New York: Funk and Wagnalls, 1970).

———. *Joseph Richardson and Family: Philadelphia Silversmiths*. Middletown, Conn.: Wesleyan University Press for the Historical Society of Pennsylvania, 1974.

Fennimore, Donald L. *Silver and Pewter*. The Knopf Collectors' Guides to American Antiques. New York: Alfred A. Knopf, 1984.

Fielding, Mantle. *American Engravers upon Copper and Steel*. Philadelphia: Privately printed, 1917.

Flynt, Henry N., and Martha Gandy Fales. *The Heritage Foundation Collection of Silver with Biographical Sketches of New England Silversmiths, 1625–1825*. Old Deerfield, Mass.: Heritage Foundation, 1968.

Forbes, Esther. *Paul Revere and the World He Lived In*. Boston: Houghton Mifflin Co., 1942.

French, Hollis. *Jacob Hurd and His Sons Nathaniel and Benjamin, Silversmiths, 1702–1781*. 1939. Reprint. New York: Da Capo Press, 1972.

Goldsborough, Jennifer Faulds. *Eighteenth- and Ninteenth-Century Maryland Silver*. Baltimore: Baltimore Museum of Art, 1975.

———. *Silver in Maryland*. Baltimore: Maryland Historical Society, 1983.

[Gottesman, Rita Susswein]. *The Arts and Crafts in New York, 1726–1776: Advertisements and News Items from New York City Newspapers*. Collections of the New-York Historical Society for the Year 1936. The John Watts dePeyster Publication Fund Series, no. 69. New York: By the society, 1938. Cited as Gottesman, *Arts and Crafts, 1726–76*.

———. *The Arts and Crafts in New York, 1777–1799: Advertisements and News Items from New York City Newspapers*. Collections of the New-York Historical Society for the Year 1948. The John Watts dePeyster Publication Fund Series, no. 81. New York: By the society, 1954. Cited as Gottesman, *Arts and Crafts, 1777–99*.

———. *The Arts and Crafts in New York, 1800–1804: Advertisements and News Items from New York City Newspapers*. Collections of the New-York Historical Society for the Year 1949. The John Watts dePeyster Publication Fund Series, no. 82. New York: By the society, 1965. Cited as Gottesman, *Arts and Crafts, 1800–1804*.

Groce, George C., and David H. Wallace. *The New-York Historical Society's Dictionary of Artists in America, 1564–1860*. New Haven: Yale University Press, 1957.

Guillim, John. *A Display of Heraldry*. 6th ed. London, 1724.

Hammerslough, Philip H. *American Silver Collected by Philip H. Hammerslough*. 3 vols. with supplements. Hartford, Conn.: Privately printed, 1958, 1960, 1965.

Harrington, Jessie. *Silversmiths of Delaware, 1700–1850*. [Wilmington]: National Society of Colonial Dames of America in Delaware, 1939.

Hindes, Ruthanna. "Delaware Silversmiths, 1700–1850." *Delaware History* 12, no. 4 (October 1967): 247–308.

Hood, Graham. *American Silver: A History of Style, 1650–1900*. New York: Praeger Publishers, 1971.

Jones, E. Alfred. *The Old Silver of American Churches*. 2 vols. Letchworth, Eng.: Arden Press for the National Society of Colonial Dames of America, 1913.

Kane, Patricia E., ed. *A Dictionary of Massachusetts Silversmiths*. New Haven: Yale University Art Gallery, forthcoming.

————. "John Hull and Robert Sanderson: First Masters of New England Silver." Ph.D. diss., Yale University, 1987.

Kauffman, Henry J. *The Colonial Silversmith: His Techniques and His Products*. Camden, N.J.: Thomas Nelson, 1969.

Masterpieces of American Silver. Richmond: Virginia Museum of Fine Arts, 1960.

Miller, V. Isabelle. *New York Silversmiths of the Seventeenth Century*. New York: Museum of the City of New York, 1962.

————. *Silver by New York Makers: Late Seventeenth Century to 1900*. New York: Museum of the City of New York, 1937.

Minutes of the Common Council of the City of New York, 1675–1776. 8 vols. New York: Dodd, Mead, 1905.

New England Historical and Genealogical Register. 1847–. Cited as *NEH&GR*.

The New-York Genealogical and Biographical Record. 1870–. Cited as *NYG&BR*.

New-York Historical Society Collections: *Burghers and Freemen*, vol. 18 (1885); *Abstracts of Wills*, vols. 25–41 (1892–1908); *Indentures of Apprentices*, vol. 42 (1909); *New-York Tax Lists*, vols. 43, 44 (1910–11); *Supreme Court Province of New York*, vol. 80 (1947); *Rivington's New York*, vol. 84 (1973). Cited as *NYHS Collections* with subtitle.

New-York Historical Society Quarterly Bulletin. 1917–79. Cited as *NYHSQB*.

New York State Silversmiths. Eggertsville, N.Y.: Darling Foundation, 1964.

Paul Revere—Artisan, Businessman, and Patriot: The Man Behind the Myth. Boston: Paul Revere Memorial Association, 1988.

Pennsylvania Magazine of History and Biography. 1877–. Cited as *PMHB*.

Philadelphia: Three Centuries of American Art. Philadelphia: Philadelphia Museum of Art, 1976.

Philadelphia Silver, 1682–1800. Philadelphia: Philadelphia Museum of Art, 1956. Originally published as *Philadelphia Museum Bulletin* 51, no. 249 (Spring 1956).

Pleasants, J. Howard, and Howard Sill. *Maryland Silversmiths, 1715–1830*. 1930. Reprint. Harrison, N.Y.: Robert Allen Green, 1972.

Prime Cards. Decorative Arts Photographic Collection, Winterthur library. These are the original file cards containing the newspaper advertisements recorded by Alfred Coxe Prime and used as the basis for his books. Gift of Mrs. Alfred Coxe Prime.

Quimby, Ian M. G. "How America Looked in 1776: Silver." *American Art Journal* 7, no. 1 (May 1975): 68–81. Cited as Quimby, "Silver."

Rice, Norman S. *Albany Silver, 1652–1825*. Albany: Albany Institute of History and Art, 1964.

Roberts, Oliver Ayer. *History of the Military Company of Massachusetts Now Called The Ancient and Honorable Artillery Company of Massachusetts, 1637–1888*. 2 vols. Boston: Alfred Mudge and Son, 1895, 1897. Cited as Roberts, *Artillery Company*.

Sewall, Samuel. *Diary of Samuel Sewall, 1674–1729*. 2 vols. New York: Farrar, Straus, and Giroux, 1973.

Sibley, John Langdon. *Biographical Sketches of Graduates of Harvard University*, and Clifford K. Shipton, *Sibley's Harvard Graduates*. 17 vols. Cambridge: Charles Williams Seaver, 1873–85; Cambridge: Harvard University Press, 1937–73. Cited as *Sibley's Harvard Graduates*.

Suffolk County Probate Records, Suffolk County Courthouse, Boston. Cited as SCPR.

Von Khrum, Paul. *Silversmiths of New York City*. New York, 1978.

Ward, Barbara McLean. "The Craftsman in a Changing Society: Boston Goldsmiths, 1690–1730." Ph.D. diss., Boston University, 1983. Cited as Ward, "Boston Goldsmiths."

————. "The Edwards Family and the Silversmithing Trade in Boston, 1692–1762." In *The American Craftsman and the European Tradition*, *1620–1820*, pp. 66–76. Edited by Francis J. Puig and Michael Conforti. Minneapolis: Minneapolis Institute of Arts, 1989.

Warren, David B., Katherine S. Howe, and Michael K. Brown. *Marks of Achievement: Four Centuries of American Presentation Silver*. New York: Harry N. Abrams in association with the Museum of Fine Arts, Houston, 1987.

Waters, Deborah Dependahl. "From Pure Coin: The Manufacture of American Silver Flatware, 1800–1860." In Ian M. G. Quimby, ed., *Winterthur Portfolio 12*, pp. 19–33. Charlottesville: University Press of Virginia, 1977.

————. "'The Workmanship of an American Artist': Philadelphia's Precious Metals Trades and Craftsmen, 1788–1832." Ph.D. diss., University of Delaware, 1981. Cited as Waters, "Precious Metals Trades."

Williams, Carl M. *Silversmiths of New Jersey, 1700–1825*. Philadelphia: George S. MacManus, 1949.

American Silver at Winterthur
Edited by Onie Rollins, copyedited by Susan Randolph
Designed and typeset on the Macintosh in Monotype Fournier
by Katy Homans and Deborah Zeidenberg
Printed and bound by Palace Press in Hong Kong